DIGITAL
COMPOSITING
In Depth

Doug Kelly

The Coriolis Group, LLC
14455 North Hayden Road, Suite 220
Scottsdale, Arizona 85260

480/483-0192
FAX: 480/483-0193
http://www.coriolis.com

Library of Congress Cataloging-In-Publication Data
Kelly, Doug
    Digital compositing in depth / by Doug Kelly.
       p. cm.
    Includes index.
    ISBN 1-57610-431-1
    1. Computer graphics 2. Image processing--Digital
techniques. I. Title
T385.K415 2000
006.6--dc21   99-052318
                         CIP

Printed in the United States of America
10 9 8 7 6 5 4 3 2 1

President, CEO
Keith Weiskamp

Publisher
Steven Sayre

Project Editor
Don Eamon

Technical Reviewer
Eric Jurgenson

Production Coordinator
Meg E. Turecek

Cover Designer
Jody Winkler

Layout Designer
April Nielsen

CD-ROM Developer
Robert Clarfield

Coventry University

 CORIOLIS

OTHER TITLES FOR THE CREATIVE PROFESSIONAL

Character Animation In Depth
by Doug Kelly

3D Studio MAX R3 In Depth
by Rob Polevoi

3D Studio MAX R3 f/x and Design
by Jon A. Bell

Photoshop 5 3D Textures f/x and Design
by Geoffrey Smith

Photoshop 5 In Depth
by David Xenakis and Sherry London

Bryce 4 f/x and Design
by R. Shamms Mortier

Canoma Visual Insight
by Richard Schrand

Flash 4 Web Animation f/x and Design
by Ken Milburn and John Croteau

Adobe ImageStyler In Depth
by Daniel Gray

To my parents, with love and gratitude.

ABOUT THE AUTHOR

Doug Kelly has written books and articles and has presented seminars on computer graphics since 1992. His publications include *LightWave 3D 5 Character Animation f/x, Character Animation In Depth*, numerous articles for *Keyframe* and *3D Artist* magazines, contributions to the manuals for several 3D programs, and his LENY '97 Character Animation seminar CD-ROM. He is currently a freelance writer and animator and is editor of *Keyframe Magazine*. You can contact him at **dakelly@earthlink.net**, or through his Web site at **http://home.earthlink.net/~dakelly/index.htm**.

ACKNOWLEDGMENTS

First, thanks are due to the crew at Coriolis who, through patience, persistence, problem solving, and perseverance, manage to get even the most troublesome books out the door (not to mention paying the author). Without these people, you wouldn't be holding this book: Don Eamon, Mariann Barsolo, Robert Clarfield, Meg Turecek, April Nielsen, Beth Kohler, Jody Winkler, Dylan Zoller, and Bob Marvin.

Many professional compositors and other digital artists contributed case studies, advice and constructive criticism to this book. Without their contributions, it would be poorer by a great deal of real-world experience and fantastic imagery. Thanks to: Eric Jurgensen, Sherry Hitch, John Allardice, Emile Smith, Steve Pugh, Chris Bond, Boyd Shermis, Christle Leonard, Jason Goodman, Stephen Baker, Tom Williamson, Dylan Crooke, Domenic DiGiorgio, Stephen Evans, Chris Jones, Tony Lay, Matt Morgan, Rob Gougher, Phil South, Lee Stranahan, David Hibsher, Chris Nibley, and Jared Bendis.

Those who build the artists' tools are also due a great deal of thanks. It's easy to lock down the code, ship the boxes, cash the checks, and go on to the next project. It's tougher to be there when users need support, reviewers have deadlines that seem to require time travel, and writers like myself ask for much and can promise little or nothing in return. This book is evidence of the faith and support of both official vendor representatives and the helpful, considerate individuals who happen to be employed by those vendors: Steve Roberts, Joanne Dicaire, Shai Hinitz, Stuart MacKinnon, Jose Velasquez, Brick Eksten, Jane Perratt, Frank White, Brad Peebler, Chuck Baker, Dan Kraus, Michel Besner, Emma Shield, Erica Schisler, Steve Kilisky, Maureen Miller, Deniz Bolbol, Julie Hill, Bob Hayes, Ron Brinkmann, Melisa Bell, Paul Griffes, Roula Idriss, Alexandra West, Richard Welnowski, Lucy Jacobs, Hans Jung, Matthias Flass, Tom McAuliffe, James Holland, Amanda Hubly, and Brian Hoffman.

Finally and most importantly, Patricia K. Kelly, Ed.D., not only proofreads, edits, and sanity-checks my writing, but keeps me healthy and sane—even when she has to drag me away from my computer to do it. For getting me through the previous book, this book, and all the future books, thank you!

CONTENTS AT A GLANCE

PART I   THE PROFESSION OF COMPOSITING

Chapter 1   Who Is the Digital Compositor?
Chapter 2   The Rest Of The Team
Chapter 3   Digital Compositing In Brief

PART II   INPUT

Chapter 4   Visual Technicalities
Chapter 5   Reel To Virtual
Chapter 6   On The Set

PART III   BASIC COMPOSITING

Chapter 7   Concepts
Chapter 8   Starting Off Easy
Chapter 9   Life Ain't Easy

PART IV   INTERMEDIATE COMPOSITING

Chapter 10   There's WHAT In The Frame?
Chapter 11   Whole Lotta Shakin' Goin' On
Chapter 12   Put It Back

PART V   ADVANCED COMPOSITING

Chapter 13   When Life Gives You Lemons
Chapter 14   A Perfect Match
Chapter 15   Timing

PART VI   OUTPUT

Chapter 16   That's A Wrap
Chapter 17   Video Out
Chapter 18   The Big Screen

PART VII   THE BUSINESS SIDE OF COMPOSITING

Chapter 19   Taking Care Of Business

Appendix A   What's On The CD-ROMs
Appendix B   Bibliography

TABLE OF CONTENTS

Introduction..**xxv**

PART I THE PROFESSION OF COMPOSITING

Chapter 1
Who Is The Digital Compositor?..3
Where Did They Come From?   4
Tasks   5
A Day In The Life   5
Qualifications   7
    Education   8
    Talent   8
    Computer Skills   9
Compositor Profiles   9
    Chris Bond, President, Frantic Films   9
    Dylan Crooke, Managing Director, Momentum Animations   12
    Sherry Hitch, Supervising Visual Effects Compositor, Foundation Imaging   15
    Eric Jorgenson, Chief Engineer, Video Workshop   17
    Tom Williamson, Visual Effects Supervisor, Computer Cafe, Inc.   22

Chapter 2
The Rest Of The Team...25
Meet The Team   25
    The Major Players   26
    Set Crew   27
    Composition And Animation   32
    Production Assistants, Gofers, And Peons   34
Working With A Team   36

Chapter 3
Digital Compositing In Brief..41
Evaluating Software   41
    Online Research   42
    Platform Wars   44
    The Test Drive   45
    Feature Sets   46

Available Compositing Software   49
   Adobe After Effects   49
   Discreet effect*, paint*   50
   eyeon Software Digital Fusion 2.53   51
   NewTek Aura   52
   Nothing Real Shake   53
   Puffin Designs Commotion   54
   Silicon Grail Chalice   54

PART II   INPUT

Chapter 4
Visual Technicalities

57

Digital Image Basics   57
   Resolution   59
   Color   60
   Packing It In   61
File Formats   63
   Format Quick Reference   64
Video And Film   67
   Film To Computer   67
   Video To Computer   67

Chapter 5
Reel To Virtual

69

Image Quality   69
   Component Separation   70
   Sampling   71
   Compression   73
Desktop Hardware Options   73
   Entry-Level Video Cards   74
   MPEG Capture Cards   79
   DV: FireWire, iLink, IEEE-1394   81
   Fast Drive Cards   81
   Dedicated Drive Cards   83
Telecine   85
   CCD Telecine   86
Film Scanners   89

Chapter 6
On The Set 93

Shooting Decisions 94
    Camera 94
    Lighting And Rigging 95
    Roto 100
Documenting The Set 100
    Clean Plate 105
    Motion-Control Cameras 112
Computer-Generated Imagery (CGI) 116
    CGI Shadow Surfaces 116
    Project 6.1: Duplicating Porch Shadow Surfaces 116
    Project 6.2: Duplicating Chessboard Shadow And Reflection Surface 117
    CGI Lighting 119
    Project 6.3: Matching CGI Lighting For Porch 119
    Project 6.4: CGI Matching Lighting And Reflections For Chessboard 122

PART III   BASIC COMPOSITING

Chapter 7
Concepts 129

Basic Compositing Theory 129
    Channels 131
    Mattes 133
    Filters 143
    Geometric Transformations Or Transforms 149
    Other Effects 151
Problems 153

Chapter 8
Starting Off Easy 161

Basic Tools 161
    The Digital Fusion Interface 162
Compositing With Alpha Channel 165
    Project 8.1: Compositing With An Alpha Channel 165
Simple Keying 174
    Project 8.2: Luma Keying Stock Footage Over A Background Element 174
    Project 8.3: Chroma Keying 179
Filters And Effects 188
    Project 8.4: Experimenting With Filters 189
    Project 8.5: Animating A Setting 190
    Project 8.6: Animating And Masking A Dissolve 192

Geometric Transformations (Transforms)   197

    Project 8.7: Animating A Flip Transform   197

    Project 8.8: Animating A Pan Transform   199

    Project 8.9: Flow Organization   201

Title Design And Character Generators   203

    Project 8.10: Animating A Credit Scroll   209

    Adding Timecode   216

    Drop Shadows And Outlines   218

    Project 8.11: Main Titles   220

    Elegant Text   224

Chapter 9
Life Ain't Easy   225

Take Out The Garbage   227

    4:2:2 Color Undersampling Problems   229

    Project 9.1: 4:2:2 YUV Sampling Correction   231

Bluescreen Problem Solving   232

    Screen Correction   233

    Project 9.2: Screen Correction   234

        Screen Correction (After Effects)   236

        Aura And Screen Correction   240

        Chalice And Screen Correction   240

        Screen Correction (Commotion)   240

        effect* And Screen Correction   242

        Shake And Screen Correction   243

    Ultimatte Screen Correction   243

    Project 9.3: Ultimatte Screen Correction   243

        Ultimatte Screen Correction (After Effects)   244

        Chalice And Ultimatte Screen Correction   246

    Silencing Noise   247

    Cleaning Up Film   250

    Project 9.4: Cleaning Up Film   250

        Cleaning Up Film (After Effects)   254

        Aura And Cleaning Up Film   259

        Chalice And Cleaning Up Film   260

        Cleaning Up Film (Commotion)   260

        effect* And Cleaning Up Film   262

        Shake And Cleaning Up Film   262

Digital Compositing Plug-Ins   263

    Zbig Demo   264

    Ultimatte Demo   264

Go With The Flow   265

PART IV INTERMEDIATE COMPOSITING

Chapter 10
There's WHAT In The Frame? **269**

Rig Removal With A Clean Plate   270
  About The Footage   272
    Project 10.1: Rig Removal With An Effect Mask   274
      Rig Removal With An Effect Mask (After Effects)   280
      Rig Removal With An Eraser (Aura)   283
      Rig Removal With An Effect Mask (Commotion)   284
      Rig Removal With An Effect Mask (effect*)   284
      Rig Removal With An Effect Mask (Shake)   286
Rotoscoping   287
    Project 10.2: Rook's Rotoscope Removal   288
      Rook's Rotoscope Removal (After Effects)   300
      Rook's Rotoscope Removal (Commotion)   303
      Rook's Rotoscope Removal (effect*)   304
      Rook's Rotoscope Removal (Shake)   305
    Project 10.3: Rotoscoping An Actor Removal   305
      Rotoscoping An Actor Removal (After Effects)   306
      Rotoscoping An Actor Removal (Commotion)   308
      Rotoscoping An Actor Removal (effect*)   308
      Rotoscoping An Actor Removal (Shake)   309
Clean Your Plate   310
    Project 10.4: Time-Shifting A Clean Plate   310
      Time-Shifting A Clean Plate (After Effects)   312
      Time-Shifting A Clean Plate (Commotion)   313
      Time-Shifting A Clean Plate (effect*)   314
A Little Makeup   315

Chapter 11
Whole Lotta Shakin' Goin' On **319**

Tracking   320
    Project 11.1: Track A Moving Object   323
      Track A Moving Object (After Effects)   332
      Aura And Tracking   334
      Track A Moving Object (Chalice)   334
      Track A Moving Object (Commotion)   335
      Track A Moving Object (effect*)   336
      Shake And Tracking   336
Stabilizing   336
  Single-Point Stabilization   336

Project 11.2: Stabilize The Box Footage   337
   Stabilize The Box Footage (After Effects)   340
   Aura And Single-Point Stabilization   340
   Stabilize The Box Footage (Chalice)   341
   Stabilize The Box Footage (Commotion)   342
   Stabilize The Box Footage (effect*)   342
   Shake And Single-Point Stabilization   344
Two-Point Stabilization   344
Project 11.3: Two-Point Stabilize Of The Match000.jpg Porch Footage   349
   After Effects And Multi-Point Stabilization   358
   Aura And Multi-Point Stabilization   359
   Two-Point Stabilize The Match000.jpg Porch Footage (Commotion)   359
   Two-Point Stabilize The Match000.jpg Porch Footage (effect*)   359
   Shake And Multi-Point Stabilization   362

Chapter 12
Put It Back   363

Using Stabilized Footage   363
Project 12.1: Rig Removal With Stabilized Footage   364
   Cleaning A Plate In Photoshop   364
   Rig Removal With Stabilized Footage (After Effects)   369
   Rig Removal With Stabilized Footage (Commotion)   372
   Rig Removal With Stabilized Footage (effect*)   372
   Rig Removal With Stabilized Footage (Shake)   374
Destabilizing   374
Project 12.2: Destabilize The Box   375
   After Effects And Destabilizing   377
   Aura And Destabilizing   377
   Motion Destabilize (Chalice)   377
   Motion Destabilize (Commotion)   377
   Destabilize The Box (effect*)   377
   Shake And Destabilizing   379
Match Move   379
Tracking For Animation   380
Project 12.3: Track Motion Path For Porch Model   381
   After Effects And Tracking Motion Paths   384
   Aura And Tracking   384
   Track Motion Path For Porch Model (Commotion)   384
   Track Motion Path For Porch Model (effect*)   384
   Shake And Tracking   385
Putting It All Together   385
Project 12.4: Match Move The Porch Model   386
   After Effects And Match Moving   399

Aura And Match Moving   400

Chalice And Match Moving   400

Commotion And Match Moving   400

effect* And Match Moving   401

Shake And Match Moving   401

Four-Point Destabilize   401

Project 12.5: Motion Destabilize   401

After Effects And Four-Point Destabilizing   407

Aura And Four-Point Destabilizing   407

Chalice And Four-Point Destabilizing   408

Motion Destabilize (Commotion)   408

Motion Destabilize (effect*)   408

Shake And Four-Point Destabilizing   409

Animating The Camera   409

PART V   ADVANCED COMPOSITING

Chapter 13
When Life Gives You Lemons 413

Missing In Action   413

Project 13.1: Replacing Missing Or Damaged Frames   414

Replacing Missing Or Damaged Frames (After Effects)   418

Replacing Missing Or Damaged Frames (Aura)   422

Replacing Missing Or Damaged Frames (effect*)   424

Tweaking Colors   427

Eyeballing NTSC Color On A Computer Monitor   428

Your Best Tool: Eyeball v.1.0   428

Normalized Values   432

Gamma   432

Keep It Legal   433

Project 13.2: Limit A CGI Element To NTSC-Legal Colors   434

Limit A Comp To NTSC-Legal Colors (After Effects)   434

Aura And NTSC-Legal Colors   434

Limit A Comp To NTSC-Legal Colors (Chalice)   435

Commotion And NTSC-Legal Colors   435

Limit A Comp To NTSC-Legal Colors (effect*)   435

Limit A Comp To NTSC-Legal Colors (Shake)   435

Super Black   435

Project 13.3: Adding Super Black To Legal Colors   435

Color Tools   437

Sampling Colors   437

Color Space Conversion   438

Project 13.4: Color Space Conversion For Noise Removal   440
    After Effects And Color Space Conversion   442
    Aura And Color Space Conversion   442
    Chalice And Color Space Conversion   442
    Color Space Conversion For Noise Removal (Commotion)   443
    effect* And Color Space Conversion   443
    Color Space Conversion For Noise Removal (Shake)   443
Color Gain   445
Brightness/Contrast   445
Isolating An Effect To A Foreground Element   446

Chapter 14
A Perfect Match   449

Digital Advantages   452
    Project 14.1: Making A Simple Matte Painting   453
Matte Painting For The Moving Camera   461
    Project 14.2: Compositing A Multiplane Pan   462
        Compositing A Multiplane Pan (After Effects)   467
        Compositing A Multiplane Pan (Aura)   469
        Chalice And Multiplane   470
        effect* And Multiplane   471
        Shake And Multiplane   471
    Project 14.3: Comping A Matte Painting Into Stabilized Footage   472
The Third Dimension   473

Chapter 15
Timing   477

Work With What You've Got   478
    Reversing Footage   478
    Project 15.1: Reversing Footage   478
        Reversing Footage (After Effects)   480
        Reversing Footage (Aura)   481
        Chalice And Timing   482
        Reversing Footage (Commotion)   482
        effect* And Reversing Footage   483
        Shake And Timing   483
    Changing Speed   483
    Project 15.2: Creating Fast-Motion Footage   483
        Creating Fast-Motion Footage (After Effects)   485
        Creating Fast-Motion Footage (Commotion)   485
        Creating Fast-Motion Footage (effect*)   486

Project 15.3: Creating Slow-Motion Footage   486
Creating Slow-Motion Footage (After Effects)   486
Creating Slow-Motion Footage (Commotion)   488
Creating Slow-Motion Footage (effect*)   488
Filling In The Blanks   489
Project 15.4: Slow Motion With Interpolation   489
Slow Motion With Interpolation (After Effects)   489
Slow Motion With Interpolation (Commotion)   492
Slow Motion With Interpolation (effect*)   492
Project 15.5: Fast Motion With Interpolation   493
Fast Motion With Interpolation (After Effects)   495
Fast Motion With Interpolation (Commotion)   495
Fast Motion With Interpolation (effect*)   496
Motion Blur   497
Project 15.6: Faking Motion Blur   497
Faking Motion Blur (After Effects)   502
effect* And Faking Motion Blur   505
Happy Trails   505
Project 15.7: Faking Strobe Lights   506
Faking Strobe Lights (After Effects)   507
effect* And Faking Strobe Lights   507
Stretching Time   507
Project 15.8: Animating A Speed Change   510
Animating A Speed Change (After Effects)   510
Animating A Speed Change (Commotion)   512
effect* And Animating A Speed Change   513
Project 15.9: Useful Spline Tricks   513
After Effects And Useful Spline Tricks   514
effect* And Useful Spline Tricks   514
Project 15.10: Do The Jerk   514
Do The Jerk (After Effects)   514
Do The Jerk (Commotion)   515
Do The Jerk (effect*)   516

PART VI   OUTPUT

Chapter 16
That's A Wrap

That's A Wrap   519
Precompositions   520
Uncompressed Image Sequences   520
Garbage And Simple Rig Removal   520

Noise And Grain Removal   521

Mattes   521

Stabilization   522

If You Don't Know What To Do, Do What
  You Know   522

In And Out And In And Out And In And Out   522

Network Etiquette   523

Memory Management   524

Project 16.1: Setting Up A Win NT RAM Drive   525

Output Issues   528

RTV Output   528

Chapter 17
Video Out   535

Streaming Internet Video   536

Downloadable Internet Video   540

Web Page Issues   541

Local Computer Playback   543

Output To Tape   549

All-In-Wonder   549

DV Master Pro   551

Perception RT3DX   552

Video Toaster NT   553

Recording Options   555

Chapter 18
The Big Screen   561

High Definition Television   562

HDTV Hardware Selection   563

Film Recorders   565

Kinescope   565

CRT Film Recorders   566

Laser Film Recorders   566

Electron Beam Recorder   572

E-Cinema   572

PART VII   TAKING CARE OF BUSINESS

Chapter 19
Taking Care Of Business   583

Starting Out   583

Self-Education   584

Just The FAQs, Ma'am   586

Schools   586

Practice   587

Best Foot Forward: Your Demo Reel   588

Quality, Not Quantity   590

Résumé, Portfolio, And Cover Letter   591

Interviews   592

Getting Hired   593

Not Getting Hired   594

Networking   594

Mentoring   595

SIGGRAPH   596

Visual Effects Society   596

VFXPro: The Daily Visual Effects Resource   597

Being An Employee   597

Now What Do I Do?   597

Make Your Boss Look Good   598

Maintaining Your Space—And Yourself   600

Collecting Your Due   601

Benefits   601

Screen Credit   602

Renegotiation Is Not A Bad Thing   602

Professional Development   603

Side Projects   604

Running Your Own Shop   604

Growing A Business   606

Setting Goals   606

Personnel   607

Financing Your Business   607

Do Not Waste, But Do Not Skimp   608

Pricing   609

Business Is Business   609

Insurance   610

Advertising   611

Protecting Yourself   612

Dealing With Clients   612

Contracts   613

Family Business Is Still Business   613

Intellectual Property   615

Choosing An Attorney   616

Legal Self-Care   618

When It Is Not Fun Anymore   618

Appendix A
What's On The CD-ROMs 621

Appendix B
Bibliography 627

Glossary 633

Index 653

INTRODUCTION

You may have picked up this book because you are a digital compositor, because you are interested in becoming a digital compositor, or just because the artwork on the cover looks interesting and you want to know what *digital compositing* means. In any case, you picked up the right book. Digital compositing is the digitally manipulated integration of at least two source images to produce a new image. This is a new, rapidly growing, and increasingly important art form. This book's cover art has all been digitally composited, either for the tutorial projects found exclusively in this book or for television or feature film productions you may have seen. This book is designed to show you how to duplicate these effects and, more important, how to create your own special effects with digital compositing tools and techniques.

What Is "In Depth" About This Book?

This book is written for anyone, at any level of expertise, who wants to become a digital compositor. If you are just starting out, the basic chapters will give you enough information to understand the technical parts of the more advanced chapters. If you are already an intermediate or advanced digital compositor, the simpler chapters will provide a useful review of what you already know, and the advanced chapters will show you how to hone your existing skills and help you develop new ones. In addition to the technical chapters, this book includes several chapters on the rest of the digital compositing business: finding a job, working in a studio, starting your own studio, making a living, and staying out of trouble.

Unlike some books on computer arts, this book doesn't stop at showing you basic techniques. The projects, advice and case studies in this book are based on real-world television and film productions. The project files on the two CD-ROMs are not compressed, cut-down or simplified versions; these are the full video or film resolution footage and data files that you can expect to use in professional productions. This book is intended to give you instruction and practice at real-world levels, using the same tools that are in daily use in television and film production houses. If you learn and practice what this book teaches, you should be able to produce digital composites at a level of quality that studios and clients are willing to pay for.

What Is In This Book

This book is divided into 19 chapters, which I have designed to be read in order. The first chapters cover basic information, and later chapters grow progressively more advanced. Here are summaries of what you'll find in each chapter:

- Chapter 1, "Who is the Digital Compositor?" This chapter provides an overview of your opportunities as a digital compositor, the kinds of work you can expect to do, and the colleagues and mentors with whom you will be working.

- Chapter 2, "The Rest of the Team." This chapter briefly introduces the other artists, technicians, and businesspeople who contribute to a typical production, from the executive producer down to the production assistant.

- Chapter 3, "Digital Compositing In Brief." This chapter gives the technical information you need to evaluate and choose your own compositing tools, including a thumbnail analysis and comparative evaluation of each digital compositing program currently on the market.

- Chapter 4, "Visual Technicalities." You need a basic vocabulary and knowledge of digital media (and their analog origins) to be a good digital compositor. This chapter presents the short course, with references for you to consult as you need them.

- Chapter 5, "Reel To Virtual." Understanding how film and video get into your workstation can make the difference between a routine composition and tearing your hair out. This chapter presents the essential digitizing knowledge you need.

- Chapter 6, "On the Set." Even if you never become a visual effects supervisor, learning how to set up or supervise an effects shoot can make your compositing work easier and can help you produce better results. This chapter takes you behind the scenes to show you what on-set factors are critical for your composites.

- Chapter 7, "Concepts." This chapter presents a visual catalog of the most important concepts and tools you will use as a digital compositor. Learning the contents of this chapter will make the rest of this book easier to understand and will enable you to communicate more effectively with other effects artists.

- Chapter 8, "Starting Off Easy." This chapter provides a tour of the basic tools that should be part of every digital compositor's kit. Projects show you how to create the composites pictured in Chapter 7 and enable you to experiment with your software tools to learn their uses and limits.

- Chapter 9, "Life Ain't Easy." As a digital compositor, you will rarely be handed an easy shot. You will more often be asked to salvage, repair, or fake something that either went wrong or was overlooked in principal photography. This chapter shows you how to do this.

- Chapter 10, "There's WHAT in the Frame?" One of the most common problems for digital compositors is the removal of people or objects that show up where they shouldn't. This chapter shows you how to remove them, as pictured on the back cover.

- Chapter 11, "Whole Lotta Shakin' Goin' On." Your ability to composite footage from a moving camera can make the difference between an easy job and one that you wish you'd never seen. This chapter explains several techniques for stabilizing footage.

- Chapter 12, "Put It Back." Restoring or simulating camera motion after compositing other effects can make the difference between a shot that sells and one that looks faked. Projects in this chapter demonstrate how to shake up stabilized footage after the rest of the composition is finished.

- Chapter 13, "When Life Gives You Lemons." This chapter shows you how to repair the worst footage that a camera mishap can drop on your workstation. Poor exposure, bad color, inadequate contrast, and missing or badly damaged frames can all result from camera problems. The scanning or digitizing process can add flaws to the footage, including dropped frames, dirt and scratches, jitter, and poor color balance. When you are called on to repair extreme damage, you need to match the repaired footage seamlessly to the adjoining footage.

- Chapter 14, "A Perfect Match." A *matte painting* is a two-dimensional image created at least partly by painting, and composited with other elements to create illusions of depth and scale. Matte paintings are used primarily for set extensions and backgrounds, and they are an important part of the digital compositor's art because they can be used in every style and genre of filmmaking. This chapter shows you how to piece together a simple matte painting, touch up the gaps, merge the painting with footage, and comp a multiplane camera move to simulate perspective shifts.

- Chapter 15, "Timing." Timing effects can be part of compositions to salvage bad footage, to create clean plates for rig removals, or to stretch or compress a shot to fit with other elements. Whether they are planned ahead as early as the first script or are last-minute changes during the final edit, you can expect to composite some of these effects on nearly every project. This chapter shows you how to handle these timing effects.

- Chapter 16, "That's A Wrap." This chapter shows how to optimize your renders, prioritize your work with precompositions, and manage your system and network resources to give you maximum creative flexibility and still make your deadlines.

- Chapter 17, "Video Out." After your comps are rendered, you need a way to deliver them to your client or audience, to record them for future viewing or reuse, and to make reference copies for your demo reel or personal archive. Knowing something about the video transfer process can also make a difference to your compositing. With the information in this chapter, you'll be able to choose the best video output for your comps.

- Chapter 18, "The Big Screen." If you can make it here, you can make it anywhere. Your comps have to look good on screens so large that every pixel is several inches square, in front of audiences with trained eyes and high expectations. If you want to succeed on the big screen, you have to understand how that screen works. This chapter presents all the information you'll need for big-screen output.

- Chapter 19, "Taking Care Of Business." When you are trying to break into the business, you need to know what employers are looking for and where to find industry information. After you land a job, you need to know how to keep it and how to avoid being exploited or disabled. You need to know even more if you want to start and run your own studio. This chapter presents answers and directs you to resources where you can learn more.

Finally, you'll find Appendix A, "What's On The CD-ROMs," and Appendix B, "Bibliography." Appendix A presents (in greater detail than you will find on the back cover of this book) information about the two CD-ROMs supplied with this book. Appendix B contains brief reviews of books that I have found useful to digital compositing and related arts.

The CD-ROM

When I compiled the CD-ROMs for this book, I tried to avoid the shortcomings of the usual "bonus CD-ROM" included with many computer graphics books. First, the 650MB available on a single CD-ROM just didn't cut it for this book because video and film footage takes a lot of space. Instead, there are two chockfull CD-ROMs with this book; I think 1.3 gigabytes, about 3,800 files, is a pretty good compilation. Second, one goal of this book is to enable you to choose your own digital compositing tools, so I included demo versions of several of the top programs for you to try out. Third, a tutorial project that you don't have the tools to complete is next to useless; therefore, I have designed most of the projects in this book so that you can complete them with one or more of the demo programs included on the CD-ROMs. I hope you have fun with the CD-ROMs; I think they contain a lot of toys, eye candy, and serious tools for you to play with and learn from.

How To Use This Book

If you are teaching yourself, turn to page one and start reading. Work through each chapter and project, in the order in which they're presented. I know that it's really tempting to jump right into the first project, but I warn you that you will lose more time—and suffer pointless frustration—if you don't read the material in order. I have heard from readers of my previous books that they tried to just follow the step-by-step instructions for projects, skipping over "the stuff in between," only to find that they made bad judgment calls, didn't understand why they were doing what they were doing, and ended up with poor results. In the end, they had to go back and read the book in the original order. I haven't written all these words just to fill up space, or because I really love to type; every word is where it is for a very good reason.

If you have the good fortune to be using this book as part of a formal class on digital compositing, congratulations! Make the best of it; you are lucky to have immediate feedback and guidance from peers and instructor(s). It's far more difficult to learn an art form without that feedback. Follow the directions of your instructor, and make the time to read the out-of-class materials and to do all the extra projects and tutorials. What you get out of the class is directly proportional to the effort you put into it. Even the most brilliant and talented slacker is not going to do well as a digital compositor; in the end, you are judged by the quality of the work you finish, not by the "promising" way you fail to finish a job.

> *"The job of the teacher is to pull everything out of the student, and the job of the student is to pull everything out of the teacher."*
> *— Sister Corita Kent*

If you have the challenge of teaching a class in digital compositing, I congratulate you on your wise choice of this book as a classroom resource <grin>. I designed most of this book's projects to be completed with the demo software and source footage included on the two CD-ROMs. The only other resource you need is student access to workstations capable of running the software. If you need to create objective written tests, I recommend culling the italicized terms of art from each chapter and consulting the Glossary for their definitions. You should be aware that multiple-choice tests on the application of compositing tools are fraught with loopholes; there are usually at least two (more often five or six) perfectly valid ways to achieve the same effect. You might do better to construct these portions of tests as short answer or, for more complex problems, short essay. If you need to test the diagnostic judgment of your students (an exercise I highly recommend), I suggest you use a video or film projector to display examples of problem footage, with the students writing brief descriptions of the problem and how they would set up a composition to correct it. If the necessary equipment is available to students, I strongly suggest that a significant part of their grades be based on the submission of their completed compositions on videotape or CD-R. This enables you to evaluate their talent (if any), mastery of the subject, and attitude toward work expectations and deadlines. If your students intend to pursue careers as digital compositors, you can't stress good work habits strongly enough.

In addition to the reading material in this book, you will find several supplementary texts listed in the bibliography. I highly recommend Ron Brinkmann's *Art and Science of Digital Compositing* as companion reading; it covers the theory and higher mathematics of digital compositing in far greater detail than you'll find in this book, but it doesn't address specific software as this book does. Finally, if you have any questions, comments, or suggestions about classroom use of this book, please email me at **dakelly@earthlink.net**. I'm always happy to help an educator.

If you are an experienced compositor, feel free to skip around. However, this book is laid out in a progressive order, with basic concepts explained in the early chapters and more difficult concepts building on those basics in later chapters. If you get lost, look for references to preceding projects that you skipped over. The odds are good that the concepts you are having trouble with are explained in those projects. If a particular word or concept is unfamiliar, look for its definition in the Glossary or check the index for the word's first appearance in this book.

About The Projects

The tutorial projects in this book are written so that you can complete them with as many different compositing programs as possible. This book covers the most popular compositing software, including After Effects, Aura, Chalice, Commotion, Digital Fusion, effect*, Shake, Ultimatte, and Zbig. The demo version of Digital Fusion that is included on the first CD-ROM can be used to complete nearly all the projects. The other programs, either demo or full version, may or may not be usable to complete one or more projects because not all programs may have all the features you need. For this reason, the primary section of each project is designed for Digital Fusion. Most projects include secondary sections that are designed for as many as possible of the remaining programs. If a particular program cannot be used to complete a project, I say so.

If you are just starting to learn digital compositing, I strongly recommend that you work through this book using the Digital Fusion demo software. If you are already using a different program, I suggest that you at least read through the primary Digital Fusion section for each project before you begin the secondary section designed for your software. If you are considering which compositing program to purchase, I hope the comparisons offered by these projects will help you make the best purchase decision for your work.

Moving On

This introduction should give you a good idea of what this book contains and the best way for you to use it. Chapter 1, "Who Is The Digital Compositor?" describes your opportunities as a digital compositor, the kinds of work you can expect to do, and the colleagues and mentors with whom you will be working.

PART I

THE PROFESSION OF COMPOSITING

WHO IS THE DIGITAL COMPOSITOR?

What are a digital compositor's working conditions? How did today's supervisors get where they are? What will this career be like in the future? Digital compositor is a job title that was completely unknown 10 years ago, outside of a handful of people doing research at Industrial Light + Magic. Five years ago, it was barely understood by most of the special effects industry, let alone the general public. Today, every effects house is expected to have digital compositors on staff. Moreover, nearly every new motion picture and many television programs roll credits for digital compositors. Digital compositing is a new, rapidly growing, and increasingly important art form. Fans of special effects, and even the general public, have begun to recognize the contributions of digital compositors to their favorite entertainment.

Unfortunately, fame has its drawbacks. Some compositors are starting to voice concerns about the future of this new profession. One fear is that digital compositing will be perceived as the next big career fad. When that happened to character animation, hordes of wannabes inundated studios with schlocky demo reels. Fly-by-night schools started up expensive animation programs with inadequate instructors and poorly designed coursework. Many graduates of these programs were disappointed to find that paying upwards of $25,000 for a piece of paper did not guarantee a job; the studios still insisted on evidence of talent and ability.

This book—particularly this chapter—is intended to help you begin or continue a career as a digital compositor. Part of that help is in telling you exactly what the work is like, what you will be expected to do, and what the drawbacks are. If you aren't cut out for the discipline and sheer hard work necessary to succeed at a professional level, you should find that out now. If you have neither the talent nor the motivation to excel as a professional digital compositor, this is the best time to recognize that fact. If, on the other hand, this chapter reinforces your determination to be a digital compositor, I hope you will be able to make better-informed decisions about your tools, training, and career. Even if you choose not to pursue a career as a digital compositor, this book should help you in your quest to enjoy digital compositing as a hobby or sideline.

Where Did They Come From?

Digital compositors working today have an incredibly broad range of experience and training as a group. Making generalizations about these people is dangerous; they are as diverse a group as you will find anywhere, with the oddest juxtapositions of talents and interests you can imagine. However, I believe a few generalizations are worth the risk, for the sake of giving you some idea of your colleagues' backgrounds.

The top names in the digital compositing business often have academic degrees, either in fine arts, computer graphics, or both. You will see these people presenting sessions at SIGGRAPH (Special Interest Group on Computer Graphics), being interviewed by *Cinefex* magazine, or being featured on the VFXPro Web site. They got where they are by being the best in their field. They started with inborn talent and developed it through practice, exploration, formal study, and more practice. These compositors contribute new insights and tools to the profession; their inventions and publications become part of the tools you will have on your desktop in the future. If you are fortunate and work hard, someday you may have the opportunity to work under their supervision and learn directly from them.

Only slightly lower in the professional hierarchy are those who have lots of experience, but little formal education. These compositors come from diverse backgrounds. Some come from video or film engineering, moving from technician to artist over a period of years and bringing a deep resource of technical knowledge. Some come from art backgrounds, translating self-taught traditional techniques into the new digital media. Some come from the traditional optical and practical effects industry, translating skills and trade secrets from film-based to digital cinematography. These people bring an invaluable fund of hard-won experience to their current positions. If a really nasty problem has you stumped, chances are excellent that one of these "old hands" will remember a traditional technique to fix it and will be able to translate that knowledge into a digital fix. If you are ever in a position to set up a studio, make sure that you hire at least one experienced compositor. If you have nothing but new blood, you will be constantly reinventing the wheel.

The newest crop of digital compositors tends to have a higher proportion of computer-based experience, simply because computer graphics software has been readily available throughout most of their education and life experience. However, the overriding criterion for their continued success is still artistic talent. Digital compositing requires mastery of both the computer-based tools and the artistic principles. CGI (computer-generated imagery) artists getting into the compositing field have the challenge of learning color theory, film, video, and other technical details to balance their computer skills. For many compositors, these technical issues are more challenging to master than any graphics software.

Tasks

Digital compositors perform a variety of tasks, even at large studios where they are highly specialized. The smaller the studio, the more generalized the work and the more varied your responsibilities. At the smallest studios, you may be responsible for dealing with the client, shooting footage, digitizing, color correcting, creating CGI elements, compositing, recording output to tape, delivering the tape to the client, and fetching your own coffee. At a larger studio, you may simply be provided all the elements and be expected to perform only the compositing work. At really huge facilities, you may be able to specialize in something like day/night reversals or adding CGI ground fog. However, for the sake of your own career, you should beware of excessive specialization and keep up your general compositing skills.

At any size studio, the more senior and skilled you are, the more interesting your work will be. At the beginning, you can expect to get the simpler assignments, such as rig removal. At a large studio, you may be doing rig removal exclusively for a long time. For example, a studio the size of ILM may have hundreds of employees doing nothing but move-matching. The really tough assignments are reserved for the senior or supervising compositors, because they have the most problem-solving experience. After they have developed a solution, the problem footage may be farmed out to other compositors, along with a recipe for the solution. If you develop a talent for solving the apparently unsolvable, you will be much more valuable to any studio. If you are good enough, you may even earn your way to a unique position like Visual Effects Researcher. Then again, you may be happy with a relatively settled career doing rig removal.

Note that I used the phrase "relatively settled." In a career that has existed for less than 10 years, in a field that has been professional for barely three generations, in a medium that didn't exist a century ago, you can't expect things to remain the same long enough for you to accumulate much time-in-grade. Do not plan to rest on your laurels at any point in your career. If you think you can coast for a while, you will most likely find yourself being supervised by some kid who blew past you on the career ladder while you were napping. The best digital compositors are constantly doing research and finding better ways to do things no one previously thought possible. You can bet they won't be caught unawares.

A Day In The Life

How the compositing work flows through your hands depends on the job, the client, your working environment, and sometimes the phases of the moon. Basically, don't expect to ever do two shots in exactly same way. There are so many variables that it is counterproductive to try to nail down an excessively rigid workflow.

However, most studios do have some sort of general workflow for compositing jobs. If at all possible, the compositor or VFX supervisor should be part of preproduction planning. Failing that, the VFX supervisor should be present at, or at least consulted before, the shoot. If the client ignores both these tenets of efficient effects production, the first stage of the compositor's job may be evaluating the footage and deciding whether to take the assignment. (Chapter 13 may be a help at this point.) The footage and storyboard may call for CGI elements to be created, additional live elements to be shot on location or in bluescreen, even a complete reshoot if the problems are too severe.

After the supervisor selects a basic course of action, the compositor may or may not be officially responsible for chasing down all the elements for the *comp* (composited end product). A good compositor always takes a share of that responsibility. Even if it is someone else's job to get you that CGI monster element, it's your comp that's going to show up late on the project time line. If you get the element late, you'll have less time to complete your work and the quality will probably suffer, even if you do make the deadline. A little diplomatic nagging is much better than last-minute blame assignment or shoddy results.

When the compositor has all the elements, the fun really begins. Undetected problems, discrepancies between the elements, corrupted files, and other manifestations of Murphy's Law rear their ugly little heads. The compositor's job is to slay these hydras as fast as they pop up, before they can spawn more problems downstream. This is where the more experience the compositors have—and the more skilled they are with the available tools—the faster and more productive they can be, which is why practice is so crucial to your development as a digital compositor. If every problem puts you into a cycle of blind guesswork, you are not going to get much work done. Case Study 1.1 shows how quick thinking salvaged a project from an unanticipated disaster.

Depending on the project's supervisor and client, the compositor's finished results may not be all that finished. Unless the compositor is extremely experienced, competent, and carries some weight at the studio, the first comp is probably not going to be the final comp. As with any commercial art form, the paying customer, the middleman, and anyone in the vicinity seem obligated to make suggestions. The supervisor and client are the ones who can insist that their suggestions be implemented, or at least seriously considered. One of the strongest justifications for the purchase of top-end, high-ticket compositing systems is that the clients with the deepest pockets are also the ones that demand unlimited tweaks in real time right up to the deadline. Compositors who can do this work can rake in some very serious cash with one of these systems—if they don't mind catering to prima donna clients and investing a quarter million dollars or so in the tools. Personally, I am perfectly happy with less money and more-reasonable clients. I think your life's work should be fun.

After the cycle of work on a shot is complete, the compositor may start on the next project, pick up where she left off on a simultaneous project, or find that the just-completed project is being resubmitted due to changes to one or more of the elements. This cycle may be repeated until the final deadline, when the compositor is rushed and has to turn in work she considers unfinished. Get used to it. This is an art form like many others, and the old saying still holds true: "A work of art is never completed, it is simply torn out of the artist's hands."

Case Study 1.1
Frantic Films' Manitoba Theatre Centre Ad For *MasterClass*

This spot was one of those flukes. Originally, the concept was to do a video dolly over props to tell a story, but the camera failed. In a pinch, it was shot on 35mm, we did a synthetic rostrum in post, and the commercial was saved. Post and animation were completed in one day.

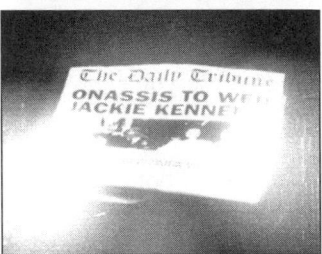

Art Direction: Doowah Design; Animation: Chris Bond; Editing/Post: Chris Bond.

Storyboard: Start slow pan over piano and over photographs of Maria Callas and the love of her life—Aristotle Onassis. Text burn-ins throughout sequence, leading to end on prop newspaper with headline "Onassis to Wed Jackie Kennedy." Flashbulbs "flash" into end tag.

Finally, perhaps many weeks or months after the compositor sees the last of a shot, she experiences one of the deepest satisfactions of this career. The shot is shown on a TV or motion-picture screen, and nobody notices. (Except for that yahoo—excuse me, digital compositor—cheering from the front row.) That's what you are aiming for: the subtle compositing effects that defy detection. If you do your work exceptionally well, you may someday pick up an award for an effect even your colleagues couldn't detect. And until then, you can enjoy one of the other satisfactions of this career: cashing a paycheck from a job you enjoy!

Qualifications

The good news is, you don't need an expensive degree to land a job as a digital compositor. The bad news is, you have to demonstrate real artistic talent and well-developed skills in the medium. More good news: You can acquire a decent set of tools for a very reasonable price (the free demo versions on this book's CD-ROMs are a good place to start). The bad news: You have to buckle down and simply practice for a long time to hone your inborn talents into marketable skills.

Education

School transcripts, diplomas, and other evidence that you attended classes have very little to do with your finding a job as a digital compositor. This is mostly because schools have a (generally unwritten, but nevertheless well-established) policy of not flunking students for lack of talent. You still may be able to get a good education in a fine art from such a school, but every dud grad makes the diplomas of talented grads less valuable. Many schools are also sorely lacking in coursework that deals with the real world. I am always exceptionally happy to visit a school that actually teaches art students how to get a job, to look after their own career and finances, and generally to stay off public relief and out of trouble. It's too bad more schools aren't like that.

Talent

Supervisors looking to hire compositors look for two things: a portfolio and a demo reel. Don't even bother to contact a studio if you don't have one or the other; preferably, you should have both.

The demo reel is less important to many studios, because standard VHS resolution is insufficient to judge the quality of a good composition. However, it can be critical to demonstrate your ability to animate motion graphics, move-match, rotoscope, and create many other compositing effects based on time and motion. Most of the software mentioned in this book can render sequences suitable for video. Chapter 17 describes your options for dumping output to tape. More information about editing, formatting, and submitting a demo reel are included in Chapter 19.

Your portfolio is where you should spend a lot of effort. Supervisors want to see that you understand color, balance, light, and shadow—all the principles you can learn in traditional art classes. Many supervisors want to see that you can express yourself visually, that you have the talent and skill to draw or paint well. Painting is especially important to many studios; the digital compositing you will be expected to do more closely resembles painting than any other traditional art form. You should also create high-resolution prints of your best digital compositions for your portfolio, especially if you are submitting a demo reel with your portfolio. A good print is the best way to show off the quality of your compositing work; the video shows off your timing.

Most studios are now (or will be soon) making the transition to HDTV production with film-level 2K resolution. They want to see that you can handle it, that you are familiar with the higher demands of the new video standards. You can't show that on a VHS tape, but you can render and make a print of it. This enables the reviewer to go over your work with a magnifying glass, seeing just how well you solved the problems of that particular shot. If possible, you should also make prints of the same quality for all the elements so the reviewer can see what you started with. If you can make an impressive-looking 2K print from really lousy footage and other elements, you have a much better chance of being hired. Most studios need digital compositors who can deal successfully with real-world flawed elements; they have no use for someone who can simply follow a recipe to assemble a theory-perfect visual jigsaw puzzle.

One of the best pieces you can include in your portfolio is an example of how you solved a major problem with color balance. A working knowledge of color space, along with related problems and methods for correcting them, is apparently one of the most needed and rarely found attributes of new compositors. See Chapter 13 for details, but plan on coming up with some original examples on your own. (Reviewers are notoriously unimpressed with canned tutorials presented as original work.)

Computer Skills

Because you are reading this book, I think I can safely assume that you understand the importance of knowing how to operate a computer. If you are looking for a job with "digital" in the title, you had better make sure you don't have to call for help because your coffee cup snapped off the CD-ROM tray in your workstation. You should know what the parts of your computer are called and (roughly) what they do. You should also have a basic understanding of how to use your computer's operating system and be able to perform simple tasks such as saving a file, formatting a diskette, sending and checking email, changing your password, and printing a document. If you have to call tech support for any of these tasks, you need to read one of those books with the word *idiot* or *dummy* in the title. It's also a really good idea for you to know how to pronounce computer and compositing jargon before you go to an interview. If you confidently mispronounce a common term of art, your credibility will suffer. You might still get the job, but starting off as a water cooler joke is probably not what you had in mind.

Compositor Profiles

Following are some biographical background, comments, and advice from professional digital compositors.

Chris Bond, President, Frantic Films

Currently fulfilling my role as a budding young VFX Supervisor and President of Frantic Films, I have been working in the field of computer graphics since 1991. I first started out as a student at the School of Fine Arts at the University of Manitoba, which promptly led to a keen interest in the newly emerging "computer art" field. After purchasing the fastest-possible PC computer (a 486-DX33 with 20MB of RAM) and choosing the best 3D software from the two packages available (3D Studio R2 DOS), I quickly threw myself into production. After a brief freelance career, I spent nearly three years at Manlab as Autodesk/Kinetix tech support and as an animator, producing everything from award-winning television commercials to interactive CD-ROMs and kiosks.

I then started working in freelance production while teaching 3D animation part-time at a local college. During that time, I worked for a short while in preproduction and demo production of the Sony PlayStation game "Crime Killer" with PixeLogic UK.

Making a quick move back into television and film, I started Frantic Films in March of 1997 with my business partner, Ken Zorniak. Over the course of 1997, I worked on some incredible local and national projects—including openers for the Woman's Television Network and commercials for the Royal Winnepeg Ballet. We finished the year by winning more awards and getting our work onto vendor's reels and having it shown at several booths at NAB (National Association of Broadcasters) and SIGGRAPH. One of the *Sesame Street* segments that I produced was purchased by the Children's Television Workshop for the next six years and will show in over 155 countries. (I'm just glad I can influence that many children with my wild ideas of "cooperation.") Recently, I wrapped up my work with Boyd Shermis on the Stephen King miniseries *Storm of the Century*, and I am looking forward to other large-scale projects.

My role models are VFX supervisors like Boyd Shermis, Richard Hollander, and others, who focus on bringing the impossible to reality on a 70-foot screen—and consistently pull it off. My favorite pieces of compositing are shots you don't know aren't real. They are the hardest to achieve, and because of their nature, the most overlooked. That being said, one really nice *Face/Off* shot of a guy flying toward a wind tunnel and *Titanic*'s engine room sequences were both done by the now-defunct VIFX. *The Matrix* had some really nice compositing work. Of my own work, my current favorite is the work we did on *Storm of the Century* for ABC. This involved heavy amounts of snow/fog/water spray on miniatures, with a heck of a lot of 3D camera moves. Fun stuff.

My daily work is always changing. Grunt work like line removal or rotoscoping is covered by trainees/interns or whoever is unlucky enough to get it. I'm handling most of the senior compositing chores, which basically means I figure out how the shots are going to be done, and then I set up a standard for the other compositors to follow. We currently have five seats of 3D and five seats of 2D compositing, and so we move things around as we see fit.

In reality, about 0 to 70 percent of my time is spent compositing, depending on the job. In a typical workweek of 60 to 70 hours, I may spend three or four days on compositing—although this all changes depending on the job. Right now, for example, I'm heavily involved in two shots where the bulk of the work is done in the 3D world and compositing will only be a small percentage of the final job. But on *Storm of the Century*, compositing was three to four times the work of the 3D CG elements. Every job is different.

We work with both outside VFX supervisors and directly with clients. Basically, one of us gets assigned to that client and works through it with them—sort of as a producer. The larger the job, the bigger the team, and the more experience the senior person has to have. Either way, it's worked well. I really think you need to have one or two central people the client can feel comfortable talking to. All financial issues go through one person, though—we don't make the artists deal with any of that.

Right now, everyone wants to be an animator. That's because it's seen as the "big" thing to do. ("Look at me! Just like Disney, mom!") But most people just don't have the talent to be animators—and most of them don't want to work that hard. I think the same thing will happen to compositing: There will be a rush to become a compositor, and more schools will have it as an option. But it's hard, critical work, and many people won't make the cut.

From the other perspective, however—from ours, as digital compositors—I think that compositing is becoming easier, so shots are becoming harder. The impossible is happening on a 70-foot screen (didn't I say that already?), and everyone is out to play make believe. And once you can do that, it's not going to go away.

Advice To Future Digital Compositors

Anyone who walks through my door and shows talent and enthusiasm has an opportunity. 3D work is a help, programming experience an asset, but it all comes down to design. Do they have a portfolio? Print? Animations? Paint? A background in film could certainly be of help, but the reality is that our world is so different from that. I don't think a filmmaker could come sit down and be any better at compositing than a 2D animator over the same amount of time. It's all about the individual, how they think and what kind of talent they have. It's all art.

I think digital compositing is all about composition (duh!) and color. Therefore, we like to take in 2D artists, probably trained in paint, although we've had some luck with some other design disciplines. For example, we have an architecture graduate working with us right now designing broadcast openers for a fashion TV series.

Traditional art training is really important because it's about composition and color; I don't think nonartists can do it. I don't really believe in formal education or training for digital compositing. It's my opinion that 99 percent of educational facilities are years behind the industry. Schools that move ahead and really do a great job (Sheridan College in Ontario) have students that command positions at top facilities—something we can't compete with (yet).

Work hard. Work with color—*lots*. Learn all about Box versus Gaussian versus Sinc versus Lanczos . . . because you have to know all this stuff. Successful digital composition is about understanding visual continuity and having an eye for detail, good color sense, enthusiasm, and of course, patience.

Digital compositing involves technical skill too. The thing we're looking for most, in my opinion, is that I'm the only one at our studio who really, truly understands gamma/multiplication, and so on, along with the issues going on behind the software, so we're really looking for people who are savvy in this area. As time goes on, our people are learning this—but it would be nice if they had a better understanding of what's going on when you do an add versus a multiply.

The hardest part to learn is all the technical stuff. It's great to have a billion types of blurs at your fingertips, but what are all those anti-aliasing features for? What are they best suited for? I don't have time in the real world to experiment with film-res composites and see how different filters perform, and from a viewing perspective, I'm tired of seeing bad post effects that use the wrong blurs for the wrong thing. (Did you see the defocus in *Star Trek: Insurrection* using a box blur? It was *so* obvious!)

Tailor your demo reel to the job or client. It's been my experience that VFX supervisors that want to hire you for CG/real composites couldn't care less about the glossy broadcast work you did for a station ID.

Frantic Films
420-70 Arthur Street
Winnipeg, Manitoba
Canada R3B 1G7
204-949-0070
204-949-0050 fax
info@franticfilms.com
www.franticfilms.com

Dylan Crooke, Managing Director, Momentum Animations

I have been involved with digital compositing for the past five years. My first taste of it was doing music videos and having to overlay 3D and 2D graphics. Simple stuff, but it taught me the basics. I was a freelance digital artist for about a year, working wherever I could, doing anything I could, as long as it was on computers and (I hoped) went on TV. After a while, I decided that I didn't really like the work that I was getting and started my own company, Momentum Animations. Hoping to focus on character animation for the broadcast market, we got off to a great start. Our first-ever job was a character animation piece for a big computer show. We had 20 layers of 3D animation that we had to composite using text-based IFL files in an early version of 3D Studio. Boy, was that painful.

But it led to our next job, an opener for a TV show called *World's Greatest Commercials*. This was a huge job for us. We had to composite TV sets on custom-made stands into locations around the studio, and we had exterior and interior shots. It was our first real go at compositing work. We

Dylan Crooke

only did locked-off camera shots, because we were pretty scared and we didn't want to mess it up. Three of us worked for two months, got the job done, and the clients were rapt.

So after that, the work started flowing in. We've since done jobs for some major commercial clients, including work for Singapore and one of our biggest jobs: four minutes of special effects for a show called *Oz Encounters*. Now, like many people, we are moving toward a feature-film project and a TV series.

I really like the compositing and effects work in *Independence Day*; it was the first stuff that I actually sat in the cinema and said "wow" out loud. The real sense of mayhem and action they created was outstanding, and the sheer amount of jets and spacecraft in the battle scenes was very impressive.

My favorite examples of my own work are some of the shots for the *Oz Encounters* program. I did one shot (I think it's the only handheld shot we did) where the camera is shaking around, looking at a huge spaceship (that we put in) with blue beams below it touching the ground. I got the motion tracking spot-on, and the final shot is really believable. Unfortunately, the editor of the show decided to cut it up into three shots, and some of the impact was lost. Oh, well.

Momentum Animations has now moved out of the effects side of things. The only compositing we do is purely for rendered 3D layers. As of this writing, we are working on a feature film project. Almost every shot is composited in some way, usually to save time re-rendering backgrounds, but also to create depth-of-field shots and desaturate the backgrounds to suit the style we want to achieve.

We don't really have standard days, as we are faced with different challenges constantly for each shot. But mostly the compositing part of our production is about 20 percent of the total workload. We use Adobe After Effects all the time. (Obviously, Photoshop is used in conjunction with it.) We chose AE because the people we had here at the time all knew how to use it, and it runs on a Mac, which is good too. It's a bit fiddly to use, but it's incredibly powerful.

Our clients generally don't know much about the technical side of what we do, but they are very clued in to the creative and aesthetic aspects of a job. We try to explain things very clearly and make sure we have good contact with them throughout production. Most of the time, you need to understand their job and what their own client wants, as well as to anticipate any problems. You have to always realize that you are responsible for the job, even if you get a client that doesn't really care what you do.

I think digital compositing is becoming a very standard tool in modern TV and cinema, and we will see more and more of it. A lot of it will no doubt be terrible and badly done, but this will make all the good work stand out even more. I think that it can only be a good thing that people are creating this kind of work. There will still be good stories to tell and bad stories to tell, so just make sure you're involved with the good ones. I certainly think that audiences will get used to the technology and, therefore, become less impressed.

Advice To Future Digital Compositors

Practice! How else are you going to get good?

If you want to work in this business, you need a strong understanding of the tools and techniques of compositing. You also need an understanding of how to get the job out to the final medium, a strong aesthetic judgment, the ability to logically and quickly set up a process for how to approach a particular job or shot, and most important, experience. You can get this by messing around in Photoshop with a lot of layers. I don't know of any courses here in Melbourne that specifically teach digital compositing. The best way to learn is to find someone who does it that you know or to do some work somewhere. Next best thing: Get on the Internet and do a search for "digital compositing." That'll keep you busy for a while.

We learned heaps by talking to people on the Internet. Most people are very accessible and easy to find. Just bug them. Let them know you are interested, and they will be more than happy to share their techniques and discoveries with you. It's quite amazing how the industry people share their knowledge. It just shows how everyone's goals are the same: to make stuff that people can go "wow" at.

I studied fine art in high school and went on to study fine art for a year at university. My opinion is that it's a total waste of time. As long as you spend your time creating visual work and studying other people's work, you should arrive at the right place and not have to bother with all that art history stuff. (Unless, of course, that's what you want.)

I think the essential part of compositing is this: You need to understand the way people use the medium that you are working in. To understand it, you must study, analyze, and criticize it. Then you must re-create it in your own way, that is pleasing to you and (hopefully) to your audience.

When we are hiring, I look for someone with a strong aesthetic sense, but mostly I look for someone who knows the tools we use and works hard and fast to create fantastic-looking shots. There's no doubt about it, a shot works or it doesn't; you don't need years of experience to see whether something is believable or not.

My only advice is that if you want to become successful in any industry, you should seek out and learn as much as possible about the industry. We've had so many people come through here complaining that there aren't any courses or that they are interested in compositing but can't find any information about it. What a load of rubbish. All they need to do is jump on the Net, go to a library, watch a bunch of films, go to some festivals, meet some filmmakers, et cetera, et cetera. Nothing annoys me more than people who don't go out and make things happen for themselves.

I'm always getting emails from people saying, "Oh, you guys are so good. I'll never be that good." What a load of crap! If everyone took that attitude, nothing would ever get made. Just three years ago, we wrote a letter to Pixar asking for information; they were *gods* to us. Last year, we made a short film called *Macca Strewth,* and it got shown in a bunch of film festivals, along with *Geri's Game*. Of course, our film was technically nowhere near *Geri's Game*, but it was totally cool being on the same screen as a Pixar production.

Momentum Animations
6 Salisbury Street
North Caulfield 3161
Melbourne, Victoria
Australia
+61-3-9500-1142
+61-3-9500-1194 fax
dylan@momentumanimations.com
www.momentumanimations.com

Sherry Hitch, Supervising Visual Effects Compositor, Foundation Imaging

I am currently a Supervising Visual Effects Compositor at Foundation Imaging. I have been with the company since 1993 and have been compositing professionally for most of that time. I attended the Herron School of Art in Indianapolis and discovered an interest in visual effects while majoring in TV/Film at Ball State University and experimenting with Cubicomp graphic computers and Amiga Video Toasters. I worked in the Video Information Service production facility at Ball State for three years, learning to create CGI animation. I was also active as a student member and officer of the National Broadcasting Society, Women in Communication, and International Television Association. I also worked as a Production Assistant (PA) for several local and network productions.

After relocating to California, I worked as a college intern on CBS's *The Young and the Restless*, researching materials, writing synopses, and assisting with all areas of production. Eventually I discovered the Henry bay on the studio lot, where I got a good look at high-end graphic systems for the first time. I then did preproduction work for a marketing firm. In 1993, I landed a job as CGI modeler on a low-budget feature that eventually "went south."

Sherry Hitch

The silver lining was that I had met Steve Pugh (currently the General Manager here) through the low-budget production and was hired on at Foundation Imaging as a PA for the first season of *Babylon 5*. Based on my previous graphics experience and Ron Thornton's approval of my student reel, I was given the chance to composite and animate screen displays during *B5*'s second season, using Photoshop and After Effects. By the end of the season, I had assisted Kevin Kutchaver and Mitch Suskin in pulling bluescreens, as well as doing split mattes, color correcting, and some roto work. Following my success in season two, I was promoted to senior digital compositor for the third season, which won a Sci-Fi Universe Award for Best Visual Effects for Television.

Following *Babylon 5*, I have worked on *Hypernauts*, *Star Trek: Voyager*, the animated film *Subzero: Batman vs. Mr. Freeze*, the NBC comedy special *steve.oedekerk.com*, the sitcom *You Wish* on ABC, the film *The Jackal*, a few shots for NBC's drama *Players*, and the kids' show *Mystic Knights of Tir Na Nog*. While moonlighting from Foundation, I worked on a few shots from the opening titles for *Men in Black*, the USA telefilm *Panic in the Skies*, and the Martin Sheen/Luke Perry film *Storm*. As of this writing, I am working on a commercial for the Sci-Fi Channel, the grand finale of *Star Trek: Deep Space Nine*, a new all-CGI television series *Starship Troopers*, a telefilm for FOX called *St. Patrick*, and the upcoming comedy film, *The Specials*.

When I saw *Jurassic Park* for the first time, I was amazed at how good everything matched to make the dinosaurs look like they were really there. I was blown away! I was especially impressed with the scenes that had a moving, sweeping camera with CGI dinosaurs and the actors. I realize a lot of people, including myself, were extremely impressed with the CGI dinosaurs and their movement—*but* a lot of their believability also has to do with the compositing. If their colors were off or the lighting was at all wrong or the shadows were in the wrong direction, we wouldn't have believed they were actually in the scene, and thus we wouldn't have believed the whole exciting movie experience.

Kevin Kutchaver is someone whom I've respected for many years now. He was the one who basically taught me a heck of a lot about After Effects and compositing. Kevin is now a partner in the visual effects house Flat Earth and has worked on many, many features and television shows, such as *Return of the Jedi*; *Ghostbusters*; *Dreamscape*; *Robocop*; *Big Trouble in Little China*; *The Addams Family*; *Honey, I Shrunk the Kids*; *Star Trek VI: The Undiscovered Country*; *Toys*; *The Shadow*; and *Blade*, just to name a few. Then there's television, such as the first two seasons of *Babylon 5*, and all episodes of *Hercules: The Legendary Journeys* and *Xena: Warrior Princess*. Kevin has created effects from the optical method through the current digital way, all with his own unique and personal style.

In my opinion, Kevin is the greatest animator of special-effects lightning in the business. Kevin also has taught me a lot about quicker methods to getting the same job done, which is essential in this day of the effects business—especially for television, where the turnaround time for effects to be done can sometimes be only a few days.

The favorite piece of work that I've done would have to be this one single shot that I did for the NBC television drama, *Players*. It was very challenging on all aspects of compositing. It had bad greenscreen, a background that needed to be stabilized and warped to match the camera lens, and lots of bright light to light the actor properly. It also needed to be color-corrected because it was supposed to be nighttime. Plus, we needed to paint some set extensions to continue the side of the building down to the street, track and change the color of the cars in the scene, and add a depth of field to the shot. I had only a few days to complete the shot, so it really got my brain cells excited! I got it done, and I have been able to use it as an example for demos for compositing.

Foundation Imaging
24933 West Avenue Stanford
Valencia, CA 91355
www.foundation-i.com

Eric Jorgenson, Chief Engineer, Video Workshop

It is fun, and if you can't appreciate the creative joy of doing it, then probably you should be doing something else.
—Eric Jorgenson

At Video Workshop, we have been doing traditional compositing for about 10 years, and we were experimenting with it before then—before we were a broadcast-quality facility. We started out with 3/4-inch tape, and we've been around for about 20 years. We were strictly industrial-quality at first. It's been interesting to follow the whole history of video special effects through the years, and it's nice to have that history as a background to give a perspective as to what's happening with computers.

We added digital compositing to our toolset about a year ago when After Effects came out for the PC. Prior to that, because we have a linear suite, we were compositing through video switchers. So we're certainly no stranger to compositing, but we were using the traditional linear edit suite techniques and multigeneration tape passes. We are now a 1-inch tape facility, which is very good as far as multigenerational tape capacity and stuff like that. So we have experimented over the years with many different layers of composited material and had very good luck with maintaining quality using traditional methods. But, of course, your palette of possibilities is much more limited when you are dealing with systems like that, and a program like AE really expands your capabilities quite dramatically.

Of course, a lot of the techniques and fundamentals remain the same. Keying and matting and all that kind of thing grows out of the motion-picture techniques that were developed back at the beginning.

The way I got into the video business was as a salesman for this company. I was the first employee and always approached things with a technical outlook. I immediately got us into system configurations. When I got into the business, there were a lot of interesting things happening—time base correction, video news gathering, color cameras, that sort of thing. So I've pretty much been in from the beginning.

When I was in college, the Video Rover Portapack from Sony was kind of the tool of the day, and I took a course, Video as an Art Form, from some crazy lady from the Manhattan art crowd. It was total guerrilla video; just try anything. It was kind of fun to have video free improvisation. There were no technical parameters at all; it was just video as a medium to express yourself. And I think it's come back to that now, really, with video being so accessible these days. It's really a fun, creative tool, and I admire people who can take advantage of that aspect of it.

I graduated with a degree in economics, which doesn't offer a whole lot of potential. In college, I worked in the AV department, carrying around projectors and that sort of thing. Fortunately, the school I went to, the University of Rochester, was fairly well-to-do, and they decided they were going to put together a little video production facility. I was really lucky. There was a guy there whose father was the vice president in charge of engineering at ABC. So he was really a bigwig, and his bailiwick was engineering. In fact, his kid used to go down to the national conventions and work, handling frequency allocations and stuff. He knew a lot about video because he had been hanging around it his whole life. I learned a lot of technical things from him, and he was a good influence on me.

I liked video, and I actually started looking for a video-related job while I was still in college. Because cable TV was just coming into Portland at that time, it was an obvious place for me to work. That is what started off the Video Workshop. At the time, I kept going to the general manager for the yet-to-be cable company and asking him about origination and public access and all that kind of thing. And he said they were not interested, that all they wanted to do was pipe the programs to people's homes and send them the bill. However, because Portland was one of the new markets that had just been opened up by the FCC, the city started making demands on the cable companies as conditions to set up the franchise. One of the conditions was to set up these public-access studios. I checked that out, realized that the cable company was going to have to do it, and actually offered these people a proposition that we would manage all their local origination and public-access facilities for them so they wouldn't have to deal with it. And that's where the Video Workshop came from, out of Maine Video Systems. Cable TV bought $100,000 worth of video equipment and put us in charge of operating it, and we actually created a private company around that. We were sort of the production end of Maine Video Systems at that time, and it paid for our equipment.

So, it was kind of lucky; we actually started the company fully equipped, with no outlay of capital, just in exchange for managing local origination and public access. Unfortunately, it was destined for failure just because of the political aspects of public TV and cable access. It turned out to be a political football, where there were a lot of vested interests (including our own). We were obviously interested in making money, and other people were more interested in getting on television, so clashes were inevitable. Sooner or later, people with enough political clout were able to terminate our agreement with cable TV. But by that time, we had established a clientele, and we were really the first people around doing that kind of thing.

From that point, we just kind of built on the base we had developed and continued on, step-by-step. A number of years later, we moved into this building; and a number of years after that, we built this suite, which was about 10 years ago. And that kind of got us into the broadcast-quality region. In the mid- to late '80s, there was really a post-production boom happening, especially in Portland, because Portland was really an advertising center. This might sound kind of funny because Portland isn't that big a city. But for northern New England, there just happened to be a lot of different interests here, and Portland was supporting 30 or 40 ad agencies at the time. Most of them were one-employee shops, but it was really amazing that there was so much activity in Portland. That all changed during the '90s. The boom went bust, primarily because the banks all merged and went out of state and because of various other factors. So things really died right down in the early '90s.

But we managed to survive because we weren't totally into broadcast. Actually, we became more of a nonbroadcast house, as far as actual percentage of work, dealing with outside producers who were into producing videos for training or whatever. Again, with our corporate connections as being a video dealer, we had all the necessary contacts. We managed to maintain a very consistent business right up to the present, and we have done OK.

And now we're interested in continuing that. We're obviously at a transition point for video right now. All the traditional analog/linear equipment is becoming obsolete. Digital is taking over, and we want to participate in that. We're not afraid of that change, even though we have a lot invested in analog technology. Actually, we did it right. Because we started 10 years ago, all this equipment is long since paid for. We're going to keep this room (the linear editing suite) pretty much intact—not as a museum, but because a lot of people still like to work this way. There are certain advantages to the traditional techniques, one being speed. It really is faster to put something together in a traditional linear suite, as long as you don't want to mess around with it and you know what you want to do. It's just a matter of queuing up the tape and editing it into a program, which is similar to digitizing your source material in the nonlinear world. In NLE, that's just the start. The tweaking process can go on interminably. But in linear, you're done.

It's sort of like with audio: You'll have some analog people who will never say die. You will never convince them that analog is inferior to digital. The same sort of sensibility exists in video. It's kind of quaint.

We're also looking not only at digital as far as NLE, but also at high definition. That's definitely coming, and we want to participate in it. We're looking ahead to that and seeing how we can make a smooth transition to high-definition production.

Regarding digital compositing, I've always been of the opinion that people are just scratching the surface of what is potentially doable. It's like when 3D computer animation first came out. You have to do the simple things first. The subtle things, the things that really have an idea behind them, I haven't seen. I haven't been blown away yet. Everything I've seen up to this point seems somewhat experimental. People are a little tentative in working out creative ideas. Every once in a while, though, you see something that impresses you.

Certainly, I've seen a lot of shots that were sort of technical tricks, and that fascinates me. But I think everyone is a little jaded by special effects at this point. It's seldom that I'm taken beyond the point where I'm emotionally involved with a scene rather than technically picking it apart. In *Contact*, the look that they imparted on the planet sequence, just the sort of overall colorization effect, really grabbed me. I thought that was really interesting; how it imparted this kind of otherworldly atmosphere and how it altered perception a little bit. I think those are interesting directions to go. To get more into the mind and mess around is, to me, a fun potential application.

Our company is a little different. We have always worked with clients directly. Clients come in here to edit. They sit down, and they want to be involved. You want to keep their interest level up, and the linear editor is great for that—spinning reels, noise, audio tape, and all that. Participating in the creative process is fun for them, and it's fun for me too. But when you're working on a nonlinear system, it tends to be much more individual. Working with clients in an NLE session (if you're doing sort of the background work, and just working things out rather than turning out finished movies), it's difficult for clients to follow, and it puts them at a distance from the whole process. They go through sensory deprivation. So anything that speeds up the creative process is great if you're dealing with clients. The ICE board is great when you're composing in After Effects, because it renders frames almost instantaneously, and you can create these tremendous atmospheric effects by adding layer upon layer of filter effects. Otherwise, you'd just be sitting around for a minute or two without acceleration.

Acceleration is also great from the client standpoint. They can see our work and compare it to a competitor's, who isn't as up to snuff as we are, and they realize it's going to get done more quickly here. And, of course, it increases our rates. But it just makes it more fun to create with these systems where you're not just twiddling your thumbs waiting for something to happen. It definitely encourages you to experiment more. Playing with blurs and fogs slows down the rendering enormously. To be able to put all that back in and still get fast feedback makes it easier to play and experiment. And with that experience, you can get more sophisticated in your use of the tools.

We don't do as much compositing as we'd like commercially because people around here are not that sophisticated. If we could instigate a lot of creative ideas, I think we could do a lot more with compositing. Clients just aren't aware of what's possible. They'll come out of left field and ask about something they may have seen on another program. Very seldom do they come up with something original. On the other hand, the producers we deal with tend to be pretty technically savvy. They know what's possible.

We've done a number of things, like the talking cow for Oakhurst Dairy. We had one spokesman who thought he was blinking too much, so we removed his blinks, which was kind of fun. We did a spot where a glass materializes out of a TV screen and flies into a woman's hand and she takes a drink. So at one point it's a 3D CGI glass and the next it's real. It was kind of fun to figure out how to do that. It would be great to get into more kinds of things like that.

However, we actually avoid getting involved in creative decisions just because we don't want to compete with ad agencies and independent producers, whom we consider our bread and butter. That's just a decision that we made, as opposed to a lot of our local competition who sell themselves as being soup-to-nuts production facilities and want to get heavily involved in creative decisions. When we are working with an agency, we see ourselves as strictly the technician or the editor or the cameraman or whatever. On the graphics we can get a little more creative. Generally, we eschew creative input.

Advice To Future Digital Compositors

I think the best thing is just to have a creative drive. I was so excited when I was a kid. I was so into getting myself into video and just immersed myself in the whole technology; I couldn't get enough of it. And I just don't see that level of excitement very often in young people now. They seem to be a little jaded. But every once in a while, you find someone who has really got the bug. And I think that someone has got to have the desire to get into this type of work. It is fun, and if you can't appreciate the creative joy of doing it, then probably you should be doing something else because it is a fun business. If you can't appreciate it, why do it? It's always fun to see your commercials on TV. That's one of the side benefits of the job.

The other thing is, it's becoming so accessible now. You can buy some of these Kai's Power Goo-like programs for 40 bucks, put them on a PC, and just mess around. I think that stuff is great, and it's going to be even more accessible in the future. Really, the technical end of the business is just going to become relatively unimportant. And maybe it's a bad thing to give too much free reign to creativity. It's like all the MIDI instruments. In a way, it took a little bit out of being a virtuoso musician—when you can just program a computer note by note to play a song. I hope the same thing won't happen to video. I don't think it will, because video is kind of starting from scratch, whereas music has been around for a long time. But just being able to grab a camcorder and go out and make your movie—it can be fantastic. There's no reason why a kid now can't go out and make a *Jurassic Park* and do a pretty reasonable job at pulling it off—as long as that kid has the knowledge base and the desire to do it. That's tremendous. It may not be quite to the level of Spielberg, but you can come up with a reasonable facsimile.

Again, compositing is like playing music. It's half studying and practicing and coming up with the knowledge base and observing. But the other half is a sort of innate ability that you really either have or you don't. There are people who are natural born directors who have the vision. That's something that's always impressed me. I see a lot of people in various situations come and go here who are interested in video in one way or another, and a lot of them are just totally crazy people. But anyone who has a vision, even if someone comes in and says something like, "I'm going to make *Beowulf*," I'll do whatever I can to help them realize that vision. I'll support all who have a vision, even if they are a little bit crazed.

To become a digital compositor, ultimately you just have to get your hands on the tools. Some kind of a school program might be nice, but it's not totally necessary. I think you have to develop an interest in the subject matter. Certainly, the most interesting things are either in feature films or in television commercials these days. So the stuff is out there for people to look at and for kids to become curious about. I think studying film and the history of film is important, because having a historical perspective helps in all this stuff. Knowing what's possible and how today's effects are built on fond memories that we developed years ago is important and can really motivate you.

Video Workshop
495 Forest Avenue
Portland, ME 04101
207-774-7798

Tom Williamson, Visual Effects Supervisor, Computer Cafe, Inc.

As Visual Effects Supervisor/VP, I manage feature film and commercial production. My responsibilities include script breakdown, budgeting, technical direction, project scheduling, and on-set supervision. I am also one of the senior artists with responsibilities including 3D animation, 3D modeling, compositing, morphing, image processing, and rotoscoping. In addition, I am lead programmer and have designed several pieces of proprietary software for use on Intel, DEC Alpha, and Windows CE devices.

My days are nuts; when I'm not on the box, I'm on the phone or in a meeting. I work with supervisors on films, and in essence, they are the client. But I also work with regular clients from agencies and private companies. Because of our location, we tend to do most of our business by phone and the Internet. With our recent opening of our Santa Monica office, however, we hope to get more face-to-face.

I started on my professional career in 1988 on the remake of *The Blob*. Back then, I was a mechanical designer for the make-up/creature effects industry. I worked for several years at various shops on over 20 feature films, such as *The Addams Family*, *Army of Darkness*, and *A Nightmare on Elm Street 5*.

I started experimenting with digital compositing in 1993. Back then, we used Amiga computers, and the software we used were solutions such as Opal Paint, Art Department Pro, and ImageFX.

Tom Williamson

About the same time, I joined forces with David Ebner, Jeff Barnes, and Ron Honn to build a small FX house on the central coast; thus Computer Cafe was born. We are presently working on our twelfth feature film, *The Crow: Salvation*. We also have so many broadcast design and commercial credits, it's getting hard to remember them all. For a full list of the Cafe's work, go to **www.computercafe.com**. For my full credit list, go to **www.best1.net/~tomcat/Pro_Page/Resume/Credits/credits.html**.

Some of my favorite compositing work was on *Star Kid*. We did some great stuff. That film was a major breakthrough for our company. We did over 213 visual effects on that movie, and it was only our second film. We also did the Sylvia sequence in *Flubber*; that turned out great. Our shots in *Armageddon* got some major exposure. They are all in every promo for the movie that I've personally seen, and they are the backgrounds on the DVD. My favorite single composite was for (dare I say it?) *Barney's Great Adventure!* I had to make a baby say "Barney." It was tough, but I came up with a pretty clever solution.

In the near future, I hope to see the merger of film, digital, and HDTV technologies. I'm looking forward to a fully digital cinematic experience, and it will increase the productivity and throughput immensely. I can't wait to be able to shuttle through film res frames like I do with video now. I know that Lucasfilm is really advancing the state of the art, and I'm working with software and hardware providers to fulfill my wish list.

Advice To Future Digital Compositors

First, get a computer. You need to know how to get around and to have a good basic knowledge of computing. Next, get a camcorder and a copy of Adobe Premiere or Macromedia Director, and start compositing and layering. Learn to make images merge together.

You need to know computers, maybe not all of the more popular operating systems, but at least one. Most of the professional compositing software is out of the price range of the private user, and that's where the schools come in. They have the gear and the software (if you can get the lab time). You can't expect to master every package out there; stick with one and learn it well. Once you know it, the others will be easy to learn later.

You need an eye for composition, color, and style. Most people tend to think of compositing as some sort of jigsaw puzzle, and you just need to figure out the order. But it is an art, and the machines need to be staffed by artists.

Traditional art training is beneficial, yes; important or necessary, no. I have no formal training. I believe you are born with artistic skill; it can't be learned, only honed. It's like going to school to be tall—you just can't.

I look for the right attitude, first of all. We are always accepting reels and résumés, and we get dozens a week. Occasionally, one comes in that really catches our eye, and we'll call that person. I personally think that a good attitude is more important than fully developed skill. We can make you a better artist, but not a better person.

The toughest part to learn? The whole film-versus-digital issue, aspect ratios, color depth, 3:2 pull-down, pull-up, key numbers, et cetera, et cetera. The whole thing's enough to give you a brain cramp. You really need to know both film and video, in addition to computers, to make them all play nice together.

Computer Cafe, Inc.
3130 Skyway Drive, Suite 603
Santa Maria, CA 93455
805-922-9479
805-922-3225 fax
www.computercafe.com

Moving On

This chapter provided you with a clear picture of your opportunities as a digital compositor, the kinds of work you can expect to do, and the types of colleagues and mentors with whom you will be working. This information should enable you to make better-informed decisions about your tools, training, and career. The next chapter introduces you to the other members of the production team—the people you will rely on and who will, in turn, rely on you.

THE REST OF THE TEAM

Digital compositing is usually only part of the production process. This chapter presents a brief introduction to the other artists, technicians, and businesspeople who contribute to a typical production.

One of the most liberating aspects of the revolution in digital cinematography is that you really can do it all yourself. Software tools exist that can assist you in doing screenwriting; storyboard and layout art; CGI modeling and animation; video and audio digitizing; record keeping; financial and scheduling project management; music composition and recording; audio and video mixing and editing; title design; compositing; and film or video recording.

The question is, do you want to handle it all? If you really have a driving, unique artistic vision that you feel only you can realize, then more power to you (just don't try to be your own agent and attorney, as well). If you prefer to concentrate on one specialty and do it well, then more power to you also. Whatever your approach, you need to know something about the other professions and trades associated with film and video production. I hope this information will help you become a more effective compositor, whether you pursue an independent career or join one of the growing number of effects houses.

Meet The Team

Most production studios have an organizational structure with similar job titles, although the actual responsibilities of the people vary from studio to studio. Generally, the larger the organization, or the bigger the project, the more people will specialize and the more specific their job titles. Because this is a relatively new field, and many shops are highly flexible, you will run across unique job titles that are difficult to fit into the traditional studio hierarchy. Following are some generalizations about the most common job titles current in the industry.

The Major Players

The following listing describes the upper stratosphere of industry jobs:

- *Executive Producer*—Whenever you hear a job title that contains the word *executive*, this generally means the bearer can execute anyone on the production. Seriously, *executive* generally means they have control of finances. An executive producer can shut down a production, or—when necessary—go to bat with the studio for additional resources. Although the exec producer is definitely one of the dreaded studio suits, this person is responsible for seeing that you get paid.

- *Producer*—A producer is the general coordinator of a production. The producer is responsible for seeing that the director and supervisors have the resources they need and that schedules and delivery criteria are met. Producers also deal with conflicts between the director and other top-echelon personnel.

- *Visual Effects Producer*—This is a relatively new title, and its place in the pecking order is not always clear. In some facilities, the visual effects, or VFX, producer actually outranks the director regarding effects production. In others, the VFX producer reports to the director but is otherwise the highest authority for effects production. Essentially, this position is a parallel to the traditional producer, who concentrates on live-action shoots. The creation of this position is in recognition that the financial and scheduling issues of effects production are materially different from those of live action and require a different kind of expertise.

- *Director*—The director is the person responsible for the overall product—for keeping the "big picture" clearly in sight. In smaller shops or on shorter projects, the director will go over the effects storyboards with you to make sure you understand the effect he or she is looking for. The director will also pass final judgment on your work. In effect, the director is a minor deity, answerable only to the executive producer or the client. Some directors will remind you of their status at every opportunity. Others will remind you of their rank only if you do something inadvisable, like continuing to disagree with them after they've made a decision. Voice your opinion once, diplomatically, then go along with whatever the director decides. Making the final decision is what the director gets paid for.

  Good directors can also be your best mentors. They generally have the most on-the-job experience of anyone on a production team, and they can be a treasure trove of knowledge and advice. Listen to their critiques carefully, consider their advice, and do your best to learn from their experience.

  The worst kind of director (from an effects point of view) is one who doesn't understand the time and effort necessary to create an effect in post-production. Occasionally, one of these directors will insist on treating effects like a live shoot, repeating "takes" until the director sees what he or she wants. If you ever have the misfortune to work for a director like this, make sure you save every version of your work. Odds are good that after wasting a lot of everyone's time, the director will come back to the first version.

- *Writer*—The writer develops the script. Unless there are rewrites, the writer has the least influence on the difficulty of your work as a compositor. In many cases, once the script has been translated to storyboards, all further development is done visually and the script is obsolete. The writer may still participate in story sessions, but any revisions from that point are collaborative efforts.

- *Storyboard Artist*—The conceptual or storyboard artist translates the written script to a series of sketches and revises, adds, or deletes sketches during story sessions. Because storyboard artists work in 2D, they can "cheat" or draw effects that are difficult to create. If you see a story sketch that is going to be a problem, point it out (diplomatically, of course) at the first opportunity. It's a lot easier to revise a story sketch than filmed elements or the finished comp.

- *Art Director*—The art director (and the entire art department, in larger organizations) is responsible for developing the overall look—the visual style—of the product. Like the storyboard artist, the art director can create 2D drawings of effects that are challenging to create; you will need to work closely with the VFX supervisor in negotiating with the art director to make sure the proposed effects can be created with available resources.

- *Visual Effects Art Director*—This position is an offshoot of the traditional art director, acknowledging that the job has become too complex for a generalist to do well. The art director still calls the shots for the overall style of the project, but the visual effects art director is responsible for those decisions as they affect VFX. This position is usually a half-notch above the VFX supervisor, because an art director can generally overrule any artist or art supervisor.

- *Visual Effects Supervisor*—The visual effects supervisor is responsible for parceling out the tasks to individual artists or teams, for supervising them in order to make deadlines and ensure quality, and to assist with troubleshooting and problem solving on the toughest problems. When an effect seems impossible, the VFX supervisor is the one who can make it happen. In recognition of their responsibilities and talents, these are the people who get to pick up an effects Oscar™ and other awards.

Set Crew

Depending on the size of the studio and the type of work it handles, there may be in-house crews for live-action set work. These include the camera, lighting, and grip departments. Shooting background plates and lock-down effects shots is simple and requires a minimum of time, personnel, and equipment. The standard camera crew is made up of at least four people, including the following positions.

- *Director of Photography*—The director of photography (DP) is responsible for the overall look of the shot and works with the director. The DP translates the director's needs into directions for the rest of the camera crew, and for the lighting and grip departments. On a major production, the DP may rarely touch the camera, leaving that work to the camera operator.

- *Camera Operator*—The camera operator actually runs the camera, switching it on and off, aiming it, and perhaps doing some maintenance as needed.

- *First Assistant Camera*—The first assistant cameraperson, or 1st AC (also called the "focus puller,") changes the camera focus during the shot, takes measurements, and does some camera maintenance.

- *Second Assistant Camera*—The second assistant cameraperson, or 2nd AC (also called the "clapper/loader") loads film into the magazines (mags), puts the clapper in front of the lens at the beginning of each shot, keeps notes on the film and camera settings for each shot, and assists in the operation and maintenance of the camera as needed.

Of course, there are a few optional members of the set crew that you may or may not see on a working set, as follows:

- *Motion Control Operator*—If the shot requires a camera move and you need multiple passes for different elements, you should use a motion-control camera rig. These rigs are expensive and require expert handling, so they usually come with their own crew. See Chapter 6 for details.

If you can use available light (the sun), you can skip the lighting department. If the shot is a lock-down, you can skip most of the grip department. Most shoots need a production assistant or two; for location shooting, make sure they drive pickup trucks.

Case Study 2.1
Sector Expander Commercial

By Lee Stranahan and David Hibsher

This case study goes behind the scenes of a commercial for an Italian watch called the Sector Expander. Propaganda, a Los Angeles/New York commercial and music video production company, produced the project. The VFX supervisor on the project was Ken Stranahan. He has a great résumé, including work on TV shows such as *Star Trek: The Next Generation*, *Space: Above and Beyond*, and *Sliders*. Propaganda producer Suzanne Preissler had put together a top-notch crew. Doug Liman, the director, had previously worked with both Ken and Suzanne on a commercial for Airwalk shoes. Liman had made a splash with the Miramax low-budget indie comedy *Swingers*. On that film, Liman acted as both director and director of photography. In fact, for much of the film, Liman was the camera operator as well. For this shoot, Liman had a solid and experienced cinematographer. Russell Carpenter had been behind the camera on *True Lies*, *Lawnmower Man*, and *Titanic*. At the time of shooting the Sector Expander commercial, Carpenter had not yet won his Oscar for Titanic, but he sure seemed like a safe bet. Ken jumped at the chance to work with him.

Commercials, like music videos, are often shot based on a treatment rather than a script. The treatment for the Sector Expander spot read more like a miniature film than a spot to hawk watches; it was a 1-minute sci-fi movie. The spot opens with the hitchhiking hero standing on

(Photo: Lee Stranahan)

Director Doug Liman (left), Visual Effects Supervisor Ken Stranahan (center), and Director of Photography Russell Carpenter.

an asteroid. A spaceship picks him up. The ship is full of pods, and each pod contains a species captured by the Alien Girl, who owns the ship. The hero is trapped but manages to break free, turns the tables on the Alien Girl by trapping her, and frees the other trapped aliens. (Doesn't that make you want to buy a watch?)

Ken hired an outside artist to design the aliens. Ken had to do this early in the production process, because some physical models of the aliens needed to be built for dressing the set. Also, the long process of modeling the aliens in LightWave and prepping them for animation (by adding bone structure, control handles, and so on) had to happen as early as possible. There were five different aliens, each of which had to look completely different from the other species.

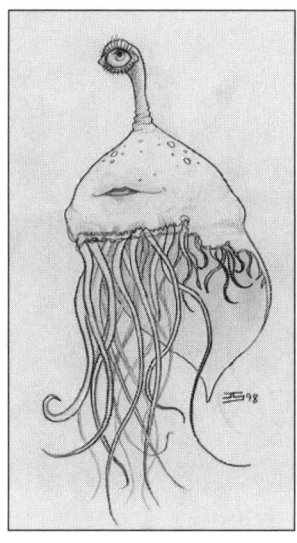 

An alien design sketch and a finished shot.

The two-day shoot was scheduled on a lot at Universal Studios in Universal City, California. There were a number of meetings to plan the shoot, which was complicated by the fact that the clients were in Europe. The design team created sketches for the set and creatures. I set up a Web site that was used for client approvals, but time and distance still caused a number of minor communication problems.

Ken and his team were involved from early in pre-production. This helped a lot, because the commercial was incredibly effects-heavy. Almost every shot had some sort of visual effect. With Ken's team being involved early, they were able to catch a lot of problems in time. Unfortunately, in production there are always things that take you by surprise.

The treatment called for one of the pods to drop down on the commercial's hero, capturing him. Originally, this was supposed to be done as a practical effect rather than using CGI elements. After the pods were built, it was obvious that the practical effect would not be possible. The pods were very heavy, and the idea of actually dropping one even a few feet brought visions of blood and gore effects not called for in the script (or covered by insurance).

There were always plans to build CGI versions of the pods (see the following images) to extend the set. It was cheaper to make the set appear larger through CGI than to rent a bigger stage, build a bigger set, and make more props. Animator David Hibsher was on set with Ken to take a look at the pods and to make notes for building the pods in LightWave. These notes included Hi-8 videotaping of the prop pods. The CGI version of the pods also had to be built in sections so they could telescope as they rose or dropped, rather than simply rising or falling as a single, rigid object. This effect would have been difficult, expensive, or impossible with a practical model.

 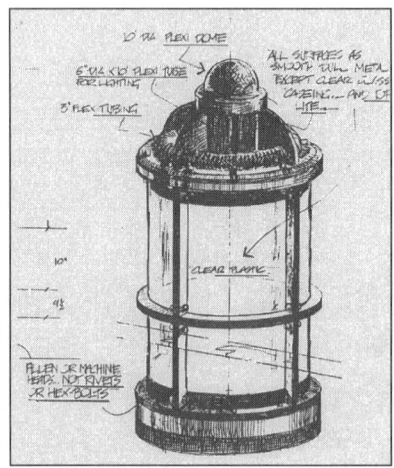 

Evolution of the pod design from concept art to blueprint to LightWave rendering.

For the set extension, Ken and David also made video notes of other parts of the set, especially the inside of the alien spacecraft, including the wall beams and windows. Another advantage of making videotaped notes is that they better capture the effects of lighting and fog than written notes can. These effects are vital to creating an effective set extension.

Photo: Lee Stranahan

VFX supervisor Ken Stranahan (left) and animator David Hibsher.

One place where written notes are a must, however, is in recording the camera data and motion. Several shots in this commercial called for live action to be composited with CGI. The LightWave camera must exactly mimic the attributes of the real camera to make the computer-generated parts appear to be on the set. The necessary camera data included the lens size, the height of the camera from the set floor, and the angle of the camera to the floor. The effects team recorded this data for every take of every shot, creating a pages-long list.

The effects team must also carefully record the motion of the camera. If the CGI camera does not faithfully reproduce the on-set camera moves, the composited objects will appear to slide around during the shot. Even slight mistakes can stick out like a sore thumb and can ruin the believability of the composite.

One particularly difficult shot called for the camera to dolly through the set while panning around a CGI pod that was composited in later. A C-stand placed on the set gave the camera operator a target during the move. This stand had to be digitally removed later. The beginning and ending camera positions had to be carefully calculated by triangulating from several reference points on the set. The position of the CGI pod also had to be calculated. The distance of the camera move and the best guess of the move's time had to be recorded, again for each take. Even with all the right data, manually matching camera moves in LightWave is tedious work.

The Alien Girl's appearance was another problem. Rather than using makeup, the director decided it would be better to give her a negative-image appearance digitally in post-production. Because it was impossible to isolate the Alien Girl from the background, this meant hours of work to draw the necessary matte. One of the effects team had to draw roto-mattes every frame or two in Digital Fusion, an extremely labor-intensive process.

This change also added to the overall complexity of the project's organization because it meant that a separate pass would be required to run effects on the Alien Girl. Suppose that a shot was planned where you could see out the windows of the spaceship, see the Alien Girl, and there was a moving pod as well. This shot would require at least three passes: one bluescreen keying pass to put the star field outside the window, one hand-roto pass to fix the Girl, and one pass in LightWave to add the animated CGI pod.

You can avoid some of these problems by very careful preproduction. However, this shoot proved that—even with experienced producers, directors, and crews—changes sometimes can and do happen at the last minute. Why? Because production days, being expensive, are limited. Preproduction allows you to solve some problems before they occur, but some problems don't rear their ugly little heads until you actually see the actors and props on a lit set. The ability to roll with the punches is an important job skill for anyone in this business. Anyone can pass blame around, but if you want to work in this industry, you need to be the kind of person who can solve problems.

Lee Stranahan (**www.stranahan.com**) is a filmmaker, photographer, visual effects artist, and teacher who has taught thousands of people how to get more out of LightWave through seminars, videos, and CDs. He lives in Pasadena, CA.

David Hibsher (**www.netcom.com/~dhibsher/**) is a freelance animator in West Hollywood, CA, who has worked on *Star Trek: Deep Space Nine*, *Conan: The Adventurer*, Airwalk commercials, and other TV projects. As a technical writer and instructor for NewTek, he contributed to the LightWave 4.0 and 5.0 documentation.

Composition And Animation

Depending on the size, complexity, and aim of a project, you'll find the following compositing- and art-related specialists:

- *Supervising Compositor*—If the project is large, you may be working under a supervising compositor. Exact job titles and authorities vary from studio to studio. Usually, these are senior compositors who act as deputies for the director or VFX supervisor. You will probably receive your shot materials from the supervising compositor rather than the director. If you are new to the profession, the supervising compositor may become your mentor, helping you out on problem shots and giving you the benefit of experience. Take advantage of the opportunity to learn.

- *Digital Artist*—There are several flavors of digital artist, and (again) the larger the studio, the more specialized the job title. In addition to compositors, some studios have roto-matte artists, matte painters, and digimatte artists. Bearing a different title is simply a matter of getting very, very good at one particular specialty within the general area of digital compositing. One more job title, Commercial Digital Artist, is a recognition that advertising work requires a special kind of digital artist who can cope with insane schedules while turning out great work.

- *Animator*—This class of artist may have its own hierarchy, from Director of Animation through Supervising VFX Animator to VFX Animator. Titles and responsibilities vary according to the size of the studio, experience of the person, and whether it's a union shop. Essentially, these artists make things move. The top artists, character animators, can create the illusion of life and performances that garner Best Picture nominations. Lower-level animators make space-craft or flying logos zoom around. There is often some overlap between 3D CGI animation and the effects animation created by compositors. It's to your advantage to understand when you can do a better job, and when the shot should go to a 3D animator.

- *Technical Director*—In most shops, the technical director (TD) builds, textures, and lights CGI models that will be rendered for you to composite. The TD may also develop custom software tools. In larger shops, responsibilities for CGI modeling, lighting, textures, and setup may be separate job descriptions. In smaller shops, you may be doing all these tasks by yourself.

  The TD will usually provide you, the compositor, with rendered CGI elements. The TD may also provide you with additional technical specs on the rendering, such as light placement, color, and intensity. This information can make your work much easier, so cultivate your TDs and treat them well. TDs tend to have more computer skills, and a more analytical and engineering approach than other digital artists do, which has led to industry stereotypes about cultural conflicts between the two "tribes."

  When you take a problem to a TD, be diplomatic (as with all team members), and attempt to understand the TD's side of the problem. It's a good idea to learn the vocabulary of CGI. People are generally more receptive to suggestions if you speak their language. As a compositor, you do not need to know absolutely everything about CGI software or the particular computer hardware you use, just as you don't need to know how to make a pencil to use it effectively. However, more knowledge can be a good thing; just as in other arts, the artist who doesn't understand how the tools function and how they are made is at a disadvantage.

  Just like any other large business, the need for development and maintenance of specialized production tools at very large studios have necessitated more detailed TD-class job titles such as Computer Graphics Software Developers, System Administrators, and System Developers. Although these positions still call for a great deal of creativity, the jobs' formal requirements generally include a four-year degree in electrical engineering or computer science. At top shops, even the artists have to be able to work in Unix.

- *VFX Research & Development*—This relatively rare position is usually reserved for TDs or senior digital artists who are so gifted, they are more valuable pursuing research than doing grunt work. The phrase "special-effects wizard" is overused; but in this case, it's the simple truth. If you ever get a chance to see what one of these people is working on, be prepared to get your mind bent.

- *Telecine or Scanner Operator/Colorist*—Filmed elements have to get into the computer somehow. Depending on the quality required, these elements might come from a telecine machine (for video) or a film scanner. Either machine needs a skilled and experienced operator to produce the best results. The operator should also be a colorist, unless you really enjoy doing a lot of color correction in your comps. For smaller studios, telecine or film scanning is done through a service bureau. Larger studios have these facilities in-house. See Chapter 5 for details on the digitizing process.

- *Motion Capture Engineer*—This job title is becoming more common at effects studios. If your studio is creating video game footage or trying to animate a large number of humanoid CGI shots, you may have a motion capture, or *mocap*, facility in-house. Getting useful data from a mocap session is still a bit of a black art, so the engineer who runs the capture gear is a highly specialized and valuable member of the effects team. If you anticipate doing any 3D work, you should familiarize yourself with the tools for transforming mocap data into useful animation curves. Mocap can be used to drive compositing effects, too.

- *Technical Assistants*—At big shops like ILM, artists aren't expected to do their own backups and other computer administrivia. Technical assistants (TAs) take care of that. As an entry-level position, I suppose it's a great opportunity to learn.

Production Assistants, Gofers, And Peons

Someone has to pick up and deliver stuff, keep track of schedules and checklists, and make sure that nothing falls through the cracks. Effects production is even more detail-sensitive than live-action cinematography. Don't underestimate the importance of—or try to complete a major project without—these invaluable assistants. Treat them well; after all, someday you might be working for them!

Case Study 2.2
Snow Crash, *Star Trek: Voyager*, "Timeless"

By Steve Pugh, General Manager, Foundation Imaging

The following image is from one of several shots that make up the dramatic crash landing of the Voyager on a frozen planet after the crew loses control of the craft at warp. The sequence was brought to us by Visual Effects Supervisor Mitch Suskin, who was overseeing all of the effects for that episode, working closely with one of our supervising animators, Rob Bonchune. Mitch came to us with a solid idea of what he wanted the shots to look like, so the actual animation of the ship was straightforward. In this instance, the "look" of the shot was his primary concern, and the realism—the ship's mass, the landscape's texture, the atmosphere—was paramount (if you'll forgive the pun).

John Teska built, textured, and lit the landscape, then worked with Rob to elicit just the right snow-blind, midday lighting effect from the glacial mountains.

To achieve the plumes of snow kicked up when the Voyager impacts the terrain and skids toward camera, we used two high-speed cameras (our 96 frames-per-second Fries-Mitchell and a rented 400-fps camera) to film elements of baking soda and fuller's earth. John Allardice and Emile Smith used all sorts of techniques—throwing heavy objects into piles of baking soda, dragging Voyager-shaped "sleds" through, and launching fuller's earth out of air mortars—to get the elements needed.

Final comp of the Voyager crash landing on a frozen planet.

We scanned these elements to tape; then Sherry Hitch and our compositing department processed them to pull mattes so we could map the elements onto polygons in LightWave. In Layout, Allardice positioned the polygons and dissolved them out until the timing of the crash called for a particular plume or explosion.

Steve Pugh is General Manager of Foundation Imaging.

Foundation Imaging
24933 West Avenue Stanford
Valencia, CA 91355
www.foundation-i.com

Working With A Team

Whenever you have a job interview, be sure to ask questions about workflow and creative opportunities—it shows you are interested in doing the work, and the answers will tell you a lot about the organization.

Every shop is different, and even the same shop can vary from project to project. An advertising project may come from a micromanaging client or agency with very specific ideas about everything, or they may ask the production team to come up with the whole concept. A project may start out very nebulous, with the creative team soliciting story ideas from everyone down to the janitor; or the director may have one of those crystalline, burning visions that dictates every detail. As a compositor, you need to stay flexible and adapt your working style to your employer or client. The compositor's portion of the work is usually late in the process and close to the delivery deadline. Therefore, you need to have your work planned, complete with alternatives that take into account problems that have occurred on similar jobs. Make sure you know how your studio works, and then think ahead!

Depending on shop policy (and your seniority), your supervisor may simply hand you the elements and tell you how to composite them. In more flexible shops, you may be allowed or encouraged to contribute ideas in story meetings, storyboard sessions, and other creative collaborations. These are good opportunities to practice your diplomacy and teamwork skills. You should also keep in mind the ground rules for these meetings, which can vary a great deal between shops, teams, and even directors.

One common approach is to separate the creative, brainstorming part of a meeting from the analytical, critical part. If a meeting is being run with this approach, the fastest way to make yourself *persona non grata* is to break the rules, either criticizing during the brainstorming session or throwing in new ideas after the analysis has begun. In any case, don't hare off on topics that aren't on the agenda, don't chime in if you don't have anything constructive to contribute, and never play devil's advocate just for the sake of starting an argument. Try not to think out loud, either; give yourself a moment to phrase an observation or suggestion as concisely as possible, and think about the effect your suggestions may have on the other people in the meeting.

If you are not sure of what you have to say, and especially if your remarks may offend someone in another department, consider making discreet suggestions through channels (such as your supervisor) after the meeting. You're better off having your supervisor take credit for one of your ideas (yes, this happens) than offending a coworker through ignorance. Diplomacy and tact are essential to all production team members. You want to build a reputation as a person of few words and good ideas, so when you do speak up, your team members will listen.

"A lot of creative people, storyboardists, art and set directors . . . and others are involved, and you have to respect the way the project works. You have to be a team player and get along with others. At times, you'll think you have the right idea, and someone else will think he has the right idea. Maybe you both do—or neither of you is close."
—Steve Bloom, screenwriter

Pay attention to the person running the meeting too. Some people run very good meetings, where most participants leave with a positive attitude, good ideas are created, and a lot of work gets done. Try to emulate these people; someday you're going to be the one leading the meeting.

The point of all this effort is usually a film or video. Sometimes there are other goals: a better job, a distribution deal, a film contract, a political statement, fame, fortune, or just getting credit for a class. Whatever your goal is, make it clear from the start, and keep an eye on it. No project ever goes perfectly, and when you have to choose what to sacrifice, you'll appreciate a clear picture of what's necessary to your goal and what can be discarded. When you're embroiled in all the details of producing an effect, it's very easy to lose sight of your original goal. Once you're no longer focused on the goal, your project can veer off into directions you won't want it to take. At the least, the execution may lose focus and not be as powerful as you intended; at worst, the project may come apart completely.

Keep an eye on your goal!

Case Study 2.3
Storm of the Century

By Chris Bond, Frantic Films

A small harbor town in Maine gets ravaged by an immense storm in this Stephen King original miniseries. For this project, Frantic Films provided digital rain, snow, water, and atmosphere effects for miniature, studio, and otherwise-peaceful plate photography. The end result, a truly nasty storm.

This one kept us busy. Of course, living in Winnipeg, we are no strangers to big snowstorms, but that didn't make the task much easier. Nearly 100 layers of 3D CG snow totaling over 40 gigabytes of data were created for the project, along with CG water spray, fire, and fog. These elements were crafted in 3D Studio MAX and then composited to our tracked and hand-rotoscoped background plates. The biggest challenge for us was making the snow look as realistic as possible while still matching the fake on-set plastic snow (see the following three figures).

Still photography by Chris Bond.

Miniature pier set during rigging.

Pier shot before CGI effects.

Pier shot with CGI snow and water spray composited.

The accompanying stills show just two of the 20 shots delivered by Frantic. In one, we watch the storm coming, rolling in over the pier as waves crash in, tossing the docked boat about. Another shows trees, telephone poles, and wires swaying in the strong wind.

Miniature forest and power line greenscreen set.

The plate photography consisted of miniatures or artificial forest manufactured by another effects house. Frantic was on hand during the miniature shoot to take extensive notes and reference photos that would help in the later stages.

Miniature forest and power line set with CGI snow composited.

Credits: VFX Supervision: Boyd Shermis. Art Direction: Boyd Shermis, Chris Bond. 3D Modeling/Animation: Chris Bond, Bob Green, Conrad Dueck. Editing/Post: Chris Bond, Darren Wall, Eva Batchelor, and Shane Davidson.

Frantic Films
420-70 Arthur Street
Winnipeg, Manitoba, Canada R3B 1G7
Phone: 204-949-0070
Fax: 204-949-0050
info@franticfilms.com
www.franticfilms.com

Moving On

This chapter presented brief job descriptions of your potential colleagues and included several case studies of how production teams have successfully dealt with real-world challenges. This information should enable you to make better decisions in your career. The next chapter will give you the technical information you need to choose your compositing tools.

DIGITAL COMPOSITING
IN BRIEF

This chapter gives you the technical information you need to evaluate and to choose your own compositing tools, including thumbnail analyses and comparative evaluations of the most popular desktop digital compositing programs currently on the market.

Evaluating Software

The worst way to choose any software is to rely on the marketing hype printed on the box, on the publisher's Web site, or in press releases. The job of the person writing that copy is to sell the product, not to give you an unbiased appraisal of the software's capabilities. When you are reading marketing materials from the publisher of compositing software, the best you can hope for is a simple statement of the program's functions and a list of film and television productions and studios that have successfully used the software.

A long bullet list of features is not an indication of how well the software actually works. The implementation of each feature, how it works, and how you can work with it determine the software's value. Bullet lists are nearly useless because it's relatively easy to add a feature just to have that bullet. If Company A makes a big deal out of having tracking and stabilization, Company B can take the wind out of A's sails by adding a simple tracker and stabilizer to its own product. That makes A's sales job much more difficult; instead of being able to say, "We have something Company B doesn't," Company A now has to explain why its feature is better. That is a very difficult thing to do when you're limited to the back of a box. To make matters worse, the comparison charts used in some software reviews simply tote up the bullet lists of all the products. This favors the unscrupulous software developer who packs the bullet list with shoddy, user-hostile features rather than making robust, user-friendly implementations of fewer features.

Magazine reviews of software can vary so widely that it's not wise to rely exclusively on one source or reviewer. Some publications are unscrupulous enough to never give a major advertiser's products a bad review. Even the most ethical publications have to deal with significant problems: impossible software shipping schedules, finding qualified reviewers who can also write intelligibly, insanely short reviewing and writing deadlines, and 60- or 90-day production cycles that can make reviews hopelessly outdated by the time the magazine hits the newsstands. It's not fun, and there are no winners when the process goes awry. Online reviews can be even worse; although they can bypass many of the delays of print reviews, they can also bypass many of the quality-control checks that prevent a poorly written review from getting through to the public. You need to consider the source. For print magazines, the integrity of the publisher, editor, and reviewer is important. For online reviews, only the integrity of the reviewer matters. When the software review process does work, a professional compositor has sufficient time to put the software through its paces and then write a concise but thorough description of the program's pros and cons. That kind of review should be one of your strongest aids in selecting your own compositing tools.

Testimonials from artists or studios who have successfully used the software are relatively fair indicators that the software actually works in a production environment. However, you need to take into consideration the fact that some artists become extremely attached to their tools, and they will defend and promote the advantages of their choices despite any amount of evidence to the contrary. The least reliable references are those who have used only one company's products, rant about how lousy everyone else's products are, or have been employed in any capacity by the publisher. If the person lauding Brand X used to be the booth monkey for Brand X at trade shows, you may consider his testimony in favor of Brand X to be unduly influenced, even if it is sincere. The most reliable references are working professionals with strings of credits in high-profile film or TV productions, who have used a variety of programs over a long period of time, and who personally own several compositing programs. These artists have a longer baseline from which to make comparisons, are intimately familiar with the pros and cons of competing programs, and are usually secure enough that they don't get emotional about their choice of tools.

Online Research

A good starting point for finding unbiased testimonials is the publisher's Web site. That may sound strange considering my earlier comments, but often the strongest testimonials come from senior compositors who state their opinions concisely and unambiguously. These make great sound bites. However, look out for too many ellipses (…) where the marketing people have edited the testimonial. Editing for brevity is reasonable, but editing out negative comments about the software, or positive comments about a competitor's software, is unethical and all too common.

Once you have a few artists' testimonials for each program you are considering, you need to do some online research to find out what's behind the marketing hype. I recommend sites such as **deja.com**, a repository and search engine for Usenet newsgroups (see Figure 3.1). There are many newsgroups pertaining to digital compositing, ranging from software-specifics to general

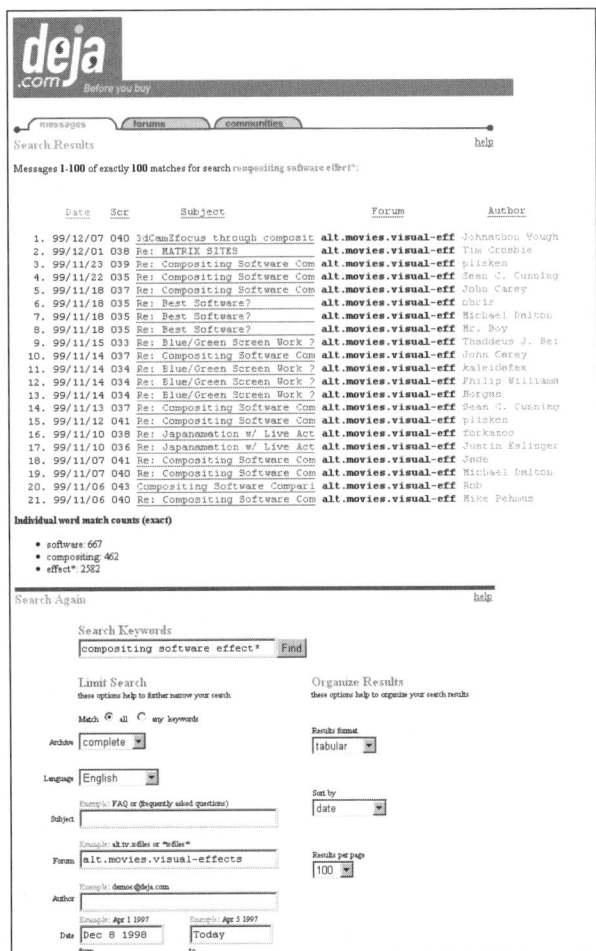

Figure 3.1

Results of a **deja.com** search for "compositing software effect*" in the **alt.movies.visual-effects** newsgroup.

cinematography and special effects—such as **alt.movies.visual-effects**. I recommend searching by the compositing software's name, the software publisher's name, and the names of the testimonial artists, both singly and in combination. One search I strongly recommend is the most common short name for the product, in combination with the words "trouble," "problem," "complaint," or "tech support." If there is a serious problem with the software, you will almost certainly find it discussed somewhere on Usenet. If you have questions or want to follow up a discussion thread, **deja.com** also enables you to post reply messages and to track future posts on particular threads. This site is a very handy tool for many people.

Pigsfly.com is another Web site that I recommend to digital compositors. This site is home to a variety of listservs or mailing lists pertaining to editing, compositing, and special effects. The Digital Fusion listserv is hosted on this site, as are those for BorisFX and Speed Razor. If you have specific questions about any of the software covered, especially competitive comparisons, this is a good place to ask. Peruse the list archives, subscribe and read a few days of messages, then post your questions according to the list rules. If you're polite and follow the rules, I can guarantee you'll get useful information. The more user-centered and responsive software publishers monitor these mailing lists, so you may even receive answers from the programmers who wrote the software you're considering. Listservs for other compositing programs do exist. Some are maintained by the software publishers, which can tend to stifle free discourse, especially regarding the shortcomings of the software or of the parent company's policies. If you can't find a listserv for the software you are investigating, try posting your question to the **alt.movies.visual-effects** newsgroup.

Platform Wars

Because some people seem to have what amounts to a religious fervor for (or against) particular hardware/operating system platforms, I believe it is necessary to include this disclaimer. In my work, I have used Amigas, Macs, SGIs, and PCs running nearly every flavor of operating system ever seen on desktop computers. I have no special interest in or bias toward one platform over another, aside from the tenet that you should use the tool that works best for you. There are demonstrable differences between platforms in the areas of user interface, stability, cost, performance, interconnectivity, market share, and vendor support. What platform you choose depends largely on which of those factors is most important to you. No single platform is the best solution for all digital compositors.

If you want to work for someone else, you need to stay flexible. Don't accept a job with the idea that you can change the organization; platform choice is not a religion, and you are not a missionary. If you love Macs but accept a job in an exclusively NT house, you will need to keep your pro-Mac opinions to yourself. I know of at least one artist who was fired because he spent too much time nagging studio management to change the core software and not enough time learning to use (or being productive with) that software.

If you are a freelance digital compositor, you are pretty much free to choose the platform that suits your own creative style. Some people love Macs; some prefer NT; some like Irix, Linux, or other more esoteric flavors of operating systems. As long as the only thing you have to share with others is standard footage formats, you can use what you like. However, if you are setting up or expanding a studio, you have to consider the working habits of others and the issues of interconnectivity. You'll have an easier time hiring compositors with experience on the most common platforms and a harder time convincing experienced professionals to change platforms to suit your personal tastes.

You also need to consider the overall cost of the workstations, software, and network you'll need for your studio. Some platforms have higher costs for the same level of performance. Some platforms will not have the software tools available that you would prefer. As of this writing, most digital compositing software has migrated (or plans to migrate) to the Windows NT platform.

The Mac OS platform is still healthy, however; and SGI still has a grip on the top-end market. If you are considering a major investment in hardware and software, you need to look at what's available now and to make your best informed guess at where the market will be in the near future, when you'll need to upgrade or replace your tools. More than one effects house has gone under in the last few years because they overinvested in the wrong platform, then were undercut by studios that made more cost-effective decisions. Losing your business because of an irrational platform preference is simply stupid.

The Test Drive

The test of a tool is in the using. You can do as much preliminary research as you like; I recommend it to save time and effort in weeding out the obvious nonstarters. However, choosing the right digital compositing software should always come down to just you and the software. Most publishers are smart enough to realize that few customers will shell out large sums of money without a test drive. The best-possible test for compositing software is to try using it with the assistance of a compositor who has experience with that program; this gives you a leg up on the learning curve, resulting in a more accurate picture of the software's capabilities, and a less frustrating and more productive test drive.

The second-best test of compositing software is to try using it by yourself, at your leisure. Digital compositing software has to be complex because of the number of different functions it has to perform. Even the best interface will take some getting used to, and if you're harried by clients and deadlines, you are less likely to have patience with learning a complex user interface. You should test the software with the same type of project you will be comping for clients, but it's not fair to demand that the software be immediately usable at full speed. Test software only when you have time to experiment, and allocate enough time to work through whatever documentation (especially tutorials) is provided with the software. You should be able to do most of your software testing with free demo versions; nearly all compositing software publishers provide some sort of limited demo version to potential customers. The best demos are fully functional versions that either time out after a reasonable test period or watermark the final output so it can't be used commercially. Less useful demos have features disabled, are limited in resolution, or can't render or save to a usable format. There are several demo software packages on this book's CD-ROMs. Other demo versions are only available from the publisher, either by registering and downloading from their Web site or by requesting a copy. I highly recommend installing and trying out as many compositing programs as possible. The more experience you have with all the available software, the more informed your final choice of tools will be. Remember, too, that you aren't limited to just one program; many compositors use several programs. One program may have an especially good tracker but substandard chroma-key tools, while another may be great at chroma key but lousy at tracking. As long as both programs can work with the same image file formats, there is no reason not to use them together.

It is not wise to evaluate compositing software only with the tutorial or demonstration footage provided with that software. At best, tutorial footage is usually massaged to make it easier to work with; that's the point of a tutorial, to be easier than the real world purely for the sake of instruction. At worst, unethical publishers may provide oversimplified, cleaned-up footage that makes their software look better than it would with more-realistic footage. Most of the tutorial footage on this book's CD-ROMs has also been cleaned up in some way, but the CineVort, CineGirl, and Match directories contain raw film and video footage that you may find useful in stress-testing compositing software and hardware. Your best course of action is to test the software on footage that you will actually be using. If you have footage from a current or past project, use that. For old footage, try setting up the same comps you used originally. Is the new software any easier or faster to set up? Does it produce comparable, worse, or better results? Does it have all the features and operations you used originally, is it missing functions you need, or does it have new features that would have saved you time and resources?

Feature Sets

Most digital compositing software, as mentioned previously, will have the same basic features—at least according to the bullet lists on the packaging. As you evaluate the software, you need to run through a checklist of the most important functions and test them to make sure they actually perform up to your expectations and needs. Following is a general checklist for compositing software; depending on your needs, you may choose to emphasize or ignore features that are more or less important for you. If you are relatively new to digital compositing, the terminology in this checklist will make more sense after you have worked through the rest of this book.

Compositing Images

The most basic feature of any compositing program is the ability to combine two or more images. These operations are at the core of almost any comp, so the ability of the software to perform these operations should be the lowest common denominator of a serious tool. If you are evaluating a program that can't perform one or more of these operations, you probably don't want to use that program in a production environment. Some of the common operations include:

- Add (A+B)
- Subtract (A-B)
- Over (A over B, using A's alpha channel)
- Under (A over B, using B's alpha channel)
- Maximum (whichever pixel value is higher)
- Minimum (whichever pixel value is lower)
- Average or Mix (average or weighted average of A and B)
- Reorder channels
- Opacity (alpha channel only)
- Z-buffer (an Over operation based on the depth or Z-axis values)

Mattes

The ability to pull a clean matte is crucial to many compositing operations. Many programs claim this ability, but it's one thing to say it and quite another to do it. Any program should be able to produce a clean matte from good bluescreen, greenscreen, or luma-key footage, or pull a difference key with a clean plate. The real test of matte tools is in how well they deal with an uneven bluescreen, a range of blacks in a luma key, or noise in a difference key. Does the software give you the ability to erode or choke the matte, to make effective spill correction, and to deal with nonstandard or oddly lit chroma-key colors?

Input/Output

If the software is going to be useful at all, it must be able to load and to render most common file formats, in both compressed and uncompressed versions, at the resolutions you need. For higher-end work, your tools must be able to handle film resolutions. The best programs have unlimited resolution, enabling the same software to comp anything from tiny 320x240 multimedia clips up to 6K VistaVision footage and magazine or poster stills. In addition, you will be able to work faster and more efficiently if you can set up a comp using lower-resolution *proxy* footage, then switch to the full-resolution footage without having to make any other changes. If your system has special video hardware or multiple processors, you should find out if the compositing software has the necessary drivers to use that hardware to best advantage.

Tracking And Stabilization

If you plan to do any work at all with live-action footage, you need software with good tracking features and at least single-point stabilization to remove unwanted camera motion from the footage. To do the best stabilization, the software must have *subpixel accuracy*, the ability to track patterns smaller than individual pixels. If you need to stabilize footage from a camera that rotates or zooms around the lens's long axis, you need software that can perform multiple-point stabilization to correct for rotation and scaling. Any software that promises stabilization features should also be able to destabilize, or restore the camera motion; without that feature, you will not be able to match the appearance of the original footage for a seamless comp.

Timing

A good compositing program should provide you with functions to perform a variety of timing operations. The most basic level of timing is to reverse, hold, drop, duplicate, or append existing frames. A more advanced program will enable you to seamlessly stretch or compress footage by interpolating or merging existing frames to create new frames, using motion blur, resampling, and other algorithms.

Video/Film

Converting from one media format to another is a common task in post-production work. The capability to convert from film to video, or from one video standard to another, is essential for any production house. Your compositing software should have the ability to swap the order of fields, deinterlace, or interlace. If you do film work, you will also need the tools to convert film to video using 3:2 pull-up, convert video to film using 2:3 pull-down, and either convert film's logarithmic color space to video's linear color space (and vice versa) or work in log color space throughout the comp process.

Customization

Does the software enable you to write mathematical expressions? Is there a software developer kit (SDK) that enables you to write plug-ins? This can be a crucial feature in a high-end production environment, where you can't afford to wait for the vendor's programmers to make the changes you need. You, or your studio's technical staff, need access to the guts of the software to customize it to your specifications.

Mathematics

Digital compositing is very sensitive to mathematical errors. A lack of accuracy can make fine-tuning a comp an exercise in frustration. The software's internal accuracy should be at least one order of magnitude better than the color depth of the final delivery medium. The best professional-level software can work in 8 bits per channel linear, 16 bits per channel linear, and 10 bits per channel logarithmic color spaces. You should also look for software that works with floating-point normalized values (0 to 1) rather than bit-depth-specific values (0 to 255, 0 to 1024, 0 to 64K).

Transformations

The ability to change the size and orientation of an element in a comp is important to most types of compositing work and is especially crucial to motion graphics. At a minimum, your software should be able to crop, scale, resize, pan, rotate, flip, flop, pin, warp, and displace elements. The difference in these functions between the basic level and the top professional tools lies in the algorithms available; this is especially important when you are comping significant resize or scale operations. Your software should present you with a range of algorithms, and you need to know which ones are appropriate to a given situation.

Image Processing

If you have worked with any image processing software (such as Photoshop), you know how powerful image processing filters can be. At minimum, your compositing software should include blur, sharpen, grain, smear, median, emboss, dilate, and erode operations. For serious professional use, the software should enable you to create your own filters, to import Photoshop or other third-party plug-ins, or both.

Color

Color space conversion is important if you are working with footage from a variety of sources, but it is also useful for the large number of effects that are easier to create in a particular color space. Your software should, at minimum, enable you to convert between RGB, HSV, HLS, YUV, and CMY color spaces. Other color operations you will need include gamma, gain, fade, contrast, brightness, saturation, multiply, divide, histograms, lookup tables, compress, expand, clamp, and set. You may not use all these features on every comp, but the more comps you do, the more you will come to rely on a full-feature set. If your software doesn't give you complete control of your color space, you will find it much harder to create top-notch comps.

Text

Creating titles and other text-based motion graphics is the bread and butter of small post-production shops. The quality of the text, the typefaces available (TrueType, PostScript, or both), and the animation and effects you can apply to the text all make a big difference in your ability to cost-effectively produce text-heavy comps. If you anticipate lots of text work, you should look very carefully at the text and animation tools in the software you evaluate.

Optimization

Your bottom line, whether on your own or as an employee, will often rest on your ability to finish a comp on a deadline. That means you need efficient tools, and the ability to control those tools to get the most work out of them in a given length of time. Your compositing software should enable you to limit time-consuming operations to a particular *region of interest*, to mask effects with mattes, and to work with lower-resolution proxy footage to speed up response time. You should also be able to render precompositions to save time downstream. Finally, the software should give you the options to allocate system resources, including memory, swap files, and network access.

Available Compositing Software

The following information was current at the time this chapter was written, in early December 1999. These brief reviews are not intended to be the last word on what digital compositing software is best for all users and circumstances. No single tool is suitable for all tasks, and every user has a different working style. These reviews are intended only as a basic survey of the most common options available at this time. New software is constantly being introduced, and the programs listed here may be improved or fall by the wayside. For the latest information on versions, prices, and features, you should visit the Web sites listed.

Adobe After Effects

After Effects is the most popular digital compositing software currently on the market, if you measure popularity by number of units sold. Adobe has the advantage of a nearly seamless tie-in with its other graphics products, including Photoshop, Illustrator, and Premiere. Because it was developed initially on the Mac platform, it is the tool of choice among Mac users. Because it has a solid development team and a good track record, it's a good choice in its NT incarnation as well. If you have used Premiere for editing and simple motion graphics, After Effects will seem very familiar. This transference of skills makes AE an extremely productive tool, right out of the box, for artists with previous Adobe experience.

After Effects' strengths lie in motion graphics. The program's capability to work with elements imported from both bitmap and vector drawing programs makes it a strong performer for comps that incorporate text and line art. AE's animation tools are also solid. Third-party support for plug-ins is outstanding; Adobe has a lot of experience and a sound policy of encouraging outside developers, with the result that After Effects has more plug-ins available than any other compositing software. AE plug-ins are becoming something of a de facto standard in the industry; other products are adapting themselves to be able to use AE plug-ins.

If you are serious about digital compositing, you will need the more expensive Production Bundle ($1,499), because the basic version ($689) is missing crucial tools such as tracking, improved keying, and expressions. Unfortunately, even at this higher level, After Effects isn't suitable for video or film work that requires complex tracking, stabilization, or destabilization. The tracker in the Production Bundle version is only so-so, and there is no simple way to reverse a stabilization to restore camera motion. There is no provision for multiple-point tracking at all, so stabilizing for rotation or scaling is simply not available. Paint tools are also absent, so you'll need some third-party plug-ins to provide those functions. Because of these shortcomings, After Effects combined with Puffin Designs' Commotion is a popular toolset for higher-end compositing work.

The documentation for After Effects is excellent. The User Guide and Production Bundle Guide are adequate introductions and references to the program's features. Adobe Press produces an excellent series called *Classroom in a Book*, and I recommend the appropriate title for any Adobe software you own. The tutorials are very good, if simple, explanations of how you can apply tools to create intermediate-level art. As of this writing, the *Classroom in a Book* for After Effects 4.1 is about to be released. There are also worthwhile third-party books, such as Coriolis' survey guide to AE plug-ins, *After Effects 4 In Depth*.

The tryout version of After Effects 4.0 is located in the Adobe directory of the first CD-ROM. This tryout version is more thoroughly crippled than most other publishers' demo versions; you will not be able to save any part of your work or output to anything but the screen display. However, the tryout does give you an idea of how the tools behave and at least a limited idea of the results you can expect.

Adobe Systems Inc.
345 Park Avenue
San Jose, CA 95110-2704
Phone: 408-536-6000
www.adobe.com
Listserv: **www.onelist.com/community/aftereffects**
Adobe-sponsored forum: **www.adobe.com/support/forums/**

Discreet effect*, paint*

Discreet's effect* and paint* products bundled together ($2,395) make good compositing companions for 3D Studio MAX. The integration of MAX's RLA output with RLA-based compositing tools in effect* make 3D effects such as depth of field much easier to comp. Effect* has always used a strong 3D metaphor, even for 2D effects; animatable lights, camera view, and raytraced shadows make this program a very capable hybrid between 2D compositing and 3D animation and rendering software.

Available for both Mac and NT platforms, effect* option 2 lags significantly behind effect* option 3, which is currently only available for the SGI platform. Option 3 appears from early reports to be a complete rewrite, sharing little beyond the name with option 2. With time, effect* users can expect more features from flame*, inferno*, and other SGI-based Discreet products to migrate down to the Mac and NT platforms. Until that time, option 2 is significantly slower in many operations than other comparably priced software reviewed here.

Effect*'s tracker is one of the best available; no surprise, because it's the same code used in Discreet's top-end flame* product. Effect*'s capability to apply tracking data to control points on a spline-based mask is currently unique among the products reviewed here. Oddly, effect* has the lowest resolution limit of the programs reviewed here—only 2000×1500.

The documentation for effect* and paint* could stand a little work. The bulk of the User's Guide is a once-over-lightly view of each program's features, with a scattering of very brief tutorials (five steps or less) for some of the more involved operations. If you want or need tutorials with greater detail, refer to the Lesson directory of the software installation or download tutorials from the Discreet Web site.

The tryout versions of effect* and paint* option 2.0 are located in the Discreet directory of the first CD-ROM. These versions include tutorials and footage, and are well worth your time to explore. The only features disabled are project saving, and a watermark red X is rendered in the middle of the screen and the final output. This is a very good demo version that lets you really experiment with the software before making a purchase decision.

Discreet
10 rue Duke
Montréal, Québec, Canada H3C 2L7
514-393-1616 or 800-869-3504
Fax: 514-393-0110 or 800-305-6442
www.discreet.com
Email: **product_info@discreet.com**
Newsgroup archives: Customers only, password-limited access on company Web site.

eyeon Software Digital Fusion 2.53

Digital Fusion has been earning popularity rapidly in both television and film production in the last few years. It offers a good combination of ease of use, efficient rendering, and broad range of features for the price. If you are compositing only for video, you can do well with the basic package at $2,495. For film work at 64-bit color depth and other high-end tools, the Post version is $4,995.

The pipes-and-tiles Digital Fusion user interface has suffered criticism in past versions, so the latest version enables users to work in either the original tile layout or the more compact (if less visually stimulating) timeline layout. My personal preference is to use the tiles to rough out a comp, then fine-tune timing and transitions in the timeline.

Digital Fusion's toolset is one of the most complete in the field today, and most features have sufficient depth to keep all but the most finicky specialist happy. If you do nothing but text-based motion graphics, you will probably be happier with After Effects; for any other kind of video or film work (and especially live-action matte work), you will do better with DF.

Digital Fusion is one of the fastest desktop compositing programs available, especially if you have multiprocessor machines. With intelligent use of proxy and cache settings, you can easily strike a balance between screen display quality and refresh speed. Optimizing for fastest rendering is simple and straightforward.

Third-party support for Digital Fusion is very good, with developers such as Ultimatte, 5D Monsters, and Zbig leading the pack. A plug-in adapter program is also available to enable many After Effects plug-ins to work within Digital Fusion.

The documentation for Digital Fusion is a little quirky, but adequate. The current version is an assembly of the 2.0 manual plus several updates for incremental releases up to 2.53. Due to this patchwork, it can sometimes be frustrating to try looking up a feature or tutorial in the paper manual. However, the PDF, HTML, and Windows Help versions of the documentation are more searchable and will usually present a solution to the problem. In addition, the eyeon Web site hosts a collection of tips that most users will find extremely helpful, and the **pigsfly.com** mailing list is a wealth of expertise and good advice.

A demo version of Digital Fusion 2.53 is located in the eyeon directory of the first CD-ROM. This is a completely functional version, enabling you to save, edit, and reload flows and really give the software a thorough test. The only limit to the demo version is the pair of Digital Fusion and eyeon software logos that are watermarked onto random corners of the final output. You should be able to complete every project in this book with the demo version of Digital Fusion.

eyeon Software
70 Valleywood Drive
Markham, Ontario, Canada L3R 4T5
800-862-0004
www.eyeonline.com
Listserv: **www.pigsfly.com**

NewTek Aura

As of this writing, NewTek is hard at work on Aura version 2.0. This is a very good thing, because Aura 1.0 was seriously shortchanged for compositing tools to make the paint and drawing tools especially powerful. On the positive side, Aura includes its own scripting language (George), and there are already many useful George scripts being traded among Aura users. The Aura 1.0 Reference Guide gives an indication of what you can expect from the program. The built-in functions tend to be very simple, but the technical reference for George and the scriptable functions show very technically minded users how to pull more advanced effects out of the program. If you are already using LightWave or the Video Toaster NT, you should take a long look at Aura. The vertical integration of NewTek products promises significant production advantages.

NewTek
8200 IH-10 West
Suite 900
San Antonio, TX 78230
800-847-6111
www.newtek.com
Old listserv: **www.lightwave-outpost.com/archives/aura/index.html**
Newer listserv: **www.onelist.com/community/AURA**

Nothing Real Shake

Shake was developed by a group of professional compositors who became frustrated with the available digital compositing tools. The first version was command line only, but the current version has a graphic user interface (GUI) that makes it more artist-friendly. It is still one of the more technically oriented compositing programs, and it definitely favors the analytically minded over the wing-it-and-see-what-happens crowd. Shake is very good at image manipulations such as color space conversion, filtering, and layering elements. However, tracking, rotoscoping, and garbage mattes are not supported in the current version. It also has a strong bias toward film work; if you only need to composite video, you might take a look at ShakeVideo, distributed by Media 100. It will also save you a few bucks: ShakeVideo 1.0 is only $2,500, but Shake 2.1 is $9,999.

Some professional compositors consider Shake to be the best 2D image-processing tool generally available. It is flexible (once you know what you're doing), fast, powerful, and reportedly stable and relatively bug-free. It has been used on many feature films, including *End of Days*. I would not recommend it as the first compositing tool for a novice to learn, but if you're an experienced professional, it's certainly worth a trial run.

The documentation and tutorials for Shake 2.0 are in the Shake directory on the second CD-ROM. The current demo version of the software is available for download from the Nothing Real Web site. Shake is currently available for Windows NT and SGI.

Nothing Real, L.L.C.
211 Windward Avenue
Second Floor
Venice, CA 90291
310-664-6152
Fax: 310-664-6157
www.nothingreal.com
Email: **sales@nothingreal.com**
Support: **support@nothingreal.com**
Listserv: **www.onelist.com/community/nreal**

Puffin Designs Commotion

Commotion is a recent port to the NT platform from its original development on the Mac. It has some excellent paint, tracking, and rotoscoping tools but it falls a little short on some of the more advanced compositing operations. It has been combined very successfully with After Effects as a Mac-based compositing solution. One of Commotion's highest-profile uses was in the previsualization stage of *Phantom Menace*. However, the current version only works in 8 bits per channel color depth, adequate for rotoscoping and tracking but inadequate for color comping in film-depth color spaces.

Puffin Designs, Inc.
80 Liberty Ship Way, Suite 7
Sausalito, CA 94965
800-401-0009
www.puffindesigns.com
Listservs: **www.toolfarm.com** and **www.postforum.com/Commotion/**

Silicon Grail Chalice

Chalice is one of those programs that everyone talks about but few have actually used. It has an extensive and impressive filmography, but very little information about it is available in third-party sources or on the Internet. The program is relatively expensive, and it has an odd pricing structure. Instead of buying the software outright, you license it for a specific length of time. This helps studios who need it on a project-by-project basis, because the studio can charge off the entire license fee to the project rather than having to depreciate a much higher purchase price across several projects. At $1,000 for a three-month license or $2,900 per year, it isn't cheap, but it does have advantages. Chalice is geared to film work, so it supports floating-point 32-bit color depth, and it requires the extra memory and processor speed to handle it. It's definitely overkill for video work, but it's a very good, flexible film tool, according to professional compositors who have actually used it.

Demo versions for IRIX, Intel NT, and Alpha NT are available for download from Silicon Grail's Web site. The manual and tutorials for version 1.6 are located in the Chalice directory of the first CD-ROM.

Silicon Grail Corporation
710 Seward Street
Hollywood, CA 90038
323-871-9100
www.sgrail.com
Email: **info@sgrail.com**

Moving On

This chapter presented the criteria and basic technical information you need to choose your compositing tools. The next chapter presents a short course in digital media, including vocabulary and references.

PART II

INPUT

VISUAL TECHNICALITIES

You need a basic vocabulary and knowledge of digital media (and their analog origins) to be a good digital compositor. This chapter presents the short course, with references for you to consult as you need them.

Any good artist is a competent craftsman first. As a digital artist, image files and software are your canvas and paints. If you do not understand their essential properties, the capabilities and limitations of your media, you cannot reach your potential as an artist. If you don't know the difference between a pixel and a pica, or you think bit depth is something your dentist worries about, you don't understand your media. You might be able to fake it for a while, but your ignorance will eventually trip you up. If you make the effort to add a few new words to your vocabulary (and understand the reality behind them), you can become a better digital artist.

Digital Image Basics

Most visual media are originally *analog*, which means that the media can change smoothly and continuously from one value to another without sharp breaks. The colors in film, mixed paints, or television screens are examples of analog media. *Digital* media are defined by numbers, so changes in value are discrete and can be very sharp. The colors produced by LCD displays and color printers are examples of digital media.

Digitizing analog media turns a smooth, continuously changing value into a series of numbers. For example, natural sound is an analog signal, like the waveform shown in Figure 4.1. To digitize it, you first decide how often to sample it, or into how many discrete pieces you will divide it. This is the *sampling rate*. Then you measure the value of the analog signal for each one of those

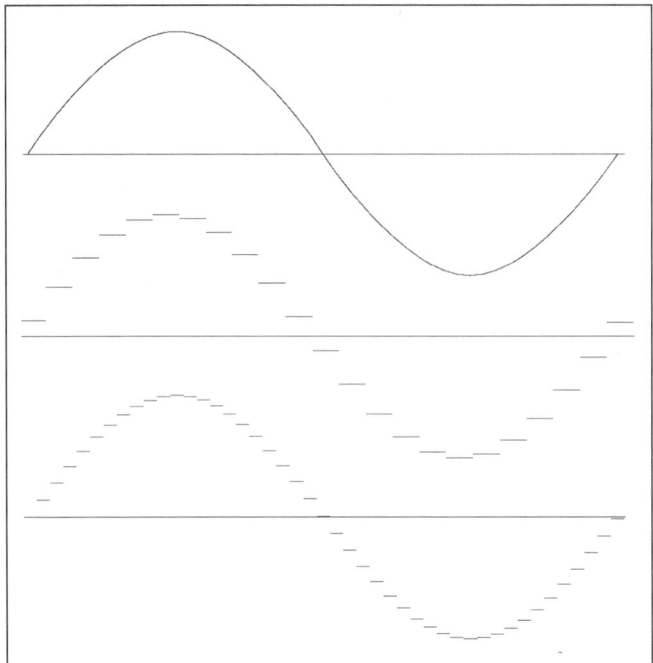

Figure 4.1
Analog waveform, low sampling rate digitized waveform, and high sampling rate digitized waveform.

samples. You end up with a series of numbers that you can plot like stair steps, which approximates (but does not precisely duplicate) the original analog signal.

The higher the sampling rate, the closer the approximation and the higher fidelity the digitization. Audio sampling rates for compact discs (CDs) are usually 44.1 kHz, or 44,100 samples per second. This enables you to capture at least two samples from a 22 kHz sound, the highest frequency most humans can hear. It is important to use a sampling rate higher than (preferably twice as high as) the highest frequency of the analog signal. If you use too low a sampling rate, you lose too much information and the digitized copy is obviously inferior.

To digitize an analog image, you have to sample it into picture elements, or *pixels*. A pixel is the smallest unit of a digital image. If you look very closely at an LCD display (for example, a laptop computer screen), you can see that it is made up of tiny rectangles. Each one of those rectangles is the equivalent of a pixel in a digital image. Digitizing a frame of film or other analog image is like laying a grid of tiny rectangles over the image, then measuring the average color in each rectangle. Like the waveform in Figure 4.1, this gives you a close approximation, but not an exact reproduction, of the original analog image.

Resolution

The number of pixels in an image is the *resolution;* for example, 720x480 is 720 columns of pixels wide by 480 rows of pixels tall. Resolution is the sampling rate for images. The higher the resolution, the better quality the image. In Figure 4.2, the width of the image is sampled 720 times, and the height of the image is sampled 480 times, creating 345,600 separate numbers that describe the color of each pixel.

The largest commonly used resolution for film work is currently 4096x3072, called 4K. This is generally used only for IMAX films and special-purpose still images; for most feature film work, 2K (or even 1K) is acceptable. Common resolutions for compositing include 4K and 2K for film work, 1K for low-end film work and HDTV, 720x480 for video, 320x240 for multimedia, and 180x120 for Internet distribution. To compare the image quality of different resolutions, refer to the first set of facing pages in the Color Studio section in this book.

The proportion between the horizontal and vertical measure of the image is the *aspect ratio.* There are many aspect ratios in use for film and video. The 4K example has a pixel aspect ratio of 4096:3072, or 4:3. The individual pixels may also have an aspect ratio. You need to be able to match and convert aspect ratios for your source and output formats. If you mismatch aspect ratios, your images will be distorted, as shown in Figure 4.3. This is especially important if you are combining elements from different sources, such as CGI, film, or video, or footage shot with different lenses.

Figure 4.2
A 720x480 digitized image.

Figure 4.3
Incorrect 16:9 aspect ratio applied to Figure 4.2.

HOW BIG IS IT?

A *bit* is the smallest piece of information a computer can work with. Eight bits make a *byte*; for example, the number 256 in binary, 11111111, is one byte. K, or kilo-, in computer jargon means 1,024, or 2 to the 10th power. Therefore, one *kilobyte* of data is 1,024 bytes. Powers of 2 are common in digital formats because they translate easily into binary mathematics, the ones and zeros that computers use. M, or mega-, is 1024×1024, or 1,048,576. Therefore, a *megabyte* of data is 1024×1024x8 bits. You do not need to memorize these numbers; you just need to understand the relative sizes: 1 bit is miniscule, 1 byte is a single character, 1 kilobyte (1K) is half a postage stamp, 1 megabyte (1MB) is a floppy disk or one frame of video, 1 *gigabyte* (1GB) is a big chunk of a hard drive or half a minute of uncompressed video, and 1 *terabyte* (1TB) is a studio's network of hard drives or a little under 10 hours of uncompressed video.

Color

Resolution defines two dimensions of the digital image. There is a third dimension: the color or bit depth. Each pixel in an image has one color, and each color can be defined digitally by a set of numbers. Each of the numbers is referred to as a *channel*. There are a variety of *color spaces*, or methods of numbering colors: HLS, YIQ, YUV, CMYK, and RGB. Most film and video compositing is performed in RGB color space.

- HLS (hue, luminance, and saturation) color space is useful for performing color corrections. Sometimes HLS is called HSB, for hue, saturation, and brightness. The hue channel is the position of the color along the spectrum. You might describe hue with a color name like "red." The luminance channel is the brightness of the color along a gradient from black to white. Higher luminance makes the difference between brick red and fire-engine red. The saturation channel is the amount of color, or *chrominance*, also along a gradient from black to white. Lowering the saturation washes out that fire-engine red to a pale pink.

- YIQ color space is taken from the NTSC television standard. Y controls the luminance channel; I controls the in-phase, or red/cyan, channel; and Q controls the quadrature, or magenta/green, channel.

- YUV color space is taken from the PAL television standard. Y controls the luminance channel, U controls the blue channel, and V controls the red channel.

- CMY (more commonly called CMYK) color space is taken from the four-color separation process used in commercial printing. Standard printing inks are cyan, magenta, and yellow. For printing, the fourth channel—K—controls the black ink.

- RGB color space uses three numbers, one each for red, green, and blue. The longer the number you can use, the more precise the color you can define. For example, 8 bits can define 256 (2 to the 8th power) levels of that color, and 16 bits can define 65,536 (64 K) levels. Add up the bits for all three colors, and you get the color or bit depth for the image: 8+8+8=24-bit, common for video work, or 16+16+16=48-bit for more demanding film or print work.

Some image formats include another number for an *alpha channel*, making an RGBA file. Color depths of 32 and 64 bits are typical for RGBA images. Just to add to the confusion, sometimes the color depth is described by the total number of bits and sometimes by the number of bits per channel. You simply have to figure it out from context; if a high-end film compositor talks about using 16-bit, you know they are not limiting themselves to 64 K colors.

The numbers that define the color space can be either *linear* or *logarithmic* (*lin* and *log*, for short). Lin color space is generally more suited to CGI elements, whereas log color space preserves more of the contrast and depth of film. Lin and log files do not mix well. If you composite a lin element with a log element, the difference in color numbering throws off all the compositing calculations and you get nasty-looking artifacts. In practice, this simply means that you need to know whether the files you are using are lin or log and keep them separated. One common solution is to translate all log elements to lin (or vice versa) and work in only one type of color space for the whole shot.

Depending on the display medium, too low a color depth can make an image show *contouring,* or *banding.* Banding, shown in Figure 4.4, means the difference in color between adjacent pixels is easily perceived by the human eye. It's generally more difficult to see banding on a computer screen, but in print or film the problem becomes more obvious. You can hide the edge of the bands by *dithering*, or mixing up the pixels along the border, but a better solution is to increase the bit depth. The higher the bit depth, the better quality the image.

Packing It In

For the best quality, you want to have high bit depth (good color) and high resolution (big picture). However, the file size of an image is the product of the resolution multiplied by the bit

Figure 4.4
The 24-bit image shown in Figure 4.2, reduced to 8-bit color that shows banding (note background).

depth, X*Y*B. A typical video image might be 720×480×24=8,294,400 bits, or about 1MB. This means you have to have 1MB of storage for every frame of video, about 30MB per second, and your system needs to be able to push that data around. The largest image files in general use for film compositing are 16-bit 4K RGBA, which can top 96MB per frame. At 24 frames per second (fps), that is *2.3 gigabytes* of data per second of film. Obviously, this isn't something you want to try compositing on your laptop.

Storing all this data and pushing it around a computer system is an expensive problem. In attempts to solve it, various organizations have developed file formats that reduce the total file size through a process called *compression*. There are several approaches to compression. Some discard information that is less important to the finished image; this is called *lossy compression*, because there is some perceptible loss of image quality. JPEG is one example of lossy compression.

Lossless compression, as you might expect, removes only information that does not affect the finished image. For example, the simplest form of lossless compression is the removal of redundant information. Suppose that one row starts off with a blue pixel, then 17 green pixels, then 42 blue pixels, and so on. Instead of describing the same color repeatedly for each pixel, you could save space by describing only the first pixel of each color and the number of identically colored pixels following it. One example of lossless compression is LZW.

There are many compression schemes, or *algorithms*, each with advantages and disadvantages. As a digital compositor, you need to know which compression algorithms are acceptable for your work and which you should avoid.

File Formats

Digital images can be stored in a variety of *file formats*, which are methods of recording the basic pixel information. Some formats can include other information, such as copyright, artist, creation date, or software used to create the image. This extra information is usually encoded in a *header* located at the beginning of the file.

UFO: UNIDENTIFIED FILE OBJECT

If you are ever in doubt about the format of a file, try opening it in a text editor and reading the file and software data from the header.

Some file formats can store sequences of images. Open video formats like MPEG, popular commercial formats like Microsoft's AVI and Apple's QuickTime, and proprietary hardware-based formats such as NewTek's RTV can all store long image sequences as single files. Most video formats offer either (or both) lossy or lossless compression options called *codecs*, a contraction of compression-decompression. Currently popular codecs include Cinepak, Indeo, and Sorenson. If you are compositing for multimedia output, selecting the best codec will be an important part of your job. Chapter 17 has more detailed information on codecs and the output process.

One of your most essential skills is the ability to efficiently translate images from one file format to another. Compositing film or video means you will be working with image sequences, sometimes thousands of frames at a time. If you take a few seconds longer than necessary to translate each image in a sequence, that adds up to a significant chunk of time between you and your deadline. It's in the best interests of your sanity and employability that you know how to handle as many file formats as possible. Most computer artists develop a collection of image utilities that

---

FINDING FILE FORMAT CONVERSION UTILITIES

One of the best places to find information about graphics utility programs is the Graphics Conversion and Display Programs section of the Graphics File Formats FAQ. This document answers many of the most frequently asked questions about graphics file formats on Usenet. It contains URLs to the most popular freeware and shareware conversion utilities, including my favorites, DISPLAY and GDS. You can find the latest revision of this FAQ at the following addresses:

- www.ora.com/infocenters/gff/gff-faq/
- www.jazzie.com/ii/internet/faqs.html
- www.cs.ruu.nl/wais/html/na-dir/graphics/fileformats-faq/.html
- www.lib.ox.ac.uk/search/search_faqs.html

or download it via anonymous FTP from

- ftp://rtfm.mit.edu/pub/usenet/news.answers/graphics/fileformats-faq
- ftp://rtfm.mit.edu/pub/usenet/comp.graphics.misc

---

efficiently and accurately translate images from one format to another. Many of these utilities are freeware or shareware. The better ones support *batch operation*, in which the software automatically translates a sequence of images.

Which file formats you use most will depend on the tools you use and the requirements of your client or employer. If you work entirely on your own, you have the luxury of choosing the file format you prefer. If you work in a studio with shared tools, however, you need to use formats that your colleagues can also use efficiently. Sometimes you have to use a format that makes your work more difficult, because it makes work easier for other members of the production team.

Format Quick Reference

The following list describes the most commonly used image-file formats for digital compositing. Where possible, I included the locations of technical information for each format. If you ever find it necessary to create programs to manipulate these files, the format specifications will be required reading. If you never get that technical, these summaries should be enough to keep you out of trouble:

- *AI*—Adobe Illustrator file format is a variant of EPS (see the following "PS, EPS" entry). As with EPS, its best use in compositing is for titles and other line art that should be resolution-independent. Visit the Adobe Web site (**www.adobe.com**) for support and technical details.

- *BMP*—Microsoft's BMP is the native bitmap format of Windows. This format stores mapped or unmapped RGB data in 1-, 4-, 8-, or 24-bit color depth, either uncompressed or compressed with a 4- or 8-bit RLE algorithm. BMP is a popular and well-supported format, at least on the Windows platform. However, it doesn't support alpha channels.

- *CIN*—Kodak's Cineon format supports 10-bit-per-channel logarithmic color space to match the color depth of film. If you plan to work with film or HDTV, your software should support this format. You can find more information at Kodak's home page, **www.kodak.com/**.

- *GIF*—The Graphics Interchange Format is an 8-bit image format that uses the patented LZW compression algorithm. This format is used primarily for Web graphics, especially the animated 89a version. Other than that, it isn't very useful for digital compositing. For technical details of the 87a and 89a versions of the GIF format, read the following documents:

    ftp://ftp.ncsa.uiuc.edu:/misc/file.formats/graphics.formats/gif87a.doc

    ftp://ftp.ncsa.uiuc.edu:/misc/file.formats/graphics.formats/gif89a.doc

- *IFF, ILBM, ILM*—Electronic Arts Interchange File Format gained great popularity on the Amiga platform and is supported today by a number of programs. IFF files may be uncompressed or use PackBits compression. For details and specs, visit the Electronic Arts Home Page, **www.ea.com/**.

- *JPG, JFIF, JPEG*—JFIF is a file format designed to use the Independent JPEG Group compression algorithm. Files are 24-bit, and the compression can vary from nearly lossless (with little savings) to extremely high compression (with poor image quality). Using JPEG compression on an image sequence can create a crawling effect due to changes in the artifacts from frame to frame. You can get the JFIF specs online from the following FTP Internet sites:

ftp://ftp.uu.net/graphics/jpeg/jfif.ps.gz

ftp://ftp.uu.net/graphics/jpeg/jpeg.documents.gz

- *MPG, MPEG-1, MPEG-2, DVD*—MPEG is an open standard for lossy compression of video. MPEG-1 is popular for multimedia and Internet distribution of short video clips. MPEG-2 is the compression algorithm used for DVD. Both forms of compression can be made with software only, but for faster commercial production, hardware compression boards are available. If at all possible, you should not work with MPEG as source files; try to use the original uncompressed video source. Although some compositing programs can load MPEG, the variation in artifacts from frame to frame can unnecessarily complicate your work. To avoid these problems, you should convert MPEGs to image sequences or uncompressed video before compositing. When you output MPEG, tweaking the compression parameters can make a significant difference in the perceived quality of the final clip. You can find the technical specs and links to shareware and freeware MPEG programs at **www.mpeg.org/**.

- *PCX, PCC*—ZSoft's Paint format is one of the oldest desktop formats, made popular by DOS paint programs in the early 1980s. PCX files may be 1 to 24 bits in depth, use RLE compression, and can be read by just about any graphics software. Unfortunately, the format's evolution has not been managed well, and you are generally better off using BMP.

- *PICT, PCT*—Apple Computer's PICT image format supports uncompressed and JPEG files. For technical details, check Volume 5 of the *Inside Mac* books, available online at **http:// dev.info.apple.com/insidemac.html**.

- *PS, EPS*—PostScript (and Encapsulated PostScript) was originally developed by Adobe as a page-description language. It is primarily useful in compositing for titles and other resolution-independent line art. EPS files can be uncompressed or can use LZW compression. You can find technical information on Adobe's sites:

ftp://ftp.adobe.com/pub/adobe/DeveloperSupport/Technotes/

www.adobe.com/

You can find the Encapsulated PostScript specs at **www.adobe.com/supportservice/ devrelations/PDFS/TN/**.

- *PSD*—This is the native bitmap format of Adobe Photoshop. The most current version supports multiple channels and up to 16-bit-per-channel color depth. You can find the format specification for PSD at **www.adobe.com/Support/ADA.html**.

- *MOV, QT*—QuickTime is an Apple Computer format that has become popular for distributing animation and video on the Internet and in multimedia CD-ROMs. Several codecs are available, and most compositing software supports the format directly or through a plug-in. Players and other support are available through the Apple home page. You can find technical details for the format at **http://dev.info.apple.com/Developer_Services/ Technical_Documentation/Inside_Macintosh/QuickTime/CompleteBookPkg/**.

- *RAS*—Sun Rasterfile is the native bitmap for Sun Unix systems. Its color space goes as deep as 32 bits, and the format supports uncompressed and a basic form of run-length (RLE) compressed files. Technical details of the format are in the SunOS include file, /usr/include/ rasterfile.h.

- *RAW*—The RAW format is simply a Photoshop PSD file with no header.

- *RIFF, AVI, BND, WAV*—Microsoft Resource Interchange File Format is a multimedia file format that includes Audio-Video Interleaved, or AVI. You can receive technical information on RIFF in the development kit, which you can download from **ftp://ftp.microsoft.com/developr/drg/ Multimedia/Jumpstart/VfW11e/DK/VFWDK/**.

- *RTV*—This is the native format for NewTek's Frame Factory video board. It is capable of recording and playing back 720x480 24-bit 29.97 fps video with a fast RAID (redundant array of independent disks). The format uses some compression, but the file sizes are still very large. At present, only NewTek's Aura paint and compositing program and LightWave 3D program support RTV. You can get more details on RTV from the NewTek Web site at **www.newtek.com**.

- *SGI, RGB*—The Silicon Graphics Image is the native bitmap file format of Silicon Graphics workstations. These files sometimes carry the extension .rgb. You can download the specs from **ftp://ftp.sgi.com/graphics/SGIIMAGESPEC**.

- *TGA*—This is often called a Targa file, but TGA is the correct usage. It was developed by Truevision, Inc., a video card manufacturer. TGA is one of my personal favorites and is arguably the most commonly accepted file format for 24-bit RGB and 32-bit RGBA images. It can contain a lot of extra data, including your own definitions. It compresses very well using PKZIP and other archive programs, and it can be used in uncompressed and RLE compressed versions. For more technical information, contact Truevision through their Web site at **www.truevision.com/**.

- *TIFF*—This format was originally developed and maintained by Aldus, and since the Adobe acquisition, the Adobe Developers Association (ADA) has maintained it. TIFF has a number of versions, which can cause compatibility problems. If you plan to work with TIFF files, make sure you know the files' version and compression. TIFF files can be uncompressed, or use PackBits RLE, LZW, JPEG, or CCITT Groups 3 and 4 compression. TIFF supports 24-bit color, but it does not support an alpha channel or deeper color space. For these reasons, TIFF is not a good choice for film or demanding video compositing. You can download the TIFF 4.0, 5.0, and 6.0 specs from the following Web sites:

    www.adobe.com/supportservice/devrelations/PDFS/TN/TIFF6.pdf

    ftp://ftp.std.com/obi/Standards/Graphics/Formats/tiff.doc.4.0.Z

    ftp://ftp.std.com/obi/Standards/Graphics/Formats/tiff.doc.5.0.Z

- *WMF*—Microsoft's Windows Metafile is not a bitmap image format like most of these other image formats. A WMF file is a collection of function calls to the Windows environment that draws the image. This means the image has no limit on resolution. WMF files are especially useful for titles and other line art. For more technical information, consult the Microsoft Knowledge Base at **ftp://ftp.microsoft.com/kb/** or download **www.microsoft.com/developr/ MSDN/OctCD/METAFI.ZIP**, which contains the Metafile Help file.

Video And Film

The image files you composite have to come from somewhere. The most common sources (as of this writing) are analog media, such as videotape and film, but digital media are rapidly gaining popularity. In this section, we'll look at the basic specifications for some of the most common media you will handle.

Film To Computer

Bringing film images into the computer is much more straightforward than the same process for video. Film data is all present at once in each frame of film, the frame rate is the same everywhere, the image quality is excellent, and the original media is relatively stable and easy to manage. The disadvantages of film are that the images can be very large, it requires 10-bit (or deeper) log color space for best results, there are many aspect ratios, and digitizing and rerecording require expensive equipment. Chapters 5 and 18 address the more technical details of working with film.

Video To Computer

Importing images from video is trickier. There are PAL, NTSC, and the new HDTV formats, depending on your physical location and the demands of your market. Video frame rates are odd numbers like 25 or 29.97. Each frame is not a single image, but an interlaced pair of fields, and either one may be dominant. Video has a fraction of the resolution and color depth of film. Videotape media has dropouts and other physical problems that can affect image quality. On the positive side, video digitizing and rerecording equipment is relatively affordable and easy to integrate into an existing computer or studio. Chapters 5 and 17 address the more technical details of digitizing and recording video.

PAL

The PAL video standard has a frame rate of 25 fps, a resolution of 625 lines, and field dominance of even field first, odd field second. A typical resolution for digitized PAL frames is 720x576, with 24-bit color depth. The PAL standard is used in most of Europe and in many other areas.

NTSC

Used primarily in the U.S., the NTSC standard has a frame rate of 29.97 fps, which is usually rounded up to 30 fps for the sake of convenience in working with short pieces. In longer pieces, precisely 29.97 is necessary for proper sync. Video resolution is 525 lines, with field dominance of odd field first, even field second. Typical digitized resolution for NTSC frames is 720x486.

HDTV

High-definition television (HDTV) is a very recent batch of standards, with no de facto dominant standard as of this writing. Generally speaking, HDTV means a screen aspect ratio of 16:9, with digitized frame resolution of 1920x1080 and color depth of at least 24-bit. This larger image size is not yet supported by all desktop compositing software. Because broadcasters in the U.S. are being required to make the transition to HDTV, if that is your market, you need to make sure your tools can handle the high-definition formats. Chapters 5 and 18 include more detailed information about HDTV hardware and media that are currently available.

Most video formats use *timecode* for synchronization. This is a normally invisible signal encoded on the videotape along with the video and audio signals. Professional video equipment can read the timecode either to a separate display or superimposed on the video monitor. The standard timecode for NTSC is SMPTE (pronounced simp-tee, the acronym for Society of Motion Picture and Television Engineers), which is usually displayed as *hh:mm:ss:ff*, or hours, minutes, seconds, and frames. Timecode is necessary when editing a comped shot back into a video sequence, to make sure the sound and video synchronize properly and that no fields or frames are dropped.

TIMECODE PAYMENT INSURANCE

Timecode is also handy to make sure you are paid. You can show the client an approval tape with timecode running across the bottom of the screen, then deliver the clean tape only in exchange for your final payment.

Moving On

You should now have a basic vocabulary for, and understanding of, the media you will use as a digital compositor. This knowledge will make the rest of this book easier to understand and will accustom you to the jargon you will use in your everyday work.

The next chapter, "Reel To Virtual," will explain the hardware and software tools you may use to digitize film and video, and to manage that data on your compositing workstation or studio network.

CHAPTER 5

REEL TO VIRTUAL

Understanding how film and video get into your workstation can make the difference between handling a routine comp and tearing your hair out. Here is the essential digitizing knowledge you need. This chapter is going to throw a lot of numbers and technical specifications at you. I wouldn't if I could avoid it; I'm not fond of memorizing numbers and arcane jargon either. However, if you want to be a competent digital compositor, you need to understand at least the basics of how the technology of your art works. Just as a sculptor needs to understand the essentials of metallurgy for chisel fabrication, you need to understand the technicalities of sampling film and video to get them into your workstation.

If you are working in a large shop, you may have the luxury of simply grabbing your footage, already digitized and ready to comp, off a network server. If you are working in a smaller shop or on your own, you may have to digitize video footage yourself, or oversee telecine or film scanning at a service bureau. The more of these processes you are responsible for, the more technical knowledge you need to perform your job well. Even if you never digitize footage yourself, you need to know what to expect and when you can ask for something to be fixed or redigitized. When there is a problem that you have to fix, knowing what caused that problem is usually more than half way to correcting it. Finally, if you stay in the business long enough, you will be supervising or managing, and you will have to make purchase decisions on hardware versus outsourcing. You need as much information as possible to make the right decisions.

Image Quality

The quality of images for digital compositing is a combination of resolution, color depth, component separation, sampling, and compression. High-resolution footage with excessively low sampling, shallow color depth, or lossy compression is worse for your purposes than lower-resolution footage with more reasonable sampling, color, and compression. Ideally, you want to work with footage that is at least the resolution of your output medium, is sampled at least one-to-one for each color component, and is compressed (if at all) using a lossless algorithm such as LZW. Unfortunately, we don't live or work in an ideal world, so you need to know which of these trade-offs you'll have to deal with and which you should avoid.

Component Separation

The lowest level of analog video recording is *composite*, which runs the entire video signal through a single wire. Composite signals use a single RCA connector—usually color-coded yellow—that you find on consumer video equipment, including bottom-end PC digitizing cards. The problem with composite video is that the parts of the video signal that contain color and luma information are combined in a way that they can interfere with each other. This shows up as a colored shimmer in black-and-white footage or in areas of saturated color. If you have to work with a composite source, your equipment should have a good comb filter to separate the signals as much as possible. The cheaper notch filter will not do as good a job.

The next level of analog video is S-Video, or Y/C. This separates the video signal into four wires, one pair carrying the luma signal and the other pair carrying the color signal. This still allows the color and black-and-white components to interfere with each other, but these errors are much less noticeable. S-Video is available on higher-end consumer-, prosumer-, and some professional-level equipment, and it is common on entry-level PC digitizing cards. The connectors can be either separate RCA jacks for Y and C, or a single four-pin connector. Incidentally, Macintosh ADB port (keyboard) cables make excellent S-Video cables.

The best level of analog video is *component*, which keeps the video signal separated into luma and two color components. Component video is only found on professional equipment, including the best PC digitizing cards, and the three connectors are usually bayonet-lug BNC.

Digital video formats bypass or reduce many common analog signal problems. As with any form of digital data, after it's "in numbers" you simply don't have to worry about crosstalk, interference, generational loss, or most other problems that plague analog recording. Instead, you have the "all or nothing" effect, where if these problems existed in the analog source, they may have no effect in the digital format until a threshold is reached, at which point catastrophic failure results. Although you can still have data dropouts, most digital data transfers use some form of error checking and correction. If the data as received doesn't precisely match the data as transmitted, the data is re-sent until it arrives correctly. Uncompressed digital is the only form of video that is exactly the same no matter how many times it has been copied. Connectors for digital video include Serial Digital Interface (SDI), IEEE-1394 (FireWire), and nearly 20 other types. Make sure your existing hardware has matching connectors for whatever new hardware you are considering.

Sampling

Computers work in RGB color space, but most video is captured and processed in YUV color space. Y is the luma component, and the U and V components are color difference signals. An RGB image must be sampled equally in all three color channels to record an accurate image. However, YUV video can be sampled at a high frequency for the luma components and lower frequencies for the color components with little loss of image quality. The ratio between Y, U, and V sampling rates is used as a shorthand indicator of video recording quality. Common ratios are 4:4:4, 4:2:2, 4:1:1, and 4:2:0.

The 4:4:4 ratio means that luma and both color components are each sampled at 13.5 million times a second (13.5 MHz), or once per pixel. This is the top-end sampling rate, but it takes up far too much storage space: So it is not used in standard recording media. 4:4:4 is generally used only for transmission or internal processing. 4:2:2 means that Y has been sampled for every pixel, while U and V were each sampled for every other pixel horizontally. This sampling level is used in D1, D5, Ampex DCT, Digital Betacam, Digital-S, and DVCPRO50 recording formats. 4:2:2 gives a 1.5:1 savings in data size over 4:4:4, so it's more reasonable to record and store. 4:2:0 means that for every four samples of Y in a 2×2 square, there is one sample each of U and V. This sampling pattern is used for MPEG, PAL DV, and DVCAM, and was also called YUV12 by Intel.

4:1:1 means that for every four samples of Y horizontally, there is one sample each of U and V. This sampling pattern is used in most digital video (DV) formats, including DVC, DVCPRO, and NTSC DV, and DVCAM. The linear pattern of 4:1:1 avoids problems that can occur with 4:2:0 sampling of interlaced video. However, if you ever have to convert a 4:1:1 sample to 4:2:0 for DTV or DVD distribution, the result will be a 4:1:0 sample that is missing half of its color information. 4:0:0 is the most efficient way of accurately sampling a composite signal. Because the luma and both color components are combined, the initial 4 Y samples include the entire signal so there are no separate U or V samples, thus the zeroes. This sampling is used in Sony/Ampex D-2 and D-3 digital formats.

The bottom end of component sampling patterns is YUV9, Intel's compressed YUV format, which provides a compression ratio of up to 3:1. The picture is divided into blocks of 4×4 pixels. For each block, 16 values of Y, one value of U, and one value of V are assigned. This sampling is too low for anything but multimedia and Web video, but it's used in most current entry-level video cards and in popular multimedia codecs such as Indeo and Sorenson Video.

Sampling is subject to *quantization* (or *quant*) errors, where the analog signal has a value that is not exactly one of the digital numbers available, so a number that is nearest in value is used. In general digital applications, this is also called a *rounding error*. These errors aren't usually visible, but they can add up through a series of sampling operations. Quant errors are smaller if you use a higher bit depth, because the additional precision of the extra bits reduces the size of any errors. For example, D-1, D-5, and Digital Betacam formats can sample at 10 bits, whereas other digital video formats sample at 8 bits. You can also minimize quant errors by sampling the analog signal only once and using the digital data throughout the rest of the compositing process.

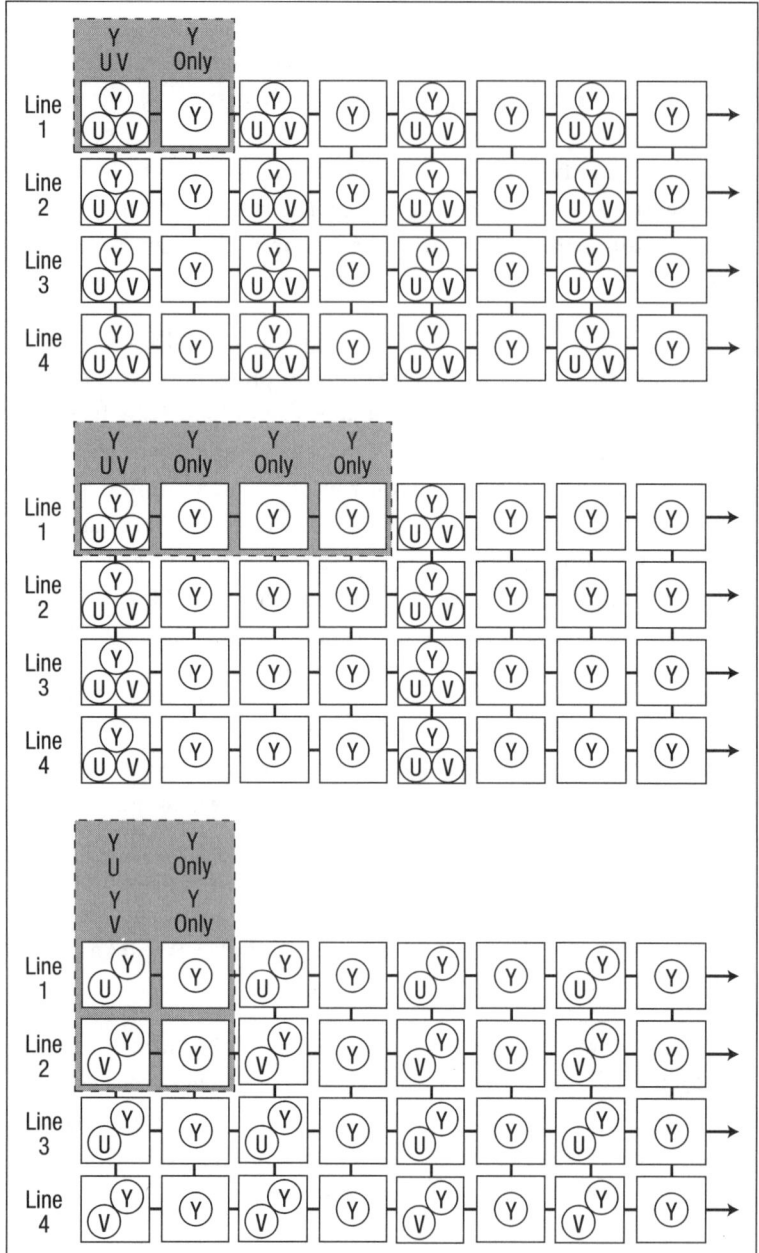

Figure 5.1
This figure shows 4:2:2 (top), 4:1:1 (center), and 4:2:0 (bottom) sampling patterns. Note that the 4:2:0 pattern samples U and V on alternate lines in each field. A frame view would show two lines of Y/U pairs, then two lines of Y/V pairs.

Quant errors also crop up when you convert color spaces. For example, most video is recorded in YUV color space, but most compositing software processes images in RGB color space. Each time you apply an operation, both the YUV/RGB conversion and RGB/YUV reconversion can add quant errors. One solution is to use software that performs all operations in YUV space. However, as of this writing, there are no YUV-native desktop compositing packages. Another solution is to convert all incoming footage to RGB, run all comps in RGB, and only convert back to YUV when dumping the finished footage to tape. The problem with this solution is that some color correction and luminance operations are best performed in YUV color space. One way to minimize quant errors in this case is to precomp all the YUV operations, then convert the precomp to RGB. This is another example of applying your knowledge as a digital compositor to anticipate and prevent problems, rather than attempting to fix them after they occur. It's much easier, less stressful, and makes a *much* more professional impression on your supervisor or client.

Compression

As a digital compositor, compression is your enemy, but one with which you will often have to negotiate. Compression can damage the images you need to work with in ways that make your work harder. On the other hand, compression can be useful to you in saving storage space and transmission time, and it's almost always necessary for transmission and distribution of the finished product. As much as possible, you should work with uncompressed original footage and reserve compression for the final step before distribution.

Sony Digital Betacam and Ampex DCT compress data by 2:1; DVCPRO50 and JVC's Digital–S compress by 3.3:1. These are relatively low compression ratios, and differences from the uncompressed source are barely visible. Any compression higher than 3.3:1, however, is going to make compositing more difficult and produce poorer results. DV, DVCPRO, DVCAM, and Digital 8 all compress at 5:1 using MPEG-2 with DCT (Discrete Cosine Transform), and Betacam SX uses it at 10:1. None of these formats is preferable for footage to be composited.

To give you an idea of the amounts of data you will have to handle, here are some comparative data rates: 295.5MBps for 2K film Cineon image sequences, 1,244MBps for 1920×1080 HDTV, 270MBps for D-1, 170MBps for D-5, 19.2MBps in MPEG-2 compression for DTV (Digital Television, one HDTV or five SDTV signals), 15MBps for M-JPEG compression, 3.6MBps for DV25.

Desktop Hardware Options

If you want to digitize video using a personal computer, you have an excellent variety of tools to choose from. The last few years have seen a dramatic decrease in the price-performance ratio for video-capture hardware and software, and a remarkable increase in the top-end quality available to desktop machines. You should be able to find a tool that fits both your budget and your image-quality needs.

Entry-Level Video Cards

The least expensive video digitizing option is to buy a video display card that also doubles as a capture card. Several manufacturers have been producing these cards for a number of years now, so you have a decent baseline of owner experience to draw upon when making your selection. These cards typically cost less than $200 and require no more expertise to install than any other video display card. They generally also produce a data stream small enough to be recorded to a desktop system's main hard disk drive (HDD), so you don't have to spring for AV-rated high-speed drives.

One of these cards is the ATI All-In-Wonder PRO. Capturing uncompressed YUV9 (4:1:0 sampling) at 640×480, 30 fps with this card requires at least a Pentium 233 MHz processor and sufficient space on a Fast IDE or SCSI drive capable of about 10MBps sustained transfer rate. At these rates, capture file storage occupies 595MB per minute, or 1.68 minutes per gigabyte, and 17,863MB for 30 minutes. Because the capture speed depends completely on the data transfer rates of the hard drive and the main bus, any other system activity during capture can cause dropped frames. If you use this hardware to capture video for digital compositing, you should carefully check every captured clip to make sure every frame is there.

The default capture resolution for this card is actually 320×240, and the larger resolution is upsampled in real time. You may want to try comping your own upsampling from a 320×240 capture for better filter selection and control or to prevent dropped frames. This card is also a decent video driver card, and inexpensive drives are available to enable it to play DVDs through your computer. If you are just getting started in digital compositing, or if your work is primarily for Web or multimedia, this board may be all the capture hardware you need.

Be aware that the video-capture function only works in Windows 95 or 98, not in Windows NT. ATI has been stalling NT users since Win 95 shipped and now simply tells them to wait for the Windows 2000 update. So, if your compositing software is NT only, the All-In-Wonder PRO is usable only if you set up a dual-boot system. Boot to Win 98, run your captures, reboot to NT, and run your comps. Awkward, but it works.

Case Study 5.1
Laptop On Set

By Jason Goodman, CEO, Multimedia Software Design

A laptop computer can be very useful to the LightWave artist on the set for testing bluescreen setups and CGI element matching. It also impresses the client, which is exceedingly important in today's "what have you done for me lately" business world.

MSD animator Stephen Baker and I went on set with a PowerBook G3 300 and an iREZ CapSure PCMCIA video-capture card. The goal of this shoot was to create an element for a larger animation, which required several newscasters to appear on a wall of over 60 LightWave-generated television sets. The PowerBook proved useful on the bluescreen set, as

LightWave laptop on the bluescreen set, operated by Stephen Baker.

shown in the following figure. It assisted us in pinpointing the subtle details of the live-action setup, and in re-creating them in our virtual set. The results were great, and the whole procedure was surprisingly easy to set up and work through.

The key to this process is the video-capture hardware in your laptop. I do not know of a laptop with built-in analog video-capture capabilities (although it may exist), so the first thing you need to do is find a suitable third-party solution. Most laptops offer expansion capabilities via PCMCIA or what is now referred to as PC Card or CardBus slots. On many laptops, one of the slots features a capability known as Zoomed Video. This is often used for MPEG or DVD decoding cards if your laptop has a DVD player. The same technology that allows these high-bandwidth devices to blast video onto your laptop screen in this case allows your laptop to capture video. If you are using one of Apple's new 400 MHz or 333 MHz G3 PowerBooks, or an iBook, you have the added option of using a USB video input device.

Image quality is not my primary fascination with the CapSure or other products like it. In this example, the footage is used merely for reference within the LightWave scene. The CapSure proved to be more than adequate for the intended bluescreen shoot. All we really needed was a still frame. You may wonder why I would not grab this with a digital camera, and there is a good reason. It is important that the still frame or clip that we capture is coming directly out of the source camera. I want to capture subtleties in the shot such as perspective created by the focal length of the camera's lens and other elements that would not be reproduced in an image captured by a separate camera.

The 300 MHz machine I used for this shoot does not have USB, which is why I opted for a CardBus (PCMCIA) iREZ CapSure card. It cost $129 and captures only at 320×240. I have since seen this same card advertised for $99. While the CapSure offers decidedly lower resolution than some other cards, it still handily met our requirements for this shoot. With new devices coming to market, I anticipate the possibility of further price reduction for this product, so it may remain a good solution for the budget-conscious. Remember that this captured footage is used only as a reference for live-action objects and lighting. The 320×240 resolution provided by the CapSure proved totally suitable.

iREZ seemed confident in the CapSure's ability to do 30 fps, so if you find yourself in a situation that requires this frame rate, it may be a good choice for this reason as well. This card also deceptively claims that it will capture 640×480, but this is merely an interpolation of its native 320×240 frame size. (Incidentally, iREZ was showing a CapSure Pro product at MacWorld that may be out by the time you read this.) Its key benefit over the card I used is its capability to capture 640×480 full-resolution frames. It also offered a small breakout box that featured S-Video input. For a more complex shot, the added quality could conceivably be a benefit. My determination to use the CapSure was more of a practical decision based on the expansion options my machine provided rather than on the features of competing products. I do not recommend either of these devices as a video professional's primary digital I/O interface, so you may find yourself in a similar situation.

To create our element, we shot an actor against bluescreen at a blue desk. LightWave was to provide the background and virtual desk to make this actor appear as if he were a news broadcaster on a high-tech set. We wanted to be able to see the lighting as it fell on both the blue desk and the actor so we could accurately mimic that lighting in the virtual set. This was the primary reasoning behind the LightWave laptop approach. The technique also served as a wonderful previsualization tool, making the client and the director feel very high-tech and confident that the shot would be a success. Again, this is important if you want to be able to charge more for your work in the future. In this particular case, it may have been slightly overkill, but we already had the laptop, and the additional hardware was inexpensive enough to make it worthwhile. The final shot was a success, and this was a contributing factor; so perhaps it was necessary. On a more complex shoot, this technique could prove to be a huge time and money saver. If you've ever had to deal with problem footage in post-production, you may find yourself wishing you had taken this step during principal photography.

On the set, the LightWave scene was modified to match the live action setup. Camera and lighting positions were easily adjusted. In this case, the camera was locked off and the actor was stationary, which greatly simplified our job. We simply ran a composite video cable out of one of the monitors on the set and fed it right into the CapSure card. This allowed us to grab QuickTime movies (useless to LightWave) and still frames that we loaded in as background images. Elements of the scene were updated in real-time as elements on the set changed.

Possibly the biggest benefit of this whole endeavor was our ability to get pertinent camera information (focal length, distance from the subject, and so on) right there on the set and to check it against our scene. These things could have easily been overlooked or recorded incorrectly had we not been checking them in real-time. This proved particularly important because setting the LightWave camera to the focal length of the actual lens did not look correct. I believe we received incorrect information about the size of the CCD in the real camera. This affects the look of a shot created by a lens of a given focal length, and in this case, made it not match the LightWave scene. This would have been potentially problematic if we had merely recorded data on set and attempted the comp entirely in post-production. Having the ability to check these parameters on the spot and modify our scene to suit the setup was fantastic.

I also took several photos with a digital still camera as a precaution, in case we needed additional information later. They proved unnecessary, but better safe than sorry. One thing we did not do that I would highly recommend: It would have been good to attempt to pull the matte on set to determine if any lighting anomalies could be corrected. We did run into this problem in post, but unfortunately, it was too late to do anything. This was not a tragedy; it just required a bit more tweaking when pulling the matte from the bluescreen background. In this case, there was both a vertical background and a horizontal surface (the blue desktop) in front of the actor, as shown in the following figure. The light striking the desk illuminated it much more than the background, making parts of it appear almost white.

The lighting setup.

Fortunately, using software such as Ultimatte allows you to use a screen correction layer, which can eliminate such problems. If you plan to use Ultimatte or a similar tool, make sure you shoot a screen correction element. This is a shot of just the bluescreen with no actors. You will use it later to drop out any abnormalities in the screen. Screen correction can be very effective and is one of Ultimatte's powerful features. This can really help problem shots, but good lighting on a bluescreen is still very important to a composite's success. Having a good gaffer or DP with a lot of bluescreen experience is a great way to avoid these types of problems. If you have not shot bluescreen footage before and intend to spend some money renting time at a bluescreen studio, I strongly encourage you to invest in the added expense of an experienced professional gaffer to set up your lights.

Once our LightWave scene was set up and saved, our job on the set was done. We took the laptop back to the studio and got ready to do the composite. This was done with a combination of After Effects and LightWave. The BetaSP tape from the shoot was digitized using NewTek's Video Toaster NT, converted to AVI format, and brought into After Effects, as shown here:

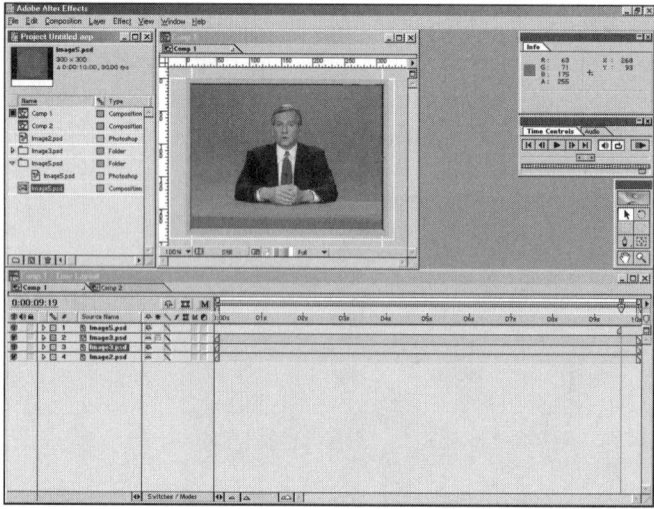

Compositing in After Effects.

In After Effects, an alpha channel was created from the bluescreen with the Ultimatte plug-in. This could have probably been done with the built-in chroma key tools in After Effects or Aura, but Ultimatte is the Cadillac of bluescreen software, and I like the results it produces. As with any project, there are many ways to achieve the same goal. This is just one of them, and it proved to be quite effective. Once the alpha channel was created for the 30-second shot, each frame was output in an IFF sequence to facilitate import into LightWave. I also converted the RBG data from our original bluescreen AVI footage into an

IFF image sequence. We work with Alpha, Intel, and Mac OS versions of LightWave, and I find the native IFF format to be the most compatible and problem-free. This becomes most apparent when dealing with ScreamerNet, really long image sequences, or generally, anything even mildly unusual.

The RGB sequence was loaded into the scene as a foreground image, with the alpha sequence masking out the blue background. The same sequence was mapped onto the desk with a high degree of transparency to create a subtle moving reflection as the actor spoke and moved his hands. The reflection is quite discrete, but it adds a great deal of realism to the final animation, as shown here.

Final composite showing correct shadows and reflections.

This technique can be easily applied to much more complex compositing shots and could really save a lot of headaches, time, and money in the long run. I hope this case study has been helpful, and I welcome input from users who exercise the technique. By the way, the iREZ card is available for the PC as well, so this isn't a Mac-only technique.

Jason Goodman is the CEO of NYC-based Multimedia Software Design. You can email him at jason@msd-nyc.com or visit the Multimedia Software Design Web site at www.msd-nyc.com.

MPEG Capture Cards

The next-most affordable digitizing option is to use one of the under-$200 consumer-level MPEG-1 capture cards. Although it's possible to successfully composite elements digitized by one of these boards, there are a number of drawbacks that make this a very poor choice. If you have other strong reasons to use an MPEG codec, you should at least use MPEG-2. Unfortunately, a decent real-time MPEG-2 capture board such as the Canopus Amber (see Figure 5.2) or Darim MPEGator II will cost you over 10 times the price of an MPEG-1 card, or about as much as an M-JPEG or uncompressed D-1 capture system. If you can't afford MPEG-2 capture, you should probably consider capturing in a different format and using the inexpensive MPEG-1 encoder only for output.

Figure 5.2
Canopus Amber for DVD MPEG-2 capture card.

The advantage of MPEG-2 is that it provides a reasonably good result with low losses and significant compression. The best examples of MPEG-2 are commercial feature film DVD releases, which are compressed in several passes using expensive software and hardware in order to maximize quality. You will not see this level of quality in single-pass, real-time compression, which is comparable to standard VHS and is what the consumer-level MPEG-2 cards are designed to produce.

The disadvantage of MPEG-2 for digital compositing is that the compression is based on frame-to-frame *deltas,* or changes in pixel values. If you were to run an operation on one frame, the following frames would look like garbage, because the deltas would no longer correspond to the new values of the pixels in the first image. An MPEG-2 video stream consists of I-frames, B-frames, and P-frames. The I-frames are intact video with DCT but no temporal compression. The B-frames reference the nearest preceding I-frame and the nearest following I-frame, and contain only the information needed to reconstruct the differences between the two I-frames. If an I-frame is missing, the B-frames can't be displayed either. The P-frames are like the B-frames, except they only reference the nearest preceding I-frame. Each P- or B-frame may contain as little as 5 percent of the information in an I-frame. If an MPEG-2 stream were all I-frames, you could composite it easily, but the video file size would be huge. Some editing systems for MPEG-2 either cut on the I-frames to preserve best quality or use one of several profiles that allow cutting on a B- or P-frame at the cost of image quality. More advanced systems such as the Matrox DigiSuite DTV can translate IPB sequences to I-frame for editing, then translate them back in real time.

If you must use an MPEG-2 source for digital compositing, you should extract a clip with complete I-frames on both ends to ensure maximum image quality and your ability to re-insert the clip after you complete the comp. You will need to render or *transcode* the MPEG-2 clip to an uncompressed image sequence or video format before you can successfully perform any compositing operations on it. Once the comp is finished, you will need to recompress the clip, using MPEG-2 parameters selected to produce results as close as possible to the original MPEG-2 source. You should expect to see a loss in image quality. Decompression and recompression with a lossy codec like MPEG-2 will never give results as good as the original. If the losses are too great, the clip will show obvious differences in the reassembled video. In this case, you may want to try sharpening or other filters on the uncompressed clip, then recompress it and assemble the video again.

DV: FireWire, iLink, IEEE-1394

Striking the middle ground between MPEG-1 and MPEG-2, a basic IEEE-1394 capture card for DV sources currently runs less than $500. With a 3.6MBps transfer rate, these cards can digitize video to most ordinary HDDs. If DV image quality is acceptable for your compositing work, this may be a good choice. However, most low-end IEEE-1394 cards have no other inputs or outputs. If you ever need to output to something other than a DV camera or recorder, you'll need a card with S-Video, component, or SDI outputs. FAST's DV Master Pro handles this issue with a breakout box containing audio and S-Video in and out, and component YUV out, but it comes with a bigger price tag, about $3,000.

What you are paying for is real-time hardware encoding. Instead of relying on software encoding that bogs your system and slows down video response, the DV Master Pro hardware uses Sony's DVBK-1 chipset to convert analog video to DV on the fly. My own experience with the DV Master Pro has been very positive. The system installed easily and has run flawlessly under NT 4.0 Service Pack 5. The Speed Razor editing software bundled with it works very well. The S-Video capture works as well as 1394, and the codec worked flawlessly with most compositing software. The capture function is especially friendly, because all the displays are updated in real time so you can catch any problems when they occur. Other systems don't refresh the computer display or the monitor pass-through accurately, so you have to wait until the capture is done before you can look for dropped frames. I'm more confident with the capture process of the DV Master Pro because what I see is what I get. The only concern I have for compositing this hardware's input is the 5:1 compression, but that's part of the DV standard. I think FAST has done a great job with this hardware, and I highly recommend it if you use IEEE-1394 sources.

Fast Drive Cards

The next level of video-capture cards produces a higher-quality, larger data stream that requires faster HDDs. Fortunately, recent technology has brought the price of AV-speed HDDs down to a fraction of the total price for a digital compositing workstation. A significant advantage of these cards is that the fast HDDs remain available for other file storage, so you can keep your audio, still, and other project files on the same drive. This makes backups and other housekeeping much simpler and therefore more reliable.

NewTek's Video Toaster NT (VTNT) shown in Figure 5.3, which lists for $2,995, is an example of a high-quality (uncompressed ITU-R-601) video-capture and -output system that enables you to use the video HDDs for other purposes. The VTNT doesn't even dictate what type of drive you can use: SCSI, IDE, whatever, as long as it has a sustained data transfer rate of at least 22MBps. The most cost-effective way to achieve this data rate is to use Windows NT's striping utility to make the computer see several smaller, slower HDDs as one large, fast HDD. For example, if you have four HDDs that can each sustain 6MBps, you can stripe them into one virtual HDD that can sustain 24MBps. This enables you to use slower, less expensive HDDs.

Installing the VTNT is simple. It is a single card with breakout cables for component video. Options are available for SDI and DV. The software bundled with the systems includes LightWave for 3D modeling, animation, and rendering; Aura for 2D paint and compositing; and Speed Razor for editing. All three applications are optimized to work with the VTNT's proprietary RTV video file format. The only downside is that the RTV format is not used by any other compositing software, so you have to output a compatible format through Aura, LightWave, or Speed Razor, then repeat the process in reverse to get the finished comp back to RTV format for real-time playback. This is a little annoying if you are trying to pop back and forth between applications, but it doesn't really affect image quality as long as you don't use any compression in any of the file format conversions. Setting up the striped HDD array is easy too. If you haven't done it before, the VTNT manual includes a step-by-step guide that had my system up and digitizing in less than an hour after I opened the box.

When you are shopping for HDDs, keep in mind that they are a commodity market. The price per unit changes frequently, and it is possible to purchase essentially the same functionality from a number of vendors. It would be useless for me to present a list of prices and model numbers

Figure 5.3
NewTek Video Toaster NT input/output card.

here, because they change on almost a daily basis. Instead, here are a few guidelines you can follow when you buy hard disk drives for your compositing workstation.

I don't recommend that you buy the latest, top-of-the-line HDD. As with most computer technology, the first run of a product is typically priced high enough to quickly recoup research and development costs, so you won't find any bargains. Also, the first run generally has a few bugs in it. If you absolutely have to use the latest hardware, you can expect to have significant downtime and data loss, and to spend enough time on the phone to develop a first-name personal relationship with the technical support personnel for the HDD manufacturer.

I do recommend that you consider the HDD next in line from the top. Generally, there is a significant drop in price once a product is no longer top-of-the-line. The manufacturer and distributors don't want to get stuck with older, slower-moving inventory, so they price it more attractively to move it faster. You can also benefit from the experience of others. If an HDD has been on the market for even a few months, you can generally find useful information in Usenet newsgroups or other online resources.

Buy more than you think you'll need. If you are following good digital compositing practice, you will need space for lots of precomps, as well as the raw footage and the final output. Think in multiples of the largest project you'll ever work with. It's generally better to have some unused capacity than to have the downtime and stress of adding capacity (or worse, running out of drive space) when you're crunching toward a major deadline.

Dedicated Drive Cards

The next step up in video digitizing performance requires exclusive control of the HDD to maintain a high data transfer rate. This performance boost comes at the price of HDDs you can't use for anything else, but that's a reasonably affordable trade-off if your compositing needs require these cards' higher performance.

One of the most popular manufacturers for dedicated-drive video-capture systems is Digital Processing Systems (DPS). The DPS Personal Animation Recorder was the first digital disk recorder priced low enough for a hobbyist or start-up studio to afford. Subsequent DPS products have consistently targeted that price point with reliable, practical systems—so successfully, in fact, that most established studios have at least one piece of DPS gear. DPS's current product line includes the Perception RT3DX (see Figure 5.4), a system of internal cards, a breakout box, and dedicated Ultra Wide SCSI HDDs. The HDDs are controlled directly by the RT3DX cards, including striping multiple drives to appear as single drives. The proprietary file system driver makes the HDDs appear as a drive letter like the regular system drives. The virtual file system enables applications to access Perception RVD video files as image sequences in TGA, IFF, TIF, BMP, PIC (SoftImage), and SGI formats. When the system accesses a particular file type, it is accessing a virtual file created only when the file is opened. The only file type that is actually stored in the Perception RT drives is the RVD file. Frames of other file types are generated as they are accessed.

Figure 5.4
The DPS RT3DX card.

The Perception RT3DX supports two channels of real-time video playback and one channel of real-time video recording. Video inputs and outputs on the breakout box include D-1, component, S-Video, and composite, with separate S-Video and composite outputs for preview or keying, and stereo audio inputs and outputs with sample rate selection up to 44.1 kHz 16-bit audio. Video and audio are synchronized in hardware. Video is digitized at full-frame NTSC (720x486) and PAL (720x576) resolutions and compressed in hardware using M-JPEG, at as low as 1.4:1 NTSC (1.6:1 in PAL) compression ratio (user selectable) or 15MBps per data stream.

Operation of the Perception RT3DX is very slick, to the point of being transparent. Digitizing clips is about as easy as operating a VCR, and when compositing on the system, you can just forget the extra hardware is there. You simply choose the frames you want in the format you prefer, and the images are there when you need them. The software runs very stably under Windows NT. The latest product announcement from DPS is dpsReality, a 4:2:2:4 sampling system that supports a full alpha channel with the video. If you are looking for a stable, robust digitizing solution for digital compositing, DPS should be the first place you look. It doesn't hurt that eyeon Software's Digital Fusion is bundled with most DPS products.

That covers the options available to digitizing most forms of video on your desktop. If you want to work in film, however, you're going to need some specialized standalone equipment: either a *telecine* or *film scanner*.

Telecine

Telecine machines cost hundreds of thousands of dollars and require skilled operators. They are not the sort of equipment you buy on a whim; until you have a strong business case for keeping a telecine busy enough to employ a full-time operator, you will be better off outsourcing your telecine transfers to a competent service bureau. However, if you want to get the best-quality transfers (not to mention the most bang for your buck), you should understand how the telecine process works.

Telecine was originally a film projector pointed into the lens of a video camera. Before videotape, this was the way everything from feature films to television shows to news footage was broadcast. Color correction was limited to adjusting the gain of the sensor tubes, originally just the three RGB colors but later a luminance tube as well. These early film-chain transfer machines were very hard on the film; besides inflicting excessive wear, they often mangled or tore the film. Needless to say, no one would risk an original camera negative in one of these machines.

Rank Precision Industries (which has since spun off its telecine business as Cintel) introduced the flying spot scanner, or FSS, shown in Figure 5.5. This approach reversed that of the original telecines. Instead of a steady light illuminating the entire film frame and the sensor tubes doing the scanning, the FSS uses a cathode-ray tube (CRT) to cast a moving 1-pixel-wide spot of light on the film frame. This provides precise placement of the spot within the frame, even when the film is moving. The flying spot scans a line while the film moves forward one line's width, and the flying spot returns to the start of the next scan line. Enabling the film to move during the scan removed the need for the pull-down claws, sprockets, and shutters of the original film chain, making the FSS system gentle enough to safely handle camera original film. After the beam passes through the film, a system of dichroic mirrors separates the beam into its primary red, green, and blue components and directs them to separate photomultiplier tubes (PMTs), which produce the RGB analog video signal. The FSS can also scan an entire frame when the film is

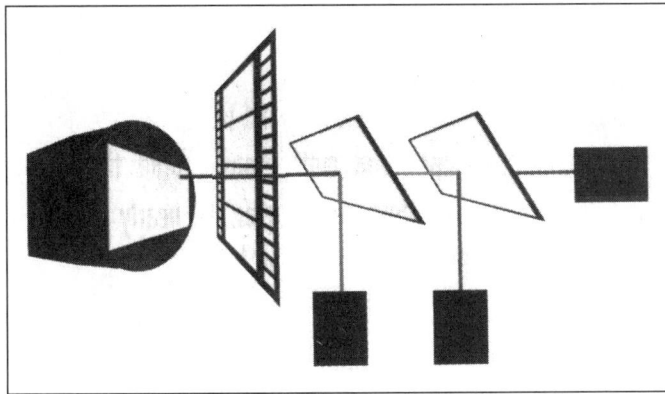

Figure 5.5
CRT flying spot scanning system.

stopped, enabling a colorist to make color corrections in real-time. To perform 3:2 pulldown, early Cintel machines ran seven different scan patches at the same time to create a 30 fps signal.

Cintel's next generation of machines, the MkIII, stored each film frame digitally at 720x488 resolution for interpolating into a 3:2 interlaced format. Color correction, however, was still based on controlling the gain on the RGB photomultiplier tubes. Cintel introduced the Mark III HD, the first 1125-line analog telecine, in 1985. A small number were used worldwide at places like Universal Studio's High Definition Telecine Center. In 1989, the next major improvement, Cintel's Ursa, used digital color controls. The Ursa converted the PMT's output into digital form at 4:2:2 sampling, making color correction and other post processing operations entirely digital. The Ursa Gold followed in 1994 with pin registration and 4:4:4 sampling at 10-bit color depth, producing full-resolution color rather than the Ursa's half-resolution sampling. Since that time, reengineering of various components by Cintel and third-party developers has increased image quality, reduced noise, increased reliability, and extended CRT life.

Cintel's latest machine, the C-Reality, shown in Figure 5.6, includes resolution options from standard definition 720×488 to HD 1920×1080 to 2K 2048×1556. Sensors are now solid-state avalanche photodiodes rather than photomultiplier tubes. An f-stop control enables the operator to correct for bowed film by stopping the lens down to keep the entire frame in focus. Internally, the C-Reality uses 14-bit color depth, but outputs 12 bits.

CCD Telecine

At the same time the Cintel MkIII was introduced, Philips brought out a telecine machine based on solid-state charge-coupled-device (CCD) technology. The FDL-60 used an array of 1K CCD elements to detect each of the RGB colors. The telecine moves the film across the CCD array, and a diffuse white light shines through the film and is channeled by a set of dichroic mirrors to the CCDs, which capture an entire row of pixels at once. This enables the film to continue moving, as in the flying spot scanner, removing the need for destructive mechanically interrupted movement of valuable film. Because the FDL-60 was designed for direct broadcast, the digital signals from the CCDs were matrixed into YUV signals. In 1990, the next-generation telecine, the FDL-90, output 4:2:2 digital video and boosted the CCD arrays to 1332 elements each. Philips' next improvement was the Quadra, with more-advanced color tools, followed by the Quadra Vision, currently Philips' top standard-definition telecine.

Philips introduced a different kind of telecine at NAB '96 with the Spirit DataCine: 1,920-pixel scanning with support for a variety of output standards derived from the scan (see Figure 5.7). The 10 custom-designed linear CCDs were developed in collaboration with Kodak, which also developed the optics for the Spirit. One advance was the use of a Xenon lamp optically converted to a diffuse source, then projected through the film via an output slit. This close confinement of the light path reduces scatter, helping to conceal scratches in the film base. Four of the CCDs, with no color filters, sample luminance for 1,920 pixels across the film frame. The other six sensors, paired for each color, sample 960 pixels, for a total sampling ratio of 4:2:2. For

Figure 5.6
Cintel C-Reality telecine.

Figure 5.7
Philips Spirit DataCine.

black-and-white film, only the 1,920 unfiltered CCD is used. The system's signal-to-noise ratios are reportedly smaller than the film grain. The Spirit's SteadiScan option uses a high-resolution camera to monitor film sprocket holes, enabling digital correction for perfect image alignment without mechanical pin registration. The success of the Spirit is probably best indicated by the fact that more than 75 of these million-dollar machines are in use worldwide.

In what would seem to be a logically inevitable marriage of technologies, Cinema Products in cooperation with Sony High-Definition Center married a Sony HDC-750 camera to a special film transport. The registration pins are controlled by electromagnetic actuators to provide fast, accurate, but gentle film handling at speeds from 1 to 60 fps. For true 2Kx1.5K capture, a digital camera with 12-bit color sampling can be swapped for the HDC-750. Cinema Products advertised the machine with the question, "Is it a film scanner with the speed of a telecine, or a telecine with the image quality of a film scanner?"

There are two criteria you should be especially aware of if you read marketing materials on high-resolution telecines: resolution and scanning speed. First, I have found a deplorable number of film professionals and telecine marketers (both of whom should know better) who are throwing around the term "2K" as a label for images that are only HD resolution. The difference is almost 14 percent, the pixel-count equivalent of a full D-1 frame. Second, I have read banner-headline claims of real-time scanning at 24 fps, followed by fine-print provisos saying they have to slow the telecine down to 6 fps to accommodate the computer's recording speed. From people using the machines on real-world projects, I have heard the necessary slow-down is more in the range of 2 to 4 fps. If a telecine manufacturer spins its marketing this way, I wouldn't buy or use one of its machines without a detailed spec sheet and independent corroboration that the machine's performance actually meets your needs. If film professionals hand you these kinds of numbers, call them on it.

Color correction is usually an important part of the telecine process, and there is a wide range of color options available. The color correction process can make the operator (or *colorist*) look like he or she is simultaneously piloting a starship and playing *Centipede*. Generally, the operator uses three trackballs with rings around the outside (see Figure 5.8) to control the gamma and color settings. If you have to key bluescreen footage that will come through telecine, you need to make sure the colorist understands that you need consistent areas of color. If color correction on the telecine will make your compositing work harder, try getting uncorrected footage so you can pull a clean matte, then apply the matte to the corrected footage. If there appear to be spill or other problems that you can correct while pulling the matte, try negotiating with the colorist to make corrections to the footage after the comps are done.

If you are compositing with the intent of output to film, you need to be aware of what telecine does to film grain: It smoothes it out! This is great for video work because it removes a lot of noise and makes it easier for you to pull a clean matte. Unfortunately, for film work, you will have to fake film grain into telecined elements in order to match footage that did not go through the

Figure 5.8
A telecine workstation.

telecine (see Figure 5.9). Also, according to Ultimatte, film grain is less of a problem to compositing than the noise generated in the telecine itself. This noise is level-dependent, and the blue channel has significantly more noise than the other channels. This is especially important if you need to pull a bluescreen matte. If you plan to telecine footage and you anticipate blue channel noise problems, you may want to shoot with greenscreen. Telecines generally inject less noise in the green channel, and the green layer of most film stocks has finer grain. In any case, you need the telecine to sample at least 4:2:2 and as deep a color space as possible, and to record to a component digital medium. Anything less will lose the color data you need to make a clean comp.

There used to be a large gap between telecine and film scanning. Telecine was strictly for video broadcasting of "film at 11" news footage, filmed studio productions or movies, or transferring film to consumer-grade videotape for distribution. Film scanners were strictly for supporting feature-film-quality digital post-production. The difference in resolution, color depth, and processing speed were worlds apart. Now telecines are available that are able to produce nearly the same level of resolution and color depth as the film scanners.

Film Scanners

When you are compositing specifically for feature film, you need images with at least 2K resolution and color depth to match the full response of film. If you are going to be playing compositing games like stabilization, match moves, or anything else that may compromise the framing, you'll need even higher resolution to provide some elbow room. 6K VistaVision is not too much to

Figure 5.9
Top: A close-up of a scanned film image showing film grain. Bottom: The same magnification of a telecined image from the same footage.

ask when the element you're tracking is all over the frame. When you need this kind of extreme imaging, nothing else will give you the performance of film scanners.

Film scanning is expensive. These are machines that take a 1,000-foot reel of film, pin-register one frame at a time, and extract up to 21 million pixels from each image. That takes a level of precision manufacturing that you don't see in your average consumer TV or fax machine, and that is why film scanners start at around a quarter million dollars and go up—way up!—from there. As with telecines, you don't buy one of these on a whim. Even the giants of the effects industry like ILM only have a few of these machines in-house. Most film scanners are owned by specialized service bureaus who can pay for the machines by keeping them running most of the time and by charging a good price for their services. Rates vary depending on how large and complex the scanning job is, but you can expect to pay around $2.00 to $5.00 per frame for top-quality scans.

You can see an example of lower-resolution film scanning in the Cineon files on the CD-ROMs and in the two-page spread in the Color Studio. These images were scanned at only 2K resolution, the level of film scanning used when you think you'll be able to stay within the frame. Even though this is "the low end," each frame is about 12MB. Full-frame VistaVision images can be nine times that size. Needless to say, you need a honkin' big workstation to handle a long sequence of film images, and even monster systems move these files around more slowly than you might prefer. Working with film images will drive home the utility of using thumbnail or *proxy* image sequences to experiment and of loading up the full-res images only when you are ready for the final tweaks.

CCD film scanners use the same solid-state sensors, one per pixel, as some telecines, just more of them in larger arrays. If you want to capture a 4K line, you need to use 4,096 CCDs. That's a pretty large, very touchy chip to manufacture. If you use multiple separate CCD arrays, you run into alignment problems. If you try to take multiple passes with a smaller CCD array, you run into even more alignment problems. Getting everything to work right, reliably, is an impressive piece of engineering.

Shown in Figure 5.10, the Imagica IMAGER XE is a film scanner with a pin-registered film transport and a tricolor linear CCD. It processes data internally at 16 bits per channel, but outputs through a 14-bit A/D converter. The IMAGER XE can scan VistaVision at 4096x6144, and standard 35mm full aperture at 4096x3112. It handles 35mm film in Academy, CinemaScope, VistaVision and Full Aperture, plus 16mm and Super16. Optimal speed is supposed to be 4 seconds per frame at 2K resolution and 11 seconds per frame at 4K, but I wouldn't use those times to schedule any important deadlines. The scanner can output files in TIFF 16/8-bit Linear, FIDO 10-bit Logarithmic, or SGI 16/8-bit Linear. The machine is run by an SGI O2 R5000 or higher, or an NT workstation. This is the first Imagica scanner to allow operation by a non-SGI workstation. I see this as one more indication that the effects industry is going NT. For more information (including a list of service bureaus that use Imagica scanners), visit **www.imagica-la.com**.

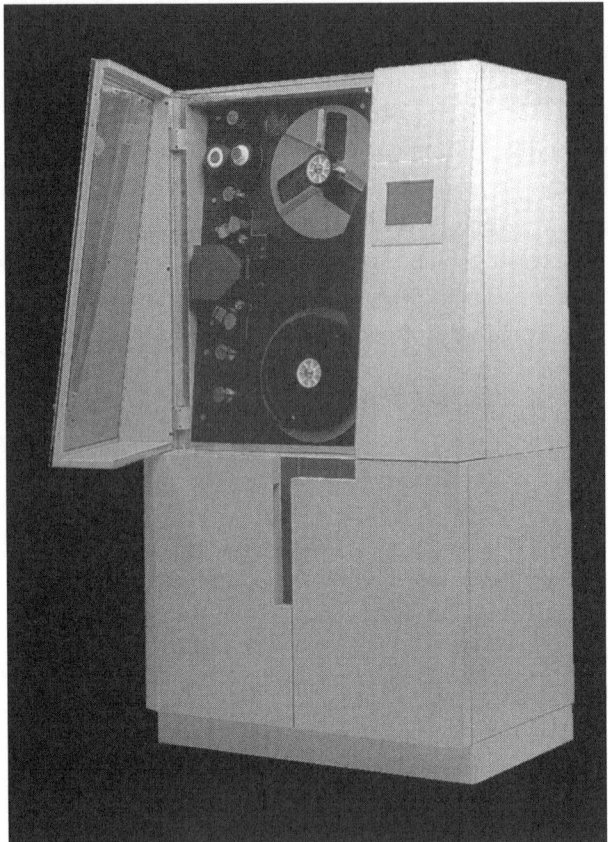

Figure 5.10
Imagica IMAGER XE digital film scanner.

Moving On

This chapter has equipped you with the knowledge you need to successfully import nearly any film or video format into your compositing workstation. Now that you know what to do with the media, you need to know what you can do to improve the quality of what gets recorded on this media type. The most careful 4K laser scan of the best film stock will be useless if the shoot was bungled. The next chapter tells you how to work with the shooting crew to get the best footage for your digital compositing.

ON THE SET

Even if you never become a visual effects supervisor, learning how to set up or supervise an effects shoot can make your compositing work easier and help you produce better results. Most of your compositing work relies on the quality of raw footage. At the beginning of your career as a digital compositor, you may be able to rely on supervisors to provide you with footage and other elements. You may be able to concentrate exclusively on compositing, without worrying about where the elements came from or how they were created. As you gain experience, you will be expected to solve or anticipate more difficult problems. To do this, you need to know how an effects shoot works and how to prevent problems on the set. This knowledge is also part of your preparation for the responsibilities of a lead compositor or visual effects supervisor. If you are a freelance compositor or you want to run your own effects company, you need to understand these issues right from the start.

For any effects shot, a visual effects supervisor should be on the set—this means either you or a trustworthy and knowledgeable colleague. Like packing a parachute, you can't trust the shooting of effects footage to anyone who won't be relying on it. If you can't supervise the shoot, at least convince the producer to hire lighting and camera people who have done bluescreen work successfully.

> *"No amount of clever post-production can undo the damage of poorly recorded source material."*
> *—Mark Christiansen*

If a client walks in with bluescreen footage and you weren't on the set, you can't afford to take his word for the quality of the bluescreen setup. The job could be anything from a quick-and-easy key to a nightmare of garbage mattes and hand-rotoscoping. If at all possible, try to key a few frames from the footage before you give the client a quote.

If you make it onto the set as visual effects supervisor, there are some people issues you need to remember. A professional crew includes a lot of people, and a definite hierarchy exists. You are an outsider, an unknown quantity. Only the director may know you, and you may be on set before the director shows up, so make sure someone makes the appropriate introductions.

Access to the camera is a big deal. Only the director and DP (director of photography) and their camera crew are allowed to look through the camera. The fact that you can, too, puts you among the highest ranks on set. Don't abuse it. Look through the camera only to check the shot for your effects, and don't disturb the camera crew while you are doing it.

You usually need to get information from the camera crew and production assistant. You also need the cooperation of most of the grips and gaffers. Anybody who touches the set, props, or lights can make your job easier or harder. Be nice, and don't ask for anything you don't need. Use the chain of command; get the director's approval in advance, then talk to the DP before you start asking the rest of the crew to do (or not to do) something.

Shooting Decisions

As VFX supervisor, you may have an influence over (or even sole responsibility for) a myriad of factors on the set. You need to have enough information to make sound decisions. On the set, with an expensive crew waiting while you dawdle, is not the time for you to start thinking about your options. Plan ahead!

Camera

Shoot in the best format you can. Even if the rest of the production will be shot or edited on a lower standard, you need a high standard to get a clean key. Film is best but is harder to justify for a broadcast or industrial video production. If you are working in broadcast, the lowest standard you should shoot is BetaSP; the higher you go, the easier and faster your work will be. DV and other heavily compressed formats cause more problems than they solve. S-Video crams the color signal through a single wire and isn't much better than composite. If possible, you should shoot with a system that enables you to get uncompressed footage straight into your computer.

If you can shoot on film, consider using Kodak's SFX 200T, which was developed to correct bluescreen fringe problems for DreamQuest's *Mighty Joe Young*. This film stock is more expensive, but if you're doing high-end feature film work, it pays for itself. For less demanding work, you can use more common film stock. If your budget is really tight, use short ends left over from larger productions. Because effects shots are rarely longer than a minute or two, you can get away with using a few hundred feet of film at a time. These short ends can cost as little as 6 cents a foot, compared to 50 cents per foot and up for longer stock. Short ends give the camera loader a little more work, but that shouldn't cripple your production schedule.

For film shoots, try to use a camera that has a video tap. You can feed the video through a low-end chroma keyer that will give you live feedback about your bluescreen setup. This makes correcting lighting problems much faster and can save time and money both on the shoot and in post. If possible, set up the keyer with a video feed of the actual background elements you will be compositing. If the backgrounds have not been completed yet, you can try using conceptual art or story sketches.

If you are shooting on video, make sure you adjust the camera's white balance before you shoot the clean plate, and keep this setting throughout the shoot. If you let the white balance wander, different takes will require different compositing settings, eating up more of your time. If the camera has any edge enhancement features, turn them down; too much can make compositing even more difficult. Don't use additional gain either; gain adds noise in proportion, so a better solution is simply to use more light on the set.

Lighting And Rigging

When everything is perfectly consistent between the clean plate and the final take, you can run a simple screen-correction pass that does more than 90 percent of your corrections. If any part of the set changes between the clean plate and the final take, you will have to fix it with more time-consuming or expensive processes. This variability is why shooting effects elements on a soundstage is generally easier; you have complete control over lighting and sets. For location shooting, all you can do is try to minimize the problems.

Changing sun angle can also create more work for you. If shooting goes long enough that the change becomes a problem, you will have to tweak the matched lighting on other live or CGI (computer-generated imagery) elements to avoid continuity problems. This is where the exact time as recorded by the production assistant or 1st AC (first assistant cameraperson) can save you some guesswork. For CGI elements, software that automatically re-creates sun angle (based on location and time) usually solves the problem. For live elements, you'll have to work with the lead gaffer to tweak the lighting for a close match.

Bluescreen

Bluescreen is a class of compositing processes based on extracting foreground elements from a monochromatic background. The weather maps on TV are a low-end example of bluescreen. The meteorologist stands before a wall that's painted and lit as a solid bright blue, and the studio engineers use a chroma keyer to replace every blue pixel coming from the camera with a pixel from the weather-map video feed. Bluescreen has been used for decades and has survived the transition from optical film processes to digital film and video. Bluescreen can be demanding to use effectively, but with all those years of shared experience, the basics are fairly well established.

Any change to the bluescreen's lighting, backlighting, or shadows causes problems. This means your goal is to prevent or control any natural influences on the bluescreen. The bluescreens should be backed with *blacks* (light-proof black screens) to prevent irregular backlighting or shadowing. All rigging should be extra solid to prevent movement. If you have to shoot on a windy day, you will find that large bluescreens make excellent sails. In that case, simply plan for a lot of corrections during compositing.

Keep sets, talent, and props as far from the bluescreens as possible. You have to put a lot of light on the bluescreen to get an even color, and blue-tinted reflected light tends to bounce off everything else, creating *spill*, as shown in Figure 6.1. One way to minimize spill is to use grazing light

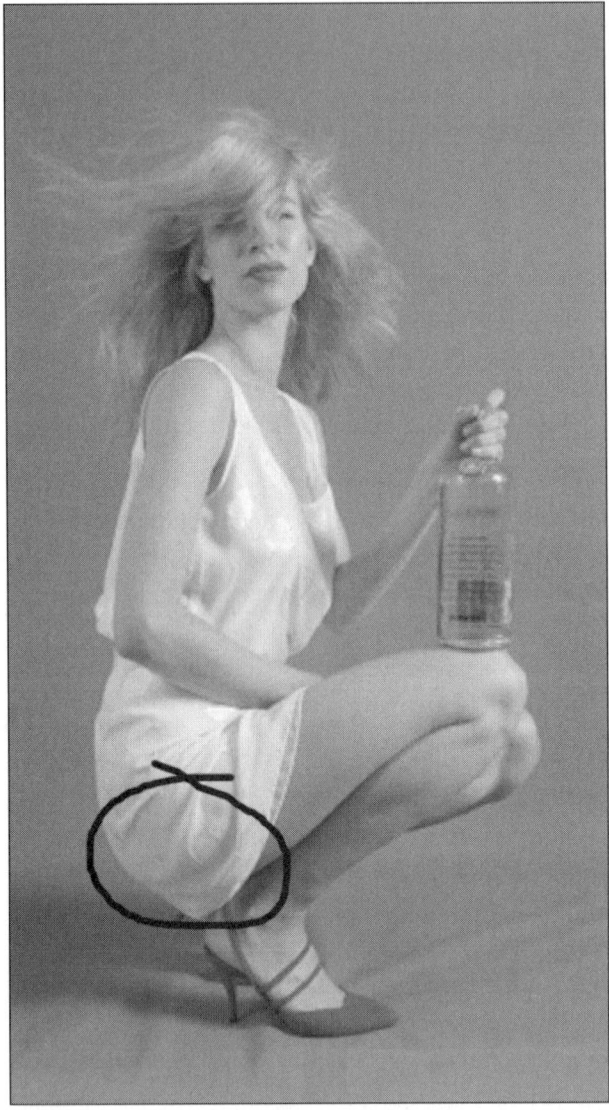

Figure 6.1
Blue spill, or light reflected from the bluescreen backdrop.

rather than direct light. Another is to use ultraviolet (UV) light; some bluescreen paints and fabrics fluoresce under UV, giving an even, bright key color without spilling on your foreground subject. If the rest of the lighting setup allows it, you can also strongly backlight the actors or use a pale yellow gel backlight to help wash out the blue spill. Don't go overboard on edge lighting, however. If you get a halo effect, the only way you can get rid of it in post is to choke the matte. If you can shoot using natural light, it will solve or avoid several of these problems.

ULTIMATTE RECOMMENDS AGAINST COLORED BACKLIGHTS

When using Ultimatte, tinted back lighting is not needed to counteract the blue spill as it is with a chroma key setup. The Ultimatte will remove the spill from the backing. Any amber light added in an attempt to counteract blue spill simply adds an amber cast to the foreground subject in the composite.

Run a light meter all over your bluescreen. The luminosity of your bluescreen should be equal to or higher than the brightest object in the scene, but no more than two or three f-stops higher than the foreground subject's hot spots. Too low and you increase your keying problems; too high and you get excessive spill and the foreground washes out. Light the bluescreen as evenly as possible. Large diffusers or *softboxes* such as Chimera's Lightbanks (**www.chimeralighting.com**) cast a soft light without distinct shadows.

If possible, stop down the camera aperture a little to prevent the edges of the frame from darkening, which can make compositing more difficult. If the subject is in sharp focus but the bluescreen is a little blurry, it will smooth over minor lighting and color inconsistencies in the bluescreen.

If you will be doing a lot of bluescreen work, you may want to equip your studio with a *cyclorama,* or *cyc*. This is usually a wall-and-floor set that has smooth curves instead of sharp corners at the joins. These curves make it easier to light the bluescreen evenly. Cycs are also used (with different colors) in conventional studio photography. For example, a white cyc is commonly used for fashion or product photography.

Choosing A Color

Colors found in nature rarely approach the pure, saturated values possible with bluescreen paints or fabrics. The larger the difference between any natural colors in the footage and the artificially saturated colors in the bluescreen, the easier it is for compositing software to extract the foreground from the bluescreen. This means you can't simply slap any old paint on your set and expect to get good results; you have to use special high-saturation paints or fabrics. At $50 a gallon or $30 a yard, you don't want to choose the wrong stuff.

The most popular colors for color keying backgrounds are blue, green, and orange, in that order. Theoretically, it is possible to key nearly any saturated color, but these are the ones proven to work best in most situations. For convenience, I will use the term *bluescreen* from here on to refer to any color used for keying.

Blue generally gives better results when you are working with skin tones, but green is better for bringing out shadows in low-light situations and is easier to work with digitally. Some older film stock worked better with blue, but this is less of an issue with current film stocks. Because of the odd chemistry of bluescreen paints, they behave differently when you apply them to sets or props. It is generally easier to get an even, solid coat with blue paint; the green paints tend to require repeated applications for an even coat, and spot touch-ups don't blend in as well. If you are using a fabric backdrop, the fuzzier materials diffuse the light better. Some software (like Ultimatte) works best with a very specific bluescreen color.

Bluescreen Suppliers

Purchasing a bluescreen is a relatively simple task. These are several of the more popular suppliers of bluescreens:

Rose Brand East
512 West 35th Street
New York, NY 10001
800-223-1624
www.rosebrand.com

Rose Brand West
10856 Vanowen Street
North Hollywood, CA 91606
800-360-5056

Wildfire
11250 Playa Court
Culver City, CA 90230-6150
800-937-8065

Markertek Video Supply
914-246-3036
www.markertek.com

Elite Video
501-321-0440
www.elitevideo.com

Make sure that your bluescreen color doesn't appear in any of your foreground subjects. If you anticipate a problem, choose a different color. Before you choose a bluescreen color, digitize still images of the costume and props for the shot. Bring the stills into your compositing or image-editing software, and sample any questionable areas for their RGB component colors. As long as they contain significant amounts of colors *not* found in the bluescreen, you'll be fine. For example, a blue foreground element with a little red and a little green will separate cleanly from a pure 0, 0, 255 blue background. Make sure that the costume, makeup, and set design people understand the color issues as early as possible. Most professionals have worked with bluescreen before, but it pays to err on the side of caution. It won't make you any friends if a costume has to be dyed or replaced, makeup removed and reapplied, or (worst case) an entire bluescreen set repainted or re-rigged to deal with a color incompatibility. Considering the expense of any of these options, you are more likely to be told to fix it in post.

Holoset: A New Alternative

Play, Inc. has recently introduced a new chroma-key system called Holoset. Listing at $1,000 for the basic kit, this includes an illuminator ring of blue LEDs that mounts to the camera lens, as shown in Figure 6.2, and a portable fabric backdrop coated with reflective microspheres. You can also buy additional reflective fabric to cover sets or props.

In use, the LEDs produce a blue light that is *monochromatic* (all precisely the same color). Because the backdrop is reflective, rather than having a color of its own, the only light reflected back to the lens is exactly the same color produced by the LEDs. The relatively low power of the LEDs prevents spill from most foreground materials. In a demonstration, bright white clothing did not exhibit spill until it was within 3 feet of the lens. Beyond 5 feet, all materials—even blues near in

Figure 6.2
A Holoset lens attachment.

shade to the LEDs' light—exhibited no spill problems. Although this technology is still too new to make any snap judgments about it, I believe the Holoset is worth considering. The time and cost savings in light rigging, cyc or set painting, and keying touch-ups should pay for the Holoset rig in short order.

Roto

Rotoscope is a patented process originally developed by the Fleischer studio to enable animators to trace over live-action film to create cel animation. Current use of the term *rotoscoping* (*roto* for short) has grown to include tracing animated matte outlines for compositing. These results are called a *roto-matte*. Because a compositor does not rely on a bluescreen in creating a roto-matte, it is possible to roto footage from ordinary set or location shooting. This has several advantages: Rigging and lighting are much easier; actors can give a better performance more easily if they don't have to pretend to be surrounded by a completely imaginary environment; and the final results often look better because there is no trace of bluescreen spill or mismatched lighting.

However, if you want to dispense with the bluescreen, you need a perfectly matched clean plate, or the roto'd element will flicker and jitter. This means you have to either lock down the camera (which annoys many directors) so there is no movement or use an expensive motion-control camera rig so the movement is perfectly duplicated in both the clean plate and the final shot. If you are shooting on film, you also need to use a pin-registered camera so the film is perfectly steady.

Finally, a roto-matte generally requires more work from the compositor than good bluescreen footage does. The best shots for roto work are short takes where the foreground elements (actors) need to be separated from, then composited back into, the same background. For example, suppose you have footage of an actor running down a street toward the camera. The director wants you to put a CGI monster into the shot behind the actor and the nearest cars, but in front of the more distant cars and buildings. You roto out the foreground elements, then composite the foreground, monster, and background elements back together.

Documenting The Set

Before you shoot the live action, you need to thoroughly document the set. After the shoot, you will need to re-create those parts of the set that other composited elements will touch, shadow, or be shadowed by. Trying to do this after the fact, when all you can measure are images from the live-action footage, is much harder. Take a few notes, measurements, and photographs now, and you'll save yourself many headaches later.

The first priority is reference points. You need to choose or create several visual references that will be easy to pick out in each frame of the footage. You will use these reference points to stabilize and match camera motion and may also have to use them to create models of shadowed or shadowing surfaces. A good reference point contrasts strongly with its surroundings and shows a consistent profile throughout camera moves. In the sample footage shown in Figure 6.3, the sidewalk, steps, and door provided a number of excellent reference points.

Figure 6.3
A frame from the sample footage.

If you can't find a good set of reference points, you may have to make your own. Ping-Pong balls painted Day-Glo green work well, and you can tack them temporarily to the set or props with putty. A solid, non-natural color from the Day-Glo palette makes it easy for you to mask the reference marks out of the footage during compositing. Spherical reference marks provide a more consistent appearance through most camera moves, making tracking and motion stabilizing much easier. An excellent example of this technique is shown on *The Making of Jurassic Park* videotape or laserdisc, in the Gallimimus stampede sequence (see Bibliography). Another example, using flat markers, is the Jurong Cobra case study later in this chapter.

Your second priority is to measure the set, including the reference points and any surfaces that CGI or other composited elements will touch, shadow, or be shadowed by. You will need to model these reference points and surfaces and add them to your CGI scenes, so you can set up and animate the scene to match. I've found the most reliable way to keep track of set measurements is to take a series of photographs or digitized video prints of the set and then write my notes and measurements directly on the prints. If you can't mark up the photos, try grease pencil on a transparent overlay. Figure 6.4 shows my notes for the porch steps in the sample footage.

You should also measure the position of any local (other than sunlight) light sources and (very important!) the starting position and attitude of the camera's focal plane. Get the lens settings too. If you are working with a commercial film crew, you can get some of these measurements from the focus puller or 1st AC. It's a good idea to crosscheck your measurements. It's much easier to re-measure on the set than to locate and correct measurement errors during post-production. The following case study shows how one production house uses sketches to record critical set information.

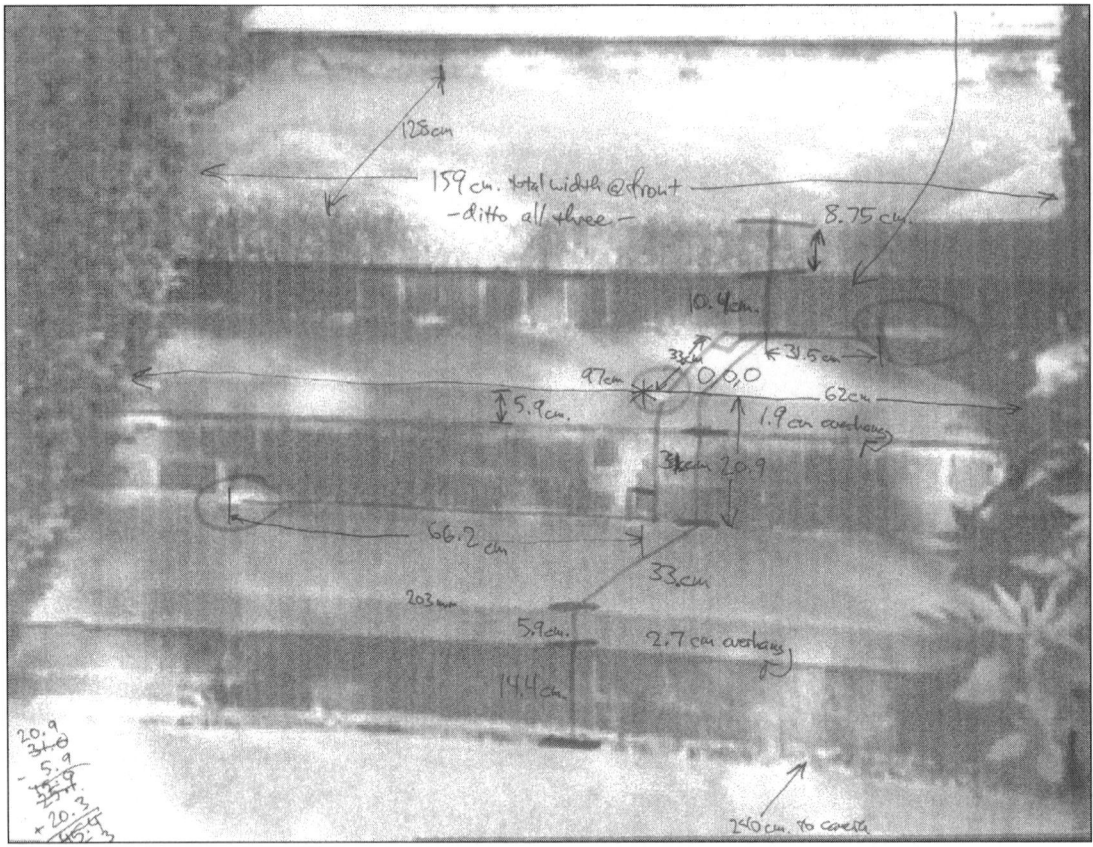

Figure 6.4
Measurements and notes on reference photo.

Case Study 6.1
Making Of Oz Encounters

by Domenic DiGiorgio, Technical Director, Momentum Animations

Oz Encounters was one of the largest projects undertaken by Momentum Animations. Close to five minutes of computer imagery and special effects were generated to re-create the close encounters experienced throughout the program. One of the underlying criteria maintained throughout the project and reinforced by Producer Debbie Burns and Director Ian Macrae was to keep the re-creations as accurate as possible and maintain their integrity. As a result, the 10-week project began well before any location shooting had taken place.

The storyboards of the re-creations by Ian, shown here, clearly outlined the composition, timing, and movement within each shot. We were able to break them down and schedule a time line for the Momentum team to work from. The storyboards also allowed us to focus our 3D model construction on what was actually going to be seen, eliminating any unnecessary detail.

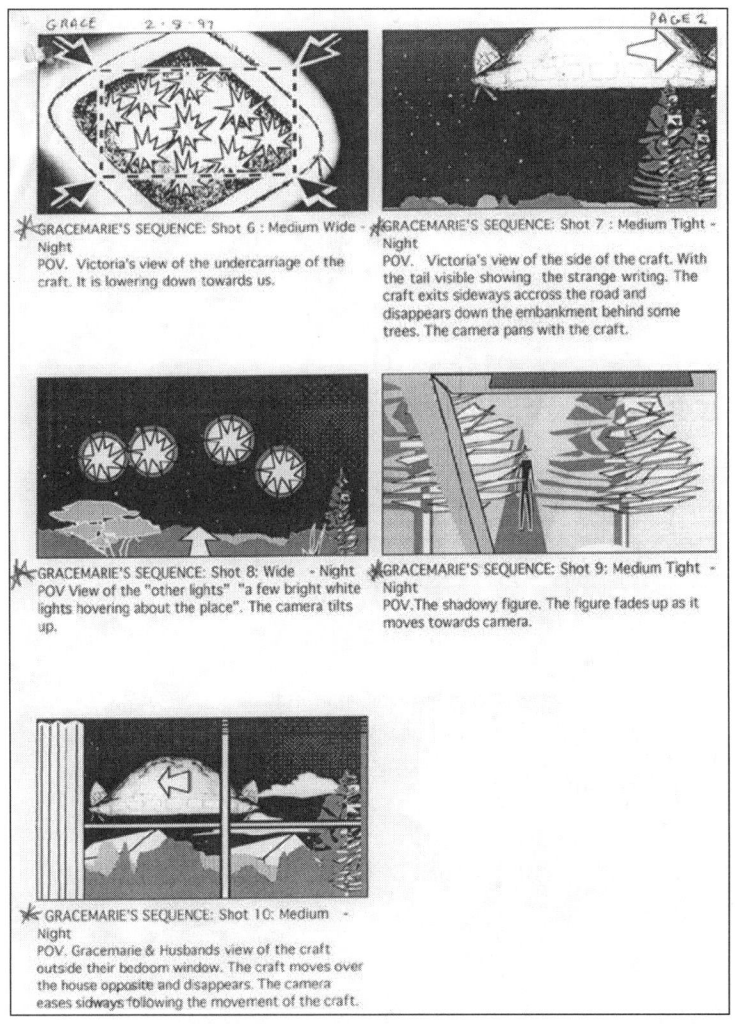

GRACE   2·9·97   PAGE 2

GRACEMARIE'S SEQUENCE: Shot 6 : Medium Wide -
Night
POV. Victoria's view of the undercarriage of the
craft. It is lowering down towards us.

GRACEMARIE'S SEQUENCE: Shot 7 : Medium Tight -
Night
POV. Victoria's view of the side of the craft. With
the tail visible showing the strange writing. The
craft exits sideways accross the road and
disappears down the embankment behind some
trees. The camera pans with the craft.

GRACEMARIE'S SEQUENCE: Shot 8: Wide   - Night
POV View of the "other lights" "a few bright white
lights hovering about the place". The camera tilts
up.

GRACEMARIE'S SEQUENCE: Shot 9: Medium Tight -
Night
POV.The shadowy figure. The figure fades up as it
moves towards camera.

GRACEMARIE'S SEQUENCE: Shot 10: Medium   -
Night
POV. Gracemarie & Husbands view of the craft
outside their bedroom window. The craft moves over
the house opposite and disappears. The camera
eases sideways following the movement of the craft.

Partial storyboard for Gracemarie sequence.

Sketches by Stephen Evans during the effects shoot allowed Dylan Crooke and me to
accurately match lighting and camera perspective within the animation packages.

Once the footage had been selected and digitized into our system, the team went to work
setting up the 3D scenes. From the collected data and analysis of the background footage,
Dylan, Chris Jones, and I were able to set up the correct lighting and camera perspective to
ensure that the 3D elements blended seamlessly into the scene. LightWave 3D was used to
create all the crafts and lighting effects. Because a number of the shots were filmed from
either a moving vehicle or a hand-held camera, a registration rig was used to provide
reference markers for the 3D elements. The reference markers allowed us to accurately match
camera movement using a combination of LightWave 3D and Adobe After Effects. This rig
was then digitally painted out to provide a clean background plate.

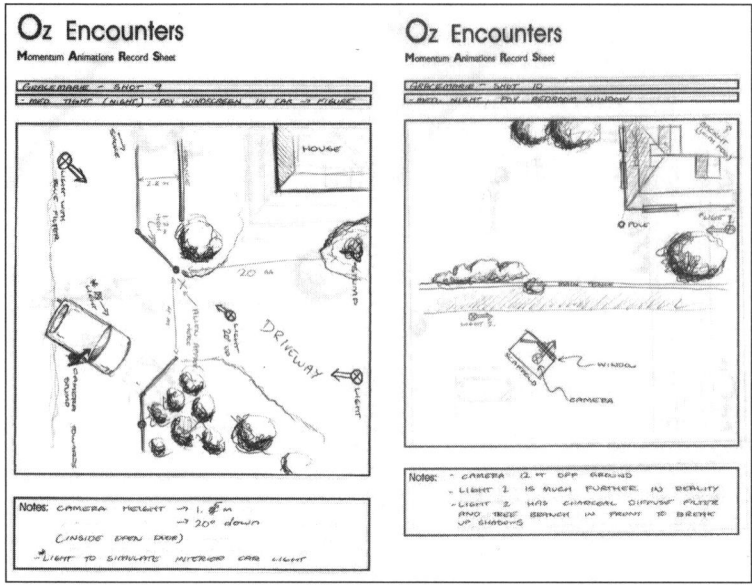

Location sketches for shots 9 and 10 (Gracemarie).

As usual, many of the required effect shots had their complications. In one case, some bright lights were required to be seen behind trees from a moving vehicle. This shot proved impossible to motion-track due to the registration rig being intermittently obscured. As a solution, Tony Lay and I reconstructed the shot from 2D elements within After Effects. A

The finished shot.

combination of motion blur, fake camera movement, and retouched images resulted in a very convincing effect.

Momentum Animations
6 Salisbury Street
North Caulfield 3161
Melbourne, Victoria
Australia
Phone: +61 3 9500 1142
Fax: +61 3 9500 1194
dylan@momentumanimations.com
www.momentumanimations.com

Clean Plate

After you've got the data you need for modeling, you can start collecting what you'll need to match the lighting, shadows, and colors. The first step is a clean plate, an image of the empty set with lighting just as it will appear in the final footage. This is the visual reference you will consult on questions of shadow and highlight density, falloff (the shadows' soft edges), and color, as shown in Figure 6.5. You may also use a series of clean plates, taken in different directions, to build environment reflection maps.

Figure 6.5
Clean plate.

The second step is to repeat the clean-plate shoot with reference lighting objects in the frame. I like to use a set of plastic foam objects that are light, rigid, and easy to move around on the set. You can make your own easily with inexpensive materials from any craft shop. The only criteria are that you be able to extract shadow and highlight colors and that you can deduce the angle of light sources from the reference shots. My own rig is a plastic foam block topped by a 1-cm grid, with a wooden dowel gnomon at one corner and a white plastic foam lighting ball (see Figure 6.6).

Just place the reference lighting objects in the frame, preferably as close as possible to the character's anticipated position, and take another clean plate (see Figure 6.7).

The goal of all this is to be able to produce an exact match between CGI elements and the clean plate, as in Figure 6.8. Note the exact match of shadow angle and density between the reference image and the final composite.

Figure 6.6
Close-up of a lighting reference object with gnomon and white ball.

Figure 6.7
Lighting reference object with gnomon and white ball.

Figure 6.8
CGI lighting reference objects and character composited into a clean plate.

Case Study 6.2
On The Set For The Jurong Cobra

by Dylan Crooke, Momentum Animations

The COBRA.MOV animation, which you'll find in the Momentum directory of the CD-ROM, was created as an advertisement for Jurong Reptile Park. This animation is a composite of a CGI snake character over live footage of a complex jungle location shot just outside of Melbourne. The live-action camera was mounted on a crane and could move along almost any axis. The final shot chosen was complex and almost an orbit of where the cobra was to be placed. Lighting was matched by placing a white and a chrome sphere in the scene and shooting them directly after the main shots. This allowed us to get a good idea of the color and direction of the light.

The live footage was dumped onto our computers from digital Betacam via a DPS Perception VR (video recorder). The raw footage (see below) was then deinterlaced, partially to give it a more filmic look and also to make it easier to paint out reference markers placed in the scene by Technical Director Domenic DiGiorgio.

Frame from the raw live footage showing markers.

Most of the scene was measured as accurately as possible by Technical Assistant Stephen Evans at the time of the live-action shoot. He was then responsible for fully modeling the CGI scene. Steven also worked out a neat way to paint out the reference points: He motion-tracked each point and placed part of the image back on top of the point, covering each nicely with a feathered edge. The results were seamless, and you would never know there were once about half a dozen markers in the shot.

Move-matching the camera was tricky. Because the movement was so unusual, it proved to be almost impossible to track accurately. The more I worked on the camera path, the more of a mess I made. It seemed that the best results were achieved by using fewer keyframes for the camera. Unfortunately, it still wasn't a perfect match.

The 3D snake character was modeled and animated using Hash's Animation:Master version 5. The CGI layers were rendered as 32-bit TGA files using the alpha channel as a matte, as shown here.

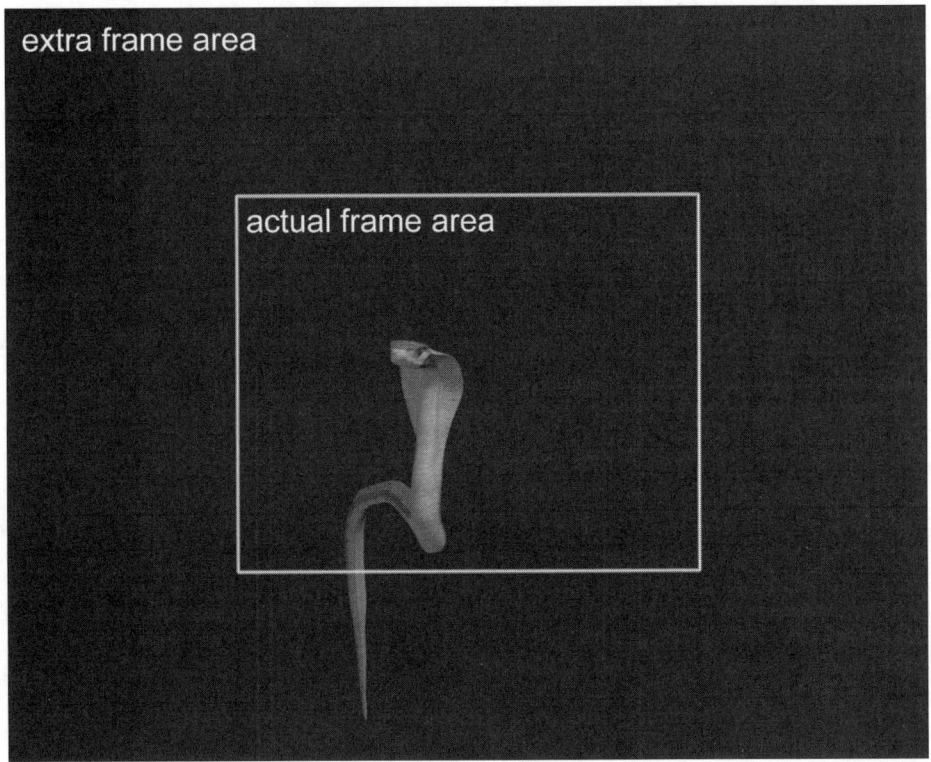

Snake character rendered with an alpha channel.

Additional color grading and noise filters were also applied to further integrate the snake into the scene. The cobra's shadow was created by making the snake inactive (invisible to the CGI camera) but still casting shadows, and by making the scene totally white. When this was rendered, a grayscale image was produced that could be used as a shadow layer in the final composite, as shown here.

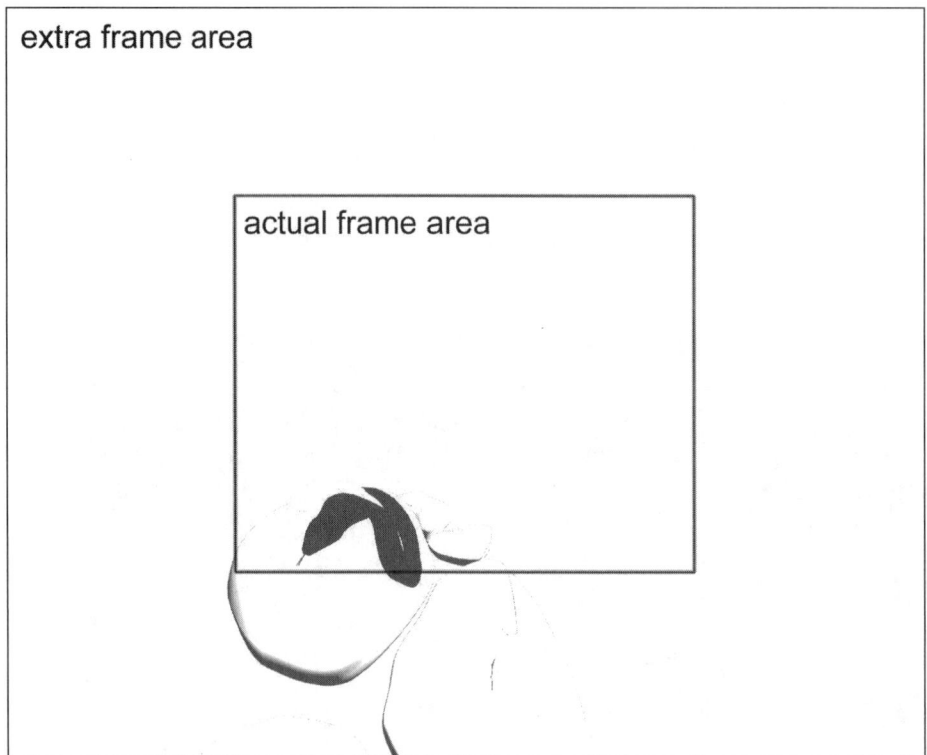

extra frame area

actual frame area

Rendered snake shadow layer.

We finally settled on a 2D solution to the move-matching problem. We rendered the footage, motion-stabilized it, then motion-tracked the stabilized footage to the live-action layer. In this case, the cobra was coming from the bottom of the screen, so extra image area around the frame was required. The frame size was doubled to allow extra image if needed. The final render had only four camera keyframes.

I rendered a single point from the scene, one of the reference markers near the bottom of the snake. This became just a single dot that moved around the screen as the camera moved. This footage was then motion-stabilized by locking on to the dot. This stabilized footage was a dot totally still in the middle of the screen with the frame moving all over the place around it, the usual result of motion stabilizing.

This "still" dot was then motion-tracked to the reference dot in the scene. The footage was replaced with the CGI snake animation, and that was how we got a perfect motion match. Then the foreground rock was masked out so the snake would appear to be behind it. The shadow footage was composited on the same layer as the snake, as shown here. Compositing and motion tracking/stabilizing was achieved using Adobe After Effects.

The final composite.

In theory, this technique has a problem in that even though the image is locked, the perspective will not be totally right. That is exactly the case, but it isn't nearly as noticeable as a badly locked composite. It worked for this project but may not work for all applications. It certainly saved us a lot of time, which was very important with the three-week timeline for four commercials.

Momentum Animations
6 Salisbury Street
North Caulfield 3161
Melbourne, Victoria
Australia
+61 3 9500 1142
Fax: +61 3 9500 1194
dylan@momentumanimations.com
www.momentumanimations.com

Motion-Control Cameras

If the shot calls for a camera move coordinated with a composited element, you can avoid the uncertainties and expense of move matching by using a motion-control camera. This is a powered and computer-controlled rig that can repeat precisely the same move time after time. Figure 6.9 shows one type of motion-control camera rig.

A rig like the one pictured enables you to shoot several takes that will register perfectly for compositing. For example, Figure 6.10 shows a set and lighting rigged by Chris Nibley for a motion-control shot. One end of the motion-control rig is visible at the bottom right of the photo.

Figure 6.11 shows three frames each from two separate passes with the motion-control camera. One pass was made with an empty chessboard, and the other with a full chessboard. With these two shots, you could easily make a controlled dissolve sequence in which one chess piece at a time materializes onto the chessboard, all while the camera moves.

Besides the two-dimensional information contained in the footage, motion-control rigs provide data on the third and fourth dimensions. The motion-control data that determines the camera movement can also be ported to CGI rendering software as a time sequence of position and rotation keyframes. This means you can precisely match the movement of your CGI camera to that of the real camera. The catch is that the Kuper software that runs the camera rig, shown in Figure 6.12, uses a different keyframe scheme and unit of measure than most CGI software, so you have to do a little translation.

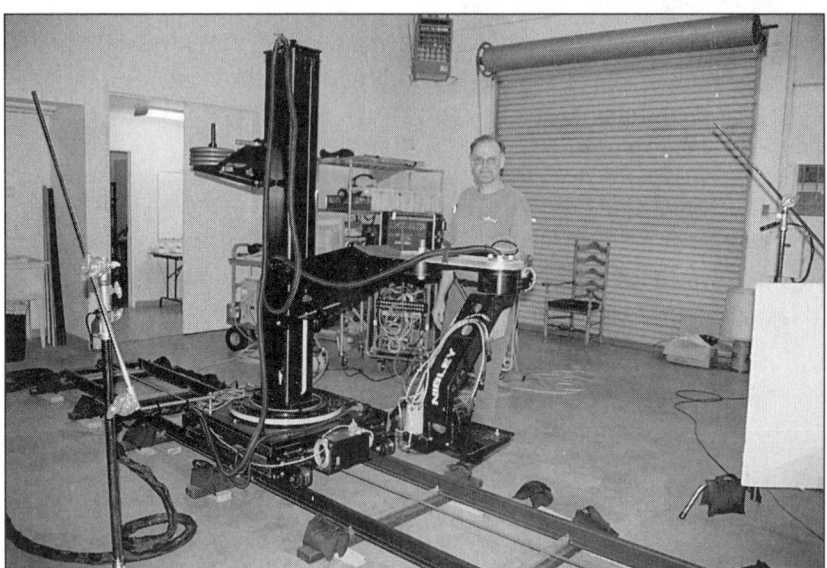

Figure 6.9
Chris Nibley of Nibley Studio and one of his motion-control camera rigs.

Figure 6.10
Props and lights set up for a motion-control shot.

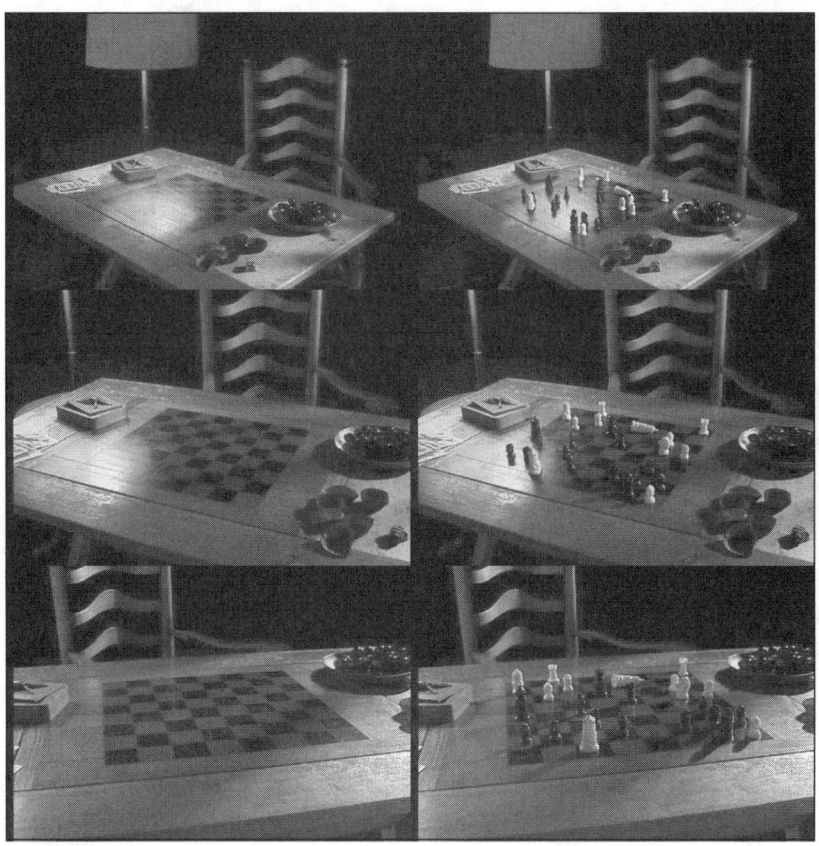

Figure 6.11
Frames 0, 139, and 277 from two motion-control passes.

Figure 6.12
Kuper software running on a motion-control computer.

You can load the Kuper data (see Listing 6.1) in a text editor to see the raw data. The first three columns record the camera's movement along the vertical, east-west, and north-south axes, in inches. The second three columns are the axes of the camera's rotation, in degrees.

Listing 6.1 Kuper data for frames 0, 1, 2, 275, 276, and 277 of chess shot.

Vtrack	VEW	VNS	VPan	VTilt	Vroll
-22.1349	44.0368	31.7283	-42.9325	-17.9018	0.0000
-22.1352	44.0350	31.7279	-42.9314	-17.9036	0.0000
-22.1360	44.0309	31.7268	-42.9288	-17.9079	0.0000
<snip>	<snip>	<snip>	<snip>	<snip>	<snip>
-29.1937	-8.1112	19.5570	14.0579	-21.5415	0.0000
-29.1947	-8.1145	19.5550	14.0690	-21.5401	0.0000
-29.1951	-8.1157	19.5543	14.0733	-21.5396	0.0000

For this example, the original data set was converted to a LightWave motion (MOT) file with a conversion utility available from **http://heimat.de/ruebe/k2l**. This produced a literal translation, but that still leaves one problem: LightWave uses metric units, and the MOT file is scaled in inches. This is relatively easy to fix in LightWave. Simply load the MOT file, open the Motion Graph Editor, and scale the X, Y, and Z axes by .0254 to convert inches to meters. The rotation data do not have to be converted because degrees aren't dependent on units of linear measure. The final tweak to this data is to shift all the keyframes up one, because the footage is numbered from frame 1, but the motion file starts at frame 0. After all these changes, the LightWave motion file should look like Listing 6.2.

Listing 6.2 LightWave motion file data for frames 0, 1, 2, 275, 276, and 277 of chess shot.

```
LWMO
1
9
278
1.118535 0.8058988 0.5622264 -42.9325 17.9018 0 1 1 1
0 0 0 0 0
1.118489 0.8058887 0.5622341 -42.9314 17.9036 0 1 1 1
1 0 0 0 0
1.118385 0.8058608 0.5622544 -42.9288 17.9079 0 1 1 1
2 0 0 0 0
<snip>
275 0 0 0 0
-0.2061083 0.496697 0.7415454 14.069 21.5401 0 1 1 1
276 0 0 0 0
-0.2061388 0.4966792 0.7415556 14.0733 21.5396 0 1 1 1
277 0 0 0 0
```

This data set enables the CGI animator to integrate rendered 3D elements with background plates with a minimum of effort and a great deal more confidence. The advantages of motion-control cameras include built-in measurements, no need to match move manually, and the capability to shoot multiple passes both for effects and for director's choice of takes. The disadvantages include higher shooting costs ($3,000 per day and up for the rig, camera, and support services), possible loss or inability to use the data, and the fact that mechanical margins of error can sometimes exceed the optical tolerances for an effect. If the machine is not tuned up properly, camera slop becomes visible in the final composite.

Remember that motion-control data set is only slightly less valuable than the footage itself. If you lose the data (and it seems to have happened to everyone at least once), you are facing that manual move-match process again and probably will blow your schedule and budget. If possible, get a floppy disk of the raw data before you leave the set. The motion-control data is digital, it doesn't lose anything in duplication, and it's usually small enough to fit on a single disk. Always be sure to make backups, and keep tabs on your motion data!

Computer-Generated Imagery (CGI)

After you've taken all the measurements and reference photos, you can use them to build shadow surfaces and lighting setups in your 3D software. If you've taken thorough and accurate measurements, you can do this by the numbers and very quickly.

CGI Shadow Surfaces

In order to perfectly composite CGI elements to live footage, shadows and reflections of the CGI elements must appear to fall on the appropriate live-action surfaces. One way to accomplish this is to model shadow-catcher or reflecting surfaces in the CGI scene. Doing this correctly can really help sell the shot; doing it badly makes the CGI element stick out like a sore thumb.

PROJECT 6.1 Duplicating Porch Shadow Surfaces

The goal of this project is to make a duplicate model in the computer of every surface that the character will cast a shadow on. This is necessary for the software to render the CGI element's shadow so it will accurately match the footage.

1. Refer to the measurements in Figure 6.4 to build a 1:1 scale model of the porch steps in the software of your choice.

   In case you can't read my scrivenings, here are the important measurements for building the model:

   • The top slab is 128 cm deep, 8.75 cm thick, and 159 cm wide. All remaining elements are also 159 cm wide.

   • The top riser is inset 5 cm and is 10.4 cm high.

   • The middle slab is 33 cm deep and 5.9 cm thick.

- The middle riser is inset 1.9 cm, and the top of the middle slab is 20.9 cm above the top of the bottom slab.

- The bottom slab is 33 cm deep and 5.9 cm thick.

- The bottom riser is inset 2.7 cm and is 14.4 cm high.

If you don't want to build the model, you can import one of the versions (PORCH.DXF, PORCH.3DS, or PORCH.LWO) I've provided on this book's first CD-ROM. I also provided models of some of the lighting reference objects (LITEREF, LITEGRID) that appear in this chapter's figures. You need to add a matte white sphere to complete Project 6.3, but then you wouldn't want me to do it all for you, would you?

2. In your animation software, load file PORCH.BMP as the backdrop image.

3. Lay out the models according to the measurements and the background image of the clean plate. Add markers for the reference points noted in Figure 6.4.

Pay especially close attention to the position of the LITEREF object. The corner with the gnomon should be precisely 97 cm from the left corner of the middle slab, and the front edge of LITEREF should be flush with the front edge of the slab. I aligned the reference object with a chip in the concrete, which I measured as a reference mark and wrote up on Figure 6.4.

If you are using LightWave, you can load file PORCH.LWS from this book's first CD-ROM to see an example of how I set up the matching scene.

PROJECT 6.2 Duplicating Chessboard Shadow And Reflection Surface

The goal of this project is to make a duplicate model in the computer of the chessboard surface visible in the motion-control footage. In addition to catching the shadow of any CGI element, the chessboard must also create matching reflections.

1. The chessboard is composed of 2-inch squares. Depending on your software, it may be easiest to create a square 16 inches on a side, with eight divisions in both length and width. If you choose not to build your own model, you can use object file BOARD.LWO from the first CD-ROM.

2. Open a new scene. Load one of the chessboard image sequences as the background.

3. Apply the motion-control file to the camera. The motion graph should look like Figure 6.13.

4. Working from the first and last keyframes, position the chessboard object in the scene to match the position and rotation of the chessboard in the background image. You should end up with something like Figure 6.14.

You may have to create several keyframes to correct for minor mechanical errors in the motion-control rig. For example, Figure 6.15 shows the motion path I created to more accurately match the chessboard object to the background image sequence. The variation was very small, only a few centimeters overall.

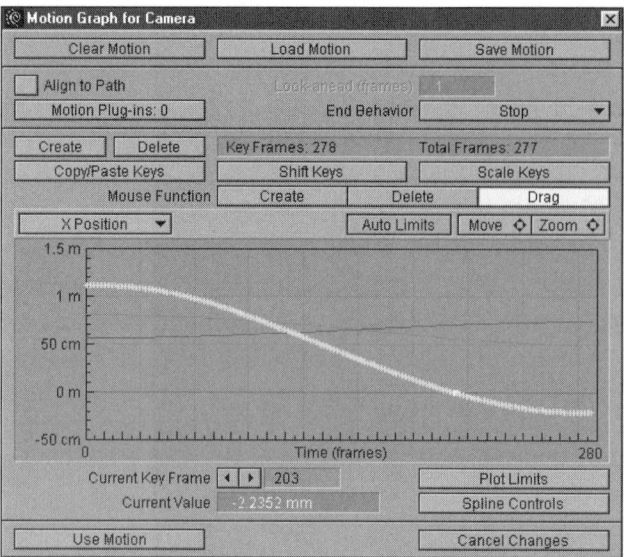

Figure 6.13

The camera motion graph, based on the Kuper motion-control data.

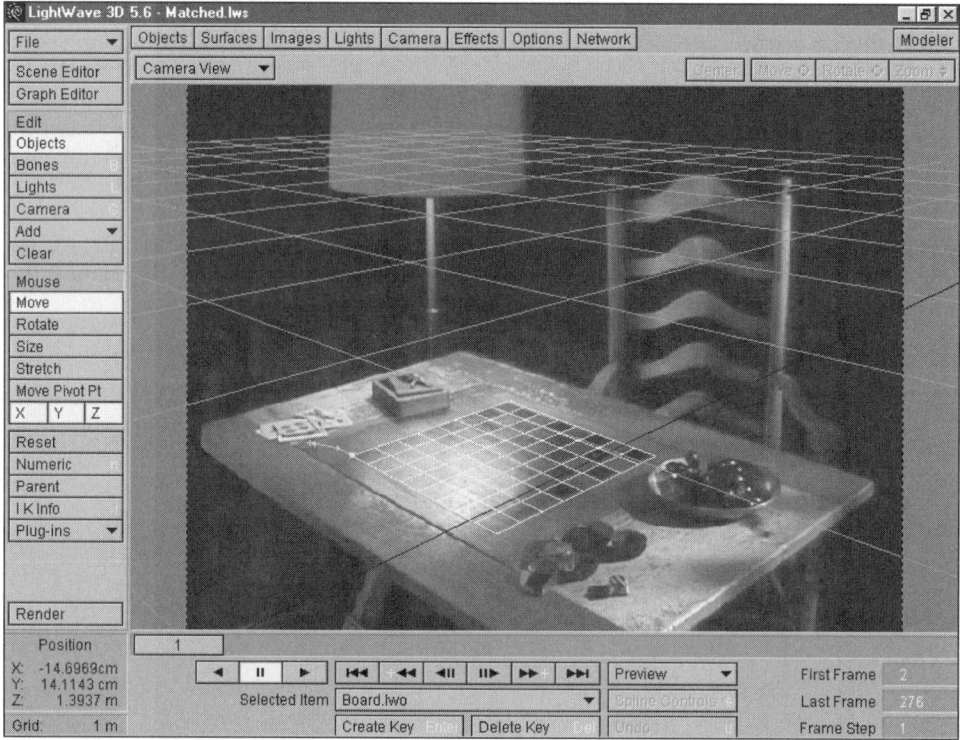

Figure 6.14

The LightWave chess scene showing the chessboard object matched to the background image.

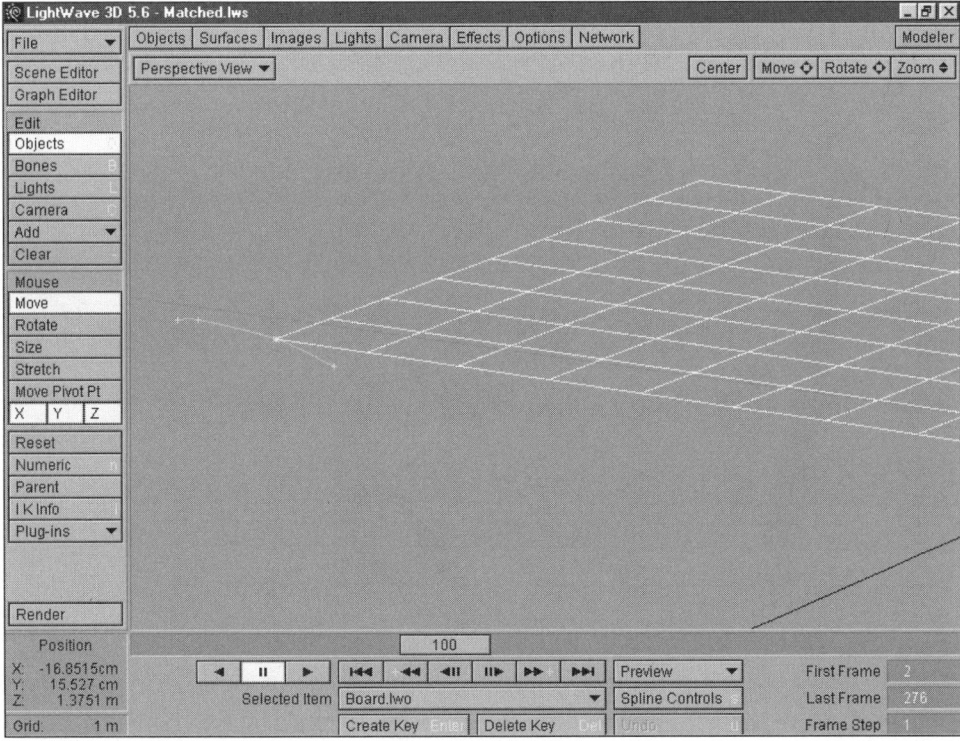

Figure 6.15
LightWave chess scene close-up showing the chessboard object motion path.

CGI Lighting

If you have to match studio lighting, then while on the set, you should have gathered complete information about light placement, colors, and intensity. A clean plate with lighting reference objects is the next best thing. If all else fails, you will have to make a series of educated guesses based on the footage you are given.

If you have to match natural outdoor lighting, you are in much better shape. It is possible to set up a default sunlight scene in most CGI software that will simulate most of daylight's effects. Tweaking the last few percentage points for a perfect match is much easier than starting from scratch.

Matching CGI Lighting For Porch

PROJECT 6.3 The goal of this project is to match the angle, intensity, color, and falloff of the light sources in the footage. It's relatively easy in this case, because the only direct light source is the sun, the shadows are distinct, and the ambient light is consistent throughout the character's area of movement.

1. In the scene you set up in Project 6.1, add a single light source at a long distance from the porch model. Position the camera to look down at the LITEREF/LITEGRID grid, as in Figure 6.16.

Figure 6.16
LITEREF/LITEGRID as rendered by the CGI camera.

2. Refer to Figure 6.6. Move the light source around, and re-render the camera view until the end of the rendered shadow appears at exactly the same grid coordinates as the shadow end in Figure 6.6.

3. Change the light falloff (if your software has this feature) to mimic the falloff of the gnomon's shadow in Figure 6.6.

The next step is to match the color of the light. This isn't just matching the color of sunlight—you have to match the color distortions produced by the video camera and the digitizing process too. The most reliable way to do this is to sample the final rendering and compare it to the same areas of the footage.

You'll need to keep Photoshop or another image-processing software open while you render and re-render the scene. If you don't have enough system memory to do this, the process will get tedious very quickly.

4. Set the light to pure white. Render a frame. Open the frame in Photoshop.

5. Use the Photoshop eyedropper to sample the image at the highlight of the white sphere. Make a note of the RGB values. Take another sample at the center of the darkest part of the shadow behind the sphere, but still on the LITEREF object's surface.

   These two samples give you the brightest and darkest color values for the light.

6. Repeat Step 5 on reference image LITETEST.TGA, which you'll find on this book's first CD-ROM.

I found the highlight sample of this image colored 239,232,238, and the shadow behind the sphere colored 14,16,16. Your results may vary.

7. Change the light's color values to match the sample you took from LITETEST.TGA. Re-render the image, and check the identical sample areas. Readjust the light and re-render until you are satisfied that the rendered color of the reference objects closely matches the original colors.

CGI Sunlight

You can make more-realistic sunlight in LightWave by setting Ambient to 0, and Parenting a starburst of Distant lights to the main (Sun) light to mimic the effect of radiosity. A rosette, for example, of eight Distant lights, each rotated on the Heading axis 45 degrees from its neighbors, with one additional Distant light pointing up and another down, gives you enough controls to mimic nearly any form of "natural" light. You simply modify each light's color and intensity to match the lighting effects seen in the clean plate. For starters, you can probably set the Sun to 200% and the color something like R=235, G=245, B=255 to match the slightly bluish tint of sunlight on film or video. Try setting the 45-degree lights to 20%, and the up/down light pair to 75%, all with the same color as the Sun light. To prevent confusing shadows and specular highlights, turn on the No Specular button and set Shadow Type to Off for every light but the Sun. Your results should look something like Figure 6.17.

Figure 6.17
Sunlight setup rendered in LightWave.

CGI Matching Lighting And Reflections For Chessboard

PROJECT 6.4

The goal of this project is to mimic the multiple lights and the reflective chessboard surface in a CGI scene. Each effect in itself is minor, but the overall effect makes the difference between a seamless composite and one that does not ring true.

1. Reload the scene you created in Project 6.2.

2. Examine the photo of the set, Figure 6.10, to estimate the approximate position and color of each light source.

3. Add a light to the scene in the appropriate position for the strongest shadow-casting light.

4. Place a null at the peak of one chess piece and another null at the peak of that piece's shadow, as shown in Figure 6.18.

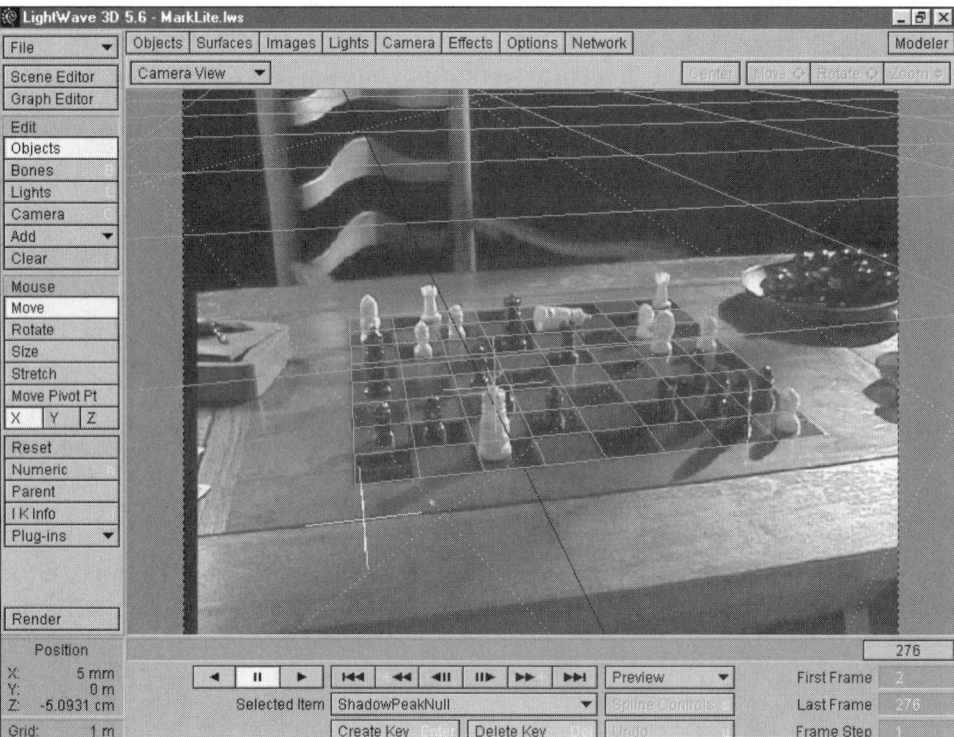

Figure 6.18
Nulls placed to mark the peak of the chess piece and shadow.

5. Target the new light at the null marking the peak of the chess piece's shadow.

6. Change to Light View. Choose the new light. Move the light until the null marking the peak of the chess piece aligns with the null marking the peak of its shadow, as shown in Figure 6.19. The selected light will now cast accurate directional shadows for any CGI objects placed on the chessboard object.

7. Place any object on the chessboard object. Refer again to Figure 6.10, and modify the light's shadow settings to match shadow falloff and density.

8. Repeat the preceding steps for the other light sources.

9. Set surface reflection attributes for the chessboard object. For example, I used the values shown in Figure 6.20.

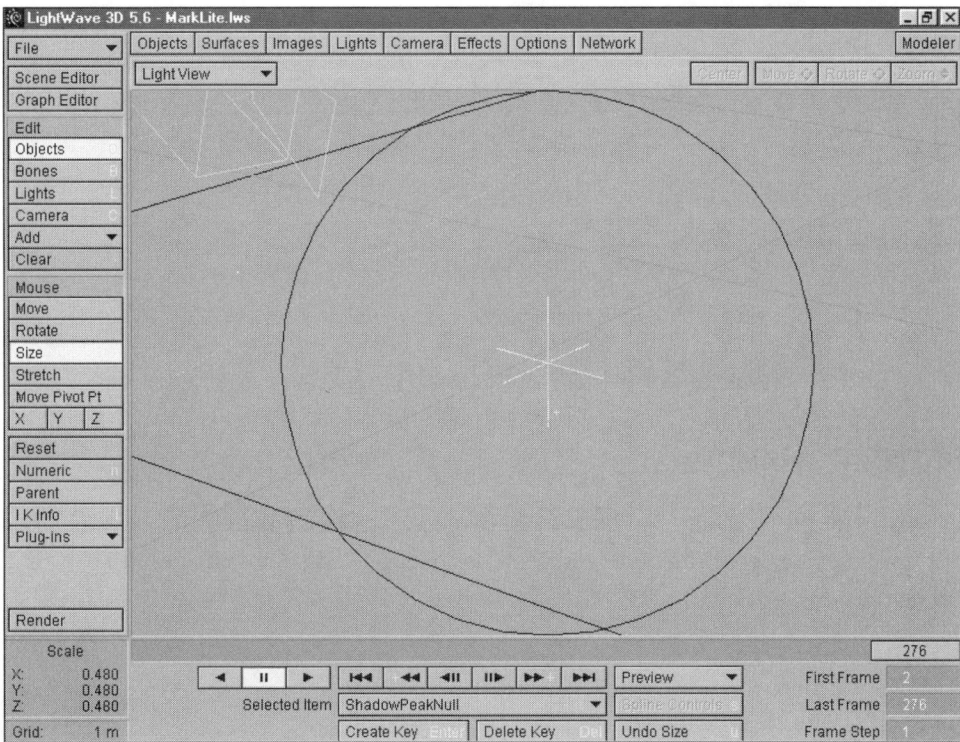

Figure 6.19
Light View aligned with nulls.

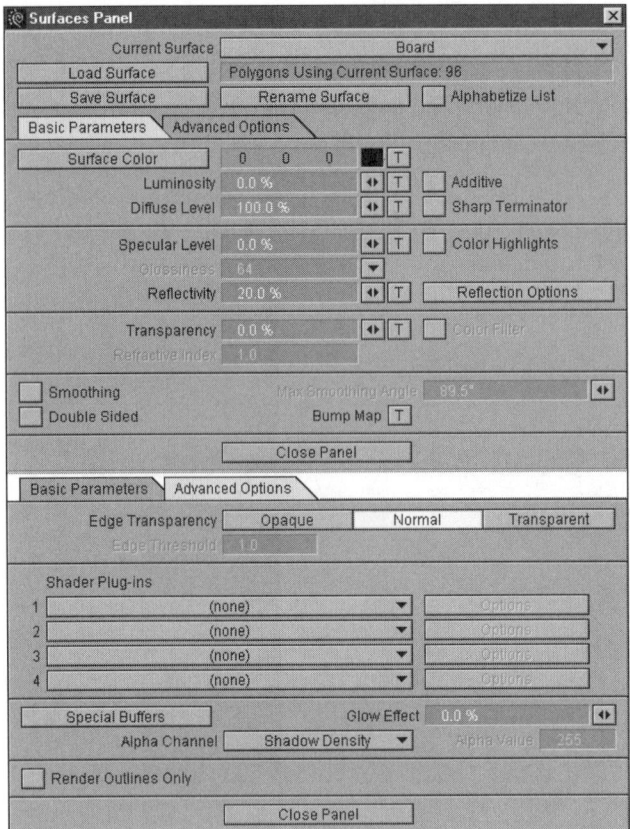

Figure 6.20
Chessboard object surface reflection settings.

If you completed all four projects, you should now be able to render CGI elements that will composite seamlessly with the appropriate background plates. Figure 6.21 shows one example of the effects you can create.

Figure 6.21
The Walker robot crossing a chessboard, with matching shadows and reflection.

Moving On

At this point, you should be able to identify and prevent the most common mistakes in a special effects shoot, so you get the best possible elements for your comps. You should also have a basic understanding of how to match set lighting and shadowed or reflective surfaces in the CGI environment. Although this does not qualify you as a visual effects supervisor, it is something you will have to master if you hope to rise that high in the profession.

Now that you know where the elements come from, the next chapter explains how they come together in the compositor's hands.

PART III

BASIC
COMPOSITING

A visual art, by definition, is difficult to put into words. It is even more difficult to learn visual arts from words, either written or spoken. For digital compositing, as for most traditional graphic arts, a picture is worth far more than a thousand words. This chapter will attempt to provide the pictures you need to view so that you'll comprehend the basic tools, processes, and concepts used every day by digital compositors. This chapter is a visual catalog of the most important concepts and tools you will use as a digital compositor. Learning the material in this chapter will make the rest of this book easier to understand.

> *Digital compositing is the digitally manipulated integration of at least two source images to produce a new image.*

The operative words in that definition are *digitally*, *integration*, and *images*. *Digitally* means we are not working directly with film or other analog media; we are using computers to manipulate digital information. *Images* means we are working with more than one image at a time; if we were working with only one image, we would simply be painting or retouching. *Integration* is the heart of compositing: The new image must appear real—completely and seamlessly integrated— as if it were actually photographed by a single camera at one instant, or the illusion of compositing has failed. Digital compositing is the art of the invisible effect.

Basic Compositing Theory

As explained in Chapter 4, the color of each pixel in a digital image is defined by numbers. These numbers can be manipulated mathematically to modify or to combine images. Most mathematical operations for compositing break down to Add, Subtract, Multiply, Divide, or combinations thereof.

One of the most basic and simple operations is Add. This simply adds the value of a pixel from the first image to the value of the corresponding pixel in the second image. In shorthand:

```
Output = A Image + B Image, or O = A+B
```

The result of an Add is shown in Figure 7.1. As you can see, an Add operation is similar to double-exposing film, with the same drawbacks. Any light areas of the background can be seen through the foreground, creating a ghostlike effect. For a clean composite, the foreground subject would have to appear over only pitch-black areas of the background. This approach was used in some of the earliest filmed special effects, but it visually isolates the foreground subject from the background, so the shot usually doesn't work for the audience.

Almost all compositing operations are based on values between 0 and 1, with 0 equal to black or the minimum value, and 1 equal to white or the maximum value. The bit depth of an image doesn't change the equations, because bit depth simply defines the number of divisions between black and white. Eight bits defines 256 divisions, 10 bits defines 1024, and 16 bits divides the 0-to-1 range into 65, 536 discrete values. Some programs can deal with negative values or those in excess of 1; others clip the excess, which can cause problems in later operations due to lost accuracy.

Exactly how these mathematical operations are performed varies from program to program. If you need to understand the technical details, you should consult your software's manuals, then experiment with the operation in question until you feel you understand it. Some programs enable you to create your own equations for more precise control of compositing. Programming

Figure 7.1
An Add operation.

useful custom filters and other image processing tools can become a lucrative career in itself, or at least make you more valuable to an employer. If you wish to create your own compositing operations, you should refer to the image processing texts listed in the Bibliography for more information about algorithms and programming.

The process of applying one or more operations to an image is called *rendering*. The result of rendering is the new image. The more complex the operations, the longer the rendering takes. Some high-end compositing systems use hardware acceleration to reduce rendering time. Others, like Digital Fusion, rely on multiple processors to share the load, providing an inexpensively scalable rendering solution. On slower systems, you may have to wait seconds or even minutes for a single frame to be rendered. On faster systems, simple operations may be rendered in nearly real time. If response speed is important for your compositing, you can always buy more processors or acceleration. See Chapter 16 for details on optimizing rendering.

Channels

A *channel* is a subset of image values from a single component of the image. A color image usually has at least three channels: R, G, B, for red, green, and blue color component information. Figures 7.2, 7.3, and 7.4 show the three color channels for Figure 7.5.

For compositing, images often use additional channels to control the transparency of the color image, indicate the depth or texture of objects, or provide other information to be used by a filter or process. Four or five total channels are common, but up to 24 are available in some compositing software.

Figure 7.2
The red color channel for Figure 7.5.

Figure 7.3
The green color channel for Figure 7.5.

Figure 7.4
The blue color channel for Figure 7.5.

Figure 7.5
A color image combining all three channels.

Mattes

A *matte* is an image in which its pixels' values are used to control the transparency of a layer in a composite. For example, open the matte file WalkM276.jpg on this book's first CD-ROM in any graphics editor. You should see a grayscale image similar to that shown in Figure 7.6.

Now open Walkr276.jpg. You should see a color image like Figure 7.7. If you use WalkM276 to control the transparency of Walkr276, the black areas around the robot will be completely transparent, the white area of the robot's body will be completely opaque, and the shaded gray areas of the robot's shadows will be partially transparent.

A more complex operation than Add is Over—the operation used most often to composite images using mattes. An Over equation looks like this:

```
Output = (Image A x Matte) + ((1-Matte) x Image B)
```

In other words, multiply Image A times the matte, multiply Image B times the inverse of the matte, then add them to get the output image.

For example, if you composite the robot image and the matte using the Over operation, with a background image like Figure 7.8, the background will show through the transparent areas with an effect like Figure 7.9. Black areas of the matte (value 0) add 0 from the robot and 1 times the value from the background, so the background shows through the black areas of the matte.

Figure 7.6
The WalkM276.jpg matte.

Figure 7.7
The Walkr276.jpg color image.

Figure 7.8
The background image.

Figure 7.9
A composite of color foreground image with background image, with the grayscale matte controlling foreground transparency through an Over operation.

White areas of the matte (value 1) add 1 times the value of the robot image and 0 times the value of the background, so only the robot appears in the white areas. The half-gray (value 0.5) areas of the matte add half the value of the robot and half the value of the background. Logical, yes?

When you are compositing long image sequences using mattes, you must keep track of the image numbering sequences and make sure all elements' numbers synchronize, or *sync*. If an element gets out of sync, edges won't match up and the composite won't work. One way to keep mattes synched to their color images is to add them to the color image as an extra channel. An example of this is the *alpha channel*—the "A" in RGBA file formats such as TGA32. An alpha channel is basically a grayscale image where darker shades signify more transparency and light areas are more opaque, just as the preceding matte example demonstrated.

An alpha channel is commonly used to composite a foreground layer over a background layer, with the alpha channel controlling how much and where the background shows through. For example, open WALKRGBA.TGA in Photoshop, Digital Fusion, or any other program that displays alpha channel information. Then open a channel display and select the alpha channel. You should see something like Figure 7.10.

Key

Key is a synonym for matte but is more generally used in reference to chroma keying for bluescreen work. *Keying* is the process of separating a foreground object from its existing background, creating a matte that then can be used to composite the foreground over a different background.

Chroma keying creates a matte by subtracting (making transparent) a particular color or range of colors. Common subsets of chroma keying include *bluescreen* and *greenscreen*, named for the background colors used. An actor filmed against a pure, saturated blue (bluescreen) background is a good candidate for chroma keying, as shown in Figure 7.11.

Luma keying creates a matte by subtracting a particular brightness value or range of values. For example, a brightly lit subject filmed in strong contrast against a black background is a good candidate for luma keying, as shown in Figure 7.12.

Difference keying creates a *difference matte* by subtracting the values of one image from those of another. For example, if you have an image of a set with no actors (see Figure 7.13), and you difference key the same set with the actors (see Figure 7.14), you can extract a matte of the difference—that is, the precise areas occluded by the actors (see Figure 7.15).

Difference keying is a powerful tool and the best reason for you to make sure you have a clean plate (remember how I harped on that in Chapter 6?). Even if you don't have a clean plate, you can often save time by making one. As long as the camera was locked down (or the footage has been stabilized) and every part of the background is visible in at least one frame, you can assemble bits and pieces from different frames to create a clean plate. The time and effort to do this

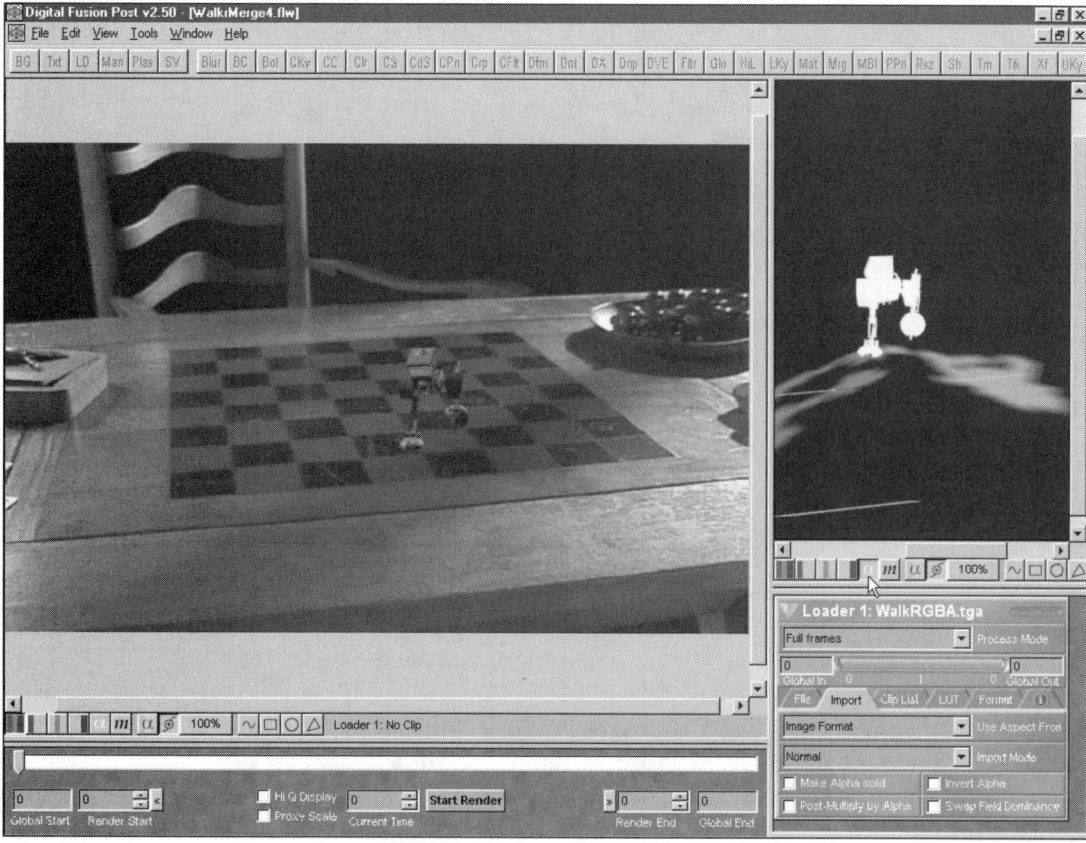

Figure 7.10
WALKRGBA.TGA loaded in Digital Fusion, displaying combined RGB channels in the Large view and the alpha channel alone in the Small view.

is generally much less than that you would expend animating a roto-matte to extract the actors from the background.

A *fixed* or *static matte* is set up at the first frame and does not change throughout the image sequence. A *traveling matte* moves but does not necessarily change shape. A traveling matte is often used on a rigid object that does not rotate or change profile during the sequence—for example, a microphone or other rig element.

An *articulate matte* is one that is animated to change shape over the course of an image sequence. Generally, a matte is articulated in order to closely follow the contours of the subject being extracted—for example, a moving object that must be removed from a background. Simple articulate mattes can be used to delineate rigid objects such as props, vehicles, and components of safety rigs, as shown in Figure 7.16. These mattes are relatively easy to animate and may require only a handful of control points and a few keyframes for the entire length of the shot.

Figure 7.11
An actor filmed against a bluescreen background for use in chroma-key compositing.

Figure 7.12
Left third: the original background image; Middle third: luma-key composited flames over background image; Right third: a frame from the Ceiling Fire clip from Artbeats Digital Film Library. The black background makes these clips easy to composite using luma keying.

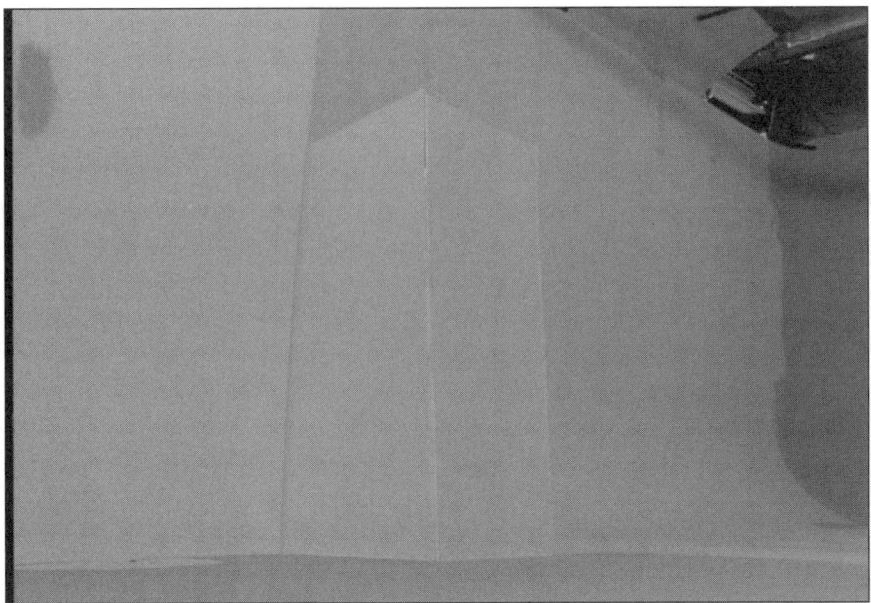

Figure 7.13
A clean background plate.

Figure 7.14
The same set as the previous figure, with actor, props, and set dressing to be composited.

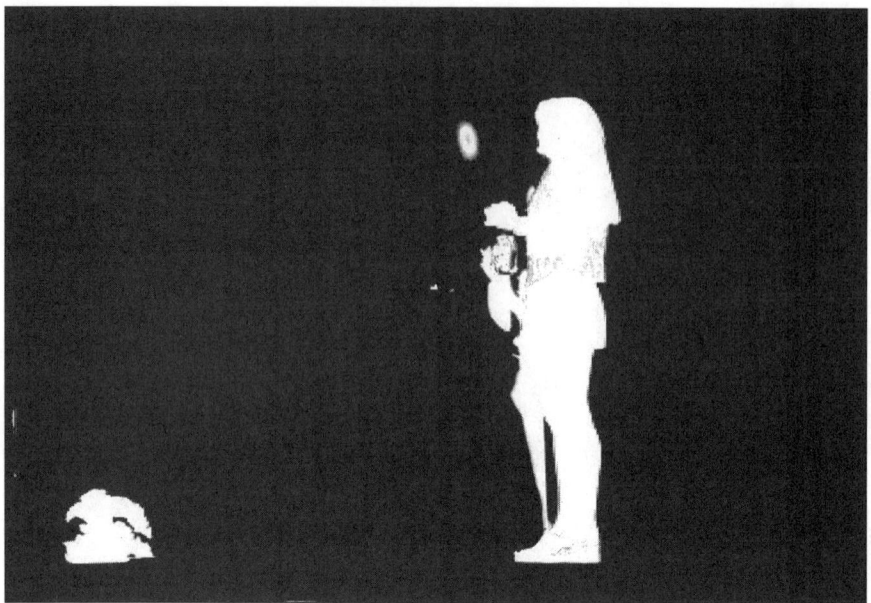

Figure 7.15
A difference matte, with subjects extracted from clean plate.

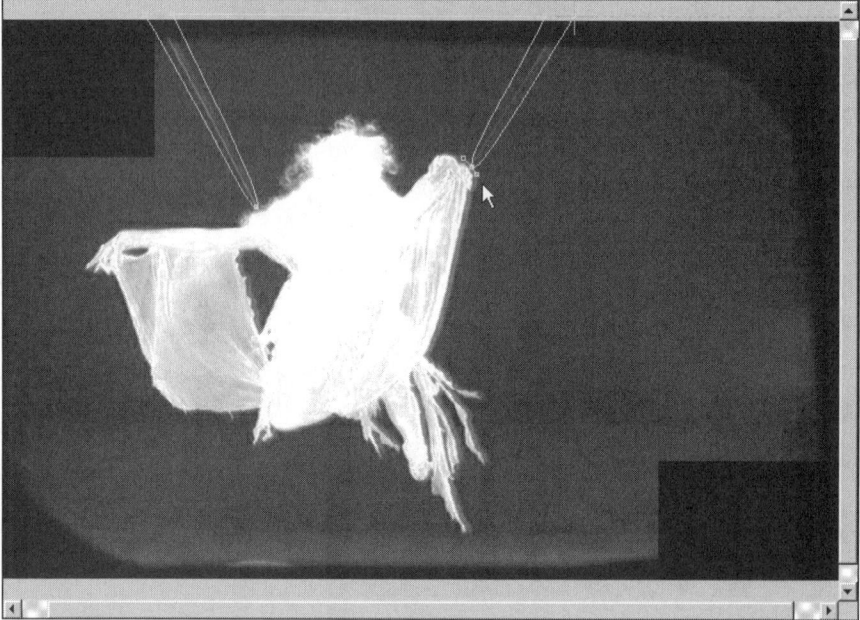

Figure 7.16
An articulate matte positioned to remove lines from the actor's flying rig. The arrow indicates an animatable spline control handle.

An extreme form of articulate matte is the *rotoscope* (or *roto-*) *matte*, which is animated frame-by-frame to extremely tight tolerances. Roto-matte work is generally reserved only for shots that have no clean plate, when the camera was not locked down or motion controlled, and when both the background and foreground are too complex for other matte extraction methods. In most cases, roto-matte work is the last resort simply because of the time and expense of having an artist tweak the matte controls on every frame. The compositing effects applied to the Alien Girl, as described in the *Sector Expander* case study in Chapter 2, required a rotoscope matte for every frame of her appearance. This required a great deal of time and effort for the compositor. A roto-matte for a single actor may have dozens of control points; multiply that by 1,440 frames per minute of film (1,800 for video) and you can see the huge amount of work involved.

A *complementary matte* is the inverse of a primary matte, having precisely opposite grayscale values for each pixel. Figure 7.17 shows a complementary matte for the WalkM276.jpg matte shown in Figure 7.6. Complementary mattes are useful for controlling effects that do not have an invert option.

A *garbage matte*, or *G-matte*, shown in Figure 7.18, is a quick-and-dirty way of blocking off part of an image with a hand-drawn polygon or bitmap shape. The portion of the image blocked off is usually rigging or other garbage, hence the name. The matte may be as simple as a triangle; the simpler and faster to draw, the better. Garbage mattes save time for the compositor by reducing the area that requires more painstaking work, and they may save rendering time as well.

An *edge matte* contains only the boundary or outline of the subject, as shown in Figure 7.19. This is a useful tool for creating either inner or outer garbage mattes that conform closely to irregular

Figure 7.17
A complementary matte for the WALKGRAY primary matte.

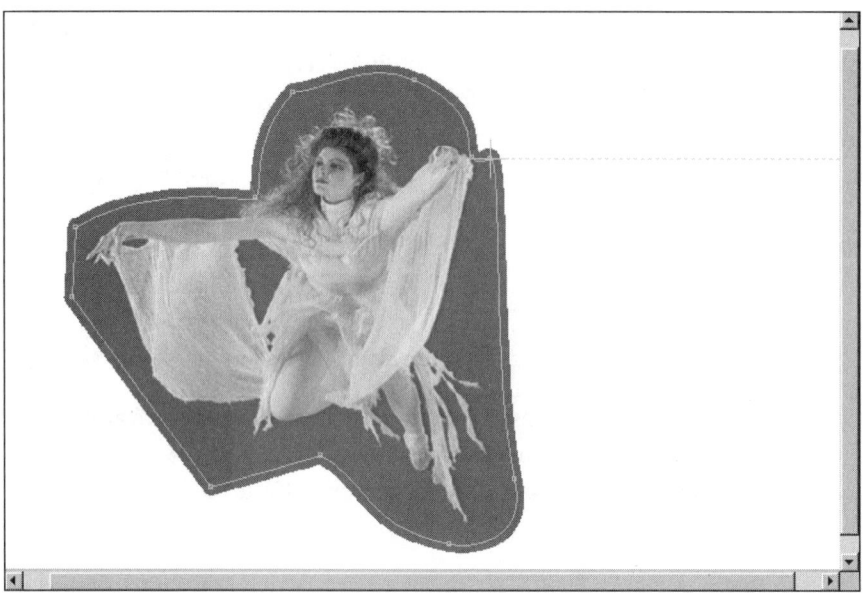

Figure 7.18
A garbage matte blocking out known transparent areas surrounding the foreground subject, making noise removal and other cleanup unnecessary for those areas.

Figure 7.19
An edge matte.

contours. Edge mattes are also handy for masking the effects of a process to the edges of a foreground element. In addition to compositing, edge mattes can be applied to a single image as the basis of energy-discharge effects such as lightning, St. Elmo's fire, or energy-weapon hits.

Mask

A *mask* is a special matte that restricts or modifies the area affected by a process, rather than separating part of an image from its background. The effect is similar to using masking tape to prevent paint from falling on areas you want to protect. A mask can have sharp or feathered edges and may be any shape, limited only by your software's masking tools. The most common use of masks is to limit keying effects to the immediate area of the keyed subject, excluding unwanted effects in the rest of the image. Masks can be animated by hand or tracked to moving patterns in an image sequence. For example, Figure 7.20 shows the beginning, middle, and end frames of a dissolve effect that uses a mask (indicated by the bright green outline) to restrict the effect. The background and foreground footage both had drifting smoke and flickering firelight, so dissolving from the full background to the full foreground would have created glaring artifacts all over the screen. With the effect masked more closely to the actors, any dissolve artifacts would be passed off as part of the "materialization."

One use of masks is to define a *region of interest*, a specific area where the mathematical operations will be especially time-consuming. Limiting this area can make major improvements in overall rendering time. For more examples of how region of interest can save you time, see Chapter 16.

Filters

A *filter* is an algorithm used to sample and modify an image pixel by pixel. There are several types of filters. A class called *spatial filters* modifies each pixel based on the values of the surrounding pixels, or *kernel*. Typical kernels are 3×3 or 5×5, but other kernel sizes are used too. For example, a median filter changes each pixel to the median value of the kernel, making individual pixels that have odd colors or brightness blend into a closer match with their surrounding pixels. This makes the median filter a good tool for noise removal. However, it also tends to soften the image if applied too strongly. Because the median filter is based on a variable mathematical operation, you have more options for fine-tuning it. Setting the filter's thresholds to limit the effect of the median filter usually removes the worst noise without excessively softening the image. See Figures 7.21 through 7.23.

A subclass of spatial filters is the *spatial convolution filter*, more commonly called a *convolve*. This type of filter uses a *weighted matrix*, which is a fixed array of numbers corresponding to the pixels in the kernel. A convolve is often used to blur, detect edges, or sharpen an image.

One of the most common uses for convolve filters is to resample an image to a higher or lower resolution. The fastest resample filter is the *impulse*, also called the *Dirac* or *nearest-neighbor filter*, (see Figure 7.24). It samples only one pixel in the original image for each pixel of the new image.

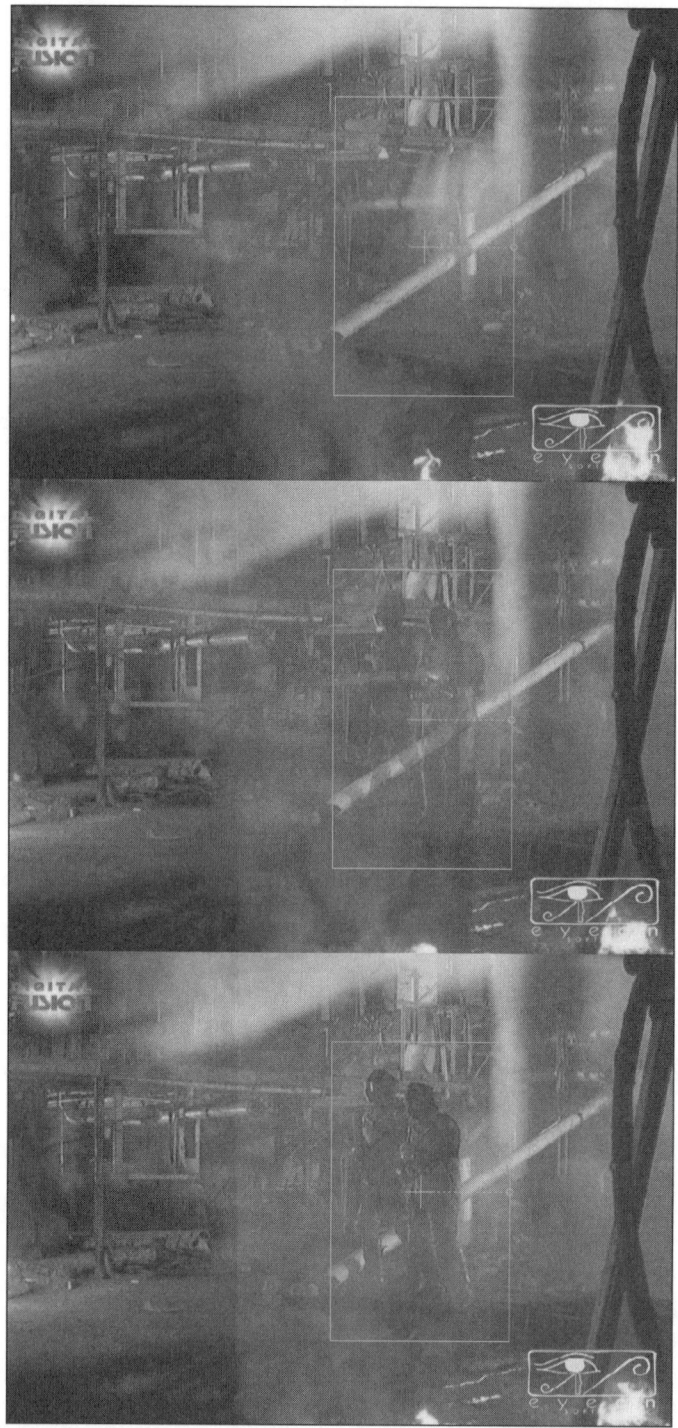

Figure 7.20
A mask restricting an animated Dissolve operation. Top: frame 0; Middle: frame 25; Bottom: frame 50.

Figure 7.21
The baseline image used to demonstrate the effects of filters and other operations.

Figure 7.22
Here, the outlined area of Figure 7.21 was enlarged to show detail.

Figure 7.23
The median filter applied to Figure 7.22.

Figure 7.24
An impulse filter applied to Figure 7.22.

The drawback is that the pixels that are sampled may be a very small fraction of the total image and may not represent the original image well. Additionally, the impulse filter tends to create a lot of noise and aliasing artifacts; it is almost never the best choice for resampling an image.

Sharpening filters work by increasing the contrast along edges, creating the illusion that the edges are sharper or have more detail, as shown in Figure 7.25. No new detail is actually created and if you overdo the sharpening, you may end up with nasty artifacts like *ringing* (see Figure 7.40 for an example).

The *Gaussian filter* (see Figure 7.26) is common to most compositing software. It creates few or no aliasing or ringing artifacts, but it tends to soften the image. The Gaussian filter is often used to blur an image or to simulate a defocus, but this filter has been used so much that it is relatively easy to spot as an effect. Its major advantage is that it is relatively fast.

The *Mitchell filter* (see Figure 7.27) is generally the best choice for resampling an image to a higher resolution. It takes longer to render than some other upsampling filters, but it sharpens the image without creating ringing artifacts.

The *sinc filter* (see Figure 7.28) is best for resampling an image to a lower resolution. It will retain more fine detail without creating too much aliasing. However, it is computation-intensive, so it tends to be slow.

Figure 7.25
A sharpening filter applied to Figure 7.22.

Figure 7.26
A Gaussian filter applied to Figure 7.22.

Figure 7.27
A Mitchell filter applied to Figure 7.22.

Figure 7.28
A sinc filter applied to Figure 7.22.

Geometric Transformations Or Transforms

Whereas a filter changes an image by modifying each pixel's color values, a *geometric transformation*, or *transform*, changes an image by moving the pixels around without changing their color values. You might think of a transform as rearranging a mosaic; all the tiles are still present, but in different places.

The most basic transform is the *flip*, an inversion of the image along the horizontal or X-axis, as shown in Figure 7.29. The flip is especially useful for reflection maps and other tricks to make a composited image appear correctly in shiny surfaces.

The flop transform is exactly like the flip, but on the vertical or Y-axis, as shown in Figure 7.30. A flop of part of an image is especially handy for creating symmetry effects, as when you need to extend a set or you want an actor to appear to be confronting himself.

A *pan transform* is when all or part of an image moves across the frame. Scrolling or crawling titles are common examples of a pan transform. Current styles in motion graphics seem to favor a large number of elements performing simultaneous pans in all directions. Personally, I find this overdone, confusing, and more than a little egotistical, but then I'm not a paying client, either. In any case, pans are useful enough that you should practice them until you are able to set one up without having to think too hard.

Figure 7.29
A flip transform.

Figure 7.30
A flop transform.

An older and no-longer-used subset of pan transforms are the *multiplane* effects, named after the camera developed by the Disney animation studio. The camera was positioned to shoot down through multiple layers of glass platens, each of which could be adjusted both laterally and along the camera axis for animated pans in three axes. Each platen held a different piece of art: The upper ones held transparent cels and the bottom ones held opaque background paintings. This enabled the camera operators to emulate perspective and depth-of-focus effects that would have been prohibitive to hand-draw. One of the best known multiplane camera shots is the London flyover sequence in *Peter Pan*, an absolutely breathtaking piece of camera work.

Digital compositing makes multiplane pans much easier. Most software enables you to animate elements separately and to use Z-channel data for complex depth moves. (The Z-channel is discussed in the next section.) Figure 7.31 shows a few frames from a multiplane pan sequence. The actor element pans right to left while the foreground element pans left to right and the background pans more slowly left to right. Note that the actor is composited to pass behind some elements and in front of others.

Other Effects

A *dissolve* is one of the oldest, most basic, and still popular effects. Although there are a plethora of variations on the basic dissolve, at core it is simply a gradual replacement of one image with another. Figure 7.20 shows a beginning, middle, and end frame from a dissolve sequence. Dissolves can be combined with other processes to create a variety of materialization effects.

A *fade* is related to a dissolve, except that the target image is usually solid white or (more commonly) solid black, as shown in Figure 7.32. Many film scripts actually end with the phrase, FADE TO BLACK. Even if none of the scene transitions are done with fades, you will generally need to do a fade to black under the end credits. The inverse, a *fade up*, is also commonly used at the beginning of a sequence. Most compositing software makes it easy to create a fade to black, white, or any other color; if there isn't a specific setup for it, you can always set up a dissolve to a solid background.

One of the common challenges in digital compositing is matching CGI elements to live footage. CGI tends to be too clean, with every surface in perfect focus. In reality, haze, dust, and other atmospheric influences tend to wash out, or *desaturate*, the colors of distant objects. This *atmosphere* is an unconscious depth cue for the audience, and if your composite does not re-create this effect, the shot will look subtly unreal. Compositing effects that mimic atmosphere generally use the *Z-buffer*, or *Z-channel*, to control the saturation of the image. A Z-channel changes luminance based on the distance from the camera. Figure 7.33 shows the Z-channel from a computer-generated rendering of a robot walking across a chessboard. The closest surfaces are dark, and distance surfaces are brighter.

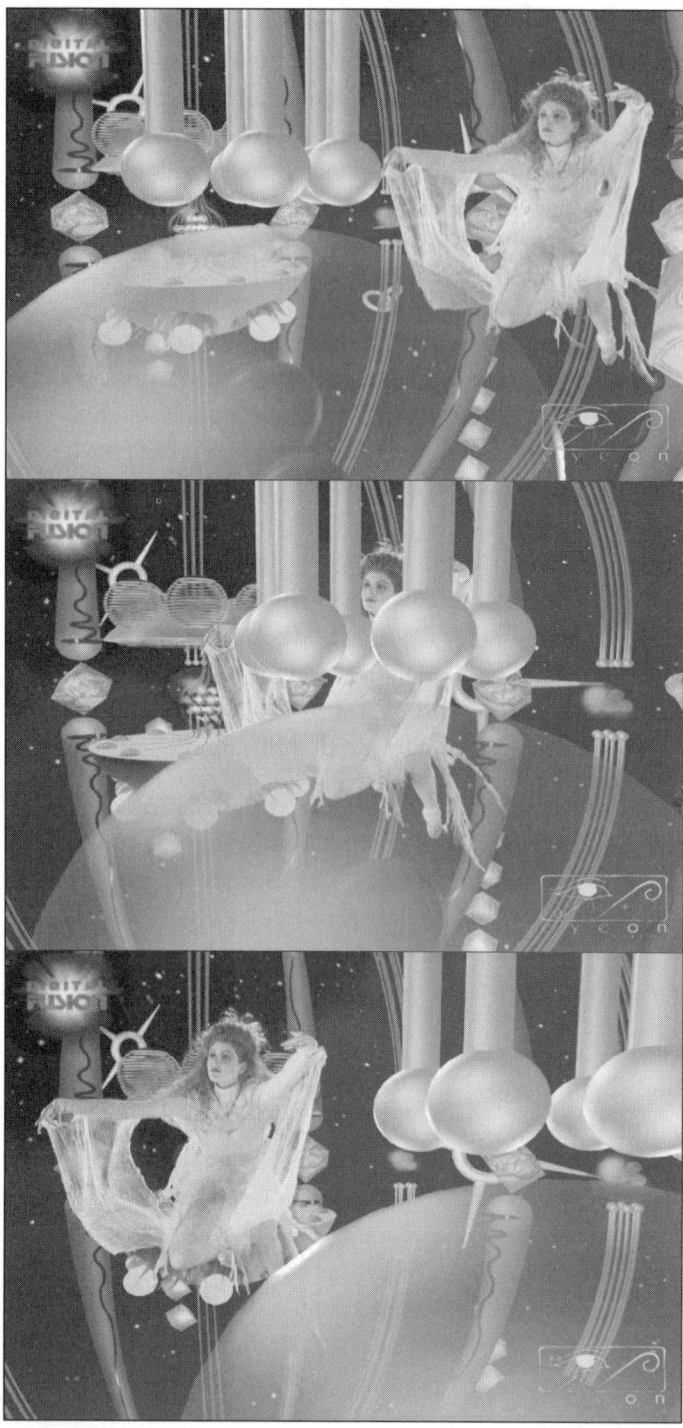

Figure 7.31
Top to bottom: three frames from a multiplane pan sequence.

Figure 7.32
Fade to black at 0%, 50%, and 100%.

Figure 7.33
A Z-channel map of distance from camera to surfaces.

A *dilate* operation enlarges the brighter areas of the image and shrinks the darker areas, as shown in Figure 7.34. An *erode* operation, the opposite of dilate, shrinks the brighter areas and enlarges the darker areas, as shown in Figure 7.35. Both effects can be used to add a halo, glow, energy discharge, or other outline-based effect to a matted subject, to create an edge matte, or to help solve matte extraction problems by enlarging or reducing the transition zone.

Problems

As a digital compositor, you must train yourself to spot problems that are too subtle for the general public to detect. There are many artifacts and mistakes that can corrupt a composition to the point where the audience no longer believes the shot, but the average audience still can't describe exactly where the illusion failed. It is your job as a compositor to detect those subconscious

Figure 7.34
A dilation of the matte for Figure 7.11.

Figure 7.35
An erosion of the matte for Figure 7.11.

giveaways and stamp them out. Here is a rogues' gallery of the most obvious blunders; treat them like Wanted posters, and keep them out of your work.

Using too low a resolution, poor-quality CGI elements, or the wrong filter when resampling an image can create hard *aliased*, or staircased, edges in the image (see Figure 7.36). Natural surfaces are always slightly irregular, and when captured on film or video, they always have soft transition zones (see Figure 7.37). You can often conceal an aliased edge by applying a small blur or median filter.

Poor choices in compression can add up to ugly artifacts. Figure 7.38 shows too high a compression factor using a JPEG codec. On the other hand, the image sequences on this book's CD-ROMs are also JPEG compressed, but with very little loss in quality. You should always evaluate your original elements and your final output for compression artifacts, and you should never apply compression to your intermediate files. After you lose the original image data to compression artifacts, you can't get it back.

If you don't tweak your mattes or keys properly, you are likely to run into *fringing* or *matte lines*. This is an outline of a different color (usually brighter) along the edge of a matte. Figure 7.39 shows an extreme fringe on the right and a better matte on the left. There are various tools to prevent or minimize fringing; see Chapter 9 for details.

Figure 7.36
An aliased image.

Figure 7.37
An anti-aliased image.

Figure 7.38
Excessive JPEG compression artifacts.

Figure 7.39
A clean bluescreen key on the left; a fringing or matte line on the right.

If you apply a sharpening filter (shown in Figure 7.25) too much, you may exaggerate the contrast along edges to the point of *ringing*. This problem can resemble a matte line, as shown in Figure 7.40. If you find this problem, simply undo the sharpen operation and try it again with a lower setting.

If you reduce the color depth of the image in order to save storage space or to accommodate a low-bandwidth delivery medium, you need to remember that you are throwing away a lot of data. You need to do it intelligently, or your work will look unprofessional. Reducing color depth without adaptive sampling, or reducing it too far even with good sampling, produces *banding*, as shown in Figure 7.41. Banding is especially noticeable in areas of continuous tone, such as human faces. Banding can occur even at 8 bits per channel if you are reducing from 16-bit or 10-bit color space. Although it's very difficult for the human eye to detect, some compositing operations can emphasize the banding. If you must use a lower color depth, choose a dither algorithm that will obscure the band edges. However, because dithering reduces the efficiency of some video compression codecs, you need to carefully weigh the trade-offs between color depth and compression.

Some programs (especially 3D CGI renderers) save RGBA images as *premultiplied*; that is, each color channel is changed by being multiplied by the alpha channel. Other software assumes that RGBA images are not premultiplied and performs the alpha channel multiplication again during the composition rendering. This reiteration of the multiplication operation creates a telltale darkening effect in the areas of the image where the alpha channel is shaded but leaves the pure black and pure white areas undisturbed, as shown in Figure 7.42. You can correct this problem by

Figure 7.40
Ringing caused by oversharpening Figure 7.22.

Figure 7.41
Banding caused by reducing the color depth of Figure 7.22 without dithering or adaptive resampling.

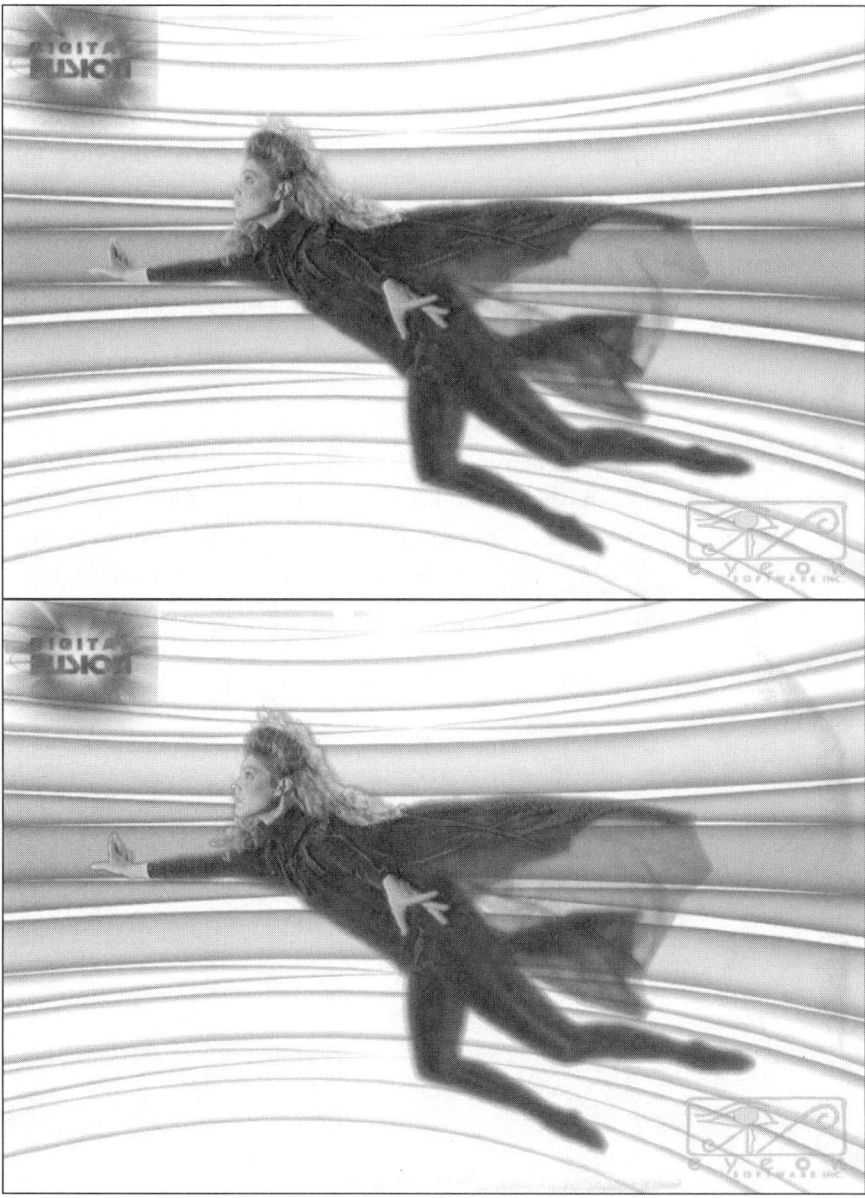

Figure 7.42
Above: correct composite; Below: duplicate multiplication of premultiplied image showing a heavy gray matte line (most visible around subject's hair).

simply turning off premultiplication when creating the source image or by disabling the duplicate multiplication in the composition.

Even if your composites don't show any of the above problems in single images, you may still find them in your final rendering. Settings and mattes that work for one frame may not work for the next. Even tiny changes between frames can make edges crawl or pop, creating *temporal artifacts*. Every one of the above problems has a temporal equivalent, and you can only detect them by rendering the image sequence. Test rendering can be time-consuming, but it's certainly better than showing your supervisor or client a shot with crawly lines all around the foreground elements.

Moving On

If you have read, examined, and understand the contents of this chapter, you'll find the text and projects in the rest of this book much easier to comprehend. You should also be able to visually identify and diagnose the problems depicted here. The next chapter will show you how to create the basic compositions pictured in this chapter, thereby introducing the tools you'll need for more complex projects in later chapters.

STARTING OFF EASY

This chapter is a tour of the basic tools in every digital compositor's kit. Projects show you how to create the compositions pictured in Chapter 7 and enable you to experiment with tools to learn their uses and limits.

This chapter takes you through tutorials designed to illustrate the concepts introduced in Chapter 7. This is an opportunity for you to experiment with the most basic compositing tools, familiarizing yourself with their operation so you are prepared for more complex problems later. If you are a beginner, you should follow each project step-by-step and carefully read the explanatory text between projects. You need to be completely comfortable with these concepts and operations before you attempt the more advanced projects in the rest of this book. If you are an experienced compositor, much of this chapter may seem to be review, but you should nevertheless read through it and familiarize yourself with the tools and project files. They will be used throughout this book, so you'll need to be able to retrieve and then apply them. Learning them now will save you time later.

Basic Tools

Before you even opened this book, you should have installed your compositing software and worked through whatever tutorials or projects were included in the official manuals. If you haven't done that, stop here, mark your place, close this book, and do it now.

In the unlikely event that you actually followed my directions in the preceding paragraph, you now have at least a basic understanding of your digital compositing software and how it works. If you insisted on jumping into the deep end, don't say I didn't warn you. In any case, keep your software manuals and CD-ROMs handy—you will probably need to refer to them now and again.

If you purchased this book to help you decide which compositing software to use, you can try any of the demo versions included on this book's CD-ROMs. As I described in detail in Chapter 3, most of the demos are disabled to the point that you can't use them to complete the projects in this book. The notable exception is Eyeon Software's Digital Fusion, which is fully enabled; it simply stamps the company and product logos randomly on your final comp so you can't use it for commercial work. For this reason, most of the projects will describe the process using Digital Fusion first and supplement where appropriate with screen shots and instructions for other programs.

The Digital Fusion Interface

You will find it easier to follow directions and interpret explanations in the rest of this book if you first familiarize yourself with the Digital Fusion (DF) interface. Throughout this book, I will use DF labels and other terminology by preference, explaining synonymous terms used in other software when appropriate. Figure 8.1 shows the basic Digital Fusion interface. You can rearrange, select, or deselect View menu options and otherwise heavily customize the DF display, so your

Figure 8.1
The Digital Fusion interface, showing a single Loader tool with the Box image sequence loaded.

screen may not look much like this. This most basic display will get you through most of the projects in this chapter. I'll explain other display options as you need them.

 The top left corner of the screen shows the program name and version—in this case, Digital Fusion Post 2.5—and in parentheses the name of the *flow*, or composition, that is currently active. You can have several DF flows open at once, which is handy when you want to adapt or to reuse a complex flow by copy-and-paste tools or settings. The next line down is the menu bar, showing the common Windows menus: File, Edit, View, Tools, Window, and Help. If you have worked with any other popular Windows applications, the contents of most of these menus should be self-explanatory; Eyeon Software did a very good job designing DF functions to behave the way Windows users expect them to.

Below the menu bar is the toolbar, which you can customize to show buttons for the tools you use most often. A DF tool performs a single operation, such as loading an image or applying a filter. Below the toolbar on the left is the Large display, and on the right is the Small display. You can view the output of any tool in either the Large or Small display; in Figure 8.1, the contents of Loader 1 are displayed in both.

Below the Large display area is the Flow Layout area. Each gray rectangle is an empty *tile*, which can hold a single tool. In Figure 8.1, a Loader tool fills the top left tile of the Flow Layout. You build your flow by arranging tools and making connections between them. To add a tool to the flow, you left-click on the tile to select it, and then either click on the desired tool's toolbar button or select the tool from the Tools menu. For example, clicking on the LD tool button will add a Loader to the flow. Figure 8.2 shows the Tools menu and the Loader/Creator submenu, with Loader selected. To help you work with your flow, you can make the tiles smaller or larger, and choose whether to display tool names or thumbnail images in Layout. You can also drag tools

Figure 8.2
Digital Fusion's Tools menu showing the Loader/Creator submenu, with the Loader option selected.

from one tile to another and change their connections. The DF displays update automatically whenever you make a change to the flow. Building a DF flow is a highly intuitive process with rapid feedback and a lot of flexibility.

At the bottom left of the screen is the Time Control area, which contains the Time slider and data entry boxes for Global Start, Render Start, Current Time, Render End, and Global End. Figure 8.1 shows the composition starting on frame 0 and ending on frame 202. The Current Time box also shows frame 202, so that is the image shown in the Large and Small displays. To the right of the Current Time box is the Start Render button; clicking on this is the same as choosing the Start Render option from the File menu. From the View menu, you can choose to display SMPTE time-code or film footage numbers rather than the frame numbers shown in Figure 8.1.

At the bottom right of the screen is the Control area. This is where you make the detailed settings for tools. Figure 8.1 shows the settings and other information for the Loader tool, including the Process Mode (Full frames), the path and file name (G:\Footage\Box\Box0200.jpg), and the in and out points for the loaded footage. Some tools have more settings than this; others are simpler. Experiment with and read about each tool when you first use it, and try out as many tools as you can whenever you have some spare time. Digital Fusion includes many tools, and additional plug-in tools are available from developers such as Ultimatte.

DIGITAL FUSION HELP

For more information about the Digital Fusion interface, refer to the Help file included with the demo software on this book's CD-ROMs. The Help files for the full version of Digital Fusion include links to video tutorials on the Digital Fusion installation CD-ROM.

USING PROJECT CLIPS AND FILES

Most of the tutorial video clips on this book's CD-ROMs are sequences of images compressed with JPEG at 100%. This format is compatible with most digital compositing software and is more efficient than most other formats, so I could squeeze in as many clips as possible. The 100% compression setting means you shouldn't have any problems with compression artifacts. Because JPEG does not support alpha channels, separate alpha channel image sequences are included for some of the clips. The alpha channel sequences have the same root name as the RGB image sequences with an "m" for "matte" appended to the end. For example, the Walker RGB footage is in the WALKER directory, and the matching matte or alpha channel is in the WALKERM directory.

JPEG images must be decompressed before they can be used. Most software does this automatically, then holds the larger uncompressed image in a temporary buffer while you work with it. This decompression can add to the rendering time of a composition. If you would like to bypass this decompression for the fastest response possible, you may want to convert the JPEG image sequences to another format such as TGA or TIFF and save them on your system's hard drive.

Compositing With Alpha Channel

The most common compositing operation is to comp a foreground image over a background image using a matte or alpha channel. As explained in Chapter 7, this process uses a grayscale image to control the transparency of the foreground, allowing the background to show through the black areas, the foreground to cover the white areas, and a proportional mixture of the foreground and background in gray areas.

Mattes or alpha channels can be created in many ways. Alpha channels are generally easiest to use when they are rendered by CGI software at the same time as the CGI color elements. The edges and gradients of a CGI rendering are precisely controlled, and because the images are digital from the beginning, there are no film scanning or video digitizing artifacts. Just to make this first project an easy one, I've provided a CGI-rendered element and alpha channel.

PROJECT 8.1 Compositing With An Alpha Channel

The goal of this project is to composite a CGI animated character—the Walker—over digitized video of a chessboard and table. Along the way, you will learn to load and save footage, add an alpha channel to RGB footage to create RGBA footage, and merge background and foreground elements using an alpha channel.

The Walker is a stock character setup included with NewTek's LightWave 3D software, which I used to render the WALKR000.JPG sequence shown in Figure 8.3 and the matching alpha channel sequence shown in Figure 8.4. The chessboard footage (see Figure 8.5) was set up, lit,

Figure 8.3
Frame 276 of the LightWave-rendered Walker RGB image sequence.

Figure 8.4
Frame 276 of the LightWave-rendered Walker alpha channel image sequence.

Figure 8.5
Frame 276 from the chessboard footage.

photographed, and digitized by Chris Nibley (**www.nibley.com**) using one of his motion control camera rigs. Later in this book, I'll explain how you can use this footage to animate your own CGI or composited elements to match the camera move.

Make sure that this book's first CD-ROM is in your CD-ROM drive or that you have copied the tutorial files to your hard drive.

1. Open Digital Fusion. It should automatically open a new, empty flow.

2. Left-click on the top left tile in the Layout area. Click on the LD toolbar button or choose the Tool|Loader/Creator|Loader menu option to add a Loader tool to the selected tile. Repeat this step for the first tile in the second and third rows of the Layout area. You should end up with three Loader tools arranged as shown in Figure 8.6, but still empty. In the next step, you'll load the image sequences pictured in the Loader tools in the figure.

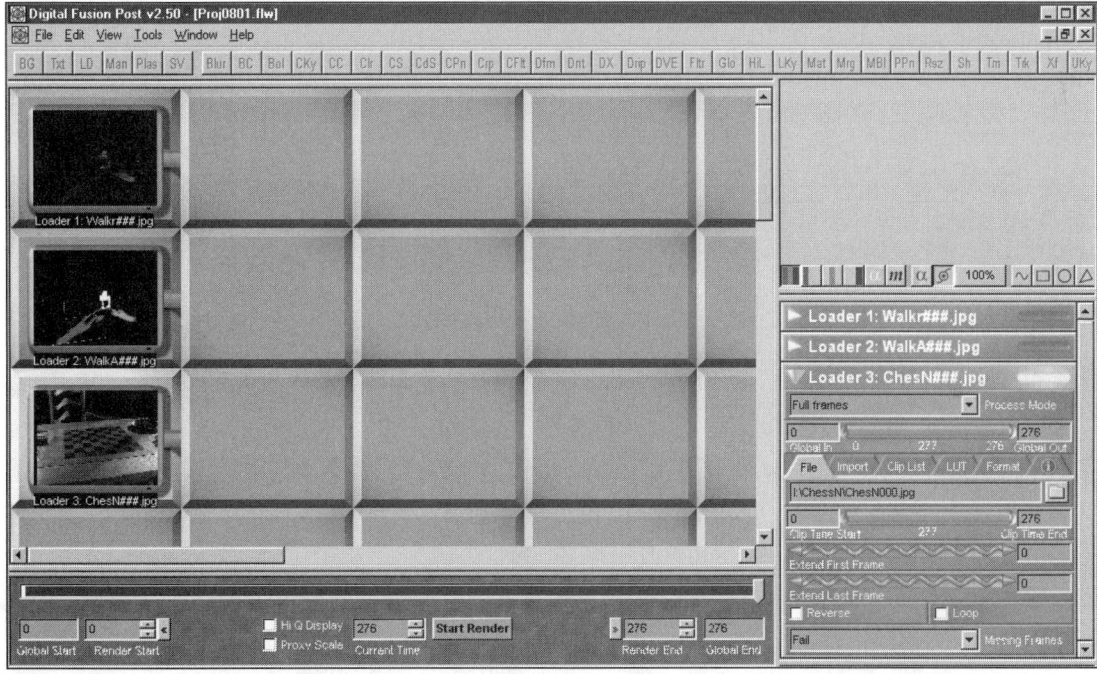

Figure 8.6
RGB, alpha channel, and background image sequences loaded in Digital Fusion Loader tools.

3. In the Control area, left-click on the yellow arrow at the left edge of Loader 3's header to open the Loader's settings. Left-click on the folder icon, and then browse your system to find and select the file ChesN000.jpg. You only have to select the first frame to load the entire sequence; Loader 3 should automatically adjust its settings to the correct number of frames, 277. Your Loader 3 should look just like the one pictured in the lower right corner of Figure 8.6. Close Loader 3 by clicking on its yellow header arrow again.

4. Repeat the preceding step for Loader 1, selecting file Walkr000.jpg. Repeat again for Loader 2, selecting file WalkM000.jpg. Close each Loader when you are done with it.

5. In the Time Control area at the bottom left of the screen, make sure that Global Start and Render Start are set to 0, and Render End and Global End are set to 276.

6. Select the empty tile beside Loader 2. Choose the Tools|Color|Channel Booleans menu option or click on the Bol toolbar button to add a Channel Booleans tool to the selected tile. Loader 2 should automatically connect itself to the Background (left side) input of the Channel Booleans tool.

7. Left-click on the red pipe on the right side of Loader 1, and drag it to the top funnel of the Channel Booleans tool. This creates a pipe or connection between Loader 1 and the Foreground (top) input of the Channel Booleans tool. Your flow should look like Figure 8.7. You can remove the connection by clicking on the funnel and dragging back to the beginning of the pipe. You may want to play with this a bit, just to get a feel for making and changing connections in DF.

Figure 8.7
The Channel Booleans tool configured to combine RGB and alpha channels into an RGBA image sequence.

8. Open the Channel Booleans tool in the Control area. In its Color Channels tab, configure it to copy the red, green, and blue FG (foreground) channels to the red, green, and blue output channels, and the Luminance BG (background) to the Alpha output channel. Your configuration should look like Figure 8.7. This configuration combines the RGB and Alpha channels from the two Loaders into a single RGBA image sequence. Because this is a straight copy of each channels' values, there is no mathematical operation, and you don't have to worry about premultiplication or other issues.

You can view the results of any tool by dragging it to either the Large or Small displays, or by right-clicking on the tool and choosing Large, Small, or All from the View On submenu. Figure 8.7 shows the Large display hidden and the Channel Booleans tool results displayed in the Small display. A row of display option buttons is located along the bottom edge of both Large and Small displays. When a tool outputs an alpha channel, you can view it by clicking on the button marked with the alpha symbol, "α", or "m" for "matte." The button marked with the alpha superimposed over the three color stripes chooses a display that adds the color and alpha channels together. The buttons with single color stripes enable you to view one channel at a time, a very useful feature for many compositing operations. The button with all three color stripes (and no alpha symbol) displays only the RGB channels, the visible color image.

9. Make a new directory on your system's hard drive, and name it WALKER.

10. Add a Saver tool to your flow, to the right of the Channel Booleans tool. The Saver should automatically connect to the output of the Channel Booleans tool.

11. Open the Saver tool in the Control area. In the Saver's Format tab, make sure Save Alpha is checked, as in Figure 8.8. In the File tab, choose your preferred file format. Make sure you choose one that supports RGBA format and one that will be compatible with your other graphics software; I recommend TGA. Choose to save to the new WALKER directory, with the root name WALKC000.TGA.

Save your flow as Walker1.flw.

12. Click on the Start Render button (bottom center of the screen), or choose the File|Start Render menu option, to begin rendering your composition to the new WALKER directory. Because you left the output of Loader 3 without a Saver, DF will display an alert dialog box warning you that some results won't be saved. Just click on Yes to continue rendering. During the render, DF will show progress by moving the frame slider and displaying the rendering frame in the Current Time box at the bottom center of the screen. A small, green light will also blink on each tool in Layout as that tool performs its operation. Depending on the speed of your system, the whole rendering can take anywhere from less than a minute to several minutes; you can either watch the pretty lights or go for a cup of coffee. When the rendering is complete, DF will trigger your system's alert sound and display the rendering's statistics.

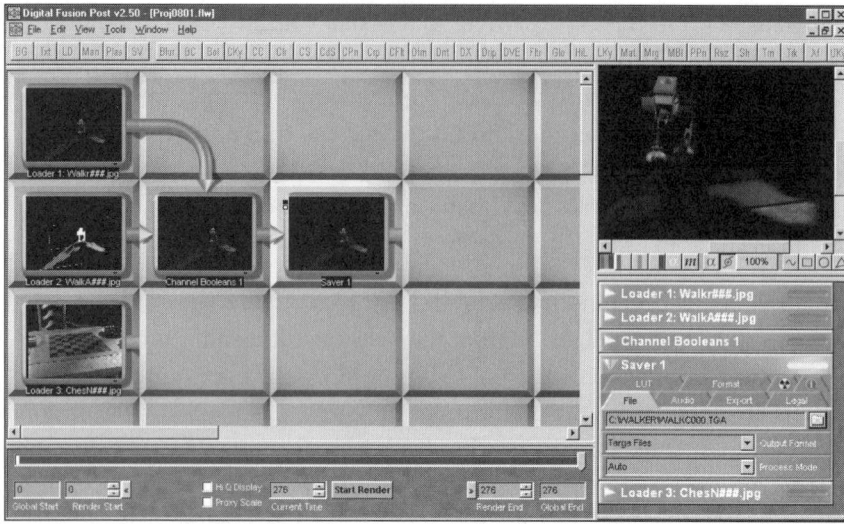

Figure 8.8
The Saver tool configured to save the alpha channel to the output image sequence. The Saver File tab settings are shown (left) and the Format tab settings (right).

After you render the WALKC RGBA sequence, you will be able to reload and then use it in other projects without having to separately load and Channel Boolean the alpha channel sequence. This will make your comps simpler and easier to manage. This is called a precomposition, or *precomp*.

ALPHA CHANNEL PRECOMPS

You can save time in other projects by precomping all the alpha channel sequences now. You simply choose the new RGB sequence in Loader 1, choose the new alpha channel sequence in Loader 2, choose a new directory and root file name in Saver, set the appropriate frame numbers to render, and render. If you have enough space in your system to store all the rendered sequences, do this now. The alpha channel sequences are located in directories that end with the letter "m" for "matte," and their matching RGB sequences are in directories with the same name but without the m.

---

13. Load the WALKC000.TGA sequence you just rendered into Loader 1, replacing the WALKR000.JPG sequence.

14. The alpha channel in Loader 2 is obsolete now, so right-click on Loader 2 in the Layout area and choose Delete. Drag Loader 3 up to the first tile in the second row.

15. Delete the Channel Booleans tool also. The Saver tool will automatically move to the second column to close up the space. Drag the Saver tool back into the third column to free up the second column again.

16. Add a Merge tool to the tile between Loader 3 and the Saver. The Loader 3 and Saver tools should automatically connect to the Merge tool. Connect Loader 1 to the Merge foreground (top) input, just as you connected it to the Channel Booleans tool earlier in this project. Your flow should now look like the Layout area in Figure 8.9.

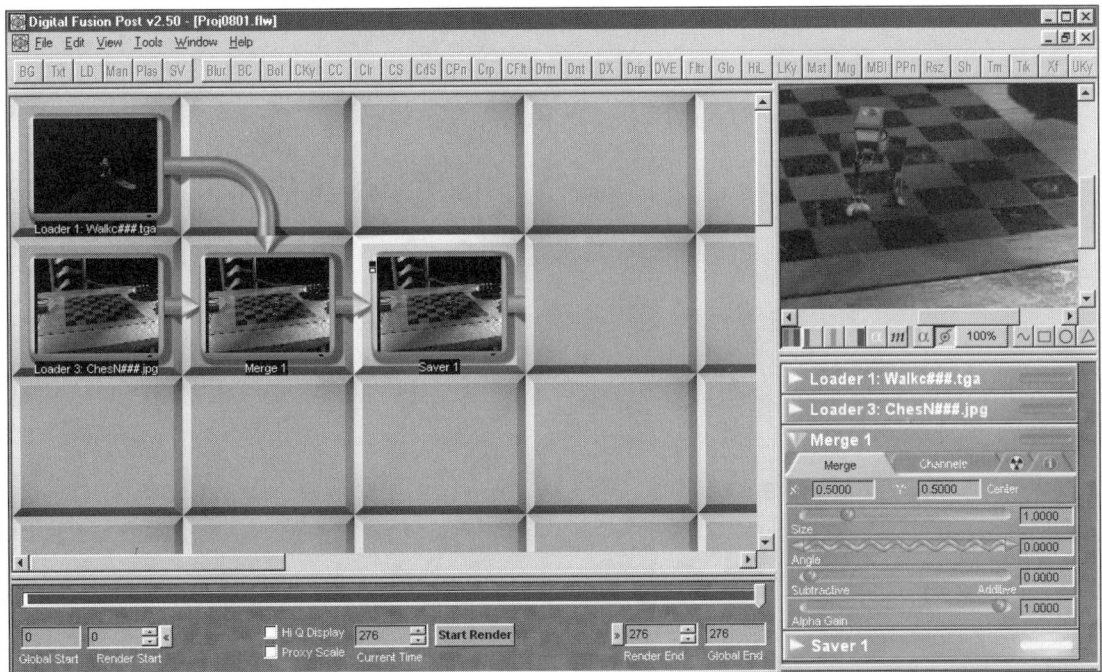

Figure 8.9
The Merge tool configured to composite the Walker foreground sequence over the Chessboard background sequence by using the alpha channel.

17. Open the Merge tool in the Control area, and make sure the settings are 1.0 Alpha Gain and 0.0 Subtractive, as shown in Figure 8.9. This Merge tool performs the Over mathematical operation described in Chapter 7. You can vary the density of the Walker's shadows by increasing the Subtractive value towards Additive, but reducing the Alpha Gain will make the Walker transparent. View the Saver's output in either the Small or Large displays, and play with the Merge tool settings to get a feel for their effects.

Digital Fusion can render a preview so you can see what the composition looks like when playing back. Simply right-click on the tool you want to preview, and choose Create/Play Preview On|Small (see Figure 8.10, left). DF will render the tool's output for the whole Render range, and then display the preview in the Small display area. A set of player controls will appear in the lower right corner of the screen, as shown in Figure 8.10, right. You can also use the frame slider in the player controls to scrub the preview faster than you can scrub the Time Control slider. This can be useful when the timing of an effect is tight and you need faster feedback to judge your work.

When you have settings you like, choose a new directory and root file name, and render the composition. You may want to choose an animation format such as AVI or QuickTime that your system can play back, rather than an image sequence.

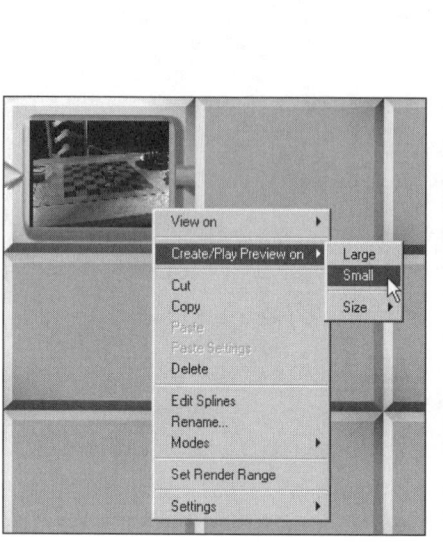
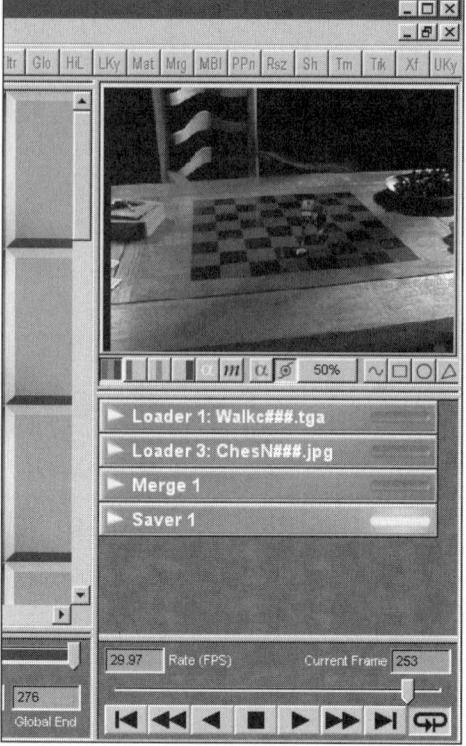

Figure 8.10
Choose Preview, left, and Preview Playback in the Small display area, right.

Sometimes, it's a good idea to preserve an alpha channel through a composition just in case you need to fine-tune the comp later. Because the alpha channel from the Merge tool is blank, you can replace it with the original alpha channel from the image sequence in Loader 1.

18. Drag the Saver tool one column to the right to leave room between the Merge and Saver tools.

19. Add a Channel Booleans tool between Merge and Saver.

20. Drag another connection from Loader 1 to the Channel Boolean's foreground (top) input. Your results should look like Figure 8.11.

MULTIPLE OUTPUT CONNECTIONS

Digital Fusion allows you to make more than one connection from a single output. This saves you the time, bother, and screen space of duplicate Loaders and other tools that feed parallel flows like this one.

---

21. Change the settings for the Channel Booleans tool to copy the background RGB channels to the corresponding output channels, and the Alpha foreground channel to the Alpha output channel, as in Figure 8.11.

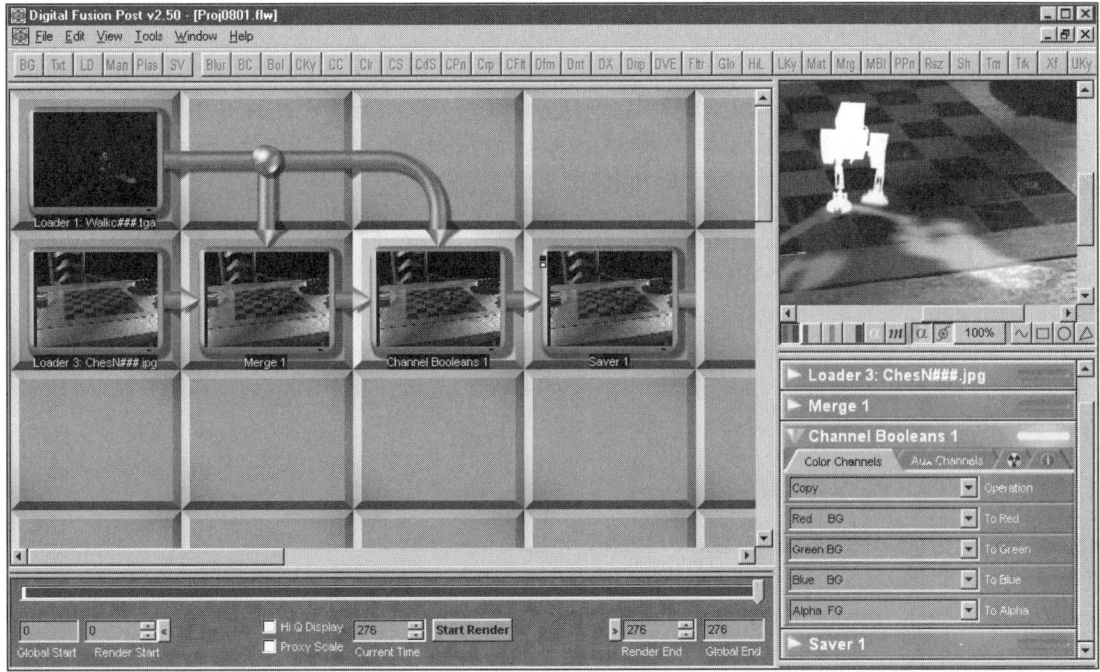

Figure 8.11
The Channel Booleans tool configured to copy the original alpha channel to the alpha channel of the final composite.

22. In the Saver, choose an output format that supports alpha channels. Then choose a directory and root file name. Save your revised flow with a new name. Finally, render your composition.

Congratulations! You've just completed the first compositing project. In this project, you learned how to:

- Add, delete, and move tools and connections to build a flow
- Load elements with the Loader tool
- Combine channels with the Channel Booleans tool
- Create a precomp
- Perform an Over composite using an alpha channel and the Merge tool
- Render a Preview
- Render the composition to several file formats with the Saver tool

You will use these new capabilities in nearly every composition you create. With a little more practice, they will become as easy and unconscious as tying your shoes.

Simple Keying

Keying is the process of separating a foreground object from its existing background. (This process is described in more detail in Chapter 7.) You will need to key, or *pull a matte,* for an element whenever you don't already have a matte or alpha channel. There are many ways to key. This section covers the two most basic: luma and chroma.

Luma keying creates a matte based on the dark and light areas of the element. All compositing software includes tools for luma keying, but some have more-refined tools than others. It is relatively simple to create elements for a luma key; you can photograph a light subject against a dark background, or a dark subject against a light background. For example, Artbeats creates much of its excellent Digital Film Library series of effects footage by filming against a black background. This makes the footage very easy to luma key.

PROJECT 8.2 Luma Keying Stock Footage Over A Background Element

The goal of this project is to use a luma key to composite a foreground element of stock footage over a background element. This will show you how to manipulate luma controls to blend the elements seamlessly. The foreground footage you'll be using is a selection from the Artbeats Digital Film Library. The Ceiling Fire JPEG image sequence, shown in Figure 8.12, is a seamlessly looping fire clip from the ReelFire 1 collection. The fire was photographed against a nearly pure-black background.

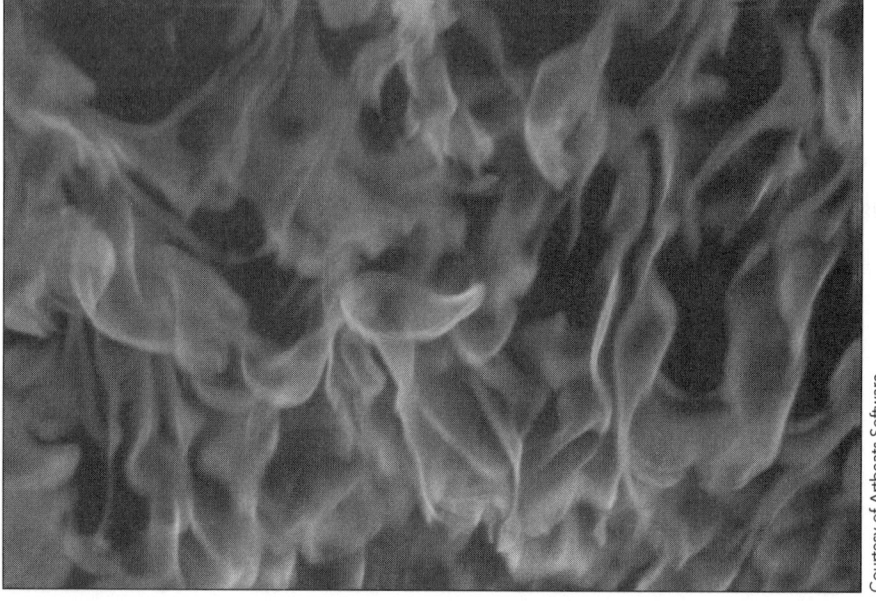

Courtesy of Artbeats Software.

Figure 8.12
A frame from the Fire0000.jpg image sequence.

Artbeats Software, Inc.
1405 North Myrtle, Suite 5
Myrtle Creek, OR 97457
(541) 863-4429
(541) 863-4547, Fax
www.artbeats.com

The background element is a shot of an actor jumping off a platform with a fireball going off in the background, shown in Figure 8.13. Although the selected elements are not a professionally perfect match, this is the type of comp you might have to do if the script called for the actor to be leaping into an area that was already on fire. For obvious safety reasons, it's best to keep actors as far from real flames as possible. It's much safer (and cheaper) to composite flames into a shot in post-production than to rig practical flames on set.

Figure 8.13
A frame from the Jump0000.jpg image sequence.

1. Open a new flow. Add a Loader tool to the top left tile of the Layout area. In the Loader control, choose Fire0000.jpg from the CEILFIRE directory.

2. Add a second Loader below Loader 1. In Loader 2's control, choose Jump0000.jpg from the JUMP directory.

3. Set the flow's Global and Render Start frames to 0, and Render and Global End frames to 102, the last frame of the Jump element.

LOOPING FOOTAGE

If the Jump clip was longer than the Fire clip, you could set Loader 1 to Loop, and the fire would repeat as long as necessary. This is why looping stock footage can be so valuable: It gives you an extra margin of safety. For example, if the original Jump element was 102 frames and the fire element was 208 frames, you'd be fine. However, if the director decided to substitute a different take of the Jump element that was 240 frames, you'd have to come up with a longer fire element. With looping footage, you're covered no matter how long the other elements run.

4. Add a Luma Keyer tool to the empty tile beside Loader 1, either by clicking on the LKy toolbar button or by choosing the Tools|Matte|Luma Keyer menu option.

The Luma Keyer tool adds the luminance, or brightness, value from all three input color channels and saves the result to its output alpha channel. It passes the input RGB channels straight through to its output. The result is the RGBA image shown in Figure 8.14, where the Luma Keyer output is sent to both Large and Small displays. Large shows the alpha channel while Small shows the RGB channels. As you can see, the transparent (black) areas of the alpha channel correspond to the dark areas of the color channels, and the opaque (white) areas of the alpha channel correspond to the bright areas of the color channels.

Figure 8.14
The Luma Keyer tool creates an alpha channel visible in the Large display area.

5. Add a Merge tool to the third tile in the second row. Connect Loader 2 to the Merge tool's Background (left side) input. Connect the output from the Luma Keyer to the Merge foreground (top) input.

6. Add a Saver tool to the tile to the right of the Merge tool. The Saver should automatically connect to the Merge tool. Your flow should now look like the Layout area in Figure 8.15.

Figure 8.15
The luma key flow showing Luma Keyer settings.

7. In the Luma Keyer controls, play with the Matte Contrast setting to find a value you like. Settings higher than 0 will make the flame edges stand out more; below 0, the flames fade to completely transparent at –1.0.

You can also tweak the key with the Low/High control, which determines the matte's low and high thresholds. The High setting should rarely go below 0.8, which means that any pixel higher than 80% luminance is completely opaque. The Low setting, generally best if lower than 0.2, makes any pixel with a lower value become completely transparent.

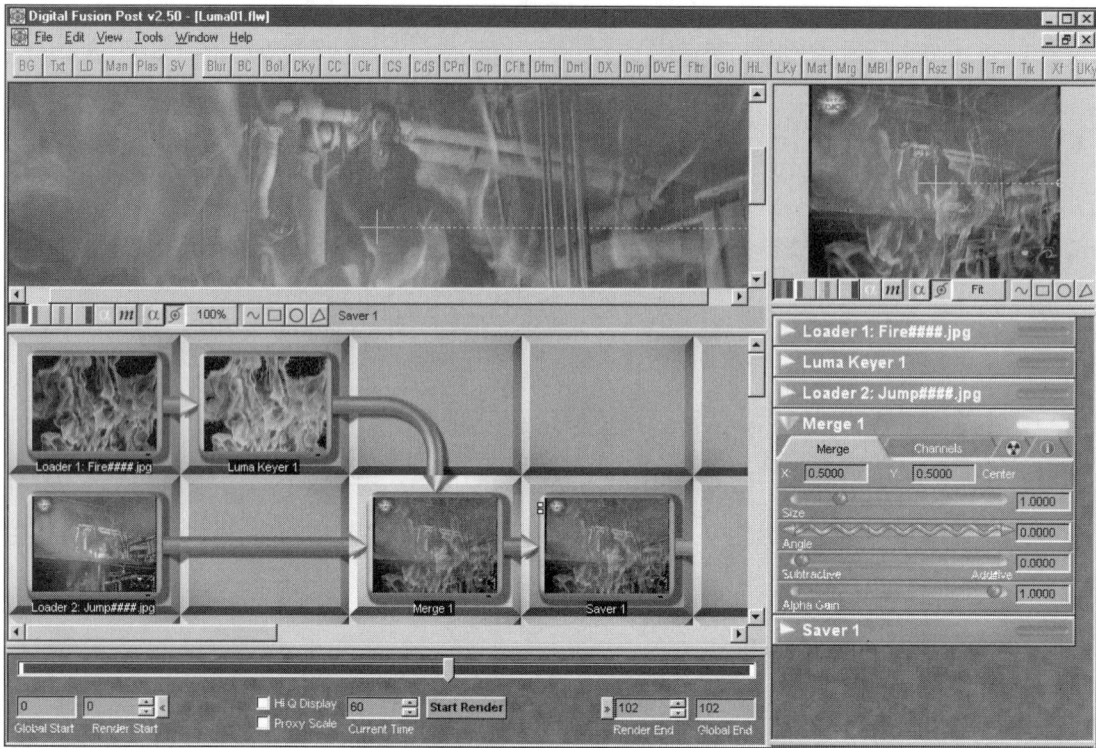

Figure 8.16
The final luma key flow showing Merge settings.

8. Open the Merge tool in the Control area, and make sure the settings are 1.0 Alpha Gain and 0.0 Subtractive, as shown in Figure 8.16. As in the previous project, this Merge tool performs the Over mathematical operation described in Chapter 7. You can vary the density of the flame edges by increasing the Subtractive value towards Additive, but reducing the Alpha Gain will make the entire fire transparent. View the Saver's output in either the Small or Large displays and play with the Merge tool settings to get a feel for their effects.

If you like, you can insert a Channel Booleans tool between the Merge and Saver, and copy the Luma Keyer alpha channel to the output alpha channel. As I mentioned in the preceding project, sometimes having that alpha channel can come in handy later.

9. When all the settings suit you, render your composition.

In completing this Project, you learned how to:

• Use the Luma Keyer tool to extract a matte from a dark background

• Fine-tune the matte using the Merge tool's Subtractive/Additive and Alpha Gain tools

Now that you've learned to pull a matte based on the single variable of luminance, let's try it with three times the variables: *chroma* or *color keying*. As Chapter 7 details, this process is also known as bluescreen or greenscreen, after the colors commonly selected for backgrounds. It's generally more useful than luma keying due to the difficulty of lighting actors and sets over a perfectly black or white background. A saturated color background is challenging to light (see Chapter 6), but at least you can put a decent amount of light on your foreground subjects.

PROJECT 8.3 Chroma Keying

This project will show you how to key bluescreen footage to extract a clean matte. Bluescreen processes can be very complex and demanding. In many ways, this project is a best-case example. In later chapters, you will apply the techniques you learn here to more-challenging keying problems. For this reason, it's important that you complete this project successfully, and that you take every opportunity to experiment with the variables and options until they are completely familiar to you.

1. Open a new flow and add two Loaders. In the first Loader, load the image sequence from the GirlSide directory, as shown in Figure 8.17. In the second Loader, load the image sequence from the TshipBG directory, as shown in Figure 8.18.

Figure 8.17
A frame from the GirlSide image sequence.

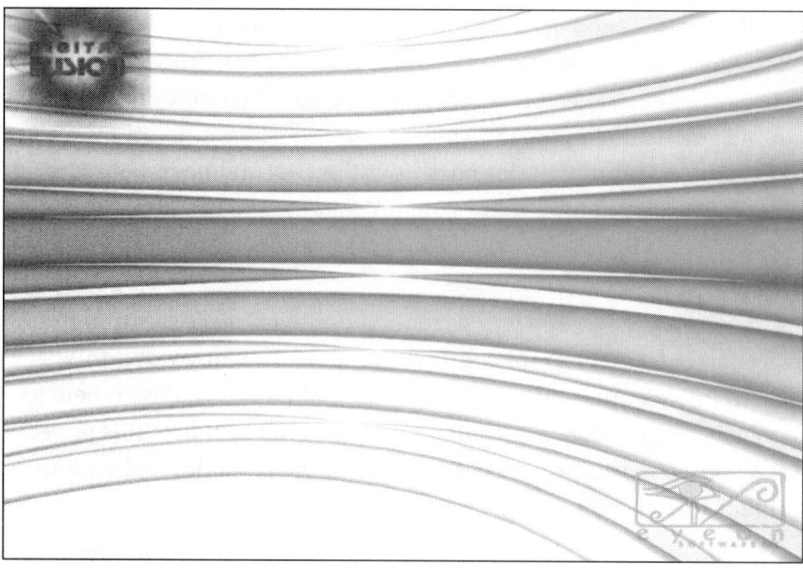

Figure 8.18
A frame from the TshipBG image sequence.

2. Add a Merge tool to the third tile in the second row, and connect it to the second Loader.

3. Select the tile beside the first Loader and then click on the UKy toolbar button, or choose the Tools|Matte|Ultra Keyer menu option, to add an Ultra Keyer tool to the flow. Connect the output of the Ultra Keyer to the Merge tool.

4. Send the Ultra Keyer to the Small display, and the Merge to the Large display. Your flow should now look like Figure 8.19.

5. The default Ultra Keyer settings will composite the actress over the background, but there is a lot of blue spill and a heavy blue outline, visible rigging lines, and clutter around the edges, as shown in Figure 8.19. To see what the default matte looks like, double-click on the alpha (α) button under the Small display. This toggles the Small view to display only the alpha channel of the Merge tool's output.

This alpha channel has rough edges, lots of noise, and variations in the density of the background (see Figure 8.20). Let's look at some tools for cleaning up this mess.

6. Open the Ultra Keyer in the Control area. The Ultra Keyer has three tabs: Pre Matte, Matte, and Image. Select Pre Matte.

7. The first control at the top is Color Background. Set this to Blue.

The next set of controls is the Red, Green, Blue, and Luminance range settings, which define the range of colors to be added to the matte as opaque. DF makes it very easy to select and to tweak these color ranges by dragging a selection box in the display showing the Ultra Keyer.

Figure 8.19
Basic bluescreen flow with default Ultra Keyer settings.

8. In the Small display, left-click and drag to select areas that you want to matte out. You can repeat this several times, adding bits and pieces to the matte each time. If you're not happy with the results, click on the Reset Color Ranges button at the bottom of the tab and try again. Make sure you don't include any of the actress, but do include the rigging wires visible above her. Don't worry if there are a few holes in the nearly transparent areas. This is just the first rough pass; you'll have plenty of chances to fix them later. When you're done, your color ranges and alpha channel should look something like Figure 8.21. Check the Lock Color Picking box to nail down the color ranges.

9. The next setting down is Pre Matte Size. Drag this over to about 10. This softens out the roughness along the matte's edges—kind of a dithering and anti-aliasing combined.

10. For now, skip Matte Separation and move on to the Image tab. First, let's suppress the pervasive blue spill on the actress's white costume. Drag the Spill Suppression setting all the way over to 1.0. Set Spill Method to Medium. These two settings desaturate any blue color to a soft gray.

Figure 8.20
The first rough alpha channel extracted with the default Ultra Keyer settings.

Figure 8.21
The alpha channel after drag-selecting portions of the Small display.

Figure 8.22
Above: The actress's left leg is partially transparent (arrow), indicating too broad a range in the matte threshold.
Below: A corrected Matte Threshold fixes the problem.

If you change the Current Time or drag the Time slider to frame 70, you can see that the combination of shadows and blue spill has made the actress's left leg partially transparent, as shown in Figure 8.22. This indicates that the matte threshold is too extensive and needs to be constrained.

11. Select the Matte tab. The Matte Threshold control is at the bottom of the tab. Drag the upper end of Matte Threshold down to about 0.8, and drag the lower end up to about 0.2. Now matte values above 80 percent are fully opaque (including the leg), and matte values lower than 20 percent are fully transparent.

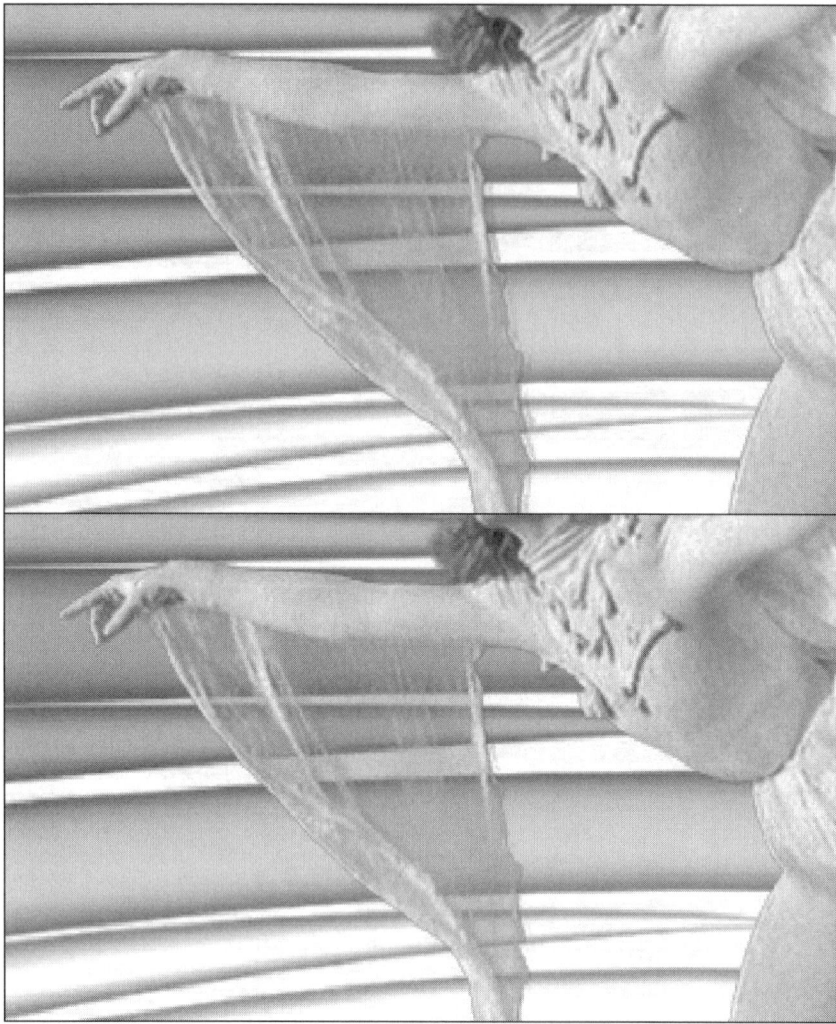

Figure 8.23
Above: The gauze is too opaque. Below: A corrected Matte Gamma fixes the problem.

12. The gauzy material trailing from the actress's right arm is too opaque, as shown in Figure 8.23. The Matte Gamma setting controls the opacity of these kinds of partially transparent areas. Drag the Matte Gamma slider down to about 0.75, or whatever seems appropriate.

13. The last step in extracting the matte from the bluescreen footage is to tweak the *fringe*, or the thin gray border around the edges of the matte. Zoom the Large display to 200% or larger, and scroll the display so you can see several problem areas of the fringe at the same time. Figure 8.24 shows a hard, thin fringe along the actress's arms, body, and trailing gauze, and a thicker but less dense fringe in her hair.

Figure 8.24
Fringe problems along "hard" edges (arrow) and in hair.

Figure 8.25
The Fringe Gamma control set to 6.0.

14. Go back to the Image tab of the Ultra Keyer control. The fringe controls include Fringe Gamma, Fringe Size, and Fringe Shape. Set the Fringe Gamma to about 6. This gets rid of most of the fringe problem, as shown in Figure 8.25.

The Fringe Size controls the width of the transition zone from foreground to background. A higher number spreads this transition out; a smaller number keeps it tight. If you already have a good matte, numbers smaller than 1.0 are best. If you push the Fringe Size too large, it starts to behave like a glow effect and washes out the edges of your foreground subject. For this example, I found a Fringe Size of 0.3 good for softening the matte edge without obscuring any of the subject (see Figure 8.26).

The last setting, Fringe Shape, is only a concern when the Fringe Size is very large. A high Fringe Shape value pushes the transition zone outward, and a small value pulls it in. Because the matte is already in very good shape and the Fringe Size is less than 1.0, you can leave Fringe Shape at the default value of 0.5. If you want to experiment, push it up to 1.5 just to see the dark fringe line it will produce. Your final matte should look like Figure 8.27.

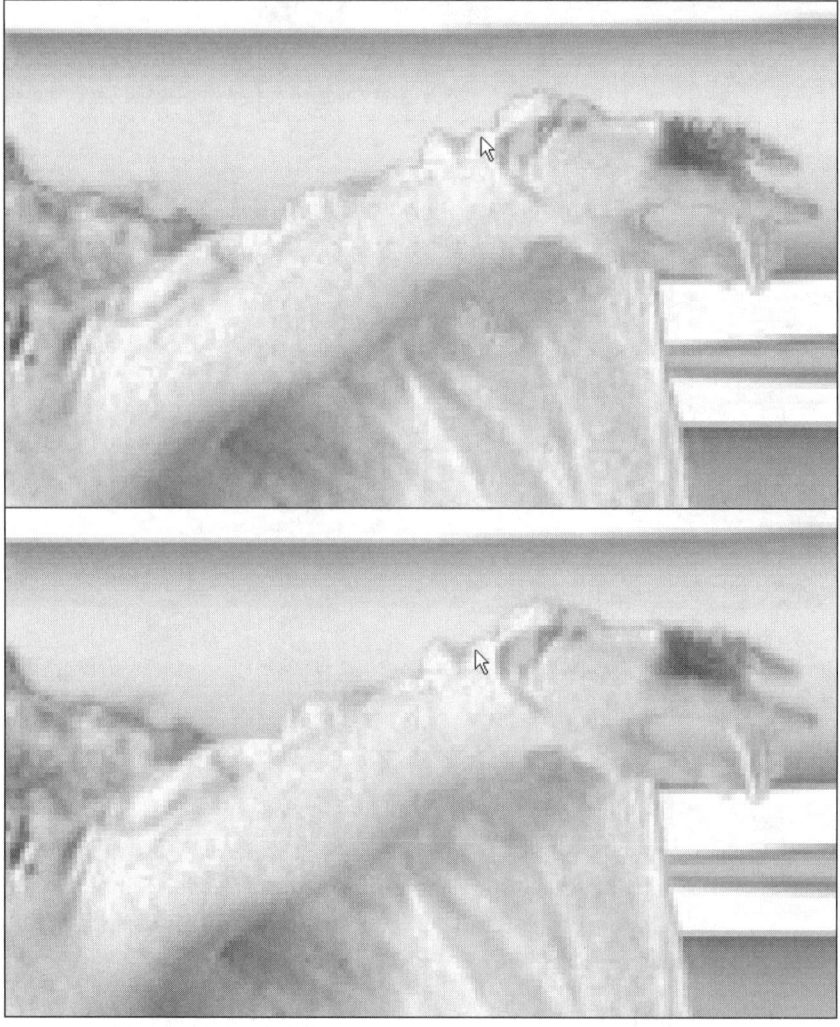

Figure 8.26
Above: The Fringe Size is set to 0.0. Below: The Fringe Size is set to 0.3.

Figure 8.27
Fringe settings in the Image tab, and the final matte.

There is still a slight but noticeable fringe of gray around the edges of the actress. This final step is where Chapter 7's discussion of premultiplication comes in. DF can make use of premultiplied images to improve the results of an Over operation.

15. Check the Post Multiply Image box at the bottom of the Image tab. Open the controls for the Merge tool. In the Merge tab, set Subtractive/Additive to 1.0. Your results should look like Figure 8.28.

16. Test your composition by adding a Saver and rendering the sequence, or by making a full-size Preview on the Large display. You need to see the sequence at full resolution with no compression to judge the quality of the matte. You should also test this composition with different background footage. How does it look with a dark background? Would you change any settings? What if the background changes? Are there any settings you would need to animate to compensate for changes in the background?

17. Save your composition as BlueScrn.flw. You'll need it for other projects later in this chapter.

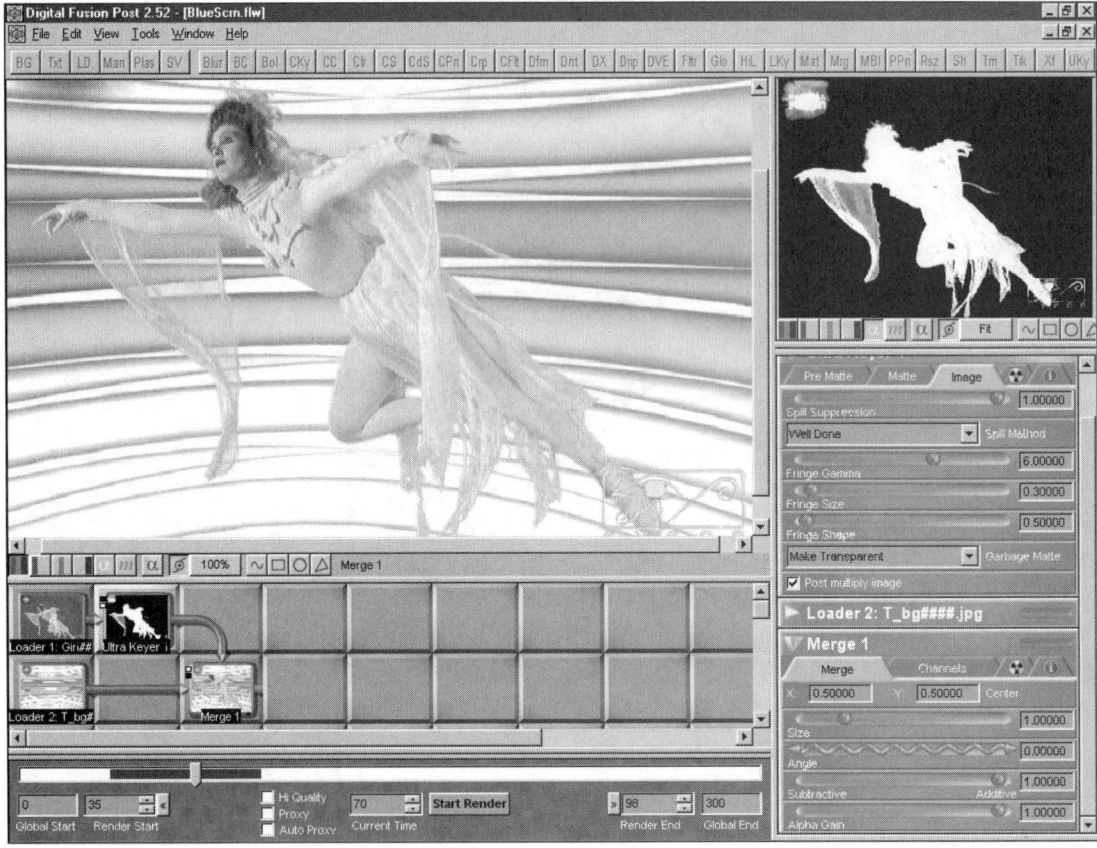

Figure 8.28
The Merge settings and the final composition.

In completing this project, you learned how to key bluescreen footage using the Ultra Keyer tool, including how to:

- Adjust color and luminance ranges
- Suppress blue spill
- Adjust matte high and low thresholds and gamma
- Fix fringe problems
- Coordinate keyer premultiplication with the Merge tool

Filters And Effects

So many filters and effects are available—with more being programmed every day—that it is more important to learn how to evaluate and choose between them than how to use any specific one. Projects 8.4, 8.5, and 8.6 show you how to set up and test a collection of filters and how to comp two of the most basic and common visual effects—the fade and the dissolve.

PROJECT 8.4 Experimenting With Filters

The goal of this project is to set up a testing flow that you can use to experiment with the effects of various filter tools. It isn't intended to be useful for rendering a finished composite, but it will save you a lot of time when you've temporarily forgotten which filter does what. It's also a convenient place to save your favorite filter settings so you can copy-and-paste them into your other compositions.

1. Open a new flow. Add a Loader to the leftmost tile in the third row. Load the Box footage from the CD-ROMs, or any other footage that has a good color range and a variety of edges and gradients.

2. Select the second tile in the second row. Choose the Tools|Filters|Blur/Sharpen menu option to add the selected filter to the flow. Connect the Loader to the filter tool.

3. Repeat the preceding step for all the other tools in the Tools|Filters submenu, arranging them as shown in Figure 8.29.

4. After all the filter tools are connected, minimize the Flow view and maximize the Large display, as shown in Figure 8.30.

You don't need to see the flow anymore, and you will want the maximum space in the Large display so you can zoom in to 400% to examine the effects of the filters closely. You can set the Small display to 100% to show the same area unmagnified.

Figure 8.29
All Filter tools are added to the flow and connected to a single Loader.

Figure 8.30
The Flow view is minimized and Large display is maximized and zoomed to 400% to show the filter effects in the best detail.

To select a filter, double-click on its Control header and send its output to the Large and Small displays by pressing the accent (') key (usually at the top left of the keyboard, just above the left Tab key and below the Esc key). By completing this project, you learned a quick, easy way to compare the effects of filters and other tools. You may want to make similar test flows for the other Tool submenus.

PROJECT 8.5   Animating A Setting

The goal of this project is to duplicate one of the most basic operations of the traditional optical printer: the fade to black. This operation and its variations (fade from black, fade to white, and so on) are used in nearly every production. The ability to animate and time a fade is a simple but essential skill for a digital compositor.

1. Open a new flow. Add a Loader, and load any footage you have handy, as long as it's more than 60 frames.

2. Add a Brightness/Contrast (BC) tool to the right of the Loader, using the BC toolbar button or the Tools|Color| Brightness/Contrast menu option.

3. Display the Loader on the Small display and the BC tool on the Large display so you can compare before and after the effect. Your screen should look like Figure 8.31.

4. In the Control area, right-click on the Brightness slider, and choose BézierSpline from the pop-up menu (see Figure 8.32).

5. Press F8, or choose View|Show Spline View, to see the Spline editing area below the Large display. You won't have to use this area in this project, but you will be able to see the effect of what you are doing.

6. At frame 0, the default Brightness setting of 0.0 is exactly what you want. Go to frame 60. Drag the Brightness slider all the way to the left, –1.0. The Large display should go black while the Small display remains unaffected.

DF automatically creates a new keyframe in the Bézier spline when you change a setting. You may have to click on the Fit button in the Spline view to re-scale the display so your new keyframe is visible (see Figure 8.33).

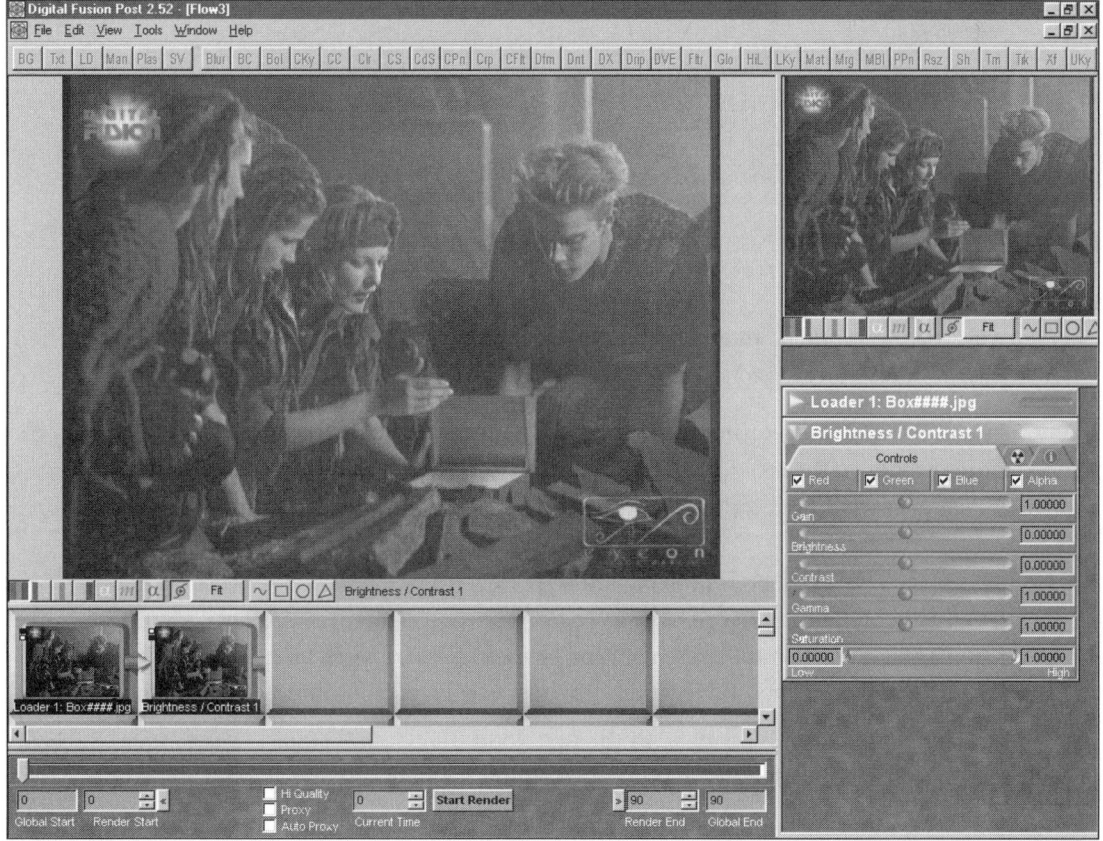

Figure 8.31
The Brightness/Contrast tool connected to Loader 1.

Figure 8.32
The Brightness slider, with BézierSpline selected as the new animation control.

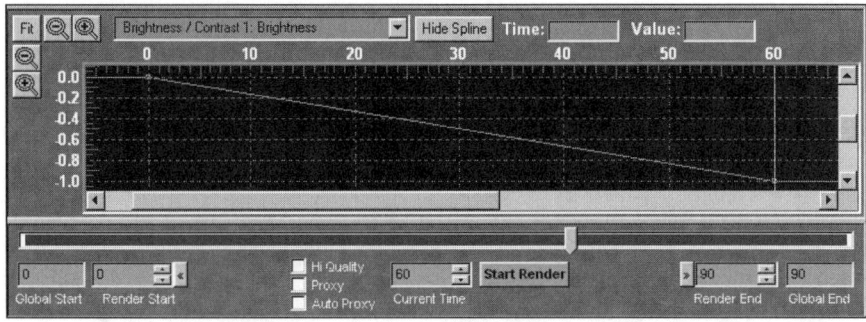

Figure 8.33
The Brightness keyframe set for –1.0 at frame 60.

7. Make a Preview or add a Saver, and render the composition from frame 0 to frame 90. When you play it back, you should see a smooth fade to black between frame 0 and frame 60.

Many DF tool settings can be animated using Bézier splines. Practice adding, deleting, and modifying keyframes both in the tool Control and in the Spline editor. This is another basic skill that you will be using every day as a digital compositor.

PROJECT 8.6 Animating And Masking A Dissolve

The goal of this project is to dissolve a foreground element over a background element. The challenge is that the foreground element is not a perfect match for the background, so in addition to the dissolve, you have to limit or mask the effect to minimize any discrepancies.

1. Open a new flow. Add two Loaders. In the first, load the BeamBG footage (see Figure 8.34). In the second, load the Beamdown footage (see Figure 8.35).

2. Add a Dissolve tool to the right of Loader 2, using either the DX toolbar button or the Tools| Composite|Dissolve menu option. Your flow should look like the one in Figure 8.36.

3. In the Dissolve control, right-click on the Background\Foreground slider and select BézierSpline as the animation control, just as you did in the preceding project.

Figure 8.34
A frame from the BeamBG footage.

Figure 8.35
A frame from the Beamdown footage.

4. At frame 0, drag the Background\Foreground slider to 1.0, full Foreground. Go to frame 50.
    Drag the Background\Foreground slider to 0.0, full Background.

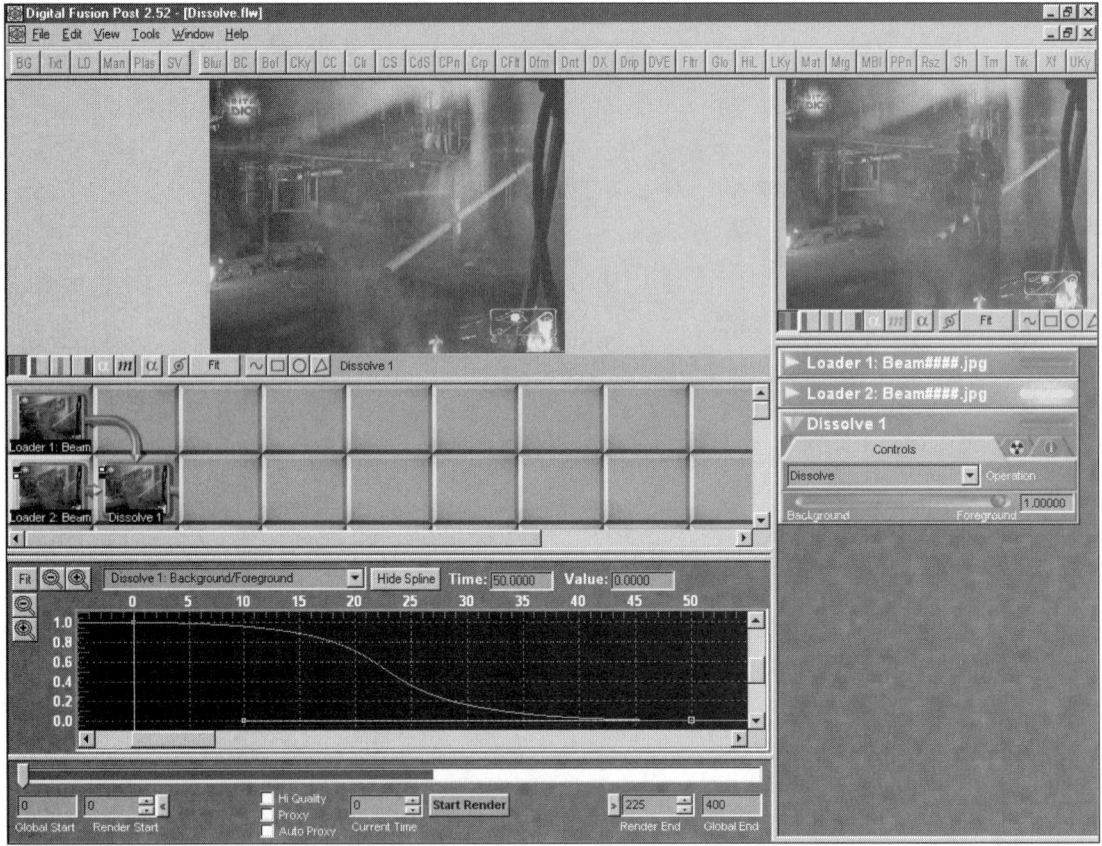

Figure 8.36
A flow showing the Dissolve spline.

5. Open the Spline view. Click on the Fit button to fit all the keyframes into the current view.

6. Click on the key at frame 50. Drag the Bézier handles to change the shape of the spline. Do the same with the key at frame 0. Try to match the shape of the spline shown in Figure 8.36. This will give a smoothly accelerating and decelerating dissolve.

The dissolve should work fine at this point, but now there is another problem. The drifting smoke is markedly different between the background and foreground elements. If you let this composition go with a simple dissolve, the whole frame will appear to be dissolving. One solution to this type of problem is to mask the effect to a small area. In this case, you'll mask the dissolve effect so that most of the frame is always the foreground element, and just enough of the background is used to cover the actors during the dissolve.

7. Make sure that your Large and Small display Options are set to Show Controls, the Dissolve tool is shown in the Large display, and the Current Time is frame 50.

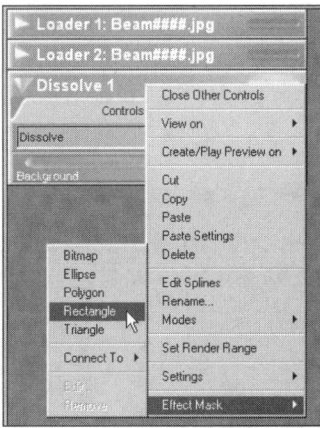

Figure 8.37
Adding a rectangular Effect Mask for the Dissolve tool.

8. In the Control area, right-click on the Dissolve 1 header, and choose Effect Mask|Rectangle from the pop-up menu (see Figure 8.37). A bright-green rectangular box with crosshair should appear.

9. You can move the mask by dragging the center crosshair, resize it by dragging the edges, and rotate it by dragging the circular handle to the right of the center crosshair. Play with this a bit to get a feel for each of the mask controls. Adjust the mask to cover the actors, with a little to spare (see Figure 8.38).

Figure 8.38
Adjusted rectangular Effect Mask.

10. This flow will do the job, but it's still a little rough. The transition at the edges of the mask is too abrupt and gives away the effect. Let's fix this. Press F10 to bring up the Mask control view. Open the Rectangle 1 control, and double-click on the *m* button under the Large display to see the mask channel (see Figure 8.39).

Figure 8.39
The control panel and the Large display of the Effect Mask.

11. In the Rectangle 1 control, drag the Soft Edge slider to about 0.07 to soften the edges of the mask, as in Figure 8.40.

12. Hide the Rectangle 1 controls, change the Large display back to normal RGB view, and save the composition as Dissolve.flw. Make a Preview or render the first 50 frames. Can you spot the edges of the dissolve?

In completing this project, you learned how to:

- Animate a Dissolve operation

- Apply an Effect Mask

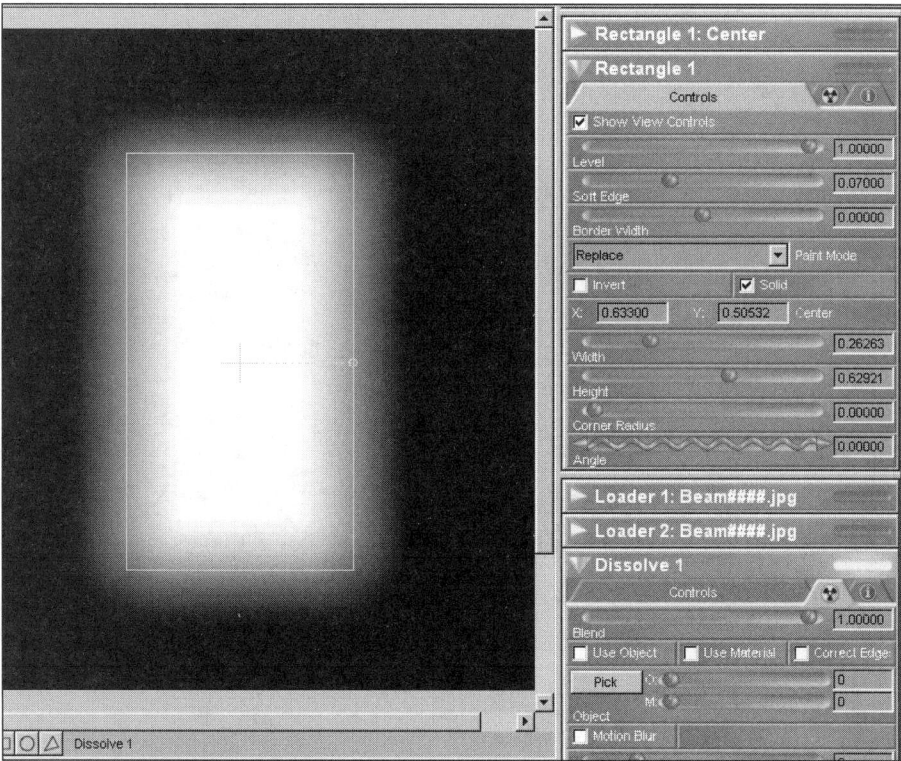

Figure 8.40
Soft Edges applied to the Effect Mask.

- Move, size, and rotate an Effect Mask
- Soften the edges of an Effect Mask

Geometric Transformations (Transforms)

Transforms are especially important for motion graphics and for comping multiple live-action elements from different shoots. The ability to tweak size, aspect ratio, direction, or rotation to match other elements, or to animate an immobile element, is crucial to everything from simple titles to top-end feature film effects. Besides, transforms are just plain fun to goof around with.

PROJECT 8.7 Animating A Flip Transform

The goal of this project is to familiarize you with the Transform tool and some of its capabilities. You can create most simple geometric transformations with this tool, so you should find it very useful.

1. Load the BlueScrn.flw composition you saved from Project 8.3.

2. Choose the Tools|Transform|Transform menu option, or click on the Xf toolbar button to add a Transform tool between the Ultra Keyer and the Merge tools.

Figure 8.41
Left: A Transform tool added to flow. Right: Horizontal flip transform enabled.

3. Open the Transform controls. Check the Flip Horiz(ontal) box. You should see an effect like that pictured in Figure 8.41.

4. Uncheck the Flip Horizontal box.

Now you want to animate the flip transform so the actress is facing left (normal) for the first 89 frames, then flips to face right for frames 90 to 179, then unflips to face left again at frame 180. This is a preliminary setup for the next project, in which you'll make the actress pan back and forth across the screen. The timing of this flip transform has to match the timing of the ends of the pan transform.

5. Set Render End to 180, or six seconds. Go to frame 89.

6. In the Transform controls, right-click on Flip Horiz and choose Bézier Spline. Add keyframes at 89, 90, 179, and 180. Figure 8.42 shows the modified spline.

7. Make a Preview or render the composition. You should see an abrupt flip at frame 90, then a flip back at frame 180.

8. Save your composition as Flip180.flw. You'll need it for Project 8.8.

In completing this project, you learned how to:

• Use the Transform tool to perform a Flip geometric transformation

• Animate a checkbox setting using a Bézier spline

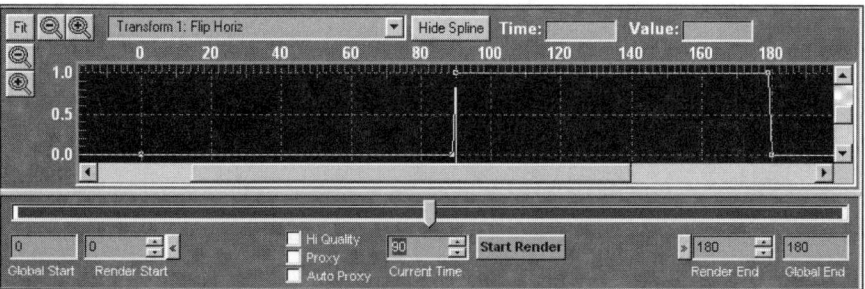

Figure 8.42
A Bézier control spline with Flip keyframes at 89, 90, 179, and 180.

Animating A Pan Transform

PROJECT 8.8

The goal of this project is to resize an element and then animate it across a background. This is a basic component of more-advanced techniques in motion graphics, move matching, and other digital compositing tasks.

1. Reload the Flip180.flw you saved from the preceding project. Select the Transform tool, and make sure the Large display options are set to Show Controls. You should see a bright green crosshair in the center of the Large view.

2. Position the mouse cursor over the center of the green crosshair in the Large display. A small pop-up label should appear, reading Transform Centre. This means you can select the Transform tool's Centre control. Right-click, and choose Transform 1 Centre|Path from the menu (see Figure 8.43).

3. In the Transform control, change Size from 1.0 to 0.3333. This makes the actress element small enough to look appropriate flitting across the background—kind of a Tinker Bell effect.

4. Click and drag Transform Centre to right, off screen, as shown in Figure 8.44.

5. Go to frame 90. Drag the Transform Centre control completely off screen to the left, as shown in Figure 8.45. This conceals the abrupt horizontal flip off screen.

6. Go to frame 180. Drag the Transform Centre control off screen to the right again (refer to Figure 8.44). This completes the Path for the Transform Centre control.

7. Make a Preview. The actress should pan across the screen from right to left, flip horizontally off screen, and pan back again from left to right.

8. Save your composition as Path180.flw. You'll need it for Project 8.9.

In completing this project, you learned how to:

• Use a Size transform

• Animate an element along a path

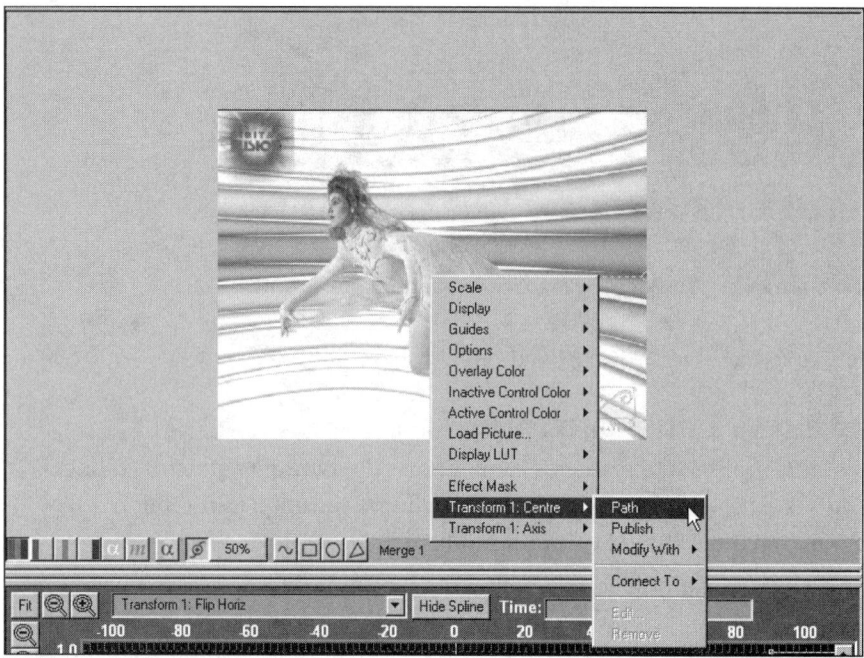

Figure 8.43
Transform 1 Centre|Path is selected.

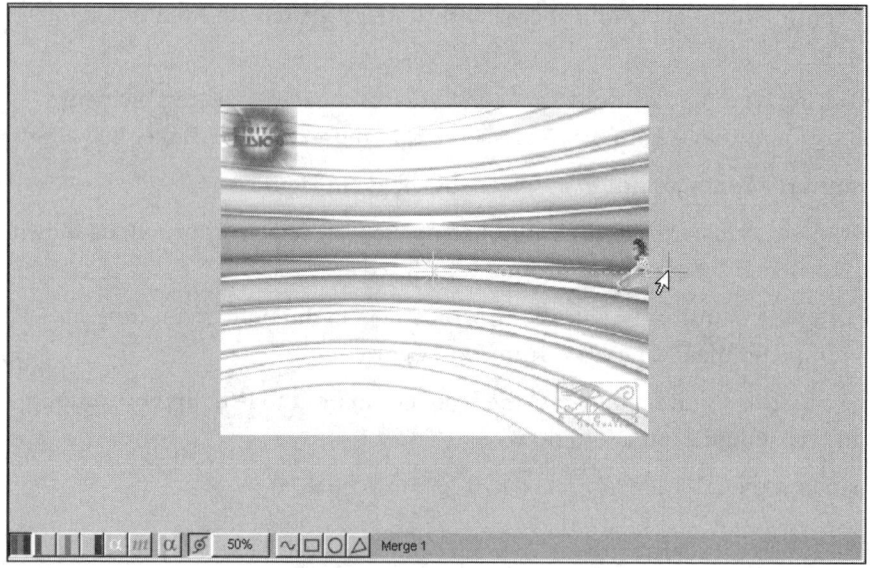

Figure 8.44
The Transform Centre dragged off screen right at frame 0.

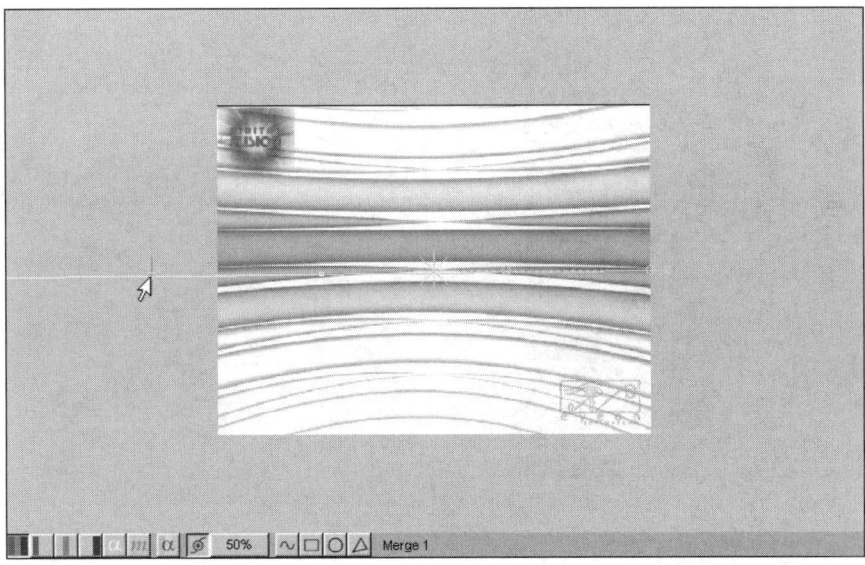

Figure 8.45
The Transform Centre dragged off screen left at frame 90.

PROJECT 8.9 Flow Organization

The goal of this project is to add two new elements to the flow: one to appear behind the actress and one to appear in front of her. The result should be that the actress appears to fly through a complex three-dimensional environment. Adding the new element Loaders and other tools in the correct operational sequence requires you to rearrange the flow to make room.

1. Reload the Path180.flw flow you saved from the preceding project.

2. Hold down the Shift key. This tells DF to maintain the tools' connections as you drag them from one tile to another.

3. Starting at the bottom, drag each tool to a lower tile until your results look like Figure 8.46.

4. Add a Loader to the top left tile, and load the TShipFG precomp you rendered in Project 8.1. You didn't render this precomp? Well, either go back and precomp it now, or load both the RGB and matte sequences and comp them with a Channel Booleans tool. If you choose the latter option, your flow is going to be about three times as cluttered and won't match the rest of the figures for this project. This is another reminder that doing things in the proper order, and in advance whenever possible, will save you time and effort later.

5. Add another Loader to the tile between Loader 1 and Loader 2. Load the TShipMG precomp you rendered in Project 8.1. Your flow should look like Figure 8.47.

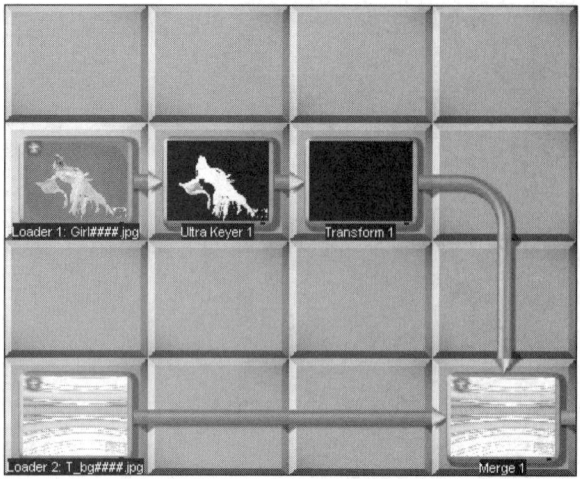

Figure 8.46
The rearranged flow with more space between the tools.

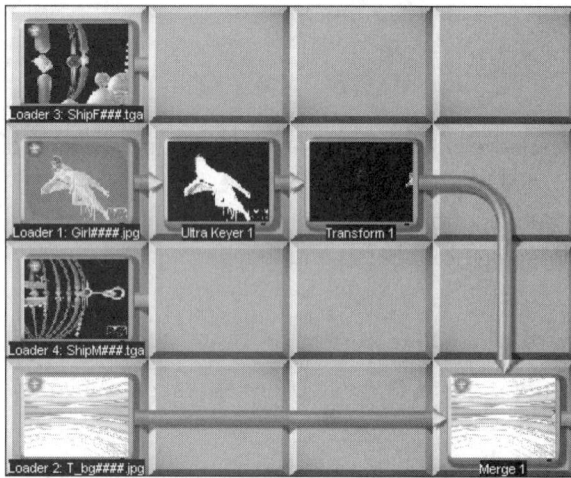

Figure 8.47
New element Loaders added to the flow.

6. Disconnect Loader 2 from Merge 1. Add a Merge tool beside Loader 2, and add another Merge tool to the right of Merge 1.

7. Connect Loader 2 and Loader 4 to Merge 2, and connect Merge 2's output to Merge 1. Connect Merge 1's output to Merge 3, and connect Loader 3 to Merge 3. Your flow should now look like Figure 8.48.

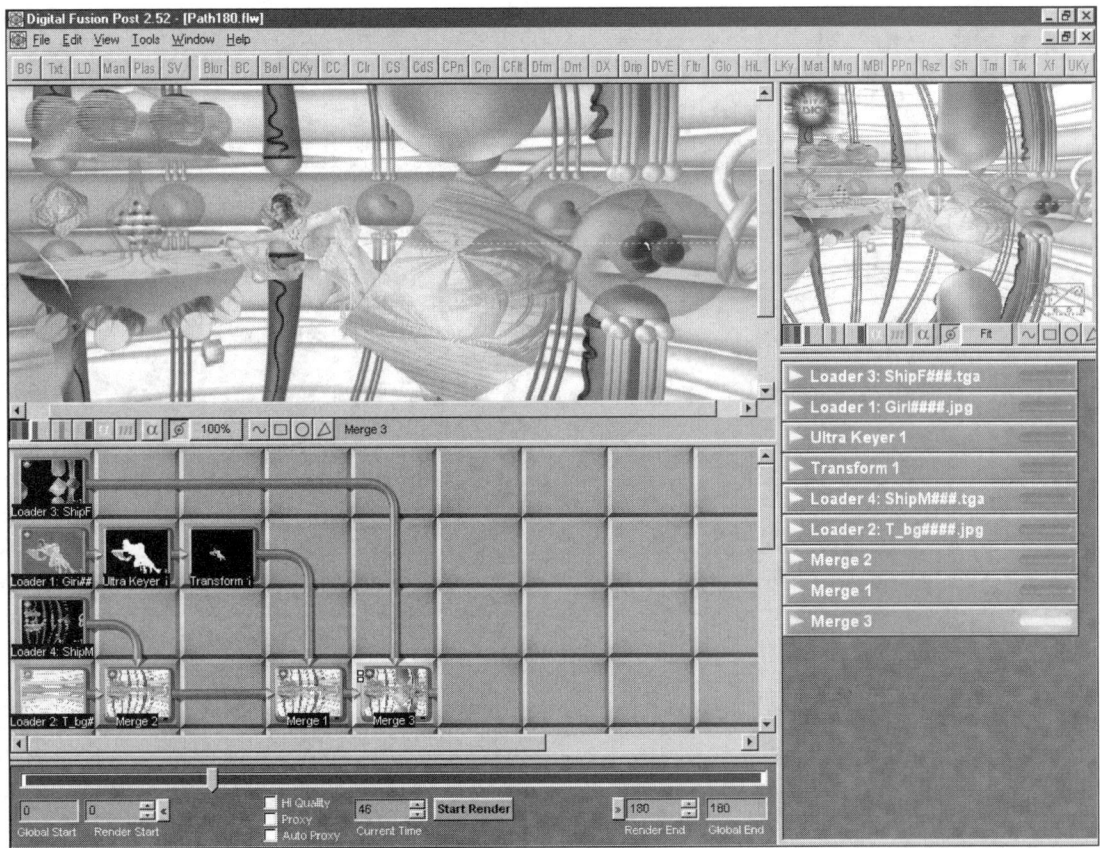

Figure 8.48
The completed flow, showing the actress element behind the foreground element, but in front of the middleground and background elements.

Technically, you could have added the new Loaders at the bottom of the flow and rearranged the connections to fit. However, you need to practice rearranging your flows and think about more logical arrangements. It can save you (and your coworkers) a lot of time and aggravation if your flows are arranged logically; they are easier to understand and modify. The flow you just constructed is arranged foreground-to-background, but another useful arrangement, background-to-foreground, is shown in Figure 8.49. How quickly can you rearrange your flow to match this one?

Title Design And Character Generators

Good title design and readable credits add to the professional appearance of any film or video production. Take the time to do them right, especially for your demo reel. Titles are cheap, quick to create, and easy to animate, but you still have to put some thought into them. They should at

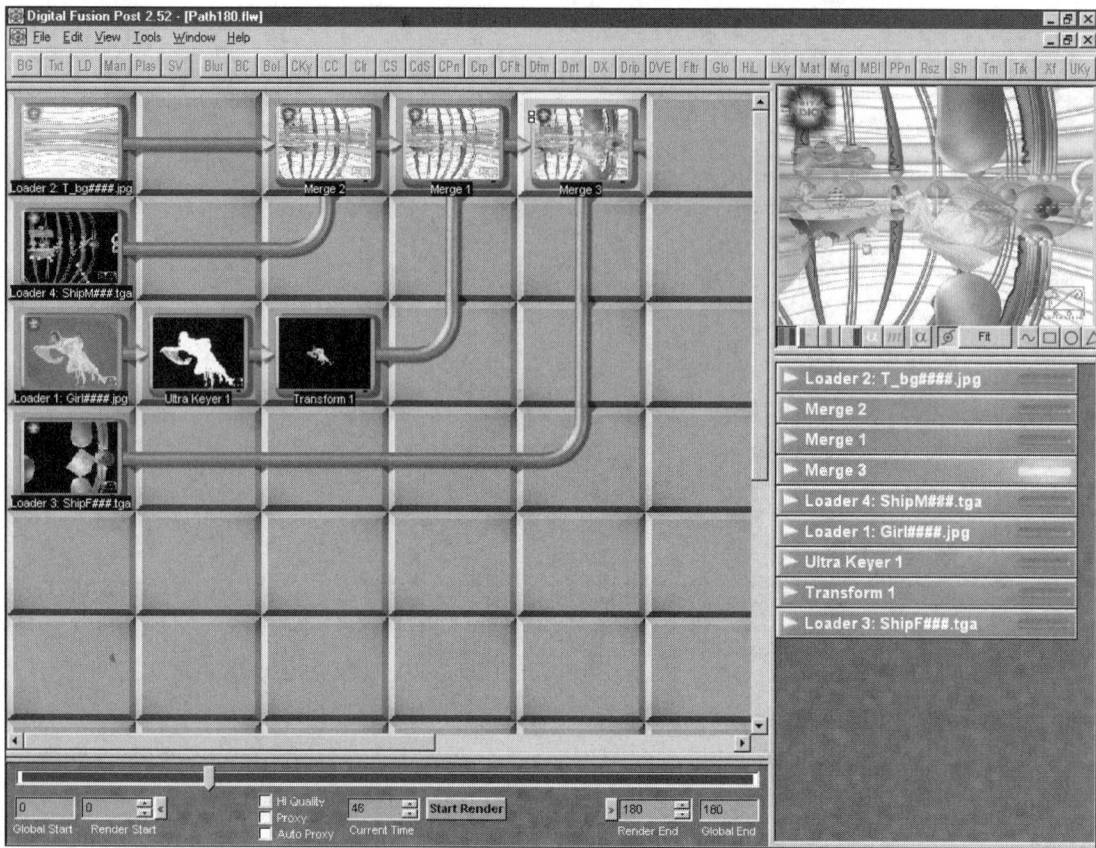

Figure 8.49

Path180 flow rearranged in background-to-foreground order.

least conform to basic principles of typographic design, because your audience has to read them. These rules are few, simple, and easy to follow.

- *Keep each title card on screen long enough for your audience to read it, at least one second for every five words.* Don't dally, though. Leaving a title card in place for too long can lose your audience's attention and may detract from the rest of the production. If you are titling for a demo reel, you should keep your titles down to the minimum time—the reviewer will probably fast-forward through them if they last longer than 10 seconds.

- *Don't move your titles around too much.* Zooming titles that fly all over the screen are the hallmark of an amateur. There are some "professional" title designers out there who should be ashamed of the titles they've done for feature film and television. Flash, glitz, and a virtuoso animation performance are just annoyances if they don't help you get your message across. A prime example of this is the horrendous title and credit work for the feature film *Spawn*, in which even the expected and well-known names in the credits are almost impossible to read because of the rapidly oscillating text and poorly contrasting colors. It looks like the optical printer's gate had been left unlocked, and the film just went through any which way. If it was designed to be disturbing, it succeeded; but if the titles were meant to be read, the design failed. Hold still, and let the words in the titles speak for themselves!

- *Don't get fancy with textures for titles.* Brushed metal and polished chrome are very much passé, and the mark of an amateur. The only circumstances under which you should texture a title are when the texture ties the titles directly to the story, when the texture isn't obtrusive or distracting, and when the text will remain easily legible. A very nice example of this is the ribbon texture for the word "Beauty" in the title sequence of Disney's animated remake of *Beauty and the Beast*. The final effect is subtle, attractive to the eye, unobtrusive to the text, and links to the story thematically by its similarity to Belle's hair ribbons.

- *If you're positive that you want to animate your titles, at least make them animate legibly in the direction the audience will be reading them.* If you bring letters on screen from right to left like a TV streamer, the audience can read them as they appear. This enables you to minimize the title's on-screen time and doesn't annoy your audience. If you bring the letters on screen in reverse order, the audience can't read them until the last (first) letter appears. Unless there's a thematic reason for doing things backwards, this is just an annoying affectation.

- *Many fonts are unsuitable for reliable reproduction in video or film.* The first disqualification is the minimum width of a stroke. Many typefaces that are designed for print have fine serifs, the thin strokes that cross the ends of the major strokes in a letter (see Figure 8.50). By comparison, sans serif typefaces have no minor strokes and tend to reproduce much more evenly for both film and television.

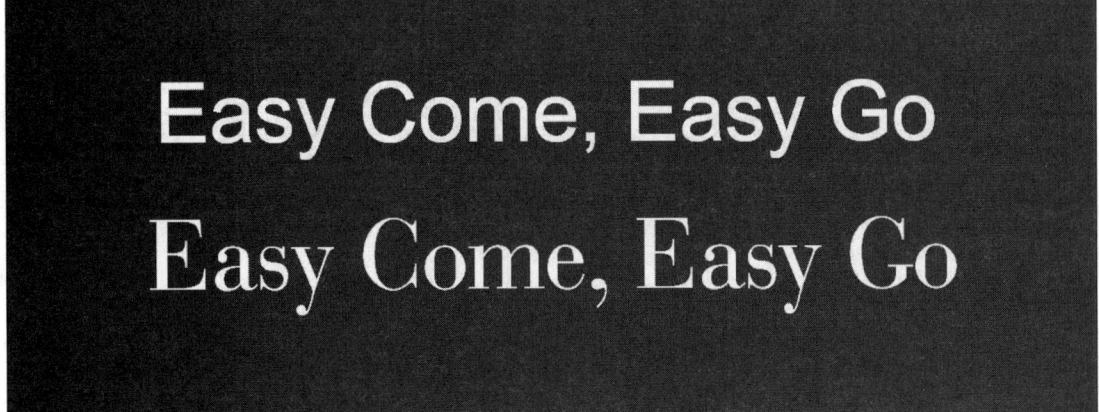

Figure 8.50
Sans serif and serif fonts.

- *Keep your delivery medium in mind when you choose a title font.* When reproduced on film, fine serifs are very sensitive to the timing of film development and can close up or bleed out. They are also sensitive to the projection environment, when low projector light can cause serifs to disappear into the background. In video, a serif that is too fine may disappear entirely or break up into a multicolored fringe effect. Fine lines (whether in on-screen type or plaid jackets) can be misinterpreted by a TV receiver as color subcarrier, a high frequency added to the video signal in the NTSC color encoding system that establishes the color saturation and hue of the picture. This is what causes the color fringing effect. Because RGB (computer) monitors don't employ the NTSC encoding system, they don't exhibit color fringing. If fringed text moves at all, this multihued border will also appear to crawl.

- *Keep your letters open.* This is closely related to the problem of serifs. Some fonts have such small letter openings that they can close up completely when reproduced on film or video. Letters like b, d, and o have less frequent problems with occluded openings, but letters like e, a, and g have smaller openings and can run into problems more easily. Letter openings are important visual cues for your audience, so choose your title fonts to make them easy to see (see Figure 8.51).

Figure 8.51
Open (top) and closed (bottom) fonts.

- *Make sure that the title letters differ enough for the audience to read them easily.* Some fonts are so heavily stylized that the letters appear almost identical, forcing the reader to search for more subtle clues to identify them. Figure 8.52 shows examples of good and inadequate differentiation.

- *Keep your ascenders and descenders as reading cues for your audience.* Ascenders and descenders are the strokes that go above the midline or below the bottom of some letters. Lowercase b, d, h, k, and l have ascenders; and g, j, p, q, and y have descenders. These strong visual cues make it easier for your audience to read your titles quickly and easily. Some stylized fonts compress

Figure 8.52
Good (top) and bad (bottom) differentiation.

Figure 8.53
Normal ascenders and descenders (top) compared to vertically compressed fonts (bottom).

the ascenders and descenders into the midline space, distorting the shape of the letter. These fonts are harder for your audience to read (see Figure 8.53), so you should avoid them. This is true of font cases. If upper- and lowercase characters are difficult to tell apart or if you run titles in all caps, small caps, or all lowercase, your audience has a harder time reading your titles. Keep your text simple and legible, and leave the storytelling and showing off to the rest of the production.

- *Use italics with caution and moderation.* A typeface that leans in odd directions is difficult to read. Choose an italic angle (if any) less than 30 degrees and preferably less than 15. Inclining the angle of a letter's major strokes changes its appearance enough to make it harder to identify. If

Figure 8.54
Normal (top) and italic (bottom) fonts.

you choose to use an italic font, at least keep the angle consistent. Once the audience identifies the italic angle, it's a little easier to read until the angle changes again. If a stylized font changes the inclination of each letter, it's confusing and difficult to read. See Figure 8.54 for examples.

• *Keep your titles consistent.* After you select a good font, use it for all your titles. Changing fonts in the middle of a title sequence requires your audience to readjust all over again, in effect reducing readability and wasting screen time. Stick to one font throughout your titles.

• *Keep in mind that your audience presumably is interested in the rest of the production, not the number of oddball fonts (see Figure 8.55) you keep on your computer.* Don't select a strange font just because it caught your eye. You don't want your audience to be so distracted with your titles that they miss the beginning of the production. Choose title fonts carefully!

• *Choose your title colors carefully.* Sometimes appropriate colors can be a nice touch, but more often, they are a bad idea. Your primary goal is to ensure that your audience can read the titles, and poor color choices can reduce the visual contrast to the point where the letters blend into the background. At the other extreme, clashing color choices create a disturbing effect that is illegible and causes most of the audience to look away from the screen. In NTSC video, using high-saturation adjacent colors that are of opposite hue (such as red-green or yellow-blue) produces *chroma crawl*, dots that seem to crawl along the contrasting edges. This is actually the subcarrier, visible now that the *dot interlace* is defeated by the 180 hue phase shift. You can minimize this effect by choosing less contrasting hues and less saturated colors. In general, plain white letters on a black background are the best title colors you can use.

• *If you are compositing titles over a background image, try to select a light primary color that contrasts pleasantly with the dominant hues of the background.* If the background image changes markedly, which is common with live footage or strong camera movements, you may have problems

Figure 8.55
Good and bad font choices for titles and credits.

getting consistent visual contrast between titles and background. In these situations, it's generally a good idea to use drop shadows or a darker outline to completely separate the superimposed titles from the background. The main title sequence from *Silence of the Lambs* is an excellent example of simple, strongly contrasting superimposed titles. Throughout a long sequence of camera moves and widely varying backgrounds, these titles never lose contrast.

- *Be careful where you put your titles in the frame.* Most compositing programs provide built-in video text-safe guidelines. For best results in all media, titles must be limited to the video text-safe area. Most televisions cut off the outer edge of the picture with a bezel over the tube's edges or rounded corners in the tube itself. Even if you are working in film, it's smart to title with eventual TV broadcast in mind. Keep your titles in the safe area, or the work will have to be retitled for broadcast—and you won't necessarily have control of the new titles!

PROJECT 8.10 Animating A Credit Scroll

The goal of this project is to create a classic credit scroll, the cast and crew listings that are shown at the end of most feature films, television programs, and videos. This relatively simple job of compositing needs to be done for nearly every production. At the least, you should be able to do good-looking credit scrolls for your own productions or demo reel. With a little practice, you should be able to do a credit scroll with about as much thought and effort as brushing your teeth.

1. Open a new flow. Add a Text tool to the upper left tile. Display the Text tool on both Large and Small display areas, and set the display sizes to Fit.

Figure 8.56
The Small display showing the Text tool contents with the Safe Title guide enabled.

2. Right-click in the Small area, and choose Guides|Safe Title. This will superimpose a bright rectangle outlining the area of the display that is safe for text (see Figure 8.56). Any text outside this area may not be legible to the audience. You will need to format your titles so they fit in this rectangle.

3. Open the Text tool in the Control area. Choose the Text tab. The white box is the data entry field for your text. You can use all the usual Windows cut, copy, and paste tools to put text in this box. To give you a realistic example of a feature film credit scroll, I've provided a text file for you to use.

4. Open Notepad or another text editor. Open the text file CREDITS.TXT from the second CD-ROM. This is an unofficial credits list for the independent film *The November Men*, copied from the Internet Movie Database at **www.imdb.com**. I've done very little cleanup on it, so if you'd like to proofread it and correct some formatting, be my guest. When you're ready, select all the text, and choose Copy from the Edit menu. Close the text editor.

5. Go back to DF and click in the entry box for the Text tool. Press Ctrl+V to paste the copied text. You should see something like Figure 8.57.

6. Scroll through the text to check for any especially long lines. The longest line you can fit inside the Safe Title guide will limit your maximum font size (and therefore the legibility of your titles). You can copy-and-paste the longest line you find to the beginning of the text file

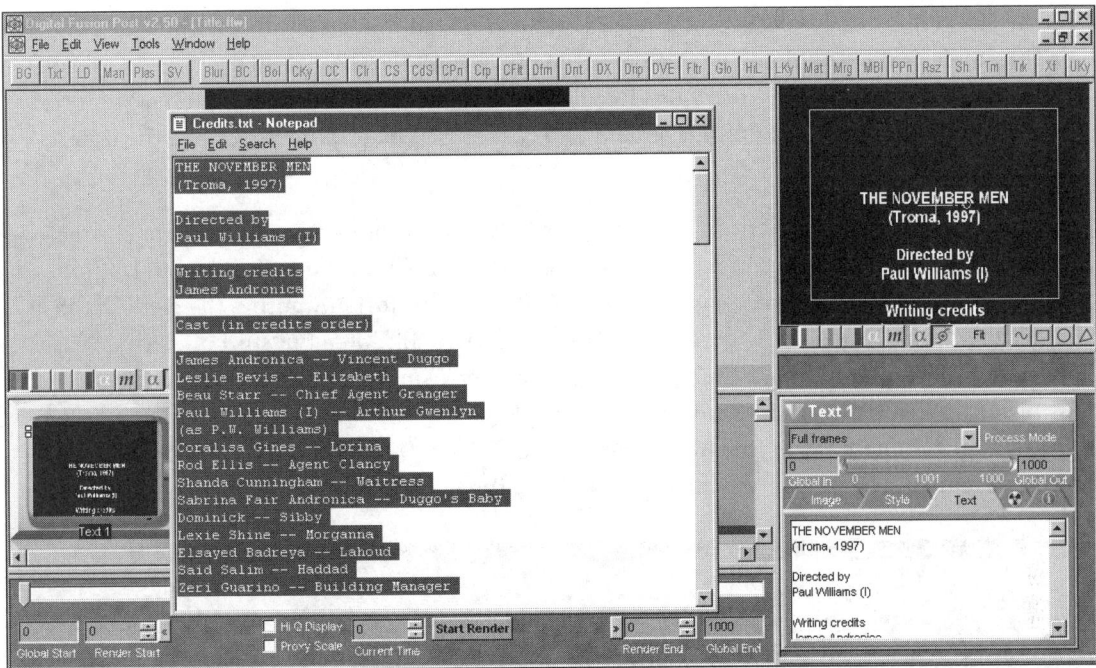

Figure 8.57

The Text tool with *The November Men* credits pasted.

to help you in the next step. (You can delete the extra line later.) The longest line in the sample text is "William Grillo—Sharpshooter Agent (Brad Lucas)".

When the formatting of the text is corrected to your satisfaction, select the Style tab. The overriding criteria for title design is legibility, so let's make sure the audience can read these credits. You need to choose a font, style, color, and size that will be easy to read.

7. At the bottom of the Style tab is the Font selector. Click on the Select button and choose a font from the TrueType fonts available on your computer. For this project, I'm using plain old Arial, but you can use anything you like as long as it's legible. Choose Bold or Italic at the bottom of the Style tab, if you prefer using either of these styles. For the Arial font, bold usually improves legibility. Unless you have a particular color scheme in mind to contrast with the credits background, I recommend you stick with the default white as the font color.

Now, work your way up through the rest of the Style tab settings. Generally, you want to keep the Justification set to Center. If you want to left- or right-justify the credits, you need to do a little more formatting of the text to keep the screen from looking lopsided. If you want to tweak the Character Spacing, Character Angle, or Line Angle, you should crank the Large display up to 100% and view your adjustments there. A reduced display doesn't show you enough detail of the text to make a good judgment.

8. The Size adjustment is critical. You need to reduce it to fit the longest line within the Safe Title guide, but keep it large enough that the text is easy to read. If you simply can't reconcile these two factors, you may have to edit your longest line(s) to shorten them so you can use a larger font size. Your results should look something like Figure 8.58. Save the flow as Credits.flw.

Most feature film credits scroll from bottom to top. A scroll is more efficient for giving a large number of people the maximum screen time; a series of dissolves would take forever. Digital Fusion makes a credit scroll very easy to animate. Before you start animating the credit scroll, you need to decide how long it should last. You can change this later, but start off with a reasonably close length. Certain roll speeds on TV inevitably look smoother than others do, due to a possible mismatch between the scanning frequency and the speed of the roll. The roll is smoother if the text moves up one scan line (or a multiple thereof) every 1/30 of a second. Other odd speeds will cause more or less of a crawling effect on the leading and following edges of the type.

Figure 8.58
The Text settings adjusted for maximum legibility of the longest line in the credits.

Anti-aliasing, sub-pixel rendering, and motion blurring are all devices that can minimize this effect, but sometimes just picking the right roll speed can clean up the look of a roll. Considering the length of the text file, I'd start with at least 900 frames. The default Centre settings in the Style tab are 0.5 for both X and Y axes, so the top of the text is centered in the display. For a smooth, centered scroll, you need to leave the X value at 0.5 and animate the Y value over that 900 frames.

9. Make sure that the Global Start, Render Start, and Current Time are set to 0, and the Render End and Global End are set to 900.

10. Right-click on the label "Centre" to the right of the Y input box in the Style tab. Choose Path. This creates a spline path that you will use to animate the Y value for the text. Press F8 or choose the View|Show Spline View menu option. This hides the Layout and reveals the Spline editor (see Figure 8.59). The selector at the top of the Spline editor shows that Path 1: Displacement is selected. This is the path you just created, along which you'll animate the displacement (movement) of the text. The longest line that you copied to the top of the text file has served its purpose, but you should go back and delete it now so you can precisely animate the final text.

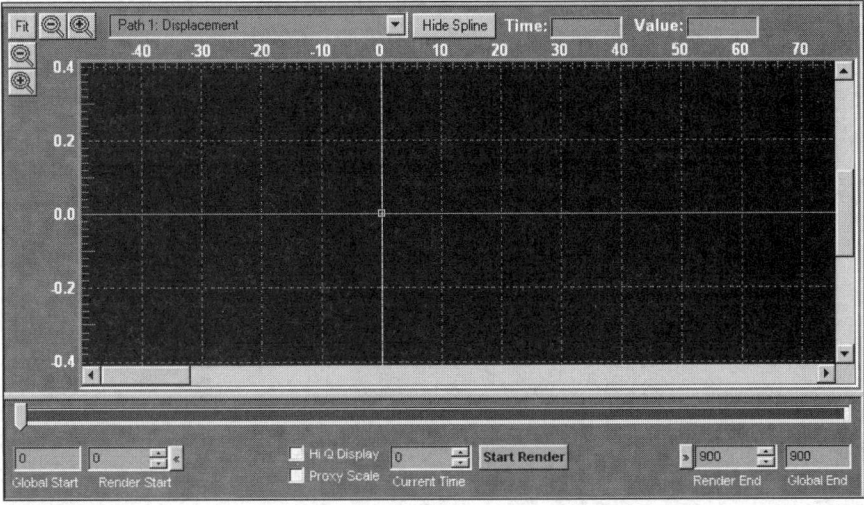

Figure 8.59
The Spline view showing the Path1: Displacement spline with a key at frame 0.

11. The Current Time should still be 0. Change the Y Centre setting to position the top of the text just below the bottom edge of the display. I found 1.1000 to work well. Typing in a new value like this automatically creates a keyframe with that value at the current frame, or it changes an existing keyframe to the new value. You really don't even have to look at the Spline editor, but I thought you might like to see what's going on.

12. Change the Current Time to 900. Change the Y Centre setting to position the bottom of the text just above the top edge of the display. I found –8.50000 to work well, but if you chose different font settings, your number may be very different.

Jumping over to frame 900 probably panned the Spline editor so far that you can't see the key at frame 0. If you want to see the whole spline, just click on the Fit button in the upper left corner of the Spline editor.

13. Drag the Time slider around or render a preview if you want to see how the text animation looks. These settings keep each credit line inside the Safe Title area for 70 frames, or about 2.33 seconds. That's a little fast for a feature film, but not unheard of for television productions. If you like, you can change Render End and Global End to 1200, and drag the second keyframe in the Spline editor from frame 900 to frame 1200. That will give each credit line about 95 frames, over three seconds, in the Safe Title area. Three seconds of screen credit isn't bad—your family can read your name. Your screen should look something like Figure 8.60.

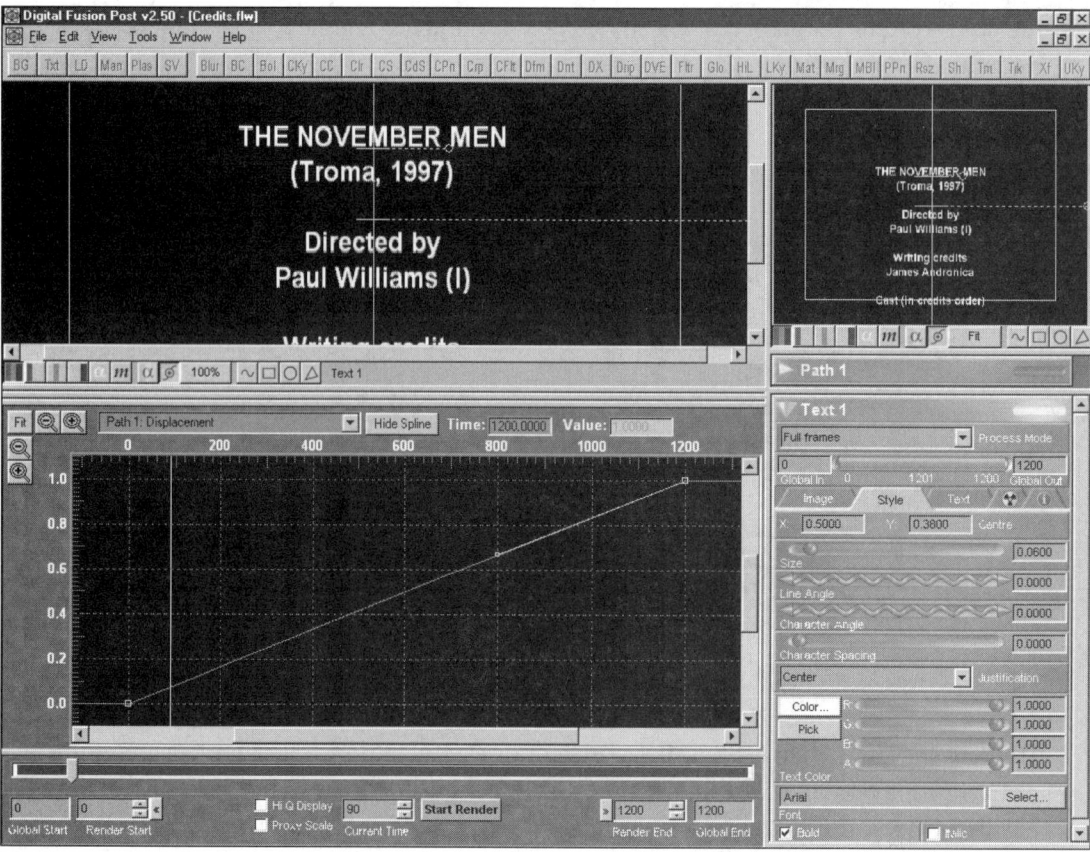

Figure 8.60
The credit scroll extended to 1200 frames, and the Spline editor view Fit to show all the keyframes.

As you can see, a simple credit scroll is relatively simple to set up in Digital Fusion once you've done it a few times. Practice making your own credit scroll, or download another credit list from the Internet Movie Database and re-create the credits of one of your favorite movies. Just for fun, you can even cast yourself in a starring role.

Credits sometimes roll after a fade to black, but often they begin over the tail end of the fade. Let's add some background footage and a fade to black to run under the credit scroll.

14. Press F6 or choose the View|Show Flow View menu option to replace the Spline editor with the Flow.

15. Select the empty tile below the Text tool. Add a Loader to the selected tile. In the Loader 1 control, choose whatever background footage you have handy. I'll use a starfield in the following figures. Make a note of the length of the footage; you'll want the fade to be complete before the footage ends.

16. Select the empty tile to the right of Loader 1. Click on the BC toolbar button or choose the Tools|Color|Brightness/Contrast menu option to add a Brightness/Contrast tool to the selected tile. You'll be animating the brightness settings to fade the background to black.

17. Add a Merge tool to the third tile in the second row. The Merge tool's Background (left side) input should connect automatically to the output of the Brightness/Contrast tool. Connect the output from the Text tool to the Merge foreground (top) input. The Text tool creates a very clean alpha channel, so you can simply leave the Merge settings at their default values to composite the text over the background.

18. Add a Saver tool to the tile to the right of the Merge tool. The Saver should automatically connect to the Merge tool. Your flow should now look like the Layout area in Figure 8.61.

19. Make sure that Current Time is set to 0, because you'll want to set a keyframe there for the Brightness setting. Open the Brightness/Contrast tool control. Right-click on the Brightness setting, and choose BézierSpline. Since you're already familiar with how to set keyframes, you don't have to open the Spline view unless you want to.

20. Set Current Time to the last frame of the fade to black. My starfield footage ends on frame 130, so I want the Brightness to start fading from the first key at frame 0 and be completely black at frame 130. I change Current Time to 130 and change Brightness to –1.0000. After you set your own ending keyframe for the fade, scrub the Time slider to confirm that the fade to black is working.

21. You can check the playback speed with a preview in the Small display, but to check the legibility of the text, you'll need to look at 100% size images in the Large display. When you're satisfied with all the flow's settings, render your credit scroll.

A main title sequence can be anything from a complex 3D light show (which is generally hard to read) to a simple series of static text dissolves.

Figure 8.61
Brightness/Contrast and Merge tools added to the flow to composite text over a fade-to-black background.

In completing this project, you learned how to:

- Import text into the Text tool

- Manage and edit text in the Text tool

- Animate a text scroll using a path

- Create and edit animation keyframes in Spline View

- Animate a control setting using a Bézier spline

Adding Timecode

Besides titles and credits, character generators are often handy for adding technical information to your compositions. For example, in Chapter 19, I advise that you put SMPTE timecode on approval footage and only hand over the clean footage after the client pays you for it. DF makes adding timecode easy. Follow the same steps as the preceding project to add a Loader, Merge, and Text tool to a new flow. Load the final footage you want to mark. In the Text tool, instead of adding text, simply right-click in the white area of the Text tab and choose TimeCode from the menu (see Figure 8.62).

Position the timecode at the bottom center of the Safe Title area as in Figure 8.63, and choose the timecode options you want from the TimeCode tool. That's all there is to creating cheap and effective payment insurance.

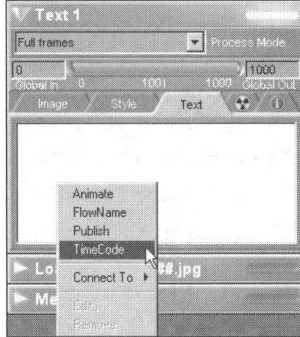

Figure 8.62
Choosing the TimeCode option for the Text tool text-entry tab.

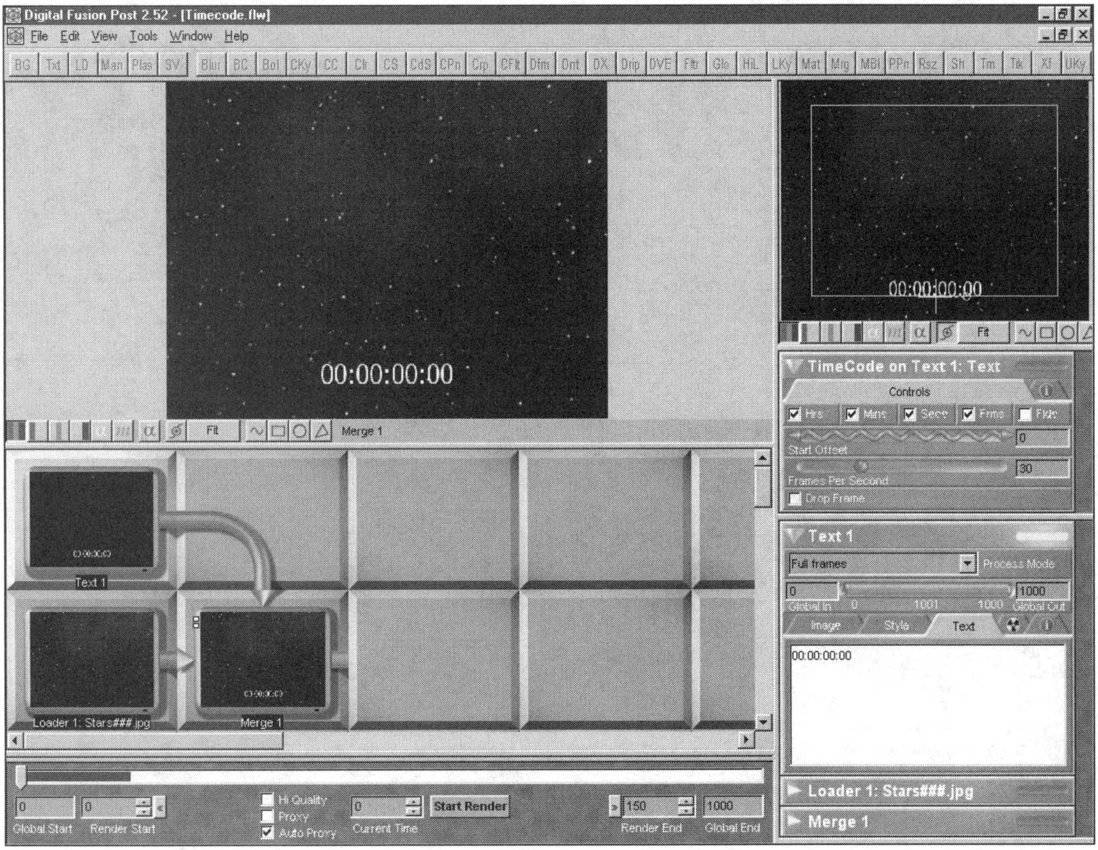

Figure 8.63
The timecode flow showing Loader, Merge, Text, and TimeCode tools, and the positioning of the timecode at bottom center of the Safe Title guide.

217

Drop Shadows And Outlines

As I mentioned previously, it is important that your titles maintain good contrast over the background. This can be difficult if the background, especially live footage, changes during the text display. One solution is to use a *drop shadow*, a contrasting copy of the text that is slightly larger and sometimes slightly offset. This creates a consistent visual contrast no matter what the background does.

You can add a drop shadow to text by adding a Channel Booleans and another Merge tool to your existing text flow, as shown in Figure 8.64. The Channel Booleans 1 tool changes the white text to black and preserves the original alpha channel, as shown in the Small display. The Merge 1 tool composites the black text with the Loader footage by using an Over operation.

The Merge 2 tool composites the original white text over the output of Merge 1. For a true drop shadow, as if the text is casting a black shadow on an underlying surface, the Merge 2 tool enables you to adjust the Center coordinates to offset the white text from the black text. This is also the

Figure 8.64
The Channel Booleans 1 tool creates a black drop shadow for the Text tool. The Merge 2 tool is added to offset the white text from 0.5, 0.5 to 0.495, 0.495.

basis for many animated text effects. Take some time to experiment with this, and think about how you can apply it to other projects.

As an alternative to a drop shadow, you can add an outline to text (or any object with an alpha channel) by adding a Glow tool to a text flow, as shown in Figure 8.65. The Glow tool enables you to control the density and size of an alpha channel around the text, so you have a lot of options, and you can accommodate almost any background to produce good text legibility.

Figure 8.65
A flow showing the addition of a Glow tool to create a black outline for the Text tool.

The Glow tool creates an expanded alpha channel based on the text, allowing the black background of the text to show through. The Merge 1 tool composites the white text with the Loader footage, using the expanded Glow alpha channel in an Over operation.

In the Glow tool controls, start with Glow at 0.90 and Glow Size between 0.0 and 1.0 for a minimal anti-aliased outline. Uncheck the Red, Green, and Blue channels and leave the Alpha channel checked.

You can create a similar outline effect by substituting a Matte Control for the Glow tool and cranking up the Matte Blur setting. However, this does not give you as much control, and I think the results don't look as clean.

If you need a different outline color, you can add a Background for the color and a Channel Booleans tool and a Merge tool to composite the new color in place of the black Text tool background (see Figure 8.66). Although it appears gray in the figure, the chosen color is green.

Figure 8.66
Background, Channel Booleans, and Merge 2 tools are added to change the outline color.

PROJECT 8.11 Main Titles

The two most common ways to handle main titles are the scroll, which you have already learned, and the dissolve. I prefer the dissolve, just because the text holds still and is therefore easier to read. This project shows you how to lay out your main titles using a series of dissolves. I'll give you a few guidelines for creating your main title sequence; however, because titles can vary so much, I'll leave the creative details to you.

1. Use whatever graphics software you prefer to create a series of grayscale images, one for each title, with light text and black background. Make the images the same size as the footage you'll use as a background, and use anti-aliased text if you can. Remember your typography, and don't make the text hard to read. Figure 8.67 is an example of a legible title image. If you prefer, you can use the images in the Titles directory of the CD-ROM.

Figure 8.67
Director's title credit from *Easy Come, Easy Go*.

2. Decide in what order you will display the title images and for how long you want each title displayed. Starting from frame 0, calculate the first frame for each title image. Don't forget to include fade-in and fade-out time too. For example, the Titles directory has 13 images. If I want them to each appear for 20 frames, with 5 frames in the fade-in and another 5 frames in the fade-out, the frame numbers for the images will be 0, 30, 60, 90, 120, 150, 180, 210, 240, 270, 300, 330, and 360. This is a little fast, but I want the numbers to be easy to remember for this project.

3. Copy the title images to your hard drive, and rename the copies according to their initial frame number. For example, the ECEG.JPG image should be first, so rename it TITL0000.JPG. The DIRECT.JPG image is next, so rename it TITL0030.JPG. The last image should be Blank.JPG, renamed to TITL0360.JPG.

4. When you have the images renamed correctly, open a new flow in DF, add a Loader, and load the image sequence, which begins with TITL0000.JPG.

5. In the Loader controls, set Missing Frames to Hold Previous. This will make TITL0000.JPG show until it is replaced at frame 30 by TITL0030.JPG, which will show until replaced by TITL0060.JPG, and so on. Set the Extend Last Frame setting to 60. This will hold TITL0360.JPG until frame 420, giving you a little working room at the end of the title sequence.

6. Add a Brightness/Contrast tool to the right of the Loader. This tool will enable you to animate the brightness of the title images to dissolve them in and out. Add a Luma Keyer to the right of the Brightness/Contrast tool.

7. Add a second Loader below the first one, and add a Merge tool to the fourth tile in the second row. Load some background footage in Loader 2. Connect Loader 2 to the Merge tool's Background input.

8. Make sure that Loader 1 is connected to the Brightness/Contrast tool, which is connected to the Luma Keyer, which, in turn, is connected to the Merge tool's foreground input. Your results should look like Figure 8.68. You can play with the settings of the Luma Keyer and Merge tools, but if your text is clean, the default settings will work fine.

9. Open the Brightness/Contrast tool. Right-click on the Brightness slider and choose BézierSpline, as shown in Figure 8.68. To see the spline, press F7 or choose the View|Show Spline View menu option.

10. You need to set three keyframes for the first title image: –1.0 at the first frame (fully dissolved, invisible), 0.0 at the fifth frame (visible), 0.0 at the twenty-fifth frame, and –1.0 at the thirtieth frame. The simplest and most direct way to do this is to set the Current Time to the desired frame and type the appropriate value in the Brightness entry box to the right of the slider. DF automatically creates the new keyframe when you change the value. You can also set keyframes and values by using the mouse in the spline view, but I did not find it as accurate and I spent more time fixing errors.

11. When you have the four keyframes set correctly, right-click in the Spline view and choose Select All. The four keyframes should highlight. Right-click again, and choose Set Loop. DF repeats the four keyframes in a loop, creating an endless cycle of 30-frame dissolves. Your final spline should resemble that shown in Figure 8.69.

The plateaus at the top represent when the title images are visible; the bottom of the intervening troughs are when the images are invisible. The change from one image to the next happens at the bottom of each trough, so the abrupt change is invisible. Because the final image is blank, the looping dissolves occurring after frame 360 are also invisible.

12. Make a preview or render your title sequence. Are the results what you expected? If you need to change the timing of the spline, you will also have to rename the image files to match the new keyframes. Because there are usually relatively few main title images, this isn't a huge chore. This approach also makes it easy to change individual title images or to resequence all the images.

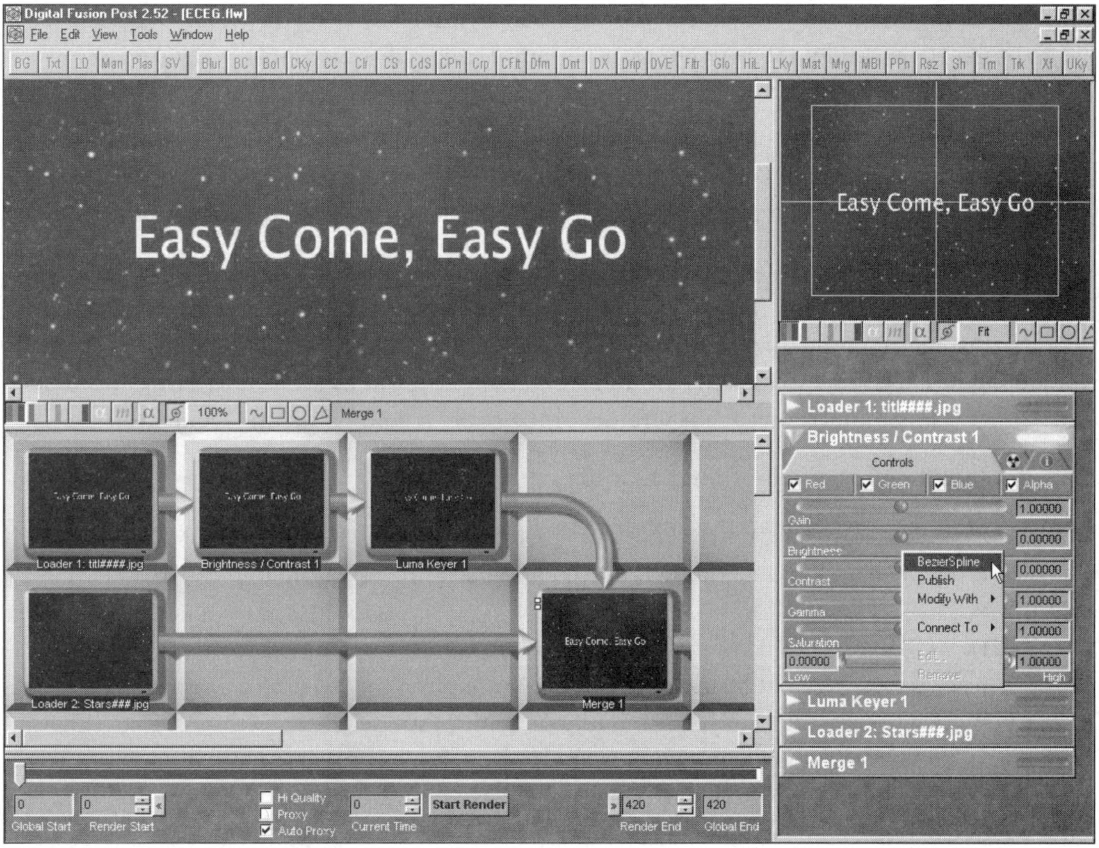

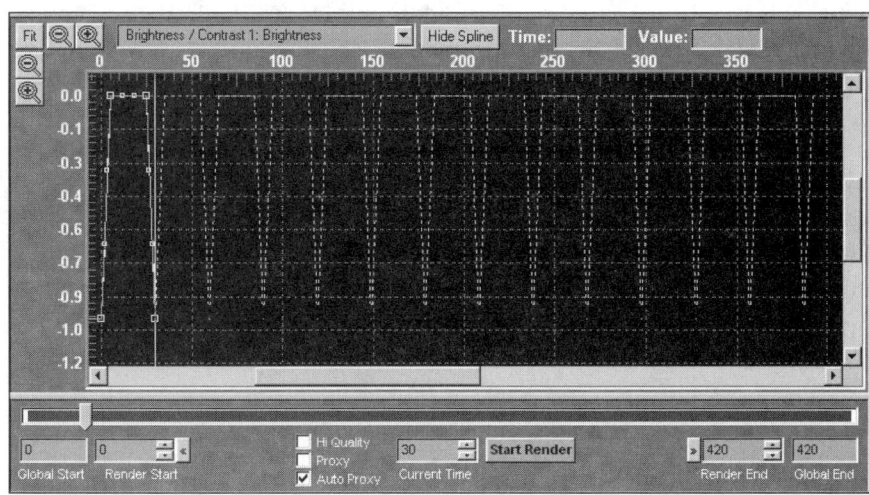

Figure 8.68

A dissolve title sequence flow.

Figure 8.69

A title sequence Brightness spline with loops set for 30-frame intervals.

13. In the Spline view, drag keyframe 5 to frame 10, keyframe 30 to frame 60, and keyframe 25 to frame 50. Note that the Loop function automatically adjusts to the new keyframes.

14. Renumber each title image to double its current number—for example, rename TITL0360.JPG to TITL0720.JPG. Reload the sequence in Loader 1 to flush the original sequence out of the buffer. Make sure that you change the Extend Last Frame setting to 120, twice the old value, and also extend the last frame for the background sequence.

Make a preview or render the title sequence. This timing gives you twice as long to read the titles, nearly two seconds each. You may have noticed that using the Loop feature requires that each image be displayed for the same amount of time. If you have titles with different display times (something that may be specified in cast and crew contracts), you won't be able to use the Loop and will have to manually set each keyframe for the entire length of the title sequence.

In completing this project, you learned how to:

• Import an interrupted sequence of images

• Loop a series of keyframes in Spline View to coordinate with sequenced images

Elegant Text

Here is a quick way to create the kind of elegant type seen in many television commercials. Rather than simply comping the type using its own alpha channel, do something with a little more depth. Route the text through two Blur/Sharpen filters—one set for a fairly high blur and the second for just a pixel or two of blur. Comp the heavy blur over the background with a 50% to 70% Additive operation. Comp the light blur over the output of the first operation with a full 100% Additive operation. Your flow should look something like Figure 8.70.

The finished render shows a subtle edge glow, similar to the soft light bleed you can see in some old black-and-white films. This beautiful and subtle effect adds a nice touch to almost any text work. This effect works equally well over live action or over a black background, as shown in Figure 8.71. You can fine-tune this effect by adding just a hint of color to the text.

Moving On

If you completed all the projects in this chapter, you should be comfortable enough with the most essential compositing tools to tackle the more challenging projects in the following chapters. Most of these advanced techniques rely on your properly executing the simpler techniques you learned here. No matter how advanced you become as a digital compositor, you should never neglect or forget your basic tools.

LIFE AIN'T EASY

Most digital compositing solutions boil down to combinations of basic tools. Even when a flow has hundreds of tools cross-linked in a matrix that appears complex beyond human understanding, each of those tools is doing one simple job. Chapter 8 guided you through the application of the most common tools for everyday digital compositing tasks, using sample footage and other elements that had been "cleaned up" or optimized specifically for those projects. That's good for learning the basics, but that's not how the real world works. As a digital compositor, you will rarely be handed an easy shot. You will more often be asked to salvage, repair, or fake something that went wrong or was overlooked in principal photography. Unfortunately, every time a compositor pulls a rabbit out of a hat and salvages another "impossible" shot, it seems to simply reinforce the directors' and producers' delusions that anything can be fixed in post. Fortunately, those delusions keep a lot of digital compositors employed and will have a big influence on the success of your career. If you want steady work, learn to fix production mistakes.

Case Study 9.1
Frantic Films' *Just a Minute*

By Christopher Bond, President, Senior Compositor, Senior Animator

This *Just a Minute* spot is a one-minute segment featuring Amirah, a little girl who discovers the wonderful world of reading. Created for WTN, this aired nationally in Canada beginning in September 1997.

Amirah was shot against greenscreen in BetacamSP. We used the resulting images as mattes, which we composited against entirely CG backgrounds. All shadows were faked, as were

Images from the *Just a Minute* spot.

other visual effects within the scene. Compositing got a little tricky due to poor lighting in some instances, but we managed to lift a reasonable key. The spaceship scene involved some tricky matte techniques, and the balloons sequence required rotoscoping a digital "rope" to Amirah's flailing hand.

Storyboard: The opening shot is of Amirah in a scene with virtual backdrops of a school and schoolyard. She touches the screen, which warps her to a new environment, a castle. From there, she speaks of all the places she can imagine, then again touches the screen. She warps to where she stands taller than skyscrapers and says, "I can be tall, or very, very small!" At this point, the camera cuts to a sequence of her jumping over a pencil on a desk and leaning against a stapler. She then turns into a comic book character, has duplicates of herself in the same scene, flies a rocket ship, sails through the air with balloons, and finally ends up in her house. Sitting on a stack of books, she explains that all of these amazing adventures can be found by reading a book: "Just make the time!"

Producer/DOP, Editing/Post/Audio: Christle Leonard.
3D Modeling/Animation, Compositing: Chris Bond.
Actress: Amirah

Frantic Films
420-70 Arthur Street
Winnipeg, Manitoba, Canada R3B 1G7
(204) 949-0070
Fax: (204) 949-0050
info@franticfilms.com
www.franticfilms.com/staff.html

Take Out The Garbage

Your first step should be to isolate the elements you want to keep and exclude any extraneous areas of the frame. This keeps both you and the software from working too hard. If you can see that an area of the frame is going to be trouble and that there is no useful subject information in that area, block it out with a garbage matte. Adding a garbage matte in DF is simple, very much like steps 7, 8, and 9 of Project 8.6. You can add a garbage matte to any matte tool. In Figure 9.1, I've added a garbage matte to exclude lighting, rigging, and other areas of the frame that won't appear in the final comp. In most live-action footage, the farther you go from the center of the frame, the more chaotic the image becomes. Lens aberrations, lighting problems, set edges, crew standing too close, mike booms, and other movable rigging all tend to creep in at the edges. If I need to reconstruct a clean plate to extract a difference key for this shot, I won't have to worry about the chaotic edges of the frame. Applying a garbage matte like this doesn't mean you have irreversibly reframed the shot either; as with most Digital Fusion operations, you can animate the position, size, and orientation of the garbage matte over time.

Along the same lines of saving work for both you and the software, you should take every opportunity to limit the amount of number crunching a comp requires. Although your workstation may not mind the extra work, it translates directly into lowered response rate and wasted time for you. No matter how fast your workstation is, you will find ways to bog it down if you are not selective about your operations.

For example, the same footage illustrated in Figure 9.1 is also going to require a tracking operation on the light bulb in the center actress' hand. Because this footage is scanned from film that was shot in low light, there is a lot of film grain. This grain can interfere with the Tracker tool's pattern recognition, slowing it down and potentially causing tracking errors. The standard fix for film grain is a blur or special plug-in like Ultimatte's Grain Killer. Either of these operations will take a lot of computation, especially on a sequence of 2K or 4K 10-bit Cineon files. However, you need the grain to be smoothed out only in the area containing the light bulb. In fact, you may

Figure 9.1
A garbage matte applied to exclude rigging and lighting artifacts.

need to preserve the film grain in order for this shot to match the rest of the footage when it is output to film again. That means you need to kill the grain just enough to get your tracking data, then put the grain back intact.

Figure 9.2 shows one way to accomplish this. I added a Blur/Sharpen tool, then applied an effect mask (Project 8.6 again) to include only the area between the light bulb's original position in the box and its final position when the actress is standing. Processing this small area to blur out the film grain will not take much time at all. To preserve the grain for a clean match to the original footage, I split the flow after the garbage matte. The original footage goes directly to the Saver tool, bypassing the Blur/Sharpen tool. The blurred footage goes to the Tracker. Motion output from the Tracker tool can be applied to elements comped over the original footage without compromising the film grain.

Figure 9.2
An effect mask applied to limit the grain-killing blur operation to the immediate area of the tracking target.

4:2:2 Color Undersampling Problems

In Chapter 5, I pointed out that the 4:2:2 sampling pattern (which is common to many video recording formats) misses half the color information. In other words, the color key will have half the effective resolution of the overall image. Because a chroma or bluescreen key is based on color differences, that missing color information can make the difference between a clean key and an unacceptable one. Figure 9.3 compares an original anti-aliased 4:4:4 RGB image to the same image converted to the 4:2:2 YUV format.

If you compare the images, you can see that the 4:2:2 image is blockier and would produce a noisier key. To prevent this, whenever possible you should try to work with 4:4:4 sampling. If you have to work with 4:2:2 footage, there is a way to improve the quality of the color sample so you can pull a cleaner matte. Figure 9.4 shows the results of processing the 4:2:2 YUV image through a series of tools that simulate the missing color information.

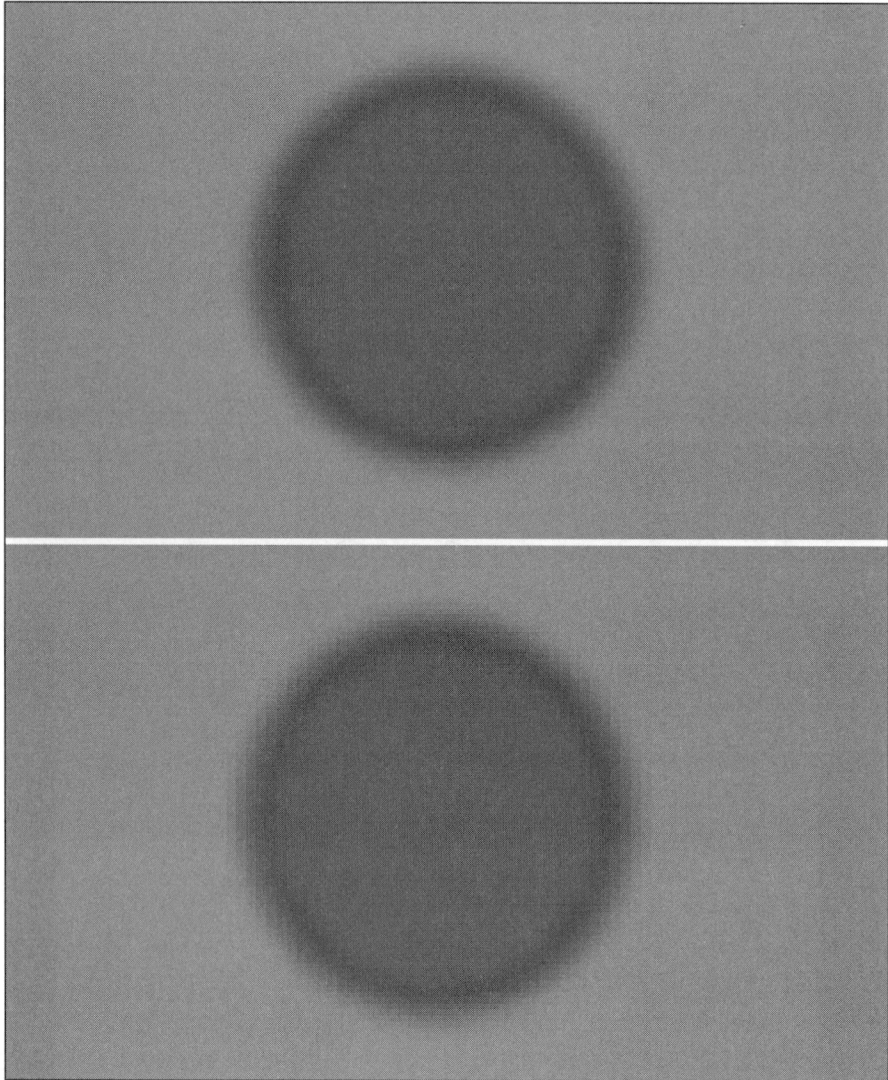

Figure 9.3
Top: Original red-and-blue image with anti-aliased transition. Bottom: Rougher, aliased transition resulting from 4:2:2 sampling in the YUV format.

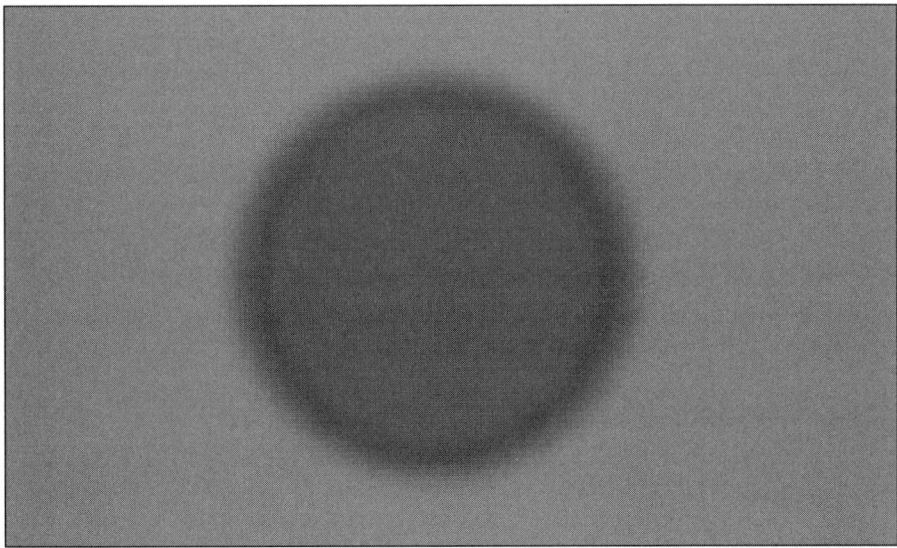

Figure 9.4
Anti-aliased transition resulting from a sequence of YUV-to-RGB-to-Custom-to-RGB-to-YUV filters.

PROJECT 9.1 4:2:2 YUV Sampling Correction

The goal of this project is to set up a simple flow that corrects the color information loss inherent in 4:2:2 YUV sampling.

1. Open a new flow. Add a Loader tool, and load the footage you want to correct.

2. Add a Color Space tool set for RGB>YUVmode.

3. Add a Custom Filter tool, and right-click on this tool's header to bring up the menu. Then you need to choose Settings|Load and select the CFLT_UV_BLEND.flt settings file, as shown in Figure 9.5.

If this file is not already in your default settings directory, you can copy it from the eyeon directory on this book's first CD-ROM. This custom filter blends the U and V color channels, interpolating them to simulate the missing color resolution.

4. Add a Color Space tool set for YUV>RGB mode. Then add a Saver tool. Your flow should look like Figure 9.5.

Figure 9.5
This flow is configured to correct for YUV format's 4:2:2 color undersampling.

Figure 9.6 shows a difference key between original bluescreen footage and the output of this flow. As you can see, most of the difference is in the edges, so it obviously has a significant effect on keying, fringe, and halo problems. You can run almost any bluescreen video footage through this filter and see a noticeable improvement in the quality of the mattes you can pull from them. Not every bluescreen shot needs this correction, but it's a good first step when you run into problems. You will probably want to keep a copy of this flow handy for correcting 4:2:2 footage as a precomp.

Bluescreen Problem Solving

As I pointed out in Chapter 6, one of the most common sources for compositing problems is a bad bluescreen. If you can't be on the set, you should be prepared for the worst when you take delivery of the footage. On the positive side, developers of compositing software have recognized this set of problems and have brought out an arsenal of bluescreen-fixing tools.

Figure 9.6
A difference key showing changes between the original footage and the 4:2:2 color sampling correction filter.

If your color keyer isn't limited to keying from a particular hue, you can correct many problems by comping your partial mattes and foreground over a solid background that is the average of the partial backing colors. For example, if you have uneven lighting, shadows, or inconsistent paint colors in the bluescreen, sample all the light, dark, and medium areas to find an average value. Your keying tools will have a better chance of working if they don't have to stretch too far, and the average color value is usually a good place to start. Set this color as the middle threshold value, and expand the upper and lower thresholds incrementally to get the cleanest possible key.

Screen Correction

Even perfectly accurate color keying can be a problem if you don't have a perfect color backing. Paint patches or fading, cracks, seams, scuffs, and dirt can all contribute to variations in the bluescreen. If your software is capable of keying hair, glass, and other problem subjects, it will also pick up these bluescreen flaws. To correct them, you can manually garbage-matte them out, reduce the accuracy of your key to blur them out, or set up a screen correction.

Screen correction enables you to correct most bluescreen flaws without sacrificing any detail in your matte. This enables you to work with an imperfectly built or maintained bluescreen set. It also enables you to light the subject for best effect, rather than light the bluescreen and then compromise on the lighting of the subject. Screen correction also enables you to compensate for problems such as glare or reflections without having to put filters on the camera. As you can imagine, screen correction is an extremely useful and popular digital compositing technique. The only serious limitation to screen correction is that you must have a clean plate. If you were not able to shoot a clean plate, you'll need to assemble one from clear areas of the footage. If the camera was moving, you'll need matching motion control footage for the clean plate. If the camera was not locked down and you don't have a clean plate, you're out of luck. If you can't salvage the footage using other keying tools, your best bet is to reshoot it.

PROJECT 9.2 Screen Correction

The goal of this project is to set up a screen correction to remove noise and clutter from the bluescreen foreground footage. To perform screen correction with Digital Fusion, take the following steps:

1. Open a new flow, add a Loader tool, and load the SC.tga image from the Ultimatte directory on the first CD-ROM (see Figure 9.7). In the Loader controls, extend the last frame to 539. This will hold the single image for the entire shot. This frame is the clean plate of a bluescreen set. The obvious flaws are uneven lighting, different paint colors, a too-short rear wall, plus minor smudges and scuffs.

Courtesy Ultimatte Corporation

Figure 9.7
Bluescreen clean plate image SC.TGA.

2. Add a second Loader tool, and load the FG_001.jpg image sequence from the Ultimatte directory. This sequence has a gap in it between frames 49 and 449, so set the Missing Frames option to Hold Last Frame. This footage shows an actress in the bluescreen set and presents the keying challenges of semitransparent lace cloth, fine light-colored hair, and curved semi-transparent glass with highlights (see Figure 9.8). Keying this footage would be challenging

Courtesy Ultimatte Corporation

Figure 9.8
Frame 539 of the bluescreen footage.

enough without the bluescreen set flaws, so you need to run a screen correction to minimize these problems.

3. Add a Difference Keyer tool to the second row. Connect Loader 1 (the clean plate) to the foreground input, and Loader 2 (the actress) to the background input. In the Difference Keyer controls, make sure Low is set to 0.0 and High is set to 0.2. This will include the entire range of both images in the difference operation. Leave Matte Blur, Contrast, and Gamma at their default settings. If you view the alpha channel for the Difference Keyer on either Large or Small display, you should see something like Figure 9.9. Note that the amount of noise would not be an acceptable matte by itself. However, because you are simply performing a screen correction, it is more important to capture all available details than it is to smooth out minor color noise. Note also that you would not want to use this matte to composite the actress over a background, as there is no shading of the shadows or transparencies; the difference key is all-or-none.

4. Send Loader 1 to the Large display. Add a Background tool to the third row of the flow. In the Background tool's Color tab, choose Solid Color Mode. Left-click on the Pick button, and drag the eyedropper cursor over the Large display to select the color of the front of the set's box, about midway up. This is where the actress' shadow, and that of the glass spray bottle, will be most critical. Whenever possible, you should correct your bluescreen color to that of the most sensitive areas. This minimizes the processing necessary to key those areas and will generally produce the best results with the least effort.

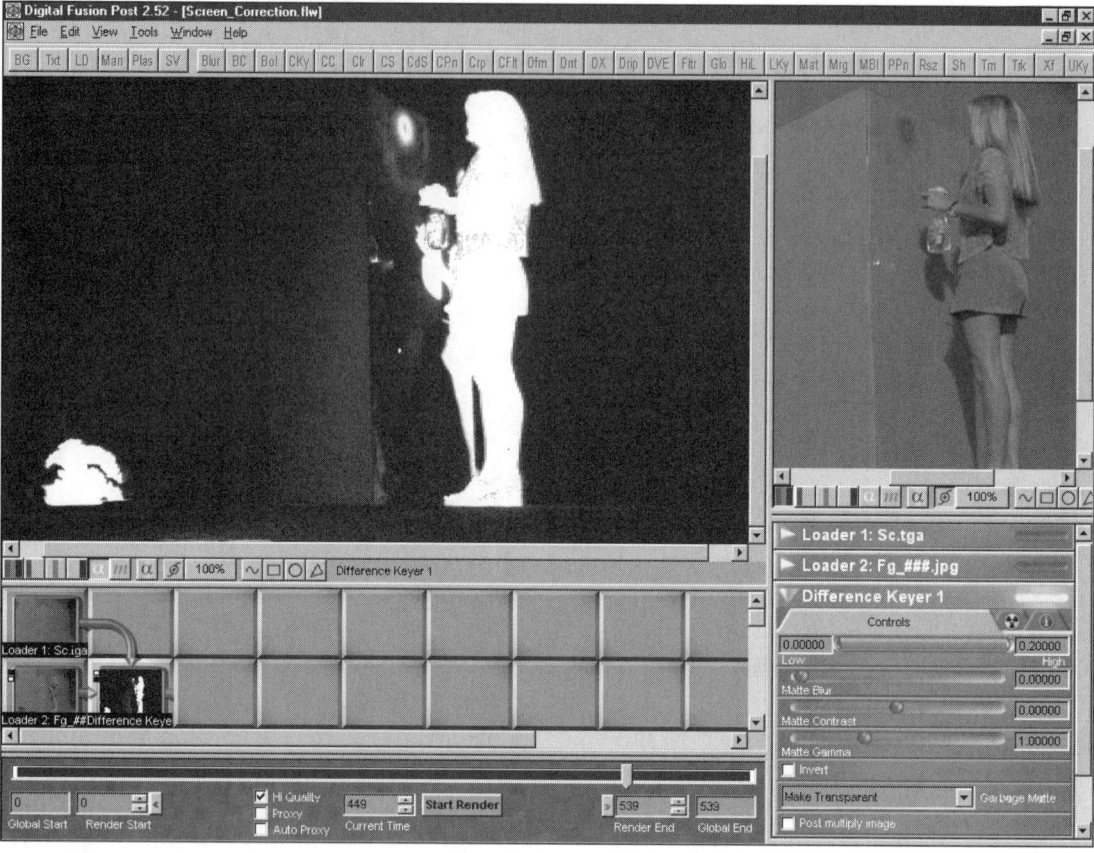

Figure 9.9
The Large display showing the difference key of the clean plate and frame 449.

5. Add a Merge tool to the right of the Background tool, and connect the Background tool to the Merge tool's background input. Connect the Difference Keyer's output to the Merge tool's foreground input. This operation replaces all the dark areas of the difference key with the median bluescreen color, and all the light areas of the key with the original actress footage. The result is shown in the Large display of Figure 9.10, contrasted with the original footage shown in the Small display. As you can see, the result is a much smoother, less troublesome bluescreen shot.

6. Add a Saver tool, and render frames 0 through 49 and frames 449 through 539 as precomps to be used later in this chapter. Save the flow as Screen_Correct.flw.

Screen Correction (After Effects)

The goal of this After Effects-based version of Project 9.2 is to set up a screen correction to remove noise and clutter from the bluescreen foreground footage. This requires the Difference Matte tool, which is only available in the Production Bundle version of After Effects. If you have the Produc-

Figure 9.10
The Large display showing frame 449 of the screen-corrected footage.

tion Bundle, you can read more details about this tool on pages 47 and 48 of the Production Bundle Guide.

1. Load the single background image SC.TGA, Figure 9.7. This will be the difference layer.

2. Load the foreground image sequence FG_XXX.JPG, Figure 9.8. This will be the source layer. The image sequence is 4.21 seconds long, so choose Composition|Composition Settings and set the Duration to 4.21 seconds.

3. Add both of the loaded elements to the Time Layout.

4. Hide the difference layer by clicking on the Video switch (the eye icon) in the Time Layout window.

5. Select the source layer. Choose Effect|Keying|Difference Matte. This opens the Difference Matte Effects Controls window, Figure 9.11.

6. In the Effects Controls window, choose View|Matte Only. This enables you to see the matte alone, so you can better judge the effects of your adjustments.

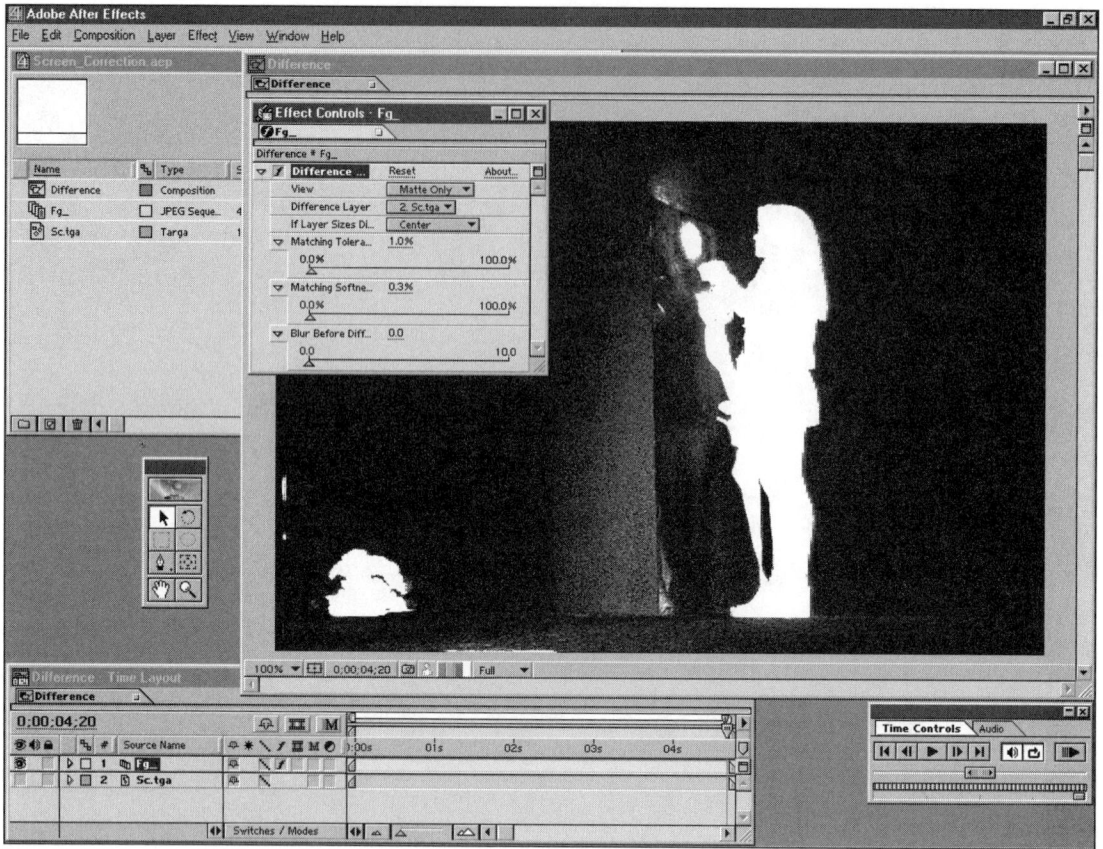

Figure 9.11

A screen correction composition, showing the difference and source layers loaded. The Effects Controls window is set for Matte Only, so the display shows only the matte, which is produced by the Tolerance, Softness, and Blur settings shown.

7. Choose SC.TGA from the Difference Layer menu.

8. Adjust the Matching Tolerance, Matching Softness, and Blur Before Difference settings to create a clean, smooth matte. Because this is a screen-correction comp, you can err on the side of caution and leave the matte noisy and open. All errors are simply replaced with the bluescreen color of the backing layer, and they can be corrected in the bluescreen comp.

9. After you have adjusted the tolerance, softness, and blur to your satisfaction, choose View|Final Output. Doing so shows the matted foreground image (see Figure 9.12). Close the Effects Control window.

10. As the next step in this process, you need to create the backing layer that will replace the matted-out areas with a solid color that is useful in a bluescreen comp. Use the Video switch to hide the source layer and show the difference layer.

Figure 9.12
The Final Output display of the difference key of the foreground footage.

11. Go to the first frame, so the new layer will extend throughout the comp. Choose Layer|New Solid. Name the new layer BlueSolid, and set it to the same dimensions as the source footage. Use the eyedropper tool to select the color from the brightest-lit area of the difference layer. This gives the BlueSolid layer a color as close as possible to the actual bluescreen backdrop color. Close the Solid Settings window.

12. Select the BlueSolid layer, and choose Layer|Send Layer To Back. Use the Video switch to hide the difference layer and show the source layer. Go to the last frame. Your comp should look like Figure 9.13.

13. Render the composition as a precomp to be used later in this chapter. My personal preference is a TGA image sequence with alpha channel and RLE compression. Save the comp as Screen_Correct.aep.

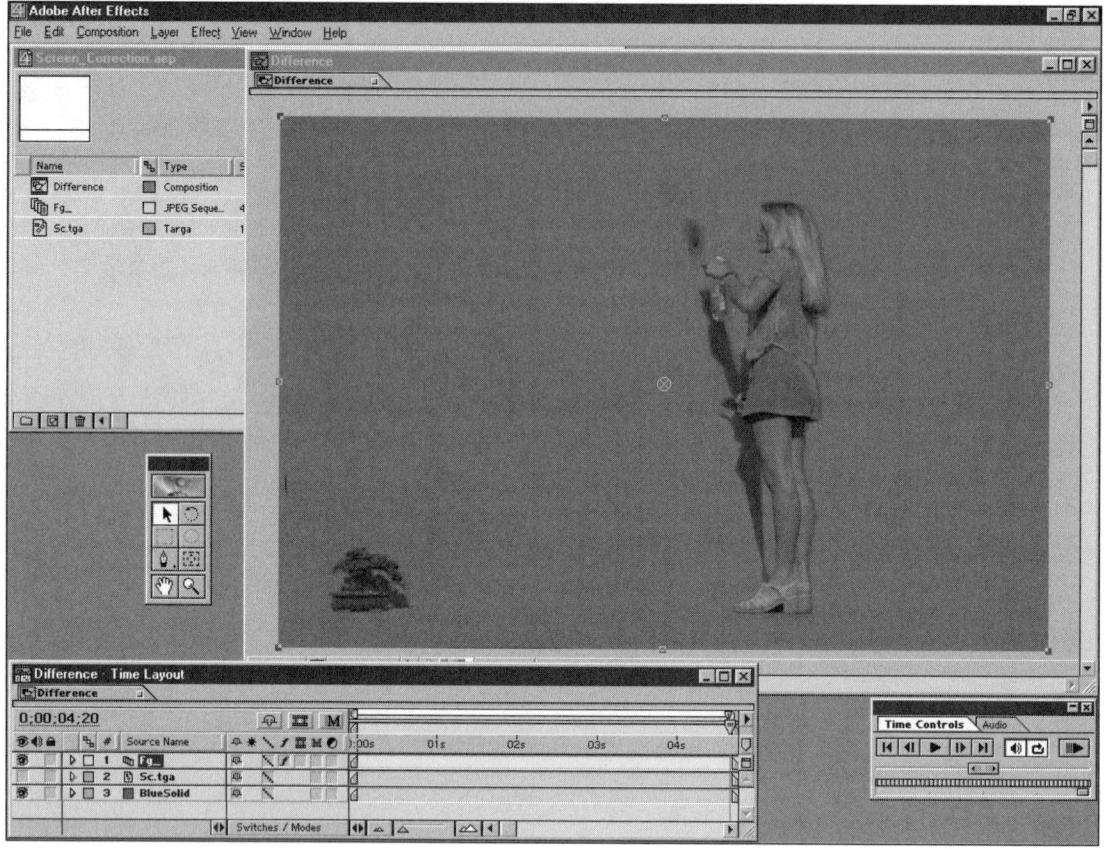

Figure 9.13
Final results of screen correction comp. Compare this to the original foreground element in Figure 9.8, and note how much easier this corrected footage will be to comp by using bluescreen operations.

Aura And Screen Correction

The tools necessary to extract a screen correction matte, or to perform a screen correction as part of a bluescreen matte extraction, are not available in Aura 1.0. If you need these features, you have to use a different compositing program.

Chalice And Screen Correction

Chalice 1.6 uses plug-ins from Ultimatte to perform screen correction. See the Chalice section of Project 9.3 for details.

Screen Correction (Commotion)

The goal of this Commotion version of Project 9.2 is to set up a screen correction to remove noise and clutter from the bluescreen foreground footage.

1. Open the single background image Sc.tga. This will be the difference layer.

2. Open the foreground image sequence Fg_450.jpg. Use this as the source layer.

3. Select Fg_450.jpg. Choose Filters|Keying|Difference Matte. The Difference Matte window appears.

4. In the Difference Matte window, set Diff Mode to RGB, set Layer To Match to Sc.tga, check Invert Matte, and set View to Matte. This will display the differences between the foreground and background images as a black-and-white matte.

5. Adjust the Min Tolerance and Max Tolerance to create an inclusive matte. You want to err on the side of including too much of the foreground rather than excluding too much of it. Remember, this is a preparatory step for a bluescreen matte extraction, not the final matte. Set Min Tolerance to 0, and Max Tolerance as low as you can get without including too much noise. Something between 25 and 40 should do. Figure 9.14 shows the effects of a setting of 33.

Figure 9.14
The foreground and background images are loaded, and the Difference Matte window shows settings for a screen correction matte.

6. When the preview matte looks good enough, change the View setting to Comp and click on OK to close the Difference Matte window.

7. Close the Sc.tga image file to free more memory. You don't need it after the Difference Matte operation is complete.

8. Choose the eyedropper tool, and select a color from a representative area of the bluescreen. Choose an area that is not affected by shadows, by reflections, or by any of the foreground elements. I found good RGB values to be 67, 98, 176.

9. Choose Calculate|Composite. In the Composite window, choose Transfer Mode as Normal, Matte as Source Image, Comp Against as Color, and Destination as Flatten. Click on the color swatch button, and set the color to the same values you sampled with the eyedropper. Your Composite window should look like Figure 9.15. Click on OK to close the Composite window.

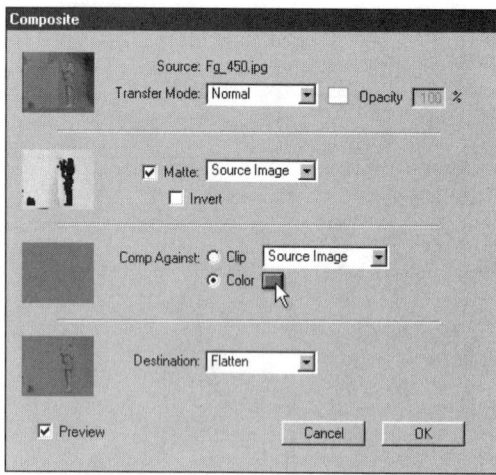

Figure 9.15
The Composite window shows settings for comping the foreground over a solid blue color, using the difference matte, to finish the screen correction.

10. Your image should now have a solid blue color replacing all the variations in the original bluescreen set, leaving the foreground elements (the actress, plant, and their shadows) ready to chroma key. Save the results to a new folder.

effect* And Screen Correction

The tools necessary to extract a screen correction matte or to perform a screen correction as part of a bluescreen matte extraction are unavailable in effect*. If you need these features, you have to use a different compositing program.

Shake And Screen Correction

In Shake 2.1, the Common function compares two images, usually a foreground and a clean plate, and extracts or hides common elements. This operator enables you to pull difference mattes, or mattes rejecting pixels that perfectly match up in both elements. The pixels are rejected if the difference between the two elements is less than the floating-point Tolerance value you set. This Tolerance setting enables you to tweak the difference matte to compensate for a better or worse clean plate. You can apply the results of the Common operation to replace an uneven clean plate or bluescreen backing with a perfectly even one, making downstream operations much easier and more efficient. If you are using Shake's GUI (graphic user interface), the Common operator is located in the Layer tab. For more details, refer to the Shake 2.1 documentation in the Shake directory on this book's second CD-ROM.

Ultimatte Screen Correction

Ultimatte has been in the keying business for a long time and is the de facto industry standard for both software and hardware. Ultimatte publishes a collection of plug-ins for Digital Fusion and other compositing software, including a Screen Correction tool. This tool goes a little further and is slightly easier to use than the previously described method using DF's own tools. There is a demo version of the plug-ins available on this book's first CD-ROM, which will work with the demo version of Digital Fusion. If you haven't already, you should stop and install the demo plug-ins now.

PROJECT 9.3 Ultimatte Screen Correction

The goal of this project is to set up a screen correction, just as in Project 9.2, but using the Ultimatte Screen Correction plug-in tool. This tool requires a clean plate or reference, just as in Project 9.2. If you like, you can reload Screen_Correct.flw and modify it for this project.

1. Repeat the initial steps of Project 9.2 to create a new flow with two Loaders, one containing the clean plate and the other containing the actress footage of the Ultimatte bluescreen set.

2. Add an Ultimatte Screen Correction tool. Connect Loader 1 to the Reference input, and connect Loader 2 to the Foreground input. In the Screen Correction Controls tab, pick a color as you did in step 4 of Project 9.2. Choose View|Corrected Foreground. Your results should look something like Figure 9.16.

You should note several important differences between this tool's results and those of the difference key. First, the upper right corner of the set is still exposed. The bluescreen color correction of this tool can't compensate for the extreme blacks visible in the stage's ceiling, so you will have to block that off with a garbage matte. The difference matte simply subtracted it, because it was essentially identical in both the clean plate and the actress footage. Second, the Ultimatte tool pulls a bluescreen matte in the same operation. If you look at the alpha channel of the tool, you'll find a very good first pass. However, the best way to finish up this comp (if you have the

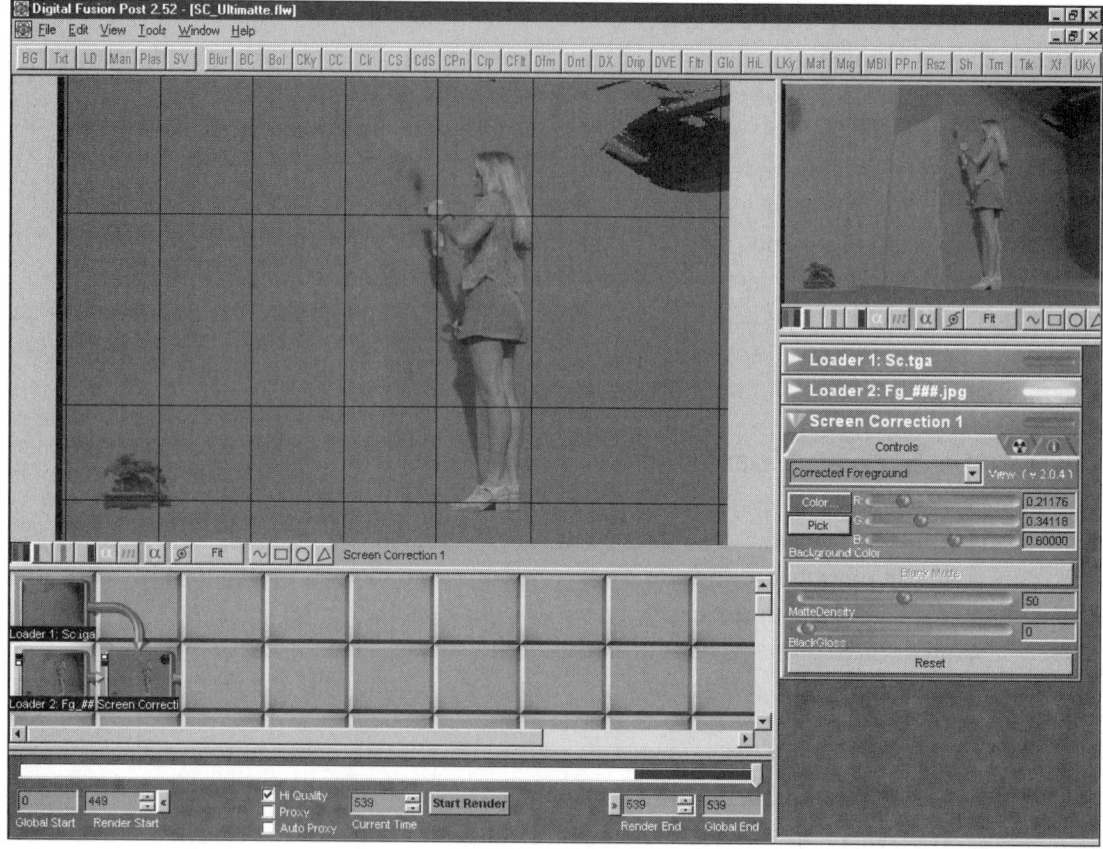

Figure 9.16
The Ultimatte Screen Correction tool applied to bluescreen footage.

Ultimatte bundle) is to apply the Ultimatte tool. Once you've picked the critical bluescreen color again, the default settings produce very nice results, shown in Figure 9.17.

Ultimatte Screen Correction (After Effects)

The goal of this After Effects-based version of Project 9.3 is to set up a screen correction, just as in Project 9.2, but using the Ultimatte Screen Correction plug-in tool. If you have not done so already, install the demo version of the Ultimatte plug-ins from the first CD-ROM into your After Effects plug-in folder. This plug-in also requires a clean plate or reference, just as in Project 9.2.

1. Reload Screen_Correct.aep. Delete the BlueSolid layer. Clear the Difference Matte effect from the source layer.

2. With the source layer selected, choose Effect|Ultimatte|Screen Correction.

3. In the Effect Controls window, choose SC.TGA from the Correction Layer menu. Click on the eyedropper tool under Backing Color and select the color from the brightest-lit area of the

Figure 9.17
The Ultimatte tool finishes the bluescreen comp.

bluescreen set (just as you did in Project 9.2). This gives the screen correction a color as close as possible to the actual bluescreen backdrop color.

4. Choose View|Corrected Foreground. The display will show the source footage as corrected by the Screen Correction plug-in, Figure 9.18.

You should note several important differences between the results of this screen correction and those of the difference matte in the preceding project. First, the upper right corner of the set is still exposed. The bluescreen color correction of the Screen Correction plug-in cannot compensate for the extreme blacks visible in the stage's ceiling, so you need to block that off with a garbage matte. The difference matte simply subtracted it, because it was essentially identical in both the difference layer and the source layer. Second, the Ultimatte Screen Correction plug-in pulls a bluescreen matte in the same operation. If you choose View|Matte, you'll see a very good first pass at the bluescreen matte. However, the best way to finish this comp (if you have the Ultimatte bundle) is to apply the Ultimatte plug-in to the source layer after the Screen Correction plug-in. Figure 9.19 shows the results of keying the source layer over the BG.TGA background image by applying the Ultimatte plug-in.

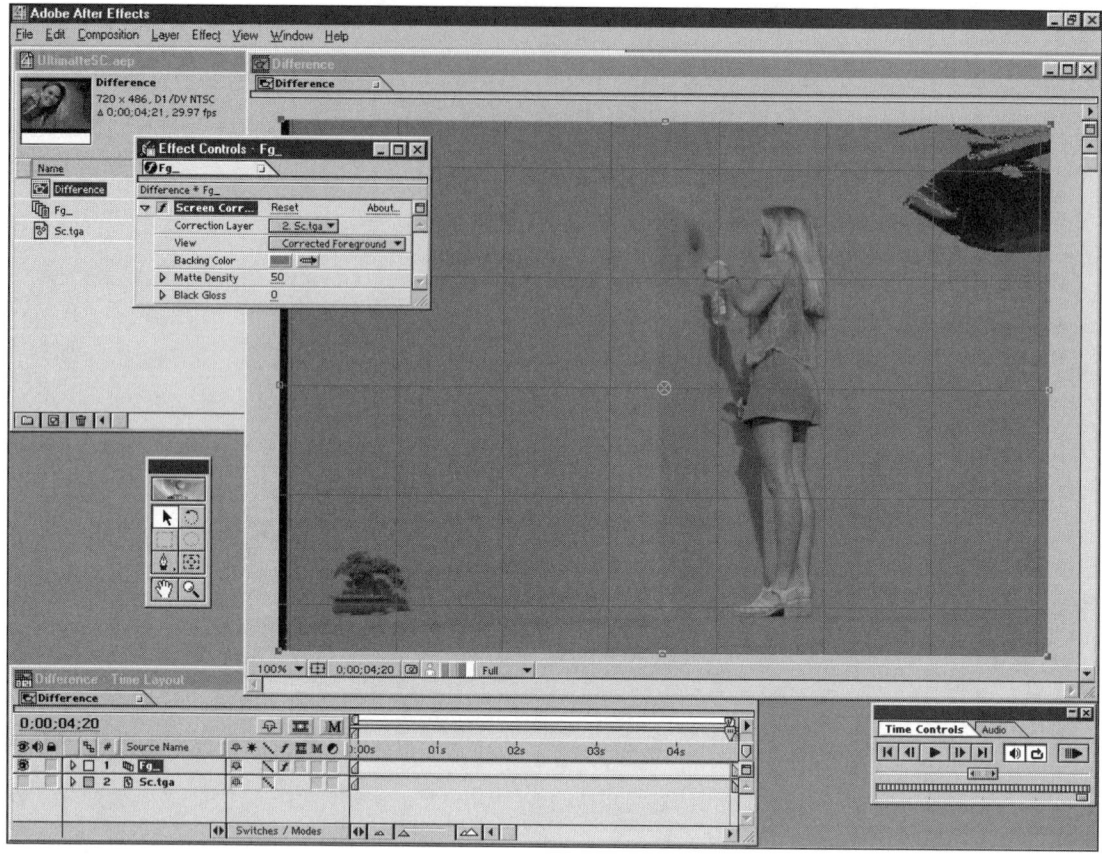

Figure 9.18
The results of applying the Ultimatte Screen Correction plug-in. Note the remaining clutter at the top right and left margin of the image.

Chalice And Ultimatte Screen Correction

There are detailed instructions for applying the Ultimatte CSC (Classic Screen Correction) Node in the Chalice 1.6 manual, pages 12.21 through 12.25. You can find the manual in PDF format in the Chalice directory of this book's first CD-ROM. Rather than repeat the efforts of the Chalice manual's authors, I recommend (if you are using Chalice) that you work through the Ultimatte CSC section in the manual, then apply the screen correction process to the background, foreground and clean plate footage in the Ultimatte directory on this book's first CD-ROM.

Several additional screen correction features are available in Chalice. The Ultimatte RSC (Roto Screen Correction) Node enables you to perform a screen correction without a clean plate. For scenes with camera motion, you can use Ultimatte RSC to correct the bluescreen, even if you don't have a motion-control clean plate. Again, full details of this process are available in the Chalice 1.6 manual, pages 12.30 through 12.41.

Figure 9.19
The foreground footage composited over a background image using Ultimatte screen correction and bluescreen keying plug-ins.

THE MORE (MATTES) THE MERRIER

If you are having trouble getting an element to comp cleanly with just one matte, try adding another matte. You can use a soft matte to bring out the element's edges and a harder matte to fill in holes that the soft matte leaves inside the subject's outline. When you add the mattes together, you will probably need to erode the hard matte to keep it from overrunning the outer edges of the soft matte.

Silencing Noise

When you need to work with bluescreen footage that has excessive noise from film grain, scanner dirt, or video digitizing or compression artifacts, you will have problems pulling a clean matte. Wherever the color of the noise approximates the backing color, the noise will poke a hole in your matte. The left side of Figure 9.20 shows an example of this problem due to film grain. The quality of the original footage showing the grain is at the top of Figure 9.21.

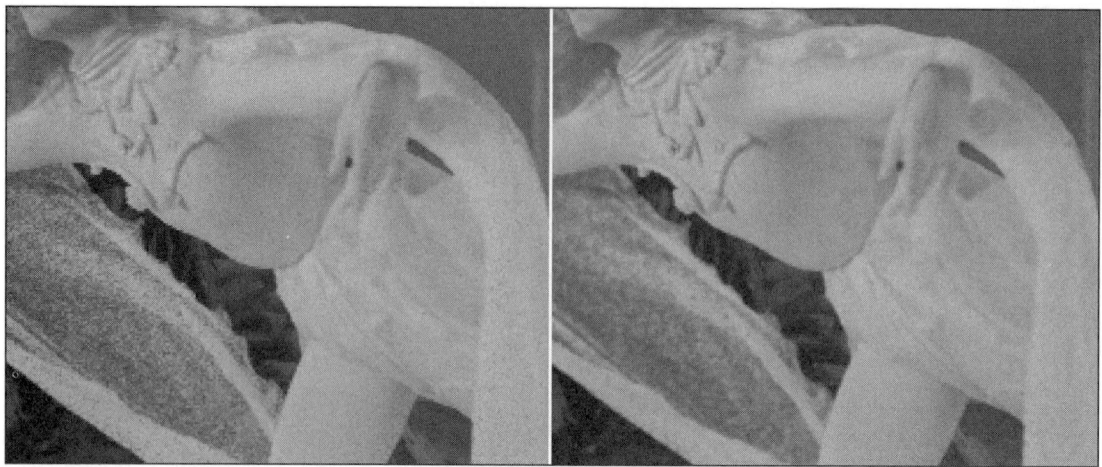

Figure 9.20
A comp of a noisy bluescreen matte extracted without blur (left) and with blur (right).

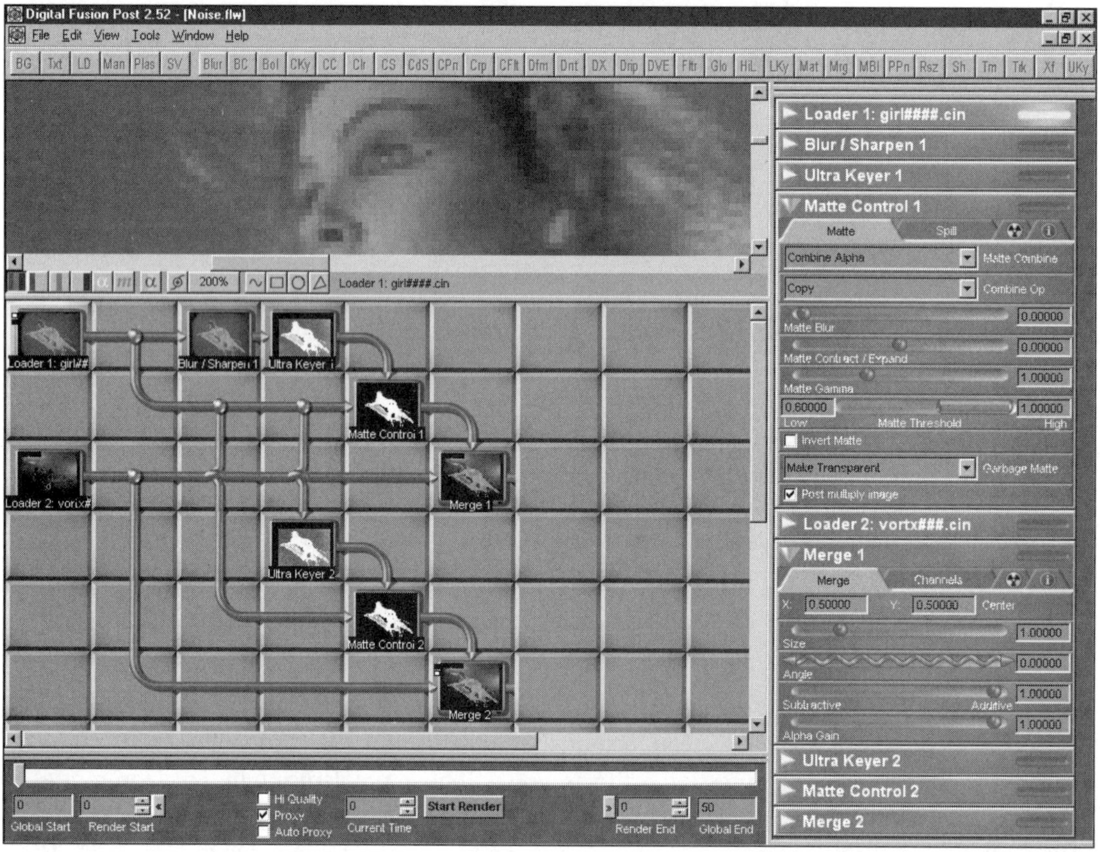

Figure 9.21
Noise-canceling comparison flow.

One way to repair this problem is to apply a slight blur to the footage, enabling you to extract a cleaner matte. To preserve the original image quality, noise and all, you can then comp the original footage using the blurred matte. One way to do this with Digital Fusion is illustrated in the flow pictured in Figure 9.21. This flow is set up to compare blurred and raw mattes, so it's roughly twice as complex as you would need for a real project. The important tools are Blur/Sharpen (set for Blur Size of 0.5), Ultra Keyer (any advanced keyer will do), and Matte Control. Note that the Matte Control tool is set to combine the alpha channel from the blurred matte with the raw footage from Loader 1. The end result is that the blurred matte has no noise-induced holes in it, whereas the noisy color details of the raw footage are preserved in the final comp.

Setting up a double flow like this is a good method of experimenting to find a solution to a tough problem. You can even compare the results of two flow branches in a single image. Just add a Dissolve tool, connect the output of the two flow branches to it, and use an Effect Mask to restrict the foreground input to one side of the screen and the background input to the opposite side of the screen, as shown in Figure 9.22. This is a good, fast-feedback way of comparing results in

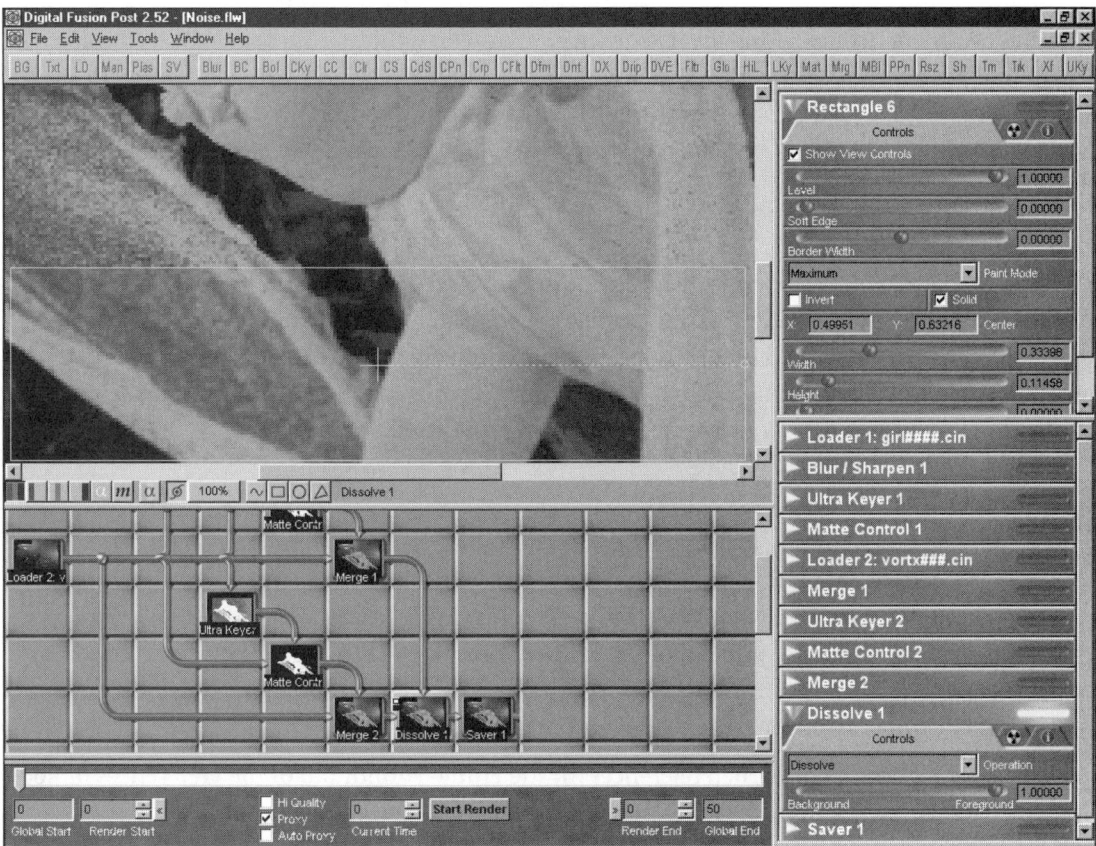

Figure 9.22
Comparison flow with Dissolve and Effect Mask.

order to find the best solution. By adding a Saver after the Dissolve, you can even render tests for your supervisor or director to use in decision making.

SEEING SPOTS

If a chroma keyer operation mistakes saturated white (bright) areas for the key color (bluescreen backing), you can use a luma key of the brightest areas to fill in the chroma key holes. This is especially useful for foreground objects that are reflective or glossy, as the intense highlights they reflect are usually saturated in all three color channels. This problem occurs with any color backing, so changing from bluescreen to greenscreen won't fix it.

Cleaning Up Film

Working with scanned film presents a set of problems that can be a headache the first time through. After you have dealt successfully with film, it shouldn't intimidate you. You should, however, develop a healthy respect for the time, resources, and talent necessary to digitally composite film footage.

Film has grain, an artifact of the layers of emulsion and dyes that create grayscale and color when light passes through the film. Different film stocks have different grain and different responses to light, so no single solution will work for all film stocks. In addition, the scanning or telecine process that digitizes the film can introduce more artifacts. If you want to minimize your headaches, you need to know (preferably well in advance) what film stock and digitizing process you will be expected to work with.

This book's CD-ROMs include some frames of film that have been scanned into 2K 10-bit Cineon files. Each image is roughly 12MB, so a second of screen time takes up 288MB. A two-hour feature film in this format would occupy a little over 2 terabytes; even one minute of film images would fill an 18-gigabyte AV hard drive. Aside from the scanning and printing costs, digital compositing of film requires a lot of expensive storage space.

PROJECT 9.4 Cleaning Up Film

The goal of this project is to extract a matte from noisy film footage by applying color correction, blur, garbage matte, and chroma key operations. Simply applying a chroma key to film footage would extract a very low-quality matte and leave a crawly, noisy matte line in the final comp. You can get much better results by masking out the worst of the garbage, smoothing out film grain with a blur operation, and color correcting to get a more pure bluescreen background for the chroma key operation to process.

1. Open a new flow. Choose File|Preferences. In the Frame Format tab of the Preferences dialog box, change the Default Format to 2K Full Aperture (Super35), as shown in Figure 9.23.

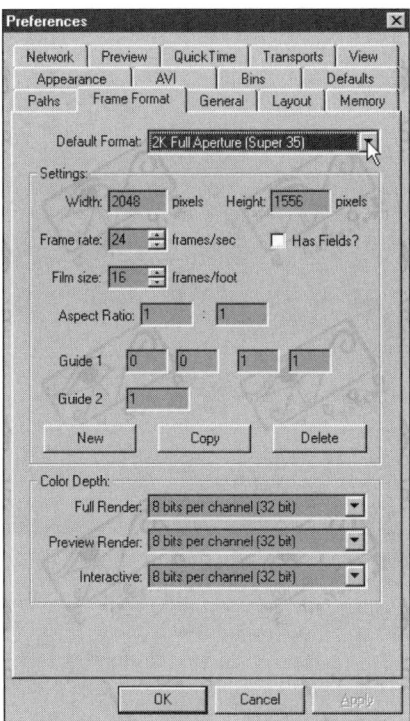

Figure 9.23
Digital Fusion Preferences dialog box showing the Frame Format tab set up for full-aperture 35mm film images.

2. Add a Loader tool, and load the girl0000.cin Cineon sequence from the CineGirl folder on the second CD-ROM (see Figure 9.24). Looks dark, doesn't it? To brighten it up, go to the Format tab of the Loader 1 controls and set Conversion Gamma and Film Stock Gamma both to 1.7. This compensates for the difference between the color space of video monitors and that of film.

3. Add a second Loader, and load the image sequence from the GirlSide folder on the second CD-ROM. This is a telecined and optimized version of the same film as the Cineon footage. The background color has been changed to make keying easier, but the skin tones are still pretty much the same (see Figure 9.25). Look closely at the difference in color range in the skin tones. This is the difference between the 256 values possible in an 8-bit per channel format and the 1,024 values possible in the 10-bit Cineon format. Film images give you much more color (as well as sheer resolution) to play with. That's a good thing; with more colors, you can make finer distinctions between foreground and background, so mattes can be cleaner and easier to pull.

Figure 9.24
Cineon film image before gamma correction.

4. Replace the footage in Loader 2 with a suitable background of the same resolution as that in Loader 1, such as the single Cineon image in the CineVort folder on this book's second CD-ROM.

5. Add a Blur/Sharpen tool and connect it to Loader 1. Apply a rectangular effect mask to limit the blur to the clear center of the frame, including all of the actress but as little of the frame as possible. Set the rectangle to Solid. This is intended to minimize the amount of processing needed to complete this comp. Make a note of the center and dimensions for this rectangle.

Figure 9.25
The Large display shows the film image; the Small display shows the telecined video image of the same subject.

6. Set Blur Size to 1.0, as shown in Figure 9.26. You may have to tweak this setting to blur the film grain enough to minimize it without completely obscuring the edge details necessary for the matte.

7. Add an Ultra Keyer tool *after* and *connected to* the Blur/Sharpen tool, as shown in Figure 9.26. Apply a rectangular garbage matte to block out the rough edges of the frame. You should be able to use the same dimensions and center as you did for the Blur/Sharpen effect mask. Set the rectangle to Solid and Inverted to pass through the center and black out the edges of the frame.

8. In the Ultra Keyer, pick a color by sampling the blue backing. Adjust the Matte Separation slider and check Lock Color Picking. Your results should look like Figure 9.26.

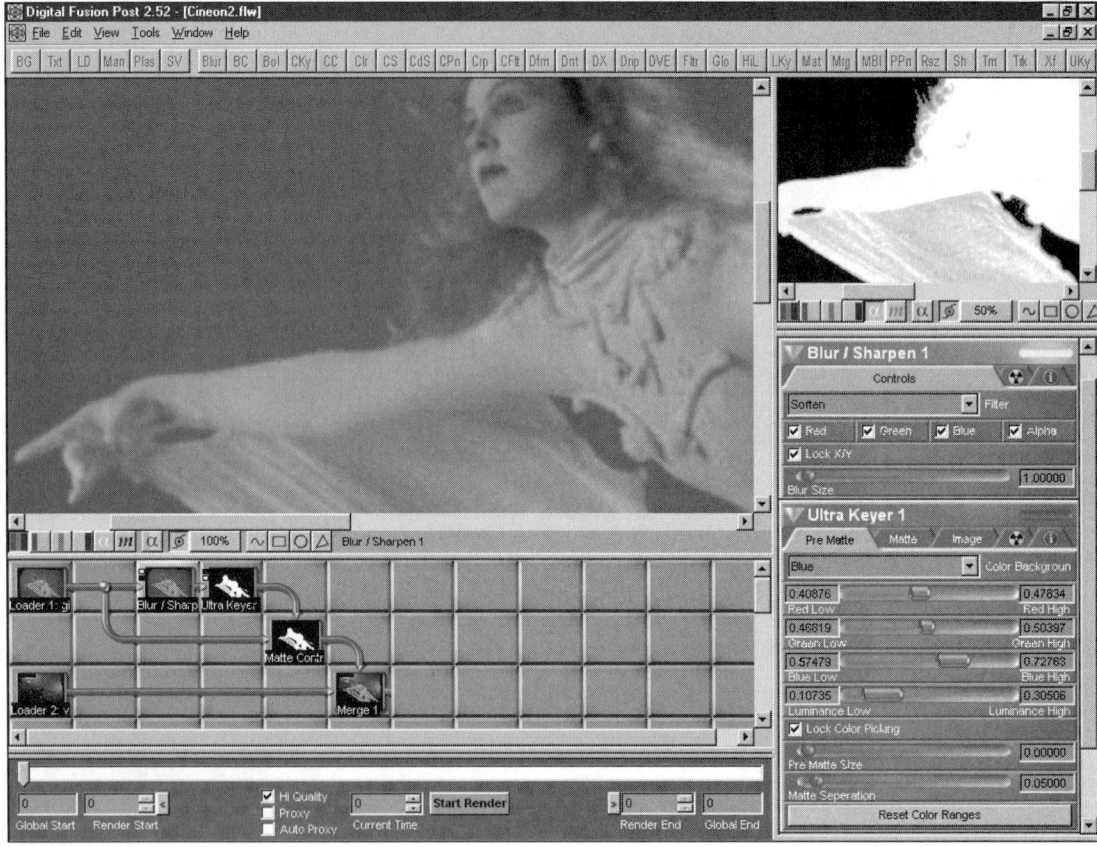

Figure 9.26
Blur/Sharpen and Ultra Keyer tool settings and results.

9. Add a Matte Control tool below and to the right of the Ultra Keyer, and connect the Ultra Keyer and Loader 1 to it. Add a Merge tool and connect the Matte Control and Loader 2 to it. Adjust the Matte Control as shown in Figure 9.27. In the Matte tab, set Matte Combine to Combine Alpha, and check the Post Multiply Image box. Pay special attention to adjusting the Matte Threshold slider. Make sure the Merge tool is set to full Additive and maximum Alpha Gain. Your results should look like Figure 9.27's Large display.

Cleaning Up Film (After Effects)

The goal of this After Effects-based version of Project 9.4 is to extract a matte from Cineon film footage by applying color correction, garbage matte, and chroma key operations.

1. Import the Cineon footage file sequence girl0000.cin from the CineGirl folder on the second CD-ROM. Select Cineon AE Format, and in the Interpret Footage dialog box, select Treat As Straight (Unmatted).

2. Make a new comp named Clean_Film, and add the Cineon sequence as the first layer.

Figure 9.27
Matte Control and Merge settings. The Large display shows part of the final comp; the Small display shows the matte.

The footage will look extremely dark and grainy and if you look at the color channels individually, only the red channel will appear to have an image because the Cineon format uses 10-bit logarithmic color space, but After Effects can read only 8-bit linear color space. Before you can see the image clearly, you have to apply an effect to convert 10-bit log to 8-bit lin color space.

3. With the girl layer selected, choose Effect|Cineon Tools|Cineon Converter. Your comp should look like Figure 9.28. There is still a lot of grain, and the image is dark, but at least you can see something.

4. With the girl layer still selected, choose Effect|Image Control|Gamma/Pedestal/Gain. In the Effect Controls window, set the effect's Red, Green, and Blue Gamma to 1.7. This brightens the image to an approximate match with the telecined footage from the same scene.

Because the Cineon Converter reduces the color depth to 8 bits per channel, much of the film grain contrast is reduced to a level that can be managed by the standard chroma key operations built into After Effects.

Figure 9.28
The Cineon-format GIRL0000.CIN image sequence loaded and converted to 8-bit linear color space with the Cineon Converter effect.

5. Import the Cineon image VORTX050.CIN from the CineVort directory on the second CD-ROM, using the same settings as for the CineGirl sequence. Apply a Cineon Converter and a Gamma/Pedestal/Gain effect, with the same settings you used in steps 3 and 4. Send the new layer to the back. This creates a compatible background layer over which you can composite the bluescreen image sequence.

6. Hide the background layer. Select the girl layer. Choose Effect|Keying|Color Key. In the Color Key area of the Effect Controls window, use the eyedropper to select a representative color from the girl layer's blue background.

7. Show the background layer. Select the girl layer. In the Color Key area of the Effect Controls window, adjust the Color Tolerance slider to refine the color key. Because of the large variation in color due to film grain, you will have to use a large tolerance value. I found 60 to work fairly well.

8. Add a Spill Suppressor effect to the girl layer. Use the eyedropper from Color To Suppress to sample the Key Color from the Color Key effect. This keeps the color operations consistent. Set Suppression to 100. Your comp should look like Figure 9.29. Save the project before you go on to the next step.

Figure 9.29
The Cineon bluescreen footage composited over a background with Color Key and Spill Suppressor effects.

There is still a lot of garbage around the edges of the girl layer, where the bluescreen was not evenly lit and where the edges of the backing and other set rigging is visible. The simplest solution to this problem is to apply a garbage mask, but After Effects' rendering order prevents that. AE renders masks first, but the Cineon Converter has to run before any masks for Cineon layers, or a rendering error will occur. There are several ways around this problem. You can render the converted Cineon footage to another format, then reload the rendered footage. Alternatively, you could move the Cineon conversion to a separate composition, with the output linked to the existing Clean_Film composition.

9. Select the girl layer. Choose Layer|Pre-Compose. In the Pre-Compose dialog box, choose Leave All Attributes. This creates a new intermediate composition and moves the selected layer with all masks, effects, and transforms to it. The new comp will become the source to the old composition.

10. The new comp, named "girl Comp 1" by default, is now represented as a single layer in the original Clean_Film comp. Double-click on that layer to open the Layer window. Maximize the Layer window; you will need as much space as possible to draw the mask. Choose a view magnification that fits the actress within the window, as shown in Figure 9.30.

Figure 9.30
The girl Comp 1 layer from the Clean_Film composition, showing the straight-line closed garbage mask.

11. Choose the Pen tool from the toolbox, and right-click repeatedly around the actress to create a straight-line garbage mask like that shown in Figure 9.30. After you add the last point, click on the first point to close the mask.

12. Choose Layer|Mask|Mode|Add. Doing so makes the inside of the mask opaque and the outside of the mask transparent. This is the effect you want for this mask; the area outside the

mask is garbage, and you want it to be perfectly transparent so the background image shows through.

13. Choose Layer|Mask|Mask Feather, and set the feather range to 12. Doing so softens the edge of the mask so it isn't as obvious when an element crosses the mask edge. This can often save you the trouble of animating the mask.

14. Close the Layer window. Choose a view magnification in the Composition window that enables you to see the entire frame. You should see a completely clean comp, as shown in Figure 9.31.

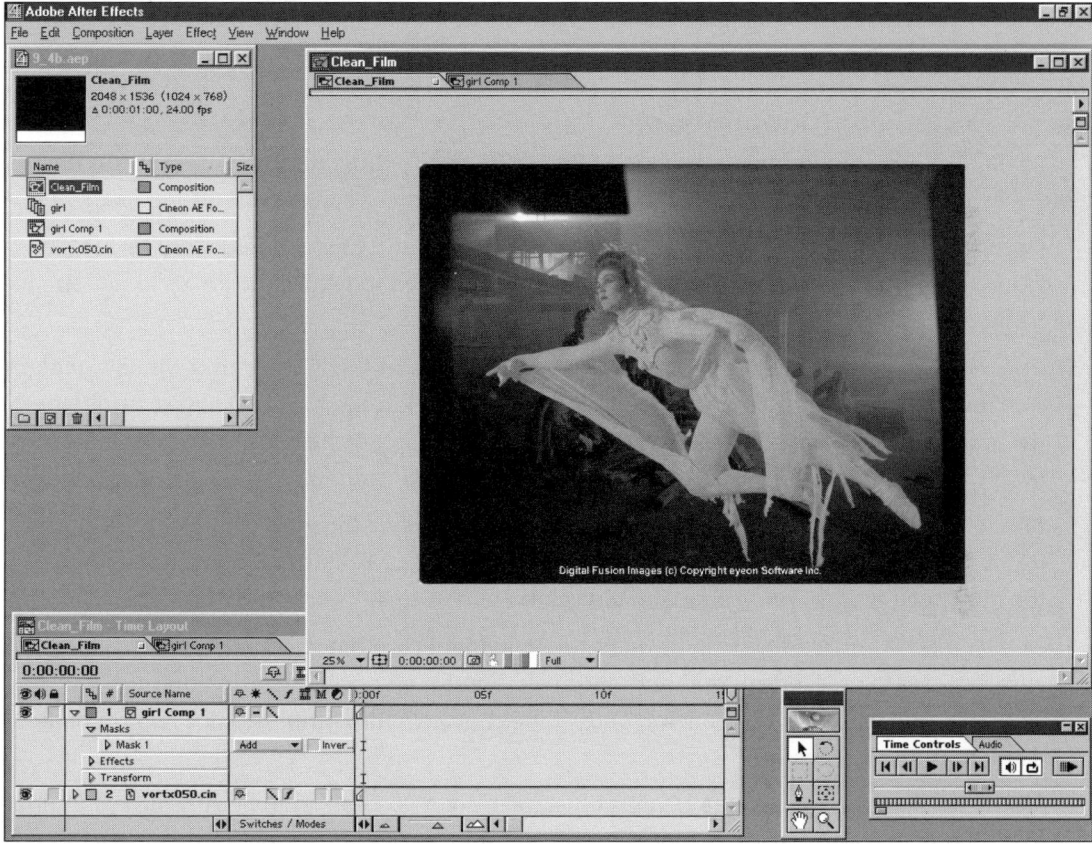

Figure 9.31
The final composite of the Cineon bluescreen footage, showing the effects of Cineon conversion, garbage mask, color key, and spill suppression.

Aura And Cleaning Up Film

Aura 1.0 cannot load Cineon-format scanned film images. If you need to work with this file format, you need to use other compositing software.

Chalice And Cleaning Up Film

If control is a measure of power, Chalice is one of the most powerful programs for working with film images. Importing and working with Cineon-format images in Chalice requires you to understand and correctly set a number of preferences through the main menu and the I/O nodes. For details, see the Chalice 1.6 manual, located in the Chalice directory of the first CD-ROM.

Color correction, bluescreen matte extraction, and the creation of garbage mattes are all covered in the five tutorials included in the Chalice documentation. Rather than duplicate the efforts of the manual's authors, I recommend that you work through the Chalice tutorials, then apply what you learn to extract a clean matte from the CineGirl footage on this book's second CD-ROM.

Cleaning Up Film (Commotion)

The goal of this Commotion-based version of Project 9.4 is to extract a matte from Cineon film footage by applying color correction, garbage matte, and chroma key operations.

1. Open the Cineon footage file sequence girl0000.cin from the CineGirl folder on the second CD-ROM. Unless your system has a lot of RAM, you'll need to reduce the proxy image size to 50 percent or less.

2. Choose Filters|Image Control|ICE Gamma/Pedestal/Gain. In the ICE Gamma window, make sure that the All Follow Red box is marked, and set Red Gamma to 1.7. Doing so brightens the image to an approximate match with the telecined footage from the same scene. Your results should look like Figure 9.32. Close the ICE Gamma window.

3. Most of the film grain is in the blue layer, so you can remove the most grain with the least loss if you blur the blue channel slightly. Choose Filters|Blur & Sharpen|ICE Channel Blur. In the ICE Channel Blur window, set the blue channel blur to 3.0. Close the window.

4. In the girl0003.cin window, step through the individual channel views and note the difference between the red, green, and blue channels. Finally, go back to viewing all three color channels, and note how the blurring of the blue channel's film grain has not removed much detail from the RGB image.

5. Set the background color to the clearest bluescreen color you can sample with the eyedropper tool. Choose the lasso selection tool. Roughly outline the marginal areas of the image, where the bluescreen color fades to black. The selection should include the entire actress and exclude the worst areas of the bluescreen background. Choose Edit|Inverse Selection. Doing so

Figure 9.32
The ICE image control filter is set to 1.7 gamma to bring the film image to an approximate match with the telecined footage from the same scene.

selects the areas you want to mask out. Press Delete or choose Edit|Delete. The selected area is deleted, leaving the background color in its place, Figure 9.33.

6. Import the Cineon image Vortx050.cin from the CineVort directory on the second CD-ROM, using the same settings as for the CineGirl sequence. Apply the same filter settings you used in steps 2 and 3. This creates a compatible background layer over which you can composite the bluescreen image sequence.

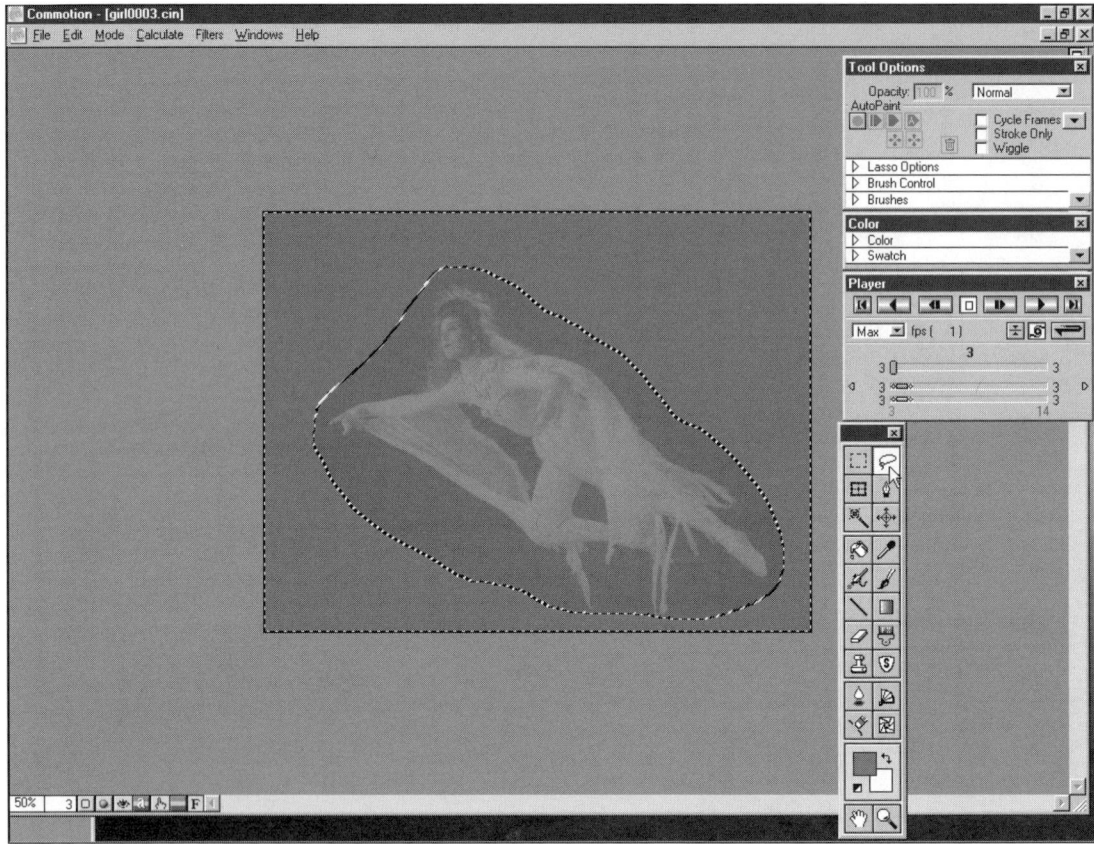

Figure 9.33
The worst areas of the bluescreen are deleted with the lasso selection tool, creating a garbage mask.

7. Select the CineGirl image. Choose Filters|Keying|BlueScreen Key. In the BlueScreen Key window, set Comp Against to Vortx050.cin, set View to Comp, and adjust the Min and Max to make a clean comp. Your results should look like Figure 9.34.

effect* And Cleaning Up Film

Unfortunately, effect* cannot load Cineon-format scanned film images. If you need to work with this file format, you need to use other compositing software.

Shake And Cleaning Up Film

The tutorials that are part of the Shake 2.1 manuals cover loading Cineon images, applying color correction, creating QuickShapes (garbage mattes), and pulling chroma key mattes. Rather than duplicate the efforts of the Shake manual authors, I recommend that you work through the Shake tutorials, then apply what you learn and extract a clean matte from the CineGirl footage on this book's second CD-ROM.

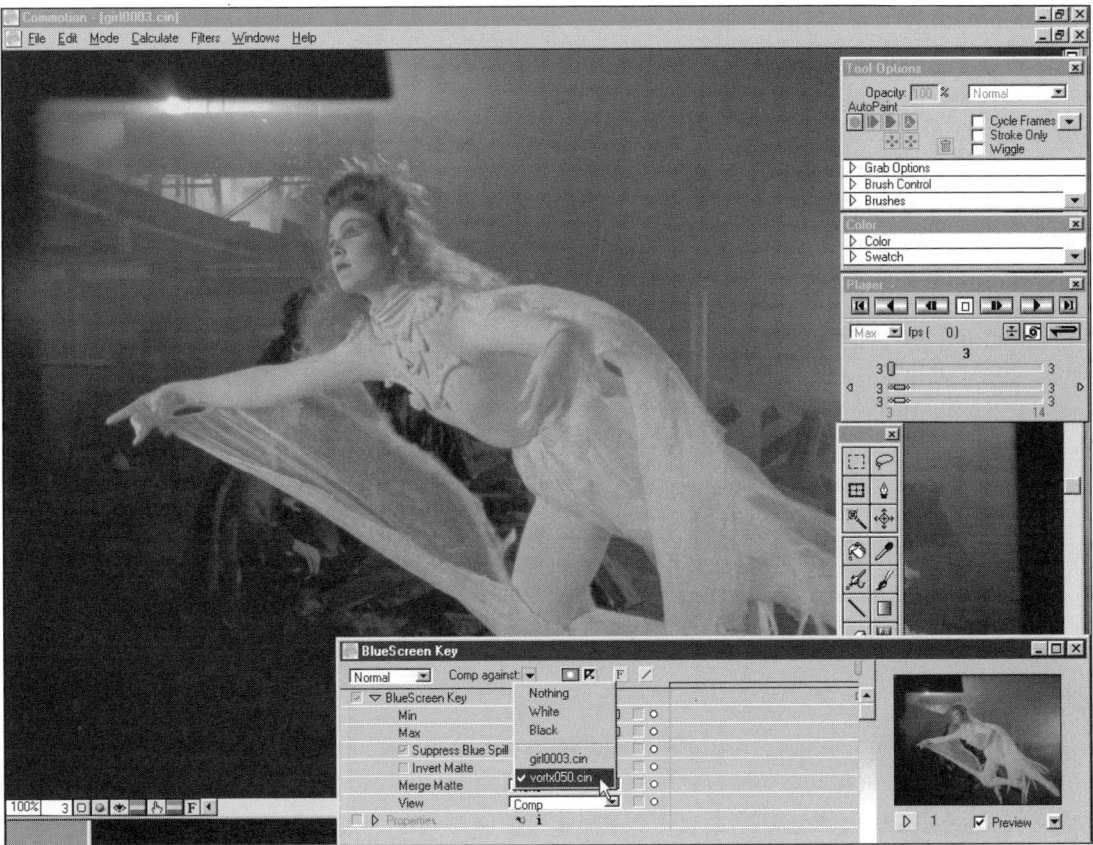

Figure 9.34
The CineGirl footage is cleaned up and comped over the CineVort footage.

Digital Compositing Plug-Ins

As I stated at the beginning of this chapter, most of your work as a professional digital compositor will boil down to variations on the same basic operations you learned in Chapter 8. You can passably solve almost any compositing problem with the basic tools provided in any professional-level software. However, solving the trickier problems may involve so many workarounds and compromises that either the results are unacceptable or the solution is cost-prohibitive. That's when you really appreciate plug-ins.

A *plug-in* is a program designed to work with your compositing software to add tools, functionality, or features. This is a good thing: it enables small specialty companies with significant technical expertise to contribute to your toolbox without having to compete with companies like Adobe or Autodesk. This is a healthy partnership for the compositing software publishers, too; plug-ins provide expertise-in-a-box that couldn't reasonably be developed in-house while remaining competitive in price and delivery schedule. In other words, if you want robust, powerful digital compositing software and you want it affordable and right now, you should appreciate plug-ins. This enables you to begin compositing with a basic program, to hone your skills with the essential tools, and to graduate to the more powerful and expensive plug-ins when you have the skill, job demands, and financial resources. If you are a student or beginner, you probably cannot afford $2,000 for a set of high-end film quality plug-ins; but then, you don't really have a demonstrated need for them either. On the other hand, a working digital compositor who has several hundred feet of film to comp and deliver in the next three weeks will not bat an eye at that price, as long as it saves time and produces a quality comp.

Most plug-in publishers make it as easy as possible for you to evaluate their products before you buy. Many publishers maintain Web sites where you can download or request CD-ROMs of free demo versions. Two of these publishers, Zbig Vision Ltd. and Ultimatte Corporation, have demo versions, tutorials, and manuals on this book's CD-ROMs. Most free demos, including those from Ultimatte and Zbig, are limited only by a random-colored grid superimposed on the plug-in's output. That enables you to apply the tool to any comp, compare the results to those produced by your existing toolset, and make an informed decision about the purchase. The grid is just to keep everyone honest, and to prevent the temptation to use someone else's intellectual property to make money.

Zbig Demo

Zbig (**www.zbigvision.com**) software is available as a standalone chroma key and compositing program, or as a plug-in for After Effects, effect*, and Digital Fusion. Zbig's strong suit is bluescreen work. In Digital Fusion, the single Zbig tool includes controls (see Figure 9.35) for every conceivable tweak you might need to repair bluescreen problems. Rather than breaking down the functions into several tools, the Zbig tool takes the foreground and background elements and performs every function necessary to composite them. This demo can be found on the first CD-ROM.

The Zbig documentation is a little light and the tutorials are very basic. However, the tool itself is so powerful, and the default settings work so well, that it's the fastest and most effective bluescreen compositing tool I've seen for the desktop. I highly recommend that you install and try out the demo version, and work through the tutorials and the rest of the Zbig online manual. As of this writing, pricing for Zbig varies from $1,300 to $9,900 depending on platform, software, and resolution; so check the Zbig Vision Web site for current prices.

Ultimatte Demo

Ultimatte (**www.ultimatte.com**) plug-ins are available for most compositing programs. At $1,495, it's not the least expensive matte tool you'll ever use, but it may be the most cost-effective. Ultimatte plug-ins are not intuitive, mostly due to the sheer number and interrelation of parameters. You need to understand what you are doing in order to use Ultimatte well, although you can get very good results simply by following the tutorial examples as recipes. The default settings are pretty good first approximations for most common bluescreen footage. The demo version on this

Figure 9.35
The Zbig plug-in in Digital Fusion.

book's first CD-ROM includes Screen Correction, Grain Killer, Ultimatte, and AdvantEdge tools, plus the Ultimatte plug-in manual for Digital Fusion and a more general overview of how the Ultimatte process works.

Go With The Flow

Most of the footage you will work with has at least one element that changes drastically in the course of the shot. The best settings for comping it may not be the same in every frame. The camera focus may change, or the subject may move. Elements may move into or out of frame. Lighting may change, shifting colors. Any of these factors (and many others) can make a good setting for one image be completely wrong for another image in the same sequence. The simplest solution (and often the best) is to animate the tool or setting that is running into trouble. This can be as simple as animating the movement of a garbage matte or as complex as coordinating the animation of every setting in the Ultra Keyer. If you're not sure whether animating settings is the most efficient solution to the problem, try configuring the best and worst frames and comparing the difference in settings. If only a few controls need to be animated, you're in good shape. If more than half the flow goes out of whack at one point or another, you should probably rethink the whole shot.

When you've finally nailed a really complex comp, don't throw it away after the final render. Save the comp itself, and save the settings of any especially difficult-to-configure tools. Give these settings file names that actually describe what they were used for, not cutesy monikers that you won't remember in a month or two when you need to find them. Even if you never reuse a particular setting exactly, being able to reuse part of it can save you a lot of time. Over the course of a busy professional career, a library of settings files can add up to a lot of on-tap expertise and many, many saved hours.

Moving On

This chapter should have given you some useful tips on fixing specific problems with challenging footage or less-than-perfect bluescreening. More importantly, I hope it has given you some strategies for solving problems and that it perhaps jogged your imagination to solve a problem with a technique you hadn't considered before. The next chapter will show you how to deal with bigger problems: objects and people who should not be in the shot.

DIGITAL
COMPOSITING
STUDIO

*On the following pages, you'll see examples
of the effects tutorials presented in this book.*

Examples Of Image Sizes

The largest image (spanning both of these pages) was scanned at 4K resolution and cropped vertically to a 16:9 aspect ratio. The full frame aspect ratio would make the image about an inch taller than this page. The next smaller image was scanned at 2K resolution at full frame aspect ratio. The next smaller image is an HDTV video frame, 1920x1180. The next smaller image is an NTSC standard video frame, 720x486. The smallest image is 320x240, commonly used in multimedia and the Internet. The largest standard 35mm film format, VistaVision, scanned at 6K resolution, would be roughly three of these pages wide and two pages tall.

320×240

NTSC 720×486

HDTV 1920×1180

2K full frame 2048×1536

4K 16:9 4096×2304

Case Study 6.2:
On The Set For The Jarong Cobra
by Dylan Crooke

A frame from the raw live footage, showing markers.

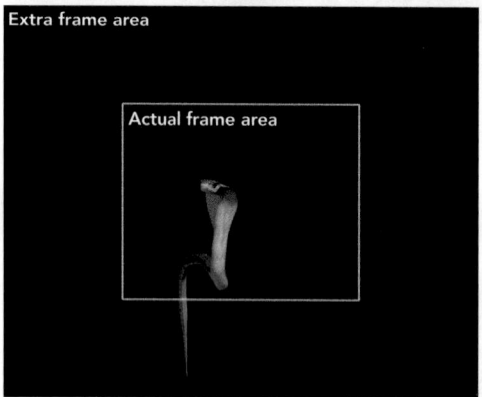

A snake character rendered with the alpha channel.

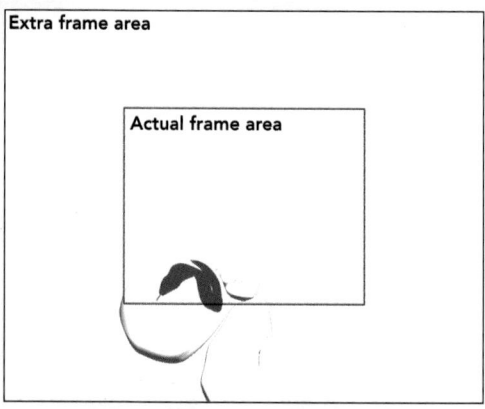

Grayscale image rendered for shadow layer in the final composite

The final composite. For details, see pages 108 through 111.

Bluescreen set clean background plate (see Figure 7.13).

A baseline RGB image (see Figure 7.2).

Same set as background plate, with actor, props, and set dressing to be composited (see Figure 7.14).

A frame from the Fire0000.jpg image sequence (see Figure 8.12).

Difference matte, subjects extracted from clean plate (see Figure 7.15).

The top image shows the original background image; the middle shows the luma key composited flames over the background image; the bottom shows a frame from the Ceiling Fire clip from Artbeats Digital Film Library. The black background makes these clips easy to composite using luma keying (see Figure 7.12).

Examples Of Filter Effects

Outlined area of baseline image enlarged to show detail.

Median filter applied to baseline image.

Impulse filter applied to baseline image.

Sharpen filter applied to baseline image.

Gaussian filter applied to baseline image.

Mitchell filter applied to baseline image.

Sinc filter applied to baseline image.

An aliased image.

An anti-aliased image.

Excessive JPEG compression artifacts.

Ringing caused by oversharpening the baseline image.

Banding caused by reducing the color depth of baseline image without dithering or adaptive resampling.

Figure 1: A close-up of a scanned film image showing film grain (see Figure 5.9).

Figure 2: The same magnification of a telecined image from the same footage (see Figure 5.9).

Actor filmed against bluescreen background for use in chroma key compositing (see Figure 7.11).

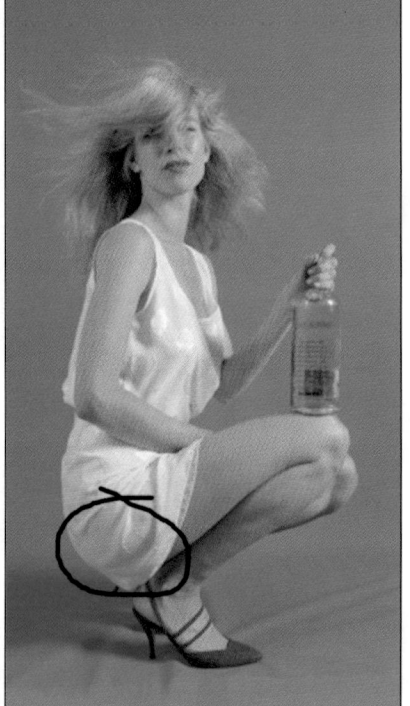

Blue spill or light reflected from the bluescreen backdrop (see Figure 6.1).

Clean bluescreen key on left half of the image, fringing or matte line on right (see Figure 7.39).

Left; the actress's left leg is partially transparent (arrow), indicating too broad a range in the matte threshold. Right; a corrected Matte Threshold fixes the problem (see Figure 8.22).

Left; the gauze is too opaque. Right; a corrected Matte Gamma fixes the problem (see Figure 8.23).

Left; fringe problems occur along hard edges (arrow) and in the hair. Right; the Fringe Gamma control is set to 6.0 (see Figures 8.24 and 8.25).

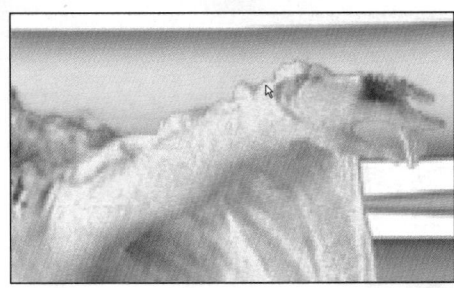 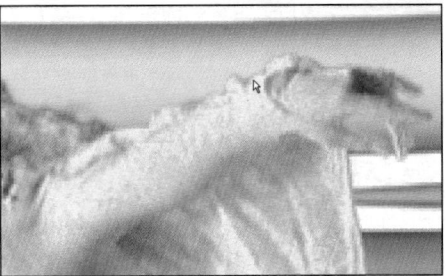

Left; the Fringe Size is set to 0.0. Right; the Fringe Size is set to 0.3 (see Figure 8.26).

Examples Of Compression Ratios

Frame 53 from sample footage, at 2X magnification.

Half-size AVI clip, as it appears in Microsoft Internet Explorer (left) and Netscape Navigator (right) browsers.

720x486 Cinepak AVI clip, compressed at a ratio of 368:1 for LAN bandwidth of 150Kbps, plays at 11.6fps. Note that compression artifacts are large enough to blot out most facial features, and the corner logo is illegible, while portions of the background that do not move show some fine detail.

720x486 Cinepak AVI, compressed at a ratio of 2700:1 for 28.8 modem bandwidth of 20Kbps, plays at 9.7fps. This clip is a waste of time and effort; all you can see are some colored blurs. It's not possible to push full-frame video through a 28.8 modem because the compression ratio goes so high above the 500:1 limit for acceptable video.

320x216 Cinepak-compressed AVI, compressed at a ratio of 154:1 for LAN bandwidth of 150Kbps, plays at 17.4fps. While fine details are still lost to compression artifacts, this is an acceptable video quality and frame rate for most Internet viewing.

320x216 Cinepak-compressed AVI, compressed at a ratio of 542:1 for 28.8 modem bandwidth of 20Kbps, plays at 10.8fps. Again, compression higher than 500:1 is unacceptable.

720x486 uncompressed AVI clip, resized to 640x480 and compressed at a ratio of 450:1 for LAN bandwidth of 150Kbps, plays at 12.6fps. The image is overwhelmed by artifacts, only gross movement is visible. Faces are nearly featureless blobs, and the corner logo is almost undetectable.

720x486 uncompressed AVI clip, resized to 320x216 and compressed at a ratio of 146:1 for LAN bandwidth of 150Kbps, plays at 16.7fps. Note that simply resizing the clip allows for much more detail and lower compression ratio for a given bandwidth. The corner logo is nearly legible, and facial features and background details are discernable.

Dissolve Example

Frame 0

Frame 25

Frame 50

Mask, restricting animated Dissolve operation (showing frames 0, 25, and 50). See Figure 7.20.

Results Of Various Compression Methods

Frame 53 of uncompressed AVI at 2X magnification.

Frame 53 of 150Kbps MPEG-1 based on uncompressed AVI, at 2X magnification.

Frame 53 of Cinepak-compressed AVI, 95% quality, at 2X magnification.

Frame 53 of MPEG-1 compressed for delivery at 500Kbps.

Frame 53 of Microsoft Video 1-compressed AVI, 95% quality, at 2X magnification.

Frame 53 of QuickTime video compressed with Cinepak codec at 95% quality, at 2X magnification.

Frame 53 of QuickTime video compressed with Sorenson codec at 95% quality, at 2X magnification.

Frame 53 of QuickTime video compressed with DV codec, at 2X magnification.

Working With Credits Text

A flow showing the addition of a Glow tool to create a black outline for the Text tool (see Figure 8.65).

Background, Channel Booleans, and Merge 2 tools are added to change the outline color of the text glow to a bright green (see Figure 8.66).

Working With Credits Text *(continued)*

Double-blurred text comped over live background (see Figure 8.71).

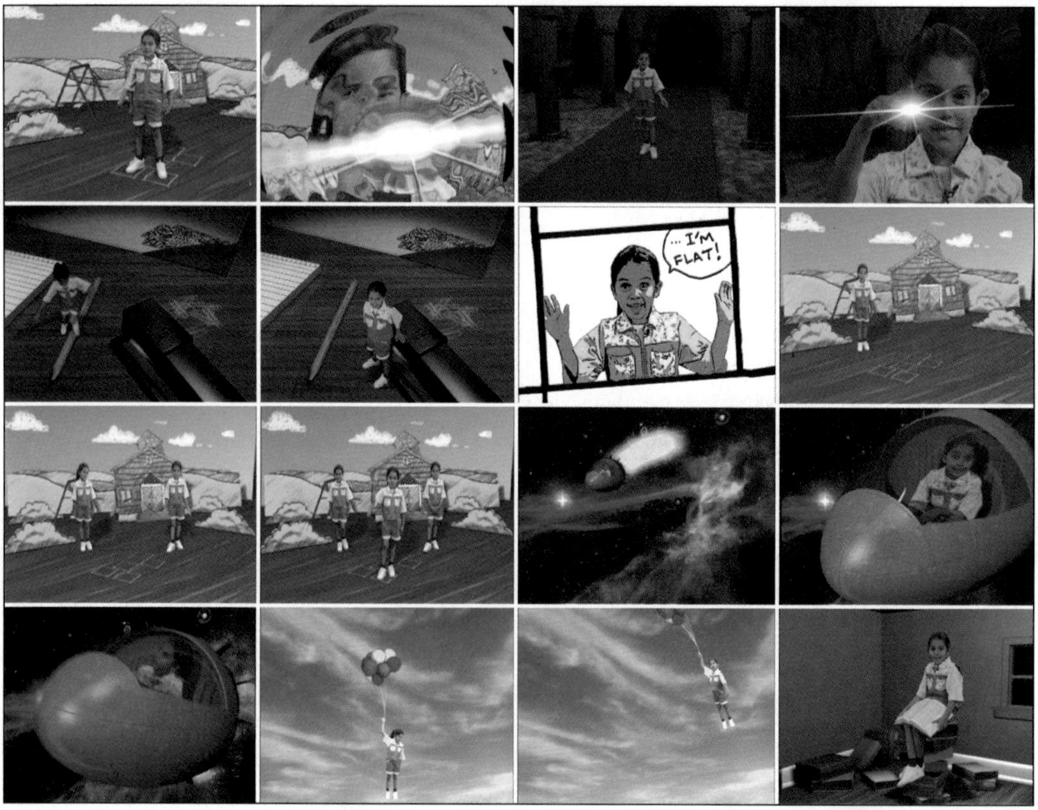

Images from Case Study 9.1, Frantic Films' *Just A Minute* by Christopher Bond.

Original red-and-blue image with anti-aliased transition (see Figure 9.4).

Rougher, aliased transition resulting from 4:2:2 sampling in the YUV format (see Figure 9.3).

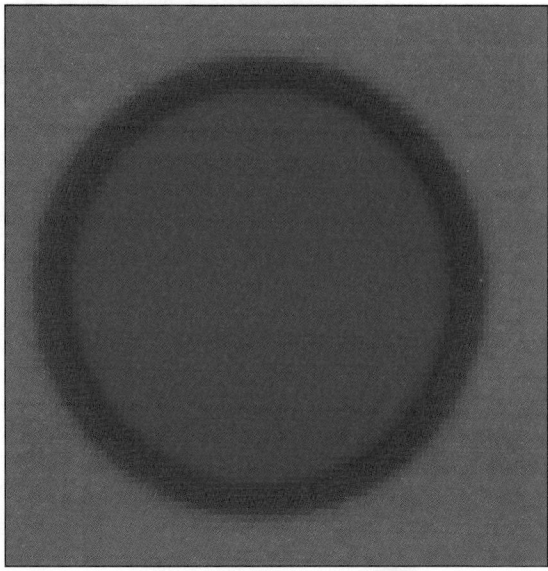

Antialiased transition resulting from sequence of YUV-to-RGB-to-Custom-to-RGB-to-YUV filters (see Figure 9.3).

Ultimatte tool finishes bluescreen comp (see Figure 9.17).

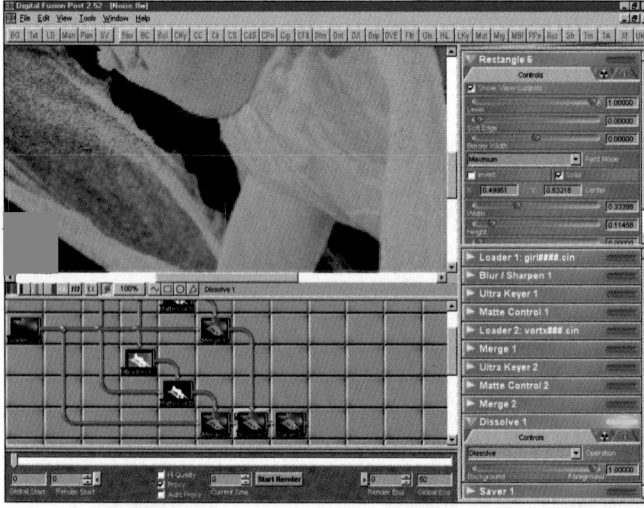

Comparison flow with Dissolve and Effect Mask (see Figure 9.22).

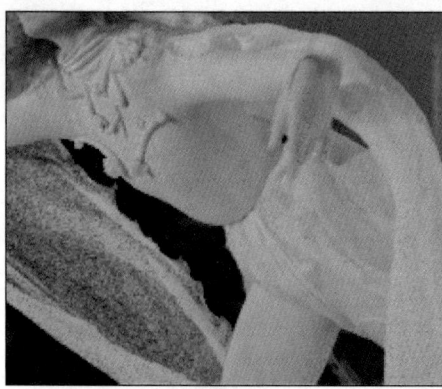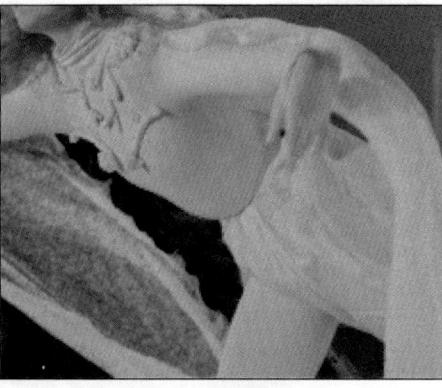

Comp of noisy bluescreen matte extracted without blur, left, and with blur, right (see Figure 9.20).

Large display shows film image. Small display shows telecined video image of same subject (see Figure 9.25).

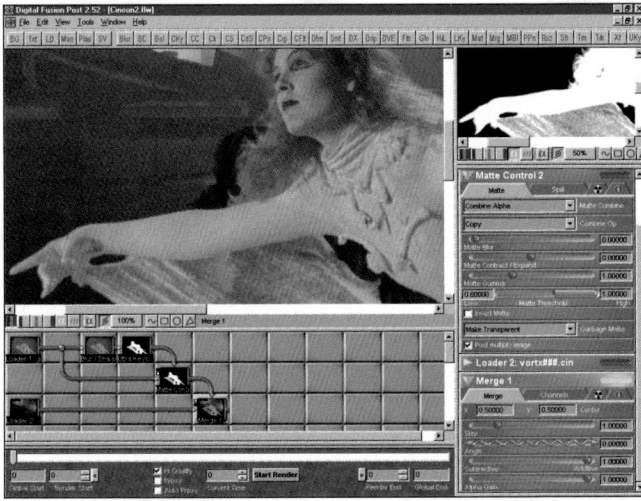

Matte Control and Merge settings. Large display shows part of the final comp, small display shows the matte (see Figure 9.27).

Zbig plug-in, in Digital Fusion (see Figure 9.35).

Rook removal: The Ellipse 1 effect mask, with Soft Edge enabled, limits the Merge operation to one white rook. Sixteen keyframes are set to keep the effect mask over the rook throughout camera motion (see Figure 10.7).

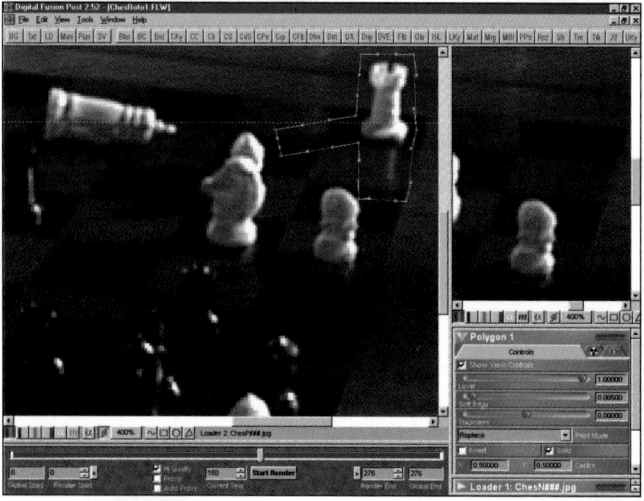

Rotoscoped rook removal: Clean plate footage is merged to remove the rook, its reflection, and shadow by the Merge 1 effect mask, Polygon 1, as shown in the small display (see Figure 10.16).

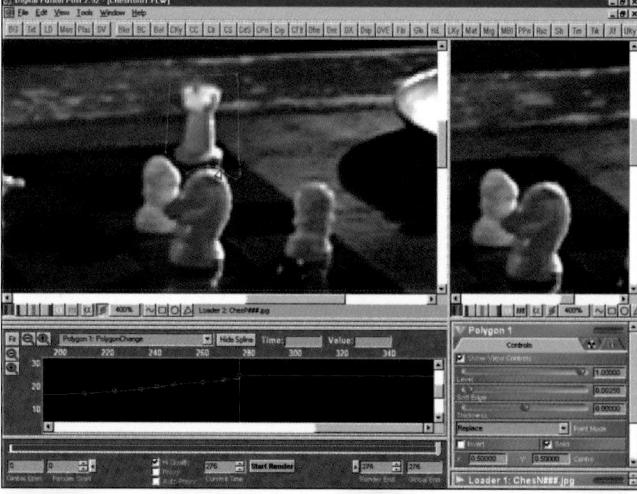

Effect mask points adjusted to remove rook, reflection, and shadow without affecting other objects (see Figure 10.22).

Case Study 2.1, *Sector Expander* commercial by Lee Strananhan. Final image showing the composited actor, set, and LightWave-rendered pods and alien. For details, see pages 28 through 32.

Above: Rendered frame from rotoscoped actor removal (see Figures 10.28).

Rotoscoped actor removal (left): Effect mask points are arranged to remove the second trooper (see Figure 10.27).

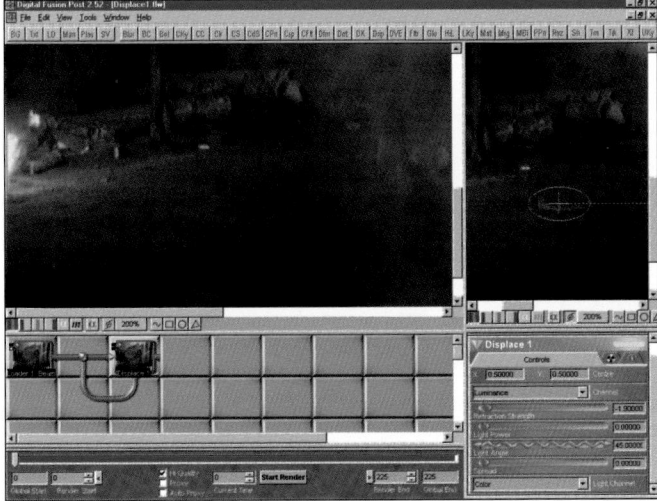

Time-shifting a clean plate: Displace warp tool with ellipse effect mask removing object from floor (see Figure 10.35).

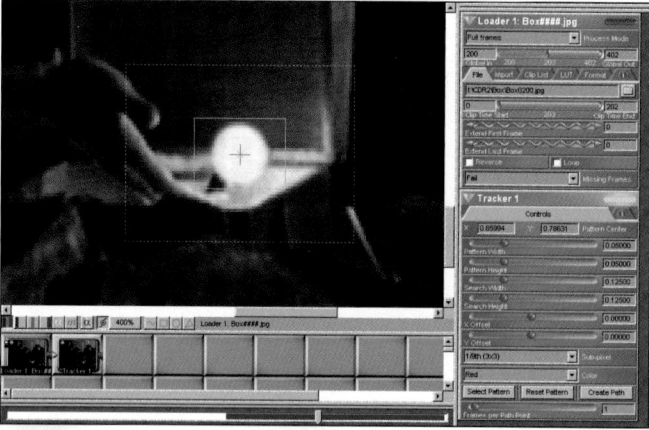

Tracker pattern selection crosshair positioned over light bulb in frame 285 (see Figure 11.5).

Clear, high-contrast pattern that will track easily and accurately (see Figure 11.3).

Muddy, low-contrast pattern that will tend to tracking loss or errors (see Figure 11.3).

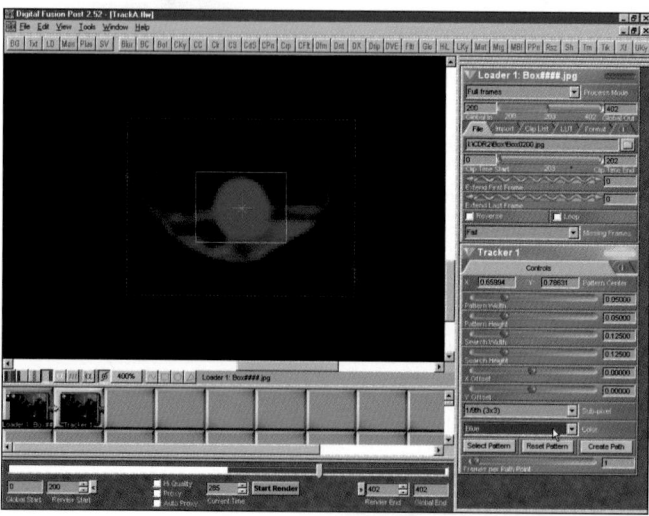

Large display and Tracker set to the blue channel for frame 285 (see Figure 11.6).

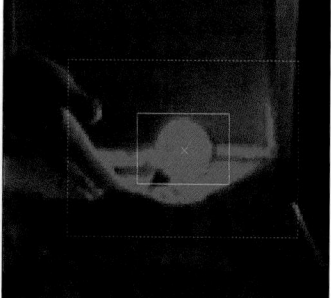

Red channel (see Figure 11.6).

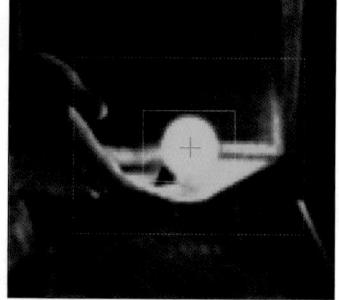

Green channel (see Figure 11.6).

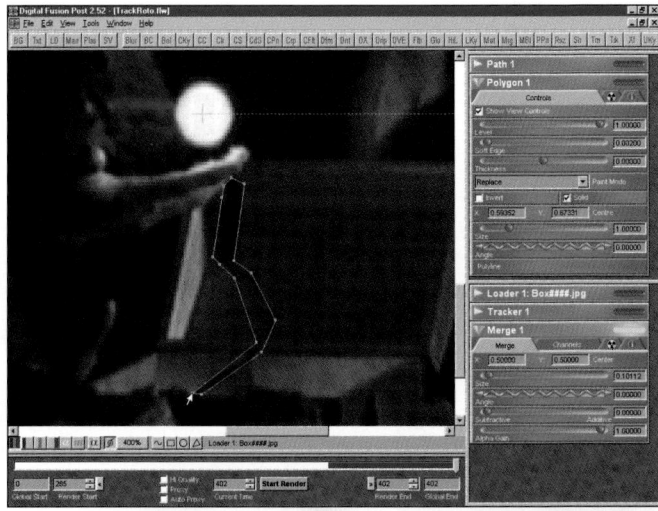

Polygon mask rotoscoped to remove light bulb wire (see Figure 11.10).

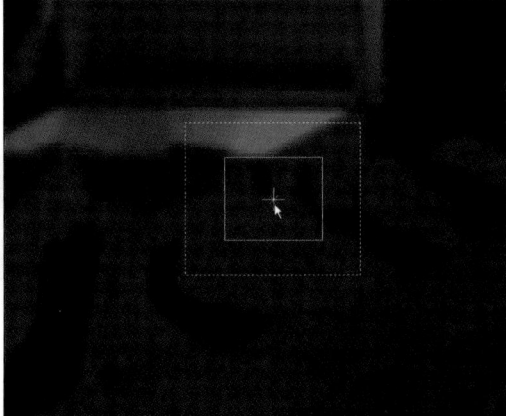

Tracker pattern selected for stabilizing Box footage (see Figure 11.14).

Every tenth frame from the Match footage (see Figure 11.2).

Frame 1, if corrected for scale and rotation to match frame 154, would only include the area inside the white rectangle. The image outside the rectangle would be lost (see Figure 11.22).

Salvaging Margins

The original frame (see Figure 11.24).

Uncropping image to triple resolution (see Figure 11.24).

Stabilized image with no margins or corners lost (see Figure 11.24).

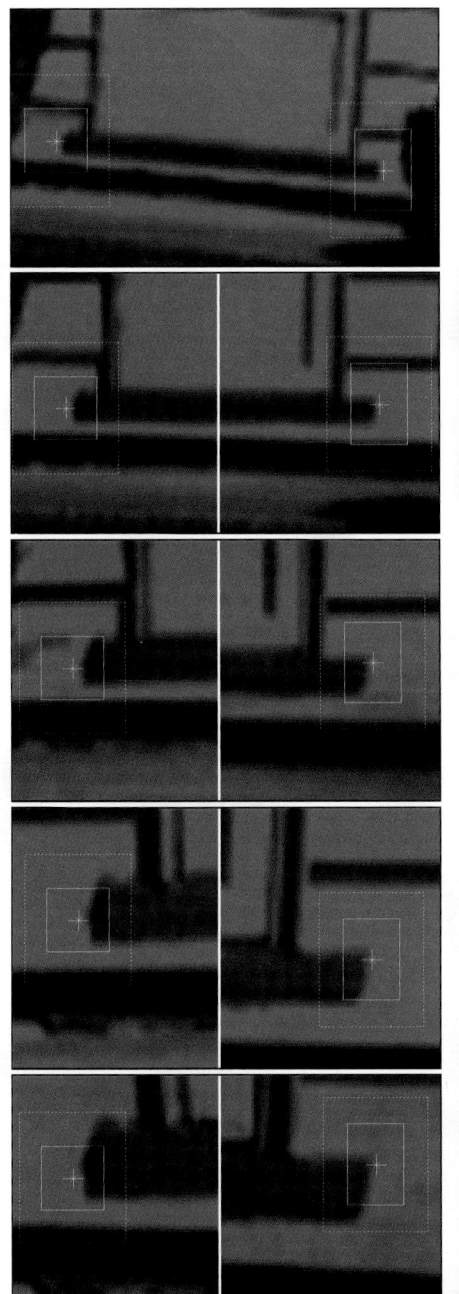

Large differences between beginning and ending tracking patterns require more than one Tracker operation.
Top to bottom: frames 1, 90, 154, 211, 265 (see Figure 11.30).

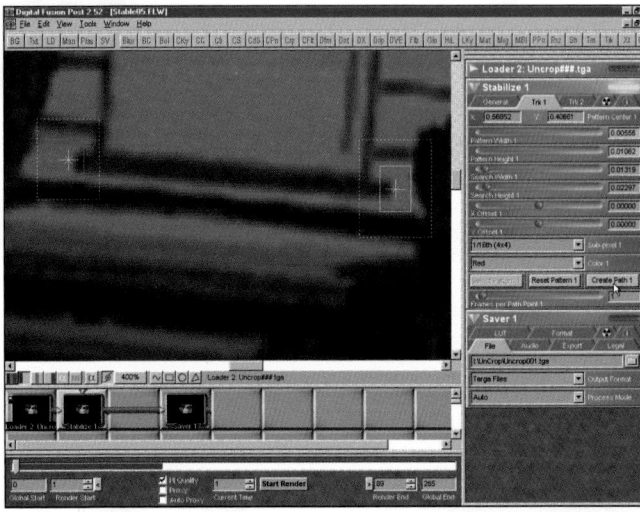

Tracker pattern selected for stabilizing frames 1 through 89 (see Figure 11.31).

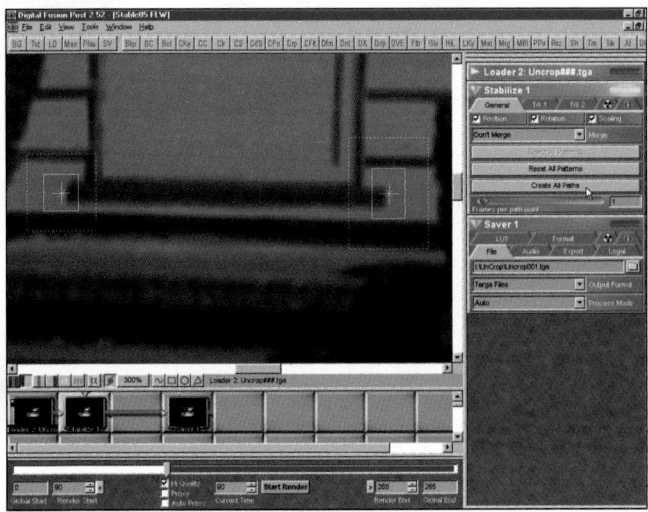

Tracker pattern selected for stabilizing frames 90 through 265 (see Figure 11.32).

Flow set up to Merge a clean plate from frames 203 and 220 of stabilized footage. Note that Loader 2's Extend First Frame is offset 17 frames in order to load image file 203 at frame 220 (see Figure 12.1).

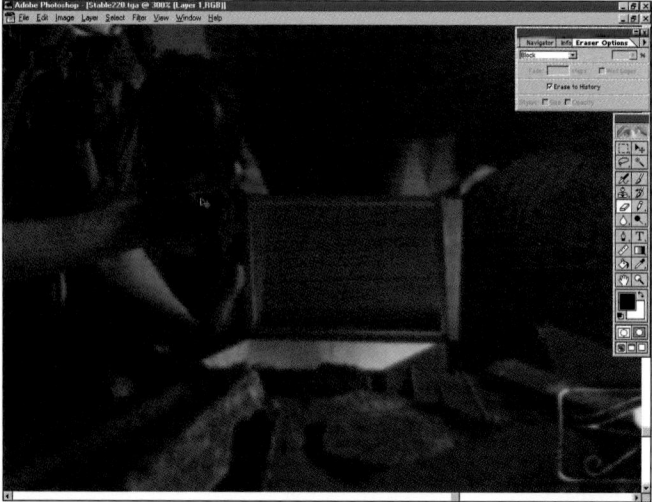

Clean plate for frame 200 created by Erase to History function in Photoshop (see Figure 12.2).

Clean plate for frame 200 created by Erase to History function in Photoshop (see Figure 12.3).

Clean plate for frame 356 created by Erase to History function in Photoshop (see Figure 12.4).

Flow showing rotoscoped wire removal in frame 365, using a Merge to the clean background plate from Figure 12.4 (see Figure 12.5).

Merge Center connected to Tracker Unsteady Position destabilizes the effects footage to precisely match the movement of the original Box footage (see Figure 12.11).

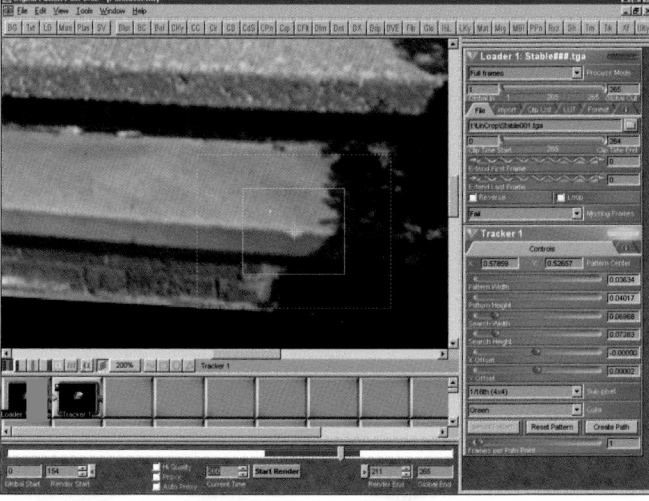

Tracker pattern defined around chip in second step at frame 200 (see Figure 12.14).

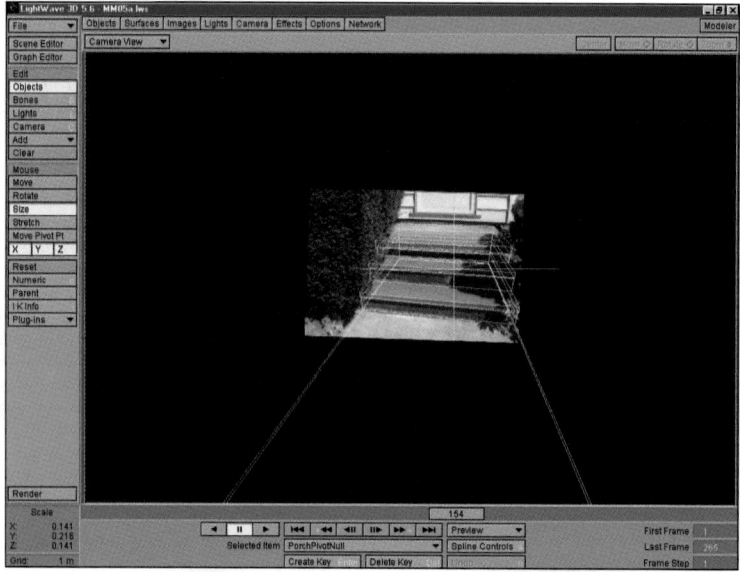

Porch aligned, and PorchPivotNull and OriginNull scaled to match background in frame 154 (see Figures 12.22 and 12.23).

Rendered test of frame 154. Note how blue polygon edges make evaluating the match much easier (see Figure 12.24).

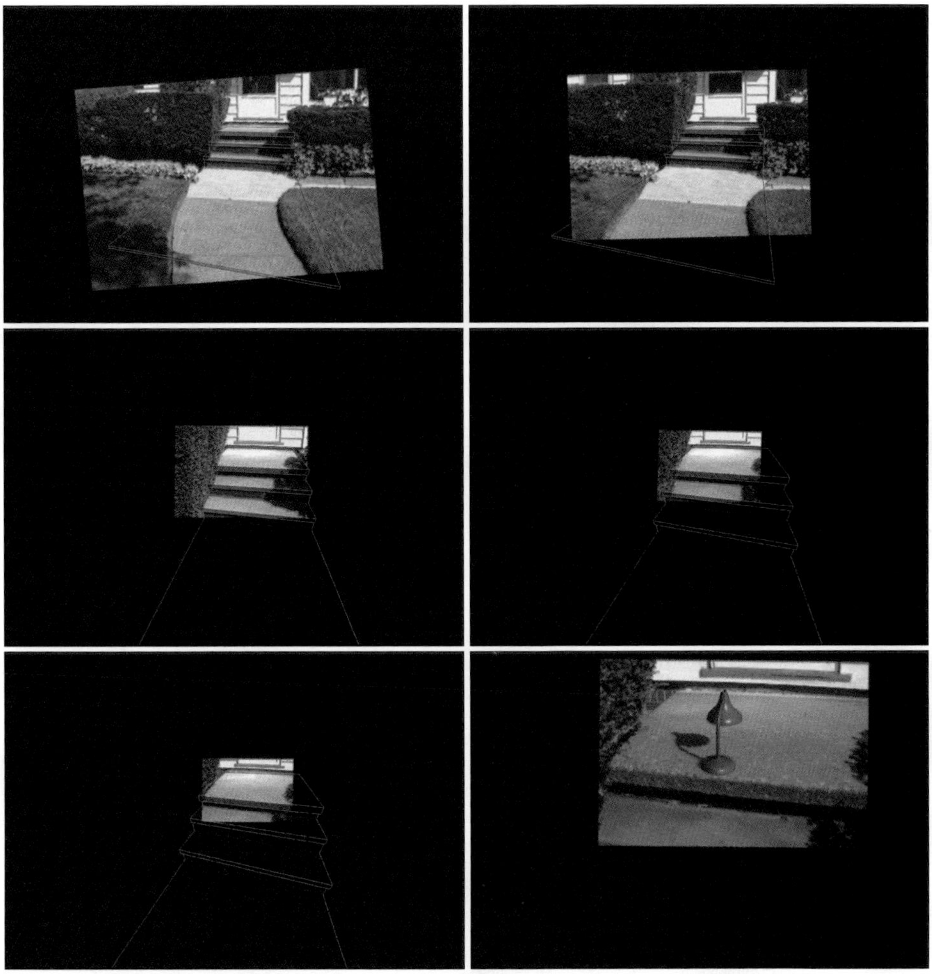

Test renderings of frames 1, 75, 180, 211, 231, and 265 (top to bottom), as shown in Figures 12.26 and 12.28.

Original footage, with destabilized effects footage Additive Merged over it (see Figure 12.33).

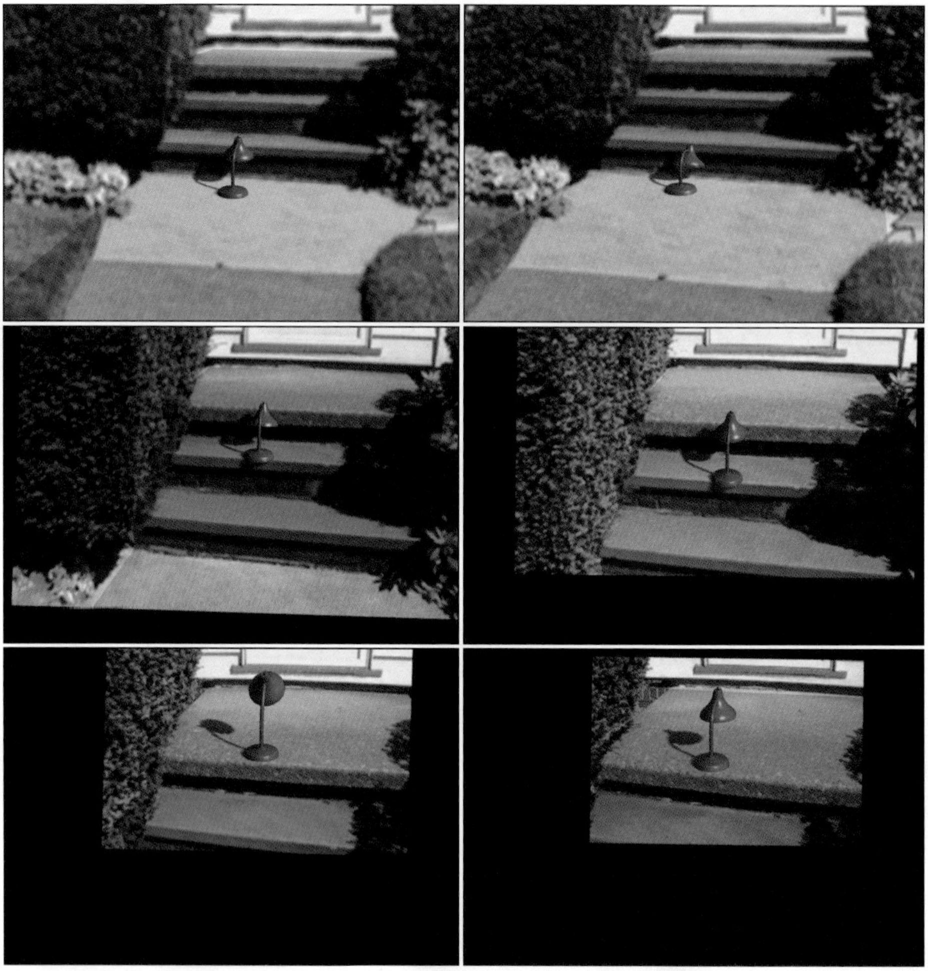

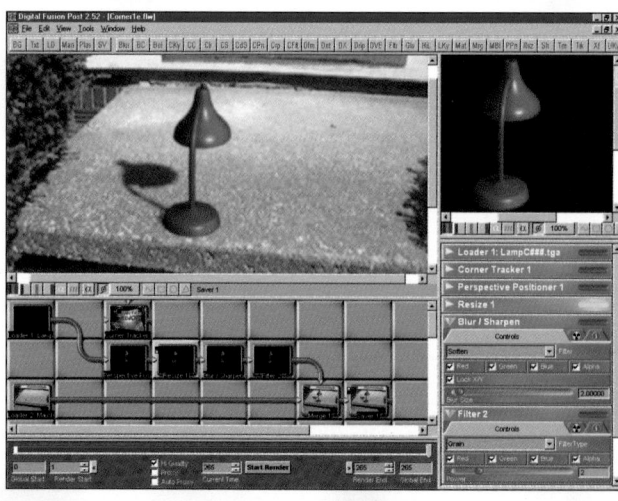

Final renderings of frames 1, 75, 180, 154, 211, and 265 with animated desk lamp and sun light added. Images are cropped to 720×486 to show detail; the full images are still 2160×1458 (see Figure 12.28).

Slight blur and grain filters added to CGI elements to match blur and noise in original footage (see Figure 12.34).

Time Speed tool configured to create missing frame by interpolating from neighboring frames (see Figure 13.3).

A non-saving branch with Color Gain and Brightness/Contrast tools added to mimic an NTSC broadcast monitor's color balance. Note that the large display shows the simulated color balance and the small display shows the Saver's actual output (see Figure 13.10).

A single frame from the Match footage on the first CD-ROM shows neutral surfaces in the concrete sidewalk, stair treads, and porch, and in the white-vinyl siding and gray-painted threshold, in contrast to the deep greens of grass and shrubbery (see Figure 13.11).

A standard color bar reference image (see Figure 13.13) to be appended to the beginning of composited NTSC video footage. Both this image and 13.12 are on the first CD-ROM, in folder Refs.

A color reference image to be appended to the beginning of composited film footage (see Figure 13.12).

Reference image 13.12 modified with a gamma of 1.7. Note that the darkest and lightest areas have not been crushed or clipped; only the midlevels have been boosted (see Figure 13.14).

The Brightness/Contrast tool's output run through a Saver for an NTSC legality check. The small display shows the illegal areas in white; the large display shows the illegal areas almost completely eliminated with very small adjustments to the Brightness and Contrast sliders (see Figure 13.25).

A Background tool added to a flow in order to sample and compare two colors. Note the eyedropper cursor over the Background's upper Pick button (see Figure 13.18).

A familiar NTSC television color adjustment problem, faked by converting from RGB to YIQ color space and using the Color Corrector tool to clip the I or red-cyan color channel (see Figure 13.20).

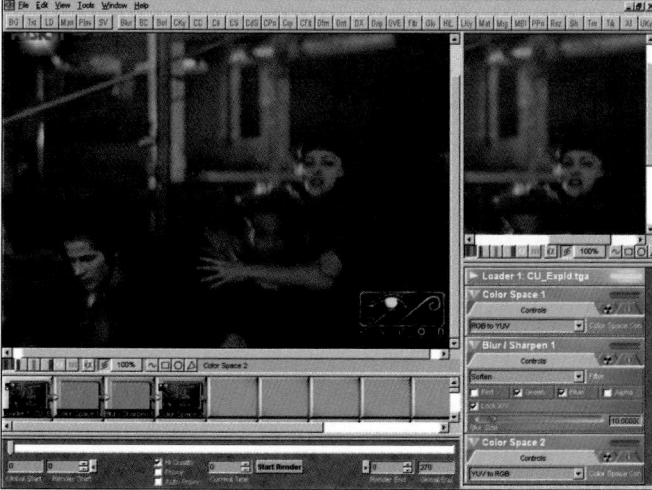

Left; the small display shows part of the original image, the large display shows a level 10.0 blur applied only to the UV channels. Right; The same level 10.0 blur as in the example to the left, applied to all three YUV channels (see Figure 13.21).

Color Studio Case Study: *The Siege* Schoolroom Shot

by Brad Carvey

I used Digital Fusion to composite four shots for a scene in *The Siege*. Joe Conti created some CGI helicopters to "fly by" a schoolroom window. The live action footage had interesting problems that complicated the helicopter and background additions. The flow for this project was simple; the complexity lay in tweaking the controls and adding the moving effect masks.

Figure 1: A frame from live-action footage showing blue spill around window frame.

First, light reflected from the bluescreen illuminated the window frame and all objects near the window. I had to remove the blue spill and replace it with white, simulated sunlight. The blue spill on the Venetian blinds, although difficult, was removed with an UltraKeyer, using maximum Well Done spill suppression, masked to window areas to prevent interference with other blue surfaces. I used a Brightness/Contrast tool to simulate sunlight, again masking it to only the window area.

Figure 2: The background image created by Joe Conti.

Next, the camera position and focus continuously changed, and because the camera was shaking, the background image had to shake in sync. Otherwise, the helicopters would seem to move erratically in the air. I tracked camera shake with DF's single-point Tracker, and connected the background and CGI helicopter elements through Transforms to the Tracker path to mimic camera motion. I also connected the effect masks to this path.

Figure 3: Frame from the final composite, showing CGI helicopter.

Third, the window frame went out of focus, so it was hard to extract a matte. Also, CGI and background elements had to be processed with an animated Blur/Sharpen tool to match the changing camera focus in the live shot, and the background image had to be altered with a Brightness/Contrast tool to simulate sunlight.
bradcarvey@hotmail.com

PART IV

INTERMEDIATE
COMPOSITING

CHAPTER 10

THERE'S WHAT IN THE FRAME?

One of the most common problems to be solved by digital compositors is the removal of people or objects that show up where they shouldn't. Safety rigging, boom microphones held too low, a grip's foot or hand, or the shadow of a production assistant can all go unnoticed until the set is struck and the most expensive talent has gone home. That makes a little post-production fix— which is your job—the most cost-effective solution. In special circumstances (such as the late Brandon Lee's tragic death during filming of *The Crow*), the ability to remove, replace, and insert people and objects can make the difference between a finished film and an abandoned film.

Not all removal problems are the result of oversights or mistakes. Most competent directors, and all experienced visual effects supervisors, have a very good idea of what digital compositors can and can't do. That means most shots that will call for digital compositing effects are planned and shot to work within your limits. However, the demands of the action film market also mean that directors will try to get every bit of the audience's adrenaline pumping, and that means more stunts, more rigging, and more removal work for you and your colleagues. That's why this type of work is called *rig removal*, even when you're removing something other than safety rigging.

If part of the production calls for bluescreen effects, the rigging can be painted with the same backing color. Most of the bluescreen rig removal can be accomplished with the keying techniques described in Chapters 8 and 9. However, a location shoot, expansive shot, lighting difficulties, or a rig that just won't take paint can all rule out bluescreen rig removal. That's when your work gets interesting. There are other digital compositing tools that can help with the simpler forms of rig removal, and I'll describe most of them later in this chapter. Sooner or later, though, you will be handed a rig removal shot that the specialized software can't handle. Your final recourse will always be a trained eye and a steady hand to paint out the offending rig one frame at a time. If you can do that, you never need to worry about being replaced by a computer.

269

Rig removal is an apparently simple but surprisingly demanding part of digital compositing. Rigging to be removed is sometimes part of a prop or set, but more often it is attached or interacting with a live actor or stuntman, so you'll have no clean transition lines and no easy choices as to where the rig ends and the actor begins. This translates into requiring your judgment when hand-painting the rig and keeping that judgment almost perfectly consistent from frame to frame. If the difference between one frame and the next is a single pixel's width, and the following frame is that same pixel's width back in the other direction, your audience will see *chatter*. Chattering is a temporal, or time-based, artifact of a roughly applied operation that fluctuates in a repeating pattern. This is a common artifact of hand-drawn film effects, including traditional cel animation. However, your job is to seamlessly and undetectably mimic reality. Line chatter may be acceptable, even stylish, for *Dr. Katz* or *Beavis and Butthead*. For live-action rig removal, however, you need perfect consistency in every frame of your comps.

Rig Removal With A Clean Plate

If you have a clean plate, you can apply a Dissolve or Merge tool with a simple mask to remove any foreground element. This is the simplest, fastest kind of rig removal and is yet another compelling reason to shoot a clean plate whenever possible.

Case Study 10.1
Out of Screen for Oakhurst Milk

By Eric Jurgenson, Technical Supervisor, The Video Workshop

This job required a simple rig removal with a clean plate, using After Effects. The job was a milk commercial for Oakhurst Milk. The script described a woman sitting in front of her computer, visiting the dairy's Web site. All this surfing is making her thirsty, so "magically" a glass of milk jumps off the computer screen and into her hand. She then takes a drink.

Initially, we considered doing a 3D model of the glass and matching the animation to the live action, but the complications involved with her gripping the glass and then drinking soon got us thinking in other directions. The idea we came up with was to use a real glass attached to a rod with a pivot that would allow us to pass the glass of milk through a "gutted" computer monitor, and yet allow the actress to grab the glass and drink.

Because this was a lockdown shot, it was an easy matter to shoot a clean plate of the set, and to remove the rod in After Effects. Finally, we added a few sparkles to the trail of the glass to enhance the feeling of magic. To make the sequence more believable, on the previous shot (a close-up of the screen) we did create a 3D model of the glass emerging from the screen toward the viewer. This was embellished with glow effects, highlights, and reflections of the environment (taken from a reverse angle shot of the actress).

A frame from the finished *Out of Screen* ad.

A frame from a closer shot, showing that the rod supporting the glass has been completely removed.

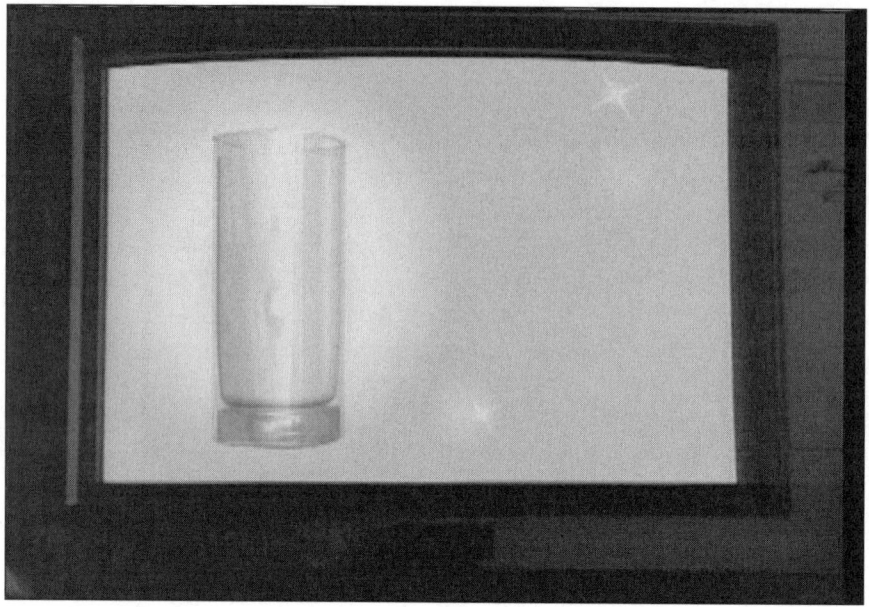

A frame showing the 3D glass emerging from the computer screen.

Graphic artist: Paul Haley
Technical supervisor: Eric Jurgenson
The Video Workshop
495 Forest Avenue
Portland, Maine 04101
207-774-7798

About The Footage

The chessboard footage used in this chapter's projects was set up, lit, photographed, and digitized by Chris Nibley (**www.nibley.com**) using one of his motion-control camera rigs. This is a powered and computer-controlled rig (refer to Figure 6.9 and the bottom center of Figure 6.10 in Chapter 6) that can repeat precisely the same move time after time. This equipment enables you to shoot several takes that will register perfectly for compositing. Figure 6.10 shows the chessboard set up and lit; you can also see one end of the motion control rig at the bottom center of this figure.

The ChesP sequence was shot with chess pieces arranged on the table (see Figure 10.1), and the ChesN sequence was shot as a clean background plate without the chess pieces (see Figure 10.2). This enables you to use the ChesN sequence as a clean plate for a rig removal of excess chess pieces. Both shots used precisely the same camera move—a complex orbit, beginning high and

Figure 10.1
Frame 276 from ChesP motion-control footage, showing chess pieces.

Figure 10.2
Frame 276 from the ChesN motion-control footage, without chess pieces. This is the clean background plate for the ChesP footage.

to the right of the chessboard and finishing lower and to the left of center of the board, with smooth acceleration and deceleration of the camera and no change in the lens settings. This exact duplication of a complex camera move enables you to use the ChesN sequence as a clean plate for a rig removal of excess chess pieces.

PROJECT 10.1   Rig Removal With An Effect Mask

The goal of this project is to remove a single foreground element by using a clean plate and a simple effect mask. These are the most basic tasks in rig removal and are used every day by professional digital compositors.

1. Open a new flow. Add two Loaders. Load the ChesN footage in Loader 1 and the ChesP footage in Loader 2.

2. Add a Merge or Dissolve tool. Connect Loader 1 to the foreground input and Loader 2 to the background input. Set the Merge controls to maximum Alpha Gain and full Subtractive. This will enable the Merge tool to replace the chess piece footage with the no-pieces footage.

3. Select the Merge tool. Set the Large display to the Merge tool and the Small display to Loader 2. Right-click on the Large display, and check Options|Show Controls from the pop-up menu. Do the same for the Small display, but uncheck the Show Controls option. This will enable you to see and manipulate the effect mask in the Large display and leave the Small display clear for you to see the results.

4. Make sure that you are in frame 0. With the Merge tool still selected, right-click on the Large display and choose Effect Mask|Ellipse from the pop-up menu to create a new Ellipse 1 effect mask. Press F10 or choose View|Show Mask View to view the Ellipse 1 controls.

5. Set Paint Mode to Replace. Using either the Ellipse 1 controls or the mouse, move the center of the effect mask over the white rook standing in the upper right corner of the chessboard. Adjust the width and height of the ellipse to just cover the rook and its shadow and reflection. Your results should look like Figure 10.3. Remember, if you want to successfully remove an object from a scene, you have to also remove any secondary evidence of that object's presence. Leaving stray reflections, shadows, or strong radiosity signatures is sloppy workmanship.

Take a close look at the Small display. If you compare the straight edges of the chessboard and the seam in the table, you'll see that the straight lines jog a little at the borders of the ellipse. This shows that there is a small misalignment between the foreground and background footage. This is common; even the most precise motion-control camera rigs aren't perfect to within a pixel. You need to be prepared to deal with these kinds of problems. Fortunately, the solution isn't very difficult.

Figure 10.3
Ellipse 1 effect mask limits the Merge operation to single white rook.

6. Because there was a very slight X-axis error in the motion-control rig, you need to add a Transform tool between Loader 1 and the Merge tool, and you need to change the X Center setting of the Transform tool from 0.50000 to 0.49500.

Your results should look like Figure 10.4. Note that the straight edges line up perfectly now.

GOING SOFT

Sometimes a badly misaligned clean plate can defy all efforts to realign it perfectly. If you can get the plate to align within a pixel or two, you can often conceal the problem by increasing the effect mask's Soft Edge setting. This action won't completely fix the discrepancy, but it will make the mismatch harder to spot. If, however, the shot is short or the subject and background are moving fast, it's often good enough.

Figure 10.4

A Transform tool is used to offset the clean plate on the X-axis to align more accurately with the chess piece footage. Note the lack of jagged lines in the Small display.

If this project were a lock-down shot, you'd be done. However, the point of using motion-control footage is that the camera moves. This means the Ellipse 1 effect mask has to move too, in order to continue to cover the white rook without covering any other chess pieces. Animating an effect mask is essentially the same process that you followed to animate the Pan Transform in Project 8.8.

7. Position the mouse cursor over the center of Ellipse 1's crosshair in the Large display. A small pop-up label should appear, reading Ellipse Center. This means you can select Ellipse 1's Center control. Right-click, and choose Ellipse 1 Center|Path (see Figure 10.5).

8. Open the Spline View (F8). Note that there is already a keyframe on frame 0 for the new path. Go to frame 276. Move the Ellipse to cover the white rook again. Note that a new keyframe is automatically added to the path. You may find that you have to change the

Figure 10.5
Ellipse 1 Center|Path is selected.

dimensions or Soft Edge of Ellipse 1 to remove the rook cleanly without removing part of the chess pieces in front of it. Your results should look like Figure 10.6.

9. Go back to frame 0 to make sure that none of your changes to Ellipse 1 have affected the rook's removal at frame 0. Reposition Ellipse 1 if necessary.

10. Go to frame 138, halfway between 0 and 276. You should be able to see that the straight-line path between the keyframed positions at frames 0 and 276 does not accurately describe the motion of the white rook around the screen. The motion-control camera was moving in an *orbit*, an elliptical pattern roughly centered on the table. The rook's perceived motion is roughly an inverse of that orbit. In any case, a two-keyframe straight line won't work, so you need to add more keyframes. To do this, you need to change the Path mode.

11. Right-click on the Ellipse 1: Center Crosshair, and choose Path 1|Insert And Modify from the pop-up menu. This mode enables you to reposition Ellipse 1 on any frame, automatically creating a new keyframe or modifying an existing one.

Figure 10.6
Ellipse 1 has been moved and resized, and has had a Soft Edge applied, at frame 276.

12. Right-click on the Ellipse 1: Center Crosshair, and choose Path 1|Linear. This makes the path follow a straight line from one keyframe to the next. The Smooth interpolation can cause odd looping behavior if you add too many keyframes, but it is useful for some kinds of animation. You can always change path keyframes from Smooth to Linear with the pop-up menu, or by pressing Shift+L for Linear or Shift+S for Smooth.

13. Still on frame 138, move Ellipse 1 to remove the white rook again.

14. Go to frame 69, halfway between 0 and 138. Move Ellipse 1 to remove the white rook again.

Do you see the pattern here? This is what is called *bracketing* a solution. You add each new keyframe halfway between the existing ones. Every time you split a segment of the path in half, you also split the size of any potential errors in half. Pretty quickly, you find that the errors have grown so small that you don't need to add any more keyframes. This is a good approach for most examples of keyframe animation. Even if the final solution ends up having a key on every frame, this bracketing approach reduces the amount of correction you have to apply to each frame.

Figure 10.7
Sixteen keyframes were set for the Ellipse 1 effect mask in order to remove the rook from every frame.

15. Keep adding keyframes and making corrections until the white rook is removed from every frame. You should end up with a path like that shown in Figure 10.7.

Note that some keyframes are closer together and others are farther apart. If you have to work around tight areas, as when the rook is directly above and behind the other pieces, you will need to set more keyframes. In other parts of the shot, the rook has plenty of open space around it so the effect mask doesn't have to be placed so precisely. In this example, I used 16 keyframes; you may need more or less.

16. Make a Preview. The white rook should be completely invisible, including its shadow and reflection.

Unless you are very good at this, you will probably see a little chatter where the rook's base passes closely behind the white knight and pawns near the end of the sequence. You may also notice that the shadow of the rook passes across the corner of the adjoining square and that the Ellipse 1 effect mask doesn't really address the shadow's removal for most of this shot.

17. Save your composition as ChesPath.flw. You'll be reusing it in other projects.

You just completed a simple rig removal. In this project, you learned how to:

- Apply an effect mask to remove a foreground object
- Compensate for minor discrepancies in a motion-control clean plate
- Animate an effect mask to match the movement of a removal subject
- Bracket keyframes to simplify and speed up hand-keyed animation
- Use Soft Edge to blend a removal seamlessly into the footage

Rig removal is one of the most basic, necessary, and common digital compositing tasks. In larger shops, the most junior compositors may comp rig removals exclusively until they've paid their dues and can move on to more creative work. Being able to comp rig removals quickly and well can keep you employed and grease your track to more challenging assignments.

Rig Removal With An Effect Mask (After Effects)

The goal of this After Effects-based version of Project 10.1 is to remove a single foreground element by using a clean plate and a simple mask.

1. Open a new project. Import the two JPEG image sequences from the ChessN and ChessP directories on the first CD-ROM.

2. Create a new composition and add both image sequences to it. Send the ChesN layer (the one without chess pieces) to the back.

3. Double-click on the ChesP layer (the one with the chess pieces) to open it in the Layer window. Change the Layer window magnification to 400 or 800 percent, and pan the window until the white rook in the upper right corner of the chessboard is centered in the window.

4. Choose the Ellipse tool from the toolbox. Drag out an ellipse mask to contain the white rook. Right-click on one of the mask control points, and choose Mode|Add from the pop-up menu. Right-click again, and select Inverse from the menu. This sets the ellipse to be transparent on the inside, allowing the background ChesN layer to show through, as shown in Figure 10.8. If you also want to remove the rook's reflection, you may want to stretch the bottom of the ellipse down a bit further. For a less obvious removal, set Mask Feather to 4 pixels to blur the mask's outline.

5. If you expand the ChesP layer in the Time Layout window, and then expand the Masks submenu to show the mask you just created, you can easily toggle the Inverse setting while examining the rook in the Composition window. If you look closely, you can see that the foreground and background layers are not perfectly aligned. This produces a slight but visible mismatch in the chessboard lines.

Figure 10.8
The ellipse mask removes the white rook from the foreground ChesP layer, replacing it with the ChesN background layer.

6. Expand the ChesN layer in the Time Layout window. Expand the Transform submenu. Select the Position setting, and change the X value from 360 to 357. Toggle the Inverse setting for the mask to observe the difference in alignment between foreground and background layers, as in Figure 10.9. Try other values for the X-axis position; 357 works for me, but your results may vary.

If this were a lock-down shot, you'd be done. However, the point of using motion-control footage is that the camera moves; the effect mask has to move too, in order to continue to cover the white rook without covering any other chess pieces.

7. If it isn't still open, open the ChesP layer in the Layer view. Drag-select all four control points for the ellipse mask.

8. Make sure that the Time Controls are set to the first frame and then in the Time Layout window, click on the stopwatch icon next to Mask Shape in the ChesP layer. This sets a keyframe for the current location of the mask.

Figure 10.9
Tweaking the ChesN layer Position X-axis value to fine-tune the alignment between the ChesP and ChesN layers.

9. Set the Time Controls to the last frame. In the Layer view, click-and-drag the mask to cover the rook. When you release the mask, it automatically creates a new keyframe at the current frame.

10. Go to the frame at five seconds and click-and-drag the mask to cover the rook again. Repeat until the mask covers the rook throughout the footage.

The rest of this process may be easier if you make the remaining keyframes on even frame numbers, for example, on each second mark. The idea is to split the difference between the keyframes that are already set. In general, this approach minimizes the number of keyframes you'll need to set to create an accurate motion path, as shown in Figure 10.10.

11. Step through or play back by using the Composition window, looking for frames where the rook is partially visible. Make corrections to the mask animation as necessary. After you are satisfied with the results, save the project as ChesPath.aep; you'll reuse it in other projects.

Figure 10.10
The mask shape is animated with 11 keyframes to remove the white rook.

Rig Removal With An Eraser (Aura)

The goal of this Aura-based version of Project 10.1 is to remove a single foreground element by using a clean plate. Because Aura 1.0 doesn't have advanced effect mask features, the easiest way to do this is by erasing the foreground element and allowing the clean plate to show through the erasure.

1. Open a new project. Import the two JPEG image sequences from the ChessN and ChessP directories on the first CD-ROM.

2. Bring the ChesP layer to the front. Go to frame 0. Choose the brush size you prefer.

3. Position the cursor over the white rook and hold down the right mouse button to enable the eraser. Move the cursor over the white rook, its shadow, and its reflection to erase them to the background ChesN layer.

4. Advance to the next frame and repeat step 3. Repeat until the rook has been erased from every frame.

Note that this process is much less forgiving and less flexible with respect to rig removal than is possible with other compositing software. If you need to do a lot of rig removal, you may want to consider using a more efficient program.

Rig Removal With An Effect Mask (Commotion)

The goal of this Commotion-based version of Project 10.1 is to remove a single foreground element by using a clean plate and a simple mask. This technique is well covered in the tutorials that are part of the Commotion manual. Rather than duplicate these tutorials here, I recommend that you work through the Commotion manual tutorials, and then apply what you learn there to remove the white rook from the ChesP footage.

Rig Removal With An Effect Mask (effect*)

The goal of this effect*-based version of Project 10.1 is to remove a single foreground element by using a clean plate and a simple mask.

1. Open a new project. Import the two JPEG image sequences from the ChessN and ChessP directories on the first CD-ROM. Send the ChesN layer (the one without chess pieces) to the back.

2. In the Main View window, zoom in until the magnification is 400 or 800 percent, and pan the window until the white rook in the upper right corner of the chessboard is centered in the window.

3. Select the ChesP layer. Choose Effects|Mask|Elliptical Mask. The Elliptical Mask window will appear.

4. In the Elliptical Mask window, click on Invert, set Feather to 1, and choose Replace from the combination mode menu. This makes the mask transparent in the first layer, allowing the second layer to show through.

5. Move and resize the elliptical mask to cover the white rook and its reflection. You should see the rook disappear in the Main View window. Your results should look like Figure 10.11.

6. Toggle the Invert setting in the Elliptical Mask window while examining the rook in the Main View window. If you look closely, you can see that the foreground and background layers are not perfectly aligned. This produces a slight but visible mismatch in the chessboard lines.

7. Expand the ChesN layer in the Timeline window. Expand the Transformation submenu. Double-click on the X Position setting, and change the X value from 0 to –3. Toggle the Invert setting for the mask to observe the difference in alignment between foreground and background layers. Try other values for the X-axis position; –3 works for me, but your results may vary.

If this were a lock-down shot, you'd be done. However, the point of using motion-control footage is that the camera moves. The effect mask has to move too, in order to continue to cover the white rook without covering any other chess pieces.

Figure 10.11

The mask for removing the white rook is visible in the Elliptical Mask window. The Timeline window shows the arrangement of the two layers. The Main View window shows the results.

8. Enlarge the Elliptical Mask window and zoom out until you can see most of the frame.

9. In the Timeline window, expand the ChesP layer, then the Effects, then the Elliptical Mask, and finally the Transformation. This reveals the X Position, Y Position, Scale X, and Scale Y parameters for the elliptical mask. These are the parameters you need to keyframe to keep the mask covering the rook.

10. Set the Frame Controls to the last frame. In the Elliptical Mask window, click-and-drag the mask to cover the rook again. When you release the mask, it automatically creates a new keyframe at the current frame. Adjust the X and Y scale of the mask if necessary. Your results should look like Figure 10.12.

11. Go to the middle frame and click-and-drag the mask to cover the rook again. Repeat until the mask covers the rook throughout the footage.

The rest of this process may be easier if you make the remaining keyframes on even frame numbers—for example, on each second mark. The idea is to split the difference between the

Figure 10.12
The mask for removing the white rook has been repositioned in the Elliptical Mask window at the last frame. Note the keyframes in the Timeline window.

keyframes that are already set. In general, this approach minimizes the number of keyframes you will need to set to create an accurate motion path.

12. Step through or play back using the Main View window, looking for frames where the rook is partially visible. Make corrections to the mask keyframes as necessary. After you are satisfied with the results, you should save the project as ChesPath.icp because you will reuse it in other projects.

Rig Removal With An Effect Mask (Shake)

The goal of this Shake-based version of Project 10.1 is to remove a single foreground element by using a clean plate and a simple mask. This technique is covered in the GUI tutorials that are part of the Shake 2.1 HTML documentation, which you can find in the Shake directory on this book's second CD-ROM. Rather than duplicate these tutorials here, I recommend that you work through the Shake GUI tutorials, then apply what you learn there to remove the white rook from the ChesP footage.

Rotoscoping

The original Rotoscope, patented by the Fleischer animation studio, was designed as a cel animation device that projected live-action film against the underside of an animation stand so the footage could be traced frame-by-frame by the animator. Because hand tracing cannot be perfectly steady, the lines tend to chatter. Because the animator is not allowed to tweak timing or pose to create a better performance, the result is usually very bad animation. Ralph Bakshi's *Fire and Ice* is a prime example. The term *rotoscoping* has been misapplied to nearly any digital effects process that requires frame-by-frame manual matching to live footage. The most commonly accepted use for the term in digital compositing is the manual matching of the outline of a mask, matte, or CG element to the outline of a live-action element. Masking the outline of an actor to separate him from a noisy background is a typical rotoscoping job.

The same drawbacks apply to digital versions of rotoscoping as they do to the original Rotoscope. Successfully rotoscoping a mask control requires both precision in the two dimensions of the initial frame, and consistency in the third dimension of time across subsequent frames. Any hand work that is not perfectly steady will create a condition known as *chatter*, a time-based artifact that fluctuates in a repeating pattern. Digital compositing tools have the advantage of blur filters and other blending tools that can mask any chatter that you encounter on the job. However, if you have a steady hand and good eye, you have the primary requirements for animating a seamless rotoscoped comp.

Case Study 10.2
Talking Cow for Oakhurst Milk

By Eric Jurgenson, Technical Supervisor, The Video Workshop

For a television commercial for Oakhurst Milk, we had to create a "talking" cow. This effect was produced in After Effects. From the original footage, we used a sequence of the cow chewing. We picked three or four chews from various head angles. The cow was turning her head during the master shot, so these angles allowed us to closely match the "chew" angles to the master shot.

By tracing out the "chews" around the inside of the mouth and the lower jaw, and then pasting them onto the master shot, we approximated the lip sync we were going after. The position of the cut-out on the master shot was determined more or less frame by frame. We might have been able to use the tracker for this, but the sequences were short, and there wasn't a hard reference for the tracker to lock to.

When we were close to getting good lip sync, we tweaked the shot by stretching the overlay horizontally and vertically around the mouth to gain a closer approximation of "human" vocal expression. The timing was refined by using Time Remapping on the overlay layer. As a final step, the edges of the matte were feathered to hide the matte lines.

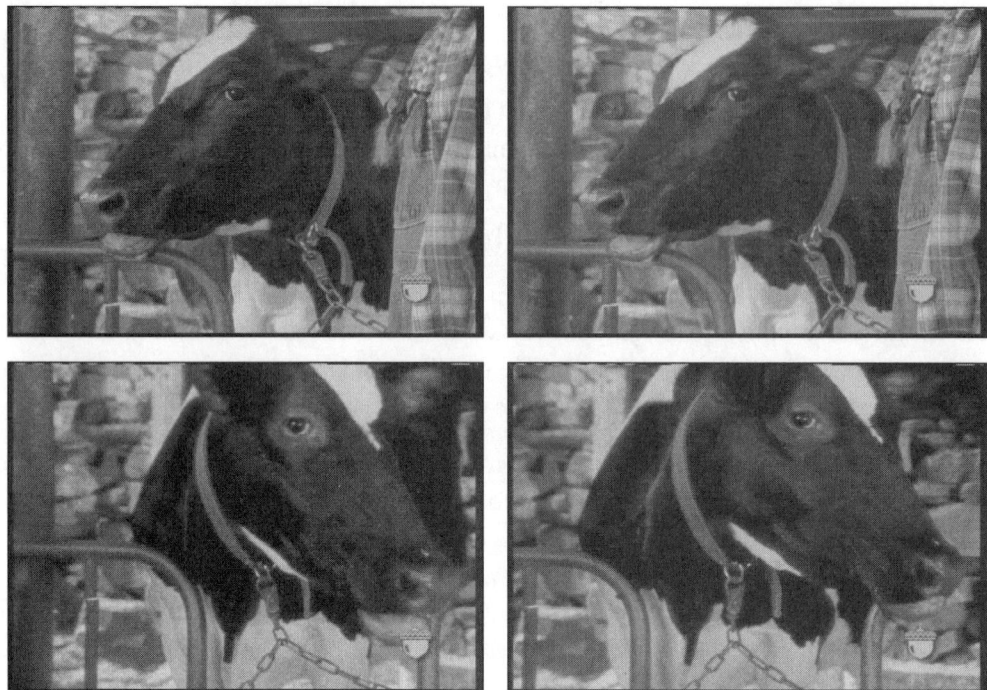

Four frames from the finished Talking Cow ad.

Graphic artist: Paul Haley

Technical supervisor: Eric Jurgenson

The Video Workshop

495 Forest Avenue

Portland, Maine 04101

207-774-7798

PROJECT 10.2 Rook's Rotoscope Removal

The goal of this project is to remove the white rook from the foreground footage more cleanly than was possible with the fixed-shape ellipse effect mask. In this project, you learn how to animate the outline of a polygon effect mask to follow complex contours.

1. Reload the ChesPath.flw that you saved from Project 10.1. In Mask View, delete Ellipse 1. In Path 1's controls, uncheck Show View Controls to hide the path. This will keep the Large display uncluttered and easier to work in.

2. Right-click on Merge 1 header. Select Effect Mask|Polygon.

3. The default mode for a polygon mask is Click Append, which adds points to the polygon with each mouse click. Center the white rook in the Large display, at 400% so you have a

clear view of its outlines. Click once slightly above and to the right of the rook's top. This will create the first point and control handles for Polygon 1. Your screen should look like Figure 10.13.

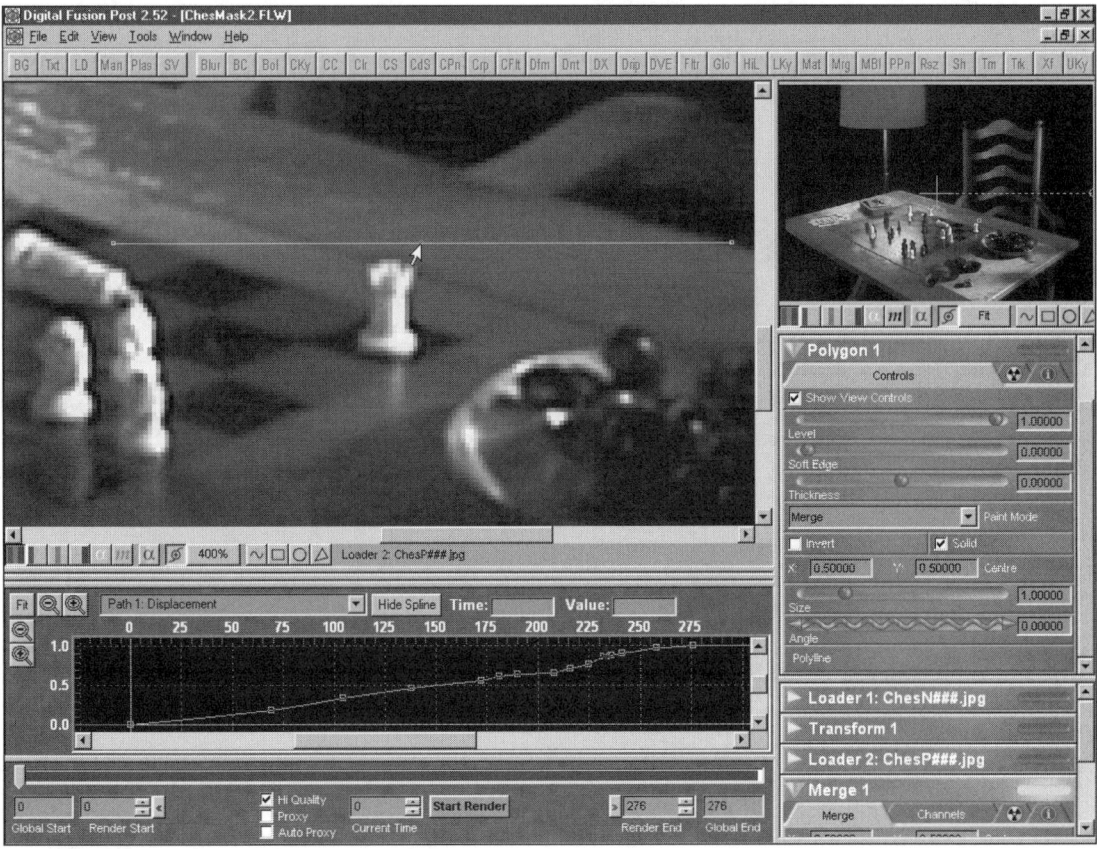

Figure 10.13
The arrow indicates the first point of Polygon 1 with control handles.

4. Click eight more times to create points around the perimeter of the rook, its reflection, and its shadow, coming back to the first point with the ninth click. Your ninth click should be exactly on top of the first point; when your cursor is located properly, a small circle will appear, as shown in Figure 10.14. If you've done everything right, the polygon will close automatically.

5. Right-click on the first point of Polygon 1, and select Polygon 1|Modify Only (or press Shift+M) to stop adding points but to still be able to animate them.

6. In Polygon 1's controls, turn on Solid and set Paint Mode to Replace. Right-click on the first point of Polygon 1 again, and select Effect Mask|Connect To|Polygon 1 from the pop-up menu. This connects the Merge operation to Polygon 1. You should see that the rook disappears in the Merge output, as shown in the Small display of Figure 10.15.

Figure 10.14

Polygon 1 with eight points set. The cursor circle indicates you're ready to close the polygon with the ninth click.

You can leave Polygon 1's center at its original location centered in the frame and simply keyframe the polygon's points to outline the rook. You also have the option of reusing the path you keyframed in Project 10.1 to position Polygon 1 over the rook. This may reduce the amount of tweaking you need to rotoscope the rook. If you want to reuse Path 1, change the Large view back to 100% or Fit so you can see the green crosshair of Merge 1 Center. Right-click on it, and from the pop-up menu, select Polygon 1: Center|Connect To|Path 1: Value. This tells the Polygon 1 center to follow Path 1. It also causes the points of Polygon 1 to pop off to the side, so you'll have to drag them back to their proper place around the rook. Press Shift+A to select all the points in Polygon 1. Drag the selected points back to surround the rook. When you have Polygon 1 located to your satisfaction, click anywhere else in the Large view to deselect the points. The remaining steps are the same whether you use Path 1 or simply keyframe Polygon 1 directly.

7. Zoom the Large view to whatever magnification you prefer. You'll be doing some finicky work in animating Polygon 1's points, so I recommend 300% or 400%. Zoom the Small view to the same magnification, and center it on the rook's square. The Small view is where you'll check to see that all traces of the rook are removed by your rotoscoped polygon.

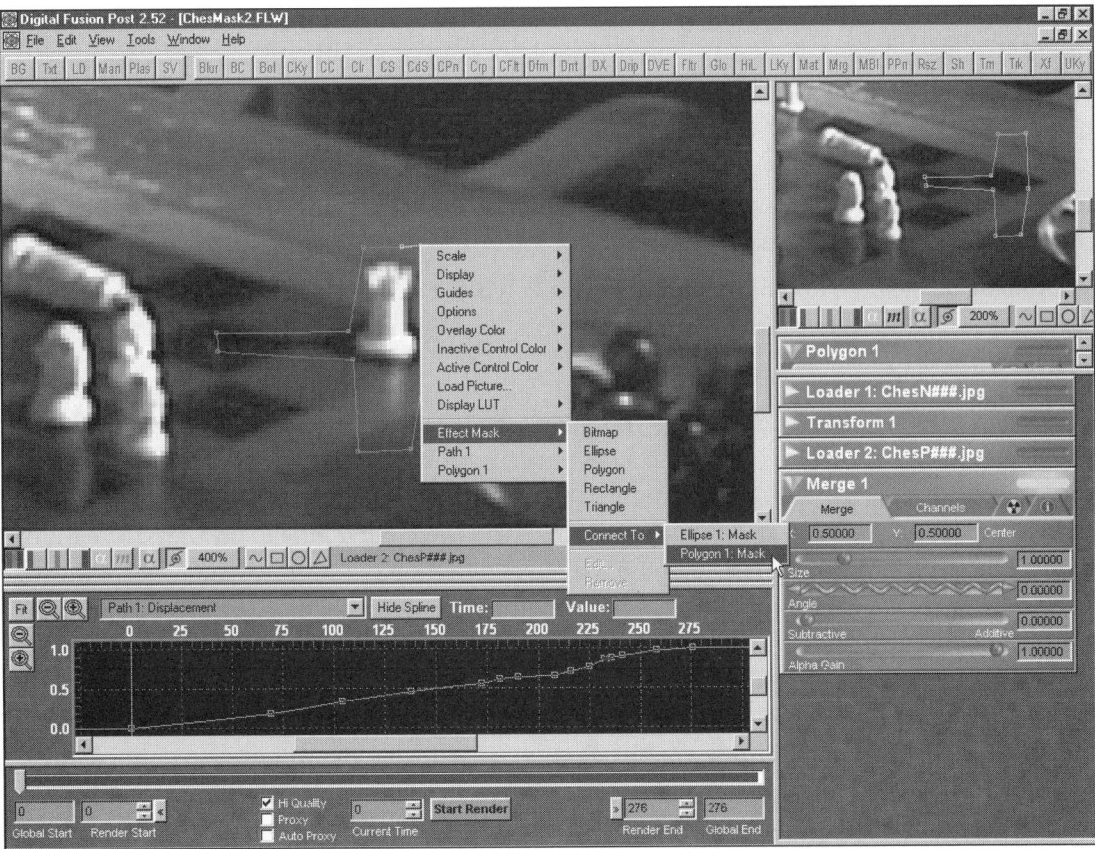

Figure 10.15
The rook is removed by the Merge 1 effect mask, Polygon 1, shown in the Small display.

You can save yourself a lot of time and trouble later on if you do a little thinking and planning now. There are two distinct portions of this footage for rotoscoping, and each requires a different level of effort. The simplest and easiest part is the beginning, where the rook, its shadow, and its reflection are unobstructed. All you have to do for this part is to match the movement of the camera and to make sure the effect mask is large enough to remove all traces of the rook. This process should require minimal keyframes and can tolerate quite a lot of slop in the placement of Polygon 1's points. The more difficult part of the rotoscoping is the end, where the rook, its shadow, and its reflection are partially occluded by the nearest white knight and two pawns. You will have to conform the polygon very closely to the outlines of these other chess pieces. This will require more keyframes and much tighter accuracy in the placement of each point, or you will be able to see chatter in the final comp.

8. Now that you know there are two parts to the footage, you need to find the dividing frame. Scrub through the footage, looking for the first frame where the rook, its shadow, or its reflection passes behind either of the other chess pieces. I found that the reflection of the rook first touches one pawn in frame 164. To provide a little clearance for the mask's soft edge, I chose 160 as the dividing frame.

To keyframe Polygon 1's shape and position for the easy part, frames 0 through 160, there are two basic approaches. One is the bracketing approach used in setting Path 1's keyframes in Project 10.1. You can follow this approach by going to frame 160, keyframing the polygon points, then doing the same at frames 80, 40, 120, 20, 60, 100, 140, and so on until you get satisfactory results. The other approach is to simply start at frame 0 and step through one frame at a time until an error is visible. Correct that error, and continue forward until you see another error. Repeat until you reach frame 160.

9. Choose a keyframe approach, and keyframe Polygon 1's outline to remove the rook, its reflection, and its shadow from frames 0 through 160. Your beginning and ending frames should look like Figure 10.16.

This is another time when you can save yourself a lot of time and trouble if you think ahead. If you look carefully at Figure 10.16, you can see that the rook does not change shape, only size, as the camera moves closer to it. This means you won't have to animate the polygon points to conform to a changing outline; all you have to do is spread them out a little to accommodate the gradual increase in the rook's size. Because the rook's reflection is a mirrored duplicate of the rook and always appears at the same angle to the camera, the same animation to account for size will remove the reflection as well. The rook's shadow is a little different; the size of the shadow increases as the camera closes in, but the angle is a function of the rook's orientation to a fixed light source rather than the camera. This means the shadow appears to change angle, making a scissors action toward the rook's reflection. This means you will need to animate the two points surrounding the far end of the rook's shadow to compensate for both increased size and vertical movement. Again, look carefully at Figure 10.16 to see these changes.

10. Limit the Render Start to frame 0 and Render End to frame 160, and make a Preview as large as possible. Set the Preview to looping playback, and watch it closely to check for chatter or other removal errors.

11. If you detect any hint of the rook, its shadow, or its reflection, stop the playback and locate the problem frames. Clear the Preview, and reposition Polygon 1's points in those frames to completely remove the rook.

12. If you have difficulty in tracking down a problem, go back to frame 0 and step one frame at a time from frame 0 to the next keyframe. Keep Loader 2 visible in the Large display and Merge 1 visible in the Small display. Have both displays zoomed to the same level, preferably 400%. As you step from frame to frame, examine the areas covered by the soft edges of Polygon 1 in the Small display. This is a more tedious but thorough quality control check. If you detect any hint of the rook, its shadow, or its reflection, you need to reposition the points in Polygon 1 to completely remove the rook.

At this point, you have successfully completed the easy part of this rotoscoped rig removal. The good news is that you have completed over half the frames. The bad news is that the remaining frames will require a lot more thought, effort, and keyframes.

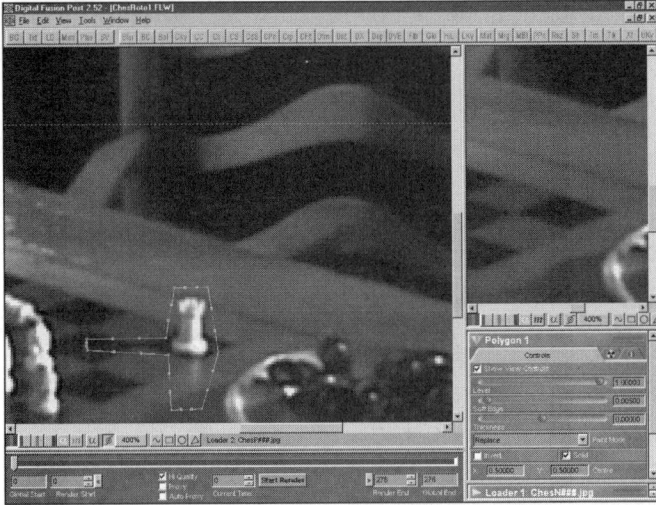

Figure 10.16
Screenshots of frame 0 (top) and frame 160 (bottom) showing clean removal of the rook, its reflection, and its shadow.

13. Scrub through frames 160 to 276, looking for critical frames. Pay special attention to the first frames where the rook, reflection, or shadow interacts with the white knight or pawns.

I found that the rook's reflection hits the lower pawn just after frame 160, and it hits the white knight just after frame 210. The reflection passes behind the white knight after frame 241. The shadow hits the upper pawn just after frame 170, but the intersection of black squares where the shadow removal is most critical is not visible after frame 223. This gives you five critical keyframes to begin the rotoscoping.

To prevent chatter, move each point as little as is possible. If you can keep a point next to a prominent feature on every frame, it will go a long way toward eliminating chatter. For example, point 2 (counting clockwise from the first point at the upper right) should be next to the right side of the rook's base in every frame. This is an excellent reference location for positioning the polygon points as a whole; simply select all points, and move the points until you have point 2 is in the right place. This will minimize the changes for most of the other points, so you can focus your attention on those points that really need to be changed. If you animate mask points to slide around an object's contours, it will practically guarantee chatter problems. For example, if you can keep point 5 at the top of the knight's head between frames 210 and 276, you'll be able to keep the edge between rook and knight more consistent at the point where chatter would be most obvious.

14. Go to frame 170, select all points, and move the points until point 2 is next to the right side of the rook's base, as shown in Figure 10.17. Note that this causes the lower left corner of

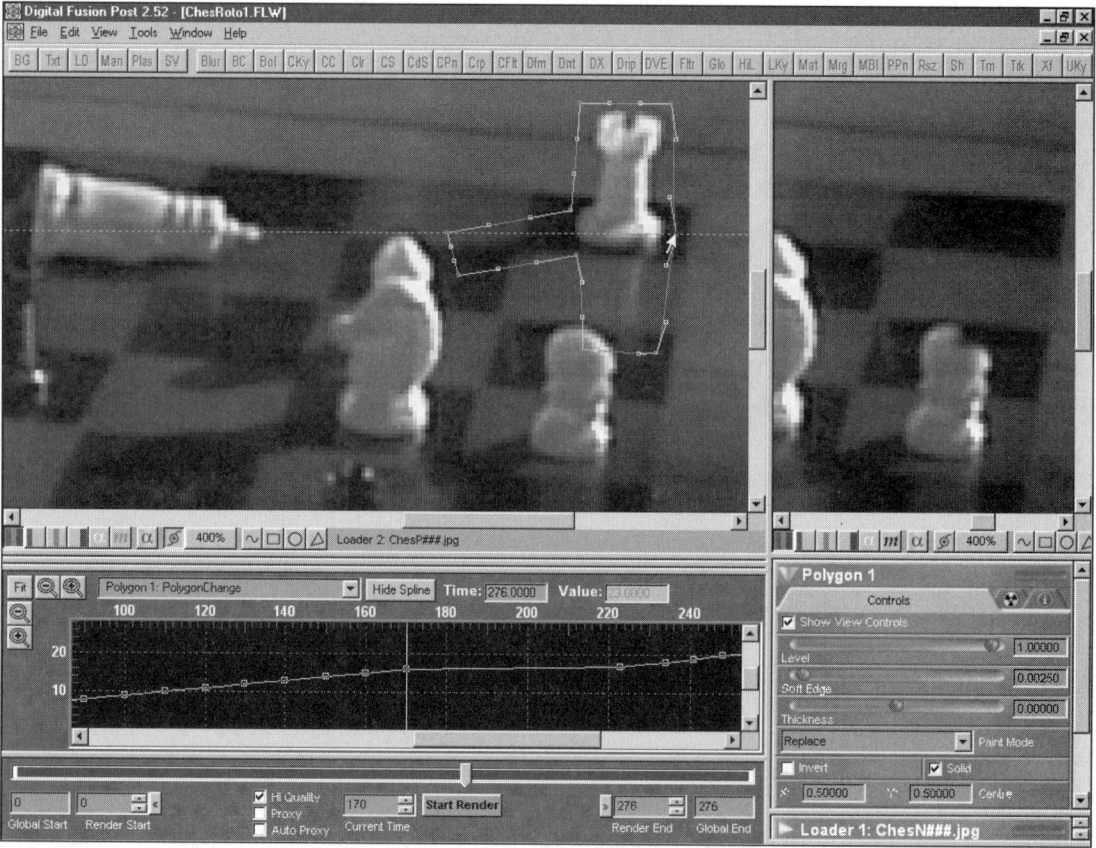

Figure 10.17
Polygon 1's point 2 is aligned to the rook's base. The lower left corner of Polygon 1 is overlapping part of a pawn and must be corrected; most other points are OK.

Polygon 1 to remove a chunk from the lower pawn's head. Adjust the other points individually to remove the rook, its reflection, and its shadow without affecting the other chess pieces. Pay particular attention to the shadow's end where it runs into the upper pawn. Your results should look like Figure 10.18.

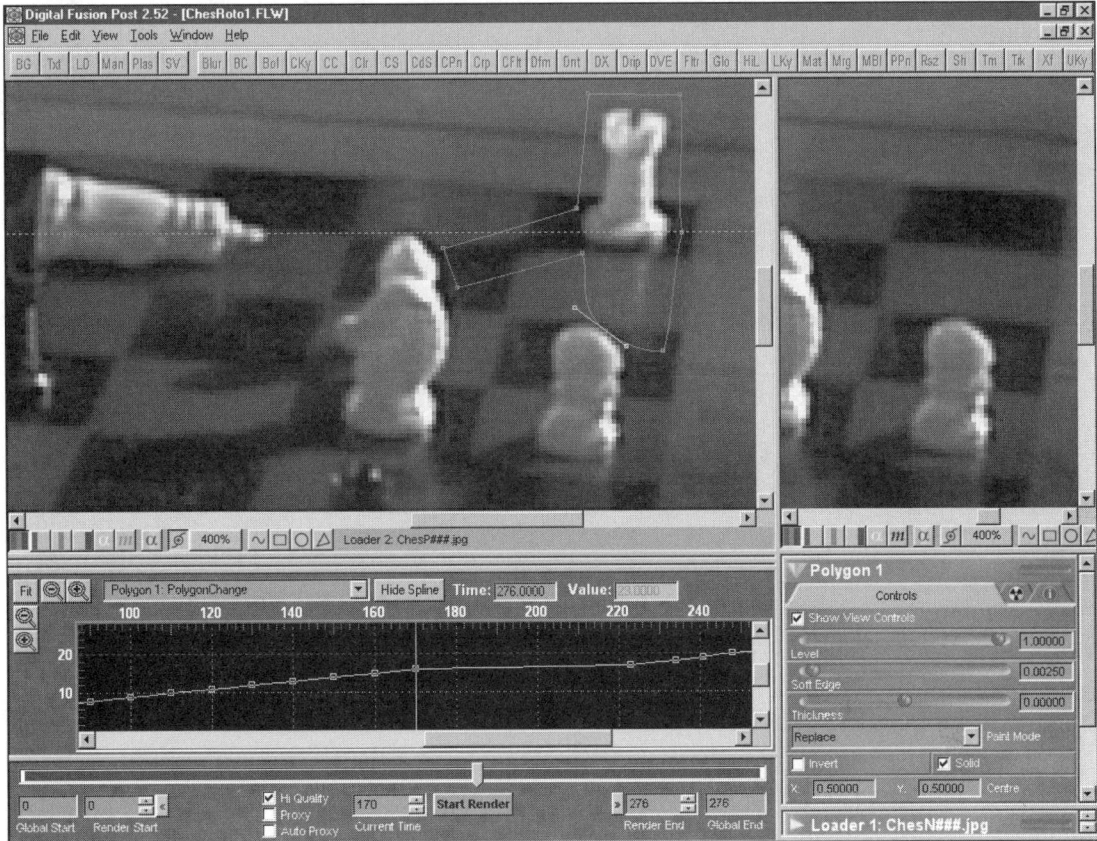

Figure 10.18

The effect mask points are adjusted to remove rook, reflection, and shadow without affecting other objects in the frame.

15. Go to frame 210. Select all points, and move the points until point 2 is next to the right side of the rook's base again. Adjust the other points individually to remove the rook, its reflection, and its shadow without affecting the other chess pieces. Pay particular attention to the reflection where it runs into the right side of the white knight. If you position point 5 at the top of the knight's head, you can keep it there for the rest of the shot. Point 4 will need some fine handle adjustments to get the spline curve to match the knight's contours. Your results should look like Figure 10.19.

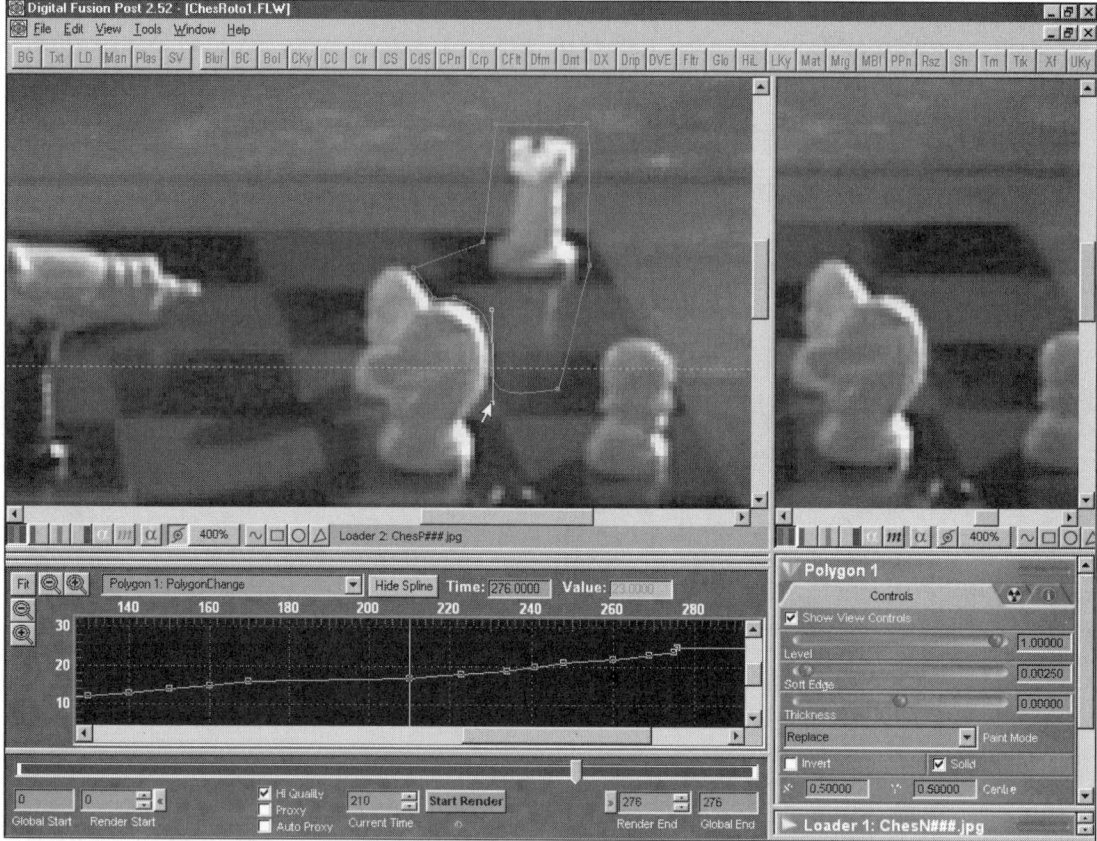

Figure 10.19
The effect mask points are adjusted to remove the rook reflection very close to the white knight.

One factor you should keep in mind when adjusting polygon mask points is that the interpolation of each point's movement is a straight line. If you set a point on one side of an object in frame 0, then position it on the other side of the object in frame 30, the point will be smack in the middle of the object in frame 15. The point doesn't know it should go around rather than through the object. DF polygon points aren't very bright; they don't know how to follow a curved path without specific instructions in the form of keyframes. If you need a point to closely follow a complex outline, you will probably have to set a key on every frame.

16. Go to frame 223. Select all points, and move the points until point 2 is next to the right side of the rook's base again. Adjust the other points individually to remove the rook, its reflection, and its shadow without affecting the other chess pieces. Pay particular attention to the shadow where it runs into the upper pawn. Your results should look like Figure 10.20.

Figure 10.20
The effect mask points are adjusted to remove the rook shadow very close to the upper pawn.

From this frame on, you don't have to worry about the rook's shadow, because the corner inter-section that showed the shadow most clearly is completely occluded by the upper pawn. The rest of the shadow falls on the black square to the left of the upper pawn, where it is effectively invis-ible and does not need to be removed. If the surface showed the shadow more prominently, it might require a second effect mask to remove it.

17. Go to frame 241. Select all points, and move the points until point 2 is next to the right side of the rook's base again. Adjust the other points individually to remove the rook, its reflec-tion, and its shadow without affecting the other chess pieces. The rook's reflection has passed behind the white knight, so you can pull up points 3 and 4. Your results should look like Figure 10.21.

18. Go to frame 276. Select all points, and move the points until point 2 is next to the right side of the rook's base again. Adjust the other points individually to remove the rook, its

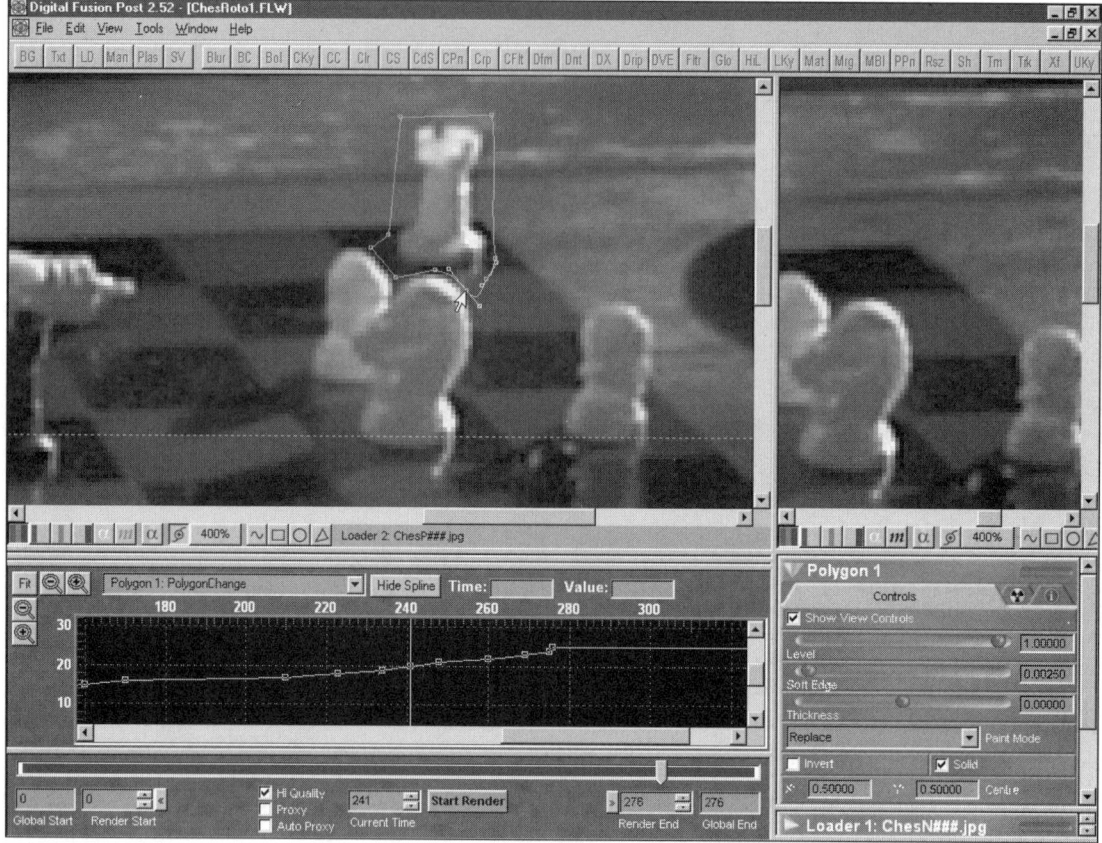

Figure 10.21
Effect mask points 3 and 4 raised after the reflection is occluded by the knight at frame 241.

reflection, and its shadow without affecting the other chess pieces. Any changes should be very small. Your results should look like Figure 10.22.

19. Go to frame 160. As you did in step 12, step one frame at a time from frame 160 to the next keyframe. Keep Loader 2 visible in the Large display and Merge 1 visible in the Small display. Have both displays zoomed to the same level, preferably 400%. As you step from frame to frame, examine the areas covered by the soft edges of Polygon 1 in the Small display. This is a thorough quality control check. If you detect any hint of the rook, its shadow, or its reflection, you need to reposition the points in Polygon 1 to completely remove the rook.

Between frames 170 and 190, you'll have to set a number of keyframes to guide points 3 and 4 around the top of the lower pawn. Remember, the points want to move in straight lines; you have to tell them with keyframes how to move around a curve. Between frames 210 and 241, you'll want to keep points 4 and 5 describing a curve very close to the white knight's outline. The tighter you

Figure 10.22
The effect mask points are arranged to remove the rook in the final frame.

draw your outline, the smaller your mask's soft edge must be. If there is only a distance of five pixels' between the removal subject and the nearest foreground object, and you run the polygon right down the middle of that distance, you still have only two pixels' worth of soft edge. If you crank the Soft Edge setting any higher, you will start to show the removal subject. However, if you zero out the soft edge, you'll have a more abrupt mask, which may chatter visibly.

20. Limit the Render Start to frame 160 and Render End to frame 276, and make a Preview as large as possible. Set the Preview to looping playback, and watch it closely to check for chatter or other removal errors.

21. If you detect any hint of the rook, its shadow, or its reflection, stop the playback and locate the problem frames. Clear the Preview, and reposition Polygon 1's points in those frames to completely remove the rook.

22. When you have the rook removed to your satisfaction, save the flow as ChesRoto.flw.

You just completed a rotoscoped rig removal. In this project, you learned how to:

- Apply a polygon effect mask to remove a foreground object
- Animate a polygon effect mask to match the movement and outlines of a removal subject
- Animate a polygon effect mask to split a precise moving edge between a removal subject and a foreground object
- Evaluate and choose keyframing methods
- Assess footage for problems and critical frames for rotoscoped rig removal

This may seem like a lot of work just to remove a chess piece. However, these same processes are used every day in television and feature film work. More often than you might believe, the only solution to a production problem or a director's last-minute inspiration is a digital compositor's skill at rotoscoping an effect mask.

Rook's Rotoscope Removal (After Effects)

The goal of this After Effects version of Project 10.2 is to remove the white rook from the foreground footage more cleanly than was possible with the fixed-shape ellipse mask. In this project, you learn how to animate the Mask Shape to follow complex contours.

1. Reload the ChesPath.aep project that you saved from Project 10.1.

2. Open the ChesP layer in the Layer window. Go to the first frame.

3. Click on Shape in the Mask Shape submenu. In the Mask Shape dialog box, click on the Rectangle radio button. This changes the shape of the mask (in the current frame only) from ellipse to rectangle. The number of control points remains the same.

4. Repeat the preceding step for each keyframe, so the mask shape is a rectangle throughout the composition.

5. Go back to the first keyframe. Magnify the Layer window to 400% or higher, and pan the window to center the mask and white rook.

6. Step through the keyframes. The difference in mask coverage between the ellipse and the rectangle should not be significant until about 5.15 seconds, at which point the lower control points of the rectangle are approaching the top of the nearest white pawn.

7. Go to the keyframe at 6.0 seconds. In the Layer window, click on one of the bottom control points of the rectangle mask. Drag the selected handle so that it is clear of the pawn, but close enough to it to mask the reflection of the rook, as shown in Figure 10.23.

8. Go to the keyframe at 5.0 seconds. Step through each frame up to 6.0 seconds, keeping a close eye on the bottom edges of the rectangle mask as they approach the top of the white pawn. If the mask covers any part of the pawn, try making adjustments to the mask shape in the 6.0 keyframe. Keep in mind that the position of each control point is interpolated as a straight line between keyframes. If you can't make the necessary corrections at the 6.0 keyframe, you may have to add a new keyframe between 5.0 and 6.0.

Figure 10.23
The rectangle mask shape is rotoscoped, one control point at a time, to remove the white rook's reflection without removing any part of the nearest white pawn.

9. Repeat the previous step for the frames between 6.0 and 7.0. This is a bit trickier because the rook's reflection is occluded by the pawn. You need to rotoscope the rectangle mask very closely to the pawn's upper edges to remove the reflection without removing any part of the pawn. You may also need to reduce the Mask Feather setting to get a finer edge on the mask.

With a little practice, you should be able to rotoscope the rook's removal with only a handful of additional keyframes. As shown in Figure 10.24, I was able to remove the rook with a total of 18 keyframes for the mask, only seven more than with the ellipse mask.

If you want to do a really thorough rotoscoped removal, you also need to remove the rook's shadow. The shadow lies diagonally across the lower left corner of the rook's square. Therefore, most of the shadow is concealed by the black squares; but at the juncture of the four squares, the shadow is more visible where it lies across the lighter squares. The shadow is almost completely occluded by other chess pieces after 7.0 seconds, but is more prominent earlier in the comp.

Figure 10.24
The rotoscoped removal of the rook required only 18 mask keyframes.

After Effects enables you to add control points to a mask at any time. When you add a control point to an existing mask, the new point exists at all keyframes. However, the new control point only has a new position keyframe at the time it is added. All the other keyframes will interpolate the new control point's position between the positions of the adjoining control points. This is very useful; you can add control points to solve a problem in one keyframe without worrying about changing the shape of the mask and causing problems in any other keyframe.

10. Go to the keyframe at 5.0 seconds and pan the Layer window to center the mask and rook. Select the Add Control Point tool (the Pen with the plus sign) from the toolbox. Click three times to add three control points along the left side of the mask just below the middle control point.

This process creates two control points that can be dragged out to the end of the shadow, plus one new control point that nails down the edge that previously connected to the middle control point. Figure 10.25 shows the new points arranged to remove the rook's shadow.

Figure 10.25
Three new control points are added to the mask and are positioned to remove the rook's shadow.

11. Using only the existing keyframes, rotoscope the new control points to remove the rook's shadow.

12. Test the removal by playing it back at 200% or higher in the Composition window. Watch carefully for any sign of the rook, its reflection, or its shadow. Make corrections as needed. When you are satisfied with the rook removal, save the project as ChesRoto.aep.

Rook's Rotoscope Removal (Commotion)

The goal of this Commotion-based version of Project 10.2 is to remove the white rook from the foreground footage more cleanly than was possible with the simple fixed-shape mask used in Project 10.1. This technique is well covered in the Rotospline tutorial (Lesson 11) that is part of the Commotion manual. Rather than duplicate that tutorial here, I recommend that you work through the Commotion manual Lesson 11, and then apply what you learn there to using Rotosplines to remove the white rook from the ChesP footage.

Rook's Rotoscope Removal (effect*)

The goal of this effect*-based version of Project 10.2 is to remove the white rook from the foreground footage more cleanly than was possible with the fixed-shape ellipse mask. In this project, you will learn how to animate the freeform mask to follow complex contours.

1. Reload the ChesPath.icp project that you saved from effect* Project 10.1.

2. Delete the Elliptical Mask effect from the ChesP layer.

3. With the ChesP layer still selected, choose Effects|Mask|Freeform Mask.

4. Go to frame 1. In the Freeform Mask window, choose the same settings you used for the Elliptical Mask in effect* Project 10.1. Draw the freeform mask to cover the white rook with a minimum number of control points, as shown in Figure 10.26.

Figure 10.26
The freeform mask control points have been arranged to remove the white rook in the first frame.

5. As you did in effect* Project 10.1, set keyframes for the position of the effect mask to cover the rook throughout the footage. Additionally, set keyframes for the position of each freeform mask control point. If you need guidelines for the mask shape, refer to the figures in the Digital Fusion and After Effects versions of this project.

6. Test the removal comp by playing it back at 200% or higher in the Main View window. Watch carefully for any sign of the rook, its reflection, or its shadow. Make corrections as needed. When you have the rook removed to your satisfaction, save the project as ChesRoto.icp.

Rook's Rotoscope Removal (Shake)

The goal of this Shake version of Project 10.2 is to remove the white rook from the foreground footage more cleanly than was possible with a fixed-shape mask. In this exercise, simply repeat the process you followed in Shake Project 10.1, with the change of using the QuickShape function (in the Image tab) to create an animatable mask shape. For details about using QuickShape, refer to the Shake HTML documentation included on this book's second CD-ROM.

PROJECT 10.3 Rotoscoping An Actor Removal

Removing one rigid, relatively simple object is a good start. But just how hard is it to do the real work of taking an excess actor out of live footage? Suppose that you are hired to comp a series of shots for a science fiction film. Part of the plot involves space troopers beaming in to an urban combat zone. After principal photography is finished and the set is no longer available, the director decides to change the script from two troopers beaming in to just one trooper. The footage is already in the can; now it's up to you to save the shot, to make the director happy, and to keep your job. If you can successfully remove the second trooper, you have the makings of a professional digital compositor.

1. Reload the Dissolve.flw file you saved from Project 8.6. This is the effect-masked dissolve, from a clean plate of a set to two actors in space trooper costumes on the same set.

2. Replace the Dissolve effect mask rectangle with a polygon. Add points to the polygon to mark the left edge of the first trooper where he overlaps the second trooper. You'll need a lot more points than you did for the rook, but try to keep them to a minimum. Close the polygon by completely surrounding the second trooper. Your results should look something like Figure 10.27.

Figure 10.27
Effect mask points are arranged to remove the second trooper.

3. Animate the effect mask polygon for the other 48 frames of the footage. Apply all the techniques you learned in Project 10.2. When you are satisfied with your work, render the footage. Your results should look something like Figure 10.28.

Rotoscoping An Actor Removal (After Effects)

Removing one rigid, relatively simple object is a good start for rotoscoping. But just how hard is it to do the real work of taking an excess actor out of live footage? Suppose that you are hired to comp a series of shots for a science fiction film. Part of the plot involves space troopers beaming in to an urban combat zone. After principal photography is finished and the set is no longer available, the director decides to change the script from two troopers beaming in to just one. The footage is in the can; now it's up to you to save the shot, make the director happy, and keep your job. This After Effects-based version of Project 10.3 details how you can solve this problem.

Figure 10.28
A rendered frame from rotoscoped actor removal.

1. Import the two JPEG sequences from folders Beamdown and BeamdnBG on the second CD-ROM. Beamdown is the foreground, and BeamdnBG is the background or clean plate.

2. Create a new composition as you did in After Effects Project 10.1, sending the background layer to the back of the comp and adding a mask to the foreground layer. Make the mask a rectangle and position it to cover the trooper on the left. Include the pipe end, where the trooper's shadow falls, within the mask.

3. Add more control points to the right side of the mask, and position these control points to closely follow the left side of the right-hand trooper. This is the same process you followed in After Effects Project 10.2 to remove the rook's shadow. This mask may require more control points due to the complexity of the removal subject. Your comp should look like Figure 10.29.

4. Animate the mask control points for the duration of the background layer. Apply all the techniques you learned in Project 10.2. When you are satisfied with your work, preview or render the footage. Your results should look something like Figure 10.28. Save your project as ActorRoto.aep.

Note that this removal technique only works with a clean plate. Because the background layer is much shorter than the foreground layer, you can't use this approach to remove the second trooper throughout the foreground layer's duration. Project 10.4 shows one solution to this problem.

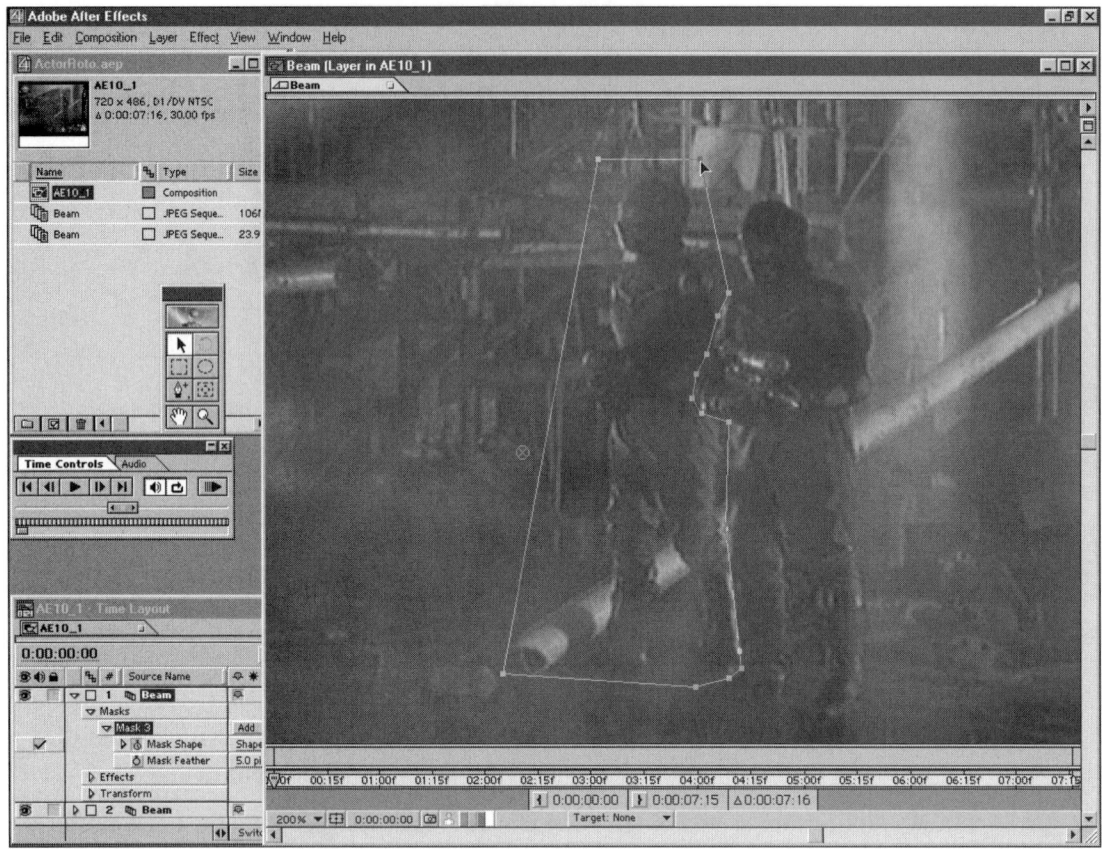

Figure 10.29
The Beamdown footage has been imported and added to a new composition, and a mask has been added to the foreground layer and positioned to remove the second trooper.

Rotoscoping An Actor Removal (Commotion)

The goal of this Commotion-based version of Project 10.3 is to rotoscope the removal of an actor, a much more complex application of Commotion's Rotospline features. This technique is clearly covered in the Rotospline tutorial (Lesson 11) that is part of the Commotion manual. Rather than duplicate that tutorial here, I recommend that you work through the Commotion manual Lesson 11, and then apply what you learn there to using Rotosplines to remove the second trooper from the Beamdown footage.

Rotoscoping An Actor Removal (effect*)

Removing one rigid, relatively simple object is a good start for rotoscoping. But just how hard is it to do the real work of taking an excess actor out of live footage? Suppose that you are hired to comp a series of shots for a science fiction film. Part of the plot involves space troopers "beaming in" to an urban combat zone. After principal photography is finished and the set is no longer available, the director decides to change the script from two troopers to just one beaming in. The footage is in the can; now you have to save the shot, make the director happy, and keep your job. This effect*-based version of Project 10.3 details how you can solve this problem.

1. Import the two JPEG sequences from folders Beamdown and BeamdnBG on the second CD-ROM. Beamdown is the foreground and BeamdnBG is the background or clean plate.

2. Create a new composition as you did in effect* Project 10.1, sending the background layer to the back of the comp. Add a freeform mask to the foreground layer as you did in effect* Project 10.2.

3. Position and shape the mask to cover the trooper on the left. Include the pipe end, where the trooper's shadow falls, within the mask. Add more control points to the right side of the mask, and position these control points to closely follow the left side of the right-hand trooper. You followed the same process to remove the rook's shadow. This mask, however, may require more control points due to the complexity of the removal subject.

4. Keyframe the mask control points for the duration of the background layer.

5. When you are satisfied with your work, preview or render the footage. Save your project as ActorRoto.icp.

Note that this removal technique works only with a clean plate. Because the background layer is much shorter than the foreground layer, you can't use this approach to remove the second trooper throughout the foreground layer's duration. Project 10.4, however, shows one solution to this problem.

Rotoscoping An Actor Removal (Shake)

The goal of this Shake-based version of Project 10.3 is to remove the second trooper from the Beamdown footage, while retaining the first trooper. This is a repeat of the process you followed in Shake Project 10.2, with the change of animating a more complex QuickShape. For details on this process, refer to the Animating QuickShape topic in the Shake HTML documentation on the second CD-ROM.

WIRE REMOVAL WITHOUT A CLEAN PLATE

You will often be asked to digitally remove wires used for flying rigs or as safety cables for especially hazardous stunts. This is simple and doesn't even require a clean plate. Load the footage, add a Merge tool, and connect the footage to both inputs of the Merge. Add a two-point polygon effect mask, and animate the points to the visible ends of the wire. Set the Merge Center to slightly off center (0.485 or 0.515 are good for starters) in a direction not crossed by the wire. The goal is to use the Merge tool to cover the wire with a thin slice of nearby pixels. Tweak the soft edge and thickness of the polygon to make a near-perfect match. You can add as many polygons as you like to the single Merge, so one pass can fix every line in a shot.

Clean Your Plate

The preceding techniques and projects assumed either that you have the required clean plate or that you didn't need one. What do you do when you don't have a clean plate, but the only options seem to require one? You make one! A number of ways exist of reconstructing or faking a clean plate. A locked shot, footage with no camera motion, is easiest to work with. If the camera is moving, you will need to stabilize the footage or manually match overlapping areas of each frame before you can extract the clean plate. Your next problem is to figure out what should be in the frame in the place of the removal subject. Generally, the replacement is an area of the set or location background. If the replacement is to include complex elements, you are best off adding them in a separate operation or comp.

If you're lucky, the removal subject doesn't cover the same area for every frame of footage. If the removal subject is moving, you can use a frame offset or *time shift* combined with a masked merge to create a clean plate. For example, if the rig is in one spot for the first 30 frames—and is not there after frame 30—you can use a –30 frame offset to merge a clean background over the removal subject.

PROJECT 10.4 Time-Shifting A Clean Plate

The goal of this project is to create clean plate footage that you can use in place of the BeamBG footage provided for Project 8.6. Suppose that the Beamdown shot was filmed without a clean plate. If you don't have the 50 frames of BeamBG footage, how would you comp the masked dissolve to "beam in" the troopers? The solution to this problem lies in the fact that the troopers move through the frame. They only stand in the beam-in location for part of the sequence; after that, the beam-in location is clear and can be used as a clean plate.

1. Open a new flow. Add two loaders and connect them with a Merge. Load the Beamdown footage into both Loaders.

2. Add a rectangle effect mask to the Merge tool. Size and position it to cover the troopers in frame 0, with enough margin to spare for a soft edge. Set the Rectangle 1 controls to match the settings in Figure 10.30.

3. You need to locate the frame where the troopers and their shadows are completely out of the effect mask. Scrub through the footage to find this frame. I found it to be about frame 160. Be especially careful about the shadows on the end of the diagonal pipe at the left edge of the effect mask.

4. In Loader 2's File tab, set Clip Time Start to the first clear frame, 160 in this case. This time-shifts Loader 2's footage to 160 frames later than Loader 1. When Loader 1 is displaying frame 30, Loader 2 is displaying frame 190. This cuts down the number of clean frames available to 65, but you need only 50 for the beam-in.

5. Set the Render Start to 0 and Render End to 65. Adjust the Merge and effect mask to make the troopers disappear completely in frames 0 through 65. Keep the soft edge as large as possible without allowing any of the troopers to show through.

Figure 10.30
The flow is set up for time-shifted actor removal in the Beamdown footage.

6. Make a Preview. Loop the Preview in playback, and see if you can spot the troopers. Fix any problems, and then render the 65 frames to a new folder.

You should end up with a 65-frame clean plate, complete with flickering flames and drifting smoke. If you'd like to test it, reload the Dissolve.flw you saved from Project 8.6 and substitute the footage you just rendered for the BeamBG footage. Your results should be identical, or even a little better, because the smoke and flames are a closer match.

If you need to comp a rig removal to create a clean plate for the full length of the footage, you might be tempted to animate the time-shifting effect mask to follow the removal subject. This is generally a bad idea, because any movement makes the mask easier for your audience to see. A better approach is a series of fixed effect masks, each time-shifting to different frames and with overlapping soft edges. You should also fade out (crank Soft Edge up to 1.0) each effect mask when the area it covers is clear; you want as few effect masks active as possible, to prevent a patchwork quilt effect.

Time-Shifting A Clean Plate (After Effects)

The goal of this After Effects version of Project 10.4 is to create clean plate footage that you can use in place of the BeamBG footage for removal and dissolve operations. You can use this process to create a clean plate when one is not already available or to correct a clean plate that has flaws. The core of this process is the reality that the troopers move through the frame. They only stand in any one location for part of the sequence; outside that, any location is clear and can be used as part of a clean plate. The trick is to time-shift a copy of the footage so a clear area is always visible through the mask.

1. Reload the ActorRoto.aep that you saved from After Effects Project 10.3.

2. Remove the background layer (because we are assuming that no clean plate is available) and replace it with a copy of the foreground layer footage. Right-click on the background footage in the Project window. Choose Replace Footage|File from the pop-up menu. Select the JPEG sequence from the Beamdown folder, the same as for the foreground footage.

3. In the Time Layout window, drag out the duration of the new background layer to match the duration of the foreground layer. Because the background layer is identical to the foreground layer, the mask shows the previously removed trooper again.

4. To make a clean plate, you need to remove both troopers and their shadows. Go to the first frame. Open the foreground layer in the Layer window and modify the mask to cover both troopers. You can simplify your work by deleting all but four control points, making the mask a much simpler polygon, as shown in Figure 10.31. Delete all the later keyframes you used to rotoscope the trooper removal in the preceding project; you will need only this first keyframe for now.

5. Close the Layer window. The Composition window still shows both troopers. To remove them, drag the background layer to the left in the Time Layout or set the In value to something near –5:15 seconds.

This offsets the background footage to a frame where the troopers have moved completely out of the masked area. The Composition window should show a clean frame, with no shadows or other evidence of the troopers, as in Figure 10.32. You can drag the background footage back and forth to find the best initial frame. Watch for the trooper's shadows on the pipe at the lower left corner of the mask; that's the last trace that you have to remove. You can crank up the Mask Feather value to help conceal the edges of the mask.

6. Render the comp as an image sequence, from the first frame to the end of the offset background layer. This comp provides just over two seconds of clean plate, with a few artifacts in lighting and smoke levels. Save the project as CleanBeam.aep.

If you need to create a clean plate for the full length of the footage, you might be tempted to animate the time-shifting mask to follow the troopers. This is generally a bad idea because any movement makes the mask easier for your audience to see. A better approach is to render as many clean plate images as you can with a series of static masks, each mask time-shifting a copy

Figure 10.31
The mask has been modified to a simple four-point polygon and repositioned to remove both troopers.

of the foreground footage to different frames. You can then assemble these image sequences, using dissolves to cover any jumps in lighting or smoke patterns, to create a single continuous clean plate that is long enough to match the foreground layer.

Time-Shifting A Clean Plate (Commotion)

The goal of this Commotion-based version of Project 10.4 is to create clean plate footage that you can use in place of the BeamBG footage for removal and dissolve operations. This is a process that you can use to create a clean plate when one isn't already available, or to correct a clean plate that has flaws. The core of this process is the reality that the troopers move through the frame. They stand in any one location only for part of the sequence; outside that, all locations are clear and can be used as part of a clean plate. The trick is to time-shift a copy of the footage so a clear area is used to cover an area that is obstructed by the moving actors. This technique is fully covered in the Clone, SuperClone, and AutoPainting tutorials (Lessons 3 and 4) that are part of the Commotion manual. Rather than duplicate these tutorials here, I recommend that

Figure 10.32
The background footage has been offset –5:15 seconds in the Time Layout window to remove the troopers from the masked area.

you work through the Commotion manual Lessons 3 and 4, and then apply what you learn there to using Clone, SuperClone, and AutoPaint to remove the actors from the Beamdown footage to create a clean plate.

Time-Shifting A Clean Plate (effect*)

The goal of this effect*-based version of Project 10.4 is to create clean plate footage that you can use in place of the BeamBG footage for removal and dissolve operations. You can use this process to create a clean plate when one isn't already available or to correct a clean plate that has flaws. The core of this process is the reality that the troopers move through the frame. They stand in any one location only for part of the sequence; outside that, all locations are clear and can be used as part of a clean plate. The trick is to time-shift a copy of the footage so a clear area is always visible through the mask.

1. Reload the ActorRoto.icp that you saved from effect* Project 10.3.

2. Replace the background layer with a duplicate of the foreground layer.

3. Revise the freeform mask (or replace it with a new mask) to include both troopers. Because the foreground and background layers are identical, the troopers will not disappear.

4. In the Timeline window, offset the background layer to the left about 125 frames. In the Main View window, you should see the troopers disappear from the area defined by the freeform mask. Adjust the offset of the background layer to replace the troopers with a clean section of the set.

5. Render the comp as an image sequence, from the first frame to the end of the offset background layer. This comp provides just over two seconds of clean plate, with a few artifacts in lighting and smoke levels. Save the project as CleanBeam.icp.

If you need to create a clean plate for the full length of the footage, you might be tempted to animate the freeform mask to follow the troopers. This is generally a bad idea, because any movement makes the mask easier for your audience to see. A better approach is to render as many clean plate images as you can with a series of static masks, each mask time-shifting a copy of the foreground footage to different frames. You can then assemble these image sequences, using dissolves to cover any jumps in lighting or smoke patterns, to create a single continuous clean plate that is long enough to match the foreground layer.

The ability to extract a clean plate from cluttered footage is definitely a skill that you will find highly useful as a digital compositor. Even with the best crew and extensive preproduction planning, something always goes wrong or is changed after the shoot. Pulling this kind of magic out of your hat can save a crucial shot, which will endear you to the director and will make the money people smile, too.

A Little Makeup

Small defects such as move-match markers (green tennis balls or glow sticks), scuffs, or a mislaid prop can be removed with a variety of simple effects. The advantage of a composited effect over a painted bitmap removal is that the effect can automatically deal with lighting and other subtle changes. A painted removal will stick out noticeably if the lighting for the surrounding area changes.

A quick-and-dirty effect for small removals is the Dent tool. This tool is great for removing small rigs, tracker targets, or paint touch-ups on bluescreens. You simply position the circular Dent over the removal subject and resize it to cover the subject with a little outside margin. With a small negative strength, the Dent 1 effect pulls in and radial-blurs the pixels around the perimeter of the circle, and shrinks the center pixels down to nothing (see Figure 10.33). This is

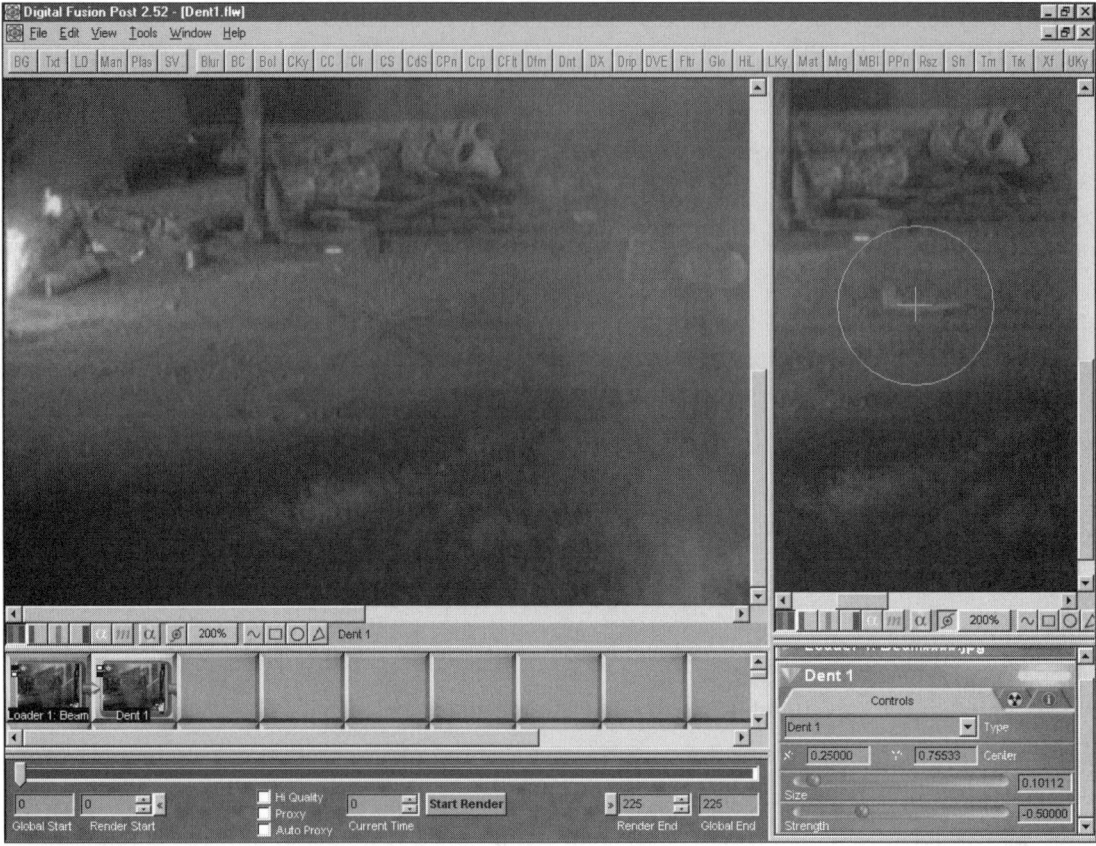

Figure 10.33
The Dent 1 tool removing an object from the floor.

great for removing small flaws in the middle of relatively uniform surfaces like walls or floors. The downside is that you'll need to fade out the effect if any foreground object passes within range of the Dent 1 circle. If you leave it active, your comp will look like you have a small black hole hiding in it.

A more versatile small removal tool is the Blur, shown in Figure 10.34. Applied with an effect mask, a variety of blurs can be used to smear adjoining pixels over the removal subject. Because the effect mask and other blur parameters can be animated, it is easier to maintain the blur removal even when a foreground subject moves across or near it. The primary disadvantage to using a Blur filter for small rig removals is that it blurs the texture of any surrounding material, so it doesn't lend itself well to removals in very complex environments.

My personal favorite for small removals is the Displace warp tool. This tool shifts the masked pixels as if they are under a refracting lens, and you can control the direction, strength, and

Figure 10.34
The Blur filter with an effect mask removing an object from the floor.

other factors to tweak the results. I think this tool does an excellent job of making removal objects disappear seamlessly. As with the Blur filter, the effect mask and other settings can be animated to deal with foreground objects passing through or near the removal area. The Displace warp tool is shown in Figure 10.35.

The last resort is one that relies entirely on your talent as a retoucher. If no filter, tool, or other compositing operation will remove the rig or other problem, you may have to paint it out frame-by-frame. Painting technique is beyond the scope of this book, but here are some general guidelines:

- Run all other removal comps first, using as many techniques from this chapter as are applicable. The more removals you can do with comps, the less you'll have to paint.

- Whenever possible, paint with patterns sampled from the footage. It's easier to get an acceptable match with patterns than with pure colors.

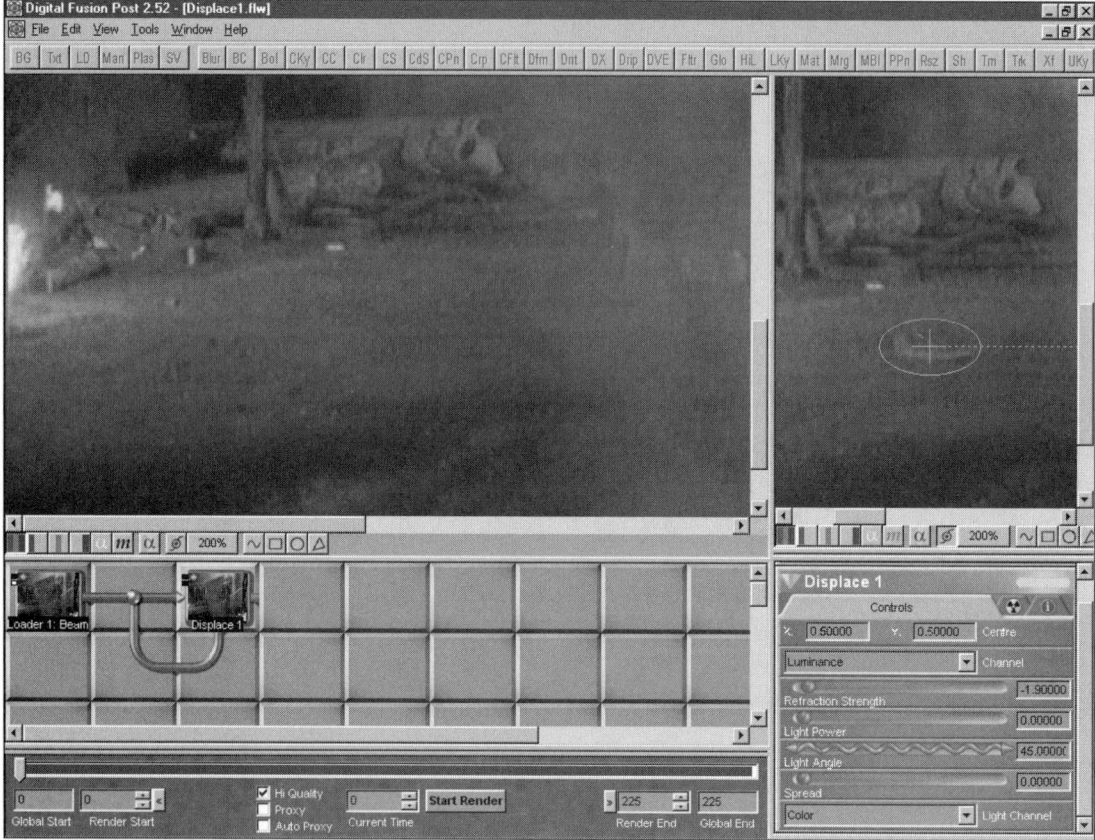

Figure 10.35
The Displace warp tool with an ellipse effect mask, removing an object from the floor.

- Copy and flip to match edges. If you copy adjoining areas on both sides of the removal subject, then flip the copied areas over the removal subject, the edges of the removal area will match perfectly. Blur or smear the seam where the flips meet to finish it.

- If you have to paint a removal with pure colors, try running a grain filter over it to conceal the effects of too-smooth painting. Live footage is always dirty and grainy, and perfect colors are a dead giveaway.

Moving On

This chapter showed you a variety of tools for removing rigging, people, and artifacts from locked-down footage. This is a very useful set of skills, but you also need to be able to handle these same problems with footage from a moving camera. The next chapter shows you techniques and tools to deal with this common set of problems.

CHAPTER 11

WHOLE LOTTA SHAKIN'
GOIN' ON

Your ability to comp footage from a moving camera can make the difference between an easy job and one that you wish you'd never seen. Any compositing operation that works with less than the full frame requires you to position at least one control. If the footage is from a moving camera, you are going to have to keyframe that control to match the camera's movement. If you're lucky, the camera move was smooth and you'll only need to set a few keyframes. If you're not so lucky, the camera move will require you to set a keyframe on nearly every frame. If the effect you are comping has many position controls, every additional control multiplies the number of keyframes you'll have to set. For a worst-case example, imagine that the footage for the actor removal in Project 10.3 was shot with a handheld camera that moved in a random direction and zoomed in or out in every frame. You might have to manually set over two dozen keys in each frame of the entire sequence. Alternatively, the locked-down footage only requires a new key on frames where the profile of the actor changes. That could be a difference in hours or days of work for you, just to correct the camera motion.

From the digital compositor's point of view, the best solution for camera motion problems is to prevent the motion in the first place. However, camera motion is an important storytelling tool, and most directors want the freedom to move the camera. That means more work for you, but that's what you're getting paid for. Camera motion can also be an artifact of unforeseen production problems. A camera mount, tripod, or other rig may have a small glitch. Someone may jostle the camera or other rigging. The equipment used to support the camera may be inadequate to hold it perfectly motionless through the entire course of a locked-down shot. Getting rid of unintentional camera motion is a salvage operation like rig removal. Your job in these situations is to salvage footage that would be difficult, impossible, or expensive to reshoot.

Figure 11.1 shows an example of a minor camera move. If you look closely at the position of the box, you can see that it is significantly closer to the bottom of the frame at the end of the footage than it is at the beginning. Sometimes a shot that is delivered to you as locked down is not, and it's up to you to spot camera movement like this before you start the comp. If you spot the problem immediately, you can discuss the camera move with the director or VFX supervisor and get a reshoot or additional time to comp the shot. If you're halfway into the comp and discover that the camera was jostled on a couple of frames, you will probably have to fix the problem on the agreed upon budget and schedule for locked-down footage. If you're freelancing or running your own business, that can mean the difference between a reasonable profit and eating the job.

Figure 11.2 shows a more obvious camera move. I shot this footage of my front sidewalk and porch with a handheld Hi8 camcorder. This is not quite worst-case videography; at least I didn't use the zoom buttons. I digitized the footage in YUV format using the ATI All-In-Wonder, the cheapest low-end option described in Chapter 5. I converted this to image sequence MATCH001.JPG through MATCH265.JPG, which you can find in the Match directory on this book's first CD-ROM. This is an example of the kind of footage you might get from lowballing clients who let their brothers-in-law shoot the footage for their used car commercials. You might also see this from someone who saw *The Blair Witch Project* too many times. More legitimately, you may see footage like this from a director who wants a "documentary" feel to the shot and who wants to preserve the camera motion as a storytelling tool. In other words, there are enough practical reasons for footage to look this bad that you should know how to work with it successfully. This chapter and Chapter 12 will show you how to deal with most forms of camera movement to make even the worst footage easier to comp.

Tracking

The most basic tool (after hand-keyframing) for correcting camera movement is the tracker. This tool uses *pattern recognition* to track a specific feature as it moves from frame to frame. In this application of pattern recognition, you tell the tracker software what the initial pattern looks like in the reference frame, and the tracker searches for that same pattern in the other frames. The tracker program may apply a variety of algorithms—anything from a simple literal template of the identical color values to advanced expert systems that can allow for variation in light, color, size, alignment, and perspective. The product of the tracker is usually a *path* of keyframes marking the center of the pattern. You can use this path for a variety of purposes. The most basic is to move an effect or tool control to precisely match the movement of the pattern.

Tracking is limited to footage with clear patterns, as shown in Figure 11.3. These patterns should be in as many frames as possible, but you can hand off the tracker from one pattern to another if a single pattern is not usable throughout the sequence. The less clear or consistent the pattern, the more work you can expect to do. Most trackers are not terribly bright and tend

Figure 11.1
Frames 200, 300, and 400 from the Box footage. Note the variation in distance from the corner of the box to the bottom of the frame, showing camera movement.

Figure 11.2
Every tenth frame from the Match footage.

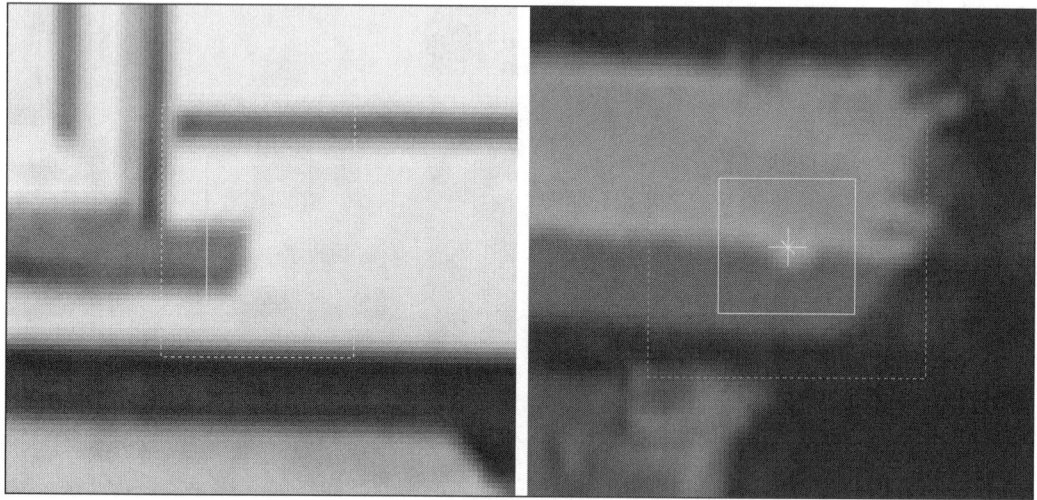

Figure 11.3
Left: Clear, high-contrast pattern that will track easily and accurately. Right: Muddy, low-contrast pattern that will tend to tracking loss or errors.

to go off the path if the pattern is too muddled in some frames. When that happens, you will have to step in and redefine the pattern or manually set a few keyframes. A varying or muddy pattern can also lead to uncertainty for the tracker, which can result in inaccurate values for some keyframes. This produces wobbly motion in the path, which you will have to manually smooth out. If the problem becomes severe, you can lose any advantage of tracking over purely manual motion correction. If you anticipate a lot of tracking work, you should evaluate your compositing software based on the ease of use and the robustness of its trackers. In addition, a number of third-party plug-ins and standalone tracking software packages are available, because solutions to this set of problems can have a significant commercial value for both studios and freelance compositors.

There are three types of trackers in Digital Fusion 2.52: Tracker, Stabilizer, and Corner Tracker. The single Tracker is the foundation of the other two, so the process of defining patterns and building a path is common to all three.

PROJECT 11.1 Track A Moving Object

The goal of this project is to track a moving pattern to create an accurate path that can be used by other tools. You will use this basic process in single- and multiple-point tracking, stabilizing, and destabilizing.

1. Open a new flow and load the Box footage from the second CD-ROM. Because I shortened this footage to frames 200 through 402, you need to set the Global In control in the Loader to 200. This will offset the footage so all the frame numbers match with the original, complete footage.

2. Add a Tracker tool from the Tools|Miscellaneous submenu and connect it to the Loader. Select the Tracker. Your screen should look like Figure 11.4.

3. The moving object you want to track is the light bulb, which isn't completely visible until frame 285. Go to frame 285.

4. Drag the Tracker crosshair over the center of the light bulb, and zoom in to 400%, as in Figure 11.5.

You want to choose a pattern with as much contrast as possible. Often, you can find a stronger contrasting pattern if you use a single color channel rather than the full RGB image. In the Box footage, the light bulb is a warm white, very strong in all three color channels, so you could use any channel. However, the interior of the box around the light bulb is strong in reds, which would blend the pattern with the background. The green channel has better contrast, but the blue channel is best; there is very little blue in this area of the frame. Figure 11.6 shows the red, green, and blue channels for frame 285.

Figure 11.4
Tracker tool ready to select a pattern from the Box footage.

5. Set the Large display to the blue channel, and set the Tracker controls' Color to Blue, as shown in Figure 11.6.

The size of the pattern you select will depend on the size of the moving object and its contrast with the background. The light bulb's appearance in the blue channel is a simple circle. Ideally, you should be able to limit the Tracker pattern to this circle and a very narrow contrasting outline. You define the Tracker pattern, with the inner box surrounding the crosshair. The image within this box will be the source for the pattern recognition algorithm to compare to all other frames.

6. Drag the Tracker crosshair to precisely center it within the light bulb's circle. Drag the inner pattern box to contain only the light bulb and a minimum dark outline, as shown in Figure 11.7.

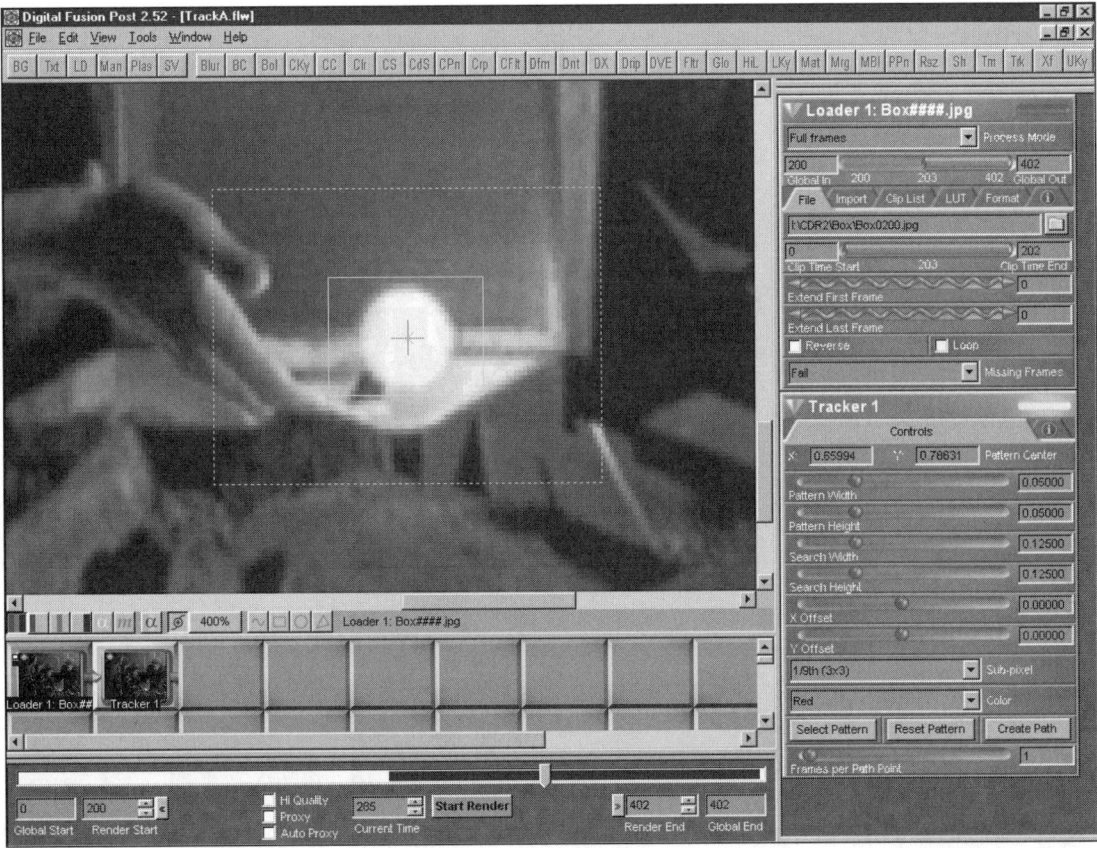

Figure 11.5
Tracker pattern selection crosshair positioned over the light bulb in frame 285.

The outer, dotted-line box defines the search area for the Tracker. That is, the Tracker will first search within the dotted lines for the pattern; if the pattern is not found, the Tracker will examine the entire frame. You should set the search area box to include the largest frame-to-frame motion of the tracked pattern, but no larger. An excessively large search area box takes longer to process and can allow the Tracker to wander off course. Keep it tight and don't confuse the Tracker. You can scrub through the footage to find the largest range of pattern motion. In the Box footage, the light bulb moves less than its own diameter between frames.

7. Resize the Tracker search area box to allow for the largest frame-to-frame movement of the pattern selected by the inner box, as shown in Figure 11.7.

8. Click on the Select Pattern button at the bottom of the Tracker controls. This sets the pattern. If you need to change the pattern, you can click on Reset Pattern, move the pattern box, and click on Select Pattern again.

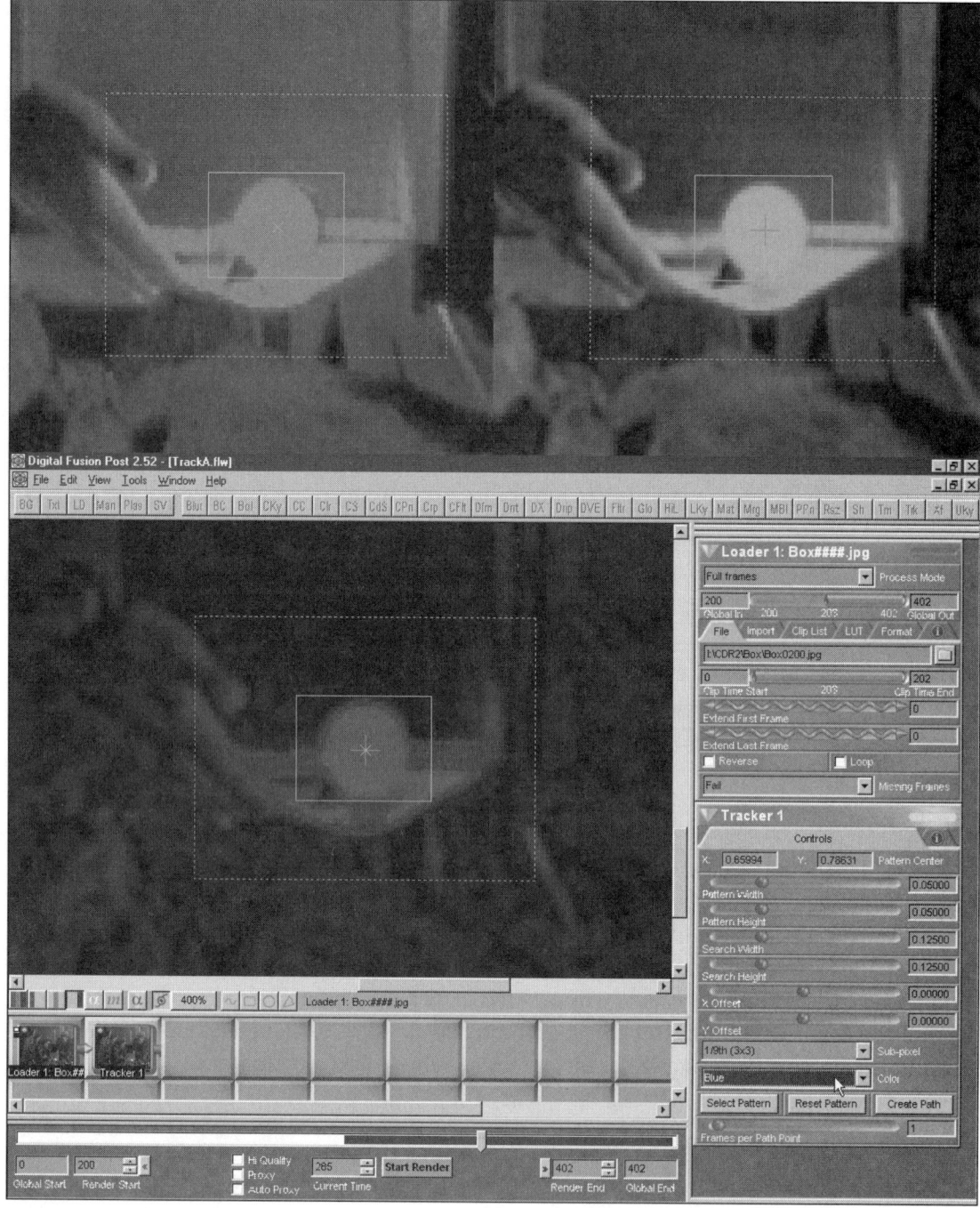

Figure 11.6
Above left: Red channel. Above right: Green channel. Below: Large display and Tracker set to the Blue channel for frame 285.

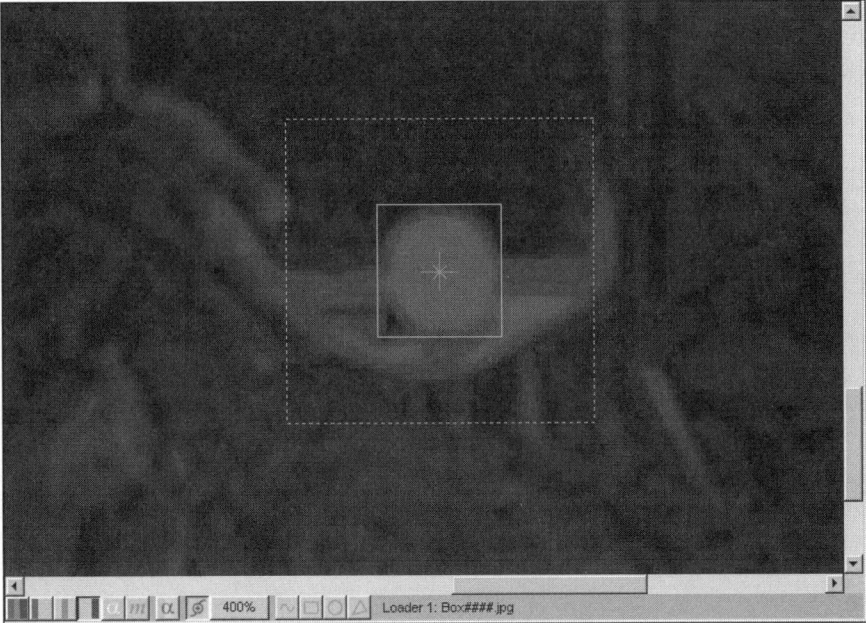

Figure 11.7
Tracker pattern box and search area box resized.

9. Set the Render Start and Render End frames for the length of path you want the Tracker to create. The Tracker will only process the frames within the Render range, beginning from the Render Start frame. Because the selected pattern doesn't exist until frame 285, set Render Start to 285 and Render End to 402.

10. Click on Create Path.

The Tracker will begin recognizing the pattern in each frame, moving the crosshairs to center on the recognized pattern, and setting the crosshair coordinates as a new keyframe in the path. This process should take only a minute or two. Watch the Tracker's progress: If it goes astray, you will need to stop the tracker, reset the pattern and render limits, and start over from the last good frame. This is a relatively simple and easy pattern, so the Tracker doesn't have to work too hard. A more difficult track, or one with multiple patterns and Trackers operating simultaneously, can take longer to process. When the Tracker is done, you should see a new Path 1 in the Mask View (F10).

Change the Large display back to full color. Open the Spline View, and click on Fit to see all the new keyframes in the path created by the Tracker (see Figure 11.8). Single-step through frames 285 to 402 to see how closely the Tracker followed the pattern. That's 115 keyframes that you didn't have to set manually.

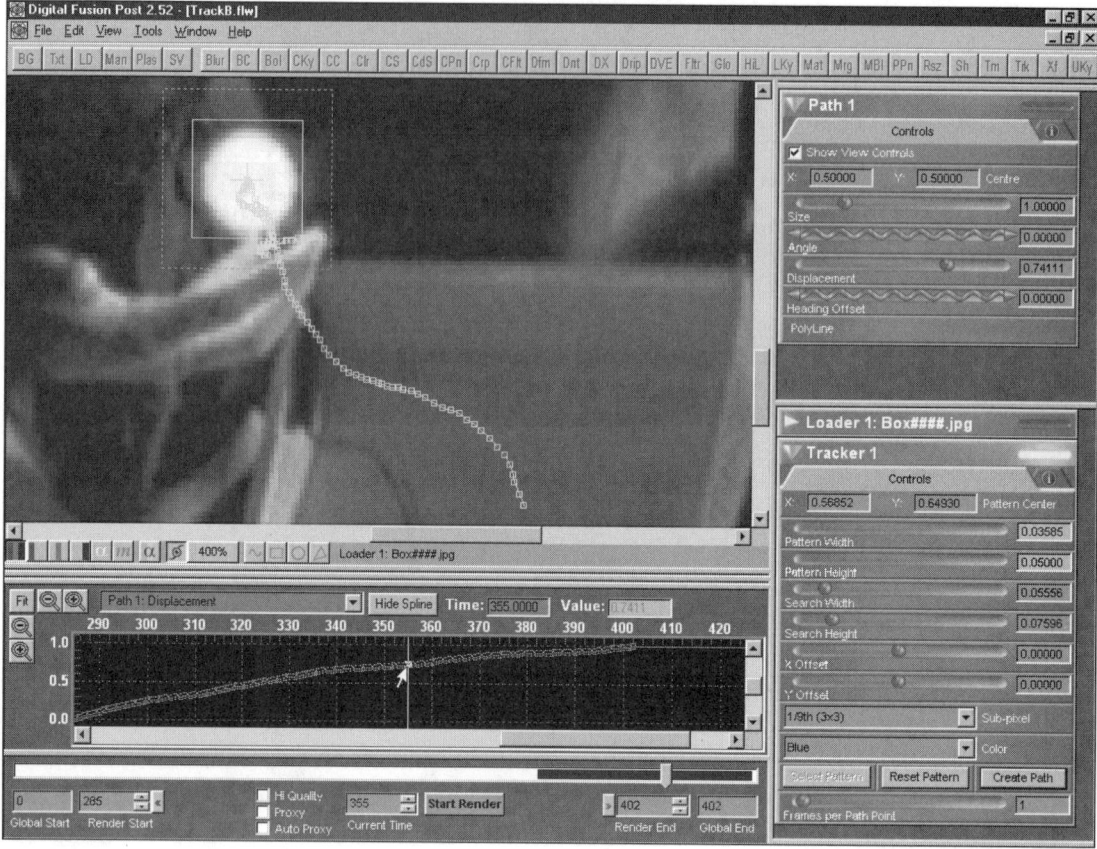

Figure 11.8
Path 1 created by the Tracker.

You now have a path that mimics the light bulb's motion for those frames where it is completely visible. So, what can you do with it? Lots of useful things! For starters, here's how a Tracker path can make a rotoscoped rig removal easier:

11. Add a Merge tool, and connect a second pipe from the Loader to the Merge foreground input.

12. Select the Merge tool. Right-click on the Merge control header, and choose Effect Mask|Polygon from the pop-up menu.

13. Right-click on the crosshair in the center of the Large display. Choose Polygon 1:Center| Connect To|Path 1:Value from the pop-up menu. This connects the center of the new polygon effect mask to the keyframed values that the Tracker recorded in Path 1 (see Figure 11.9). That means the center of Polygon 1 will automatically match the movement of the light bulb.

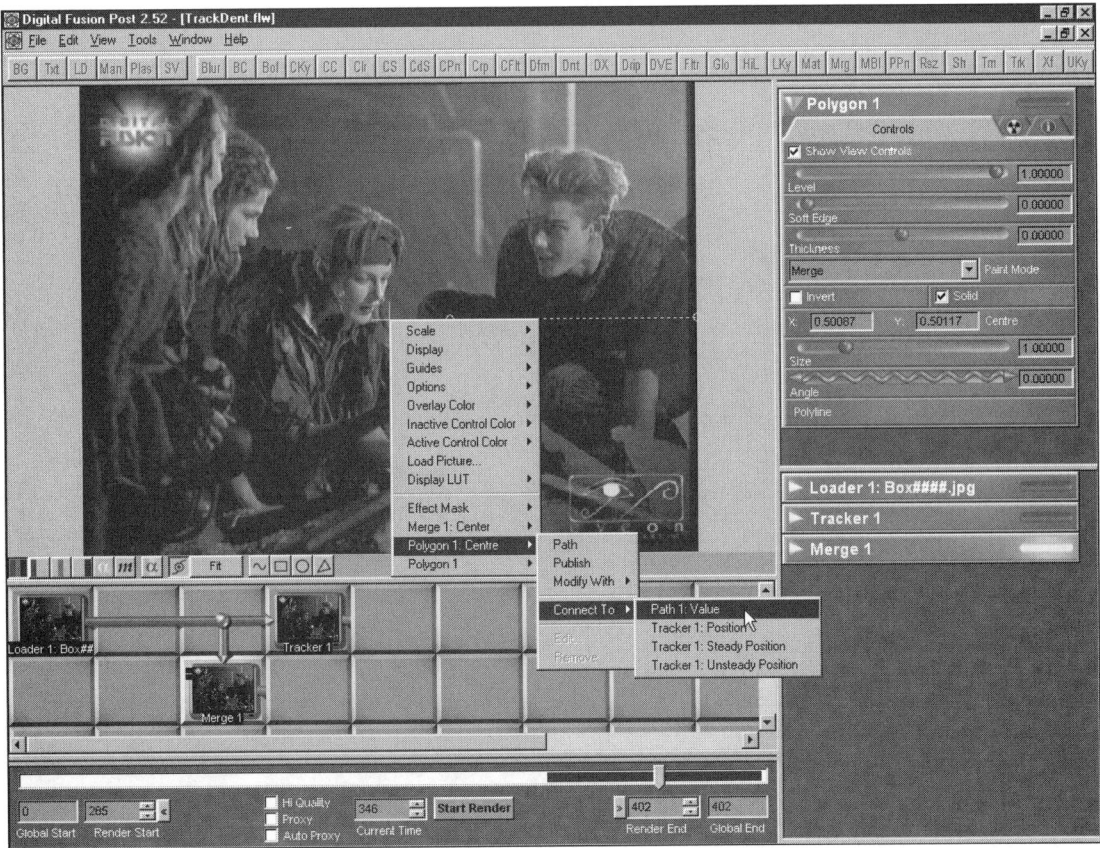

Figure 11.9
Polygon 1 connected to Path 1.

With Polygon 1 automatically matching the movement of the light bulb, you will only have to set keyframes to animate the shape of the polygon effect mask (see Figure 11.10). Contrast this to the rotoscoped rook removal in Project 10.2. If you refer back to the text around Figure 10.12, you see that the steps required to align the polygon mask to the base of the rook in each frame could be replaced by a Tracker-drawn path. That's a lot of time and effort saved, and a good track will eliminate a lot of the potential for chatter, too. If you'd like to test this, repeat Project 10.2, but apply a Tracker to the rook and connect the roto polygon mask to the Tracker's path. Similarly, using a Tracker could make Project 10.3, the rotoscoped actor removal, much easier. If you can track a pattern near an actor's center (try for a belt buckle or other centrally located costume element), you can reduce the need for keyframes to only the changes in the actor's profile. This is an especially big help when rotoscoping stunt jumps and other fast-moving actions.

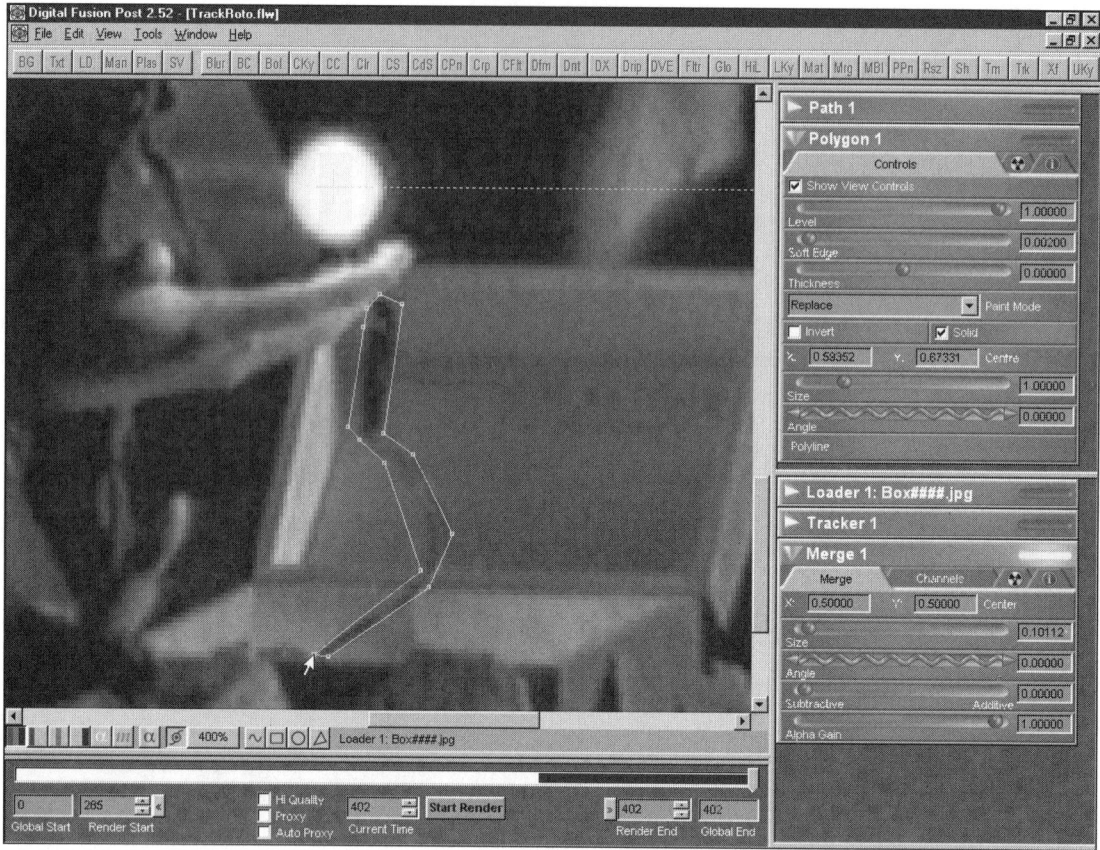

Figure 11.10
Polygon mask rotoscoped to remove the light-bulb wire.

You can connect almost any effect or element to a path created by a Tracker. You might review the last three figures at the end of Chapter 10 for ideas. With the right effect, a Tracker can make simple rig removals into complete no-brainers.

After the Tracker is finished with a path, you can edit that path manually to add keyframes. This is useful for smoothing out the beginning and end of tracks where the pattern changes or disappears. One of the most common tracking problems is when the tracking pattern begins off screen, moves across the frame, then exits. To solve this problem, you need to track the pattern in as many frames as possible, then:

14. Turn on Path 1's Show View Controls. Turn off Polygon 1's Show View Controls. Go to the first empty frame (284, if you have been following directions exactly).

15. Left-click and drag the first keyframe box to the exact center of the light bulb, where the Tracker crosshair would have been if this frame had been tracked accurately. Because there was no key set for this frame, Path 1 automatically gets a new keyframe for the coordinates you set.

16. Go to the next frame down, and repeat the click-and-drag to set new keyframes. After the light bulb is concealed by the side of the box (around frame 270), you can jump down to frame 200 and set a final keyframe.

You can estimate an appropriate location for keyframes for a hidden pattern by extrapolating from the last Tracker keyframes. In this case, the general direction of the light bulb was down and to the right, as it appeared to be resting in the back right corner of the box before the actress picked it up. Path 1 has a fairly smooth, relatively straight line from frame 289 to 285. Just make your manual keyframes align with that line, and the resulting motion will blend in well with the Tracker's. Your finished path should look something like Figure 11.11. Being able to eyeball an extrapolated motion path is a useful skill that you can develop by practice and study. An understanding of the principles of acceleration, deceleration, and slaloms in feedback systems can come in handy. However, the final authority on motion paths is the audience: It is more important that the motion "look right" than that it be perfect according to the laws of physics.

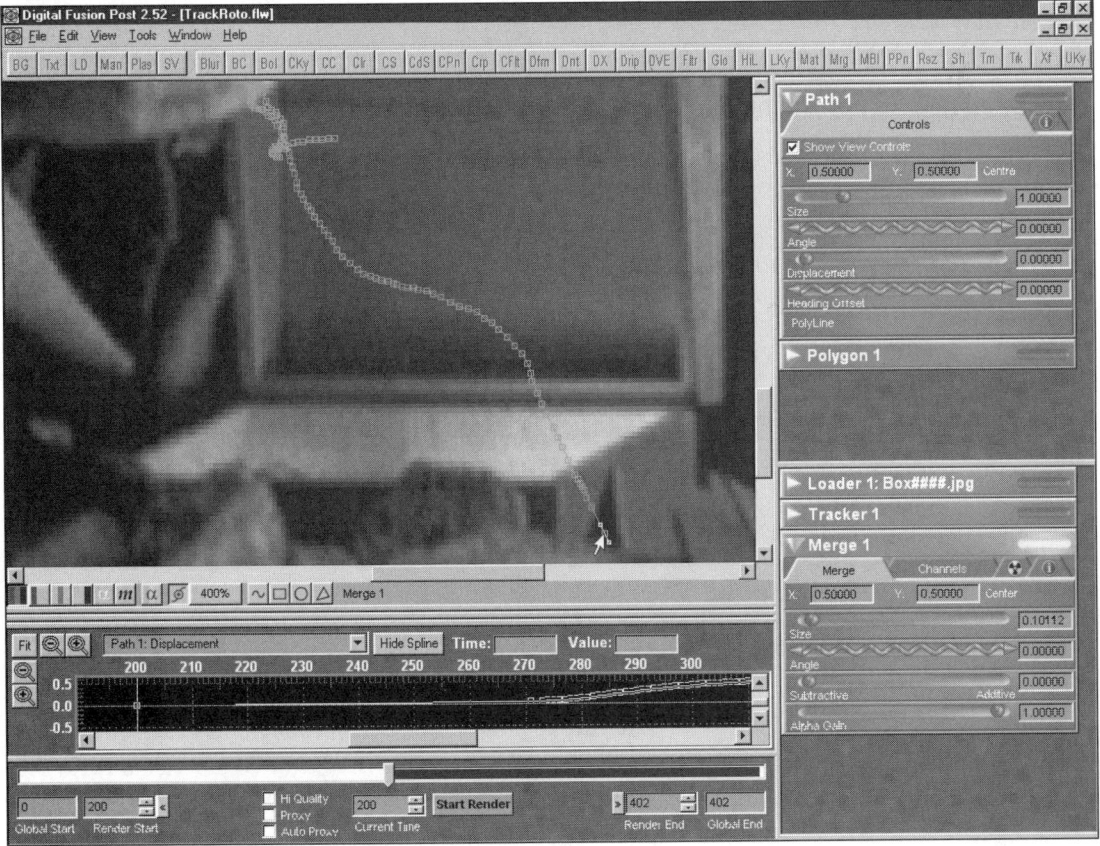

Figure 11.11
Path 1 keyframes added manually where the Tracker could not see a complete pattern, frames 200 through 284.

If a Tracker has problems following a pattern, you can try filtering the footage to make the Tracker's job easier. You can pipe the footage through a Blur/Sharpen filter or Brightness/Contrast color tool to boost the contrast and edges of the pattern. You don't have to worry about preserving image quality for other operations, because once you extract the path with the Tracker, you can go back to the original unfiltered footage.

In completing this project, you have learned how to:

- Apply a Tracker to create a keyframed path

- Manually add keyframes to an incomplete path

- Connect an effect mask to a tracker's path

- Select the best channels for a clear Tracker pattern

Track A Moving Object (After Effects)

The goal of this part of the project is to use After Effects to track a moving pattern and attach an effect to that tracked pattern. This is the basic process you will use in single-point tracking and stabilizing. After Effects' tracking features are available only in the Production Bundle version.

1. Open a new project and import the Box footage from the second CD-ROM. Create a new comp, and add the Box footage to it.

2. Import the Gship.tga image from the root directory of the first CD-ROM. You must have at least two layers in the comp before you can begin tracking. Add the Gship image to the comp, and bring its layer to the front.

3. Select the Box layer. Choose the Layer|Keyframe Assistant|Motion Tracker menu option. This opens the Motion Tracker window.

4. In the Motion Tracker window, set the In and Out points for the tracking operation. Drag the time slider to 3:00 seconds, and click on the In button (left brace) to set the current time as the starting point for the track. Drag the time slider to the last frame, 6:22 seconds, and click on the Out button (right brace) to set the end point for the track.

5. Press the I key to snap the time slider to the starting point for the track. Choose Track Position from the drop-down menu of tracking types.

The Motion Tracker window shows three markers in the center of the Box image. The small crosshair is the track point, which will become the location of any effect or layer that the track is applied to. The small inner square is the feature region, which defines the boundaries of the tracked pattern. The larger outer square is the search region, the area that is searched during the track operation in order to locate the pattern that matches the feature region.

6. Drag the track point to the center of the light bulb. This point is where you want the Gship to appear after the tracking operation, covering the light bulb.

7. Move and resize the feature region to just touch the edges of the light bulb at top, bottom, and sides. This provides a distinctive and easy-to-track pattern.

8. Move and resize the search region to include the entire area traveled by the light bulb.

If the tracked pattern (the light bulb) passes beyond the edges of the search region, the tracking operation will fail. However, too large a search region can significantly slow the tracking operation. To fine-tune the search region, you can temporarily drag the time slider to the last frame to observe the final position of the light bulb. You will need to return the time slider to the In point before you can move or resize the search region. Your results should look something like Figure 11.12.

9. Click on the Options button to open the Motion Tracker Options dialog box. Choose the Gship.tga layer from the Apply Motion To menu. Choose RGB from Track Options:Use, set Track Adaptiveness to 50%, and choose 1/16 from the Subpixel Matching drop-down menu. Click on OK to close the dialog box.

Figure 11.12
The Motion Tracker window, showing the settings for the In and Out frames, and the positions of the search region, feature region, and track point.

Unlike Digital Fusion and other compositing software, After Effects doesn't enable you to track patterns in only one color channel. This feature would make this track more accurate because the reddish surroundings could be eliminated by tracking only the blue channel. If difficult tracking operations are a regular part of your digital compositing work, you may want to consider using software other than After Effects.

10. In the Motion Tracker window, click on Track. Keep an eye on the tracking to make sure it doesn't wander off the target pattern. If it does, press any key to stop the track, then correct the problem and start the track over.

11. When the track is completed to your satisfaction, click on Apply to close the Motion Tracker window and to apply the tracking data to the Gship layer.

12. In the Time Layout window, expand the Gship layer. Under Transform, you should find that the Position variable has a keyframe on each frame between 3:00 and 6:22, the In and Out points of the tracking operation.

13. Set the In point of the Gship layer to the In point of the tracking operation. This hides the Gship until the first frame that includes tracking coordinates. Set the Gship layer's Transform|Scale to 10 percent. This reduces the Gship to a size slightly larger than the light bulb.

14. Play back the composition. For the tracked portion, you should see something like Figure 11.13. Save the project as BoxTrack.aep.

If you like, you can manually set keyframes for the motion and scale of the Gship layer to make the Gship cover the light bulb from its first appearance. This kind of manual keyframing is often necessary to smooth the rough edges of a tracking operation.

Aura And Tracking

Aura 1.0 has no tracking features. If you need these features, you must use a different compositing program.

Track A Moving Object (Chalice)

Silicon Grail's Chalice package includes a PDF version of the manual and several tutorials, plus footage for completing the tutorials. These files are available for download from the company's Web site (www.sgrail.com) and are also located in the Chalice folder of this book's first CD-ROM. One of these tutorials demonstrates Chalice's tracking features, with far greater detail than I have room to do here. Rather than having you repeat the efforts of this tutorial's designers, I recommend (if you are using Chalice) that you work through Tutorial 4, Track And Pin, and then repeat the tracking process by using the Box footage from this book's second CD-ROM.

Besides the tutorial, pages 10.18 through 10.24 of the Chalice 1.6 manual (in PDF format in the Chalice folder) cover the tracking process. If you're using Chalice, I highly recommend reading its manual before going further in this book. If you are considering downloading the demo version,

Figure 11.13
The results of the tracking operation, showing the Gship layer tracked to the light bulb.

I suggest you read the manual and tutorial instructions thoroughly, so you can maximize the time you have to experiment with the program.

Track A Moving Object (Commotion)

Puffin Designs' Commotion package includes tutorial footage and instructions for several tracking projects. Rather than repeat the efforts of the tutorials' designers, I recommend (if you are using Commotion) that you work through Lesson 8, the first tracking tutorial, then repeat the tracking process using the Box footage from this book's second CD-ROM.

Besides the Lesson 8 tutorial, pages 260 through 279 of the Commotion Manual cover the tracking and stabilizing process thoroughly and concisely. Lee Croft, lead writer on the manual, did an excellent job. If you are using Commotion, I highly recommend reading its manual before going further in this book.

Track A Moving Object (effect*)

The demo version of Discreet effect* (located on the first CD-ROM) also includes tutorial footage and instructions for a tracking project. Rather than having you duplicate that effort, I recommend that you install the effect* demo, work through the demo tutorial projects, and then repeat the tracking process by using the Box footage from the second CD-ROM.

Besides the demo tutorial, Chapter 12 of the effect* User's Guide has an excellent functional overview of tracking and stabilizing operations. If you are using effect*, I highly recommend reading the User's Guide material before going further in this book.

Shake And Tracking

Shake 2.1 has no tracking features. If you need these features, you need to use a different compositing program.

Stabilizing

Tracking patterns within the frame is adequate for compositing effects that only interact with the tracked patterns. A more difficult challenge is footage that requires full-frame effects such as removals to a clean plate. For example, the Box footage requires rig removal to hide the electrical wires leading to the light bulb, plus whatever effect is going to replace the light bulb. The most effective option would be removal to a clean plate, or a time shift, as described in Chapter 10. However, the Box footage is from a moving camera. Without a motion-controlled clean plate, no easy way exists to match the camera move to create a clean plate. A time shift also runs into problems because the background will be visibly offset with any time shift longer than a frame or two.

The solution to these and similar problems is to *stabilize* the footage. This means using a Tracker and other tools to extract the camera movement, then applying the reciprocal of that motion to the footage. The result is footage that looks like it was shot with a solidly locked down camera. Extracting a clean plate, comping time shifts, and many other operations are much simpler with stabilized footage.

Single-Point Stabilization

The simplest form of stabilization uses a single tracking pattern similar to the one you set up in Project 11.1. This is called *single-point stabilization*. It is useful for footage where the camera does not dolly in or zoom, and it simply moves (or *translates*) up, down, left, or right. Single-point stabilization is a good solution to unintentional camera motion, as when someone hits the camera or a tripod head has a glitch. This stabilization is also called *translational correction*.

Stabilize The Box Footage

The goal of this project is to stabilize the Box footage so you can use a clean plate or time shifting to remove the light bulb and wires.

1. Repeat the first 11 steps of Project 11.1, but track on all frames and use the corner of the box as the Tracker pattern, as shown in Figure 11.14.

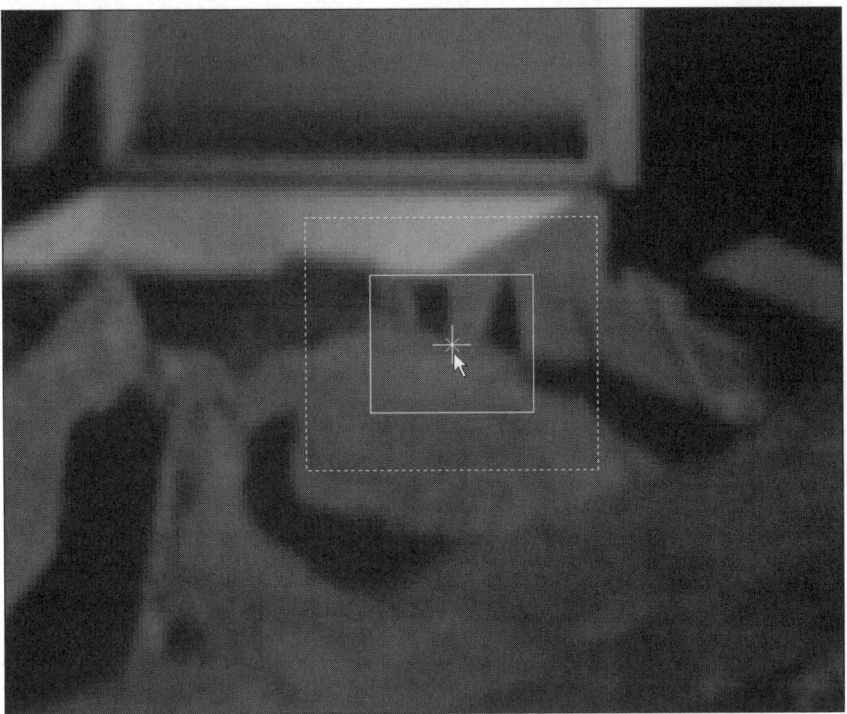

Figure 11.14
Tracker pattern selected for stabilizing Box footage.

This pattern is most visible in the Red channel and does not change appreciably as the light bulb moves around. Other areas of the box change appearance drastically as the light bulb moves, which can interfere with the Tracker.

Your Tracker results should look like Figure 11.15. Note that noise, digitizing, or compression artifacts that make small changes to edges within the pattern can cause the Tracker to make very small movements. This can actually add more jitter to the footage than it removes. You can prevent some of this motion by applying a Blur filter, Grain Killer, or other noise-reduction process as described in Chapter 9. Again, you have to do this only for the Tracker; the original footage can still be used for any downstream operations.

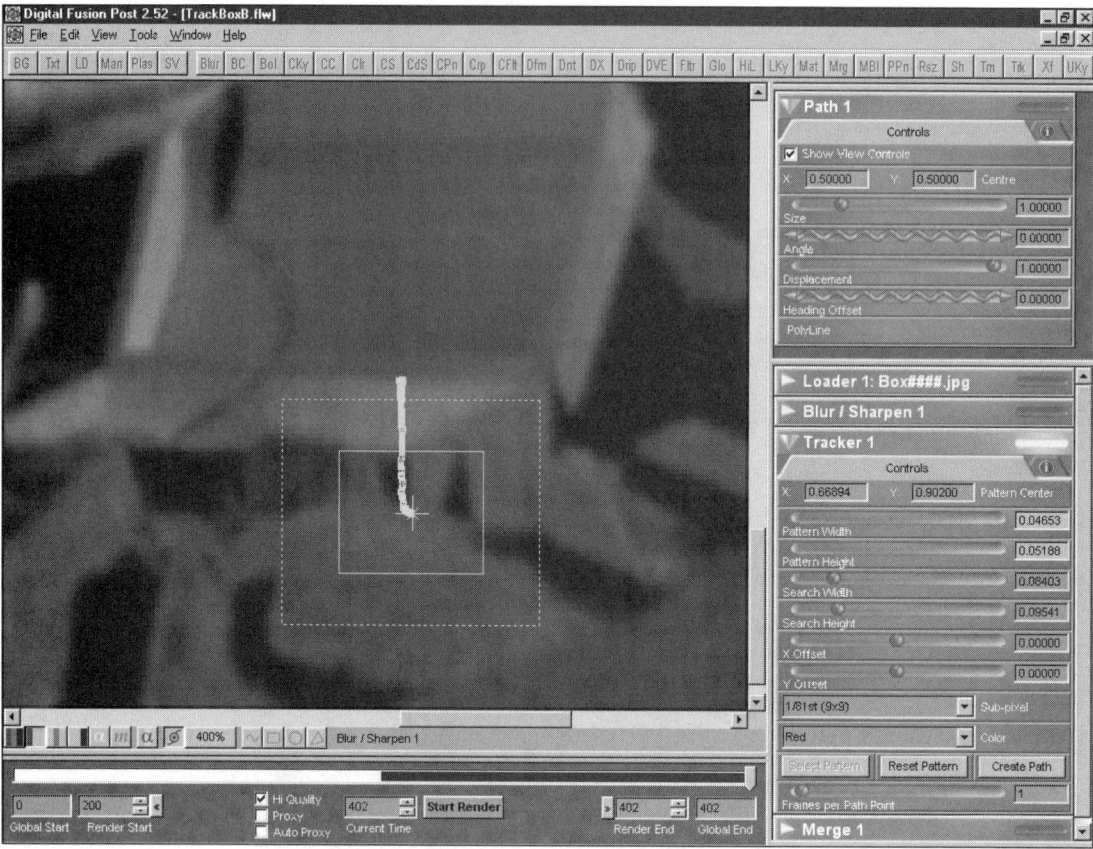

Figure 11.15
Tracker keyframes for stabilizing the Box footage.

2. Select the Merge tool. Right-click on the Merge Center control, and choose Connect To|
   Tracker 1: Steady Position, as shown in Figure 11.16.

This moves the foreground Merge input to match the reciprocal of the movement of the Tracker,
with the effect that the footage appears to be nailed down solidly. This is different from connecting to the path, and the two approaches have different uses. Connecting an effect or tool to a
path enables you to add or modify keyframes to change the motion. This enables you to use a
path to follow motion that begins or ends off screen, as you did in the preceding project. However, that path's keyframes have fixed values that won't update to accommodate any changes
you make upstream in the flow. Connecting an effect or tool to the Tracker's Steady Position
doesn't allow you to add, delete, or modify keyframes, because the final values depend on the
state of the flow at the time you initiate the final render. When you render out the flow, the
Tracker calculates the Steady Position based on the current inputs. If you have tweaked some
filters or other settings to clarify the footage, the Tracker will take advantage of that.

Figure 11.16
Tracker 1 Steady Position connected to Merge 1 Center.

3. Add a Saver and connect it to the Merge tool's output. Render the entire sequence as an AVI or other animation format that your system can play back at full frame rate. Play back the animation, and look closely at the box's movement.

You shouldn't see any movement of the box at all, at least in the center of the pattern area. You need to render the output at full resolution to check the Tracker's stabilization, because the approximations used to render previews will show a lot of jitter that doesn't appear in the final render. If you don't remember this, you may find yourself in a very frustrating loop of tracking, previewing, tweaking, and tracking again in a vain effort to remove motion that is not actually there. It's just an artifact of the preview-rendering process.

In completing this project, you have learned how to:

• Connect an effect mask to a Tracker's Unsteady Position output

• Stabilize camera motion perpendicular to the lens

The most significant advantage of using the Tracker's Steady Position is that it is precisely reversible with the Unsteady Position output. That is, footage rendered from the Steady Position can be brought back into the flow through a Loader and Merge connected to the same Tracker's Unsteady Position, and it can be given the precise camera movement that the Steady Position removed from the original footage. This is a critical ability if the camera move was a deliberate choice by the director. If you can't destabilize a shot you stabilized, you may have a dramatically shortened career. Chapter 12 has more extensive information about the Tracker's Unsteady Position tool and other destabilization tools.

Stabilize The Box Footage (After Effects)

The goal of this project is to stabilize the Box footage so you can use a clean plate or time shifting to remove the light bulb and wires. After Effects' stabilizing features are available only in the Production Bundle version.

1. Open a new project and import the Box footage. Create a new comp and add the Box footage to it.

2. In the Time Layout window, right-click on the Box layer and choose Keyframe Assistant|Motion Stabilizer from the pop-up menu. This makes the Motion Stabilizer window appear.

3. In the Motion Stabilizer window, click on the Options button to open the Motion Tracker Options dialog box. Choose Track Options:Use|RGB, set Track Adaptiveness to 50%, and choose 1/16 from the Subpixel Matching drop-down menu. Click on OK to close the dialog box.

4. In the Motion Stabilizer window, make sure Stabilize Position is selected from the stabilization type menu. The first 2:15 of the Box footage is stable, so the stabilization needs to be applied only between 2:15 and 6:22. Set the In and Out points accordingly.

5. A good pattern for stabilization is the near right corner of the lower half of the box. Set the search region and feature region as shown in Figure 11.17.

6. Click on Stabilize. After Effects will track the feature region and calculate the offset to stabilize the Box layer. Keep an eye on the stabilization; if the feature region is creeping off the target, stop the process and correct the problem.

7. When the stabilize operation is complete, click on Apply to close the Motion Stabilizer window and apply the stabilization to the Box layer. Your results should look like Figure 11.18.

8. Render the comp as a TGA image sequence named Stable###.TGA. You'll need this stabilized image sequence in the next chapter. Save the project as BoxStable.aep.

Aura And Single-Point Stabilization

Aura 1.0 has no stabilization features. If you need these features, use a different compositing program.

Figure 11.17
The search and feature regions are set up for the position stabilization of the Box footage.

Stabilize The Box Footage (Chalice)

As I stated in Chalice Project 11.1, the PDF version of the manual and several tutorials, plus footage for completing the tutorials, are available for download from the company's Web site (**www.sgrail.com**). These tutorials are also located in the Chalice folder of this book's first CD-ROM. Rather than repeat the efforts of the Silicon Grail staff, I recommend (if you are using Chalice) that you work through the tutorials and then apply what you've learned to stabilize the Box footage from this book's second CD-ROM.

Besides the tutorials, pages 10.18 through 10.24 and 14.3 through 14.8 of the Chalice 1.6 manual cover the stabilizing process. If you're using Chalice, I highly recommend reading at least these portions of its manual before going further in this book.

Figure 11.18
The Composition window shows the Box layer after stabilization. Notice the black border at the bottom edge of the image: The Time Layout window shows the Anchor Point keyframes of the stabilization between 2:15 and 6:22. The original footage is stable up to 2:15, so no keyframes were necessary up to this point.

Stabilize The Box Footage (Commotion)

As was stated in Commotion Project 11.1, the Commotion package ships with tutorial footage and instructions for several tracking projects, including single-point stabilization. Rather than repeat the efforts of the tutorials' designers, I recommend (if you are using Commotion) that you work through Lesson 8, the first tracking tutorial, and then repeat the single-point stabilization process using the Box footage from this book's second CD-ROM.

Stabilize The Box Footage (effect*)

Chapter 12 of the effect* User's Guide has an excellent overview of tracking and stabilizing. If you are using effect*, I highly recommend reading the User's Guide material before going further in this book. If you are using the demo version included on this book's first CD-ROM, you should complete the preceding effect* Project 11.1 before attempting this project.

1. Load the Box footage.

2. Choose Effect|Stabilize|Stabilize 1 Point. The Stabilize 1 Point effect palette appears.

3. Click on the Stabilize Point Pick button to activate the crosshairs. The crosshairs will appear in the Composition window.

4. Set the Mode to Shift, set the Borders to Use Color, and set the Border Color to black.

5. On the Tracker palette, click on the Position button. In the Composition window, a tracker box appears on the Stabilize effect crosshairs.

6. Position the tracker on a reference point for stabilizing. A good pattern for stabilization is the near right corner of the lower half of the box.

7. On the Tracker palette, click on the Analyze button. The Tracker will analyze the movement of the tracked patter, as shown in Figure 11.19.

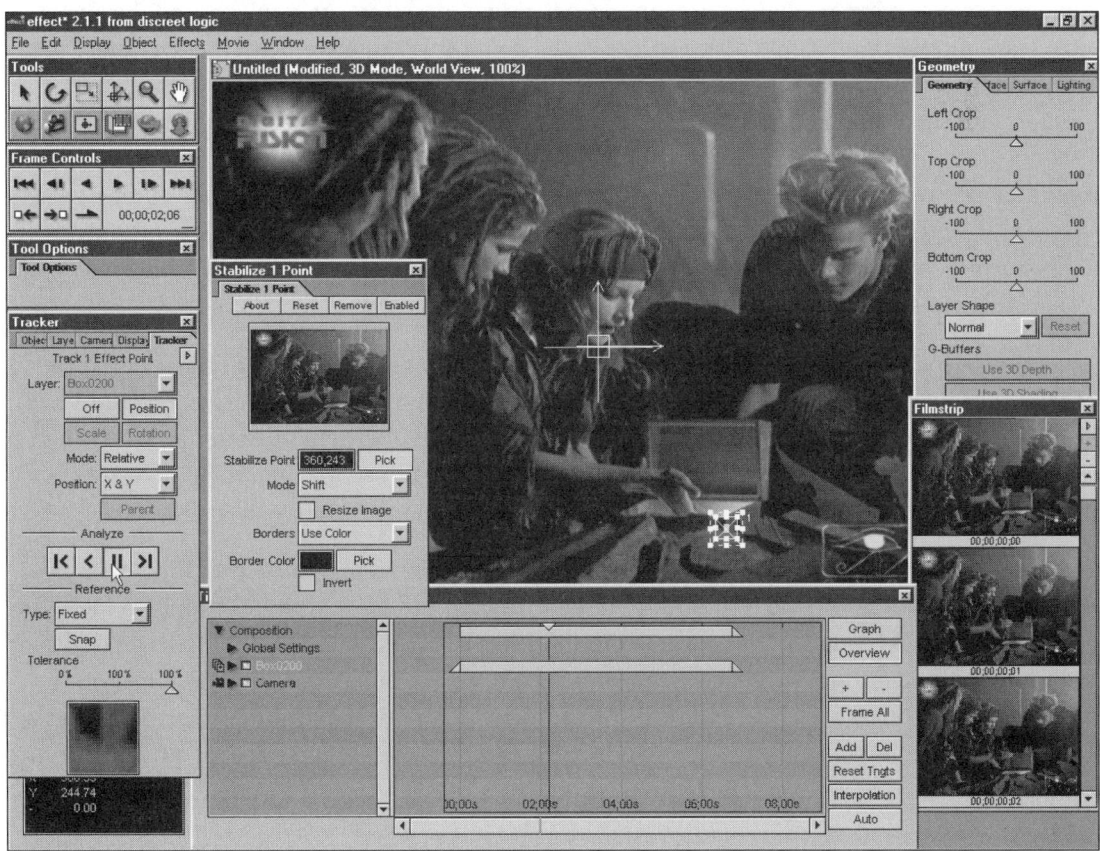

Figure 11.19
The effect* Tracker is analyzing the motion of the Box footage.

8. When the analysis is complete, click on the Enabled button in the Stabilize 1 Point effect palette. The Stabilize effect moves the Box footage according to the position of the tracker, making the box stay in one place, or *stabilize*. Note that the motion of the image exposes a black border at the bottom of the image.

9. Render the comp as a TGA image sequence named Stable###.TGA. You'll need this stabilized image sequence in the next chapter. Save the project as BoxStable.icp.

Shake And Single-Point Stabilization

Shake 2.1 has no stabilization features. If you need these features, you have to use a different compositing program.

Two-Point Stabilization

Single-point stabilization is good enough for translation corrections for simple camera jitters, but cameras can also move in or out, they can zoom in or out, and they can bank around the lens axis. These motions can't be stabilized with a single point; they require at least *two-point stabilization*. With a second tracked reference point, the software can extract scaling, perspective, and rotation corrections in addition to the translation corrections possible with a single tracked point. This stabilization of camera movement in all three axes of movement and rotation makes matching a CGI element to a complex camera move much easier. Load the Match footage or refer to Figure 11.2, and try to imagine how you would animate a CGI element to match the movement of the porch and steps. A good two-point track can remove over two-thirds of the keyframes you would otherwise have to set in a purely manual match move.

Correction of scaling means that the reference points' appearance in close-up frames (see Figure 11.20) are matched to frames with more distant (closer together) reference points (see Figure 11.21) by enlarging the more distant frames. This means the margins of the enlarged frames will be lost. Correction of rotation means that the frame will be rotated to match the alignment of the reference points. Again, the margins of the frame may be lost, as shown in Figure 11.22.

One way to preserve a full frame of image through the stabilization process is to shoot with oversized framing. That is, instead of framing the shot through the camera as it is supposed to appear in the final production, you frame the shot with a large enough margin to cover any stabilization or other framing effects (see Figure 11.23). For example, the CineVort folder on the second CD-ROM holds a 2K film image that was framed with plenty of margin. The higher resolution of film means you can stabilize and destabilize a video-resolution window out of this shot without worrying about running out of image area.

Figure 11.20
In frame 154, the threshold reference points appear farther apart when closer to the camera.

Figure 11.21
In frame 1, the threshold reference points appear close together when distant from the camera. The left point appears rotated about five degrees clockwise, relative to the right reference point.

Figure 11.22
Frame 1, if corrected for scale and rotation to match frame 154, would include only the area inside the white rectangle. The image outside the rectangle would be lost.

Another way to preserve a full frame is to shoot on an oversized format. In film production, this is commonly done using the VistaVision format, as described in Chapter 5. By filming the image sideways on standard 35mm film, you can get 6K by 4K resolution from some film scanners. This gives you the same capabilities for final 2K film framing as is shown for video framing in Figure 11.23.

> *"In the end, VistaVision is safety—you can always blow things up or reposition them in post. It's funny; after my first year of working with the VistaVision cameras at ILM, my impression was 'God, these things are horrible.' But there are times even today, in the era of 'digital magic,' when VistaVision will save your ass."*
> *—Mark Dippé, director, Spawn*

If you will be destabilizing the footage after the match move and other effects are done, there is a third way to preserve the margins of the frame. You simply "uncrop" or add a black border, wide enough to accommodate all stabilization changes, around the original footage. This gives you enough elbow room for your stabilizations to keep every image intact. For example,

Figure 11.23
A flow showing the capability to crop a smaller, lower-resolution image from a film-resolution frame, with plenty of margin left for stabilization and destabilization.

Figure 11.24 shows the original frame, an "uncropped" rendering of the same frame, and the stabilized rendering of the uncropped frame. When this image is destabilized again and cropped back down to the original resolution, the results will look like the original image with no missing margins or corners. The disadvantage of this approach is that the uncropped images are huge and will require more storage space and processing time. A good starting point is to triple the frame size, on the theory that any reference point within the frame can move no more than the full width or height of the frame. Sometimes overly large scaling corrections can push the margins of the frame even farther, but generally, 3X is a good safety margin. With experience, you will learn to estimate more closely the maximum frame size you will need. The closer you can estimate the necessary resolution, the faster and more efficiently your comps will run.

Figure 11.24
Salvaging margins. Top: Original frame. Middle: Uncropping the image to triple resolution. Bottom: Stabilized image with no margins or corners lost.

Unfortunately, two-point stabilization with Digital Fusion's Stabilizer tool can't be destabilized easily, because there is no equivalent to the Tracker's Unsteady Position connection. Chapter 12 will demonstrate one method of working around this, with a project designed to destabilize the Match footage after a match move and CGI element compositing.

PROJECT 11.3 Two-Point Stabilize Of The Match000.jpg Porch Footage

The goal of this project is to stabilize the Match footage to prepare this shot for a manual match move project in Chapter 12. The best results will minimize the number of manual keyframes you will need to set in that project. The final product of these combined projects will be a CGI element perfectly move-matched to the original, unstabilized Match footage.

1. Open a new flow. Add a Loader, and load the Match footage from the first CD-ROM.

Scrub through the footage, looking for stabilization problems and possible Tracker patterns. Keep in mind that you will be trying to animate a CGI camera and models of the porch steps, as described at the end of Chapter 6, to match this footage. Figure 11.25 is a reference photograph of the porch steps with measurements and reference points drawn on it. On-set sketches like this can greatly reduce the difficulty of a match move.

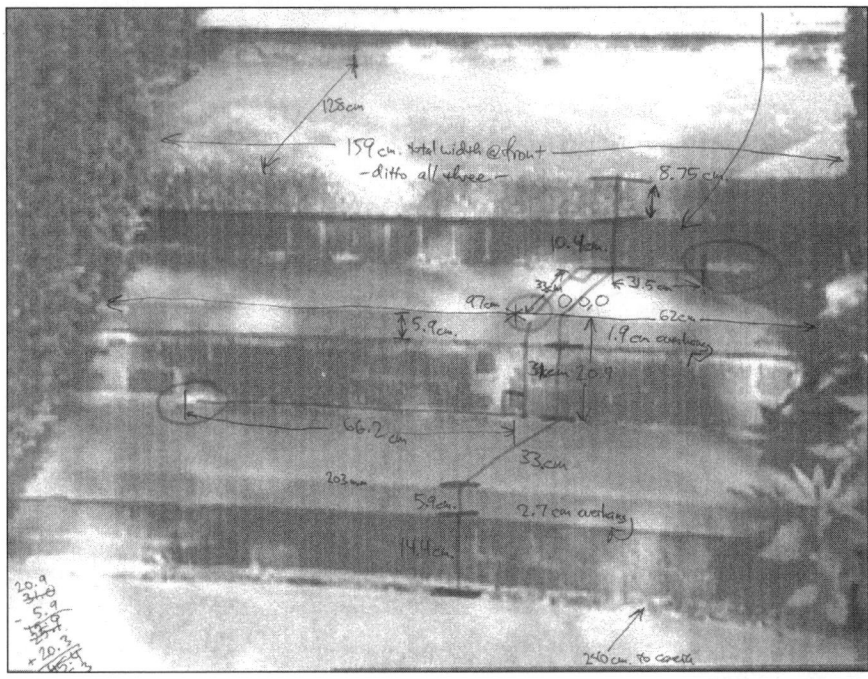

Figure 11.25
Photograph of porch steps with measurements and reference points marked on it.

From examining the footage and sketch, you might conclude that the right-side and left-side door threshold ends, as shown in Figure 11.26, are good Tracker patterns. Because the threshold is painted gray and the siding is white, any color channel will get nearly the same pattern. However, the bushes and grass are green, and therefore brightest in the green channel and darkest in the red channel. For best overall contrast, track this footage in the red channel.

Figure 11.26
Representative frame showing good candidate areas for Tracker patterns.

2. Choose a reference frame for the tracker targets.

Here are some criteria you should keep in mind:

- The change in distance between the targets determines the scaling correction.

- The change in alignment between the targets determines the rotation correction.

- The change in position of the targets determines the translation correction.

- The clarity of the targets *in all frames* determines the ease and success of tracking.

- The reference frame determines the size of your working area for comped elements.

The larger your working area, the easier it is to fine-tune a match move or other manually animated effect. A larger working area will also produce a higher-resolution image after destabilization. If the stabilization stretches the image, the destabilization will shrink the image. This effectively reduces the size and visibility of any flaws in your comp. The reverse is also true: A reduced stabilized image gives you a small, cramped working area, and the destabilization will stretch out and magnify any errors in your comp. Ideally, you could simply choose the reference frame to maximize your working area. In the Match footage, this would mean choosing frame 265 (see Figure 11.27), because that's where the porch surface is largest. Unfortunately, this is

Figure 11.27
Frame with maximum working area for match-moving CGI elements to the porch surface.

also the frame with the fewest options for other Tracker targets, a lot of rotation and translation correction, and the maximum possible scaling correction. In other words, you would get a nice big working area, but every other part of creating this comp would suffer.

You need to strike a balance among the most important criteria. For example, the plan is to do a manual match move with this footage. From the sketches and photos, it is obvious that the strong horizontal lines in this footage could be an important asset for matching shadow surfaces and any CGI characters that would move over them. With that in mind, I went looking for a reference frame that would stabilize the step and porch edges as close to perfectly horizontal as possible. I also wanted to have as many additional Tracker targets as possible. That means something below frame 212, where the chip at the edge of the second step, a central marker for the critical areas, disappears. Finally, I wanted to keep the scaling and translation changes to a minimum to reduce the size of the uncropped images. I finally settled on frame 154 of the Match footage as my reference frame.

3. Add a Crop tool to the flow, and connect it to the Loader.

4. Set the Crop controls' X Size to 2160 and Y Size to 1458, or three times the resolution of the source footage. Check Keep Aspect and Keep Centered.

Figure 11.28
The flow is set up to render the Match footage with a safe border for two-point stabilizing and destabilizing.

5. Add a Saver, and choose an output format and directory. I like to use the compressed TGA file format for this operation. The TGA files are very small because the black areas compress well. An uncompressed image at this resolution is about 12MB; with compression, it's less than 1.5MB, about the size of the original D1 image. Save the alpha channel; you'll need it for the destabilization process. Your flow should look like Figure 11.28. Render the footage.

6. Load the Uncrop footage into a new flow. Add a Stabilizer tool, and connect it to the Loader. Add a Saver. Your flow should look like Figure 11.29.

The Stabilizer tool incorporates two Trackers, plus controls to select the stabilization of position, rotation, and scaling. Most of the controls should be familiar from the preceding Tracker project. The only significant change is that you need to select two patterns.

Figure 11.29
The flow is set up to stabilize the Uncrop footage.

There is such a change in the relative size of the tracking pattern from beginning to end, as shown in Figure 11.30, that you will probably not be able to track the whole sequence in one pass. My best results came from two passes, frames 1 through 89, and 90 through 265.

The pattern for the first 90 frames should be smaller (see Figure 11.31), but the pattern for the latter half of the footage can be slightly larger (see Figure 11.32). This limits the edges of the patterns to the plain white surface of the siding, keeping the threshold corners in the middle of the pattern. This provides a comfortable level of slop in the pattern, an important consideration for this footage. With this amount of Z-axis camera movement, the apparent size of the siding boards changes appreciably on every frame. If the boards' edges were included in the tracker pattern, the tracker could only recognize a reliable pattern on a handful of frames at a time. On the other hand, the pattern of the threshold corners on a plain white background is consistent for over a hundred frames at a time.

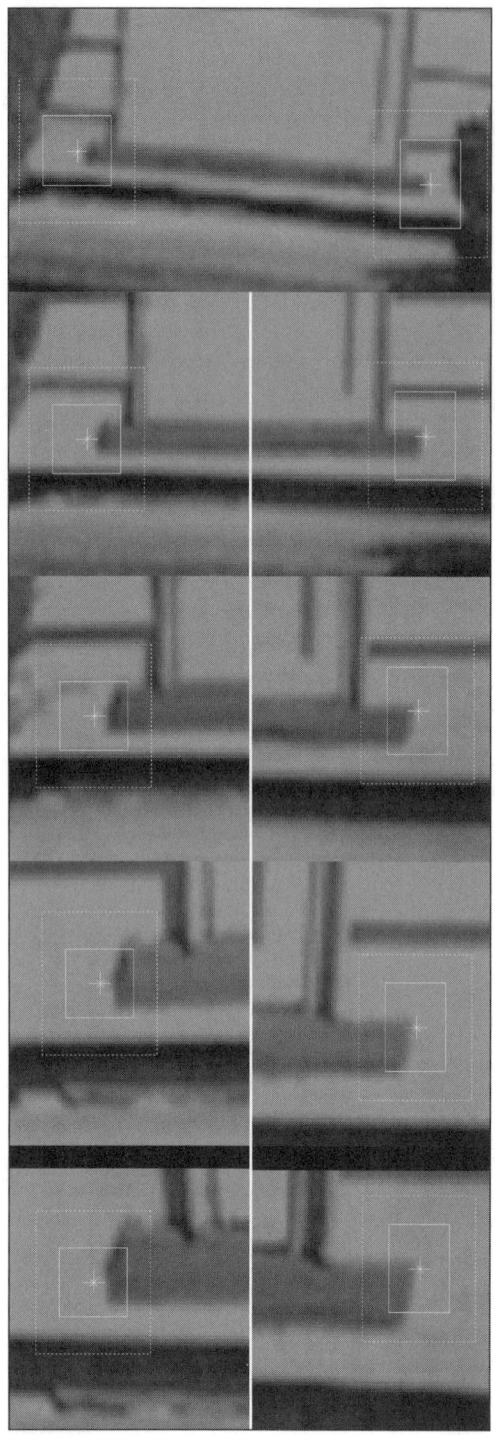

Figure 11.30
Large differences between beginning and ending tracking patterns require more than one Tracker operation.
Top to bottom: Frames 1, 90, 154, 211, 265.

Figure 11.31
Tracker pattern selected for stabilizing frames 1 through 89.

7. Go to frame 1. Select patterns for Tracker 1 and Tracker 2, as shown in Figure 11.31. Track in the Red color channel. Set Render Start to frame 1 and Render End to frame 89.

8. When both patterns are selected, go to the General tab and click on Create All Paths.

The Stabilizer will run both trackers simultaneously. This will take a minute or two. You should watch the process closely; if one of the trackers goes off course, you need to stop the track, reset the patterns, and restart the track from the last good frame.

9. When the first track is done, you need to set up and run the second track. Go to frame 90. Set Render Start to frame 90 and Render End to frame 265. In the General tab of the Stabilizer, click on Reset All Patterns.

10. Resize, but do not try to reposition, the inner box and search area box for each Tracker. Use the same sizing criteria you did for the first pair of patterns; you are making these changes simply to allow for the larger size of the patterns in the latter part of this footage. Your results should look like Figure 11.32.

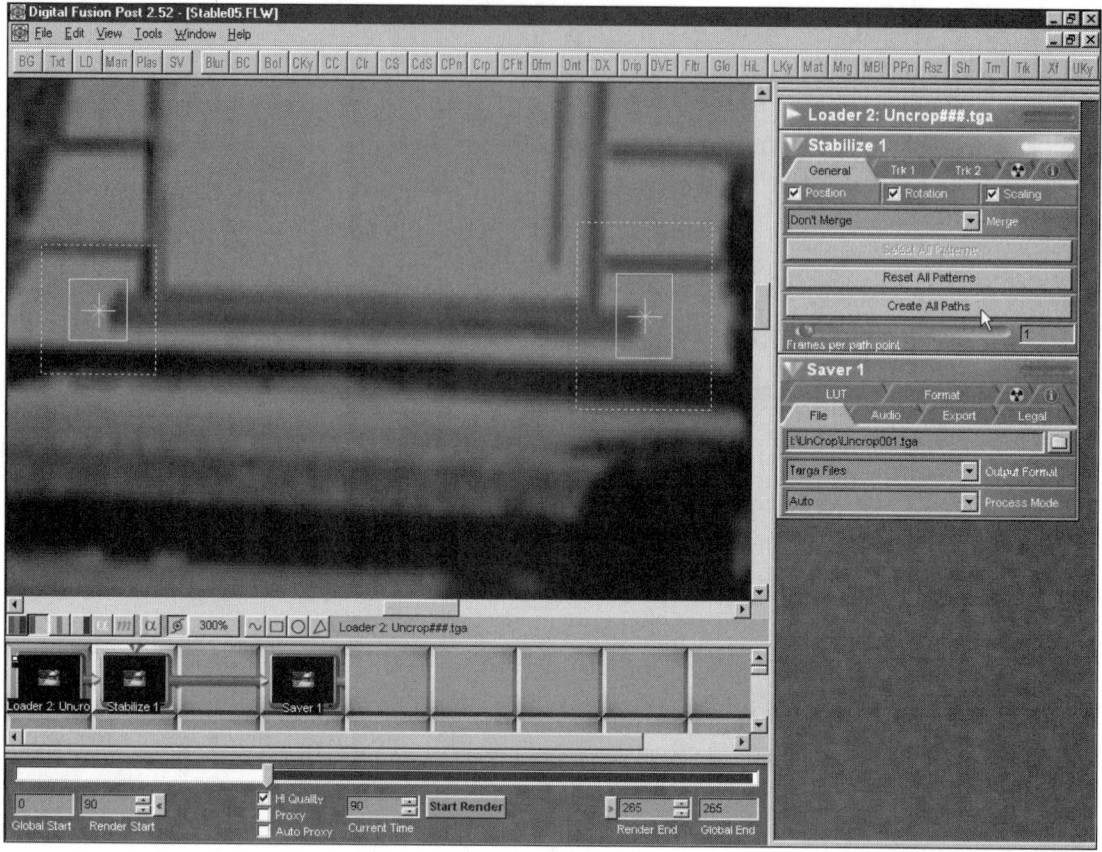

Figure 11.32
Tracker pattern selected for stabilizing frames 90 through 265.

11. When both patterns are modified to your satisfaction, go to the General tab and click on Select All Patterns, then click on Create All Paths.

Again, both trackers run simultaneously. If this track is successful, you can go on to the next step. If the trackers run into trouble, stop the track, reset the patterns, and restart the track from the last good frame. Your results should look like Path 1 and Path 2 in Figure 11.33. The final step for the stabilization process is selecting a reference frame. As I mentioned before, this is a compromise based on a number of factors. For this footage, frame 154 is a good reference frame.

12. Go to frame 154. In the Stabilize tool's General tab, click on Select All Patterns.

This tells the Stabilizer that the current frame is the benchmark that all other frames must match. In other words, the spacing, location, and alignment of every other frame will be modified so each frame's tracker pattern is in the exact location of the patterns in frame 154.

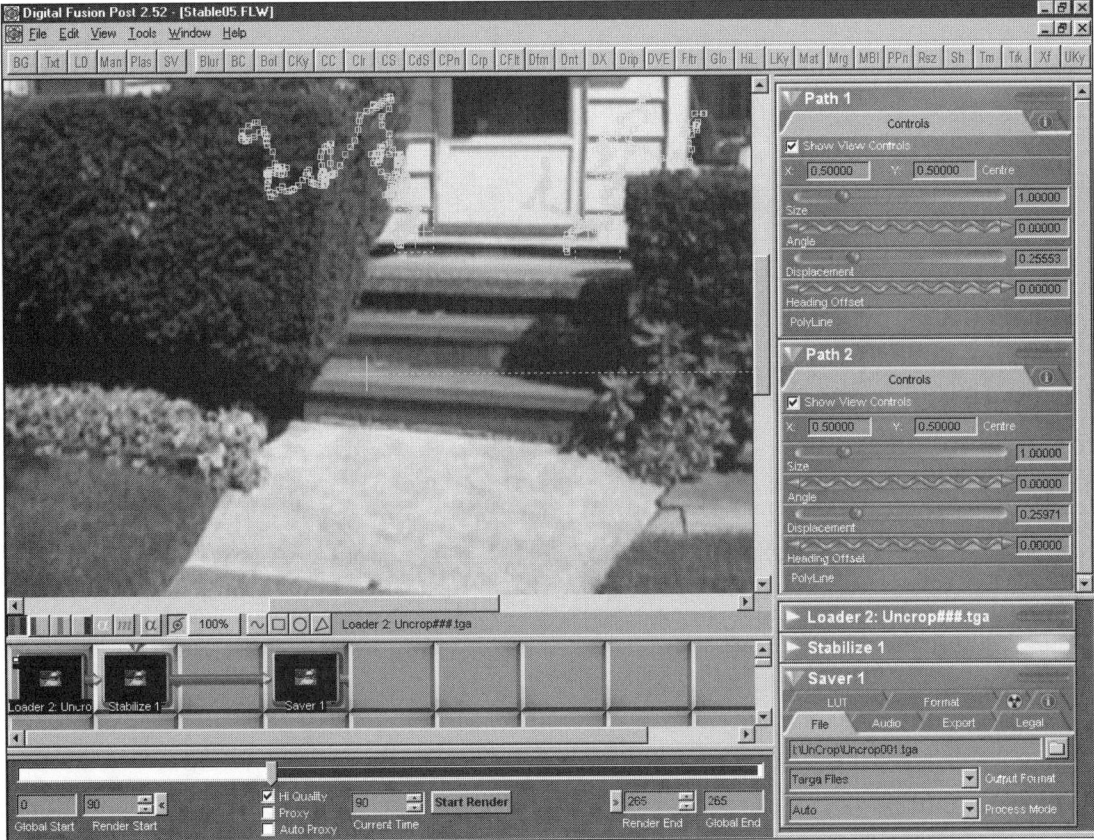

Figure 11.33
Completed stabilizing paths for frames 1 through 265.

13. Show the Stabilizer in the Large display, set to Fit. Scrub through the footage, examining the difference between the loaded Uncrop frames and the stabilized frames.

You should see the largest difference between the beginning frames (see Figure 11.34) because the Stabilizer had to scale them up to match the reference frame, and the ending frames because they had to be scaled down to match frame 154. If you want, you can experiment by repeating step 12 for different reference frames and by observing the difference it makes for the other frames. You may even find a reference frame you like better. However, please set the reference frame back to 154 before you render the final output. The destabilization projects in Chapter 12 depend on an exact match, and they are configured for reference frame 154.

14. Render the results to a compressed TGA image sequence, including the alpha channel. Save the flow as Stable.flw.

Figure 11.34
Frame 1, stabilized to reference frame 154.

In completing this project, you have learned how to:

- Choose reference frames for two-point stabilization

- Render oversize "uncropped" footage to provide safety margins for stabilization

- Assemble a complete track from several partial tracks

- Select tracker patterns for two-point stabilization

- Render stabilized footage that can be destabilized

After Effects And Multi-Point Stabilization

After Effects doesn't have the capability to destabilize footage once it has been stabilized, nor can it perform a true multi-point track to produce stabilized footage like the final results of Project 11.3. This means that After Effects can't be used to complete this project or the several related projects in Chapter 12. If you need to stabilize footage using multiple points, you should consider using a different compositing program.

Aura And Multi-Point Stabilization

Aura 1.0 has no multi-point stabilization features. If you need these features, you have to use a different compositing program.

Two-Point Stabilize The Match000.jpg Porch Footage (Commotion)

As in the preceding Commotion projects, stabilizing for scaling and rotation is covered by the tutorial lessons included in the Commotion Manual, so I'm not going to waste time and space by repeating the process here. If you use Commotion, the official manual is your best resource for learning the program. Incidentally, Commotion can also export multi-point tracking data in a form that can be used by After Effects. For this and similar reasons, the combination of After Effects and Commotion is becoming a popular digital compositing toolkit.

Two-Point Stabilize The Match000.jpg Porch Footage (effect*)

The goal of this project is to stabilize the Match footage to prepare this shot for a manual match move project in Chapter 12. The best results will minimize the number of manual keyframes you will need to set in that project. The final product of these combined projects will be a CGI element perfectly move-matched to the original, unstabilized Match footage.

Chapter 12 of the effect* User's Guide contains an excellent overview of tracking and stabilizing. If you are using effect*, I highly recommend reading the User's Guide material before going further in this book. If you are using the demo version included on this book's first CD-ROM, you should complete the preceding effect* Projects 11.1 and 11.2 before attempting this project.

1. Import the Match footage.

2. Set the Composition Settings to Custom, 2160x1458. Render the composition as a TGA image sequence, using RLE compression, to a temporary directory. This will triple the resolution of the footage, creating a black border that provides a safety margin for the two-point stabilization. Without this border, part of the original image might be expanded beyond the edge of the frame by the stabilization's position, rotation, or scaling operations.

3. Clear the comp. Import the temporary footage, the 2160x1458 image sequence with the black border that you rendered in step 2. Keep the comp resolution set to 2160x1458 for the rest of the stabilization process.

4. Go to time 05:04, frame 154. The reasons for this frame's selection are discussed in detail in the Digital Fusion version of this project.

5. Choose the Effects|Stabilize|Stabilize 2 Points menu option. The Stabilize effect palette appears.

6. Click on the Stabilize Point 1 Pick button to activate the crosshairs for point 1. The green Point 1 crosshairs will appear in the Composition window. Drag the crosshairs over the left threshold end, as shown in Figure 11.35.

7. Set the Mode to Shift, set the Borders to Use Color, and set the Border Color to Black.

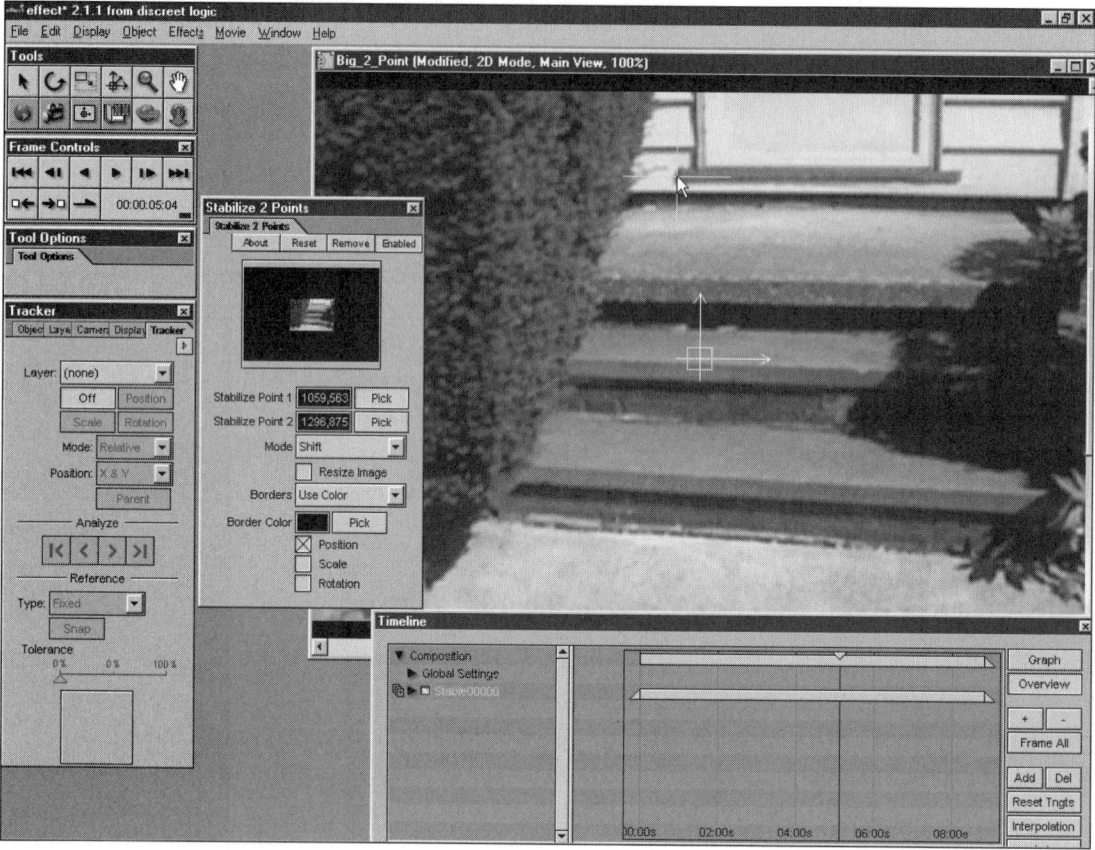

Figure 11.35

The Stabilize Point 1 crosshair is positioned over the left end of the door's threshold.

8. Select the kind of movement that you want to remove from the clip. In this case, you want to remove all three: Position, Scale, and Rotation.

9. In the Tracker palette, click on the Position button. You need to check only the Position button (the Scale and Rotation buttons are grayed out) because the Tracker is not actually tracking the rotation and scaling. The Stabilize 2 Points effect will correct the scaling and rotation based on the position data from the Tracker. In the Composition window, a tracker box appears on the Stabilize effect crosshairs.

10. In the Tracker palette, click on the reverse button under Analyze. This starts the tracking process, working backward from the 05:04 reference frame. The first reference point is tracked, and the shift data is applied to the first crosshairs. As with the previous Tracker projects, keep an eye on the Tracker's progress. Pause, delete bad keyframes, and repeat the analysis as necessary until you get a clean, continuous track. The effect* User's Guide and online help contain some good tips on this topic.

11. When the backward track is complete, repeat the process by working forward from the 05:04 reference frame.

12. When the entire track is complete, click on the Off button in the Tracker palette to turn off the tracker.

13. Click on the Stabilize Point 2 Pick button to activate the second crosshairs. The Point 2 crosshairs appear in the Composition window. Drag the crosshairs over the right threshold end.

14. Repeat steps 9 through 12 to analyze the second reference point. The shift data from the second point is applied to the second crosshairs. After analysis, the unwanted movement in the clip is applied to the Stabilize effect crosshairs. The Stabilize effect applies an opposite movement to the image to stabilize the clip. Your results should look like Figure 11.36.

15. Render the comp to a compressed TGA image sequence, including the alpha channel. Save the project as Stable.icp.

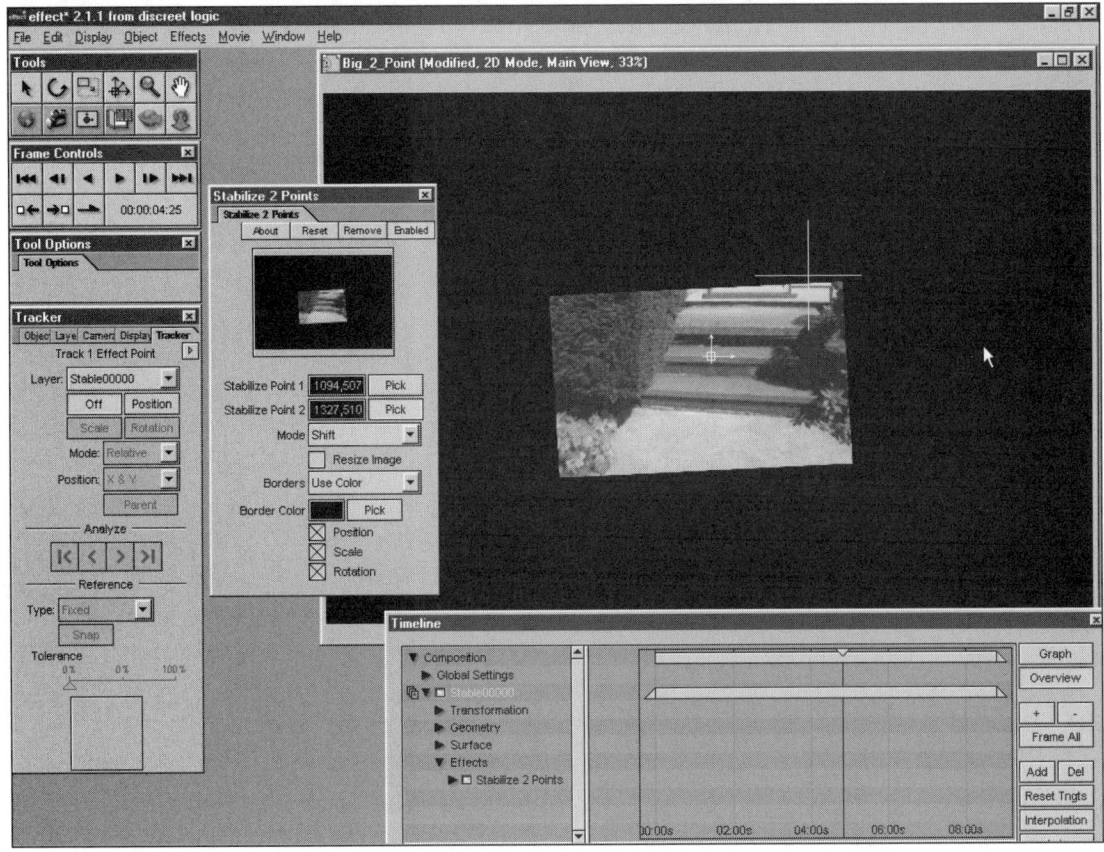

Figure 11.36
The result of the two-point stabilization on frame 04:25.

The multi-point tracking and stabilizing functions in effect* gave some of the best results of all the trackers I used in writing this book, and the tracking process was very stable and robust. After you get used to the way effect* works, tracking and stabilization goes very quickly. If you do a lot of tracking and stabilization, I highly recommend effect*, especially if you also use 3DS MAX to create CGI elements. The Discreet products are well integrated and can make match move and other complex processes much less tedious.

Shake And Multi-Point Stabilization

Shake 2.1 has no stabilization features. If you need these features, you need to use a different compositing program.

Moving On

This chapter has shown you how to nail down shaky footage. That's good; stabilization is the first step in many digital compositing tasks. However, the tougher part is often how you get that footage to shake again, in a controlled and deliberate way. That's where Chapter 12 takes up, showing you how to match move, comp CGI elements, and bring it all back to that documentary-style handheld camera look.

PUT IT BACK

Restoring or simulating camera motion after comping other effects can make the difference between a shot that sells and one that looks faked. Camera motion is part of many directors' and cinematographers' visual style, and the locked-down look of stabilized footage can stand out from that style. Restoring the motion enables the comped footage to blend seamlessly into the original footage, which is your goal as a digital compositor. Simulating camera motion can also be an effective way of adding motions that weren't in the original footage but to add to the impact of the shot. For example, a relatively static shot of a street scene is viscerally boring, even after you comp in the 30-foot-tall CGI monster. But that same footage hits your audience on a deeper, unconscious level if the camera appears to shake from the impact tremors of the creature's footsteps.

Using Stabilized Footage

Between the stabilizing processes you learned in Chapter 11 and the destabilization techniques you'll learn later in this chapter, you need to comp the effects that made stabilization necessary in the first place. These effects may include anything motion-related that a simple tracker could not accomplish.

In particular, the creation of a clean plate for rig removals and foreground object dissolves is much easier with stabilized footage. Creating a clean plate requires the selection of parts from several frames. If all the frames don't line up, piecing together a clean plate can be nearly impossible. A clean plate is needed most in exactly those frames with the most camera movement, because the alternate method of time-shifting would reveal the disparities most strongly in those frames. With stabilized footage, assembling a clean plate is as easy as from locked-down camera footage.

◢◣◤◥ Rig Removal With Stabilized Footage
12.1

The goal of this project is to comp a rig removal on the stabilized footage from Project 11.2, including the process to create several clean plates. It is possible to assemble a clean plate from two or more foreground images from within Digital Fusion. This is a good approach for a simple plate with consistent lighting and foreground subjects that move enough to reveal the entire background in the course of the footage.

1. Add two Loaders, both with the stabilized footage. Set Global In to 200, to match the frame numbers to the file name numbers.

2. Connect both Loaders through a Merge. Add a Saver tool to the Merge's output.

The goal is to remove the actress's hand, the light bulb, and the wiring. In frame 203, the actress's hand is covering the upper half of the left edge of the box lid. That same area is clear in frame 220. You should therefore be able to substitute part of frame 220 for that part of frame 203 to create a clean plate for the box.

3. In Loader 2, change Extend First Frame to 17. This will offset Loader 2 so that frame 203 will be loaded at frame 220.

4. Add an Effect Mask Rectangle to the Merge tool.

5. In frame 220, position and size the effect mask to cover the actress's right hand wherever it conceals part of the box. Your results should look like Figure 12.1.

6. Render frame 220, and save it as Clean200.tga. You will use this image as a clean plate later in this project.

There are several ways to extend this method to more demanding clean plates. You can use a polygon effect mask to select a more complex shape. You can also cascade more than one set of Loader and Merge tools to enable you to merge pieces from several different frames. However, this quickly gets cumbersome, and you are generally better off doing a complex cleaning in a paint program such as Photoshop.

Cleaning A Plate In Photoshop

One quick method for assembling a clean plate from two foreground images is to use Photoshop's Erase To History option for the Eraser tool. This enables you to paste one image over another, then use the Eraser tool to selectively remove parts of the pasted image to reveal the original image.

1. In Photoshop, open both frames 203 and 220 of your stabilized footage.

2. With frame 203 active, Select All, Copy, then Close.

3. With frame 220 active, select Paste.

4. In the toolbar, double-click on the Eraser tool icon. The Options dialog box for the Eraser tool will appear. Turn on the Erase To History option.

Figure 12.1
A flow set up to merge a clean plate from frames 203 and 220 of the stabilized footage. Note that Loader 2's Extend First Frame is offset 17 frames in order to load image file 203 at frame 220.

5. Select the type of Eraser tool you prefer. If you want smooth transitions rather than sharp edges, you might prefer the airbrush. For precision around edges, the pencil is best. For large area removal (like this project), I prefer the block.

6. Erase the actress's hand from in front of the box lid.

Try to erase only her hand and any nearby pixels colored by light or shadows from her hand, as shown in Figure 12.2. Work carefully, one stroke at a time, and check the results of each stroke before you make the next one. If you make a mistake, use Undo to restore the erased pixels. If you erase too much at one time, an Undo will delete more of your work and force you to spend more time repeating the erasure.

7. Your results should look like Figure 12.3. When you have a clean box and safe area around it, flatten the image and save it as Clean200.tga.

Figure 12.2
A clean plate created by the Erase To History function in Photoshop.

This clean plate is only a perfect match for frames 200 to 316. The box lid hinges back during frames 317 to 355, then holds at a more obtuse angle for frames 356 to 402. In addition, the lighting of the interior box surfaces changes drastically as the light bulb moves. This will require more work to create additional clean plate frames and to coordinate changes between them.

8. Make a second clean plate for frame 356.

Remove as much of the light bulb, hand, and wiring from the box as you can. I pieced together the clean plate shown in Figure 12.4 based on frame 400 with bits and pieces from frames 394, 356, and 327. In addition to the Erase To History function, I used the Blur, Eyedropper, and Pencil tools to clean up the plate. This is one example why you need a good paint program (and why you need to know how to use it) to be a digital compositor.

9. Repeat the process you learned in Projects 10.1 and 10.2 to perform a rotoscoped rig removal on the light bulb's wires, using the stabilized footage and the clean plates. Your results should look like Figure 12.5.

Figure 12.3
A clean plate for frame 200 created by the Erase To History function in Photoshop.

Figure 12.4
A clean plate for frame 356 created by the Erase To History function in Photoshop.

Figure 12.5
A flow showing rotoscoped wire removal in frame 365, using a Merge to the clean background plate from Figure 12.4.

A rotoscoped rig removal on frames 200 through 316 can use the clean plate for frame 200, and the clean plate for frame 356 can be used for frames 356 through about frame 370. However, box lid movement in frames 317 to 355, along with the lighting changes in frames 365 to 402, make the removal mask harder to hide.

The box lid movement can be concealed by dissolving between two clean plate images, 200 and 356, over the course of frames 317 to 355. Figure 12.5 shows Loader 200 and Loader 356, each of which is set exclusively to that frame. The Dissolve 1 tool is set to perform an additive mix from foreground (200) to background (356) between frames 317 and 356.

10. Load Clean356 and Clean200 in separate Loaders, and connect them to Merge 1 through a Dissolve tool, as shown in Figure 12.5. Animate the Dissolve to gradually change from Clean200 to Clean356 over the course of frames 317 to 355.

Creating a clean plate for frames 370 to 402 is more challenging. The lighting of the interior box surfaces is subtle, affected by the glowing light bulb, and shadows of the hand and wiring. The wooden surfaces also have complex patterns, so paint tools are difficult to use without flattening the colors. You will need to create at least several frames; the more frames you can clean, the better the results but the more effort you will have to invest. As in step 10, you can set up a dissolve between cleaned frames to conceal gradual changes. You may find it useful to precomp a series of cleaned individual frames and animated dissolves into a continuous clean plate. This will make your effects comps much simpler and faster to work with.

11. Create additional clean frames and animated dissolves to build a complete clean plate for the stabilized footage. Render the clean plate as a precomp.

12. Load the clean plate into your flow, and remove the extra Loaders and Dissolve(s).

13. Connect the clean plate Loader and the stabilized footage Loader through the Merge tool containing the rotoscoped rig removal you set up in step 9.

14. Adjust the rotoscoped rig removal until you are satisfied with the results. Add any other effects you like. Render the sequence; you'll use it in the next project.

In completing this project, you have learned how to:

- Clean up a frame in Digital Fusion using a Merge and effect mask
- Clean up a frame in Photoshop using the Erase To History function of the Eraser tool
- Combine two or more frames to create a clean frame
- Dissolve between clean frames to conceal gradual changes
- Precomp a clean plate, then apply it to the original footage

Rig Removal With Stabilized Footage (After Effects)

The goal of this version of Project 12.1 is to use After Effects to comp a rig removal on the stabilized footage from Project 11.2, including the process to create several clean plates. It is possible to assemble a clean plate from two or more images from the same footage, loaded as separate layers in After Effects. This approach is good for a simple plate with consistent lighting and foreground subjects that move enough to reveal the entire background in the course of the footage.

1. Open a new project. Import the stabilized image sequence that you rendered in Project 11.2.

2. Create a new composition and add the stabilized image sequence to it twice, making two layers.

3. Double-click on the front layer to open it in the Layer window. Change the Layer window magnification to 200 percent, and pan the window until the box is centered in the window. Go to time 00:03.

The goal here is to remove the actress's hand from the area of the box. At 00:03, the actress's hand is covering the upper half of the left edge of the box lid. That same area is clear at 00:20. You should therefore be able to substitute part of 00:20 for that part of 00:03 to create a clean plate for the box.

4. Choose the Rectangle tool from the toolbox. Drag out a rectangle mask to contain the actress's hand where it covers the box lid, as shown in Figure 12.6. Right-click on one of the mask control points and choose Mode|Add from the pop-up menu. Right-click again, and check Inverse from the menu. This sets the rectangle to be transparent on the inside, allowing the background layer to show through. For a less obvious removal, set Mask Feather to 4 pixels to blur the mask's outline.

5. Drag the background layer (or set the layer's In point) to –00:17, to place a clear portion of the box lid behind the mask, as shown in Figure 12.6.

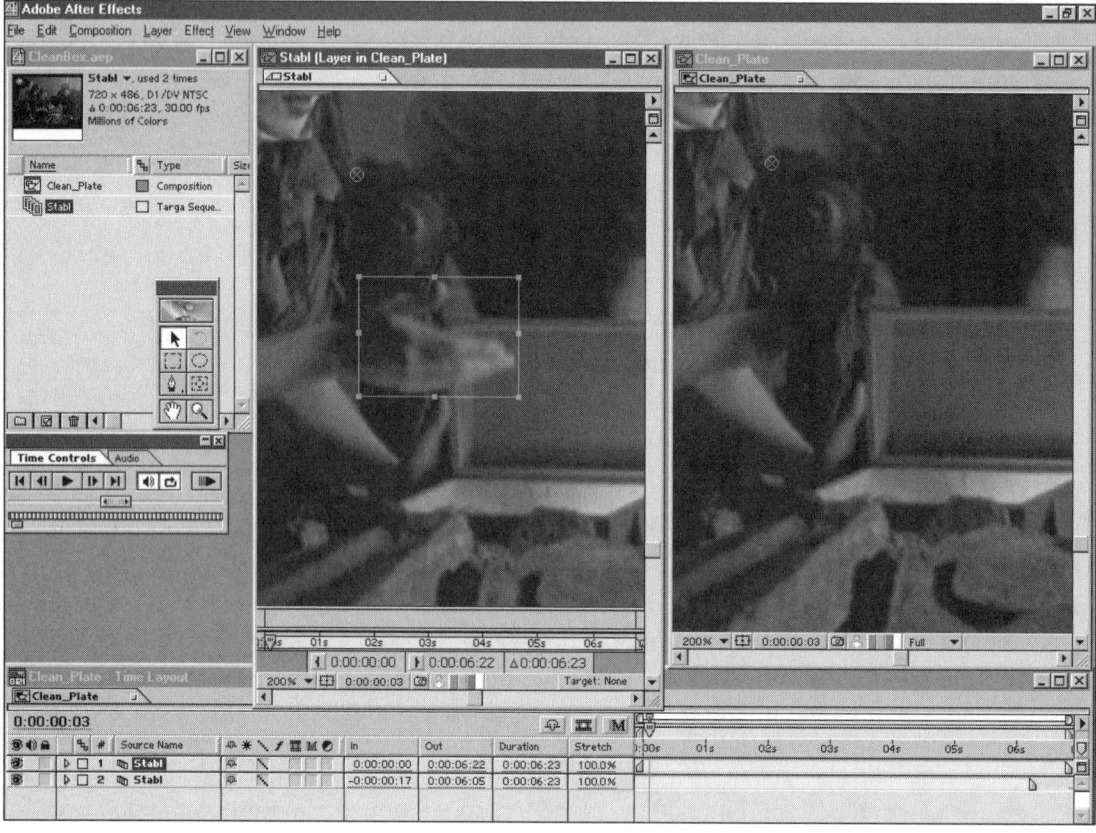

Figure 12.6
The rectangle mask removes the hand from the foreground layer, replacing it with a clear portion of the offset background layer.

6. Choose the Composition|Save Frame As|File menu option, and save the frame as a Photoshop document, Clean_Plate03.psd. You will use this image as a clean plate later in this project.

7. If you haven't already done so, go back to "Cleaning A Plate In Photoshop" earlier in this chapter and create clean plates for the other critical frames.

8. Repeat the process you learned in After Effects Projects 10.1 and 10.2 to perform a rotoscoped rig removal on the light bulb's wires, using the stabilized footage and the clean plates.

A rotoscoped rig removal up to 03:29 can use the Clean_Plate03.psd image, and a clean plate created for 05:08 can be used from 05:08 through about 05:23. However, box lid movement between 03:29 and 05:07, and lighting changes after 05:23, make the removal mask harder to hide. The box lid movement can be concealed by a crossfade blend between two clean plate layers.

9. Add a Blend effect that uses the crossfade mode between each pair of clean plate layers, and keyframe the crossfades from 100 percent to 0 percent across each gap in coverage between the clean plate images. Figure 12.7 shows the rig removal composition with animated crossfade blends set up between clean plate images Clean203 and Clean356, and between Clean356 and Clean402.

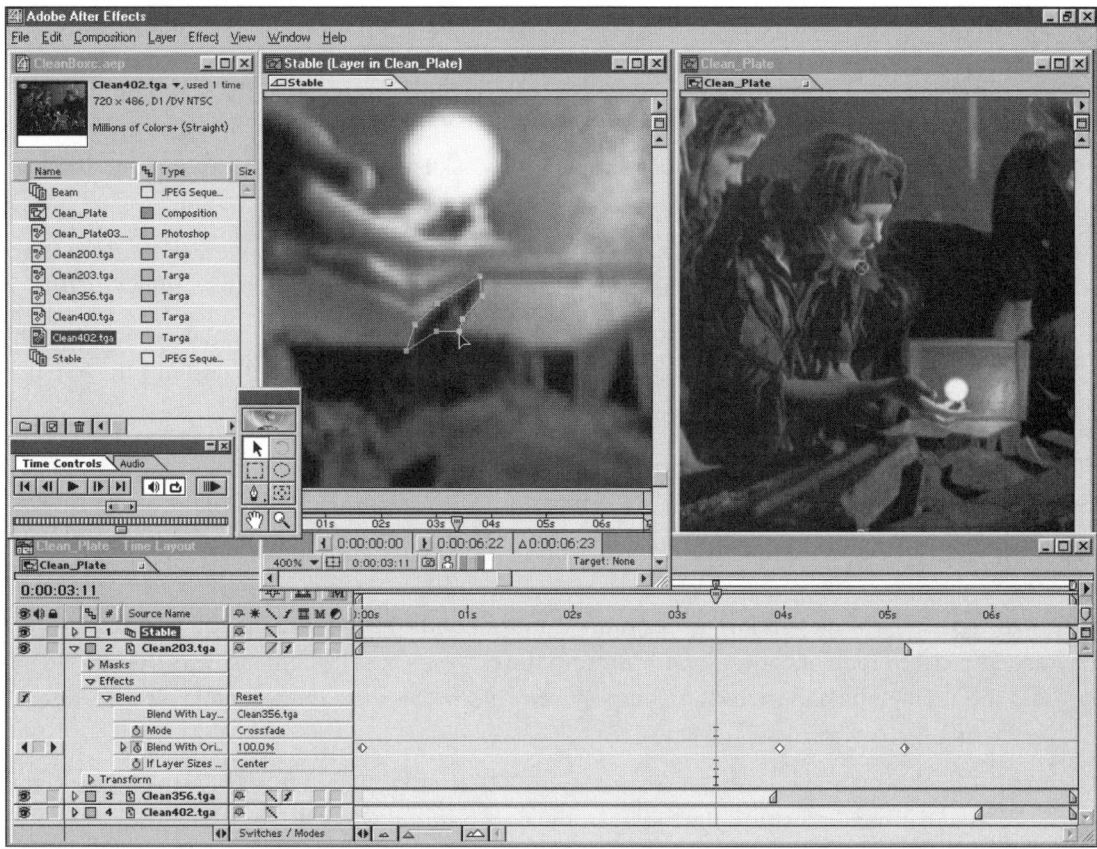

Figure 12.7

The keyframed polygon mask for removing the light bulb's wire is visible in the Stable Layer window. The Time Layout window shows the arrangement of the 2 crossfade blends between the 3 clean plate images. The Composition window shows the results.

Rig Removal With Stabilized Footage (Commotion)

Puffin Designs' Commotion package includes tutorial footage and instructions for several rig removal projects. Rather than have you repeat the efforts of these tutorials' designers, I recommend (if you are using Commotion) that you work through Lessons 8 and 11 in the manual, and then apply the stabilization and rotospline rig removal processes to the Box footage on this book's second CD-ROM.

Rig Removal With Stabilized Footage (effect*)

The goal of this project is to comp a rig removal on the stabilized footage from effect* Project 11.2, including the process to create several clean plates. It is possible to assemble a clean plate from two or more images from the same footage, loaded as separate layers in effect*. This approach is good for a simple plate with consistent lighting and foreground subjects that move enough to reveal the entire background in the course of the footage.

1. Open a new project. Import the stabilized image sequence, Stable###.TGA, that you rendered in effect* Project 11.2.

2. Copy and paste the Stable000 layer to create a duplicate layer.

3. Select the first Stable000 layer. Choose the Effects|Mask|Freeform Mask menu option. The Freeform Mask window will appear.

4. In the Freeform Mask window, click on Invert, set Feather to 1, and choose Replace from the combination mode menu. This makes the mask transparent in the first layer, allowing the second layer to show through.

5. Zoom in and pan the Freeform Mask window until the box is centered in and fills the window. Go to timecode 00:03.

The goal is to remove the actress's hand from the area of the box. At 00:03, the actress's hand is covering the upper half of the left edge of the box lid. That same area is clear at 00:20. You should therefore be able to substitute part of 00:20 for that part of 00:03 to create a clean plate for the box.

6. In the Freeform Mask window, click on the Control Points button and use the Edit Mask tool to add a closed loop of control points around the actress's hand where it covers the box lid. You should see no changes in the Composition window, because the second layer is identical to the first.

7. In the Timeline window, drag the second Stable000 layer to the left to –00:17, to place a clear portion of the box lid behind the mask. In the Composition window, you should see the change in the area defined by the freeform mask, as the actress's hand is replaced by the clean background of the second layer (see Figure 12.8).

8. Render the frame as a single image, Clean000.TGA. You will use this image as a clean plate later in this project.

Figure 12.8
The mask for removing the actress' hand is visible in the Freeform Mask window. The Timeline window shows the arrangement of the two layers. The Composition window shows the results.

9. If you haven't already done so, go back to "Cleaning A Plate In Photoshop" in this chapter, and create clean plates for the other critical frames.

10. Repeat the process you learned in effect* Projects 10.1 and 10.2 to perform a rotoscoped rig removal on the light bulb's wires, using the stabilized footage and the clean plates.

A rotoscoped rig removal up to 03:29 can use the Clean000.TGA image, and a clean plate created for 05:08 can be used from 05:08 through about 05:23. However, box lid movement between 03:29 and 05:07, and lighting changes after 05:23, make the removal mask harder to hide. The box lid movement can be concealed by a crossfade blend effect between two clean plate layers.

11. Select the first clean plate layer, then choose Effects|Channel|Blend. In the Blend window, choose the Crossfade method, and select the target layer from the Layer menu. Keyframe the crossfade from 0 percent to 100 percent across the gap in coverage between the first and second clean plate layers. Repeat this step for each clean plate layer pair. Figure 12.9 shows the Timeline with animated crossfade blends set up between clean plate images Clean000 and Clean356, and between Clean356 and Clean402.

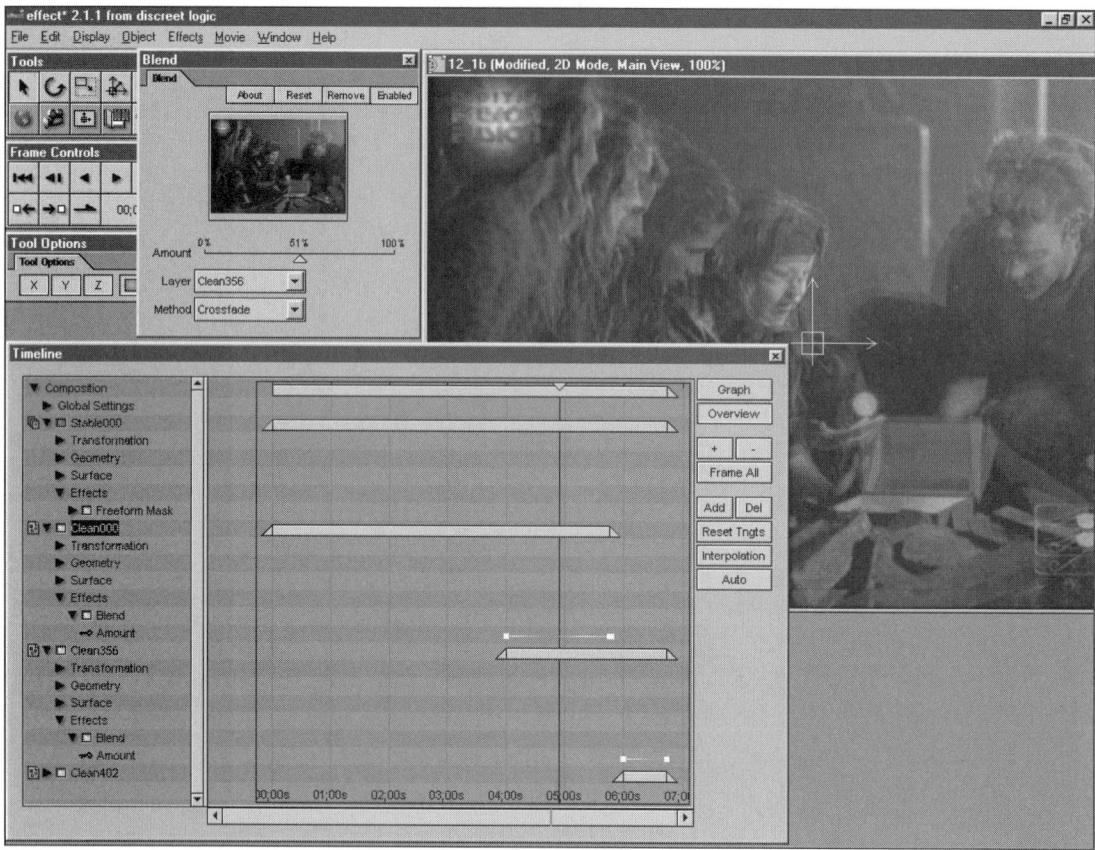

Figure 12.9
The Timeline window shows the arrangement of the 2 crossfade blend effects between the three clean plate images. The Composition window shows the results halfway through the first crossfade, with the front layer disabled.

Rig Removal With Stabilized Footage (Shake)

The documentation for Shake 2.1 includes Tutorial 2: More Swank Stuff, a masking tutorial that covers essentially the same functions as rig removal. Rather than repeat the efforts of this tutorial's author, I recommend (if you are using Shake) that you work through Tutorial 2, and then apply the masking process to the stabilized Box footage you created in Project 11.2.

Destabilizing

Destabilizing can be as complicated as simulating the motion of a vehicle-mounted or handheld camera, or as simple as undoing a stabilize comp that you applied yourself. Destabilizing is usually one of the last comps in a match move or stabilize process, and it's also one of the easiest. However, you still need to pay attention to details; overlooking a slight mismatch at this point can blow the rest of the shot.

PROJECT 12.2 Destabilize The Box

The goal of this project is to destabilize the footage you rendered in Project 12.1 to match the original Box footage you stabilized in Project 11.2. This is the simplest form of destabilizing, but the same basic principles apply to more complex operations.

1. Open the flow you saved at the end of Project 11.2. Loader 1 should contain the original Box footage.

2. Add a new Loader and load the effects footage you rendered at the end of Project 12.1.

3. Add a Merge tool, and connect Loader 1 to its background input and Loader 2 to its foreground input.

4. Add a rectangle effect mask to the Merge tool, and move and scale the effect mask to include the box and a safe area around it. Set the rectangle to Replace paint mode, Solid, and set the Soft Edge to something around 0.002. Your results should look like Figure 12.10.

Figure 12.10

The stabilized effects footage is merged with the original Box footage using a rectangle effect mask. Note the mismatch at the rectangle's edges in the Large display. Connecting the Merge Center to Tracker Unsteady Position corrects this mismatch.

375

5. Right-click on Merge Center, and choose Connect To|Tracker 1: Unsteady Position, as shown in the lower right of Figure 12.10.

Connecting the Merge to the Tracker's Unsteady Position causes the foreground footage (the rendered effects footage) to move inversely to the Steady Position. That is, the Unsteady motion cancels out or destabilizes the Steady motion you applied in Project 11.2. This results in a perfect match between the effects footage and the original footage, as shown in Figure 12.11.

Figure 12.11
Merge Center connected to Tracker Unsteady Position destabilizes the effects footage to precisely match the movement of the original Box footage.

6. Check your destabilize comp by zooming in the Large display, then by making a preview. During playback, examine the area around the edges of the rectangle.

You should look for misalignments across the rectangle's edges. If there were any errors in the Steady/Unsteady process, you may need to edit the Merge tool's Offset to correct them. Generally, if you are using the original Tracker data, you will have a perfect match.

7. When you are satisfied with your results, save the flow.

In completing this project, you learned how to:

- Merge stabilized footage with original footage using an effect mask
- Destabilize footage to match original footage using the Tracker's Unsteady Position

After Effects And Destabilizing

After Effects has no destabilizing features. If you need these features, use a different compositing program. One possibility is to use Commotion's Tracker to generate the destabilization motion, and then export the motion file in a format that can be used by After Effects.

Aura And Destabilizing

Aura 1.0 has no destabilizing features. If you need these features, use a different compositing program.

Motion Destabilize (Chalice)

Silicon Grail's Chalice package includes a PDF version of the manual and several tutorials, plus footage for completing the tutorials. These files are available for download from the company's Web site (**www.sgrail.com**). These files are also located in the Chalice folder of this book's first CD-ROM. One tutorial demonstrates Chalice's tracking features, but nowhere in the documentation does it discuss how to reverse a stabilize operation. I believe destabilization may be possible by creating an expression. If you want to tackle this problem, I suggest you start with Tutorial 4, and then read the manual sections on the Track and Apply Track nodes, followed by the manual's Appendix B, "Chalice Expression Language."

This requires a great deal of expertise, or an extraordinary amount of effort for a less experienced user. For these reasons, Chalice isn't my first choice of compositing software for beginners; if you are just learning, I recommend a different program.

Motion Destabilize (Commotion)

Puffin Designs' Commotion package includes tutorial footage and instructions for several tracking projects, including destabilization to reverse a single-point stabilize operation. Rather than repeat the efforts of these tutorials' designers, I recommend (if you are using Commotion) that you work through Lesson 8 in the manual, and then apply the same process to the Box footage on this book's second CD-ROM.

Destabilize The Box (effect*)

The goal of this version of Project 12.2 is to use effect* to destabilize the footage you rendered in effect* Project 12.1 to match the original Box footage you stabilized in effect* Project 11.2. This is the simplest form of destabilizing, but the same basic principles apply to more complex operations.

1. Open the BoxStable.icp file you saved at the end of effect* Project 11.2. The first layer should contain the original Box footage with a Stabilize 1 Point effect applied to it.

2. Select the Box layer. Choose File|Replace footage, and replace the original Box footage with the stabilized removal footage you rendered from effect* Project 12.1.

3. Open the effect controls window by double-clicking on the Stabilize 1 Point line in the Timeline window.

4. In the Stabilize 1 Point effect controls window, click on Invert. This applies the reverse of the stabilization to the footage, giving the removal footage the same movement as the original Box footage before the stabilization.

5. Change Borders to Transparent. The Transparent setting allows the background to show through any areas revealed by the movement of the foreground layer, as shown in Figure 12.12.

6. Import the original Box footage and move it to the back of the comp (see Figure 12.13).

Figure 12.12
The Timeline window shows the replacement of the original Box footage with the removal footage from the effect* portion of Project 12.1. The Stabilize 1 Point effect control window shows the settings for destabilizing the removal footage. The Composition window shows the destabilized removal footage, revealing the background at the upper edge of the window, as indicated by the cursor arrow.

Figure 12.13
The Timeline window shows the addition of the original Box footage as a background layer. The Composition window shows the background layer matching perfectly to the foreground layer at the upper edge of the window, as indicated by the cursor arrow.

7. Render the destabilized footage to RAM. Play back the rendering, looking for flaws and mismatches around the edges of the stabilization borders. After you are satisfied with your work, save the comp as BoxDestable.icp.

Shake And Destabilizing

Shake 2.1 has no destabilizing features. If you need these features, use a different compositing program.

Match Move

The single-point stabilization and destabilization you practiced with the Box footage is useful for a variety of relatively simple 2D compositing effects. More-complex effects are possible when 3D CGI elements can be precisely matched to complex camera movements. This process is called a *match move*. Prior to the production of *Jurassic Park*, all CGI compositing was done with footage from a locked-down camera, because it was simply too difficult and expensive to match elements to a moving camera. When Steven Spielberg challenged the *JP* effects team to allow him to shoot from a handheld camera, they came up with the basic techniques used in most effects houses today.

> *"On something like* The Mask, *I would be working there, taking tape measurements and working out some of the rough marks for doors and windows, which worked pretty well. No motion control was used because, with 45 shooting days, it was a tight shooting schedule. Every scene with a moving camera required a 3D match move on the computer. All the scenes with computer graphics masks for Jim (Carrey) or the dog had to be tracked frame by frame in 3D space so their CG heads would match."*
> —*Scott Squires, VFX Supervisor,* The Mask

A good 3D match move is possibly the most convincing way of integrating a CGI element into live footage. Combining complex camera movement with matching lights and shadows makes it much easier for the audience to buy the shot.

Your first goal in setting up a match move is to automate as many variables as possible. You have to perfectly coordinate the movement and rotation of the camera in all three axes, plus setting the lens parameters. That's at least eight variables, any one of which can be changing on every frame. The more variables you can track, measure on set, or otherwise nail down in advance, the easier and more accurate your match move will be.

When you have automated as many variables as possible, prioritize the remaining ones in order of frequency of change, lowest first. For example, the frequency of change in the Box footage was fairly high on the Y-axis, much lower on the X-axis, but practically zero on the Z-axis. That would put the Z-axis at the top of the priority list for a match move. The idea is to manually keyframe the lowest-frequency motions first. This eliminates one more variable with a minimum of effort and makes keyframing the remaining higher-frequency variables easier by removing ambiguities between related variables. For example, an increase in the apparent size of an object could be the result of a Z-axis move (dolly in) or an increase in lens length (zoom), and is therefore ambiguous. If the lens is fixed or has already been animated according to the focus puller's information, you can automatically assume that the change is caused by a Z-axis move and animate the CGI camera to match. You will also find that setting one variable's keyframes often reduces (or even eliminates) the need for keyframes for another variable.

Tracking For Animation

The two-point stabilization you performed in Project 11.3 still leaves a lot of movement in the footage; the farther from the reference points, the greater the motion. You will need to animate the CGI elements (camera and objects) to match this motion, either with additional trackers or by manually keyframing the XYZ translations; pitch, bank, and heading rotations; and camera lens parameters. Some digital compositing programs provide a means of exporting a tracker's path to a 3D motion file. This motion file can be used to animate a CGI object or camera. When applied correctly, this approach can automate a large percentage of the keyframes necessary for a successful match move.

PROJECT 12.3 Track Motion Path For Porch Model

The goal of this project is to create a motion path that can be used to animate the high-frequency XY-plane movements of the porch steps relative to the camera. This requires another Tracker operation, plus the exporting of the tracked path data in a form that can be used by 3D CGI software.

1. Open a new flow.

2. Add a Loader, and load the oversized "uncropped" footage you rendered in Project 11.3.

3. Using the process you learned in Project 11.1, track the light-colored chip in the front edge of the second porch step between frames 0 and 211. Your flow should look like Figure 12.14.

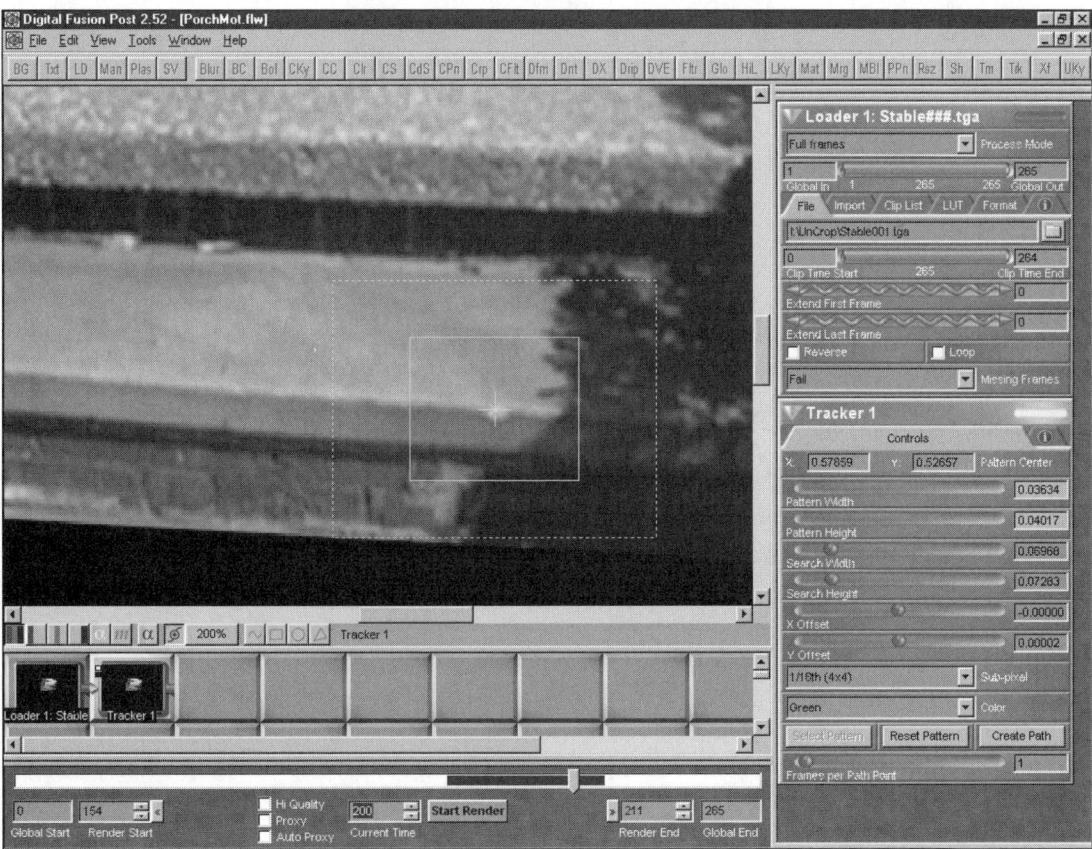

Figure 12.14
The Tracker pattern defined around the chip in the second step at frame 200.

The chip is not visible after frame 211, and it becomes very small and hard to track in earlier frames. You will probably have better results if you track the chip backwards, starting with a pattern defined in frame 211 and initiating the track at the earliest frame in which the Tracker can still recognize the pattern. You may find it necessary to track as few as 10 frames at a time. The cycle of stopping the Tracker, resetting the pattern, and restarting the Tracker becomes very easy with a little practice, and it goes quickly. As the chip becomes too small to track by itself, you should expand the pattern box but continue to keep the chip centered in the pattern. You should end up with a path like that shown in Figure 12.15.

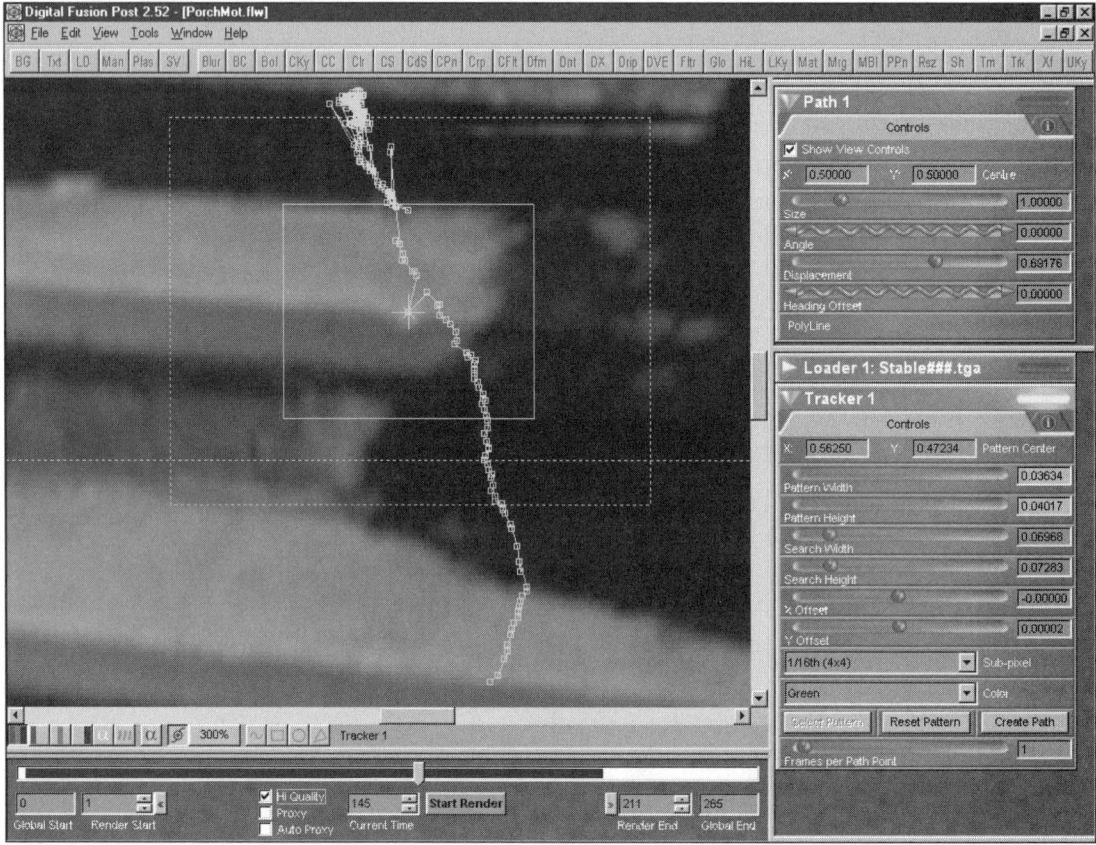

Figure 12.15
The Tracker path for frames 1 through 211.

4. Save the flow as PorchMot.flw. You may need to use it again if you run into problems when using the tracked motion file.

5. Right-click in the Large display, and choose Path 1|Export Path|LightWave MOT from the pop-up menu, as shown in Figure 12.16. Save the motion file as TrackerNull.mot.

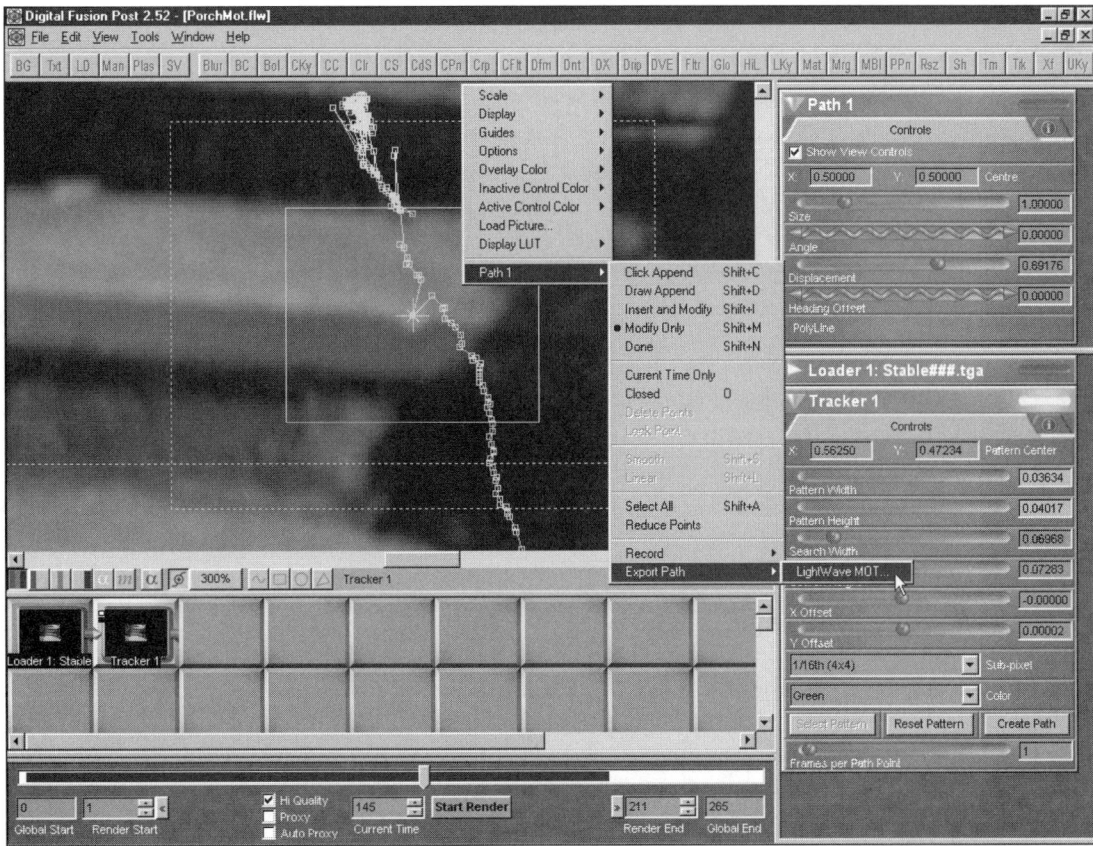

Figure 12.16
Exporting the tracker path as a LightWave-compatible motion file.

This export operation creates a text file in the LightWave motion format excerpted in the following example. After the four initial lines of the header, a selection of the first three and last three keyframes is shown. The first line of each keyframe is the change in the X coordinate, and the second is the change in the Y coordinate. Note that these numbers are changes, not absolute measures, and they are relative to the default original coordinates of 0.5, 0.5, the center of the tracked image. You will need to remember this in the next project, when you apply the motion file to a CGI object. The second line for each keyframe begins with the frame number. This is a simple text file that can be modified in any text editor, but you shouldn't fool with it unless you really know what you are doing:

```
LWMO
1
9
212
0.056829 0.062124 0 0 0 0 1 1 1
0 0 0 0 0
```

```
0.056829 0.062124 0 0 0 0 1 1 1
1 0 0 0 0
0.055671 0.062124 0 0 0 0 1 1 1
2 0 0 0 0
<frames 3 through 208 omitted>
0.076389 -0.037547 0 0 0 0 1 1 1
209 0 0 0 0
0.075347 -0.040634 0 0 0 0 1 1 1
210 0 0 0 0
0.074306 -0.041834 0 0 0 0 1 1 1
211 0 0 0 0
```

The ability to export tracker motion data to other applications can be extremely useful. For example, extracting camera motion with a tracker can enable you to feed that data back to a motion control camera rig, making it possible to shoot matching footage for a camera that was not originally motion-controlled. You may not need to use it very often, but it's a good technique to keep in your back pocket.

After Effects And Tracking Motion Paths

After Effects can't export single-point tracking data in a form compatible with LightWave. If you need this feature, use a different compositing program.

Aura And Tracking

Aura 1.0 has no tracking features. If you need these features, use a different compositing program.

Track Motion Path For Porch Model (Commotion)

Puffin Designs' Commotion package includes tutorial footage and instructions for several tracking projects. Rather than repeat the efforts of these tutorials' designers, I recommend (if you are using Commotion) that you work through Lessons 8 and 9 in the manual, and then apply the tracking process to the stabilized Match footage. You can export the tracking data in a variety of formats. Your choice will depend on the 3D software you use in Project 12.4 to complete the match move. The highest-quality option is to export all the tracking data to Electric Image, but you can also export to After Effects or one of several other text formats that are readable by a variety of 3D applications.

Track Motion Path For Porch Model (effect*)

The goal of this project is to create a motion path that can be used to animate the high-frequency XY-plane movements of the porch steps relative to the camera. This requires another Tracker operation, plus the exporting of the tracked path data in a form that can be used by 3D CGI software.

1. Open a new project. Import the oversized "uncropped" footage you rendered in effect* Project 11.3.

2. Using the process you learned in effect* Project 11.1, track the light-colored chip in the front edge of the second porch step between timecode 00:01 and 07:01.

3. When the tracking operation is complete, choose the Tracker submenu option Export|Track. The Export Tracker window will appear.

4. In the Export Tracker window, choose the file name and location to save the track file. This will be a simple ASCII text file, readable in any text editor such as Windows Notepad.

5. Open the track file in the text editor of your choice. You should see something like the excerpt here:

PorchChip.asc excerpt for frames 199 through 212.

```
199.0 : +1247.65, +560.83
200.0 : +1249.25, +560.52
201.0 : +1251.97, +559.38
202.0 : +1253.69, +557.83
203.0 : +1254.21, +554.81
204.0 : +1253.86, +551.09
205.0 : +1255.45, +547.80
206.0 : +1258.34, +543.34
207.0 : +1259.21, +535.41
208.0 : +1261.11, +526.20
209.0 : +1264.74, +517.85
210.0 : +1264.78, +504.85
211.0 : +1266.30, +502.00
212.0 : +1266.30, +502.00
```

Whether or not you can use the effect* Tracker data depends on your 3D application. The track data format is relatively simple to parse, so it is simple to convert to other formats. The first number is the frame, the second number is the absolute horizontal position of the track point, and the third number is the absolute vertical position of the track point.

Shake And Tracking
Shake 2.1 has no tracking features. If you need these features, you need to use a different compositing program.

Putting It All Together
In previous chapters and projects, you learned how to measure the set; construct CGI models for shadow-catching surfaces; stabilize footage in translation, rotation, and scaling; and extract camera motion from a tracked reference point. These are all parts of a complex puzzle, the match move, and now you're ready to put it all together. Being able to do a match move is a valuable job skill for digital compositors. This is a job that even the most advanced software tools can only partly perform. Human artists are still necessary to put the final polish on a match move, even at top-end effects houses like ILM.

"Our job was to create a computer camera move that matched what the cameraman did on the set. If there were reference points such as tennis balls or glow sticks, we'd match-move to them. Otherwise, we'd use blueprints and measurements from the actual set or location to build rough 3D models to represent people and props in the plate. The idea is to move the computer camera around until it locks into the actual cameraman's view of the set. When we had an accurate match-move program, we'd deliver that information to the animator, who would use it as a guide to lock the choreography of the creatures to the live-action plate."

—Charlie Clavadetscher, ILM 3D match move team member

PROJECT 12.4 Match Move The Porch Model

The goal of this project is to animate a shadow-catcher object in LightWave to precisely match the tracked pattern in the background footage. You will use the TrackerNull.mot file you exported in the preceding project, the footage you stabilized in Project 11.3, and the shadow surfaces and lighting you created in Chapter 6. If you didn't build the models and lighting scenes, you can use the files provided on this book's CD-ROMs.

1. Open LightWave and clear the scene. Set the Last Frame to 265.

2. Set the Camera to 0 on all axes of rotation and translation, and set a key on frame 0. Switch to Camera View.

3. Open the Camera panel. The camcorder I used to record this footage has a 1.6 to 3.6 focal length zoom lens. I shot this at approximately 1.0 zoom factor, so set Lens Focal Length to 2.4 mm as a first approximation. Set Film Size to 1/2" CCD. Turn on Custom Size, and set Width to 2160 and Height to 1458, to match the resolution of the stabilized footage. Close the Camera panel.

4. Open the Images panel. Click on Load Sequence, and choose the two-point stabilized image sequence you rendered in Project 11.3. Close the Images panel.

5. Open the Effects panel. In the Compositing tab, select the image sequence as the Background Image. Close the Effects panel.

6. Open the Options panel. In the Layout View tab, turn on BG Image For Layout Background. If you want to see the background in color, turn on OpenGL In Layout View Graphics. Close the panel. In frames 1 through 265, you should now see the stabilized footage; there is no frame 0 in the image sequence, so the background is blank on that frame. Your scene should look like Figure 12.17.

7. Add a null and name it OriginNull. (First person to make a pun gets 30 whacks with a wet noodle.) Parent the Camera to this null.

8. Load object 1_meter.lwo, located on the first CD-ROM. This is your reference frame, a simple 1-meter square. Parent this object to the OriginNull. Move 1_meter to 2.0 meters on the Z-

Figure 12.17
Stabilized footage loaded as background image in LightWave.

axis, and set a key on frame 0. This 2.0-meter offset isn't completely arbitrary; it's a rough estimate of the distance from camera to tracker pattern in frame 154.

9. The 1-meter object is used strictly for reference during the match move and should not appear in the final rendering. Open the Objects panel, and in the Appearance Options tab, turn on Unseen By Rays and Unseen By Camera and turn off all three shadow options. This will make the object invisible to the Camera during rendering. Close the Objects panel.

10. You only need to see the reference frame as a wireframe object. Open the Scene Editor, and change 1_meter to wireframe display. Close the Scene Editor.

11. Add a null. Name it TrackerNull, and parent it to 1_meter. This is the object that will move to follow the tracker pattern.

12. With TrackerNull still active, open the Graph Editor. Click on Load Motion. Choose the TrackerNull.mot file you created in the preceding project. Now click on Use Motion. Your scene should look like Figure 12.18.

Figure 12.18
Tracker motion file applied to TrackerNull, which is parented to the 1_meter reference frame. Note the motion path trailing below null.

You will notice that TrackerNull is not positioned anywhere near the second-step chip that was the tracking pattern. Tracking is based on XY plane movement of the tracker pattern. The motion file's XY coordinates are expressed as fractions of the image dimensions; that is, a pattern in the center of the screen would have the coordinates 0.5, 0.5. No value can be lower than 0.0, 0.0, and no value can be higher than 1.0, 1.0, because those coordinates are off the screen where the tracker could not follow the pattern. These coordinates are precise to six decimal places. The catch is that they are intended to match an image with the same proportions as the tracked footage. That means you need to resize the reference frame, the 1_meter object, to fit the boundaries of the background image as it appears in LightWave's Camera View. This is easy to tweak with the Numeric input.

13. Select 1_meter, and change the size until its edges precisely match the boundaries of the background image in the Camera View, as shown in Figure 12.19. Use the Numeric panel to tweak the size in X and Y axes to at least three decimal places. Set the Z value equal to the X value. Take your time and get it right; this will affect every other step in the match move.

Figure 12.19

Resizing the reference frame, which is barely visible as a narrow border around the background image, scales the motion of TrackerNull to match the tracker pattern's position.

When you are satisfied with the size, set a key at frame 0. If you step through the frames now, the TrackerNull should precisely match the chip in the second step.

14. Add another null, name it PorchPivotNull, and parent it to TrackerNull.

15. Load the Porch.lwo object from the first CD-ROM. Parent it to the PorchPivotNull. In the Scene Editor, set the Porch to full wireframe display. The nulls and reference frame can be bounding box wireframes, but you'll need to see all the Porch's edges in this project.

16. With the Porch object selected, open the Surfaces panel. Select the PorchSurface surface, set its color to black, and click on the T button next to Surface Color to open the Color Texture subpanel. For Texture Type, select the stabilized footage as a Front Projection Image Map. Set Texture Opacity to 100%, and close the subpanel to return to the Surfaces panel. This will make the Porch render as nearly invisible except for shadowing effects.

17. In the Advanced Options tab, set Alpha Channel to Shadow Density. This will make the porch surface a shadow-catcher for any other objects you animate over it. Close the Surfaces panel.

18. With the Porch object still selected, open the Objects panel. Turn off Self Shadow and Cast Shadow. In the Appearance Options tab, turn on Polygon Edges and set the Edge Color to bright blue. Close the Objects panel.

This will make the wireframe outline of the Porch visible in your test renderings, making it much easier for you to evaluate the matching of edges to the background image. The critical details of the background image can be very small and difficult to see in some frames, and the wireframes in Layout can obscure those details. The rendered Polygon Edges make a very good visual aid. Just remember to turn off Polygon Edges before you start the final rendering!

Child objects inherit the scaling of their parent objects. We don't want the Porch object to be scaled to match the background image's aspect ratio, so we need to resize the PorchPivotNull to counteract the scaling of the 1_meter object.

19. Resize the PorchPivotNull to the inverse of 1_meter's scaling. Figure 12.20 shows 1_meter object's scaling to be 6.345, 4.260, 6.345. Dividing 1 by each of these numbers gives a scaling correction of 0.1576, 0.2347, 0.1576. Apply these scaling corrections to PorchPivotNull.

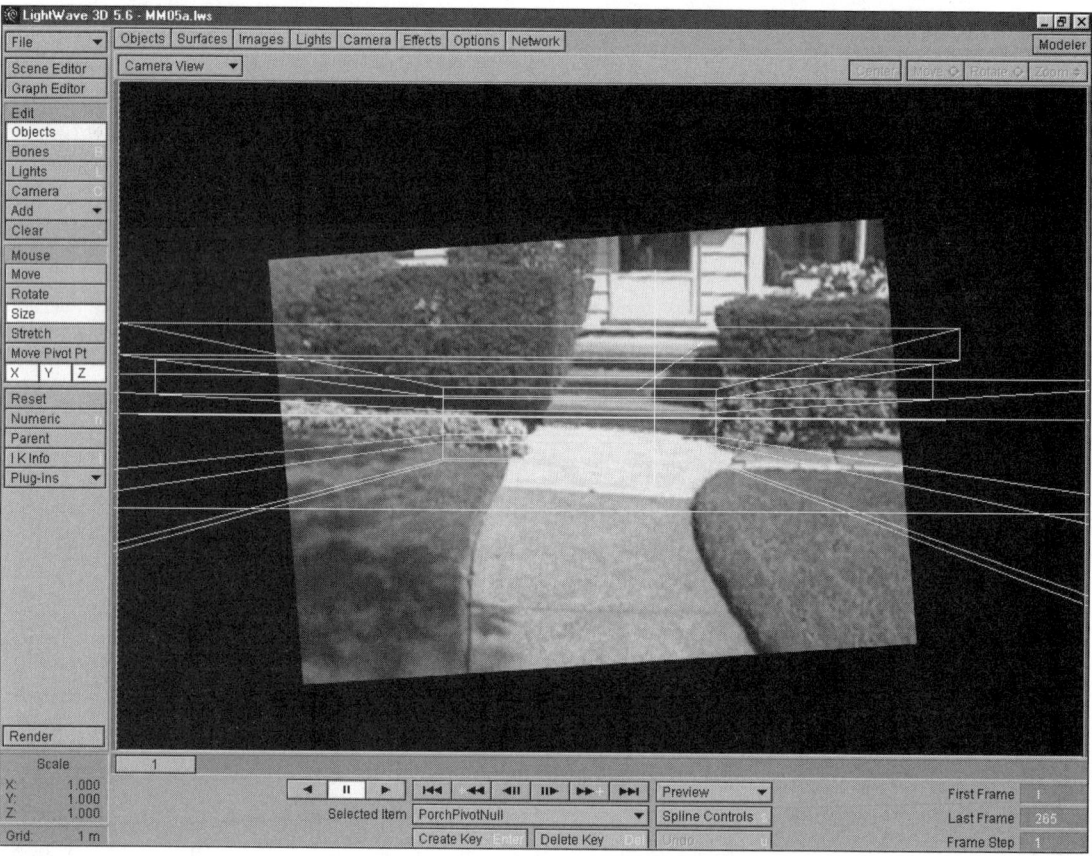

Figure 12.20
Porch object and PorchPivotNull scaled by TrackerNull's scaling, 6.345 X, 4.260 Y, and 6.345 Z.

Your results should look like Figure 12.21. You can check the scaling correction, if you like, by loading another copy of the Porch object and positioning it to match the first one. You'll have to give it the vector sum XYZ translations and HPB rotations of all the parent objects to get a precise alignment for your comparisons. When you're done with the check, delete the duplicate Porch object.

Figure 12.21
PorchPivotNull scaled to correct for the TrackerNull's scaling, 0.3748 X, 0.5 Y, and 0.3748 Z. The Porch object remains at 1.0 scaling on all axes.

The Porch object is constructed according to the sketch in Chapter 11 (see Figure 11.25), with its pivot point set at the location of the chip in the second step that was used as a tracking pattern. This means that applying the XY motion of the tracker to this model will automatically make it match the XY motion of the real object in the background footage with no offsets.

The stabilization of the footage, combined with the tracker-derived XY animation of the model, takes the place of two-thirds of the animation of the camera. The only positional variable left to animate is the Z-axis distance between the camera and the model. In order to animate the Camera, you would have to animate the 1_meter reference object's scaling to keep it exactly matched to the edges of the background image in the Camera View. You would also have to animate the counter-scaling of the PorchPivotNull to keep the tracker motion accurate. That's the reason for all the nulls and parenting; you can simply scale the OriginNull to adjust the distance between Camera and target, and the 1_meter reference object automatically scales to match. You still have to counter-scale the PorchPivotNull, but because everything is proportional, you can do that with a single click-and-drag.

In the example footage, the camera moves in a complex path, partially orbiting the porch steps. This is fairly difficult to animate. However, the camera-and-porch relative motion can also be described as a comparatively simple set of rotations of the porch around the pivot located at the tracker pattern. That's why the Porch object is built with the pivot point in that location.

The camera's focal length determines the amount of parallax at any given distance. With the model located at the appropriate distance from the CG camera and positioned over the background image, you can adjust the CG camera's focal length to match the parallax of the CG model to that of the original object. If you have an accurate measure of either the camera-to-target distance or the camera's focal length, finding the missing measurement is not difficult. However, if you have neither the focal length nor the camera-to-target distance, you have to twiddle and tweak until you find a usable setting. This is why it is so important to record this information when you are on set, and why you should be especially nice to the focus puller. Fortunately, for the purposes of this project, the initial setting of 2.4 mm is usable.

With this setup, you need to animate only a few, low-frequency variables to complete the match move:

- Size of the OriginNull to approximately match the distance from Camera to target, substituting for Camera Z-axis motion
- Size of the PorchPivotNull in all three axes to control the height, width, and depth of the Porch
- Rotation of the Porch in all three axes

As I mentioned previously, a useful strategy is to animate the lowest-frequency variable first. That means animating the OriginNull scaling first; you may only need a handful of keyframes because you can be pretty sloppy with this variable, and it doesn't change very quickly. The interaction of the PorchPivotNull scaling and the rotation of the Porch object means that you will have to animate these variables pretty much simultaneously.

20. Go to frame 154. Because this was the reference frame for stabilizing the footage, there should be no position, rotation, or scaling distortions in this frame. The distance from the tracker pattern (the chip in the second step) to the camera in this frame is roughly 2 meters, so you don't need to scale the OriginNull. With no scaling of the OriginNull, you shouldn't have to make major scaling corrections with the PorchPivotNull.

21. Rotate the Porch object so the line representing the upper front edge of the second step, which passes through the pivot point, is aligned with the upper front edge of the second step

in the background image. Modify the Heading, Pitch, and Bank values so as many as possible of the horizontal lines in the model align with horizontal references in the background image. Your results should look something like Figure 12.22. Set a key for the Porch at frame 154.

Figure 12.22
The Porch object aligned with the horizontal background lines in frame 154.

The Porch still appears a little too large. Tweak PorchPivotNull size. Try all three axes at once first, then tweak individual axes to adjust width, height, and length. You may find that you need to go back and tweak the Porch rotations to get a more precise alignment with the background. When you think you have matched the background's scale and rotations as closely as possible, set keyframes for the Porch, PorchPivotNull, and OriginNull. Your results should look like Figure 12.23.

You can check your work by rendering the frame with the same settings you will use for your final renders. With Polygon Edges still turned on for the Porch object, your results should look something like Figure 12.24.

Figure 12.23
The Porch aligned and PorchPivotNull and OriginNull scaled to match the background in frame 154.

Repeat the above steps for the other keyframes in a bracketing pattern, as described in Chapter 10. I suggest frames 1, 75, 180, 211, and so on.

- First, size the OriginNull. Examine the background image, and make your best estimate of the distance from the chip pattern to the camera. Divide that estimate by 2 (remember, 1.0 for the OriginNull is 2 meters' distance), and enter the result as the size of OriginNull.

- Second, rotate the Porch to align its horizontal lines with the corresponding horizontal edges in the background image.

- Third, size PorchPivotNull to bring the width, depth, and height of the Porch into alignment with the background image.

- Finally, go back and tweak Porch rotations and PorchPivotNull size to correct any remaining errors. Set keys for all three elements, and go on to the next frame.

The fewer the keyframes, the smoother the motion and the less likely you will make errors that produce chattering. With every keyframe you set, the discrepancies to be corrected in the adjoin-

Figure 12.24
Rendered test of frame 154. Note how blue polygon edges make evaluating the match much easier.

ing keyframes become smaller. It's up to you when to stop the tweaking; on a short deadline, "good enough" may be only the six initial keyframes. With a longer production schedule, you may have time to tweak a couple dozen keyframes.

For frames 212 through 265, you have a slightly harder job. Because the chip on the edge of the second step is no longer visible in the background image, you don't have tracker data in the imported motion file. That means you don't know where the Porch is supposed to be located in the XY plane. That adds those two variables to the list you have already animated, and the inter-dependencies between all these variables can be a very demanding juggling act. This is where you practice your interpolation skills. Your first step is to eyeball what variable settings you can, simply by looking at the background image for frames 212 through 265. The most obvious candidate is the OriginNull scaling.

22. Go to frame 212. In the Scene Editor, choose Hide All Objects. This gets the wireframes out of your way so you can see the background better.

23. Scrub through frames 212 to 265, looking only at the distance between the camera and the porch. At what frames does the camera stop moving toward or away from the porch? Ignore side-to-side, pitch, bank, or heading changes; concentrate on that Z-axis motion. By my estimate, the camera stopped moving closer to the porch on frame 231.

24a. Go to frame 231, or whichever frame you think is correct. Estimate the distance from the camera to the estimated position of the tracker pattern. You'll have to extrapolate the leading edge of the second step. Divide that estimate by 2 (remember, 1.0 for the OriginNull is 2 meters' distance), and enter the result as the size of OriginNull. Set the same value for a key on frames 232 and 265. That nails down the Z-axis motion for the rest of the match move.

24b. Another approach is to select the OriginNull and open the Graph Editor. Choose the X Scale, and look at the curve. You should be able to see a definite shape to the curve and estimate pretty closely the value that will extend the curve to frame 231, as shown in Figure 12.25. Click on Use Motion to close the Graph Editor.

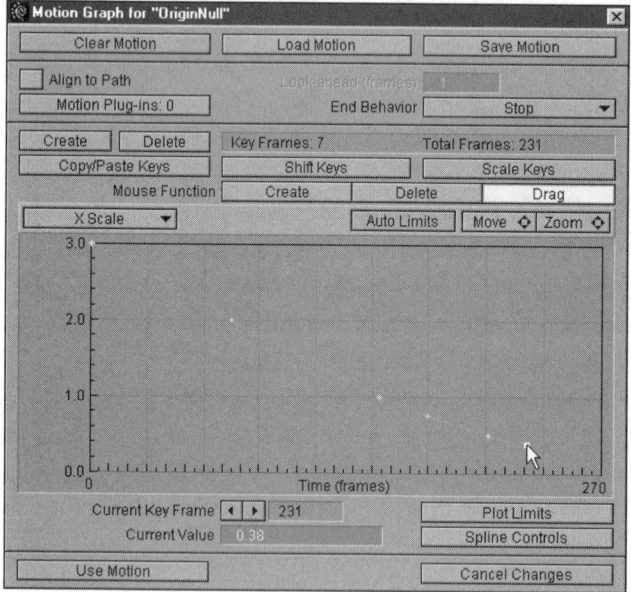

Figure 12.25
OriginNull scaling key set at frame 231, with a value that extrapolates from the slope of the preceding curve segments.

25. The scaling of the OriginNull directly affects the scaling corrections for the PorchPivotNull. Set keys at OriginNull's keyframes for the scaling of PorchPivotNull. As a first approximation, keep the same PorchPivotNull scaling as in frame 211.

26. The next lowest-frequency variable is the Porch object's Bank rotation. In the Scene Editor, make the Porch object visible as a full wireframe. On frames 231 and 265, adjust the Porch object's Bank rotation to align the horizontal edges of the Porch object with the nearest horizontal edges in the background image.

27. On frame 231, move the TrackerNull on its X and Y axes to match up the rear edge of the second porch step with the corresponding line in the background image. Cross-check this with the alignment of the front edge of the object's step and the estimated front edge of the step in the background image. If you can't get the two alignments to reconcile, you may need to change the PorchPivotNull scaling and try again.

From this point on, you will need to simultaneously tweak the PorchPivotNull scaling on all three axes, the TrackerNull X and Y position, and the Porch rotation on all three axes. An error on one variable affects the other seven. That may seem like a lot of variables to juggle at once, but remember that any remaining changes should be very small. By this time, any remaining errors in alignment, scaling, or position should only be the width of a pixel or two on your screen.

28. When you have frame 231 matched to your satisfaction, do the same for frame 265.

Because frame 231 marks the end of the camera's movement in several axes, I recommend that you copy the settings for Porch rotation, PorchPivotNull scaling, and TrackerNull position to frame 265. This will accomplish over 95 percent of the necessary tweaks for you; the remainder is relatively easy. Your final results should look like Figure 12.26.

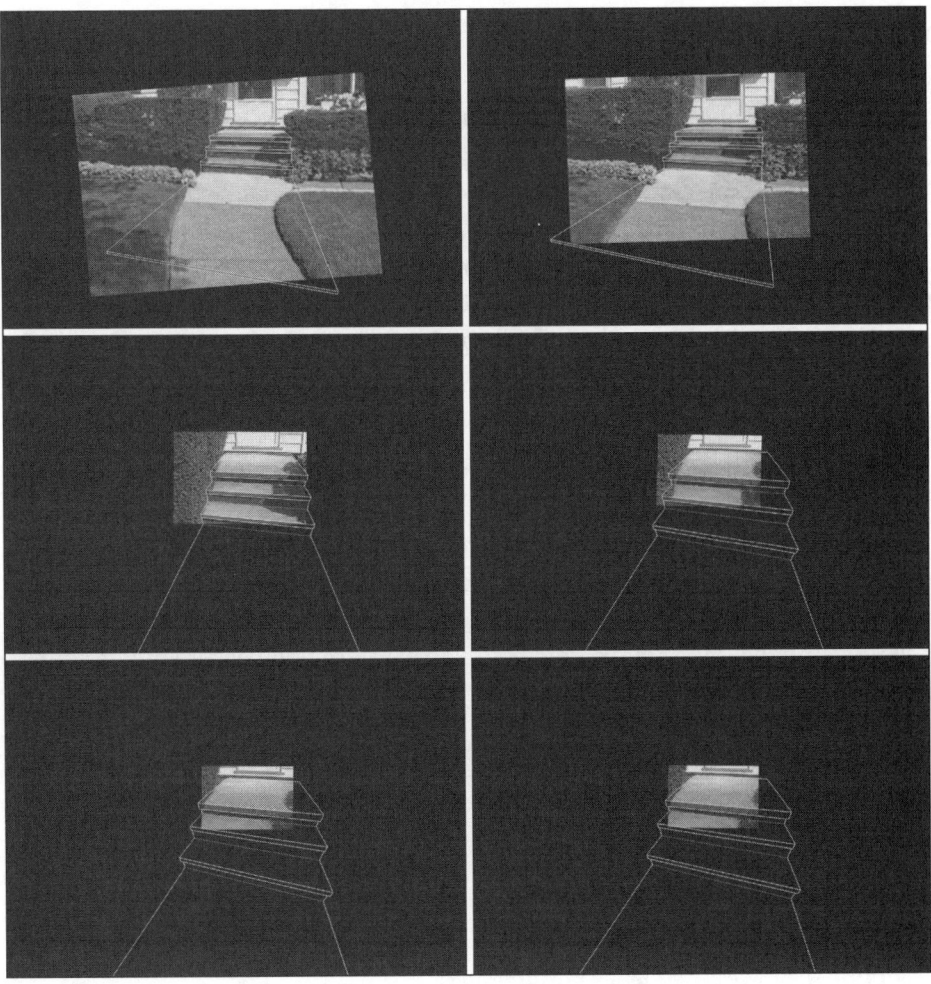

Figure 12.26
Test renderings of frames 1, 75, 180, 211, 231, and 265.

29. Now you need to step through the entire animation, looking for the frames where discrepancies peak. Wherever the match is off enough that it will show in the final rendering, create a set of keyframes to correct the problem.

Some variables will require more keyframes than others will. OriginNull and PorchPivotNull scaling should require the fewest (and identical number of) keyframes. Porch rotation will require slightly more keyframes. TrackerNull may require a key for every frame after frame 211, when the tracked motion file runs out. The XY plane movement of TrackerNull is the highest-frequency variable in this match move, and therefore the one that you will spend the most time and effort tweaking. Your manual keyframing between frames 212 and 265 should look very much like the tracker motion of frames 1 through 211, with tiny changes on most frames and the occasional larger jump.

30. When you have completed the match move, add an animated character or other moving CGI element, parented to the Porch object.

This doesn't have to be complicated, just something that casts a moving shadow over the steps and upper surface of the Porch object to show how well you've match moved the shadow-catching surfaces. If you like, use Load From Scene to add objects, motions, and lights from the LampHop.lws scene file in the Scenes folder of the first CD-ROM. This is a desk lamp object that I animated to hop up the porch steps. After you Load From Scene, you will need to delete the default Light, leaving the SunLight imported from the LampHop scene. You will also need to parent both the desk lamp object and the SunLight to the Porch object so they inherit the match move, as shown in Figure 12.27.

31. You may want to leave Polygon Edges on to check the first set of renderings with the character added; after that, turn off Polygon Edges so you can accurately judge the lay of the character's shadow over the edges of the Porch object.

32. When you are satisfied with the test render results, render the entire image sequence. If you plan to comp a subtractive merge, you can leave the PorchSurface and background image as is. Your results should look something like Figure 12.28. If you prefer to comp an additive merge, you should drop the image maps from both PorchSurface and background, resulting in a completely black frame except for the desk lamp.

Congratulations on finishing this project! In doing so, you learned how to:

- Apply a tracker motion file to position an object relative to the background image
- Match camera distance and focal length
- Divide the position, rotation, and scaling variables among several objects to enable the use of fewer keyframes
- Choose and keyframe the lowest-frequency variables first
- Set keyframes in a bracketing pattern to minimize the total number of keyframes

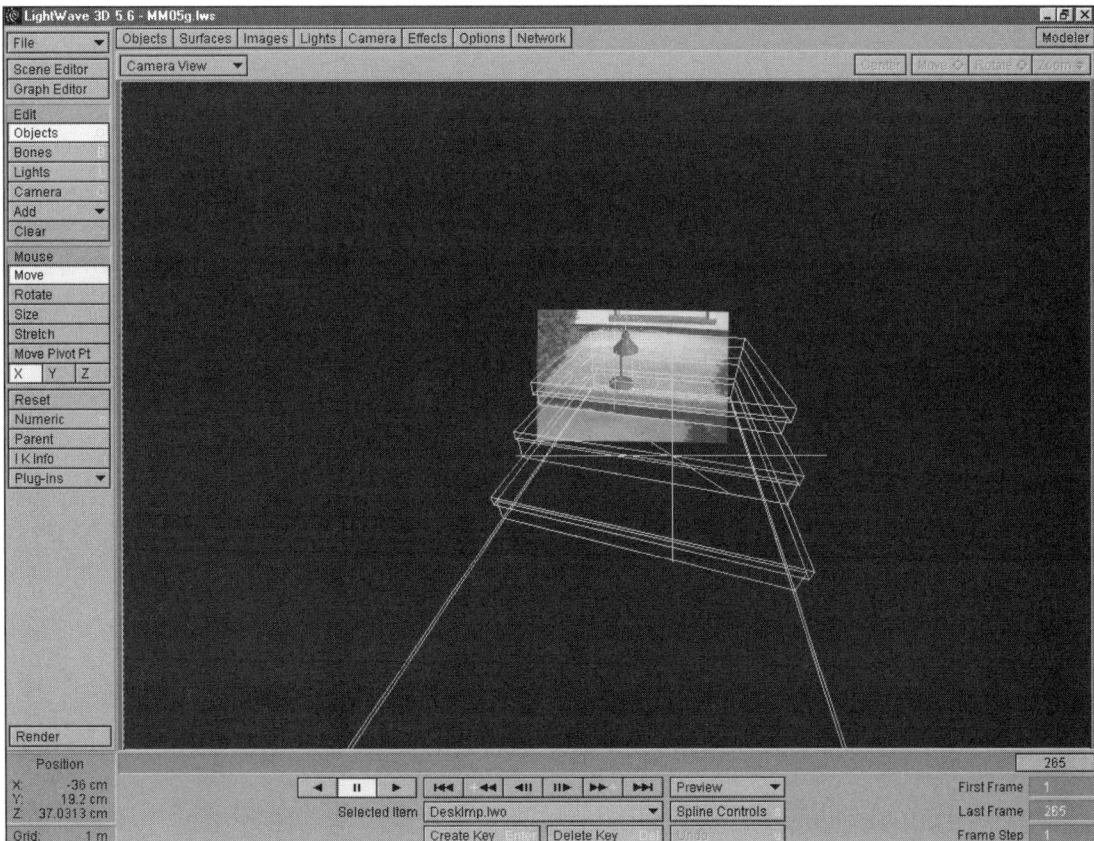

Figure 12.27
Match move scene with desk lamp added.

- Coordinate the interrelating variables of rotation, scaling, and position

- Extrapolate a new value from the slope of the existing motion graph

- Check your alignments in a test render by using Polygon Edges

Completing a match move takes a lot of effort and attention to detail, but with practice, you will accumulate techniques and shortcuts that make it faster and easier. After you have a match move locked down, you can use it to render separate shadow, ambient, specular, and Z-buffer passes. This can greatly increase your options for compositing effects and can make comping the CGI elements seamlessly into the live footage much easier.

After Effects And Match Moving

After Effects is designed as a 2D animated graphics program, and it lacks several of the tools necessary to perform 3D match moves. If you need these features, you need to use a different compositing program.

Figure 12.28
Final renderings of frames 1, 75, 180, 154, 211, and 265 with animated desk lamp and sunlight added. Images are cropped to 720×486 to show detail; the full images are still 2160×1458.

Aura And Match Moving

Aura 1.0 is designed as a 2D paint and compositing program, and it relies on LightWave (another NewTek product) for the 3D tools necessary for match moving.

Chalice And Match Moving

Chalice is designed as a 2D compositing program, and it lacks several of the tools necessary to perform 3D match moves. If you need these features, use a different compositing program.

Commotion And Match Moving

Commotion 2.1 is designed as a 2D compositing program, and it lacks several of the tools necessary to perform 3D match moves. However, it does contain most of the tools you need to track and stabilize footage in order to prepare it for use in a 3D program. Specifically, the Save All Trackers feature gives you the option of exporting tracking data for 3D Pan And Tilt, in the format of Electric Image Motion. This data can be imported directly into Electric Image to greatly reduce the amount of manual keyframing necessary to create an accurate match move. If you are using either Commotion or Electric Image, you should definitely consider this combination as a solution for your match move needs.

effect* And Match Moving

Although effect* has a number of 3D tools in addition to its 2D compositing features, it is not intended to be a full 3D CGI rendering program. As such, it lacks several of the tools necessary to perform 3D match moves. If you need these features, you have to use a different compositing program. If you use effect* and need to create 3D match moves and other 3D CGI elements, you should consider Discreet's companion product, 3D Studio MAX.

Shake And Match Moving

Shake 2.1 is designed as a 2D animated graphics program, and it lacks several of the tools necessary to perform 3D match moves. If you need these features, use a different compositing program.

Four-Point Destabilize

The final step in the match move process is to put all that live-action camera jitter back in, restoring the appearance of a handheld camera and making the CGI element that much more realistic. This process may appear complex, but it is really just a series of processes you have already learned in previous projects. Pay attention to the details, and the following four-point destabilize process will be easy to master.

PROJECT 12.5   Motion Destabilize

The goal of this project is to reverse the effects of the stabilizing you did in Project 11.3. This destabilizing restores the handheld appearance to the composited footage, so it doesn't appear overly smooth like a SteadiCam or motion control camera. Because the Stabilize tool does not have an easy reversal option like the Tracker's Unsteady Position, this process is a little more complex to set up.

1. Open a new flow. Add a Loader, and load the stabilized footage you rendered at the end of Project 11.3. Set Global In to 1, to compensate for the footage beginning with frame 1 rather than frame 0.

2. Show Loader 1 in the Large display, and set it to display the alpha channel.

3. Add a Corner Tracker (under Tools|Miscellaneous) two tiles to the right of Loader 1, and connect the Loader to it.

4. Change the Color in each of the four Tracker tabs to Alpha. The alpha channel is the easiest, most accurate channel for tracking the corners of the stabilized image.

5. In frame 1, set each four Corner Tracker to a corner of the white rectangle in the Large display, working clockwise (and numerically) from top left, Trackers 1, 2, 3, and 4.

This is the same basic Tracker procedure you followed in Project 11.1, and again with the Stabilize tool in Project 11.3. Be careful to get each pattern crosshair precisely centered on the corner of the white rectangle. Your results should look like Figure 12.29.

Figure 12.29
The flow configured to corner track the stabilized footage from Project 11.3.

6. When you have the patterns set to your satisfaction, click on Select All Patterns in the Corner Tracker control's General tab.

7. Set Render Start to 1 and Render End to 265. In the Corner Tracker control's General tab, click on Create All Paths.

The Corner Tracker tool will process all frames in the render range, creating four paths, one for each tracker. If any of the trackers go off-pattern, stop the process, reset the patterns, and start again from the last good frame. Depending on the processing speed of your workstation, this may take a while. The Corner Tracker has to process each oversized, stabilized image, looking for a pattern four times over. Be patient, and don't wander off; you need to keep an eye on the process to make sure you catch any hiccups that could foul up your comps later.

The scale and position stabilizer changes won't affect the tracking; the white corner on a black background's tracking patterns remain the same, no matter the size or position of the rectangle as a whole. Unless your original footage is from a camera that spins on its own lens axis, the Corner Tracker should also be able to deal with any rotational stabilization. However, the frames where the image is rotated most are also the frames with the highest chance of error. The corner patterns can change from a 90-degree corner nearly parallel to the edges of the frame to a 90-degree triangle at a significant offset from the original pattern alignment.

8. When the Corner Tracker finishes rendering, you should have four paths like those shown in Figure 12.30. Save the flow as Corner1.flw.

9. Disconnect Loader 1 from the Corner Tracker. Once the paths have been rendered, you won't need to modify or re-render any parts of them. If something goes wrong, you will need to reconnect the trackers and re-render the entire paths.

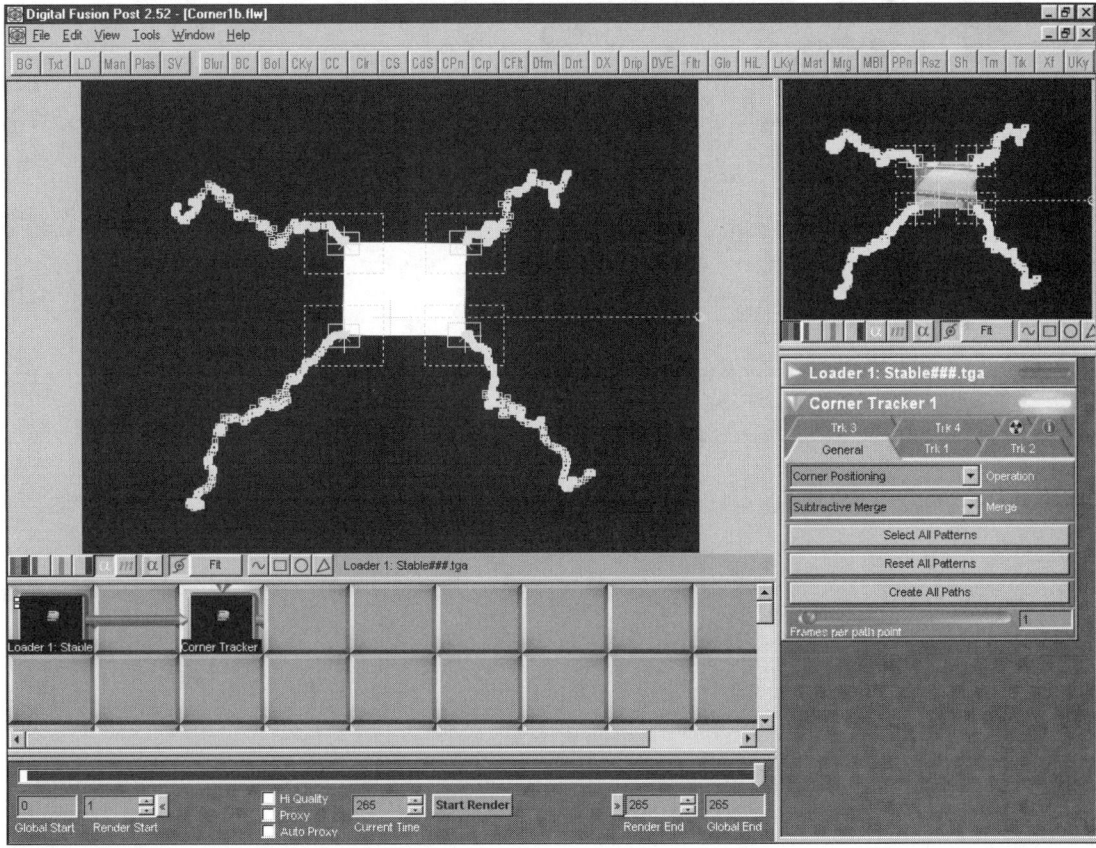

Figure 12.30
The Corner Tracker's paths.

10. Replace the footage in Loader 1 with the match move footage you rendered at the end of Project 12.4.

11. Add a Perspective Positioner tool (from the Tools|Warp submenu) and connect it to Loader 1, as shown in Figure 12.31.

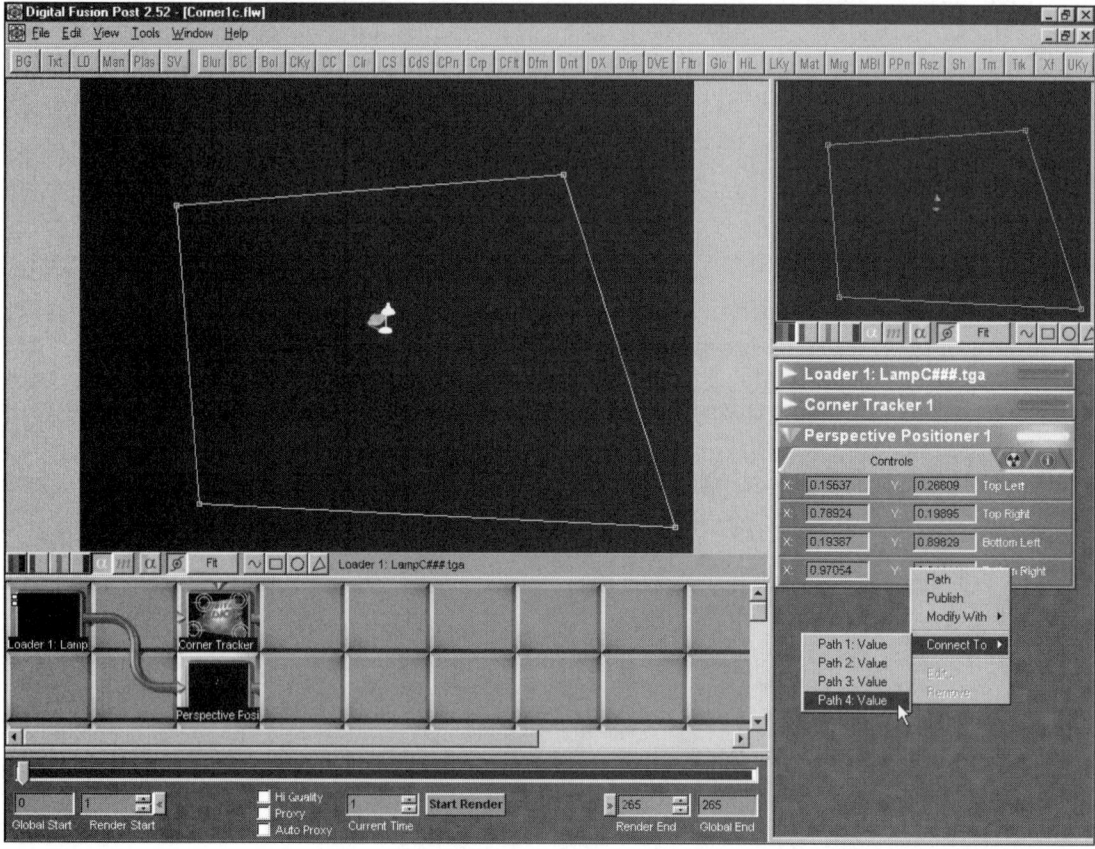

Figure 12.31
Perspective Positioner added to the flow with top left, top right, and bottom left corners connected to the Corner Tracker's path values.

12. In the Perspective Positioner controls, right-click on Top Left and choose Connect To|Path 1 Value. Repeat for Top Right and Path 2, Bottom Left and Path 3, and Bottom Right and Path 4. This connects the positioner's corners to the corresponding tracked paths of the Corner Tracker, as shown in Figure 12.31.

The Perspective Positioner will stretch the stabilized image out to fill the entire frame, as shown in Figure 12.32. This removes the rotation, scale, and position stabilizing, but leaves the frame at too high a resolution.

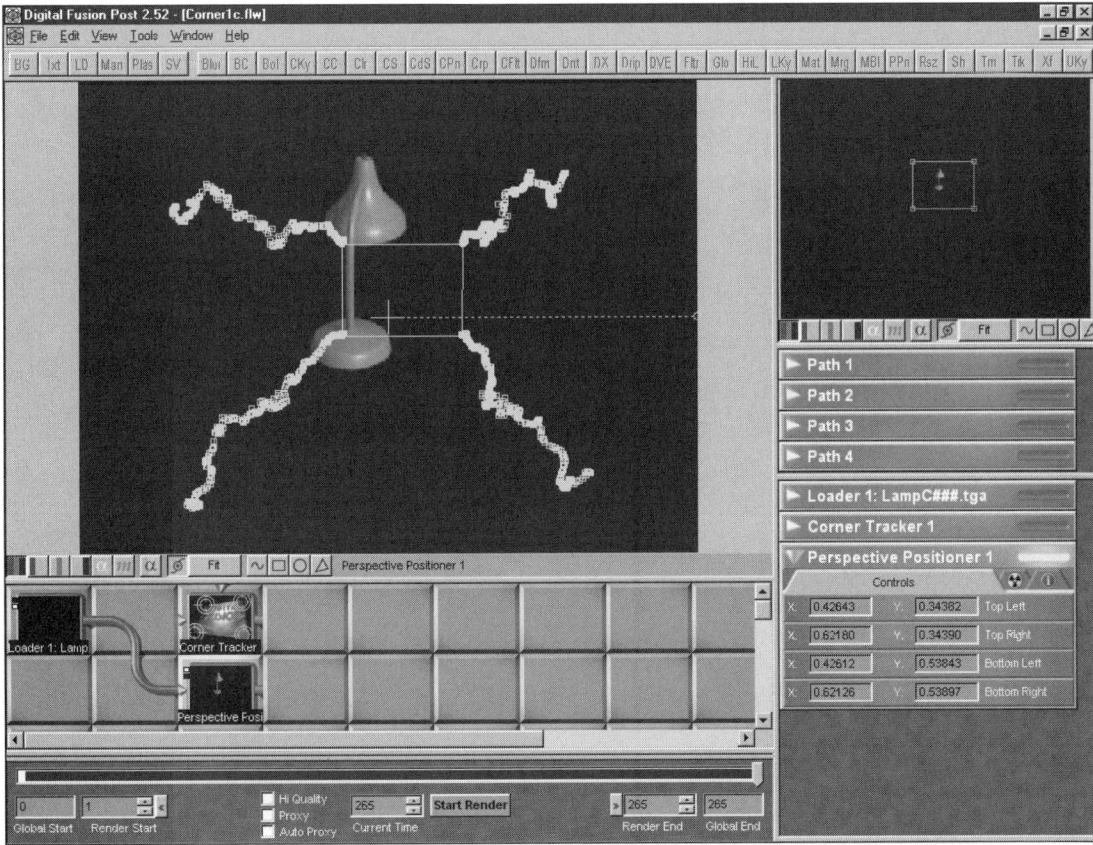

Figure 12.32
Destabilizing effect of Perspective Positioner connected to Corner Tracker's path values.

13. Add a Resize tool and attach it to the output of the Perspective Positioner. Set it to 720x486, the resolution of the original footage. Because the resize operation can be very time-consuming on such large images, choose Nearest Neighbor as the resize method until you are ready to render a final image sequence. At that time, you can change it to Sinc or one of the other more accurate downsampling algorithms.

14. Add another Loader and load the original Match footage.

15. Add a Merge tool, and connect the Resize output to its foreground input and Loader 2 to its background input, as shown in Figure 12.33. If you rendered black surfaces and black background in Project 12.4, use Additive as in Figure 12.33. If you rendered the stabilized footage as the background image and front projection image map in Project 12.4, use Subtractive.

To tweak the appearance of the CGI elements to match the footage more closely, you may want to add a blur, noise, or grain filter, or some combination of them (see Figure 12.34). Many CGI programs such as LightWave have rendering effects that can add dirt, noise, and other realistic

Figure 12.33
Original footage with destabilized effects footage with Additive Merge over it.

surface characteristics. Almost anything that will take the too-clean, perfectly rendered polish off the CGI elements is a good idea. One goal is to match the visual textures of disparate elements, so the final comp is internally consistent. A good comp should look like it was simply photographed, that every element was actually there at the same time.

16. When you are satisfied with your comp, change the Resize tool to Sinc downsampling, save your changes, then render the destabilized image sequence.

If all goes well, the final rendered animation should show your character accurately composited to the steps, with the original jerky camera motions and the correct lighting and shadows. Don't be disappointed if your first attempt doesn't turn out as well as you'd hoped. Like most processes in digital compositing, match moving takes practice and attention to detail. Try again, and I think you'll be pleasantly surprised at how quickly your results improve.

Figure 12.34
Slight blur and grain filters added to CGI elements to match blur and noise in the original footage.

In completing this project, you learned how to:

• Apply the Corner Tracker

• Apply the Perspective Positioner

• Destabilize multiple-point stabilized footage

• Merge a CGI-rendered element over original footage

• Filter a CGI-rendered element to match blur and noise in original footage

After Effects And Four-Point Destabilizing

After Effects has no corner tracking or destabilizing features. If you need these features, you have to use a different compositing program.

Aura And Four-Point Destabilizing

Aura 1.0 has no corner tracking or destabilizing features. If you need these features, use a different compositing program.

Chalice And Four-Point Destabilizing

One of the Chalice 1.6 tutorials demonstrates Chalice's tracking features, but nowhere in the documentation does it discuss how to reverse a multi-point stabilize operation. I believe destabilization may be possible by modifying the four-corner track-and-pin process described in Chalice Tutorial 4. You will need to track the four corners of the stabilized footage, then pin those corners to the corner coordinates of the original Match footage. If you want to tackle this problem, I suggest you start with Tutorial 4, and then read the manual sections on the Track and Apply Track nodes, followed by the manual's Appendix B, "Chalice Expression Language."

As I stated previously, this requires a great deal of expertise, or an extraordinary amount of effort for a less experienced user. For these reasons, Chalice is not my first choice of compositing software for beginners; if you are just learning, I recommend a different program.

Motion Destabilize (Commotion)

Puffin Designs' Commotion package includes tutorial footage and instructions for several tracking projects, including destabilization to reverse a multi-point stabilize operation. Rather than repeat the efforts of the tutorials' designers, I recommend (if you are using Commotion) that you work through Lessons 8 and 9 in the manual, then apply the destabilization process to the match move footage rendered in Project 12.4.

Motion Destabilize (effect*)

The goal of this version of Project 12.5 is to use effect* to reverse the effects of the stabilizing you did in Project 11.3. This destabilizing restores the handheld appearance to the composited footage, so it doesn't appear overly smooth like a SteadiCam or motion control camera. Because effect*'s Stabilize 2 Point effect doesn't have an Invert option like the Stabilize 1 Point effect, this process is a little more complex to set up.

1. You need a clear pattern of two diagonally opposite corners to track. The easiest way to do this is to render an alpha channel from the original stabilizing comp you saved from effect* Project 11.3. The result should be a white rectangle over a black background, providing very clear tracking patterns for all four corners.

2. Import the alpha channel sequence to a new project in effect*.

3. Run a two-point stabilization, just as you did in effect* Project 11.3, using the top left corner as Stabilize Point 1 and the bottom right corner as Stabilize Point 2. Make sure you use the same reference frame as in the original stabilization. As a check, the rectangle at the reference frame should be 720×486, and it should be perfectly level and centered.

4. When the stabilization is finished, the white rectangle should be centered and have dimensions of 720×486, the same as the original footage, throughout the comp. Scrub through the comp and look for tracking errors, and repair them by hand-keyframing the stabilization if necessary.

5. Replace the alpha channel with the match move color footage from Project 12.4. The results should exactly match the oversized footage you rendered from step 2 of effect* Project 11.3.

6. To remove the black safety border, choose Effect|Distort|Resize. In the Resize effect control window, set Corner 1 to 720,486 and set Corner 2 to 1440,972. Choose Crop from the Method menu.

7. Choose File|Composition Settings. In the Composition Settings window, change Format Options to the original D-1 NTSC setting. This restores the comp to the resolution of the original Match footage.

Shake And Four-Point Destabilizing

Shake 2.1 has no corner tracking or destabilizing features. If you need these features, you need to use a different compositing program.

Animating The Camera

Steadying and unsteadying existing camera motion can be challenging and can require some inventive solutions, but the process is essentially technical. A more artistic part of modifying camera motion is adding motion that was never in the original footage.

> "We frequently used the match-move software MM2 to add 2D camera movement to any shot that seemed static. When a dinosaur clomps through a scene, we'd add camera bounce as if the photographer were responding to the earth-shaking impact of the creature as its foot hit the ground. Even just the slightest move helps give the impression that there's a person behind the camera. It's always that last ten percent of finessing that takes a pretty good comp to the level of a photorealistic comp."
> —George Murphy, ILM technical director, Jurassic Park

When you have all the elements comped to your satisfaction, you can add XY-plane camera motion by running that footage through a Merge with its center animated by a path. If you have enough margin for reframing the shot, you can even animate Z-axis movement or rotation with the Size and Angle controls. This is another reason to shoot on VistaVision or otherwise capture a larger frame than you plan for the final production. The more margin you have, the more creative you can be with post-production camera moves.

To create realistic camera motions, you should study the original sources. Practice with real handheld footage from broadcast news and sports, "reality TV," and documentaries. The footage you can collect from helmetcams, skicams, carcams, and other sports broadcasts will cover just about every extreme of camera motion you can imagine. Military gun-camera footage from the Gulf War and other conflicts is invaluable if you are trying to simulate combat footage. Shots of earthquakes, volcanic eruptions, and other disasters are worth study, too. Load this footage into your compositing software, and try to track and stabilize it as you did in Projects 11.1, 11.2, and 11.3. Study the resulting tracker paths, and save the most important parts for reuse in simulating your own camera motions. With a little time and effort, you can build up a library of stock camera moves that can save you hours of hand-keyframing and produce pulse-pounding results from static footage.

SHAKE 2.1 CAMERASHAKE FUNCTION

This macro function adds noise to the Pan values of Move2D. It's a good example of how to use noise to mimic natural motion. For more details, see the Shake documentation on the second CD-ROM.

Moving On

This chapter wraps up the processes begun in Chapter 11. You should now be able to comp effects to deal with almost any type of camera motion, whether it requires a simple one-point track or full stabilization. The next chapter introduces another class of problems you will be expected to solve: footage with bad color, contrast, and other photographic flaws.

PART V

ADVANCED
COMPOSITING

WHEN LIFE GIVES YOU LEMONS

This chapter shows you how to make palatable lemonade out of the most sour, bitter footage that a camera mishap can drop on your workstation. When something goes wrong with the camera or digitizing process, the digital compositor is usually called upon to fix the problem. A camera operator's oversight, a simple accident, or a hostile action by the ubiquitous camera gremlins can produce footage with severe photographic flaws. Poor exposure, bad color, inadequate contrast, and missing or badly damaged frames can all result from camera problems. The scanning or digitizing process can add flaws to the footage, including dropped frames, dirt and scratches, jitter, and poor color balance. Again, some of this can be blamed on the equipment, some on the operator, and some is simply bad luck. If you are comping elements from film or CGI sources for output to video, you may also have to correct any colors that are beyond broadcast limits.

Remember that digital compositing is the art of the invisible effect. When you are called upon to repair extreme damage, you need to match the repaired footage seamlessly to the adjoining footage. This is especially important for comped footage that will be intercut with raw footage. You will have to preserve or restore the original color balance, jitter, grain, and other film or video artifacts in addition to any comped effects. It's not enough that you make damaged footage look perfect: You have to make it better than perfect by giving it enough artificial imperfections that it accurately mimics reality.

Missing In Action

One of the worst things that can happen to raw footage is a camera or processing accident that destroys a frame in the middle of a crucial shot. Some of these accidents occur during principal photography, but they are not discovered until the film is developed. The camera lens may be struck by flying debris or otherwise temporarily occluded. Typical examples might include flying debris from an explosion, airborne debris that impact a vehicle-mounted camera lens, and dirt kicked up by a vehicle or actor in the course of a stunt. This is most common in remote-controlled or unattended cameras, especially those placed to capture a high-speed stunt or effect. For handheld cameras, anything can happen. Even the camera crew can make a mistake, momentarily occluding the lens with a hand or piece of gear in a particularly frantic moment. This works to your advantage, because fast-moving action footage typically has a lot of natural motion blur that you can simulate to fake a replacement frame.

Less common problems are the result of physical damage to the film somewhere between the camera and your workstation. Although most scanning and telecine equipment is designed to be very gentle with the camera negative, accidents do happen. It's possible to lose a frame due to operator error, equipment failure, or those pesky gremlins again. Video footage can suffer similar problems and, unfortunately, is more prone to them. Dirt on the recording or playback heads, worn or damaged media, noise in the equipment, and the ever-popular operator error or simple accident can drop or damage a video frame.

Less severe versions of these problems can be solved by some of the techniques described in Chapters 9 and 10. A little dirt on the lens can be removed just like any other rig removal; a partial occlusion of a frame can be patched from a clean plate or adjoining frame. However, too much damage within a single frame can rule out rig removal and similar methods, because there is simply not enough of the damaged frame left to use.

Identifying severely damaged or unusable frames is relatively easy; you can spot them as soon as you see them. A more challenging problem is to detect and replace frames that are dropped from a video source. If the camera or an object in the scene is moving, you can detect missing frames by a sudden jerk in the movement.

PROJECT 13.1 Replacing Missing Or Damaged Frames

The goal of this project is to replace frames that were dropped in a video digitizing process. The general approach is to identify the missing frames, to renumber the image sequence to leave gaps for the missing frames, then to comp new frames into the gaps in the image sequence.

1. Create a new folder named "Complete" for the corrected footage.

2. Open a new flow. Add a Loader, and load the footage to be repaired. For this project, I'll use the Match footage used previously in Chapters 11 and 12.

3. Run a single-point Tracker, as you did in Project 11.1, on a prominent marker in the footage.

I recommend either the left or right threshold corner, as both are visible throughout the footage and they have easy-to-track patterns. You will probably have to run the track in several stages because the scaling is so extreme.

4. Maximize the Spline Editor, and click on Fit to show the entire spline. You should see a Path: Displacement graph like Figure 13.1. Select all points, and choose Linear interpolation. This will make the graph easier to read for the purpose of spotting missing frames.

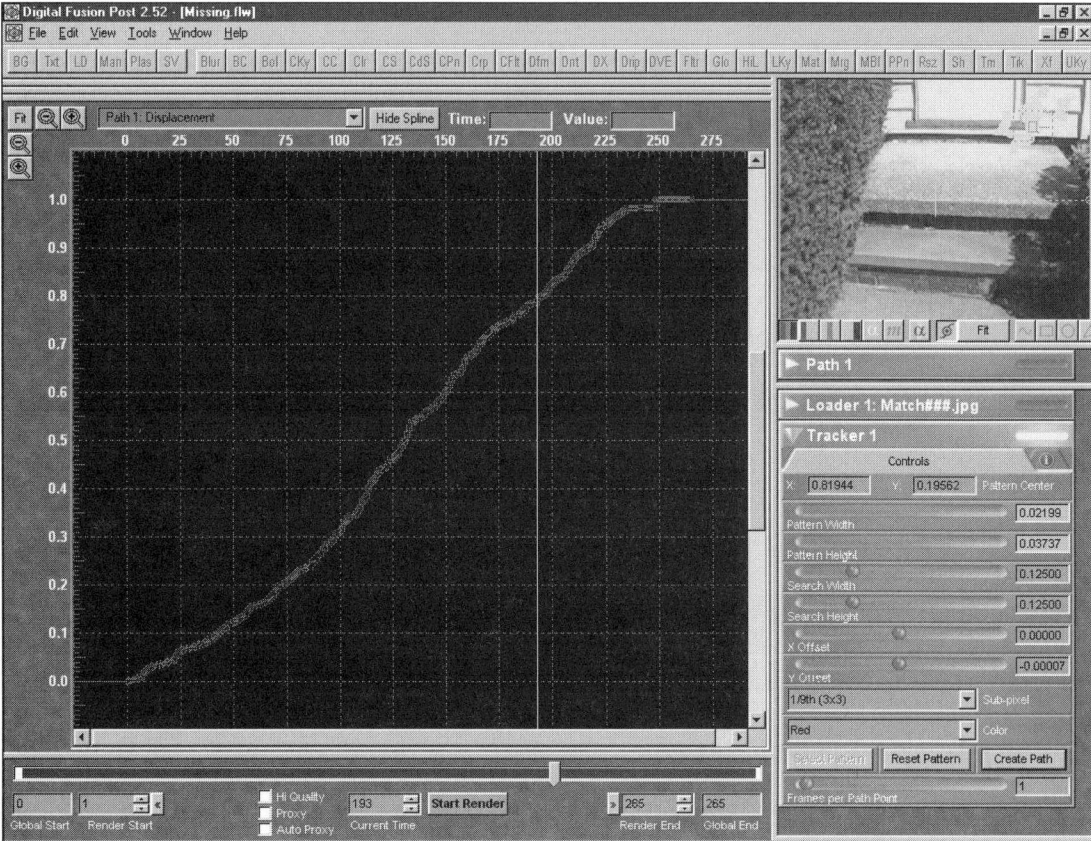

Figure 13.1

The Spline Editor showing tracker path displacement. This spline will show missing frames by sudden jumps in a relatively smooth spline.

5. Set the Current Time to frame 1, and zoom in the Spline Editor until you can easily see the slope of the spline between points.

6. Search for the first dropped frame. You are looking for a sudden doubling of the slope between two frames, like that shown in Figure 13.2. Some small variation between frames is to be expected from an unsteady camera, but a single sudden jump out of proportion to the surrounding frames is a reliable indicator of a missing frame. The larger the jump, the less likely it is that the camera could move so far in 1/30th of a second and then continue along the original relatively smooth curve. If a jump is exceptionally large, it may indicate that more than one frame was dropped.

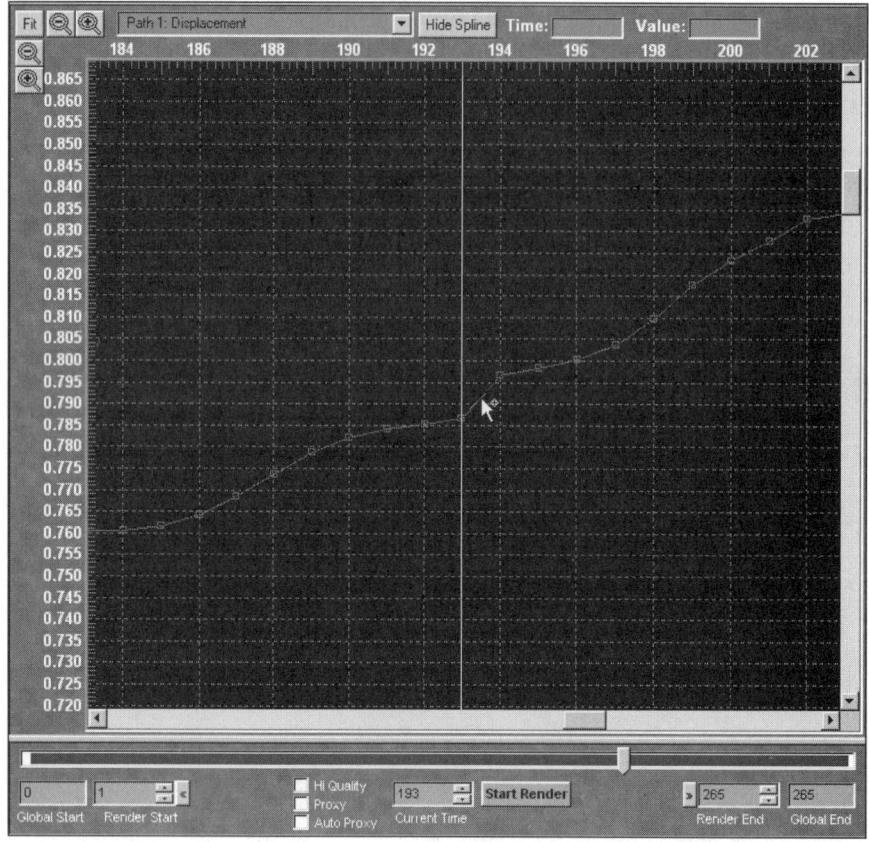

Figure 13.2

The Spline Editor showing a missing frame by a sudden jump between frames 193 and 194.

7. After you have found the first dropped frame, make a note of the adjoining frame numbers. Scroll through the rest of the spline, looking for other dropped frames. Make a list of the adjoining frames for all the dropped frames. My list indicates a single frame dropped after frames 101, 110, 128, 193, and 219. Your results may vary, but the rest of this project will be based on these frames. If you choose to replace your own list of missing frames, you will have to make the appropriate alterations.

When your dropped frame list is complete, the next step is to renumber all the existing frames to leave space for the replacement frames.

8. Copy all the frames preceding the first missing one (0 through 101) to the Complete folder.

9. Replace the Tracker with a Saver. Set the Saver to the Complete folder, with identical parameters to the footage in the Loader. The goal is simply to copy and renumber the existing frames.

10. In the Loader, increase Extend First Frame by 1.

11. Set Render Start to two frames higher than the last frame in the Complete folder (103 for this first example). This will offset the footage to leave a one-frame gap for the missing frame. Set Render End to the next frame number in the list, plus the Extend First Frame number (110+1 for this first example). This will render only the frames between the missing frames, with an offset to renumber the rendered frames appropriately.

12. Click on Start Render. Because this is a simple copy operation, the rendering should go almost as quickly as the Loader and Saver can run.

13. When the rendering is done, check the contents of the Complete directory. It should contain all the frames through the last Render End, with a gap for each missing frame.

14. Repeat steps 10 through 13 for the remaining missing frames.

After you are finished, the Complete folder should contain 266 image files numbered from 0 to 270, with gaps for the dropped frames at 102, 112, 131, 197, and 224. The next step is to create the missing frames.

15. Open a new flow. Add a Loader. Load the footage from the Complete folder.

16. Add a Time Speed tool (from Tools|Miscellaneous), and connect it to the output of the Loader.

17. Add a Saver, and connect it to the output of the Time Speed tool. Set the Saver to the same settings as the Loader, so it renders images into the Complete folder.

18. In the Time Speed controls, check the Interpolate Between Frames box. Set Sample Spread to 0.5. These settings make the Time Speed tool interpolate a new image for the current frame, composed of 50 percent each from the adjoining frames. Even though the current frame is missing, it will have no effect.

19. Set Start Render, Current Time, and Render End to the first missing frame. Click on Start Render. The Time Speed tool will render a new frame like that shown in Figure 13.3.

20. Repeat the preceding step for the remaining missing frames.

21. When you are finished, the Complete folder should contain 271 images numbered from 0 through 270, with no gaps. To test your replacement images, make a preview from the Loader and play it back.

You should find it difficult to identify the new frames just by watching the playback. The interpolated replacement images should blend into the existing footage nearly seamlessly. The Time Speed interpolation is a very quick and easy way to replace frames, but sometimes this double-exposure effect is not the result you need. You can use other techniques to create replacement frames or to fine-tune a Time Speed interpolation. Review the techniques you learned in Chapters 9 and 10, and look for ways to apply them to creating replacement frames. Some of the timing techniques in Chapter 15 can also be applied to create replacement frames, or to smooth out the Time Speed interpolation.

Figure 13.3
The Time Speed tool, configured to create the missing frame by interpolating the "next-door" neighboring frames.

The same process that replaced missing frames in the preceding project can be applied to replacing badly damaged frames. Sometimes it is a more effective use of your time and other resources simply to toss out a badly mangled frame, then to replace it with a new one created by a combination of missing-frame interpolation and rig removal, hand-painting, or other image repair techniques.

One disadvantage to replacement frames is that most techniques involve blurring or double-exposure, which makes reference patterns for tracking much more difficult to use. If you have to replace a frame in footage that will be tracked or stabilized, you should plan on manually adjusting the tracker keyframes for each replacement frame.

Replacing Missing Or Damaged Frames (After Effects)

The goal of this After Effects-based version of Project 13.1 is to replace frames that were dropped in a video digitizing process. The general approach is to identify the missing frames, to renumber the image sequence to leave gaps for the missing frames, then to comp new frames into the gaps in the image sequence.

After Effects doesn't give direct visual access to the tracker's output, so you can't use a spline view to help pinpoint missing frames. Instead, you have to eyeball it.

1. Create a new folder named "Complete" for the corrected footage.

2. Open a new project. Import the footage to be repaired. For this project, I'll use the Match footage used previously in Chapters 11 and 12. It's easier to work with frames rather than timecode, so choose File|Preferences|Time and click on the Frames radio button. Close the Preferences window. Add the footage to a new layer in the Time Layout window.

3. Step through the raw footage one frame at a time, looking for the sudden jump that indicates the first dropped frame. Some small variation between frames is to be expected from an unsteady camera, but a single sudden jump out of proportion to the surrounding frames is a reliable indicator of a missing frame. The larger the jump, the less likely it is that the camera could move so far in 1/30th of a second and then continue along the original relatively smooth motion. If a jump is exceptionally large, it may indicate that more than one frame was dropped.

4. After you find the first dropped frame, make a note of the adjoining frame numbers. Scroll through the rest of the footage, looking for other dropped frames. Make a list of the adjoining frames for all the dropped frames.

My list indicates a single frame dropped after frames 101, 110, 128, 193, and 219. Your results may vary, but the rest of this project is based on these frames. If you choose to replace your own list of missing frames, you have to make the appropriate alterations. When your dropped frame list is complete, the next step is to renumber all the existing frames to leave space for the replacement frames.

5. Copy all the frames preceding the first missing one (0 through 101) to the Complete folder.

6. In the Time Layout window, select the Match layer. Choose Effect|Time|Echo to add an Echo effect to the Match layer.

7. In the Effect Controls window, set Number Of Echoes to 1, Starting Intensity to 1.00, and Decay to 0.50. Choose Minimum from the Echo Operator menu. This will blend half of the preceding image with the current image, creating a simulation of a double-exposure as shown in Figure 13.4.

This double-exposure might be acceptable for a new frame, but you can get even better results by adding a motion blur to the image. Doing so smoothes the blended images, creating an effect closer to that produced by leaving the camera shutter open during rapid movement.

8. With the Match layer still selected, choose Effect|Blur|Motion Blur to add a Motion Blur effect to the Match layer.

9. In the Effect Controls window, turn off Motion Blur. You need to see the image clearly to make the Direction setting. Look closely at the echoed images in the Composition window. You should be able to see two distinct copies of each high-contrast detail, such as the corners

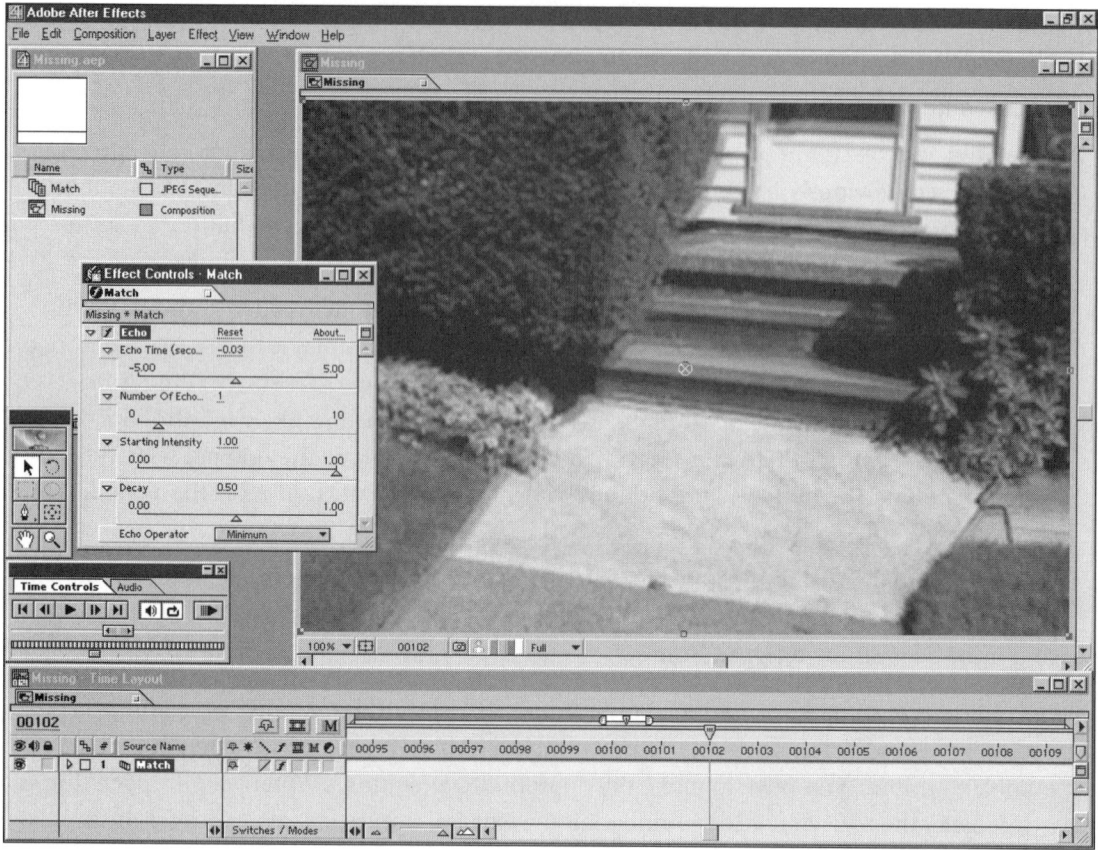

Figure 13.4

The Echo effect blends the preceding frame with the current frame to create a double-exposure effect.

of the threshold. Note the angle between these two copies, and set the Direction of the Motion Blur effect to match. For frame 102, I set this angle to 150 degrees.

10. Turn on Motion Blur. Adjust Blur Length to blur the echoed images, but not so much that the entire image is too fuzzy to see details. For frame 102, I found that a setting of 5.0 worked well. Your results should look like Figure 13.5.

11. When you are satisfied with the results of your effects settings, choose Composition|Save Frame As|File, and render the current frame to the Complete folder as a JPEG image with the same parameters as the original footage. In the Output Module Settings window, make sure that you change Format to JPEG, and Starting # to the desired frame number, in this case 102. Your results should be a new file added to the end of the image sequence in the Complete folder.

12. Turn off both Motion Blur and Echo effects. In the Time Layout window, drag the footage layer to the right one frame. This creates the one-frame offset needed to leave room for the new frame you just created.

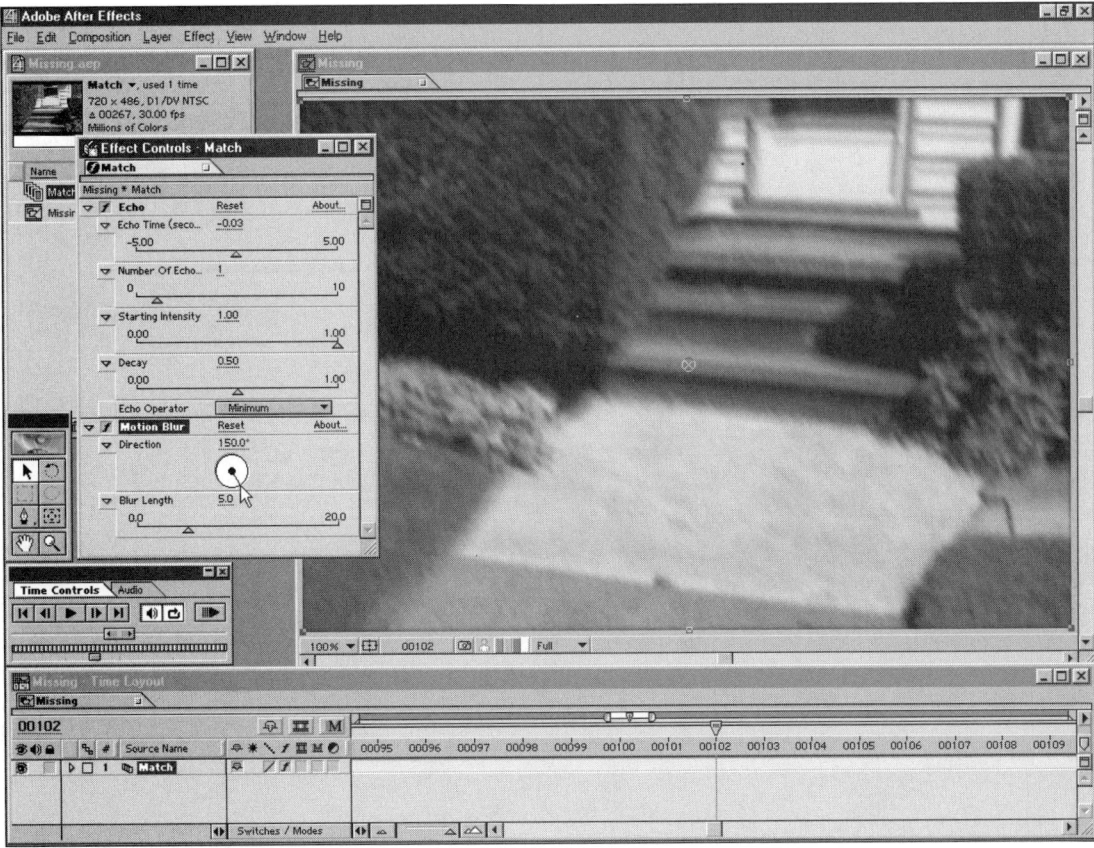

Figure 13.5
The Motion Blur effect added to the Echo effect more closely simulates the results of a fast camera move with an open shutter.

13. In the Time Layout window, limit the working area to the range from one frame *after* the current missing frame, to one frame *before* the next missing frame, taking into account the offset you added in step 6. If your first missing frame is after 101 and your second missing frame is after 110, your working area should be frames 103 through 111.

14. Send the comp to the Render Queue. Set the Render Options to the Complete folder, with identical parameters to the original footage. The goal is simply to copy and renumber the existing frames. Under Render Settings, the Time Span should be set to Work Area. To keep the numbering consistent, you need to set the Start Frame in the Output Module to the same number as Start in Render Settings. The default Start Frame is 0, which would cause the rendering to overwrite the files already in the Complete folder. The Output To string should be set to duplicate the file-name structure of the original footage—in this case, "Match[###].jpg" to create file names Match103.jpg, Match104.jpg, and so on. Your screen should look like Figure 13.6.

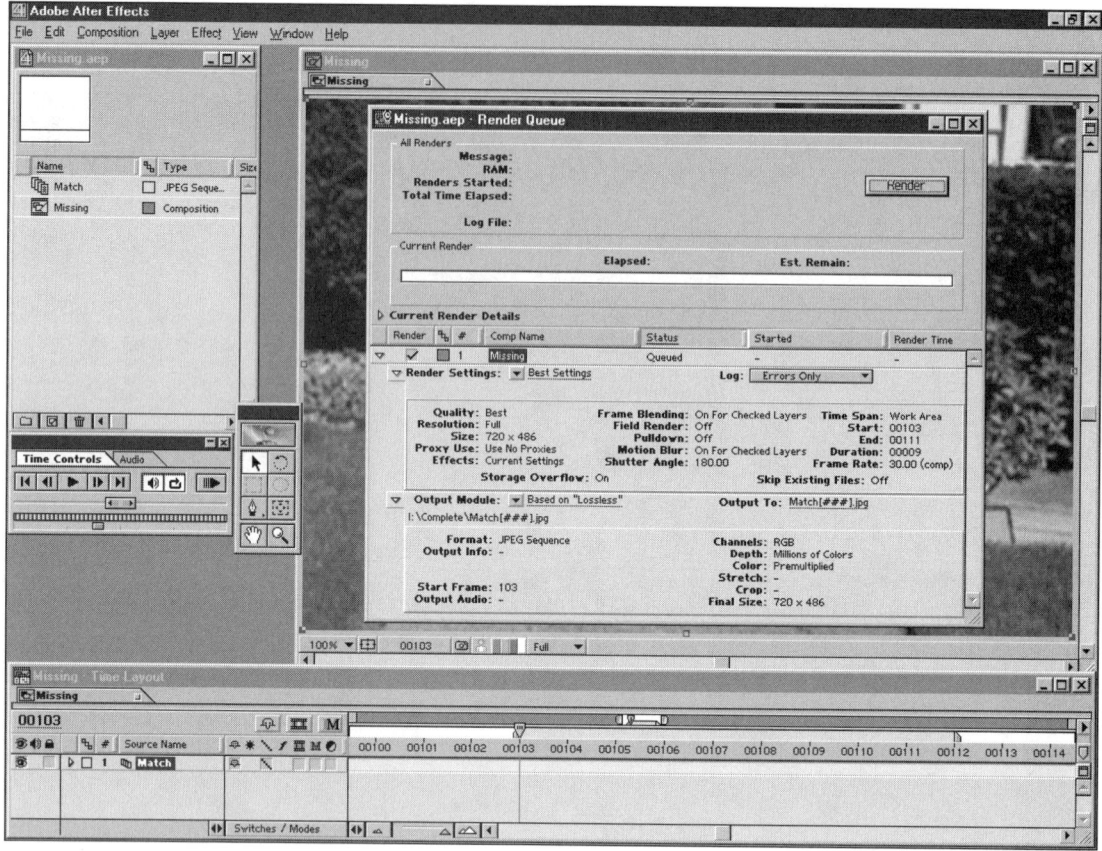

Figure 13.6
The Time Layout and Render Queue windows are set to renumber existing frames to create a space for the first missing frame.

15. Render the comp. Your results should be copies of the frames within the working area, re-numbered to frames 103 through 111.

16. Turn on Echo and Motion Blur again, and repeat steps 9 through 15 for the remaining missing frames. When you are finished, the Complete folder should contain 271 images numbered from 0 to 270, with new images for the dropped frames at 102, 112, 131, 197, and 224.

The footage in the Complete folder will play back with smoother motion now that the missing frames have been replaced. However, the echo and motion blur used to create the new frames will make it harder to perform tracking operations on this footage. If you have to track this footage, you should be prepared to hand-keyframe the tracker over the new frames.

Replacing Missing Or Damaged Frames (Aura)
The goal of this Aura-based version of Project 13.1 is to replace frames that were dropped in a video digitizing process. The general approach is to identify the missing frames, to renumber the

image sequence to leave gaps for the missing frames, then to comp new frames into the gaps in the image sequence. Aura doesn't have a tracker, so you can't use a spline view to help pinpoint missing frames. Instead, you have to eyeball it.

1. Follow the first four steps of After Effects Project 13.1 (never mind the timecode/frame conversion in step 2).

You should end up with a list of the adjoining frames for all the dropped frames. My list indicates a single frame dropped after frames 101, 110, 128, 193, and 219. Your results may vary, but the rest of this project is based on these frames. If you choose to replace your own list of missing frames, you need to make the appropriate alterations. When your dropped frame list is complete, the next step is to renumber all the existing frames to leave space for the replacement frames.

2. Select the frame just before the first missing frame (101). Press i to insert a frame. This duplicates the selected frame and inserts the duplicate after the selected frame, bumping all the following frames down to make room.

3. Select the frame just before the second missing frame, taking into account the offset you just added (111). Press i again. Repeat for frames 130, 196, and 223. You should end up with a sequence of 270 frames.

4. Render the comp as a TGA image sequence into your temp directory, with the root name TEMP###.TGA. This has the effect of renumbering the entire sequence as if the missing frames had never been dropped. However, the new frames are simply duplicates of the preceding frames; the next step is to make the new frames a better approximation of the missing frames.

5. Clear the old comp and open a new one. Import the single image TEMP102.TGA. Import the single image TEMP103.TGA. You will fade between these two frames to create a more accurate substitute for frame 102.

6. Change both layers to Anim layers, and stretch both layers out to cover frames 0 through 2. This gives you frame 1 in the middle for the 50/50 value of the fade to create the image you want.

7. Select all frames in the first layer. Choose Filters|Transitions|Fade|Fade. In the Fade window, set From to 0% and To to 100%. Click on Apply Fade. Your screen should look like Figure 13.7.

8. The fade from frame 0 to frame 2 creates a 50/50 mix of the two layers in frame 1. Select frame 1, and choose File|Export|Image and export the image as TEMP102.TGA. An alert dialog asks if you want to replace the existing TEMP102.TGA; answer Yes.

9. Repeat steps 5 through 8 for the remaining frame pairs: 112/113, 131/132, 197/198, and 224/225.

After you have created 50/50 fade replacements for all the missing frames, you can use the TEMP###.TGA image sequence as substitute footage for any other project in this book that calls for the Match footage. With the replacement frames in place, this footage may reduce or eliminate problems caused by the missing frames.

Figure 13.7

In this Aura comp, layers TEMP102 and TEMP103 are faded together in frame 1 to create the image in the large window. This isn't a perfect replacement for the dropped frame, but it's close enough for most purposes.

Replacing Missing Or Damaged Frames (effect*)

The goal of this effect*-based version of Project 13.1 is to replace frames that were dropped in a video digitizing process. The general approach is to identify the missing frames, to renumber the image sequence to leave gaps for the missing frames, then to comp new frames into the gaps in the image sequence.

1. Follow the first five steps of After Effects Project 13.1. For step 2, choose File|Preferences|General, and then in the Display Time As list, select Frames (from 0).

You should now have a list of the adjoining frames for all the dropped frames. My list indicates a single frame dropped after frames 101, 110, 128, 193, and 219. Your results may vary, but the rest of this project is based on these frames. If you choose to replace your own list of missing frames, you have to make the appropriate alterations. After your dropped frame list is complete, the next step is to renumber all the existing frames to leave space for the replacement frames.

2. Drag the Match layer to the right one frame. This is the offset that will leave room for replacement frame 102.

3. Choose File|Render or press Ctrl+R. In the Render Animation window, set Start to 103 and End to 111. Click on the Output Options button to open the Output Settings window. In the Output Settings window, set Format to JPEG Sequence, Frame Start # to 103, and Frame Increment to 1. Your screen should look like Figure 13.8.

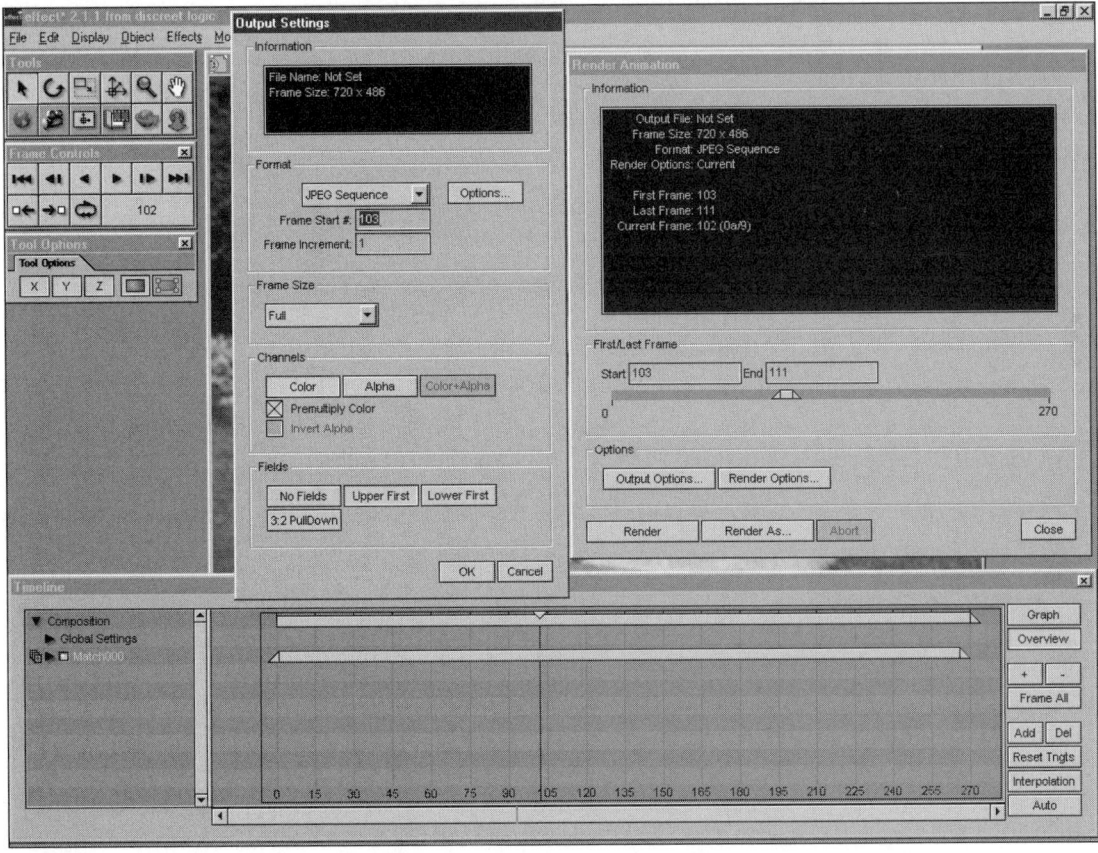

Figure 13.8
The Render Animation and Output Settings are configured to renumber frames 103 through 111.

4. Render the frame range to the Complete directory. This directory should now contain files Match000.jpg through Match111.jpg, with only Match102.jpg missing from the sequence.

5. Repeat steps 2 through 4 for image ranges 113–130, 132–196, 198–223, and 225–270. You should end up with the Complete directory containing an image sequence Match000.jpg through Match270.jpg, missing only frames 102, 112, 131, 197, and 224.

6. Clear the comp and open a new one.

7. Import the single frames Match101.jpg and Match103.jpg, bracketing the first missing frame, into separate layers.

8. Add a Blend effect to the first layer, and set it to 50 percent crossfade with the other layer. Your screen should look like Figure 13.9.

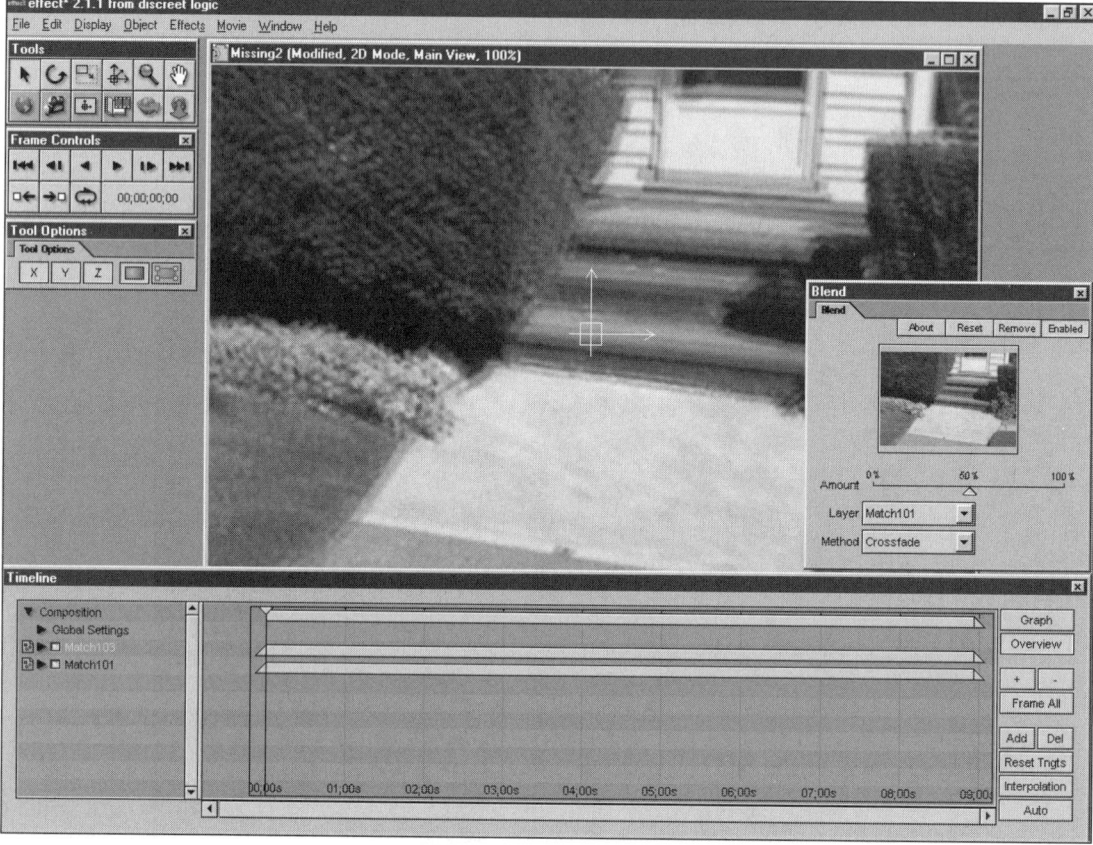

Figure 13.9
Frames 101 and 103 are blended using a 50/50 crossfade to create a replacement for the missing frame 102.

9. Render a single frame from the comp to the Complete folder as file Match102.jpg.

10. Repeat steps 7 through 9 for image pairs 111/113, 130/132, 196/198, and 113/225.

You should end up with the Complete directory that contains an image sequence Match000.jpg through Match270.jpg, and no missing frames. You can use this image sequence as substitute footage for any other project in this book that calls for the Match footage. With the replacement frames in place, this footage may reduce or eliminate problems caused by the missing frames.

Tweaking Colors

Poor lighting, errors in running the camera or telecine, or mistakes in film developing or video digitizing can present you with footage with bad color balance. In top-end studios, a colorist will control the telecine or film scanning and will do most of the color correction. In a smaller studio or independent production, you may have responsibility for color correction on the footage for your comps. Even if someone else is technically responsible for color correction, you should know how to do it in a pinch. You should also know how to discuss color correction intelligently with a colorist so you can clearly communicate your intent on a comp. There are few things more annoying to a colorist than mistakenly removing a color effect because the digital compositor didn't say, "That's not a color problem; that's supposed to be there." Taking some art classes in color theory is a good starting point; you should follow that up with technical reading on the differences between film and video color.

Before you begin adjusting the color balance in comped footage, you need to know what colors you are actually seeing. Colors appear brighter when surrounded by darker colors, and they appear darker when surrounded by lighter colors. Colors appear more saturated when surrounded by their complementary colors. When in doubt, use a sampling tool such as Photoshop's eyedropper to give you the exact color values for comparison.

The perception of color, brightness, and contrast is also strongly influenced by the viewing environment. A brightly lit environment can fool your eye into seeing more contrast in an image, while a darker environment creates the illusion of less contrast. For these reasons, it's important to control the visual aspects of your compositing environment. One approach is to remove all color from the surrounding environment, even to the point of setting your desktop colors to neutral grays. You should certainly control the intensity and color of your work lighting. Cheap fluorescent lighting, low-wattage incandescent bulbs, and other strongly colored light sources can skew your perception of color. If possible, use daylight-corrected task lighting in your workspace, and keep all extraneous light away from your monitors. Some high-end monitors have a hood to shade the monitor from overhead lights, but you can easily make one from cardboard or foamcore and paint it neutral gray.

The physical medium has a major effect on your perception of color. The difference between the phosphorescent colors of a monitor and the colors of projected light bouncing off a theater screen make color balancing for film particularly difficult. One tool you may consider is a *calibrated monitor*, one that includes a feedback sensor and special stabilizing circuitry to keep the displayed colors as precise as possible. The additional expense may be a good investment if color correction is important to your work. For video work, you should always display color corrections on a broadcast-quality monitor. For film work, you should output *wedges*—sequences of images with progressive changes in color, brightness, and contrast settings. When these wedges are output to film and developed, you will be able to choose the settings that most closely match the final results you want. At a minimum, you should print a wedge for each new film stock with which you work. To be absolutely safe, print a wedge for each lighting and lens setup if you can afford the time and expense. Each change in position, color, and number of lights on the set, and any change in the camera's lens settings will affect the color, contrast, and brightness of the footage.

Eyeballing NTSC Color On A Computer Monitor

Although a better option is to display your output on a broadcast monitor, it is possible to display a comp on your computer screen in a way that roughly simulates a broadcast image. Using Digital Fusion, you can add a branch off any comp just before the final Saver tool, run that branch through color correction, and send the results to the Large display to show an approximation of the effects of broadcasting the original comp. Every computer monitor is a little different, so these numbers are just a starting point. You will need to experiment on your own to find the best match for your own monitor. Even if you get a pretty good match, be wary of telling a client that this is what the broadcast will look like. You are better off using a weasel word or two, like "approximate" or "close," rather than "exact."

The first tool after the branch is a Color Gain. Red and green gain should start at 0.9775, blue at 1.0500. Alpha channel gain and gamma should both be unchanged at 1.0. Red, green, and blue gamma should start at 1.225. Red and blue saturation should start at 1.4, and green saturation at 1.5.

The second tool, after Color Gain, is Brightness/Contrast. This is the tool you send to the Large display. Brightness should start at –0.0125, and Contrast at 0.13. The threshold range should be full, from 0.0 to 1.0. The gain, gamma, and saturation should remain at the default value of 1.0. Your results should look something like Figure 13.10. Save this flow and keep it handy; it's one of those utility flows you will find yourself using often.

Your Best Tool: Eyeball v.1.0

After you calibrate your workstation, your most important remaining guides to adjusting color are your own eyes and trained judgment. Digital compositors, like any other artists, start out with untrained eyes. With practice and experience, you learn to make accurate color evaluations. Some people are fortunate to inherit a better-than-average sensitivity to color, akin to perfect pitch among musicians, but almost anyone can learn to have "a good eye" for color. A combination of experience, common sense, and normal color perception will enable you to adjust for consistently good color.

When adjusting color, look for elements that should have neutral tones in the original footage. *Neutral* means having a balanced triplet, where the red, green, and blue values are as nearly equal as possible. Most naturally neutral materials are shades of gray, because pure white and pure black are rare in nature and even more rare in film and video. Materials to look for include sidewalks, cinder block, brick mortar, and almost anything made out of undyed concrete. If your notes or reference photos from the set indicate that a surface is white or gray, it is safe to use that surface as a neutral reference. If you shot a clean plate with neutral-colored reference objects or a

Figure 13.10
A nonsaving branch with Color Gain and Brightness/Contrast tools added to mimic an NTSC broadcast monitor's color balance. Note that the Large display shows the simulated color balance and the Small display shows the Saver's actual output.

gray card, as recommended in Chapter 6, you can measure the colors of those objects for an accurate comparison to their colors in the footage. Neutral surfaces provide good indicators when something is wrong with the color balance. For example, a neutral concrete sidewalk bordered by green grass, as shown in Figure 13.11 (although it probably will not be evident from this grayscale image), should not be tinged with red, green, or blue. Any excess of a color in a neutral surface immediately tells you which channel you need to reduce to achieve a better balance.

Look out for *memory colors*, colors that are so well-known that most people can immediately detect any difference from the standard. This is especially important if you are doing commercial work; corporations like Coca-Cola spend fortunes establishing the exact color of their products and packaging, and they can be fanatical about color balance. The precise caramel shade of Coca-Cola, and the red of the Coke trademark, are memory colors. So are "John Deere green," "McDonald's yellow," and "IBM blue." Any variation in a memory color should trigger mental alarms that the footage's color balance is off.

Figure 13.11
A single frame from the Match footage on the first CD-ROM, showing neutral surfaces in the concrete sidewalk, stair treads, and porch, and in the white vinyl siding and gray-painted threshold, in contrast to the deep greens of grass and shrubbery.

As a visual artist, and in working with other visual artists, you may feel pressure to make colors more intense, to get them to "pop" off the screen. This problem is especially evident in artists from a print background where the working color range is more inclusive. However, overly saturated colors are more difficult to match in motion picture distribution prints, and they suffer all the problems mentioned earlier in relation to NTSC- or PAL-legal color limits for video. Remember that colors do not need to be excessively vivid for an image to affect the audience; the overall composition, framing, and a proper color balance will do the job.

Human facial skin tones are some of the most challenging and crucial colors you will have to balance. The natural human response to almost any image is to look at any human faces first. In film or video, a shot may be so brief that the audience never has time to examine anything but the faces. If you tweaked the color to perfection on the background, but left a color imbalance in the skin tones, your good work would go unnoticed and your mistakes would be obvious. In addition to being your top priority, skin tones are very fussy. People learn, consciously or subliminally, to recognize very small changes in skin tones as indicators of mood and health. A yellow cast may mean liver disease; blue tones indicate cold or cardiovascular problems; and red can mark anger, embarrassment, overheating, or intoxication. If your skin-tone color balance is off, your audience will identify the skin tones as unhealthy and will be uneasy, whether they realize it or not. Although this can be effective in a horror film, you should leave the issue of altering skin tones up to the cinematographer and makeup artist, and balance the footage for precisely natural skin tones.

Whenever you make significant changes to the color balance, you should append a standard reference image like Figure 13.12 or 13.13 at the beginning of the output footage. This enables the person who is performing color timing on the whole production to see what your adjustments

Figure 13.12
A color reference image to be appended to the beginning of composited film footage.

Figure 13.13
A standard color bar reference image to be appended to the beginning of composited NTSC video footage. Both this image and Figure 13.12 are on the second CD-ROM, in the Refs folder.

are supposed to look like. This is especially important for effects sequences that drastically change the color balance from the original footage; the natural tendency of the colorist is to reverse the changes, making the effects footage match the original. These misunderstandings can be frustrating, time-consuming, and expensive for everyone, so make the intent of your changes clear by including that reference image.

Normalized Values

As explained in Chapter 4, 8 bits per channel gives a range of values from 0 to 255, but 10 bits per channel gives a range of 0 to 1,023. The same color represented in two different bit depths will have two different *triplets* (a set of three numbers, one for each color channel). If you were setting up a comp with mathematical operations, you would have to formulate a different operation for each bit depth to get the same results. However, a single comp may include elements from both 8-bit and 10-bit sources, so it is necessary to have some means of managing multiple bit depths with the same operations. The most common way to do this is to *normalize* all pixel values to floating-point (noninteger) numbers in the range of 0 to 1. This means that, in any bit depth, an RGB triplet of 0.0 for each color channel is black, 1.0 is white, and 0.5 is a mid-level gray.

Normalized values also make many mathematical operations easier. For example, multiplying any number by 1 produces the original number; multiplying any number by 0 produces 0. As long as the variable is also in the range of 0 to 1, normalized values automatically limit the results of a multiply operation to the image's existing range of black to white.

Gamma

The gamma operation is one of the most useful compositing operations for color correction. In general, it is used to brighten or darken an image by changing the middle-range values without changing the highest and lowest values. The actual function raises the input to the power of the reciprocal of the gamma variable. That is, for a gamma of 1.7, the output would equal the input raised to the 1/1.7, or 0.588235, power, or 0.66. In equation form:

$O = I^{1/\Gamma}$

One reason the gamma operation is so popular is that it doesn't alter the white or black limits of the image even when the gamma is over 1 or below 0. If you substitute 1.0 or 0.0 for the input, you will find that any gamma value will still produce 1.0 or 0.0, respectively, for the outputs. With the gamma operation, blacks never wash out and bright colors don't get clipped to pure white. With the gamma's safety, you can brighten or darken the image to extreme levels without worrying about losing details at either end of the color space. Images processed with a gamma operation also tend to look more natural, because the falloff of the effect at each end of the color space mimics the response curves of normal vision. Figure 13.14 shows a sample image modified with a gamma of 1.7.

Figure 13.14
The reference image in Figure 13.12 modified with a gamma of 1.7. Note that the darkest and lightest areas have not been crushed or clipped; only the mid-levels have been boosted.

Keep It Legal

Different methods of reproducing images have different capabilities for displaying color. Film has a very deep color space, video color space is much shallower, and computer screens fall somewhere in between. When you are working in one color space, but will be sending the final output to another color space, you need to be aware of these limits and how the conversion will affect the final image quality.

One of the most common color space problems is exporting film or CGI elements to NTSC or PAL video. Broadcast video color space is limited partly by the nature of the radio frequency or *RF* television signal. At worst, a color or luma signal that is too intense can interfere with the sync pulse and thereby cause the receiving televisions to temporarily lose their horizontal sync. Short of that, a saturated color will cause *bleed* at its edges. An NTSC or PAL television signal is analog waveform, not a digital string of numbers; it cannot change value as abruptly as a computer monitor can. A sharp transition from one extreme color value to another will take a little longer, which shows up on an analog TV screen as a thin but noticeable bleed or transitional color line.

NTSC-legal colors have luma levels between 7.5 and 100 *IRE*, a measure of the brightness of the image, with chroma saturation of only 75 percent of the RGB color space. RGB 8-bit colors range from 0 to 255 per channel. NTSC-legal colors should be limited to a maximum of 235 in each channel to prevent oversaturation and bleed. This is especially important for CGI-rendered elements and text generated by the computer. Elements that have been digitized from video sources usually have legal color limits built in; illegal colors in digitized video are usually artifacts from the digitizing process and may be indicators of more serious problems.

 # Limit A CGI Element To NTSC-Legal Colors

PROJECT 13.2

The goal of this project is to make a CGI-rendered element legal for NTSC broadcast. In Digital Fusion, the legal color options are available in the Saver tool.

1. Open a new flow. Add a Loader, and load the Walker RGBA precomp you rendered from the Walker and WalkerM footage on the first CD-ROM. This footage was originally rendered in LightWave to the full RGB color space. The black levels are below 7.5 IRE, and the blue of the walker's windshield is saturated enough to peak above the legal limit of 235.

2. Add a Saver, and connect it to the Loader.

3. In the Legal tab of the Saver controls, choose NTSC from the Video Type pull-down menu, choose Adjust To Legal from the Action pull-down menu, and choose 100% Saturation 75% Amplitude from the Adjust Based On pull-down menu, as shown in Figure 13.15.

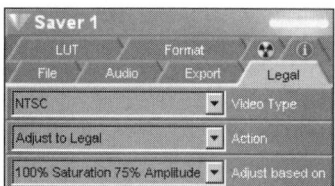

Figure 13.15
Saver controls set to limit colors to NTSC-legal levels.

If you rendered the footage from this Saver, the 0 0 0 black pixels would be converted to 19, 19, 19, and other colors exceeding the legal values would be similarly adjusted. The difference is barely perceptible to an untrained eye, but it makes all the difference for a clean broadcast signal. If you want to see which areas of the image are adjusted, choose Indicate As White from the Action pull-down menu. In a lighter-colored image, you might choose Indicate As Black for better contrast. Previewing the effects of the Legalize operation can warn you in advance of trouble areas. When you're done, return the Action setting to Adjust To Legal.

4. Save the flow as NTSC.flw. You'll need it for the next project.

Limit A Comp To NTSC-Legal Colors (After Effects)

Keeping an After Effects composition within legal color limits is very easy, as this After Effects-based version of Project 13.2 shows. After you have the rest of a composition completed to your satisfaction, select the front layer and choose the Effect|Video|Broadcast Colors. The Broadcast Colors effect gives you several options to limit the color saturation and luminance to keep your rendered output within legal limits. The After Effects User Guide has more information on the Broadcast Colors effect.

Aura And NTSC-Legal Colors

Aura 1.0 doesn't have filters to limit color output to NTSC-legal levels. If you need this feature, you need to use other software.

Limit A Comp To NTSC-Legal Colors (Chalice)

Limiting a Chalice grail to NTSC-legal color limits is simply a matter of adding the Video Safe Node to the completed grail. For more details, see the Chalice 1.6 manual, pages 13.15 and 13.16.

Commotion And NTSC-Legal Colors

Commotion 2.1 doesn't have filters to limit color output to NTSC-legal levels. If you need this feature, you need to use other software or plug-ins.

Limit A Comp To NTSC-Legal Colors (effect*)

Keeping an effect* composition within legal color limits is easy if you don't expect much, as this effect*-based version of Project 13.2 shows. When you have the rest of a composition completed to your satisfaction, select the top layer and choose Effects|Color Correction|NTSC Colors. This effect is an all-or-nothing color filter with no options to control how it changes your images, but it does keep your color legal.

Limit A Comp To NTSC-Legal Colors (Shake)

Limiting the output of a Shake script to NTSC-legal levels is simply a matter of adding the VideoSafe node to the completed script, as this Shake-based version of Project 13.2 shows. This node, located in the Color tab, clips off illegal values for PAL or NTSC video. You can also set the node for either luminance or saturation. For details, see the manual in the Shake directory of the second CD-ROM.

Super Black

Super black, also called *zero black*, means a luma value of 0 IRE rather than the 7.5 IRE of a legal NTSC signal. Super black is used by some on-air switchers to key text or graphics over live video. For broadcast use, it is sometimes necessary to provide both super black and NTSC-legal chroma and luma levels in the same footage.

PROJECT 13.3 Adding Super Black To Legal Colors

The goal of this project is to restore super black to the appropriate areas of the Walker footage that the preceding project converted to NTSC-legal levels. The super black is needed because an on-air switcher cannot use the walker's alpha channel. Instead, the black areas of the matte will be converted to super black, and the remaining areas of the matte will remain limited to NTSC-legal colors.

1. Reload the NTSC.flw flow you saved from the preceding project.

2. Set Saver 1 to save rendered files to your system's TEMP directory. The root file name isn't important, because the rendered files will be discarded later. This Saver is used only to apply the Legal function to the loaded footage. Make sure that the Save Alpha box is checked in the Format tab; the merge won't work without the alpha channel.

3. Add a Merge tool. Connect the output of Saver 1 to the foreground input of the Merge tool.

You may not have used it this way before, but the Saver tool has an output just like other Digital Fusion tools. This enables you to place a Saver into the middle of a flow to save separate alpha channels and other elements in addition to the usual end-of-flow images.

4. Add a Background tool. Set it to Solid Color, and set the color and alpha channels to 0, super black. Connect the output of the Background tool to the Merge tool's background input.

5. Add another Saver, and connect it to the output of the Merge tool. Set Saver 2 to save rendered files to the directory and root file name you prefer. Your flow should look like Figure 13.16.

Figure 13.16
A flow designed to restore super black to NTSC-legalized footage.

6. Render a few frames as a test.

7. Load the rendered images in Photoshop or some other paint program that enables you to sample colors to view their RGB values. Sample the darkest areas of the background, the shadow edges, and the walker's blue windshield.

You should find NTSC-legal values everywhere but the walker and its two shadows. If you like, load the first Saver's output from your TEMP directory and compare it. You should find an NTSC-legal black value of 19, 19, 19 throughout the background and shadow areas of the image. This would be impossible for the on-air switcher to use in keying the walker over live footage without losing all of both shadows and much of the darker areas of the walker.

Color Tools

There are various color controls and tools in any digital compositing software, and most of their functions are adequately explained in the software's reference manuals. The Windows-standard color picker, shown in Figure 13.17, uses RGB and HSL color spaces with 8-bit, 0 to 255 values. Digital Fusion's color sliders, common to most of the color tools, are based on the 0.0 to 1.0 normalized values. This can cause some confusion, and the conversion from 8-bit to normalized values may introduce rounding errors. In general, you need not worry about the difference between a 128 gray and a 0.50196 gray; the difference is not visible to the naked eye, and no compositing operation is going to go haywire on a discrepancy that small.

When you are looking for a neutral color, memory color, or reference plate color, you may find it helpful to sample or to pick a color from the footage for comparison. This enables you to compare color values by the numbers and is especially useful while you are training your eyes. An experienced colorist may be able to eyeball the difference between a 0.502 gray and a 0.500 gray; at least at the beginning of your career, however, you will probably need to rely on the color tools.

Sampling Colors

One easy way to put a color picker into a flow is to add a Background tool that is not connected to anything else. With the image to be corrected in the Large display, and the Background in the Small display, you can use the Background tool's Pick function to select colors from the Large

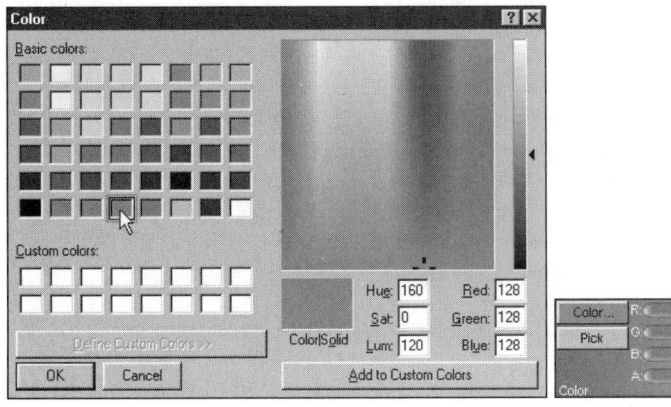
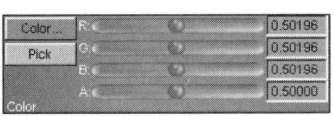

Figure 13.17
A Windows-standard color picker and Digital Fusion's RGBA color sliders.

display. Simply left-click on the Pick button, and the cursor will change to an eyedropper shape. Drag the eyedropper cursor over the Large display, and the color sliders in the Background tool and the background color in the Small display will interactively change to the color values of the pixel under the mouth of the eyedropper. If you need to examine a single color, set the Background Mode to Solid Color. If you need to compare two colors, you can set the Background Mode to horizontal, and the Small display will show a gradient between one sampled color and another, as shown in Figure 13.18. You should keep the Small display scaled to 100% to avoid sampling errors; you can scrub the horizontal slider to move between the two color extremes. This physical scanning can also help you discern the difference between the colors, because it is easier for the human eye to perceive color changes in motion than in a static display.

Color Space Conversion

Computers generally work in RGB color space, but video and film are created and broadcast in other color spaces. For some color corrections and effects, it is much easier and more accurate

Figure 13.18

A Background tool added to a flow in order to sample and compare two colors. Note the eyedropper cursor over the Background's upper Pick button.

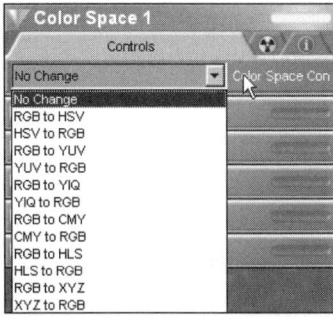

Figure 13.19
The options available for converting color spaces in Digital Fusion.

to use alternate color spaces. Figure 13.19 shows Digital Fusion's Color Space Control's conversion options.

For example, you might receive footage from an NTSC video source based on YIQ color space, where Y is the luminance, I is the in-phase or red-cyan color channel, and Q is the quadrature or magenta-green color channel. If the footage has a drift or flutter in the I channel, it would be tedious or difficult to correct this problem in RGB color space. If you converted the footage to YIQ color space, you could adjust or animate a single control to correct the problem. Contrariwise, you can fake badly adjusted NTSC video effects applied to clean footage, as shown in Figure 13.20. If you convert the footage to YIQ color space and animate either the I or Q channels, you can mimic color problems that will be familiar to anyone who has had to nurse an ancient TV set through "just one more show."

You should not apply multiple color space changes if you can avoid it. Each conversion carries the possibility of rounding errors and other discrepancies that can make the output a less-than-perfect copy of the input. If you have to convert footage to a different color space, try to do it only once. If you have footage that needs more than one YIQ-space correction, convert from RGB to YIQ once, make all the YIQ corrections, then convert back to RGB for output. Don't convert to YIQ, make a single correction, then later in the same flow convert to YIQ again for a separate correction. Minimizing your color space conversions also simplifies and optimizes your flow, so it will update and render more quickly and efficiently.

The HSV color space is particularly useful for color correction. The S or Saturation channel enables you to adjust between a desaturated grayscale image and fully saturated "posterized" image with a single control. This can be very useful when animated to produce stock effects such as a black-and-white photograph "coming to life" or a saturated sequence bleeding off color to mimic the view through a video camera's black-and-white viewfinder. For corrections and adjustments, the saturation can be boosted to give more vivid colors. This is common for television ads or music videos, where the clients like the colors to "pop." Just don't forget to legalize them afterwards.

Figure 13.20
A familiar NTSC television color-adjustment problem, faked by converting from RGB to YIQ color space and using the Color Corrector tool to clip the I or red-cyan color channel.

Color Space Conversion For Noise Removal

PROJECT 13.4
The goal of this project is to remove excessive noise from the color channels of an image while preserving the details of the luma channel. This is an especially important technique for working with video footage sampled at 4:2:2 or lower. As explained in Chapter 5, when you have half or less the original color information, the effects of noise or missing samples are multiplied. The following technique can be used to correct some video color sampling problems. This technique works best on bright footage with good color contrast.

1. Open a new flow and add a Loader. Load image CU_Expld.tga from the first CD-ROM. This is a single frame selected from a longer sequence.

2. Add a Color Space tool, and connect it to the Loader. Set the Color Space control to RGB To YUV.

The YUV space is useful because the Y, or luma, information is separate from the UV, or color, information. As explained in Chapter 5, the YUV color space is used by many video digitizing systems. The 4:2:2 sampling ratio refers to 4 samples of Y, and 2 samples each of U and V.

3. Add a Blur/Sharpen tool, and connect it to the Color Space tool. In the Blur controls, uncheck the Red and Alpha boxes.

No alpha channel exist for this image, and the Red channel corresponds to the Y of the YUV color space. Only Green and Blue, corresponding to the U and V channels, are affected by the blur operation. This limits the blur to the color information only, leaving the luma information intact.

4. Set the Blur controls to Soften and Size to 10.

5. Copy the Color Space tool, and paste it to the right of the Blur/Sharpen tool. Set the second Color Space tool to YUV To RGB, reversing the conversion of the first Color Space tool.

6. Send the Loader to the Small display and Color Space 2 to the Large display. Your flow should look like Figure 13.21.

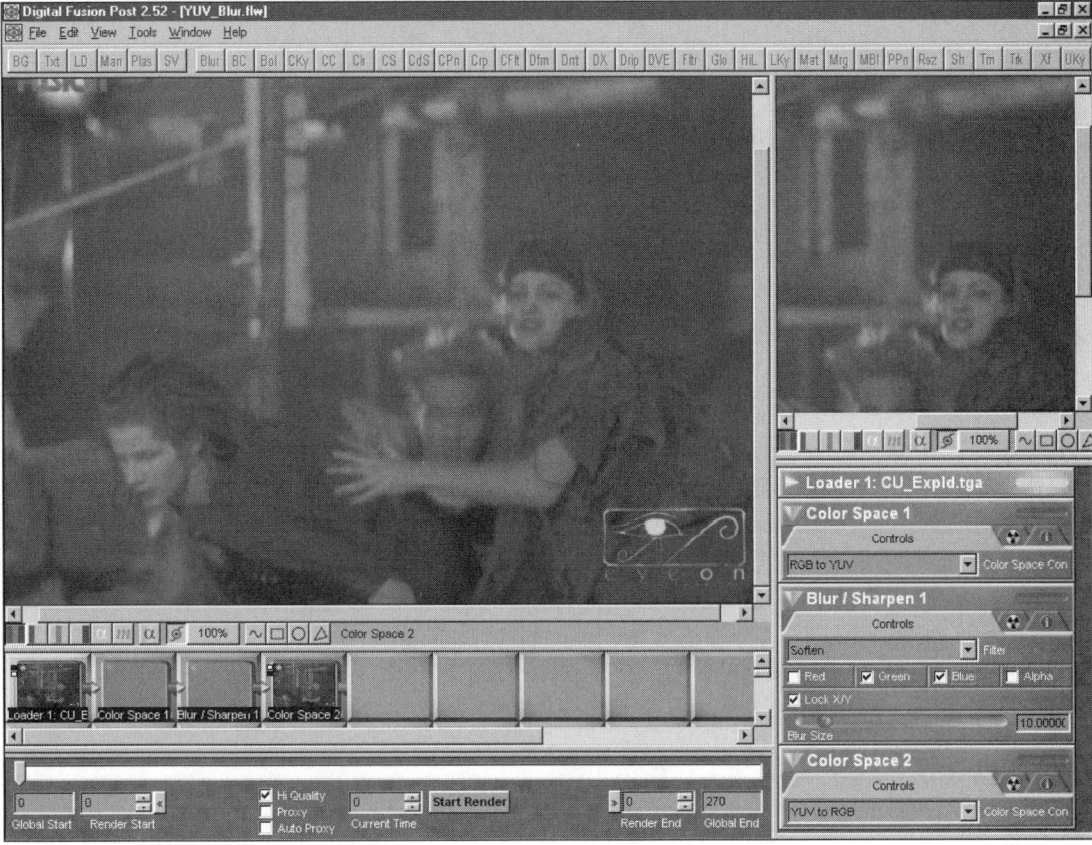

Figure 13.21

The Small display shows part of the original image; the Large display shows a level 10.0 blur applied only to the UV channels.

Compare the Large display to the Small display. The Large display doesn't seem blurred at all, just very slightly smoothed so the noise or film grain is not as obvious. This effect is an indication of how important the luma channel is for the apparent sharpness of YUV footage, and why most video digitizers sample it twice as often as the UV color channels. The differences between the Large and Small displays may not be obvious, but if you want to make truly seamless comps, you need to develop an eye for subtle details like this. If you want to see just how strong the blur is, check the Red box in the Blur/Sharpen tool and observe the resulting change in the Large display. Your results should look like Figure 13.22.

Figure 13.22
The same level 10.0 blur as in Figure 13.21 applied to all three YUV channels.

After Effects And Color Space Conversion
After Effects doesn't allow you to convert to most other color spaces, including YUV. If you need this feature, you have to use a different compositing program.

Aura And Color Space Conversion
Aura 1.0 doesn't allow you to convert to most other color spaces, including YUV. If you need this feature, you have to use a different compositing program.

Chalice And Color Space Conversion
Chalice 1.6 works in floating-point RGB, HSV, or HSL color spaces and automatically converts incoming images from YUV color space to RGB. Chalice doesn't allow you to convert to most other color spaces, including YUV, for compositing purposes. If you need this feature, you need to use a different compositing program.

Color Space Conversion For Noise Removal (Commotion)

The goal of this Commotion-based version of Project 13.4 is to remove excessive noise from the color channels of an image while preserving the details of the luma channel. This is an especially important technique for working with video footage sampled at 4:2:2 or lower. As explained in Chapter 5, when you have half or less the original color information, the effects of noise or missing samples are multiplied. The following technique can be used to correct some video color sampling problems. This technique works best on bright footage with good color contrast.

1. Open a new project. Import image CU_Expld.tga from the first CD-ROM. This is a single frame selected from a longer sequence.

2. Choose Filters|Blur & Sharpen and apply the ICE Blur filter.

3. In the ICE Blur controls, choose Channels|Chroma. This applies the selected blur to the In Phase Chrominance (I) and Quadrature Chrominance (Q) channels, leaving the Luma (Y) channel intact.

4. Experiment with the ICE Blur controls to vary the kind and amount of blur. Note that the blur is only applied to the color channels, and that the luma channel remains sharp. You can apply a fairly strong blur amount, but a small amount is usually sufficient to remove noise.

The filtered image should not seem blurred at all, just slightly smoothed so the noise or film grain isn't as obvious. This effect is an indication of how important the luma channel is for the apparent sharpness of YIQ/YUV footage, and why most video digitizers sample the luma twice as often as the IQ/UV color channels. The differences between the original and filtered images may not be obvious, but if you want to make truly seamless comps, you need to develop an eye for these subtle details. To see just how strong the blur is, choose RGB in the Channels menu and observe the resulting change as the blur is applied to all channels.

effect* And Color Space Conversion

effect* doesn't allow you to convert to most other color spaces, including YUV. If you need this feature, you need to use a different compositing program.

Color Space Conversion For Noise Removal (Shake)

The goal of this Shake-based version of Project 13.4 is to remove excessive noise from the color channels of an image while preserving the details of the luma channel. This is an especially important technique for working with video footage sampled at 4:2:2 or lower. As explained in Chapter 5, when you have half or less the original color information, the effects of noise or missing samples are multiplied. The following technique can be used to correct some video color sampling problems. This technique works best on bright footage with good color contrast.

1. Open a new script. Add a File In node and import image CU_Expld.tga from the first CD-ROM. This is a single frame selected from a longer sequence.

2. Add a RGBToYIQ node. Shake's RGBToYIQ function converts the channels in RGB (Red, Green, Blue) to standard NTSC YIQ (Luminance, Chroma1, Chroma2). Any operations connected downstream from this function will be processed in YIQ rather than RGB.

3. Add a ColorX node. This function breaks out the R, G, B, A, and Z channels and enables you to assign mathematical expressions to them individually. This makes it possible to run operations on only the IQ channels (corresponding to the GB channels, after the conversion in step 2).

4. Add a YIQToRGB node. This reverses the color space conversion of step 2, returning the image to normal RGB color space. Your script should look like Figure 13.23.

Figure 13.23
A Shake script configured to convert an RGB image to YIQ color space, to perform operations on independent channels, and then to convert back to RGB color space.

5. In the ColorX node, apply blur or median filter expressions to channels G and B. This affects only the IQ portions of the image, blurring the color channels while leaving the luma or Y channel intact.

You can find more information about ColorX and mathematical expressions for Shake in the documentation, located in the Shake directory of this book's second CD-ROM.

Color Gain

Whether you stay in RGB or convert to another color space, Digital Fusion's Color Gain tool will probably be your best all-around color correction tool. The three tabs of this tool contain slider controls for gain, gamma, saturation, and balance, either separately for each channel or with RGB channels locked together (see Figure 13.24). The gain controls perform linear color scaling, affecting the channels' brightness. You need to be careful with high gain, as it will easily exceed the legal limits for broadcast video, and a corrective legalizing operation may clip too much of the image. The gamma controls, as described earlier, apply a nonlinear color scaling that leaves the high and low ends relatively untouched, and can therefore be applied more strongly without any risk of creating illegal colors. The balance controls provide some of the controls available through color space conversion, such as removing or adding a YIQ imbalance to fake a TV receiver that is out of tune.

Brightness/Contrast

One of the most basic color manipulators is the Brightness/Contrast tool. It contains sliders for gain, brightness, contrast, gamma, and saturation, as do some of the other tools previously mentioned. However, it doesn't enable you to manipulate each channel independently; the most you can do is to disable channels you don't want to affect. The Brightness/Contrast tool is a simple, direct tool for simple problems, but it should be used with care if you need to make subtle corrections. It's all too easy to push the gain, brightness, or contrast to create illegal video colors or clip

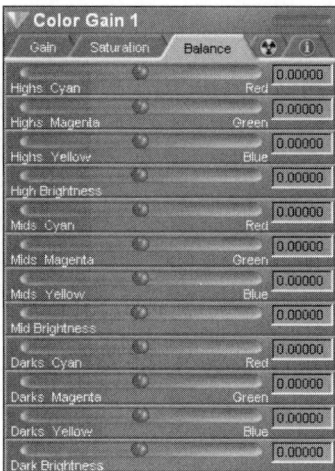

Figure 13.24
The Color Gain tool's Gain, Saturation, and Balance tabs.

the top and bottom off the luma range. If you are comping for video output, I recommend that you always use this tool in concert with a Saver set to legalize the video, and watch the Indicate As Black/Indicate As White results as you make your adjustments. For an example of the use of the Brightness/Contrast tool, see Figure 13.25.

Isolating An Effect To A Foreground Element

One of the most challenging problems in poor footage is when the actor or foreground elements are very dark, and the background or set is much brighter. You can't simply brighten the entire frame without losing the background; sometimes even a gamma operation won't get the color correction you need.

Figure 13.25

The Brightness/Contrast tool's output run through a Saver for an NTSC legality check. The Small display shows the illegal areas in white; the Large display shows the illegal areas almost completely eliminated with very small adjustments to the Brightness and Contrast sliders.

You can salvage poorly exposed footage like this by applying some of the masking and matte extraction techniques you learned in Chapters 8, 9, and 10. You can use a clean plate (if available) to extract a difference matte, soften the matte's edges, then apply the matte as a bitmap effect mask. With the background masked off, you can adjust the foreground for contrast and brightness without affecting the background. This can make the difference between an expensive reshoot and usable footage.

Moving On

This chapter showed you the basic tools and some useful techniques for color correction and damage repair to exceptionally bad footage. These tools and processes should enable you to deal with the majority of problems that are caused by the camera, scanner, or digitizer. The next chapter shows you how to piece together a simple matte painting, touch up the gaps, merge the painting with footage, and comp a multiplane camera move to simulate perspective shifts.

A PERFECT MATCH

A *matte painting* is a two-dimensional image created at least partly by painting, rather than photographic techniques, and composited with other elements to create illusions of depth and scale. Matte paintings are an important part of the digital compositor's art because paintings can be used in every style and genre of filmmaking. Fantasy, science fiction, and historical films use matte paintings to create environments that are long gone or that never existed. Matte paintings, however, are also used for such prosaic or modern-day environments as distant landscapes uncluttered by power lines or microwave relay towers; city streets with no visible advertising or staring spectators; or a runway crowded with more service and emergency vehicles, aircraft, and people than a reasonable budget could provide.

The matte painting is one of the oldest methods of special effects filmmaking. Originally, the painting was done in oils or other paints on a solid backdrop; later, it was applied to glass to allow translucent or transparent areas in more complex shapes than could be cut out of an opaque backing. Large matte paintings could be the size of theatrical backdrops and were used in much the same way. Smaller matte paintings were designed to be mounted in front of the camera lens, with cut-out or transparent areas through which the live action could be filmed. This enabled the composition of the matte painting and live action to be performed on the original film in the camera, rather than with two separate layers of film in an optical printer. The result of this *in-camera effect* was a first-generation camera negative without any additional film grain.

Although digital painting tools have largely replaced the traditional process of paint-on-glass for matte painting, the same basic processes are still used, and the same level of artistic talent is still required. More than any other part of digital compositing, the creation of matte paintings requires a high level of talent and a great deal of practice in traditional draftsmanship and painting. For feature film work, every painting is a *trompe l'oeil* that must fool the audience even when projected on a 40-foot screen. Matte paintings for film or video work have previously required only an impressionistic style, not photorealism. The difference between reality and the impressionistic painting has been concealed by film grain or video artifacts; more accurate details would be a waste of time and effort. However, the lack of grain or noise in e-cinema (see Chapter 18) may require matte paintings to be executed in a more photorealistic style in future productions.

Matte paintings are used primarily for set extensions and backgrounds that would be impossible or prohibitively expensive to build, either as practicals or in the computer. A painted background gives the director complete control over lighting, weather, and other elements that are difficult to control during location shooting. Painted backgrounds enable the director to shoot in a more predictable location or on a soundstage where every detail is under control. This makes even the most elaborate and expensive matte painting a bargain in terms of time, money, and overall control of production. A painted set extension also gives the director the freedom to shoot from more-inclusive camera angles. A limited production budget may confine practical set construction to only the ground floor of buildings, and only false fronts rather than all sides. Without set extension, the director would not be able to shoot from any camera angles that would reveal the edges of the set. If those practical sets can be extended in post-production with matte paintings, the director has the same freedom of choice in camera angles as if the practical set had been built completely in-the-round.

Case Study 14.1
Mystic Knights Cave Shot

By Sherry Hitch, Foundation Imaging

This case study shows how a production can economize on practical set construction if a matte painting can be added in post-production to substitute for part of the set. The script for an episode of Saban's *Mystic Knights of Tir Na Nog* called for a large cave interior, which would have been expensive and time-consuming to build and light. Instead, a set was built and lit for only part of the cave. The set was lit with a flickering light to mimic a fire. This variable lighting had to be matched in the matte painting.

Using Photoshop, I painted on a few different layers and was able to re-create the look, lighting, and feel of the cave. When I brought the painting into After Effects, I imported it as a comp and sandwiched the live-action element between a few painted layers. Using a soft-edge, feathered garbage matte around the live-action sequence also helped to blend the two elements seamlessly. I then adjusted the light levels for the painting on *every* frame to match the light levels for the live-action sequence.

The final comp shows matching light levels, as well as an overall match of softness, colors, and film grain throughout the entire frame.

The original plate of the cave set, showing the set edges and blacked-out areas to be filled in by matte painting.

The matte painting in progress in Photoshop.

The final matte painting with matched lighting and CGI dragons.

Sherry Hitch, Supervising Visual Effects Compositor
Foundation Imaging
24933 West Avenue Stanford
Valencia, CA 91355
www.foundation-i.com

Digital Advantages

In the traditional optical process of compositing a matte painting with live-action footage, it was too difficult to incorporate any live action that crossed the *matte line*, the edge between the painting and the live-action area. The process would require an optical rotoscope, with the intruding portion of every frame carefully traced by hand by a skilled artist. Digital compositing software makes this much easier; if an actor or other live-action element crosses the matte line, you can rotoscope an effect mask around the intruding element much more quickly and easily, and you can undo mistakes with no severe penalties in time or materials. The ability to efficiently create rotoscoped masks makes it possible to conceal the matte line within the action, making the comp much harder to detect and making the shot more believable.

One of the most significant advantages of digital over traditional matte painting is the greater ability to cut, paste, distort, mirror, and otherwise manipulate photographic elements to build a kind of digital collage. This approach can often provide over 95 percent of the finished matte painting, with manual touch-up required only for the seams and gaps in the collage.

PROJECT 14.1 Making A Simple Matte Painting

The goal of this project is to create a matte painting of a frame from the Match footage, but without the door. This is a very simple example of matte painting that illustrates the basic techniques. This process goes a little beyond rig removal by requiring you to paint by hand those areas you can't cover by copy-and-paste operations.

1. Open a frame of the Match footage (from the first CD-ROM) in Photoshop. Choose a frame that includes enough of the upper part of the wall that the shadow of the overhang is visible. You need this shadow to correctly duplicate the shadow that falls on the wall after the door is painted out. For this project, I chose frame 59.

A good rule of thumb for digital matte painting in Photoshop is to work at 400 percent, but check your work at 100 percent. It's easier to work more precisely at 400 percent, but some of the fine details you can see aren't important; however, it is important to preserve the aliased "stair steps" and other large-scale video artifacts that you can see more clearly at 100 percent. It's very important that you don't make your matte paintings too clean. A total lack of artifacts is an unnatural condition that makes the matte too clean and, therefore, unrealistic.

2. The first step to creating a matte painting is to "clean the canvas" by cutting out what you want to remove. Sample a representative background color—in this case, sample the color of the most brightly lit area of the house siding. Set this sampled color as the background color in Photoshop, as shown in Figure 14.1.

Figure 14.1
Frame 59 from the Match footage, loaded in Photoshop at 400%. The color of a brightly lit area of the house siding has been selected as the background color.

3. Use the Lasso tool to outline what you want to remove, including shadows, reflections, and any other evidence. You can delete a little at a time for more complex removals, but removing the door is pretty well defined, and you should be able to do it with a single selection. When the Lasso selection is complete and accurate, delete the selection. The door and its shadow should be replaced by the background color, as shown in Figure 14.2.

Figure 14.2
The door, threshold, and shadows deleted from the painting.

The next step in this project is to duplicate any repeating patterns from the remaining untouched areas that should also be present in the deleted areas. This image is a very good candidate for this step, because the regular lines of the siding edges form a consistent pattern with well-defined repetitions due to video aliasing.

4. Select an area of siding shadow, copy and paste it, and position the pasted layer in the deleted area so that the siding shadows line up as shown in Figure 14.3. You can get some idea of the length of the repeating pattern by looking at the bottom edge of the siding just above the porch. The regular pattern of highs and lows is not actually present in the siding; it is an artifact of the video format.

5. If you selected the copied area carefully, you should be able to paste and align it repeatedly to cover most of the deleted area, as shown in Figure 14.4. This gets a lot of the painting done very quickly. The remaining areas, though smaller, will require more problem-solving and careful painting.

Figure 14.3
An area of siding shadow copied and pasted in the deleted area, positioned to match the adjoining shadow.

Figure 14.4
The selected area pasted repeatedly to cover most of the door area. Note that the repeating aliasing artifacts in the pasted areas are consistent with the aliasing artifacts at the bottom edge of the siding, just above the porch.

6. Some of the remaining areas have only the siding shadows, whereas other areas have more complex shadows. You can cover the remaining siding shadow areas by sampling carefully from the left edge of the deleted area, as shown in Figure 14.5. This area will provide a better match than the right edge.

Figure 14.5

The left edge of the deleted area is filled in by copy-and-paste selections from the left edge. The shadow of the overhang is duplicated across the deleted area, preserving the angle and mimicking aliasing artifacts.

7. Copy and paste the overhang shadow, from the upper right of the image, across the top of the deleted area. Be careful to offset the pasted samples up a pixel or two, to match the aliasing artifacts of the siding edges.

The slim section of dark shadow at the upper left of Figure 14.5 requires more pasting than the previous steps. The area available for sampling is much smaller, so more samples will have to be used to cover the same area.

8. Select a strip of the shadowed area, and paste it repeatedly, as shown in Figure 14.6. Offset the rightmost samples downward a pixel or two, to mimic the aliasing artifacts. Don't select the sample all the way down to the edge of the board. There is a narrow band of lighter color between the deepest shadow and the lower edge of the siding, which will require extremely careful painting.

9. Refer to the original frame 59 and note how far the shadows pasted in Figure 14.6 should extend to the right. Continue pasting the shadow sample to fill in the appropriate area.

10. Select, copy, and paste the shadow-light-shadow pattern immediately below the area pasted in Figure 14.6. Your results should look something like Figure 14.7. Take your time; this is a very fussy area. Flip between 100% and 400% magnification to see if the details you are copying look all right at the resolution at which they will be displayed.

Figure 14.6
The shadowed area sampled and duplicated. Note that the rightmost three sample strips have been offset to mimic the video aliasing artifacts of the other shadows.

Figure 14.7
Duplication of the shadow-light-shadow pattern at the edge of a siding strip.

11. Copy and paste the angled end of the overhang shadow, and position it at the right edge of the area pasted in Figure 14.7. Double-check the placement of this shadow against the appearance of a similar shadow on the original door. Your results should look like Figure 14.8. Make sure you get this corner piece positioned correctly; the remainder of the paste-ups will depend on it.

Figure 14.8
The overhang shadow angle is duplicated and pasted in the deleted area.

12. Paste the corner shadow sample repeatedly to meet the lower edge of the overhang shadow that was pasted in Figure 14.5. Paste copies of the shadow stripe from Figure 14.6 to fill in to the left of the corner shadows, as shown in Figure 14.9.

Figure 14.9
Repeated corner shadows and shadow strips fill in the remaining shadow areas.

13. The remaining deleted area and copy-and-paste artifacts need to be covered with hand-painted pixels or to be blurred out with filter operations. This can be the most time-consuming part of creating a collage matte painting, and it's important that you know when to stop tweaking.

14. Use the Eyedropper and Pencil tools to add single pixels of the appropriate colors where needed. Select areas with copy-and-paste artifacts and apply Blur filters to obscure the artifacts. Your results should look something like Figures 14.10 and 14.11.

Figure 14.10
A close-up of the final painted and blurred areas.

Figure 14.11
The final matte painting, assembled mostly as a self-collage with less than 5 percent actual painting. Can you tell where the original image ends and the painting begins?

By completing this project, you learned how to:

- Create a simple matte painting
- Select, modify, and assemble photographic elements into a collage
- Paint over the gaps between collage elements
- Apply filters to hide artifacts in the finished painting

These are the same basic skills that professional digital compositors use to create matte paintings for television and film productions. However, these collage techniques are just the beginning of the skills you need to create truly professional matte paintings. To master the principles of forced perspective and photorealistic painting, I strongly recommend traditional art classes at a reputable art academy or under the personal instruction of a good art teacher.

Case Study 14.2
Saint Patrick Abbey Shot

By Sherry Hitch, Foundation Imaging

This case study is based on a shot for Fox's *Saint Patrick* telefilm, due to air St. Patrick's Day 2000. The original location footage was shot around a real abbey, which is somewhat the worse for a few centuries' wear and tear. Most of the windows are gone or severely damaged, the roofs have fallen in or are entirely missing, and many of the walls have missing or damaged sections. In addition to repairing all this damage to make the abbey appear nearly new, the producer felt that more windows and crosses were needed to better match the time period and story line.

Steve Burg used Photoshop to do the matte paintings for this show. He painted them to film resolution so that in the comp, we had enough working space to do a camera move. Can you pick out all the changes between the original plate and this painting?

Location shot of the actual abbey.

Abbey matte painting by Steve Burg.

Final composite by Beth Roy, including rotoscoped actors crossing matte lines.

In the final shot, we used After Effects to isolate the actors moving within the scene and actually rotoscope them if they crossed the matte line in that area of the shot. To rotoscope the actors, Beth Roy, the compositor on this shot, created Bézier curves around the actors at the places where they intersected the matte painting. As with the *Mystic Knights* cave shot, matching of color balance, lighting, and film grain needed to be addressed throughout the scene.

Sherry Hitch, Supervising Visual Effects Compositor
Foundation Imaging
24933 West Avenue Stanford
Valencia, CA 91355
www.foundation-i.com

Matte Painting For The Moving Camera

Correct perspective has to be carefully built into matte paintings to create a convincing illusion of depth. A pan (lateral), crane (vertical), or dolly move, or a lens zoom will break this illusion of perspective. For this reason, cameras used for compositing with matte paintings were made immovable or *locked down,* beginning with their first use in the late nineteenth century. These static compositions severely limit the director's options for camera movement. However, if a particular camera move is carefully planned, a specially distorted painting can be created to mimic the necessary changes in perspective. Unfortunately, that painting would be useless for any other camera move.

A more flexible approach is to create several separate paintings for the distant background, middle ground, and foreground. This enables the camera operator or compositor to move each painting independently to simulate shifts in perspective. This method was the basis of the Disney studio's *multiplane camera,* developed in rough form in the mid-1930s and used in several films, such as *The Old Mill.* A more advanced version of this camera was used to create the breathtaking sense of depth in the London flyover sequence of *Peter Pan.* The multiplane camera enabled many pan, crane, dolly, or combination camera moves, but it still prohibited any change in the camera's angle to the flat, 2D paintings. A few degrees of swivel instantly breaks the illusion of depth built into the forced perspective of the matte painting.

PROJECT 14.2 Compositing A Multiplane Pan

The goal of this project is to set up a flow to simulate the panning abilities of a multiplane camera. This illustrates a useful technique for creating the illusion of correct 3D perspective shifts using only 2D images. In addition, this project will show you the basic steps necessary to applying mathematical expressions to your comps.

1. Load the Path180.flw comp that you saved from Project 8.9. If you didn't save it, you should be able to quickly re-create it by now, repeating the directions in Projects 8.3, 8.7, 8.8, and 8.9, or by mimicking the flow shown in Figure 14.12.

2. In Loaders 2, 3, and 4, limit the footage to the first frame by changing Clip Time Start and Clip Time End to 0, and turning on the Loop checkbox. This removes the animation built into the footage, so that you are essentially working with one still image in each Loader that is repeated for the length of the comp.

3. Loader 1 should still contain the 180-frame sequence of the flying actress filmed against bluescreen. Because that footage is already animated by a pan transform, don't change Loader 1, Ultra Keyer, or Transform 1 at all.

4. Add a Transform tool between Loaders 2, 3, and 4 and their respective Merge tools. It will be easier to remember which Transform tool goes with which Loader if you number them identically—that is, Transform 4 is linked to Loader 4.

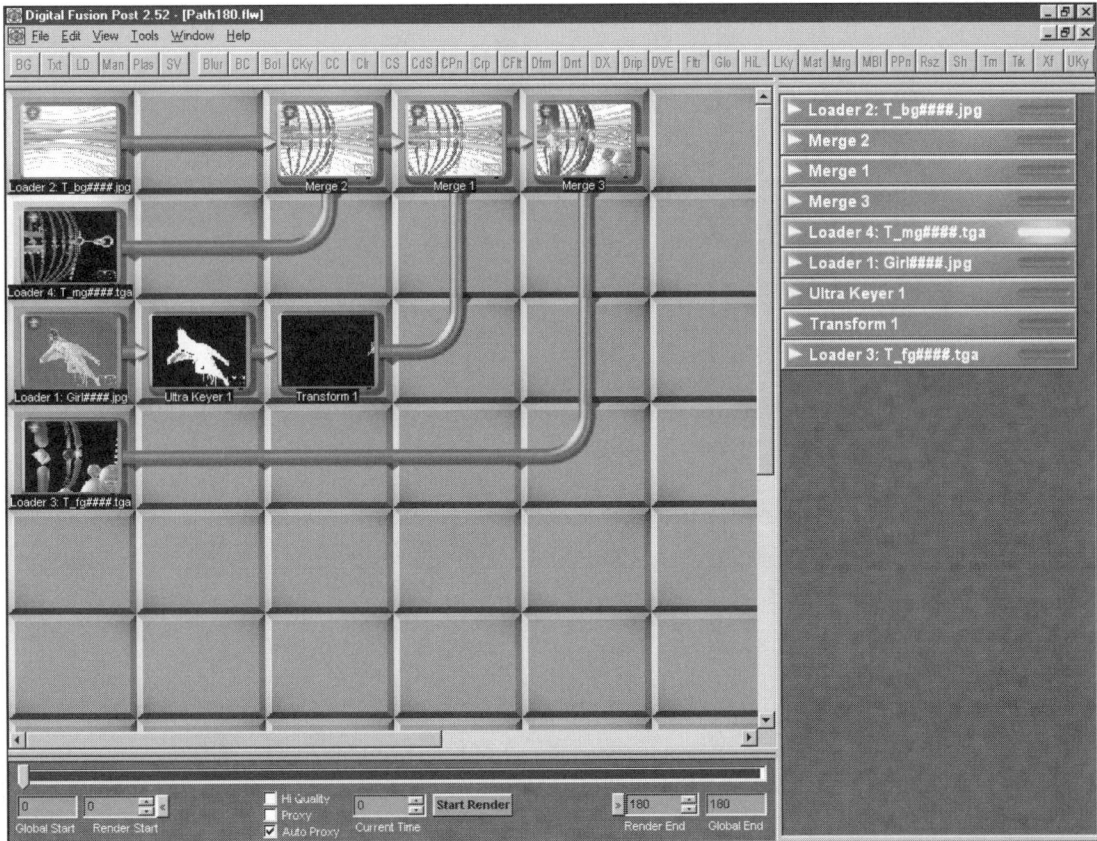

Figure 14.12
The Path180.flw composition from Project 8.9.

5. Select Transform 3, and in its controls, right-click on the Centre control and choose Modify With|Expression from the pop-up menu, as shown in Figure 14.13.

6. A new Expression 1 control will appear, as shown at the top right of Figure 14.13. Choose the Point Out tab.

7. The Transform Centre control that is affected by this expression has two parameters, X and Y. In the Point Out tab, the upper blank space controls the X-axis, and the lower blank controls the Y-axis. In the upper blank, type the formula "0.5–(0.5(Time/180))". In the lower blank, type "0.5".

The lower expression will keep the Transform at a constant height. The upper expression will cause the Transform to pan from right to left for one-half the width of the image between frames 0 and 180. The expression accomplishes this movement by subtracting one-half of the fraction Time (the current

Figure 14.13
Three Transform tools have been added to the flow, and the Transform 3 tool has been configured with a Point Out expression.

frame number) divided by 180 (the total number of frames) from the original rest position, 0.5. As the frame number increases, the value of the fraction increases from 0.0 to 1.0. One-half of this fraction therefore increases from 0.0 to 0.5. Subtracting this from 0.5, the original X-axis value of the Transform 3 Centre control, gives a linear change from 0.5 at frame 0 to 0.0 at frame 180. This expression is specifically written for the length of this comp. If you change the length of the comp, you will also have to retype the new ending frame value in place of 180.

THE ADVANTAGE OF EXPRESSIONS

Mathematical expressions are possibly one of the most powerful, and are certainly the least-used and most poorly understood, tools for digital compositing. Applied properly, you can control any parameter with any other parameter, or set up a complex operation with a single line of simple arithmetic that would otherwise require painstaking keyframe animation. If your compositing software enables you to use expressions, you owe it to yourself to learn how to use them. If your software does not support expressions, you should consider switching software.

The pan transform of the foreground element reveals the right edge of the image. This image was not designed for a pan transform and is precisely the width of the frame. A matte painting intended for a multiplane pan operation like this would usually be rendered at several times the frame width, to allow plenty of room for pan transforms. This is another example of why you should always shoot or digitize in an oversize format, so you'll have the extra room you need for transforms or reframing.

8. Right-click on Expression 1, and choose Copy from the pop-up menu. This copies both the Expression control and the control's settings. This is the easiest way to duplicate complex expressions that you want to use or modify for other controls.

9. Select Transform 4, and in its controls, right-click on the Centre control and choose Modify With|Expression from the pop-up menu. Expression 2 will appear.

10. In the Expression 2 controls, choose the Point Out tab. Right-click on the Expression 2 control header, and choose Paste Settings from the pop-up menu, as shown in Figure 14.14. This will copy the expression you typed in Expression 1 into the same spaces in Expression 2.

11. In the Expression 2 controls' Point Out tab, change the formula in the upper blank to 0.5–(0.25(Time/180)).

Figure 14.14
Pasting settings from the Expression 1 controls to the Expression 2 controls.

Note that the change from 0.5 to 0.25 will halve the movement of Transform 4 as compared to Transform 3. This means that the foreground element, panned by Transform 3, will move twice as far as the middle-ground element that is moved by Transform 4. That mimics the perspective shift that would be visible if these elements actually existed in three-dimensional space, and the foreground element was halfway between the camera and the middle-ground element.

12. If you like, add an Expression to Transform 2's Centre control and paste the settings from either Expression 1 or Expression 2. Try changing the multiplier to a very small value, 0.05 for example.

A distant background should move very little in a camera pan; at the horizon line or vanishing point, it should not move at all. You can fine-tune the perspective shift in a multiplane comp by tweaking the multiplier value. If you would like a more interactive means of adjusting the multiplier, you can substitute a numeric variable in place of the multiplier, then interactively manipulate the appropriate numeric slider in the Number In tab, as shown in Figure 14.15.

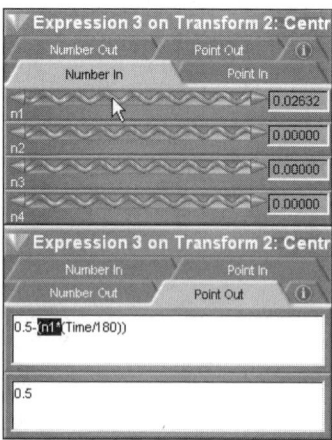

Figure 14.15
Below, the numeric variable n1 is substituted for the multiplier in the X-axis formula for Point Out, and above, using the mouse to vary the n1 slider in the Number In tab.

When you are satisfied with the pans produced by your expressions, render the output or create a preview, and examine the results. Is the 3D perspective shift convincing? What could you change to improve it?

By completing this project, you learned how to:

• Set up a multiplane pan transform

• Adjust the pan transforms to mimic 3D perspective shifts

• Apply mathematical expressions to controls

Compositing A Multiplane Pan (After Effects)

The goal of this After Effects-based version of Project 14.2 is to simulate the panning capabilities of a multiplane camera. This illustrates a useful technique for creating the illusion of correct 3D perspective shifts using only 2D images. Additionally, this project shows you the basic steps necessary to applying mathematical expressions to your After Effects comps using Motion Math.

1. Import the first frame only from the TShipbg, TShipmg, and TShipfg sequences that you comped with their corresponding alpha channels in Chapter 8. If you haven't done this, do it now. You'll find the separate JPEG color and alpha channel image sequences on the second CD-ROM.

You don't need the animation built into these image sequences; you only need the first frame from each sequence to create the desired multiplane effect.

2. Create a new comp, and set it for a 5-second duration. Add the three images to it so the foreground is layer 1, middle ground is layer 2, and background is layer 3 (see Figure 14.16).

Figure 14.16

The TShip multiplane project with all images imported and added to the comp. Note the layered appearance of the Composition window, due to the alpha channels of the foreground and middle-ground images.

3. Expand the first layer and expand the Transform submenu. In the Position variable, set a keyframe at the first frame for the default value of 360, 243 and another keyframe at the last frame for 120, 243. This keeps the foreground layer centered vertically while moving right to left across the screen over the course of the comp.

Notice that this movement exposes the cut-off right margin of the foreground. If this were a real comp for a paying client, you would need to have an extra-wide image to avoid this problem. This is another example of the usefulness of VistaVision or widely framed footage; they give you more latitude for panning and other layer motions, without losing image quality by upsampling standard-size images.

4. Select layer 2, the middle ground. Choose Layer|Keyframe Assistant|Motion Math. This opens the Motion Math dialog box.

5. In the Motion Math dialog box, load the Parallax (parallax.mm) script from the MMScript folder in your After Effects home folder. In the script, change the scale_factor to 0.40. Make sure that the middle ground is the first layer and the foreground is the second layer. Both layers' Property should be set to Position, and both layers' Channel should be set to X. Click on the Sample At 30 Samples Per Second radio button. Your dialog box should look like Figure 14.17.

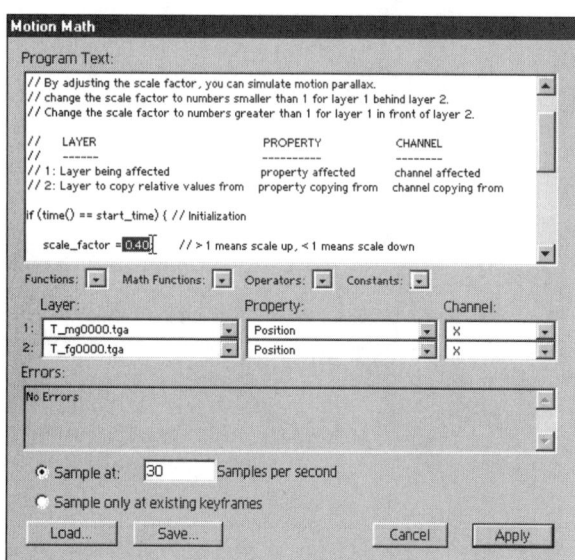

Figure 14.17
The Motion Math script and settings that moves the middle ground layer at 40 percent of the speed of the foreground layer.

This script will move the middle ground layer at 40 percent of the speed of the foreground layer, in the same direction and along the same axis. This mimics perspective shift, creating the illusion that the middle layer is some distance between the foreground and background layers.

6. Repeat steps 4 and 5 for the background layer, but change the scale_factor to 0.05. This makes the background move very slowly, as if it were very distant from the middle and foreground elements (see Figure 14.18).

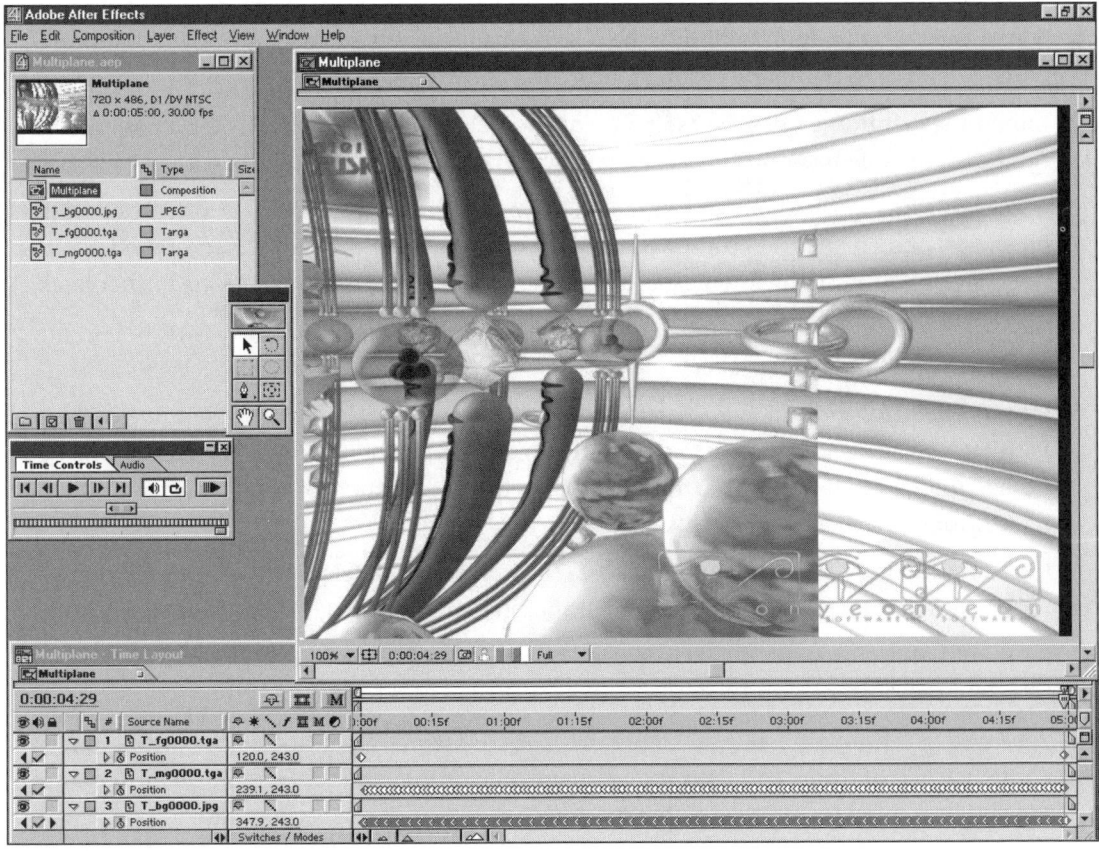

Figure 14.18
The last frame of the multiplane comp shows the differential motion of the three layers, simulating parallax. Compare this frame to the Composition window of Figure 14.16.

This is actually more convincing than leaving the background immobile. Human vision has evolved to judge distances all the way to the horizon by using the relative motion of parallax; any object closer than the vanishing point should move, even if only a tiny amount. Because the changes in each layer's position from one frame to the next are very small, you should always set each visible layer's Quality level to Best. This enables subpixel accuracy, producing smoother and more accurate movement and rendered edges.

Compositing A Multiplane Pan (Aura)

The goal of this Aura-based version of Project 14.2 is to simulate the panning capabilities of a multiplane camera. This illustrates a useful technique for using 2D images to create the illusion of correct 3D perspective shifts.

1. You need the first frame only from the TShipbg, TShipmg, and TShipfg sequences that you comped with their corresponding alpha channels in Chapter 8. If you haven't done this, do it now. You'll find the separate JPEG color and alpha channel image sequences on the second CD-ROM.

You don't need the animation built into these image sequences; you need only the first frame from each sequence to create the desired multiplane effect.

2. Import the first frame from the Tshipbg sequence. Drag out the layer to 150 frames, and right-click on the layer and choose Make Anim to convert it to an anim layer.

3. Choose File|Import|Brush and select the first frame of the Tshipmg sequence. You import the middle-ground brush first because you need to paint the brushes over the background in order from back to front, so the foremost brush layers are on top of the brush layers further back.

4. Right-click on the T_bg layer and choose Select All. This enables the brush operation to affect all the images in the anim layer.

5. Choose Filters|Animated|Keyframer. In the Keyframer window, go to the first frame and set Position X to 360 and Y to 243, to center the brush over the background layer. Go to the last frame, and set Position X to 160 and Y to 243 to move the brush toward the left side of the screen. Your screen should look like Figure 14.19.

6. Click on the Apply To Layer button to paste the keyframed brush over the selected frames of the background layer. When the filter operation is complete, close the Keyframer window.

7. Make and play a preview. If the keyframed brush motion isn't what you intended, undo the filter and repeat steps 5 and 6 until you are satisfied with the results.

8. Repeat steps 3 through 7, but substitute the Tshipfg foreground image for the brush, and set Position X to 0 at frame 150. This makes the nearer, or foreground, layer move farther than the middle ground layer, creating the illusion of parallax or perspective shift.

9. When you are satisfied with the results, render the comp and save the project.

You can vary the Position X value at frame 150 to modify the apparent distance between the foreground and middle ground images. The X values I suggest here are simply a good starting point. You can also create a multiplane pan by writing a George script, Aura's system for incorporating mathematical expressions into compositions. This approach, once it is set up, has the advantage of being more controllable with less effort. For details on using George scripts, see the Aura Reference Guide.

Chalice And Multiplane

The Chalice 1.6 documents include tutorial elements and instructions for several projects. Tutorial 3, The Basics, deals with comping multiple masked and layered elements to create the illusion of depth. Rather than duplicate that tutorial here, I recommend that you work through the Chalice 1.6 basic tutorials, then repeat the multiplane animation process using the TShipbg, TShipmg, and TShipfg sequences from the second CD-ROM.

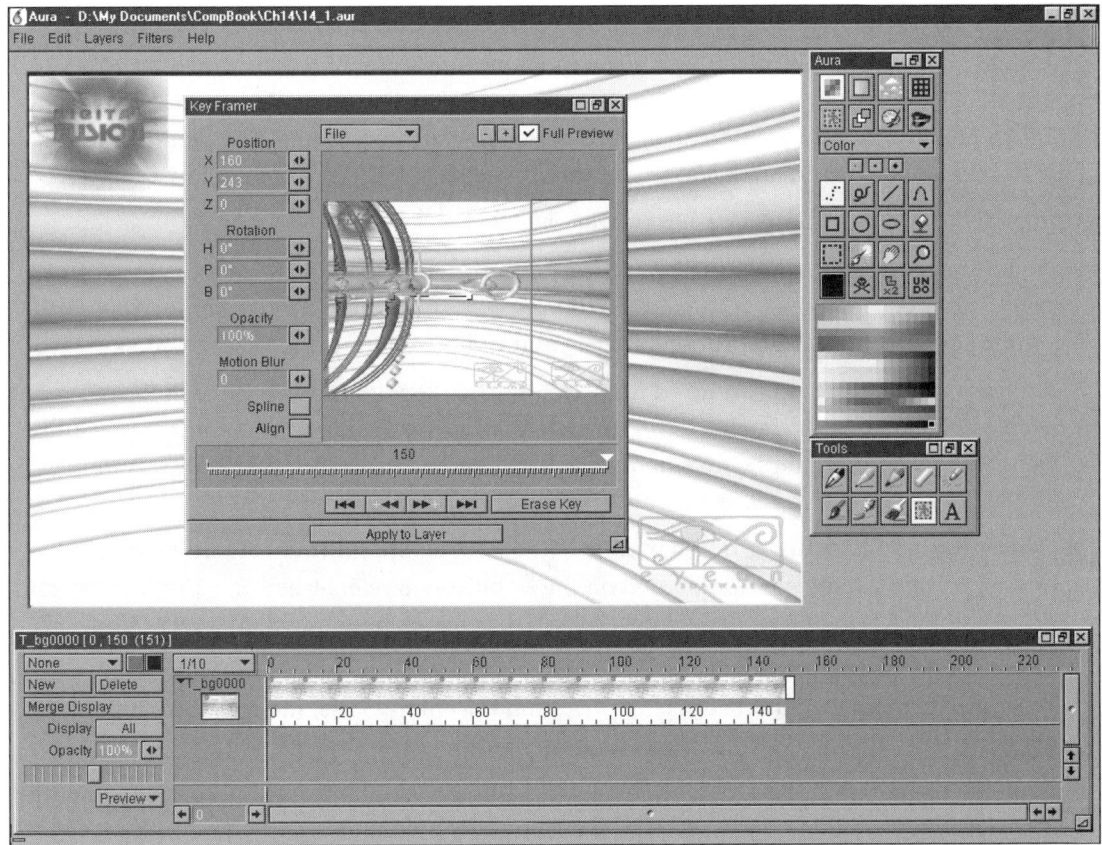

Figure 14.19
The Keyframe filter is set to animate the Tshipmg brush over the Tshipbg background layer.

effect* And Multiplane

The demo version of Discreet effect* that is located on the first CD-ROM also includes tutorial footage and instructions for several projects, including one on composition that deals with a moving 3D camera and multiple spaced elements. Rather than duplicate that tutorial here, I recommend that you install the effect* demo, work through the demo tutorial projects, then repeat the multiplane animation process using the TShipbg, TShipmg, and TShipfg sequences from the second CD-ROM.

Shake And Multiplane

The Shake 2.1 documents (on the second CD-ROM) include tutorial elements and instructions for several projects. The GUI Intermediate tutorial deals with comping multiple masked and layered elements to create the illusion of depth. Rather than duplicate that tutorial here, I recommend that you work through the Shake 2.1 tutorial projects, then repeat the multiplane animation process using the TShipbg, TShipmg, and TShipfg sequences from the second CD-ROM.

PROJECT 14.3 Comping A Matte Painting Into Stabilized Footage

The goal of this project is to incorporate the matte painting you created in Project 14.1 into the stabilized footage you produced in Project 11.3. Properly stabilized footage requires only one matte painting, which can be stabilized to match the reference frame. The painted-over area of the stabilized footage is then dissolved out with an effect mask, just like a removal subject.

1. Load the UnCrop flow you saved from Project 11.3.

2. In the Loader, substitute the matte painting for the original footage. Render the first frame only. This produces a copy of the matte painting with the oversized black border necessary for the stabilization/destabilization process from Chapters 11 and 12. Close the flow.

3. Load the Stable.flw comp you saved from Project 11.3. Replace the footage with the matte painting image you just rendered. Change the Extend First Frame setting to the frame number of the matte painting's source image. If you followed Project 14.1 precisely, this will be frame 59.

4. Render the matte painting's frame from the Stable.flw comp, shown in Figure 14.20. If you chose to create a matte painting based on the stabilization reference frame, the "before" and "after" stabilization images should be identical, but there's no sense in taking chances.

5. Set up a rig removal dissolve using a polygon effect mask, as you did in Project 10.2, with the mask defining the outline of the removal subject—in this case, the door, threshold, and shadows.

6. Load the original stabilized footage you rendered in Project 11.3 as the background, and the stabilized matte painting as the foreground. Your flow should look like Figure 14.21.

The results from this flow should look like Figure 14.22. Because the matte painting is only a single frame, it cannot simulate the temporal artifacts of the original footage. To create a truly seamless composite, you will need to apply a noise or grain filter to the matte painting to simulate these video artifacts. These filters should be applied either between the matte painting's Loader and the Dissolve or after the output of the dissolve but within the same effect mask. This will prevent the noise filter from affecting the background footage, which would have the effect of interfering with or doubling the original video artifacts.

Even with the added noise, the fact that the matte painting exhibits none of the small movements of the background footage would make it stick out like a sore thumb. The solution to this problem is destabilization. You should always plan to destabilize footage that includes a matte painting (or any other still element). Leaving a matte painting perfectly stable makes the painting much easier to spot, and it ruins the illusion of even an otherwise perfect comp. Restoring the original camera motion (or adding artificial motion) to the final comp enables the combination of noise, blur, and an accurate track to conceal the matte painting's appearance.

Figure 14.20
Two-point stabilizing the matte painting to match the footage from Project 11.3.

By completing this project, you learned how to:

- Merge a matte painting with stabilized footage
- Conceal matte painting temporal artifacts with noise and grain filters

The Third Dimension

If you need to produce realistic perspective shifts throughout complex camera moves, there is another alternative for digital matte paintings. With the right 3D rendering software, it is possible to map a two-dimensional painting onto a three-dimensional surface. Mapping a painting onto a 3D model means that the model doesn't have to contain all the details represented in the painting, and that the painting doesn't have to create the perspective shifts required by the camera move. For example, you could apply one of the frames from the Match footage to the Porch model. The model is simply a collection of rectangular blocks, but the image mapped onto it will

Figure 14.21
The matte painting dissolved into stabilized footage through an effect mask.

provide the shadows, color, and apparent texture of brick, mortar, and concrete. As long as no unmapped surfaces are exposed to the camera, the mapped model presents an exact illusion of the three-dimensional reality.

In Steven Spielberg's *Hook*, for example, a matte painting of Neverland was mapped onto a simplified 3D computer model of the island, to allow camera motions that demanded realistic perspective shifts in the painted landscape. A painting-and-model that balances the trade-offs between modeling and painting complexity is faster and more efficient to create—and therefore more cost effective—and provides a greater degree of freedom to the director.

Figure 14.22
Representative frames of matte painting dissolved into stabilized footage. Extremes of rotation and scaling contribute to visible artifacts.

Moving On

This chapter showed you how to paint and composite matte paintings. The next chapter shows how to comp timing effects to salvage bad footage, how to create clean plates for rig removals, and how to stretch or compress a shot to fit with other elements.

CHAPTER 15

TIMING

The ability to change the timing of footage is an important part of the digital compositor's toolkit. Timing effects can be part of comps to salvage bad footage, to create clean plates for rig removals, or to stretch or compress a shot to fit with other elements. Whether timing effects are planned ahead as early as the first script or are last-minute changes during the final edit, you can expect to comp some of these effects on nearly every project.

Timing effects can also be powerful storytelling tools. The freeze frame isolates and emphasizes the moment. Slow motion gives even frantic actions a choreographed, balletic precision, and it can be applied to emphasize a romantic, action, or horror shot equally well. Fast motion amplifies the startled humor of slapstick comedy. Reverse motion can be part of crucial effects that would be prohibitive to create using other techniques. These and other timing effects are standard parts of the cinematic language, and directors and other industry professionals will expect these effects to be part of your digital compositing repertoire.

Most timing effects are possible with the optical printer and other traditional film-based tools, which have been around for most of the past century. Digital compositing solves or avoids many of the traditional timing effect problems, such as mechanically coordinating multiple layers and generations of film and then dealing with the resulting film-grain artifacts. Some timing effects are extreme enough to surpass the abilities of the traditional optical technology. Slow-motion photography, pushed to extreme speeds, loses the color and brightness of normal photography. Digital compositing tools can work with footage shot at more normal speeds to create the most extreme slow-motion effects without compromising image quality.

477

Work With What You've Got

The most basic timing effects simply rearrange the frames that already exist. This is possibly the easiest type of comp to create, and it is also the most common. For that reason, you need to be able to retime these simple comps with no more effort or thought than you take to file your nails. This is a basic task that you should be able to perform on any digital compositing software or hardware within minutes of your first practice session.

Reversing Footage

The simplest timing change for footage is a *reverse*. This post-production effect is commonly used in combination with on-set practical effects, to produce results such as water flowing backwards or broken objects reassembling themselves. Some types of stunts are commonly shot in reverse. For example, it's easier for an actor to make an apparently superhuman leap to a precise landing on a high ledge if a character is actually filmed in reverse, stepping back off that ledge to fall into a safety bag.

PROJECT 15.1 Reversing Footage

The goal of this project is to reverse the Jump footage, making the actor appear to leap backwards onto the platform.

1. Open a new flow.

2. Add a Loader and load the Jump footage from the second CD-ROM.

3. In the Loader controls, check the Reverse box, as shown in Figure 15.1.

Figure 15.1
The Reverse box checked in the Loader controls to reverse the loaded footage.

4. Set the render range to start at 0 and end at 102. Create a preview, and play it back.

The Loader's footage is reversed. Playback begins with the last frame of the footage and ends with the first frame of the footage. You can also reverse footage with the Time Speed tool.

Figure 15.2
A flow set up to reverse footage.

5. Uncheck the Reverse box in the Loader. Add a Time Speed tool (from the Tools|Miscellaneous menu) to the right of the Loader and connected to it, as shown in Figure 15.2.

6. In the Time Speed controls, set Speed to –1.0.

When the Speed value is positive, the footage plays forward. When the Speed value is negative, the footage plays backward.

7. Uncheck the Interpolation checkbox. Your flow should look like Figure 15.2.

8. The Time Speed tool offsets by one frame when you reverse the footage. Set the render range to start at 1 and end at 103. Create a preview, and play it back. It should look exactly like the preview you rendered in step 4.

9. Save the flow as Timing.flw. You'll need it for other projects in this chapter.

Reversing Footage (After Effects)

The goal of this After Effects-based version of Project 15.1 is to reverse the Jump footage, making the actor appear to leap backwards onto the platform.

1. Open a new project. Import the Jump JPEG sequence from the second CD-ROM. Create a new composition with a length of 03:13 to match the Jump sequence, and add the Jump sequence to the Time Layout window.

2. In the Time Layout window, select the Jump layer. Press Ctrl+Alt+R. Play back the comp.

This reverses the footage for the entire duration of the comp. If you need to reverse only part of the footage or if you want to have finer control of the reversal's timing, you can use time-remapping.

3. With the Jump layer still selected, press Ctrl+Alt+R again to undo the reversal. Press Ctrl+Alt+T to enable Time Remapping for the Jump layer. Expand the Jump layer (and the Time Remap menu within the layer) to show the Value and Velocity graphs. Double-click on the Jump layer to open the Layer window. Your screen should look like Figure 15.3.

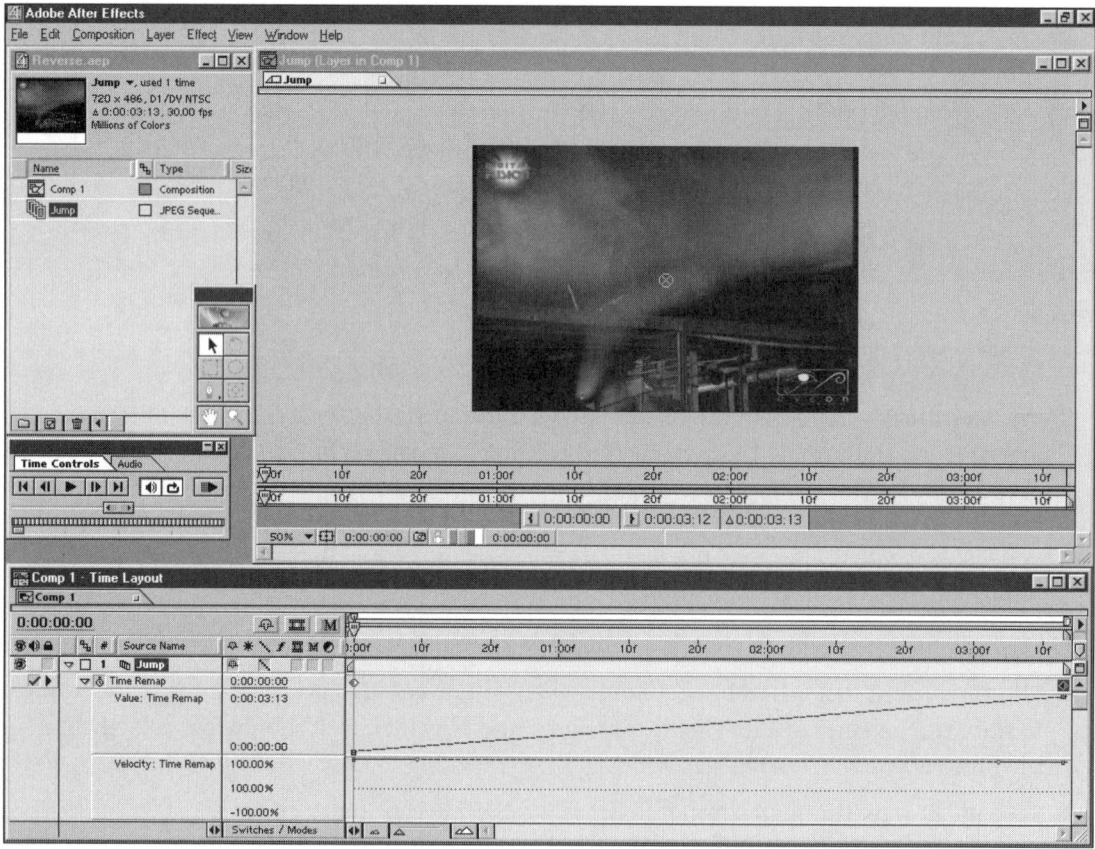

Figure 15.3

The Jump composition with the Layer window and Time Layout window configured for time remapping.

In After Effects, you can use either the Time Layout window or the Layer window to remap the timing of a layer. The Layer window provides a visual reference of the footage, while the Time Layout window shows keyframed graphs for value and velocity. If you are remapping based on visual cues in the footage, use the Layer window; if you need to remap time based on specific times or speeds, use the Time Layout window.

4. In the Value graph in the Time Layout window, there are keyframes at the beginning and end of the comp. The first keyframe is set to 00:00, the beginning time, and the second keyframe is set to 03:13, the end time. Drag the first keyframe up to the top of the graph window. Drag the second keyframe to the bottom of the graph window. Your graph should look like Figure 15.4.

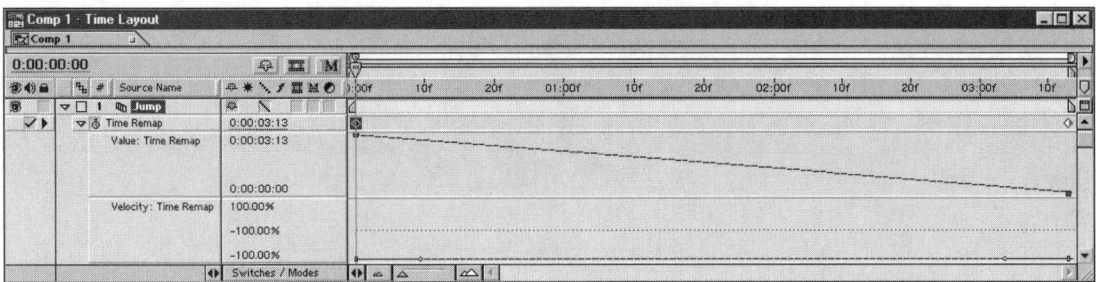

Figure 15.4
The keyframes in the Time Remap Value graph have been modified to reverse the Jump layer.

This reverses the layer, duplicating the effect you created in step 2. However, Time Remapping gives you many more options to control the timing of a layer, with fast feedback and easy-to-use tools. The After Effects User Guide has more information on Time Remapping.

5. Save the project as Remap.aep. You'll use it later in this chapter.

Reversing Footage (Aura)

The goal of this Aura-based version of Project 15.1 is to reverse the Jump footage, making the actor appear to leap backward onto the platform.

1. Launch Aura with NTSC preferences. Import the Jump image sequence from the second CD-ROM.

2. Open the Layer control panel and select the Jump layer.

3. From the Jump layer submenu, choose Select All.

4. From the Jump layer submenu, choose Reverse Selection. Your screen should look like Figure 15.5.

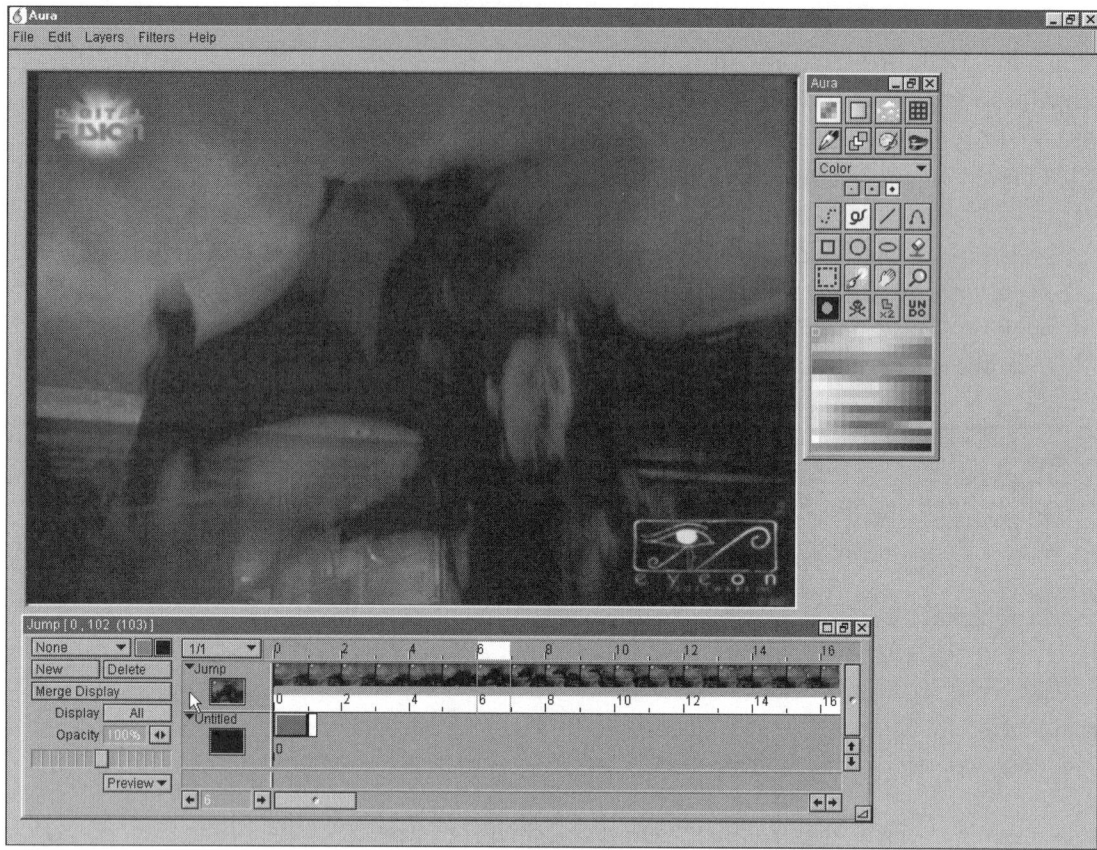

Figure 15.5

The Reverse Selection menu option has been applied to reverse the Jump layer.

Unfortunately, Aura 1.0 isn't really designed for timing manipulation. It just doesn't have the tools you need for the rest of the projects in this chapter. If you want more powerful timing tools for your digital compositing work, you need to use other software.

Chalice And Timing

Many of the timing operations described in this chapter can be executed in Chalice by using the Range parameters of the Disk Input Node. The Range parameters enable you to resequence the frames in the imported footage. You can set new starting and ending frame numbers and skip frames by changing the Increment value. Additionally, you can use the other Range parameters to change the order in which the frames are accessed and to add holds and loops. For more details, see the Chalice 1.6 documentation located in the Chalice folder on the first CD-ROM.

Reversing Footage (Commotion)

The goal of this Commotion-based version of Project 15.1 is to reverse the Jump footage, making the actor appear to leap backward onto the platform.

1. Open a new project. Import the Jump sequence from the second CD-ROM.

2. Choose Calculate|Time|Time Adjust to open the Frame Time Adjust window.

The Time Adjust window contains a graph showing the frame numbers of the footage along one axis and the frame numbers of the comp along the other axis. The original timing of the footage is represented by a diagonal line from the lower left to upper right corners of the graph. You can add, delete, and adjust control points in the graph to vary the timing of the footage. This window is Commotion's primary timing control, and you will use it in most of the projects in this chapter.

3. Drag the leftmost control point to the top of the graph, and drag the rightmost control point to the bottom of the graph. This reverses the slope of the graph, making the footage play back in reverse.

effect* And Reversing Footage

Believe it or not, nothing in the effect* documentation, tutorials, or courseware mentions anything about reversing footage. If you need to reverse footage, you'll need to use Discreet's companion editing software, edit*, or another compositing program.

Shake And Timing

You can perform most of the timing projects in this chapter by creating scripts that use Shake's TimeX function. Refer to the Shake 2.1 documentation in the Shake folder on the second CD-ROM for details on how to write scripts and apply this function.

Changing Speed

Slow-motion or *slo-mo* effects are created in film production by speeding up or *overcranking* the camera. If you shoot film at 48 fps, then project that film at the normal 24 fps, the action will appear to take place at half speed. Cameras used in feature film production can be modified to shoot up to 400 fps, and special high-speed cameras can shoot at even higher rates. Slow-motion effects are common in action films, where the fast action of a fight sequence, explosion, or stunt would otherwise pass far too quickly for the audience to catch it. A less common effect is to *undercrank* or slow down the camera, or to project the film at a faster rate than the film was shot. One familiar use of this fast-motion effect is the city scene of traffic and pedestrians, where the speeded-up footage conveys the sense of modern urban life careening out of control.

Digital Fusion can create both over- and undercranked effects with the Time Speed tool. This can be used to speed up, slow down, reverse, or delay footage.

PROJECT 15.2 Creating Fast-Motion Footage

The goal of this project is to change standard footage into fast-motion footage. This is the simplest approach to shortening footage. This effect is appropriate where you want the final effect to mimic film that is projected at double speed.

1. Load the Timing flow you saved from Project 15.1.

2. Set the Time Speed to the Large display, and set the Loader to the Small display.

3. In the Time Speed controls, uncheck the Image Interpolation box. Set Speed to 2.0 to change the footage to double speed. Set Render Start to 0 and Render End to 51, half the footage's original length. Your flow should look like Figure 15.6.

Figure 15.6
A flow set up to double the speed of the loaded footage.

This will double the apparent speed of the footage by leaving out every other frame of the original footage.

4. Save the flow as Timing2.flw. Render a preview and play it back.

The action won't appear jerky because it is going by so fast, but the missing frames do take away some of the motion blur that is a subliminal cue of speed for your audience. With that small loss of realism, the impression of the fast-motion footage is comic rather than dramatic. This is why dramas that want to convey a sense of speed use slow motion (*The Six Million Dollar Man*) and why productions that use fast motion do better with a humorous tone (*The Flash*).

Creating Fast-Motion Footage (After Effects)

The goal of this After Effects-based version of Project 15.2 is to change standard footage into fast-motion footage. This is the simplest approach to shortening footage. This effect is appropriate where you want the final effect to mimic film that is projected at double speed.

1. Reload the Remap.aep file you saved in After Effects Project 15.1.

2. Move the current-time marker to a frame in the middle of the comp, around 1:22. Click on the keyframe navigator box to add a keyframe at the current time.

3. Drag the new keyframe to the top of the graph, so its value is 03:13. Drag the first keyframe to the bottom of the graph, to value 00:00. Your graph should look like Figure 15.7.

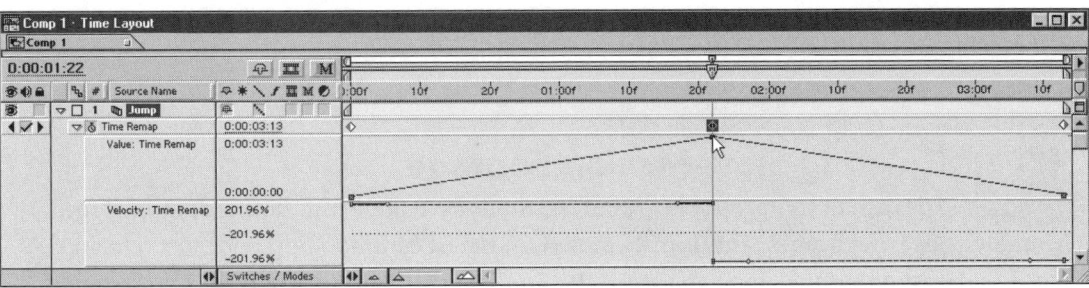

Figure 15.7
The keyframes in the Time Remap Value graph have been modified to accelerate and ping-pong the Jump layer.

This graph makes the Jump layer play back at double speed up to 01:22, then reverse and play back to the beginning at double speed. If you need only the forward portion of the playback, you can delete the keyframe at the right end of the comp and shorten the comp to 01:22. For now, leave the comp at the current length and save it again, to use in the next project.

Creating Fast-Motion Footage (Commotion)

The goal of this Commotion version of Project 15.2 is to change standard footage into fast-motion footage. This is the simplest approach to shortening footage. This effect is appropriate where you want the final effect to mimic film that is projected at double speed.

1. Open a new project. Import the Jump sequence from the second CD-ROM.

2. Choose Calculate|Time|Time Adjust to open the Frame Time Adjust window. The default graph should be a straight diagonal line from lower left to upper right.

3. Add a new control point to the middle of the graph. Drag the new control point to the top of the graph.

This makes the footage play back at double speed, compressing the entire length of the footage into the first half of the comp. This technique doubles the apparent speed of the footage by leaving out every other frame of the original footage.

4. Save the project as Timing2.

Creating Fast-Motion Footage (effect*)

The goal of this effect*-related version of Project 15.2 is to change standard footage into fast-motion footage. This is the simplest approach to shortening footage. This effect is appropriate where you want the final effect to mimic film that is projected at double speed.

1. Open a new project and import the Jump footage from the second CD-ROM.

2. Select the Jump layer. Choose Object|Stretch Layer and enter 50 for the stretch percentage. The Timeline will automatically update.

This technique doubles the apparent speed of the footage by leaving out every other frame of the original footage.

3. Save the project as Timing2.icp.

PROJECT 15.3 Creating Slow-Motion Footage

The goal of this project is to change standard footage into slow-motion footage by repeating the existing frames. This is the simplest and most common approach to stretching footage and is appropriate where you want the final effect to mimic film that is projected at half speed.

1. Reload the Timing2 flow you saved from Project 15.2.

2. In the Time Speed controls, uncheck the Image Interpolation box. Set Speed to 0.5 to change the footage to half speed. Set Render End to 204, double the footage's original length. Your flow should look like Figure 15.8.

If you uncheck the Image Interpolation box, the Time Speed tool will simply duplicate the preceding frame as many times as necessary to fill the new frames. This produces the same effect as projecting the footage in slow motion: each frame is simply held longer.

3. Save your flow as Timing3.flw. Render a preview and play it back.

There is no interpolation or blurring in the new frames to smooth out the slowed-down action, so any fast action may appear stuttered or jerky. Sometimes this is the desired effect, but more often, you will be asked to smooth it out.

Creating Slow-Motion Footage (After Effects)

The goal of this After Effects-related version of Project 15.3 is to change standard footage into slow-motion footage by repeating the existing frames. This is the simplest and most common

Figure 15.8
A flow set up to halve the speed of the footage. Note the Time Speed control with the Speed variable set to 0.5.
This effectively doubles the length of the footage by holding each original frame for two frames.

approach to stretching footage and is appropriate where you want the final effect to mimic film
that is projected at half speed.

1. Reload the Remap.aep file you saved in the preceding project.

2. Press Ctrl+K or choose Composition|Composition Settings to open the Composition Settings
   dialog box. Change the Duration from 03:13 to double, or to 06:26. Click on OK to close the
   dialog box.

3. In the Time Layout window, drag out the length of the Jump layer to cover the full new
   length of the comp.

4. In the Jump layer, delete the Time Remap keyframe at 03:13. Go to 06:26 and create a new
   Time Remap keyframe. Drag the 06:26 keyframe to 03:13, and drag the 00:00 keyframe to
   00:00. Your graph should look like Figure 15.9.

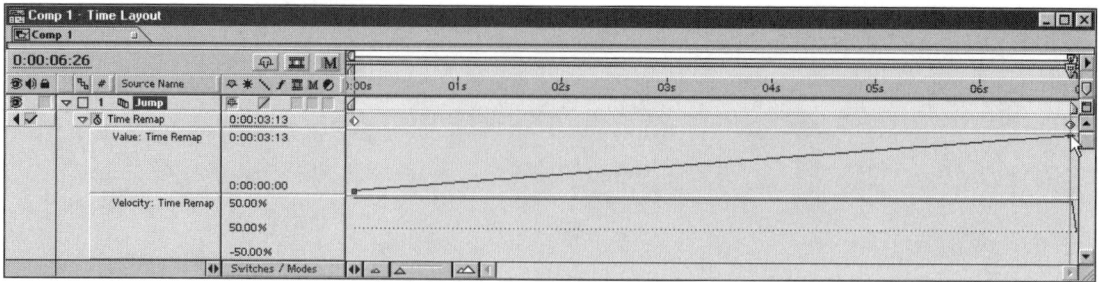

Figure 15.9
The Time Layout window, configured to double the length of the Jump footage to produce slow-motion footage.

5. Play back the comp. Each original frame is held for two frames to create the slow-motion effect. However, there is no interpolation or blurring in the new frames to smooth out the slowed-down action, so any fast action may appear stuttered or jerky. Sometimes this is the effect you want, but more often, you will be asked to smooth it out.

6. Save the project as SloMo.aep. You'll use it in other projects later in this chapter.

Creating Slow-Motion Footage (Commotion)

The goal of this Commotion-related version of Project 15.3 is to change standard footage into slow-motion footage by repeating the existing frames. This is the simplest and most common approach to stretching footage and is appropriate where you want the final effect to mimic film that is projected at half speed.

1. Open a new project. Import the Jump sequence from the second CD-ROM.

2. Choose Calculate|Time|Time Adjust to open the Frame Time Adjust window. The default graph should be a straight diagonal line from lower left to upper right.

3. Drag the leftmost control point from the bottom to halfway up the graph.

This makes the playback start with the middle frame of the footage, stretching out the second half of the footage to cover the entire length of the comp.

4. Save the project as SloMo.

Creating Slow-Motion Footage (effect*)

The goal of this effect*-based version of Project 15.3 is to change standard footage into slow-motion footage by repeating the existing frames. This is the simplest and most common approach to stretching footage and is appropriate where you want the final effect to mimic film that is projected at half-speed.

1. Reload the Timing2.icp project you saved from Project 15.2.

2. Select the Jump layer. Choose Object|Stretch Layer and enter 200 for the stretch percentage. In the Timeline window, drag the right clip marker to the right to fill the dotted outline.

This change simply duplicates each existing frame as many times as necessary to fill the new frames. This produces the same effect as projecting the footage in slow motion: Each frame is simply held longer.

3. Save the project as Timing3.icp.

Filling In The Blanks

The preceding section showed you methods to rearrange or duplicate existing frames to create simple timing effects. More advanced timing effects can require you to interpolate, blend, or otherwise draw from existing frames to create new images that the camera never saw.

The Time Speed tool's Image Interpolation function merges preceding and following frames into the current frame. When stretching footage, this interpolation creates a strobed effect that can simulate the natural motion blur that would have been visible in footage shot with an overcranked camera.

PROJECT 15.4 Slow Motion With Interpolation

The goal of this project is to add image interpolation to the slow-motion footage created in Project 15.3. This will more closely simulate the motion blur present in actual overcranked footage.

1. Reload the Timing3 flow you saved from Project 15.3.

2. In the Time Speed controls, check the Image Interpolation box.

3. Set Speed to 0.25. Set Sample Spread to 0.25.

The strength of the merged frames is controlled by the Sample Spread setting. A setting of 0.5 would merge 50 percent of the preceding frame and 50 percent of the following frame with 0 percent of the current frame. A setting of 0.25 merges 25 percent of the preceding and following frames with 50 percent of the current frame. For stretching footage, you usually want the current frame to be at least 50 percent of the image, so keep the Sample Spread under 0.25.

4. Set Render End to 408. In the Loader, make sure that Missing Frames is set to Hold Previous. Because the image interpolation needs a following frame to interpolate from, your flow needs to provide a frame beyond the end of the footage. Your flow should look like Figure 15.10.

5. Save your flow as Timing4.flw. Render a preview and play it back.

Slow Motion With Interpolation (After Effects)

The goal of this After Effects-based version of Project 15.4 is to add image interpolation to the slow-motion footage created in After Effects Project 15.3. This will more closely simulate the motion blur present in actual overcranked footage.

Figure 15.10

The Large display shows an interpolated frame at a Sample Spread of 0.25, with visible strobing rather than smooth motion blur. The Small display shows the original frame with natural motion blur.

1. Reload the SloMo.aep file you saved from After Effects Project 15.3.

In After Effects, image interpolation is called Frame Blending. This is a proportional mix or blend of the color values of adjoining frames, used to create the new interpolated frames for slow-motion effects. Frame Blending is controlled for an entire comp by the middle icon button in the top row of the Time Layout window, or in the Time Layout Options menu that can be accessed by the right-arrow button at the top right of the Time Layout window. Frame Blending for individual layers is controlled by the Frame Blending switch in each layer's row, directly below the Frame Blending icon button.

2. In the Time Layout window, turn on Frame Blending for the composition, and turn on Frame Blending for the Jump layer.

3. Go to 06:07. Make sure that the Quality switch for the Jump layer is set to Best. In the Composition window, you should see an image resembling Figure 15.11.

Figure 15.11
The Composition window shows the double-exposure effect of Frame Blending for fast-action footage. Note that the comp's Frame Blending button and the Jump layer's switch are both on, and the Quality switch for the Jump layer is set to Best.

4. Go to 04:01. The Composition window shows an interpolated image with much closer overlap, creating a closer approximation of a true motion blur. This is possible because the lower speed of movement created a difference between the original frames that covered a much smaller area.

As you can see, the interpolation of After Effects' Frame Blending feature creates a double-exposure effect when the footage contains very fast action. Unfortunately, there is no built-in option or effect that will increase the sampling to include other frames. This means that a 50/50 blend of the preceding and following frames is the only interpolation available, unless you have third-party plug-ins that can provide more interpolation options.

5. Save your work as SloMo2.aep. You'll need it for another project in this chapter.

Slow Motion With Interpolation (Commotion)

The goal of this Commotion-based version of Project 15.4 is to add image interpolation to the slow-motion footage created in Commotion Project 15.3. This will more closely simulate the motion blur present in actual overcranked footage.

1. Reload the SloMo file you saved from Commotion Project 15.3.

In Commotion, image interpolation is called *Blending*. This is a proportional mix or blend of the color values of adjoining frames, used to create the new interpolated frames for slow-motion effects. Blending is controlled by a checkbox in the Time Adjust window.

2. Choose Calculate|Time|Time Adjust to open the Frame Time Adjust window. In the Time Adjust window, turn on Blend.

As you can see, the interpolation of Commotion's Blend feature creates a double-exposure effect when the footage contains very fast action. Unfortunately, there are no built-in options or effects that increase the sampling to include other frames; the fixed blend of the preceding and following frames is the only interpolation available, unless you have third-party plug-ins that can provide more interpolation options.

3. Save your work as SloMo2. You'll need it for another project in this chapter.

Slow Motion With Interpolation (effect*)

The goal of this effect*-based version of Project 15.4 is to add image interpolation to the slow-motion footage created in effect* Project 15.3. This will more closely simulate the motion blur present in actual overcranked footage.

1. Reload the Timing3.icp file you saved from effect* Project 15.3.

In effect*, image interpolation is called *Frame Blending*. This is a proportional mix or blend of the color values of adjoining frames, used to create the new interpolated frames for slow motion effects. Frame Blending is controlled for all layers of an entire comp by a single Frame Blending menu option.

2. In the Display menu, check the Frame Blending option.

3. Go to 06:07. In the Composition window, you should see an image that resembles Figure 15.12.

4. Go to 04:01. The Composition window shows an interpolated image with much closer overlap, creating a closer approximation of a true motion blur. This is possible because the lower speed of movement created a difference between the original frames that covered a much smaller area.

As you can see, the interpolation of effect*'s Frame Blending feature creates a double-exposure effect when the footage contains very fast action. The interpolated frames at 200 percent are each a 50/50 blend of the preceding and following original frames. If you stretched the footage to 400 percent, Frame Blending would create three new frames based on 25/75, 50/50, and 75/25

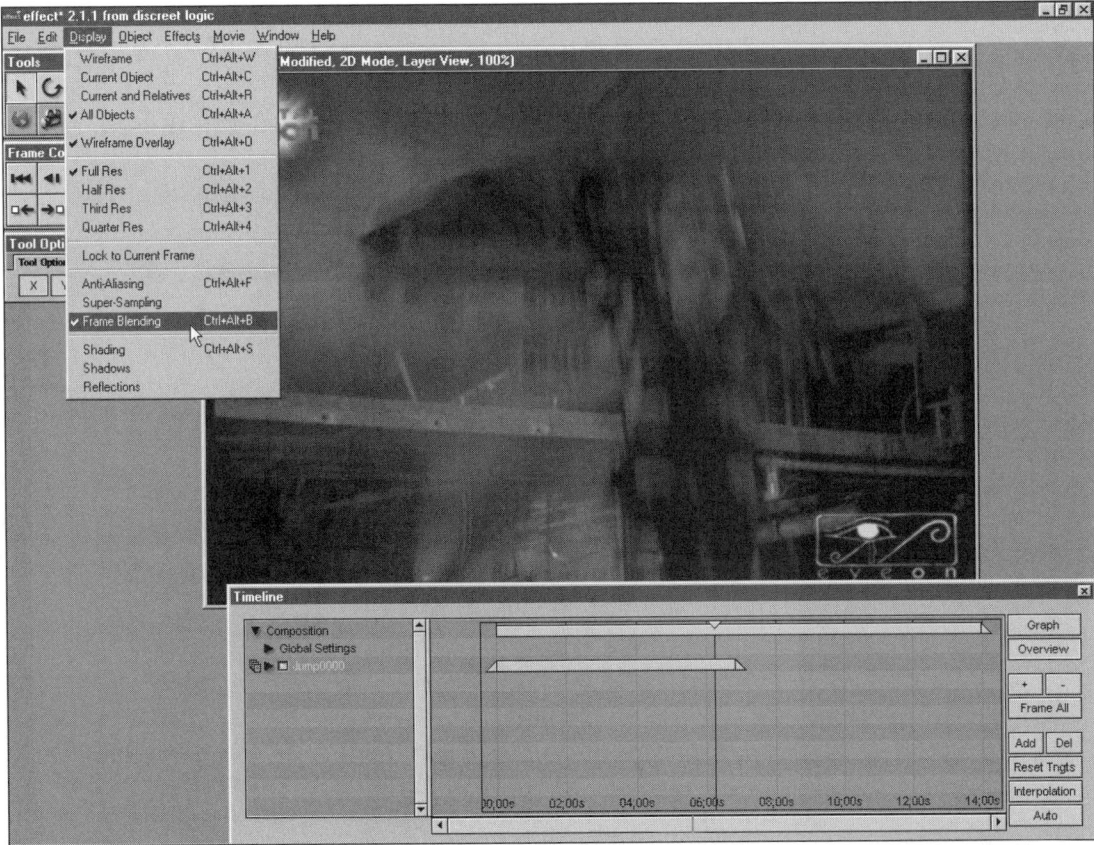

Figure 15.12
The Composition window shows the double-exposure effect of Frame Blending for fast-action footage.

blends of the adjoining original frames. Unfortunately, there is no built-in option or effect that increases the sampling to include other frames. A fixed proportional blend of the preceding and following frames is the only interpolation available, unless you have third-party plug-ins that can provide more interpolation options.

5. Save your work as SloMo2.icp. You'll need it for another project in this chapter.

PROJECT 15.5 Fast Motion With Interpolation

The goal of this project is to add image interpolation to the fast-motion footage created in Project 15.2. This will smooth out the stuttered motion created by dropping every other frame and will more closely simulate the motion blur present in actual undercranked footage.

1. Reload the Timing2 flow you saved from Project 15.2. In the Loader, make sure Missing Frames is set to Hold Previous. Because the image interpolation needs a following frame to interpolate from, your flow needs to provide a frame beyond the end of the footage.

2. In the Time Speed controls, check the Image Interpolation box.

3. Set Speed to 2.0. Set Sample Spread to 0.20.

As you learned in Project 15.4, the strength of the merged frames is controlled by the Sample Spread setting.

4. Set Render End to 51. Your flow should look like Figure 15.13.

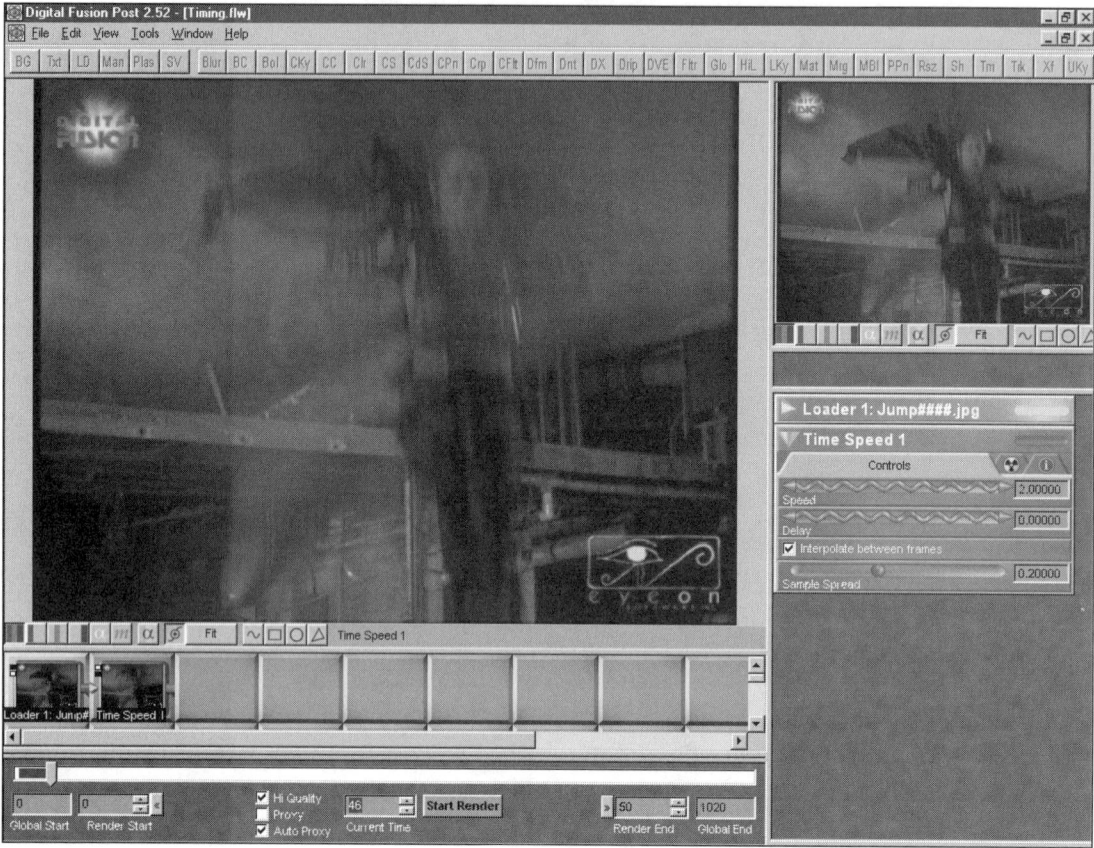

Figure 15.13
The Large display shows an interpolated frame at a Sample Spread of 0.20 for a fast-motion effect.

5. Save your flow as Timing5.flw. Render a preview and play it back.

The interpolated blending of the frames is not as obvious in this fast-motion comp as it is in the slow-motion comp in Project 15.4, but it does add a little more professional finish to the effect, compared to the results of Project 15.2. It only takes a few minutes more to set up and render, and in most cases, the results will be worth that extra time.

Fast Motion With Interpolation (After Effects)

The goal of this After Effects-based version of Project 15.5 is to add image interpolation to the fast-motion footage created in After Effects Project 15.2. This will smooth out the stuttered motion created by dropping every other frame and will more closely simulate the motion blur present in actual undercranked footage.

1. Reload the project file you saved from After Effects Project 15.2.

Frame Blending can be used for fast-motion footage as well as slow motion. The controls are the same, but the results are generally better than for slow motion.

2. In the Time Layout window, turn on Frame Blending for the composition, and turn on the Frame Blending switch for the Jump layer. Make sure that the Quality switch for the Jump layer is set to Best. Go to 01:17. Your screen should look like Figure 15.14.

As you can see, the interpolation of After Effects' Frame Blending feature creates a triple-exposure effect when speeding up the original footage. This is the result of a 25/50/25 percent blend of the two adjoining frames that are omitted, and the single retained frame. This is a little closer to real motion blur. Unfortunately, there is no built-in option or effect that will vary the sampling percentage of the frames or that will include other frames; this is the only interpolation available, unless you have third-party plug-ins that can provide more interpolation options.

Fast Motion With Interpolation (Commotion)

The goal of this Commotion-based version of Project 15.5 is to add image interpolation to the fast-motion footage created in Commotion Project 15.2. This will smooth out the stuttered motion created by dropping every other frame and will more closely simulate the motion blur present in actual undercranked footage.

1. Reload the Timing2 file you saved from Commotion Project 15.2.

2. Choose Calculate|Time|Time Adjust to open the Frame Time Adjust window. In the Time Adjust window, turn on Blend.

The interpolated blending of the frames isn't as obvious in this fast-motion comp as it is in the slow-motion comp in Commotion Project 15.4, but it does add a little more professional finish to the effect compared to the results of Commotion Project 15.2. It only takes a single setting change, and the additional rendering time will probably not be significant. In most cases, the results will be worth that extra time.

3. Save your comp as Timing5.

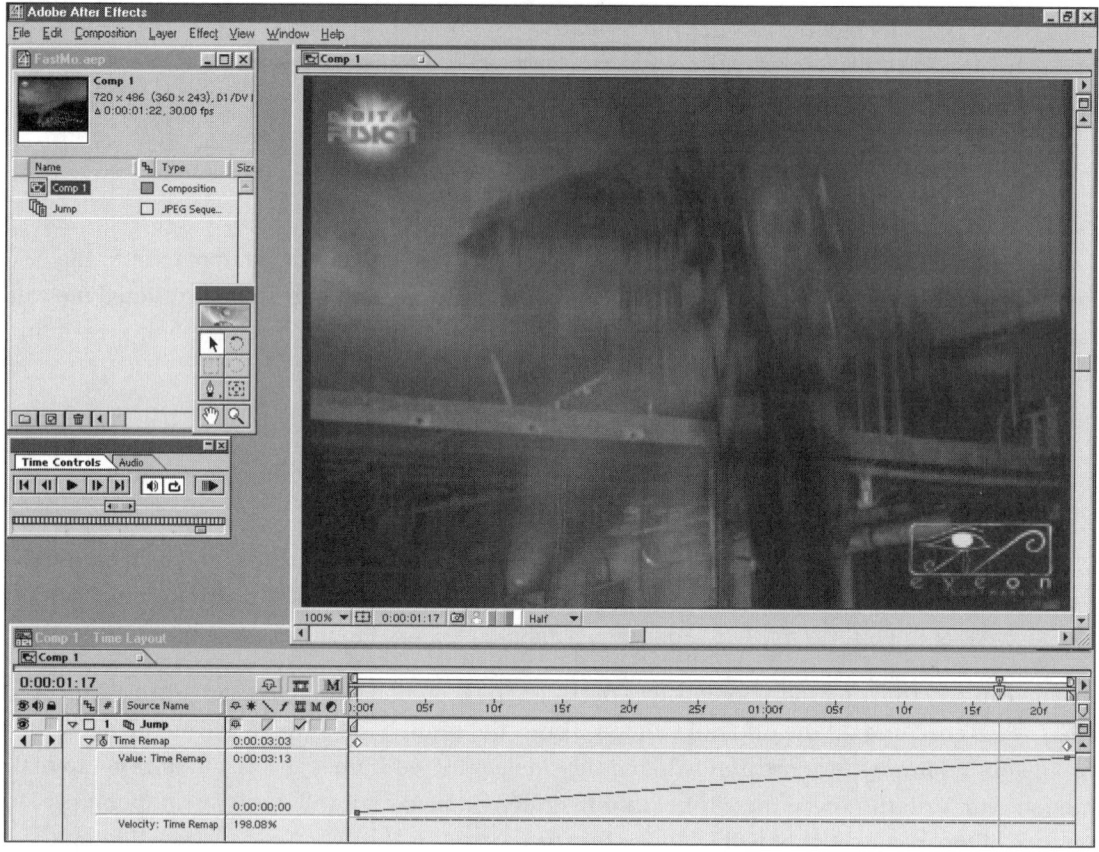

Figure 15.14
The Composition window shows the triple-exposure effect of Frame Blending for images interpolated to create fast-motion footage.

Fast Motion With Interpolation (effect*)

The goal of this effect*-based version of Project 15.5 is to add image interpolation to the fast-motion footage created in effect* Project 15.2. This smoothes out the stuttered motion created by dropping every other frame and more closely simulates the motion blur present in actual undercranked footage.

1. Reload the Timing2.icp file you saved from effect* Project 15.2.

2. Enable the Frame Blending option by either pressing Ctrl+Alt+B or choosing Display|Frame Blending.

3. Save your comp as Timing5.icp. Render the comp to RAM and play it back.

The interpolated blending of the frames is not as obvious in this fast-motion comp as it is in the slow-motion comp in effect* Project 15.4, but it does add a little more professional finish to the effect compared to the results of effect* Project 15.2. It only takes a single setting change, and the additional rendering time will probably not be significant. In most cases, the results are worth that extra time.

Motion Blur

Whenever an object is moving faster than the shutter speed of the camera, that object appears blurred in the film or video image. This is called *motion blur,* and it is an important visual cue for the speed and direction of an action. Whenever you are comping a timing effect, you should try to simulate motion blur.

One very important factor in simulating motion blur is to blur only those portions of the image that are actually moving. Static backgrounds and other elements that are near, in front of, or behind the moving objects should not be affected by the blur. This can be a challenge, especially with complex elements such as actors. It isn't usually feasible to resort to pulling a matte or hand-rotoscoping a mask solely for the purpose of adding motion blur to a timing effect. Instead, you should know at least one way to fake a motion blur with a minimum of effort.

PROJECT 15.6 Faking Motion Blur

The goal of this project is to add motion blur to only the moving objects in a slow-motion comp, leaving the static background in sharp focus. The motion blur will smooth out the strobed appearance of the image interpolation used in Project 15.4.

1. Reload the Timing3 flow you saved from Project 15.3.

2. In the Time Speed controls, check the Image Interpolation box.

3. Set Speed to 0.5. Set Sample Spread to 0.5.

This is the maximum Sample Spread setting, which replaces the current frame with 50 percent of the preceding frame and 50 percent of the following frame. If you direct the output of this tool to the Large display and go to frame 182, you should see something like Figure 15.15.

4. Set Render End to 204. In the Loader, make sure that Missing Frames is set to Hold Previous. Because the image interpolation needs a following frame to interpolate from, your flow needs to provide a frame beyond the end of the footage.

5. Add a second Time Speed tool below the first one, and connect a second branch from the Loader to this second Time Speed tool.

6. In the Time Speed 2 controls, set Speed to 0.5 and uncheck the Image Interpolation box. The output from this tool should look like Figure 15.16.

7. Add a Channel Booleans tool in the third column to the right of the Time Speed 2 tool. Connect Time Speed 1 to the foreground input, and connect Time Speed 2 to the background input. In the Channel Booleans control, set Operation to Difference. The output of the Channel Booleans tool should look like Figure 15.17.

Figure 15.15
Frame 182 output from the Time Speed 1 control, showing its 50-50 merge of preceding and following frames.

Figure 15.16
Frame 182 output from the Time Speed 2 control, showing no interpolation from adjoining frames. Note the amount of natural motion blur present in this footage.

Figure 15.17
The output from the Channel Booleans tool shows the color differences (movement) between the interpolated Time Speed 1 and the original footage from Time Speed 2.

8. The next step is to convert this color difference into a matte that can be used to limit the area affected by the motion blur. Add a Luma Keyer to the right of the Channel Booleans tool and connected to it.

9. Send the Luma Keyer output to the Large display, and choose the alpha channel viewing option for the Large display. In the Luma Keyer controls, adjust the gamma, contrast, and threshold to get a clear matte of the movement. Your flow should look like Figure 15.18.

10. Add a Dissolve tool two columns to the right and one row below the Time Speed 2 tool. The output of the Dissolve tool should look like Figure 15.19. Connect Time Speed 2 to the foreground input, and connect Time Speed 1 to the background input, as shown in Figure 15.20. In the Dissolve controls, set Operation to Dissolve and set the Background/Foreground slider to 0.5.

11. Add a Blur/Sharpen tool to the right of the Dissolve tool and connected to it.

12. In the Blur/Sharpen controls, right-click on the control header and choose Effect Mask|Bitmap from the pop-up menu. A Bitmap mask control appears in the effect mask area, as shown in the upper right corner of Figure 15.20.

Figure 15.18
A motion blur flow showing Time Speed, Channel Booleans, and Luma Keyer controls.

13. Open the Bitmap 1 controls. Halfway down is a slot marked "Drop Tools Here." In the Flow area, left-click and drag the Luma Keyer tool, and drop it in the Drop Tools Here slot of the Bitmap 1 controls. Still in Bitmap 1, set the Channel control to Alpha.

The actions that you took in step 13 tells the Blur/Sharpen tool to use the alpha channel of the Luma Keyer as an effect mask. Only the light areas of the Luma Keyer's output will be blurred, and the dark areas will remain in sharp focus.

Figure 15.19
The output of the Dissolve tool for frame 182. Note the strobing effect of the interpolated frames, especially the actor's arms.

14. Adjust the Blur/Sharpen controls until you're satisfied with the quality of the blur. You may want to toggle the Invert box in the Bitmap 1 controls, just to compare the blur effects in different areas of the mask. Your final rendered results should look something like Figure 15.21.

If you want a more precise blur control, you can substitute the Motion Blur tool for the Blur/Sharpen tool. The Motion Blur tool enables you to adjust and animate the direction and length of the blur for more realistic results with little additional effort.

If setting up this flow seems like too much bother, and you've got the cash, you might want to look at the 5D Monster MoBlur plug-in (**www.5-d.com**). It produces results (like the demo example shown in Figure 15.22) straight from the Time Speed 2 output. The downside (other than cost) is that each frame averaged 19 seconds to render with the MoBlur plug-in, versus 6 seconds with this project's flow. However, the controls for the MoBlur plug-in give you a great deal of flexibility in balancing output quality against rendering time.

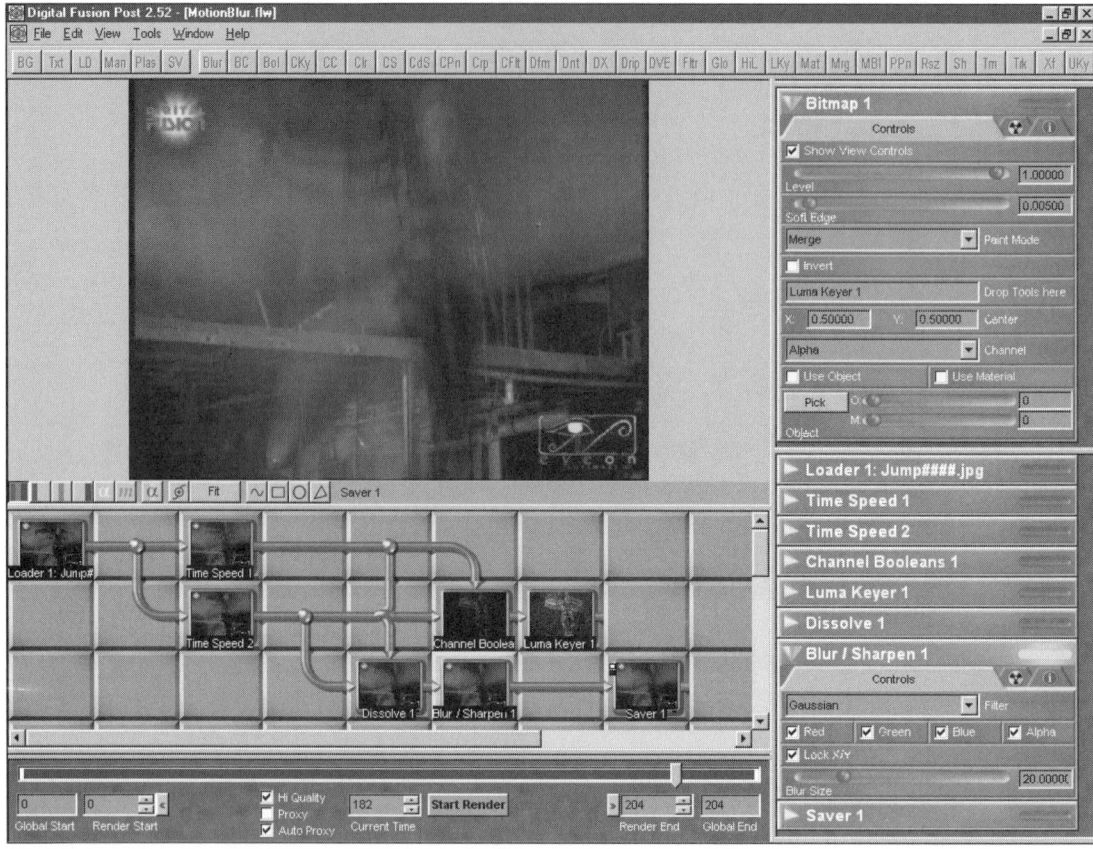

Figure 15.20
The completed motion blur flow, showing Bitmap and Blur controls.

Faking Motion Blur (After Effects)

The goal of this After Effects-based version of Project 15.6 is to add motion blur to only the moving objects in a slow-motion comp, leaving the static background in sharp focus. The motion blur will smooth out the strobed appearance of the image interpolation used in After Effects Project 15.4.

1. Reload the SloMo2.aep file you saved from After Effects Project 15.4.

2. Copy and paste the Jump layer in the Time Layout window, creating a second layer that is a duplicate of the first layer. This will provide a difference layer for the original Jump layer.

3. Drag the new layer to the left two frames, creating a single-image offset between the layers. This creates a difference between the current frame in the first Jump layer and the offset frame in the duplicated layer. Your Time Layout window should look like Figure 15.23.

Figure 15.21
The final interpolated, difference-masked, and blurred rendering for frame 182.

Figure 15.22
Output of 5D Monster MoBlur plug-in for frame 182.

Figure 15.23
The Time Layout window showing an offset duplicate of the Jump layer.

4. Select the first Jump layer. Add a Difference Matte effect. In the Effect Controls window, select View|Matte Only. Choose 2.Jump from the Difference Layer menu and adjust the Matching Tolerance to around 5.0 percent. The difference matte between the first and second Jump layers should be visible in the Composition window, as shown in Figure 15.24. The purpose of this matte is to black out as much of the background as possible and to leave in as much of the actor as possible. The noisy background with drifting smoke and variable lighting makes this blocking more difficult, but 5 percent is a good tradeoff.

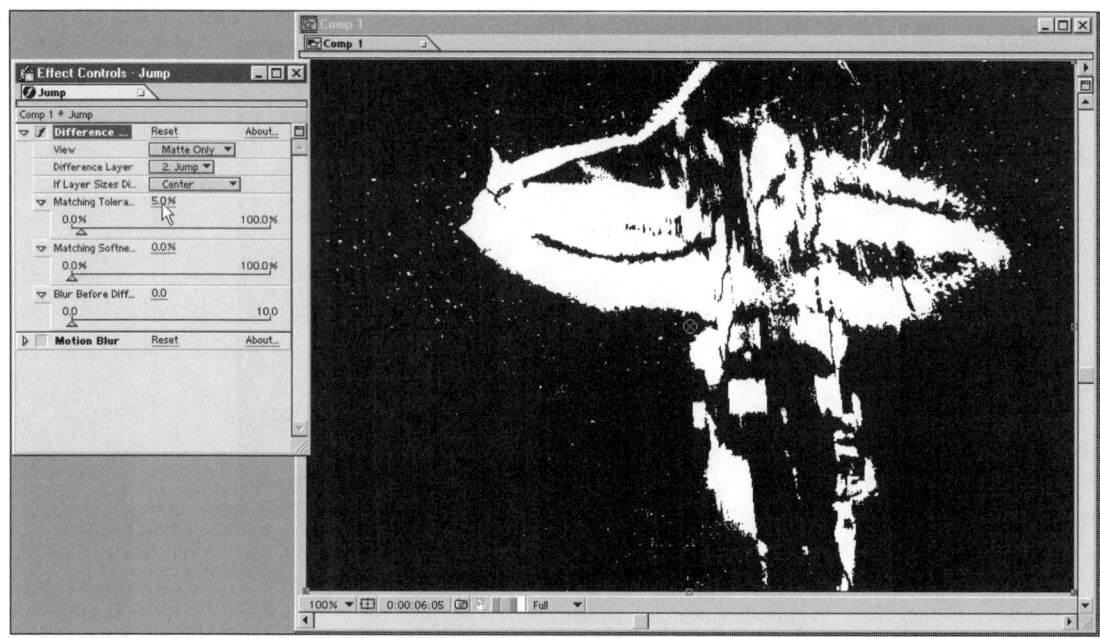

Figure 15.24
The Effect Controls window shows the Difference Matte effect settings, and the Composition window shows the results of a difference matte between the original and offset Jump layers.

5. Add a Motion Blur effect to the first Jump layer. In the Effect Controls window, set the Direction of the blur to about 165 degrees, the direction of the actor's fall. Set the Blur Length to the maximum of 20. Set the View option in the Difference Matte controls to Final Output. Your results should look like Figure 15.25.

Figure 15.25
The Effect Controls window shows the Motion Blur effect settings, and the Composition window shows the results of the motion blur applied only to the difference between the original and offset Jump layers.

Note that the motion blur is restricted to the area of the difference matte, leaving the rest of the image unblurred. The results aren't a perfect simulation of true motion blur, but they are very close. With fast-moving footage, it would take a well-trained eye to spot the difference.

6. Save your work as MoBlur.aep.

effect* And Faking Motion Blur

Discreet effect* does not currently support the type of difference matte extraction necessary for this project. If you need this feature, you need to use other software.

Happy Trails

One mark of a truly professional artist is to turn a problem into a solution. The interpolation stuttering "problem" described in Project 15.3 is exactly the effect you want if you are called on to simulate the images produced by series-fired strobe lamps. This effect has been used to simulate drug-induced hallucinations, connote superhuman speed, accent modern dance performances, and illustrate documentaries that include rapid motion.

PROJECT 15.7 Faking Strobe Lights

The goal of this project is to add strobe lighting effects to the action, creating a trail of partial images blended from past frames.

1. Open a new flow, add a Loader, and load appropriate footage.

This effect looks better if the moving foreground elements are well lit and in high contrast to a darker background. A locked-down (or, at most, slowly moving) camera is best. The faster the foreground object moves, the stronger the strobing effect and the fewer Time Speed tools you will need. For this project, I rendered 70 frames of the GirlSide footage with a right-to-left pan transform.

2. Add a Time Speed tool to the right of the Loader, and connect it to the Loader.

3. In the Time Speed controls, set the Delay to 2, check Interpolate, and set Sample Spread to 0.25.

4. Copy and paste the Time Speed tool twice to the right of the first one, and connect all three Time Speed tools in series. Set the last Time Speed tool to the Large display. Your flow should look like Figure 15.26.

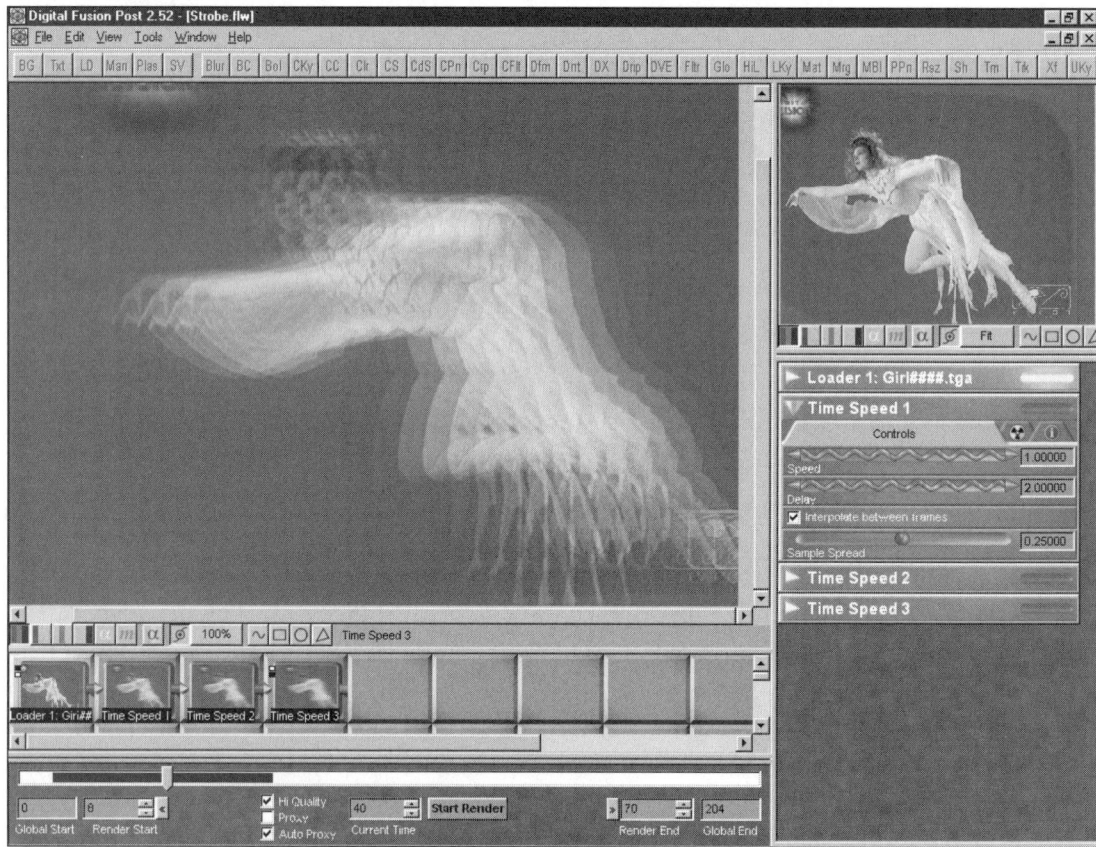

Figure 15.26
Strobe lighting effect simulated with a series of Time Speed tools.

Each Time Speed tool contributes two interpolated images to the flow, but the two-frame offset between each tool makes some of the interpolated images overlap. You should be able to pick out all six interpolated images if you look closely. You can use this effect as a precomp, then comp it behind the original footage to leave a "trail" behind the moving subject. You can also use this effect as is, especially for footage with subjects that accelerate and decelerate. When an object slows, the interpolated images move closer together; when an object speeds up, the trail spreads out.

This effect is extremely Loader-intensive, because each Time Speed tool tasks the Loader for the current frame, the offset frame, and the frames before and after the offset frame. If the Loader is also decompressing the image or loading from a CD-ROM, those tasks are multiplied as well. For these reasons, this effect is best rendered as a precomp, and the source footage should be located on a local, fast hard drive in an uncompressed format.

Faking Strobe Lights (After Effects)

You can add strobe lighting effects to action footage, creating a trail of partial images blended from past frames, simply by applying the Echo plug-in included with the standard After Effects program. You can set up to 10 echoes and vary the initial intensity and decay (fade-off) of the sampled images' effect on the current frame. Depending on the effect you want, you may prefer this plug-in to the interpolation and motion blur effects you explored in After Effects Projects 15.5 and 15.6.

effect* And Faking Strobe Lights

Discreet effect* doesn't currently support the multiple-frame interpolation necessary for this project. If you need this feature, you need to use other software.

Stretching Time

The Time Speed tool is useful for timing changes that are consistent throughout a flow. However, there are many circumstances in which you will want to animate timing effects. Those comps call for a more powerful timing tool, the Time Stretcher. The Time Stretcher tool, like the Time Speed tool, causes all tools preceding it in a flow to repeatedly load and process for the current, offset, and interpolated frames. Therefore, you should always render Time Stretcher effects as precomps. The Time Stretcher is similar to the Time Speed tool in several other ways. The Interpolate checkbox and the Sample Spread slider function the same as in the Time Speed tool. As before, keep Sample Spread under 0.25 for smoothest interpolation in most cases, and turn off Interpolation if you want a strong strobe or stutter effect.

The Source Time screw control can be set to a particular value, but a more versatile control of this Time Stretcher parameter is to animate it using a Bézier spline. Figure 15.27 shows the Spline Editor containing the spline for Time Stretcher 1: Source Time. The vertical numbers on the left side of the graph represent the source time, the original frame numbers of the footage in the

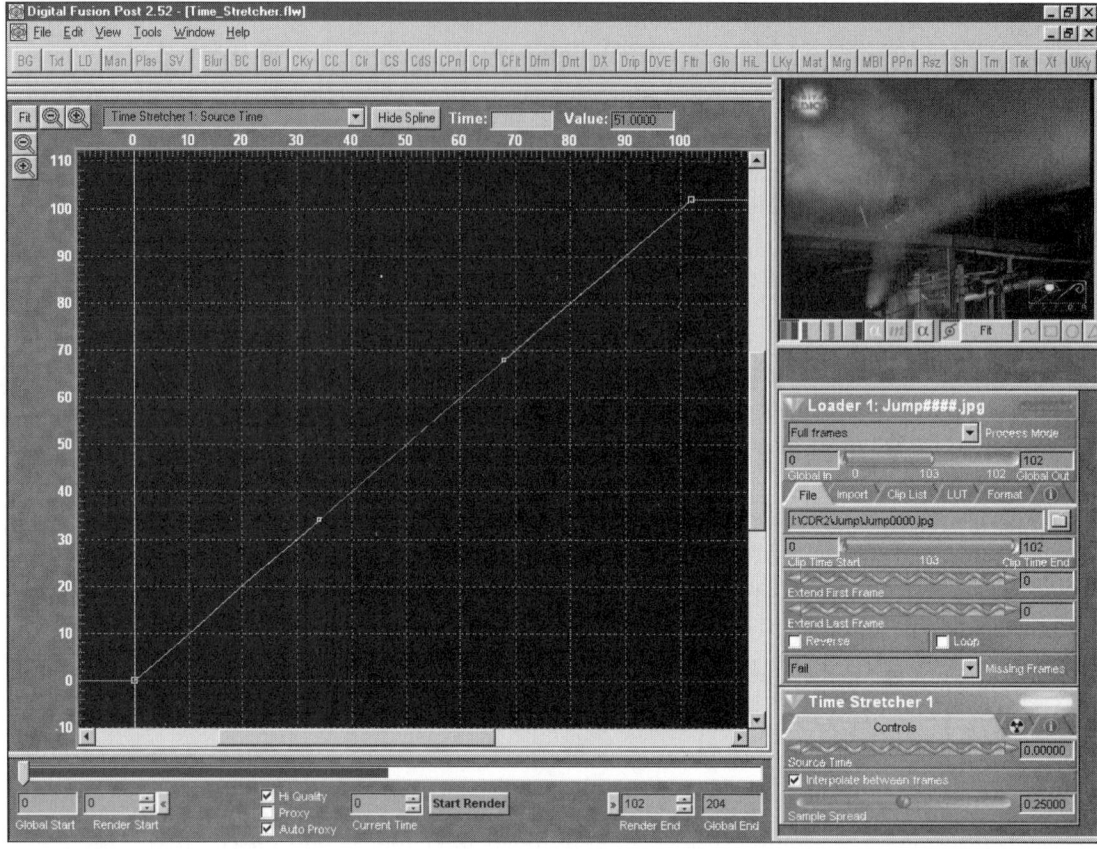

Figure 15.27
The Spline Editor showing Linear, one-to-one slope of Time Stretcher 1: Source Time spline from frame 0,0 to frame 102,102, which means no change in the speed of the input footage.

Loader. The horizontal numbers across the top of the graph represent the current time, the frame numbers that are output by the Time Stretcher tool. If the Time Stretcher is not making any changes to the timing of the footage, the vertical and horizontal numbers in the Spline Editor should correspond one-to-one, making the spline a straight 45-degree line, as shown in Figure 15.27.

You can select control points in the Spline Editor by left-clicking on individual points, or by dragging a selection box around several points. If you want to select all the points in a spline, you can press Ctrl+A, or right-click and choose Select All from the pop-up menu. The spline between the control points is shaped either by Linear, or straight-line, interpolation or by Smooth interpolation. Linear produces results like Figure 15.27. Smooth produces splines like Figure 15.28.

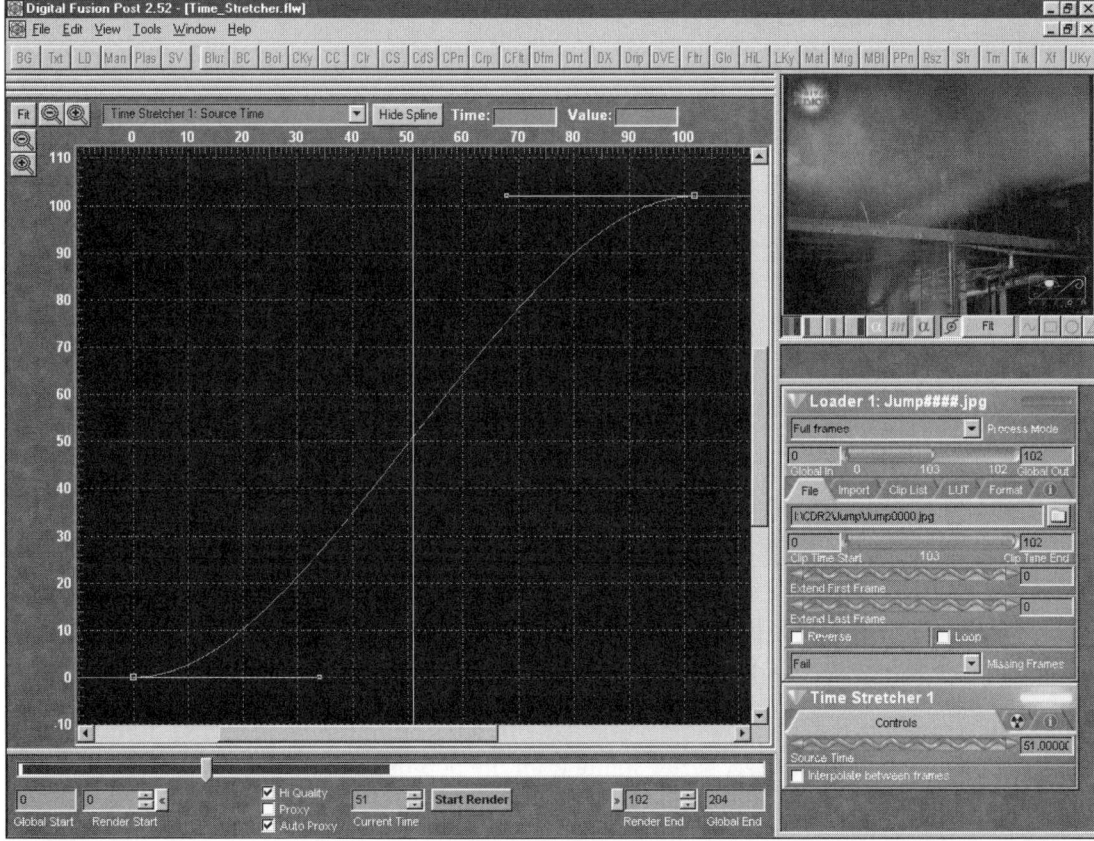

Figure 15.28
The Spline Editor showing Smooth interpolated slope of Time Stretcher 1: Source Time spline. The gradual upward curve to the right of frame 0 means slower output time at the beginning of the footage. The output time exactly matches the source time at frame 51, the halfway point. From frame 52 to around frame 90, the output time is running faster than the source time, then slows at the top of the curve to match the source time again at the last frame.

You can also change the interpolation of a control point by grabbing the control point's handles and moving them with the mouse. This automatically changes Linear to Smooth interpolation, and it enables you to interactively shape the spline by changing the angle and length of the handle.

UP IS FAST, SIDEWAYS IS SLOW

For a Time Stretcher in the Spline Editor, a vertical spline speeds up the footage; a horizontal spline slows it down.

PROJECT 15.8 Animating A Speed Change

The goal of this project is to maintain the speed of the Jump footage up to the beginning of the jump, then to slow the jump to half-speed.

1. Open a new flow. Add a Loader, and load the Jump footage from the second CD-ROM.

2. Add a Time Stretcher tool to the right of the Loader, and connect it to the Loader.

3. Right-click on the Time Stretcher control header, and choose Edit Splines from the pop-up menu.

4. Press F8 to maximize the Spline Editor View. Send the Time Stretcher output to the Small display.

5. In the Spline Editor, set keyframes at 0, 0; 72, 72; and 132, 102.

These keyframes will maintain the source speed up to frame 72, at which point the actor is jumping. The source keyframe of 102 is stretched to frame 132, making the remaining 30 source frames cover 60 frames and thereby making the jump appear to have been filmed in slow motion.

6. Select all keyframes and choose Linear interpolation.

7. Set Render End to 132, and leave Render Start at 0. Your flow should look like Figure 15.29.

You can also animate the Interpolation check mark and the Sample Spread setting. Simply right-click on either control, then select Bézier Spline from the pop-up menu. This can be very useful if you are dealing with footage with a variety of timing changes.

8. Animate the Interpolation check mark to be Off in frames 0 through 72, and On in frames 73 through 132.

Alternatively, you could animate Sample Spread to be 0.0 in frames in the normal-speed segment, and 0.25 in the slow-motion segment. Either way, you will preserve the sharp image of the source footage in the early portion of the output footage and provide the necessary interpolation to reduce strobing in the slow-motion portion.

9. Save your flow as Time_Stretcher.flw.

Animating A Speed Change (After Effects)

The goal of this After Effects-based version of Project 15.8 is to maintain the speed of the Jump footage up to the beginning of the jump, then to slow the jump to half speed.

1. Reload the SloMo.aep file you saved from After Effects Project 15.3.

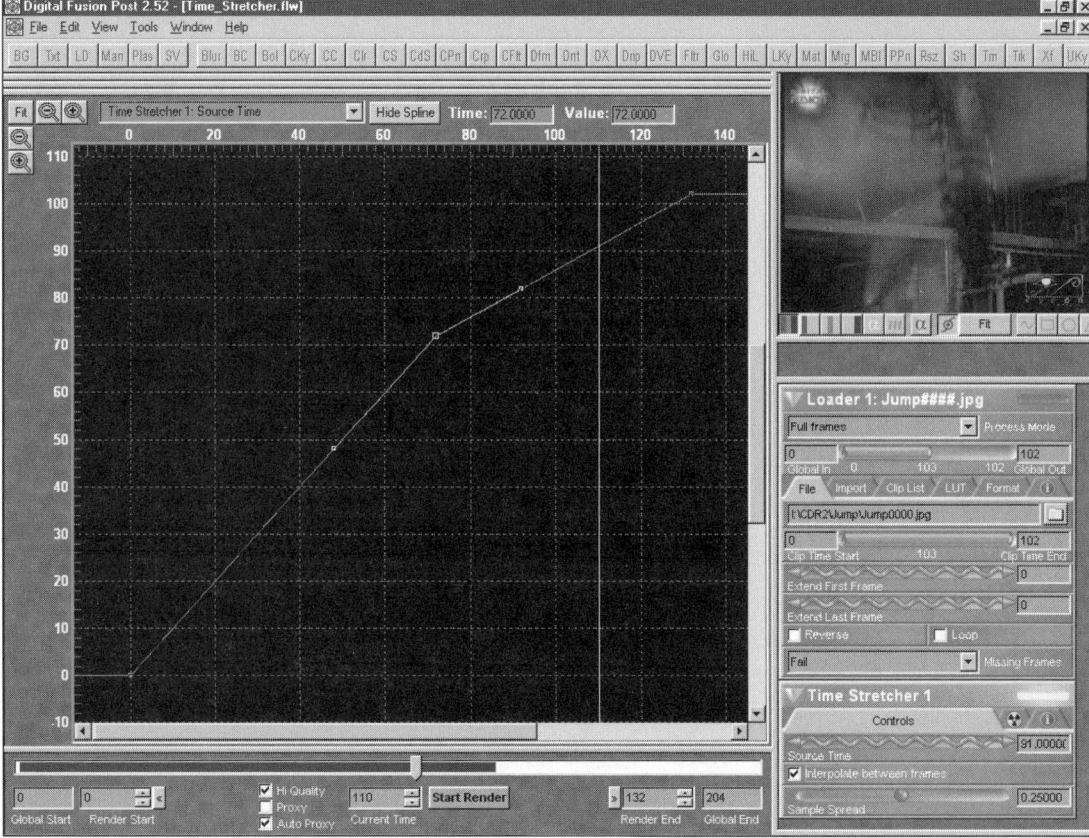

Figure 15.29
The Spline Editor shows the keyframed slope of the Time Stretcher 1: Source Time spline. The output time exactly matches the source time from frame 0 through frame 72. From frame 72 to frame 132, the output time is running half as fast as the source time. The effect is that the actor runs full speed to the edge, then jumps in slow motion.

2. In the Time Layout window, go to time 03:13. Expand the Jump layer. In the Time Remap row, drag the final keyframe marker (which should be located at 06:26) to 3:13. This restores the timing of the original footage, then holds the last frame until the end of the comp. Your Time Layout window should look like the top image in Figure 15.30.

3. Scrub the time control to find the frame when the jump starts. I found it to be 02:10, but your results may vary. With the time control slider at your chosen frame, click on the keyframe navigator to set a new keyframe. The new keyframe automatically assumes the current value of the graph line; it's like sticking a thumbtack through a string to keep it in place. Your graph should look like the middle image of Figure 15.30.

4. Drag the last keyframe from 03:13 back to 06:26. This makes the footage after the 02:10 keyframe run at slow-motion speed. Your graph should look like the lower image in Figure 15.30.

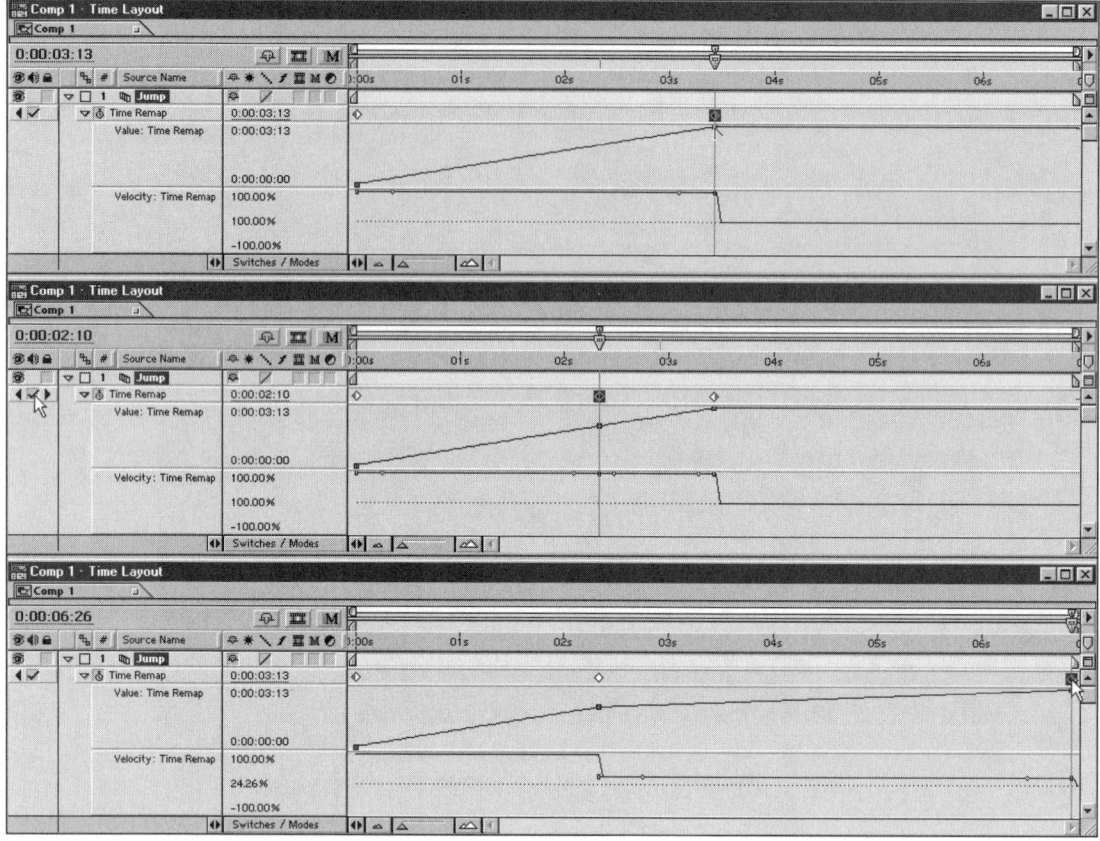

Figure 15.30
Top, the Time Layout window with the timing of the Jump footage restored. Middle, 02:10 keyframe set to nail down the start of the jump. Bottom, the frames after 02:10 set for slow-motion speed.

5. Play back the comp. You can adjust the timing of the slow-motion transition by dragging the middle keyframe horizontally to different times or by dragging the Value:Time Remap handle vertically to different values. When you are satisfied with the timing of the comp, save your work as Variable.aep.

Animating A Speed Change (Commotion)

The goal of this Commotion-based version of Project 15.8 is to maintain the speed of the Jump footage up to the beginning of the jump, then to slow the jump to half speed.

1. Open a new project. Import the Jump sequence from the second CD-ROM.

2. Choose Calculate|Time|Time Adjust to open the Frame Time Adjust window.

This window is Commotion's primary timing control. The original timing of the footage is represented by a diagonal line from the lower left to upper right corners of the graph. You can add, delete, and adjust control points in the graph to vary the timing of the footage.

3. Scrub the time control to find the frame when the jump starts. I found it to be frame 69, but your results may vary.

4. Add a control point to the Time Adjust graph to nail frame 69 at its original location. The graph slope from frame 1 to frame 69 should remain unchanged.

5. Drag the last frame's control point down halfway to the level of frame 69. This makes frames 70 and higher play back in slow motion.

6. Play back the comp. Experiment with adding and rearranging control points in the Time Adjust window to vary the speed and direction of the footage.

effect* And Animating A Speed Change

Discreet effect* currently doesn't enable you to animate or modify the stretching of a layer over time. If you need this feature, you need to use either Discreet's companion editing software (edit*) or another compositing program.

PROJECT 15.9 Useful Spline Tricks

When you have a complex spline animation set up and want to repeat it, you can copy and paste the spline keyframes to create looping animations.

1. Press Ctrl+A or drag a selection box over all the points in the spline to be looped.

2. Hold down the Ctrl key, then left-click and drag the leftmost point on the spline. You should notice that the mouse cursor changes to the barred circle NO symbol. This tells you that you can't drop the copied keyframes on the current frame.

3. Keep dragging the copied keyframes to the right, beyond the last keyframe of the existing spline. As soon as you pass the last keyframe, the mouse cursor changes to the "Add Document" symbol.

4. Release the copied keyframes on the desired frame.

5. You have now duplicated the animation once. Zoom out, if necessary, to see all the keyframes. Repeat steps 2 through 4 as needed to create as many iterations of the animation as you wish.

In addition to the looping animation you just created, you can make an animation parameter "ping-pong" or alternate between forward and backward iterations.

6. After you paste a duplicate set of keyframes as in step 4, press V or right-click and choose Reverse from the pop-up menu.

The selected keyframes will reverse themselves. Incidentally, this is an excellent way to get a symmetrical spline. Simply set the keyframes for the first half of the spline, copy and paste them, and invert the copies.

After Effects And Useful Spline Tricks

The After Effects User Guide has several helpful sections on copying, pasting, and modifying individual keyframes and entire graphs, including the use of Bézier spline handles for fine-tuning Velocity graphs.

effect* And Useful Spline Tricks

Discreet effect* does not use splines to control the timing of layers. If you need this feature, you need to use Discreet's companion editing software (edit*) or another compositing program.

 ## Do The Jerk

On occasion, you may be asked to mimic the effect of stop-motion animation. Animation is commonly shot "on twos"—that is, every image is repeated twice. Limited animation is sometimes shot "on fours," which means that every image is held for four frames. You can mimic this effect fairly easily with the Time Stretcher.

1. Open a new flow. Add a Loader, and load the Jump footage. Set Global Out to 100 to limit the footage to frames 0 through 100.

2. Add a Time Stretcher, and connect it to the Loader. Add a second Time Stretcher, and connect it to the output of the first one.

3. Turn off Interpolation for both Time Stretchers.

4. At frame 0, set a keyframe for the Source Time of Time Stretcher 1 with a value of 0. Repeat for Time Stretcher 2.

5. At frame 25 (one fourth of the footage length), set another keyframe for the Source Time of Time Stretcher 1 with a value of 100 (the full clip length).

This will speed up the output footage of Time Stretcher 1 to be four times faster than the source footage from the Loader.

6. At frame 100, set a keyframe for the Source Time of Time Stretcher 2 with a value of 25. Your flow should look like Figure 15.31.

This will slow down the output footage of Time Stretcher 2 to be four times slower than the source footage from Time Stretcher 1. Because there is no interpolation, and only one in four frames is passed through Time Stretcher 1, Time Stretcher 2 will output each source frame four times in succession. This duplicates the limited animation technique of shooting "on fours." You can experiment with different holding rates by changing the keyframes and values in steps 5 and 6. If you keep the values and keyframes in a reciprocal relation, your results should be consistent.

Do The Jerk (After Effects)

Occasionally, you may be asked to mimic the effect of stop-motion animation. Animation is commonly shot "on twos"—that is, every image is repeated twice. Limited animation is sometimes shot "on fours," which means that every image is held for four frames. You can mimic

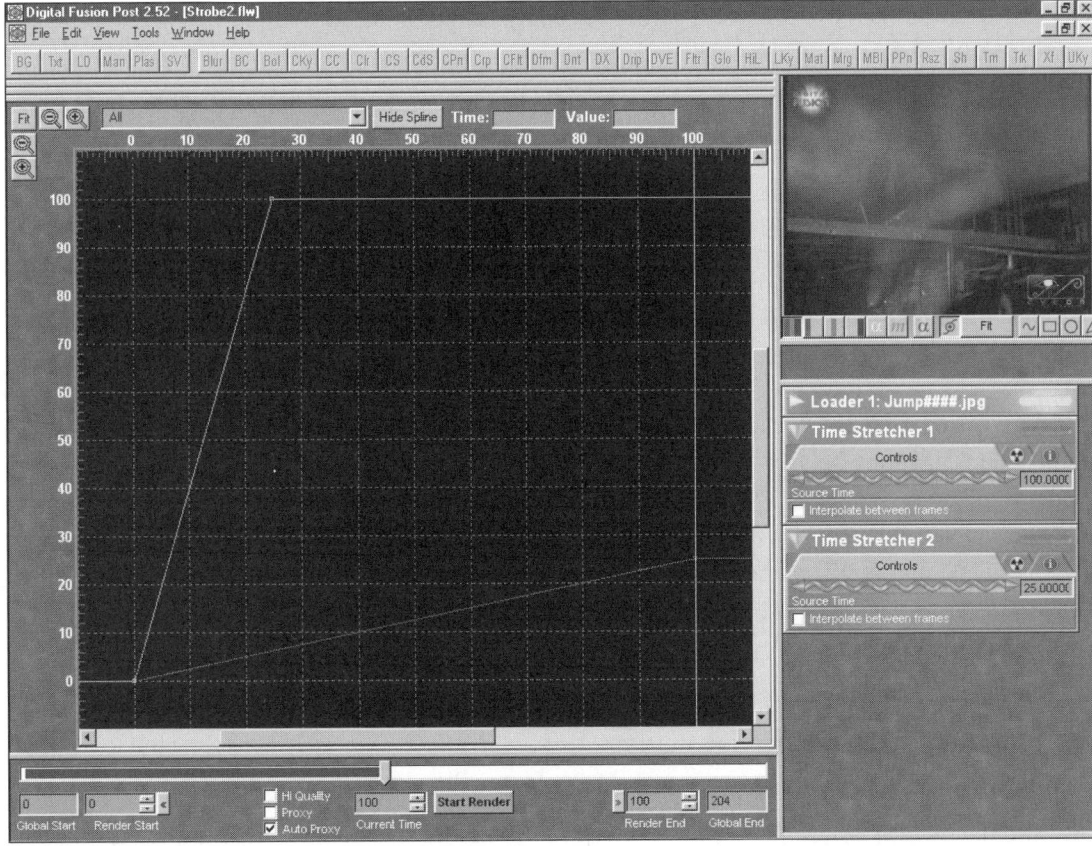

Figure 15.31
The Spline Editor shows the splines of Time Stretcher 1 and Time Stretcher 2 keyframed to create four-frame holds.

this effect fairly easily with After Effects' Time Remap. Here's the After Effects-based version of Project 15.10:

1. Follow the Time Remap procedure you learned in After Effects Project 15.2 to speed up the Jump footage by a factor of 4. Render the comp to a temporary directory.

2. Follow the Time Remap procedure you learned in After Effects Project 15.3 to slow down the footage you rendered in step 1 by a factor of 4.

This has the effect of dropping every second, third, and fourth frame from the original footage, creating the same jerkiness as animation shot "on fours."

Do The Jerk (Commotion)

Occasionally, you may be asked to mimic the effect of stop-motion animation. Animation is commonly shot "on twos"—that is, every image is repeated twice. Limited animation is sometimes shot "on fours," which means that every image is held for four frames. You can mimic this effect fairly easily with Commotion's layer stretching. Here's the Commotion-based version of Project 15.10:

1. Follow the layer stretching procedure you learned in Commotion Project 15.2 to speed up the Jump footage by a factor of 4. Leave Blend turned off. Render the comp to a temporary directory.

2. Follow the layer stretching procedure you learned in Commotion Project 15.3 to slow down the footage you rendered in step 1 by a factor of 4. Leave Blend turned off.

This has the effect of dropping every second, third, and fourth frame from the original footage, creating the same jerkiness as animation shot "on fours."

Do The Jerk (effect*)

On occasion, you may be asked to mimic the effect of stop-motion animation. Animation is commonly shot "on twos"—that is, every image is repeated twice. Limited animation is sometimes shot "on fours," which means that every image is held for four frames. You can mimic this effect fairly easily with effect*'s layer stretching. Here's the effect*-based version of Project 15.10:

1. Follow the layer stretching procedure you learned in effect* Project 15.2 to speed up the Jump footage by a factor of 4. Leave Frame Blending turned off. Render the comp to a temporary directory.

2. Follow the layer stretching procedure you learned in effect* Project 15.3 to slow the footage you rendered in step 1 by a factor of 4. Leave Frame Blending turned off.

This has the effect of dropping every second, third, and fourth frame from the original footage, creating the same jerkiness as animation shot "on fours."

Moving On

This chapter presented a number of techniques for changing the timing of footage. You should now be able to apply these techniques to solve problems, to prepare for other compositing effects, or to make a storytelling point more effectively. This chapter completes Part V of this book. The next part shows you how to wrap up your comps in a finished production, then output them to tape or prepare them for the big screen.

PART VI

OUTPUT

THAT'S A WRAP

Even the most talented and creative digital compositors may not be capable of meeting deadlines and delivering the final product if they don't plan and optimize their work. Difficult or ambiguous comps can eat up your time until, even when the comp is set up, you don't have enough time to render it before the deadline. This chapter will show you how to optimize your renders, prioritize your work with precomps, and manage your system and network resources to give you maximum creative flexibility and still make your deadlines.

Planning your comps may seem tedious, but it can be critical to maintaining a timely flow of delivered work. You will be tempted just to leap into a challenging new comp, especially when you have a flash of inspiration. However, inspiration can turn to unemployment if you consistently run late because you failed to plan your comps. When you first receive a shot, preview all the source footage and other elements, and make notes about file size, server locations, and any problems that are immediately apparent. Pay particular attention to problems that are time-consuming, either in rendering time or in head scratching and experimenting. Make a list of the tasks you know you have to accomplish to deliver the comp, and post it beside your monitor as a reminder. I like to use 3-x-5" Post-It® pads for this. With practice, this task list should take only a few minutes to create. As you finish each task, or discover a new one, cross it out or add it to the list. The value of the task list is that you have an immediate reminder of the remaining time to complete the comp and can therefore give your supervisor a more accurate estimate of when you can deliver it. When deadlines get crazy, it's difficult to remember every little detail; the task list can save you from a landslide of last-minute overlooked tasks. If you pull the completed task list off your monitor and stick it in a notebook or schedule planner, it also provides a paper trail of your work. This can come in handy when a shot needs to be recomped, or when your boss asks what you've been doing all week.

A task list can also be a big help in prioritizing your comps. There are many individual operations that you can apply immediately, while you are still figuring out exactly how you will comp the rest of the shot. Rendering these precomps can help you cope with last-minute emergencies by having as much work done in advance as is possible.

Precompositions

Precomps are the best way for you to conserve resources. You can save time, money, and aggravation if you precomp wisely. On the other hand, a lack of planning for and use of precomps can force you to buy expensive equipment or services you didn't need, can cause you to lose jobs or bonuses, and can generally drive you crazy. Precomps are not difficult to plan. There are several general categories of precomps, and each category has trade-offs that place it higher or lower in the precomp priority order.

Uncompressed Image Sequences

If the raw footage is delivered to you with any kind of compression, you should convert it to an uncompressed format that your compositing software can read directly. Compressed footage is uncompressed every time it loads. On a fast machine (or one with hardware decompression), this may not take long for a single frame, but the delays can add up quickly for a long sequence. In addition to slowing down your final rendering, the decompression time slows down your system's feedback while you are setting up the comp. You will work faster with uncompressed footage. Finally, if the compositing process decompresses and then recompresses footage repeatedly, each pass adds generational losses and artifacts. Working with uncompressed footage prevents these problems.

One exception to this is when your system doesn't have the mass storage to accommodate the footage in an uncompressed format. This is not a good excuse; the price on large hard disk drives is pretty low already, and if your time is worth anything at all, the extra storage space will be a good investment.

Another exception is when a shared network is running close to its limits, and the difference between compressed and uncompressed formats may mean the difference between a network that works and one that crashes. Again, you should throw money at this problem, but meanwhile, you may have to compromise loading and decompression time for the sake of your network's continued operation.

Garbage And Simple Rig Removal

This is a no-brainer; when you look at the footage and spot a microphone boom dangling into the top of the frame, or notice that one of the crew is standing just within the left frame margin, you know those mistakes have to be removed before the shot is finished. Masking off screen-margin garbage and fixed rigging is relatively quick and easy, especially on a lock-down shot where the garbage isn't moving and you have a clean plate. If you don't already have a clean plate, well, you know you'll eventually need one; so piece it together now using the techniques described in Project 12.1. Make sure the clean plate works for the whole shot, pay attention to placing and sizing the dissolve mask as shown in Project 10.1, and render the precomp. Now you'll have garbage-free footage to use in whatever comps are necessary to complete the shot.

Noise And Grain Removal

The decision to remove film grain, video noise, or any other artifact of the image capture process is a judgment call. If the footage to be comped is only part of a shot, the final comp will have to precisely match the original footage, noise and all. That can mean a lot more comp work to restore noise. In that case, you should only precomp a noise and grain removal operation for use in pulling mattes and other noise-sensitive comps. However, if all the footage will go through the same process, or the final output is destined for video that smoothes out the film grain anyway, you should definitely precomp a noise and grain removal. Grain killer filters, or video noise re-moval comps like Project 13.4, can take a long time to render; making a precomp can save that time for you downstream, when you're closer to deadline and have less time to play with. As with any comp, you should still preserve the original footage, but the cleaned-up precomp footage is going to be much easier to work with and will most often produce cleaner results.

Mattes

The best digital compositing software can handle RGBA image sequences, automatically syn-chronizing the matte or alpha channel to the color image. Live footage, of course, has no alpha channel originally, but you can save time and effort by pulling a matte and precomping it with the original footage to create an uncompressed RGBA image sequence. This saves load-ing time over compressed footage or separate RGB and A sequences, and it simplifies keeping track of footage.

Pulling a clean matte can involve many operations. A single bluescreen matte extraction may require garbage matte, color correction, chroma key, spill suppression, erode, and choke opera-tions to fine-tune it, and that's still a fairly ordinary example. The result of pulling a matte is a simple grayscale image sequence. Precomping that sequence to the original color footage as an alpha channel enables you to eliminate the half dozen or more matte extraction tools from your final comp, with no loss in flexibility or quality. If you need to tweak the matte to accommodate last-minute changes in the background footage, most professional software includes a tool like Digital Fusion's Matte Control that will provide adequate control without cluttering up the comp.

Difference mattes, luma keys, and the other varieties and flavors of matte extraction tools can also be rendered as precomps and added to the source footage as an alpha channel. The only reason not to precomp a matte extraction is if the matte itself is the core of the problem and is likely to be debated and changed by your supervisor or client. Whenever pulling the matte is just another part of the job, precomp it.

Stabilization

As I pointed out in Chapters 11 and 12, there are many comp operations that are simpler, easier, and produce better results when the source footage is stable. If you receive footage that is unstable, one of the more productive precomps you can render is a single-point stabilization, as described in Project 11.2. Of course, you should save the stabilization comp and tracking data, just in case you need to destabilize the footage for the final comp.

A more complex stabilization, such as the two-point process described in Projects 11.3 and 12.5, can be a real resource hog. Before you commit to rendering footage at triple resolution, warping the frame with rotation and scaling factors, and generally filling up drives and monopolizing the network, make sure you really need to do it. A two-point stabilization is a legitimate candidate for a precomp, but it isn't something you want to do without a good reason.

If You Don't Know What To Do, Do What You Know

When you are trying to find a solution to a particularly tough compositing problem, sitting and staring at the monitor is sometimes not the best way to spend your time. Most people's minds do a lot of processing on the unconscious level, especially the "outside the box" thought processes that produce unconventional solutions to new problems. If you focus all your conscious processes on the problem, you tend to block your unconscious processes. A more productive use of your time may be to take a walk, check your email, or perform some other more routine task. This temporarily distracts your conscious mind and lets your unconscious work on the problem for a while.

Precomps are one of the best ways to distract your conscious mind and still be doing productive work. Any problem that is complex or difficult enough to temporarily baffle you is almost certain to have parts or processes that are obviously going to be necessary parts of the final solution. Anything that would have to be comped later, and that you can do immediately—pulling a matte, rig removal, noise removal, stabilizing—is a productive use of your time. This is especially true if you are working under a busy supervisor or director or if you are the junior compositor on a busy team. If you have to ask for help later, at least you can say, "I precomped the parts I could figure out, but this last problem has me stumped." This demonstrates a much more professional and conscientious work attitude.

In And Out And In And Out And In And Out

Loading source elements into your comps and writing out the comped footage can occupy a large portion of your system or network bandwidth. This input/output, or *I/O*, limitation is especially true of film—or HDTV-resolution footage. Some operations, especially motion blurs and time-shifting, repeatedly access several images for each rendered frame, multiplying the input load on your system. When the input or output load on your system or network becomes too heavy, your rendering slows down and may even halt or crash. To prevent these problems, you need to manage your comps and your system resources wisely.

Network Etiquette

When you are working in a networked environment, a problem on your workstation can affect everybody else. The network is a shared resource, like the water cooler or restrooms, and everyone has a responsibility to clean up after himself and not leave messes for others. Network etiquette becomes more important as more of a studio's functions are funneled through the network. In some studios, when the network goes down, *nothing* works, from the receptionist's appointment book to the individual artists' paint software. If you work in such an environment, and a thoughtless or selfish action on your part leads to a network failure, you can expect to receive some well-deserved criticism. It won't help your job tenure if this happens more than once.

If you aren't certain what demands your comps or workstation place on the network, ask the system operator, or *sysop*. Windows NT has a variety of network and workstation monitoring tools, and the sysop can show you what tools you can use safely and what their readouts mean. If you have a comp that is going to be especially network-intensive, you should consult with the sysop before you start the render. Just like telephone or power lines, there are times when the network is heavily used and other times when it has plenty of bandwidth to spare. If you have a comp that will strain the network, the sysop may ask that you render it during *off-peak* hours when no one else is using the network.

If a comp includes a lot of I/O, you may want to copy the source footage from the network server onto your own workstation, if you have the space. This enables you to work as I/O-intensively as you like, without bogging the network down with constant read/write operations. If you don't have the space for both the source files and the final rendering, direct the output to a network drive. The read operations can be repetitive and occur at more frequent intervals, while the final write operations are usually spaced farther apart and at more regular intervals, so the network can more easily accommodate the load.

If you need to set up a network render, it is even more important that you coordinate your actions with the sysop. There are few things more likely to enrage your colleagues than to find that the comps they set up to render overnight were all preempted by the networked comp you set to take over every machine in the shop, all night long. Sometimes such an action is necessary to make a crucial deadline, but (unless you're the boss) you are not the person to make that call. Get the sysop's go-ahead, and make sure everyone knows what's going to happen. It's your comp, so it's your responsibility to notify everyone. It is much better to negotiate for resources with forewarned colleagues than to have them discover unpleasant surprises the following morning. And last but not least, if you have to change any configurations on anyone else's workstations, document what you do as you do it, leave a copy of that documentation on the workstation, and come back and undo the changes before the workstation's owner needs to use it again. This is a kindergarten rule: clean up your own messes.

A popular pastime in some shops is the playing of networked games such as *Quake*. This is a nice fringe benefit for gamers, because the video quality of the workstations and the enormous bandwidth available in graphics studios makes the gameplay the best you can find outside of high-end specialty arcades. However, you need to keep network gaming in perspective. If this is an after-hours or off-peak activity, someone may be waiting to run a heavy comp or other network process and can't use the full network bandwidth until all the gamers log off. Be considerate, and follow whatever network gaming rules the sysop establishes. Remember, the studio equipment is not your private arcade; playing network games is a privilege, not a guaranteed fringe benefit of your employment. If you abuse the network with unsanctioned games, you may bring down the wrath of the sysop (and higher brass), with the result that all game play may be banned. Your game-playing colleagues would really like you for that, wouldn't they?

Memory Management

Most digital compositing software has a preferences or options dialog box where you can set rendering parameters. The exact setting you use will depend on your system's resources, the demands of the comp, and the network (if any) used by your studio.

In Digital Fusion, all the important parameters are set in the Preferences dialog box. Choose File|Preference and select the Memory tab, as shown in Figure 16.1. If you have enough RAM available, you should keep the cache settings for Always Cache Tools, Simultaneous Branching, and Cache Static Tools turned on. This keeps images loaded in RAM, so they don't have to be reloaded from the network or your workstation's drives. This has a major effect on your comp's feedback and rendering speed. For example, I loaded the CineGirl 2K film footage from the second CD-ROM and ran a simple motion blur on it with the Memory preferences shown in Figure 16.1. On my system, the average rendering time per frame was 1.03 seconds. With the cache and simultaneous branching options turned off, the average time per frame was 1.3 seconds. With Render set to 1 frame instead of 6, the average time per frame was 1.78 seconds. Multiply that difference by a dozen or so operations in a typical comp, for hundreds of frames, and it starts to add up.

Unless you have gigabytes of RAM in your workstation, you will quickly find a point of diminishing returns along the Render slider. With my system's barely adequate 128MB of RAM, setting the slider to 7 frames, with all caches enabled, brought render times to 4.37 seconds per frame. At the maximum of 10 frames, render times were up to 10.44 seconds per frame. This increase in render time is caused by the operating system running out of available RAM and resorting to the slower access of a swap file on a hard disk drive. The thrashing sound of a hard disk drive with a heavily accessed swap file is a dead giveaway that you need to lower your cache settings for more efficient rendering and feedback.

In most cases, your compositing software and the Windows NT cache manager will do the best job of managing RAM. However, if you find that a particular comp is thrashing your HDDs, you may want to temporarily place the problem files in a RAM disk. A RAM disk is a section of your

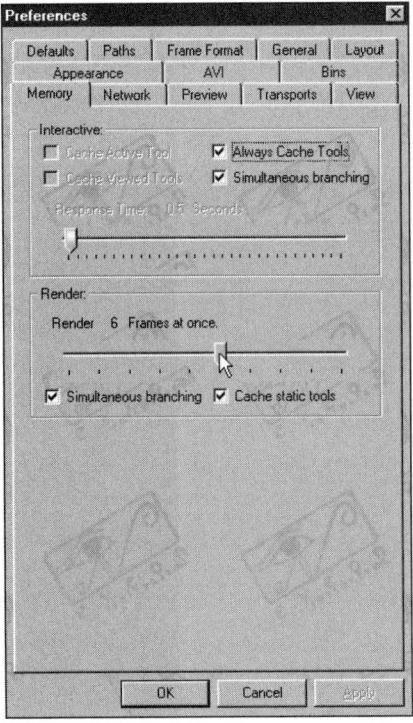

Figure 16.1
The Digital Fusion Preferences dialog box, showing the Memory tab set for optimum rendering speed of a simple 2K-resolution comp on a PII-400 with 128MB of RAM.

computer's chip memory that is set aside and handled as if it were a disk drive. Loading files from a RAM disk reduces wear and tear on your other drives and may reduce the loading element of your comp's rendering time. However, if anything goes wrong and your system shuts down or reboots, any data on the RAM disk will be lost.

PROJECT 16.1 Setting Up A Win NT RAM Drive

You can set up a RAM disk in Windows NT 4 by using a Microsoft software-only device driver that is included on the first CD-ROM. This is old code (1994), and although it works for me, you should think hard about whether the benefits are worth the risks to your own system. If you are not comfortable using RegEdit (or don't know what this term means), you should not try this:

1. Copy the self-extracting archive NTRamdsk.EXE from the first CD-ROM to your default TEMP folder. For most systems, this will be C:\TEMP.

2. Run NTRamdsk.EXE by double-clicking on it. It will self-extract into four files: RAMDISK.SYS, RAMDISK.INI, REGINI.EXE, and README.TXT.

3. Read the README.TXT file before you go further. If you have any doubts about what the next steps may do to your system, stop now and delete the extracted files from your TEMP folder.

4. Copy RAMDISK.SYS to your system's 32-bit driver folder, most commonly C:\WINNT\ SYSTEM32\DRIVERS.

5. From the Start menu, choose Run. In the Run dialog box, type the path to your TEMP folder, followed by \REGINI.EXE RAMDISK.INI, as shown in Figure 16.2. Click on OK.

   The REGINI program will make entries and changes to your system's Registry, based on the values in the RAMDISK.INI file. These include the drive letter V for the RAM disk and an allocation of 2MB.

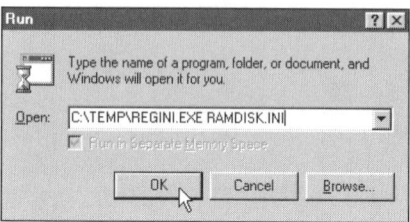

Figure 16.2
The Run dialog box ready to execute REGINI to configure a RAM disk.

6. Reboot your system. When it comes back up, you should see a new V: drive with a file size a little less than 2MB.

   If you need to change the size of the RAM disk or the drive letter assignment, you can use RegEdit directly. Keep in mind that you can severely cripple your operating system by making a mistake in the Registry. If you are not confident of your ability to edit the Registry, don't try this.

7. From the Start menu, choose Run. Type "REGEDIT" and click on OK. The Registry Editor will appear, as shown in Figure 16.3.

8. Press Ctrl+F, or choose the Edit|Find menu option. In the Find dialog box, type "DiskSize", then click on the Find Next button. When the first (and only) instance of DiskSize is found, the Registry Editor should look like Figure 16.3.

9. Right-click on the DiskSize parameter, and choose Modify from the pop-up menu. A dialog box entitled Edit DWORD Value will appear.

10. In the Value data field, type the desired RAM allocation for the RAM disk, then click on OK.

11. If you would like to change the drive letter, right-click on the DriveLetter parameter, choose Modify, and in the Edit String dialog box, type the new drive letter. Be sure you are choosing a drive letter that will not conflict with either drive-ordering or an existing drive letter. If you have any doubts, leave the parameter as is.

12. Close the Registry Editor. Reboot your system.

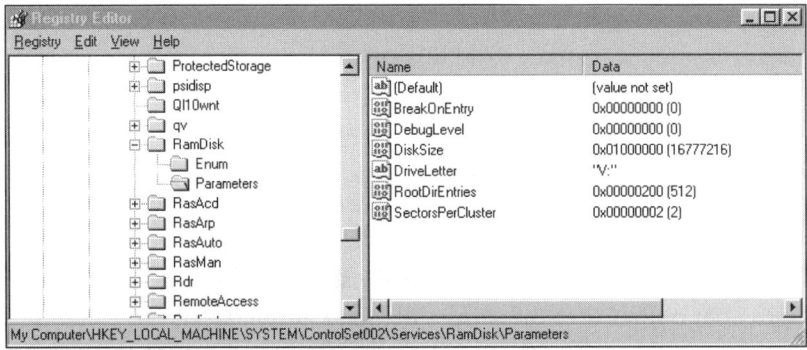

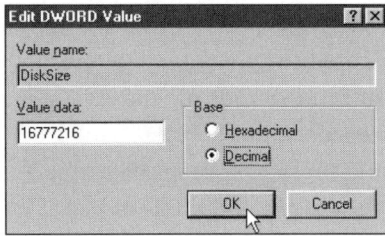

Figure 16.3
The Registry Editor (RegEdit) ready to edit the DiskSize parameter for the RAM disk. The Value data is set to 16MB in decimal notation.

If all went well, your system should now have a RAM disk with the size and drive letter you set, as in Figure 16.4. This can be a handy location for files that require very fast access, such as animations, video clips, and large sound files. However, you should remember that a RAM disk keeps

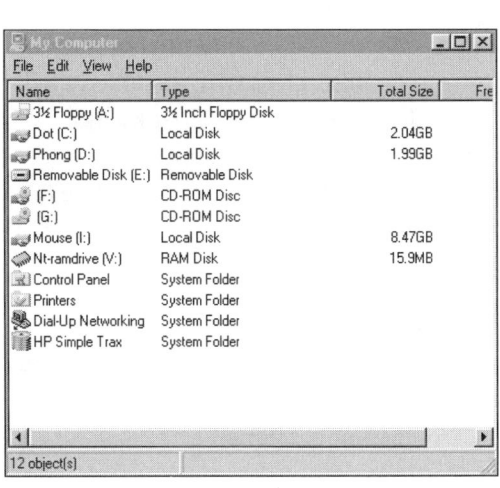

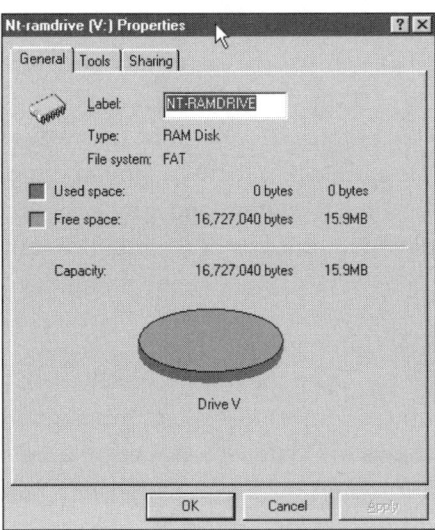

Figure 16.4
The appearance and properties of the 16MB RAM disk.

the rest of your operating system from using that block of chip memory. Unless you have far more RAM than you ever need, you should keep the RAM disk as small as possible. Remember also that the RAM disk is volatile memory; if the system hangs or reboots, the contents are gone. For this reason, you should never use a RAM disk as an output location, and you should always retain a backup copy of any file you place in a RAM disk.

Output Issues

Your comp's final output is the only evidence your client or supervisor will have that you did anything worth your pay. Treat your output with the same care and planning that you would devote to a pile of cash equivalent to your pay for the time you spent working on the comp. I have found more than one software manual that recommends rendering to RAM to save time. Personally, I'd rather juggle razor blades blindfolded; at least half the time, I wouldn't get hurt. In my experience, those odds are better than for the reliability of RAM storage of your final work. If you value your comps at all, render your final output to a safe, reliable HDD as an un-compressed image sequence. Adding compression is one more time-consuming step that can go wrong. Rendering to AVI, QuickTime, or other video clip format risks losing the whole render if the last frame goes bad. Rendering to RAM is asking for trouble. If your final delivery medium requires compression or a video clip format, you can easily and quickly compile that from the uncompressed image sequence, secure in the knowledge that your rendered images are safely available for revisions and tweaks during the compression process. Keep in mind that some of today's most popular distribution media, including DVD and streaming video, look best when derived from clean image sequences.

RTV Output

If you are using NewTek's Video Toaster NT (VTNT) for output, you will need to render your final comps through one of NewTek's applications: LightWave, Aura, or the VTNT version of in-sync's Speed Razor. As of this writing, no other applications can output the RTV format used by the VTNT to play back 30 fps D1 video. The most efficient way to do this in LightWave is to load the image sequence and set it as the Background image in the Effects panel, then render the full sequence at the same resolution and interlace settings as the original comp to an RTV file on your VTNT drive. With the correct settings, this minimizes the rendering time to approximately a copy-and-paste operation, roughly one second per frame.

LightWave RTV Conversion

Launch LightWave. Open the Images panel. Click on Load Sequence, and select the image se-quence you want to convert to RTV. For this example, I'm using the Box footage from the second CD-ROM, as shown in Figure 16.5. To keep the frame numbers consistent, leave Frame Offset set to 0. This avoids confusion in setting the render range. Close the Images panel.

In Layout, set First Frame and Last Frame to the first and last frames of your footage. For the Box footage, these are 200 and 402. Open the Effects panel. In the Compositing tab, set Background Image to the loaded footage, as shown in Figure 16.6. This will make the footage automatically

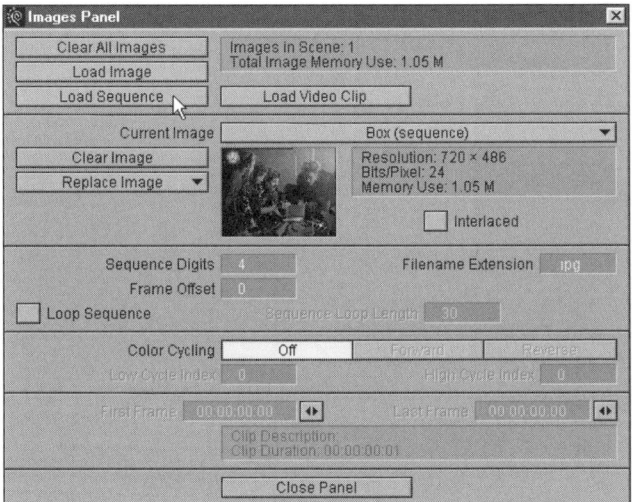

Figure 16.5
Loading the Box footage in the LightWave Images panel.

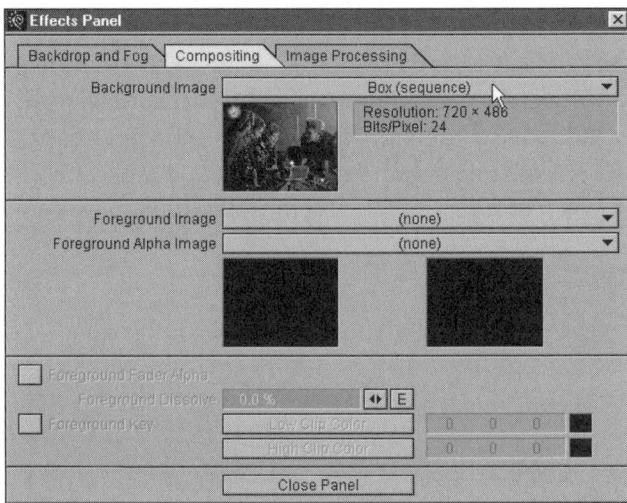

Figure 16.6
The LightWave Effects panel showing the Box image sequence selected as the Background Image.

match the Camera's field of view and aspect ratio, preventing the distortion or misalignment that would be possible if you simply mapped the image to a plane object and positioned it in front of the Camera. Close the Effects panel.

Open the Options panel. In the Layout View tab (see Figure 16.7), set Layout Background to BG Image. This enables you to check your Camera and render range settings, but you will want to change this setting back to Blank before you begin rendering. If you leave the BG Image turned

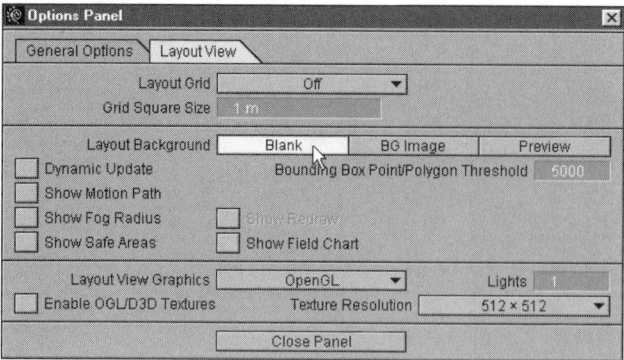

Figure 16.7

The Layout View tab of the LightWave Options panel, showing Layout Background set to Blank for the best rendering speed. To check the setup before rendering, Layout Background should be set to BG Image, then reset to Blank for rendering.

on during rendering, LightWave will take the extra time to load each image in the sequence into Layout's background. This can nearly double the rendering time and doesn't provide any useful feedback. Close the Options panel.

Open the Camera panel. Set Basic Resolution to Medium and Pixel Aspect Ratio to D1 (NTSC). These are the correct values for VTNT output. To minimize rendering time, set Segment Memory to 9MB and Antialiasing to Off, and turn off Adaptive Sampling. This allocates enough RAM to render each frame in one segment and disables rendering enhancements that don't make any difference to the footage. Your panel should look like Figure 16.8. Close the Camera panel.

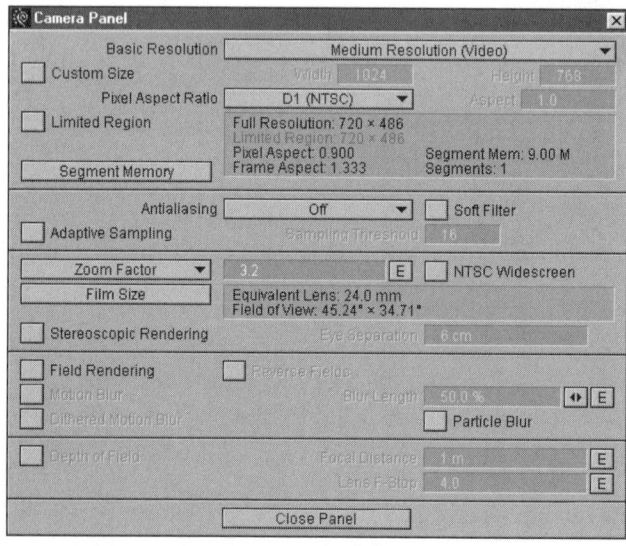

Figure 16.8

The LightWave Camera panel with the correct settings for resolution, pixel aspect ratio, segment memory, and antialiasing to produce a VTNT RTV video clip.

In Layout, go to the frame preceding the first frame of the loaded footage. The background should remain blank. Step forward one frame. The first frame of the footage should appear in the background, as shown in Figure 16.9. Go to the last frame; the last frame of the footage should load to the background. If everything checks out, go back to the Options panel and change Layout Background to Blank. If the frames don't match up, recheck your image sequence file names and the Frame Offset setting in the Images panel.

Open the Render panel. Set Rendering Mode to Wireframe, the fastest mode. You won't need any other rendering options because you only need the background image. Set Render First Frame and Render Last Frame to the first and last images of the footage, and turn on Automatic Frame Advance. Make sure Show Rendering In Progress is turned off, and Render Display is set to (none). This disables time-consuming display options that you don't need for this rendering. Set Animation Type to LW_NewTek-RTV-NTSC. Click on the Save Animation button, and choose the path and file name to save the RTV file to your VTNT drive. Your Render panel should look like Figure 16.10.

Figure 16.9
The LightWave Layout view with the first frame of footage displayed as the Background image. Note that the frame counter, 200, matches the frame number of the loaded image.

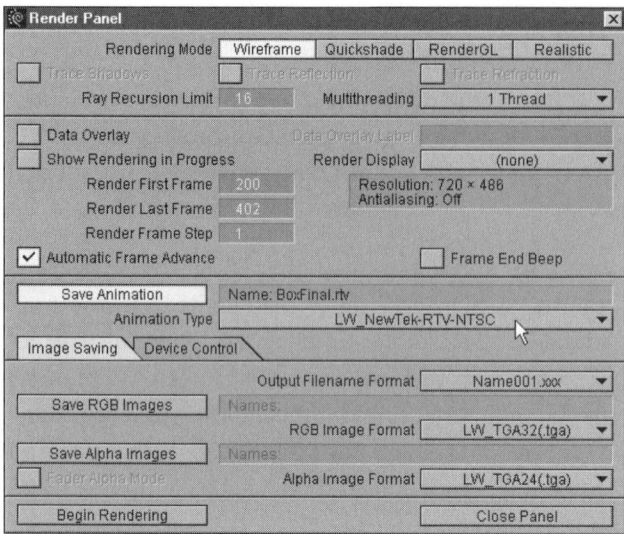

Figure 16.10

The LightWave Render panel with Automatic Frame Advance selected, all display options disabled, and the correct frame range, the Animation Type selection, and the path set to render the Box footage as a VTNT RTV clip.

Click on Begin Rendering. Each frame should take only a second or two to render. Most of this time is consumed in loading and saving files to the drives, with a little time taken to copy each pixel's value. Using a powerful program like LightWave simply to translate file formats is a little like swatting mosquitoes with a sledgehammer, but it gets the job done, and if you are using VTNT, it's a tool you already own.

Aura RTV Conversion

Launch Aura. In the startup options, choose NTSC CCIR to match the 720x486 resolution of the Box footage. Choose File|Import|Sequence. In the Load Sequence dialog box, choose the first frame of the Box footage from the second CD-ROM, and click on OK, as shown in Figure 16.11.

In the Loading Sequence dialog box, confirm that the Mark In and Mark Out frame numbers match the footage numbers, the Width and Height match Aura's current working resolution, and Full Frames is checked as shown in Figure 16.12. Click on OK.

Choose File|Mode|D1 RTV. This tells Aura that you want to work in the same mode that the VTNT displays. Choose Export|Sequence. The Interlace Fields dialog box pops up. Choose None, and click on OK. The Save RTV Clip Sequence dialog box pops up. Choose the path and file name to save the RTV clip to the VTNT drive, as shown in Figure 16.13. Click on OK.

Aura saves the RTV file to the specified drive and displays a progress bar during the save. Translating an image sequence to RTV format with Aura is a little less complicated than with LightWave, but it takes about the same amount of time to export the RTV clip as LightWave does to render it.

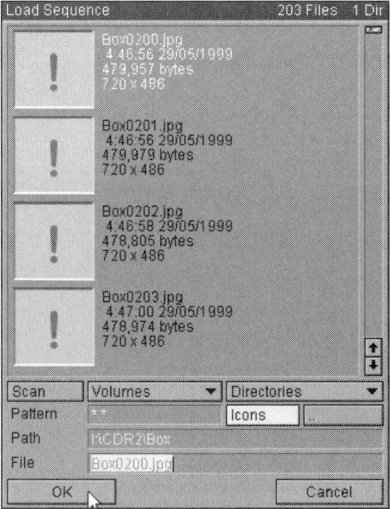

Figure 16.11
The Load Sequence dialog box with the Box footage selected.

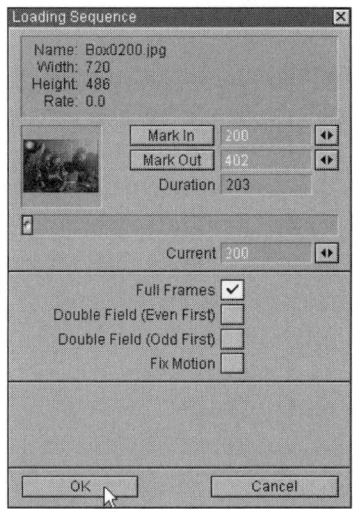

Figure 16.12
The Loading Sequence dialog box with the first frame of Box footage loaded for you to double-check the loading parameters.

CHAPTER 16

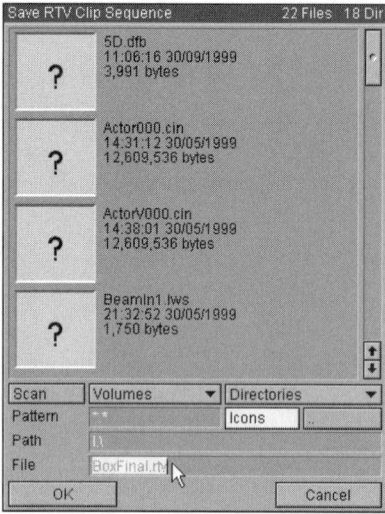

Figure 16.13
The Save RTV Clip Sequence dialog box with the new file name and the path to the VTNT drive selected.

Moving On

This chapter has shown you the basics of how to plan your work, prioritize precomps, manage your system and network resources, and optimize your renders to make the best use of your time. No amount of planning can completely prepare you for impossible deadlines and last-minute changes, but I hope this chapter will help you to make most of your deadlines and remain sane. Chapter 17 will show you how to transfer your finished comps to video and multimedia formats, and Chapter 18 will show you how to get them onto the big screen.

Even a perfectly comped shot is useless if you can't get it off your workstation and in front of your audience. After your comps are rendered, you need a way to deliver them to your client or audience, to record them for future viewing or reuse, and to make reference copies for your demo reel or personal archive. If you are working in a large studio and doing comps exclusively, your responsibility for the shot probably ends when you render the final comp to the network server. Someone else handles the technical details of editing your work into the final production, dumping it to tape, and delivering it. However, knowing something about the final transfer and delivery process can make a difference to your compositing. You'll kick yourself if you spend days tweaking a comp that ends up so reduced and compressed that you couldn't see a fringe if it was four pixels wide. On the other hand, comp shortcuts you could get away with for streaming video will look like the dog's breakfast on broadcast TV. You should also understand the transfer process if you ever hope to be a supervisor or to start your own studio. You need to understand the options available so you can make the right choices for media, hardware, and workflow.

Playing back video, whether it is on a computer, the Internet, or analog or digital television systems, requires a big enough pipe to shove all that data through without clogging up. That pipe is called *bandwidth*, and it is the single most important limit to delivering your finished production. The first factor in bandwidth is the resolution and frame rate of the end-use media. This can range from postage-stamp-size 15 fps video clips for Internet distribution at slow modem speeds all the way up to 2K 24 fps film or e-cinema files for theatrical display. This chapter will cover low-end multimedia up to the best of standard definition television (SDTV). Chapter 18 will cover high-definition television (HDTV), film, and e-cinema.

The sample footage used for comparisons in the rest of this chapter was originally a 158-frame sequence of images at 720x486 resolution and 24-bit color depth, with a total file size of 159MB in uncompressed TGA format. This footage was selected because it has a mix of locked-down and moving camera, varying light levels, motion of both human skin tones and organic textures, complex inorganic background objects, a patch of nearly saturated red, and a fixed corner graphic with both fine and thick lines. This presents some tough problems for compression and is a pretty fair test for all the codecs. Figure 17.1 shows frame 53 from this sequence, at 2X magnification so you can compare it to artifact patterns from other figures in this chapter.

Streaming Internet Video

Streaming video is a compressed video signal transmitted through the Internet and played back in real time. The smallest video bandwidth in common use is a 28.8Kbps modem connection. This tiny pipe requires very high compression and the smallest resolution your production can get away with. Streaming compression ratios range from a minimum of 200:1 up to 500:1. Resolutions of 320×240 or even 160×120 are not uncommon, especially if the production is a "talking head," a spokesperson who doesn't move much in a head-shot close-up. Most compositing artifacts, such as fringe, are nearly invisible at these low resolutions, so you don't have to spend as much time tweaking mattes to perfection. Your biggest problem is going to be making titles and text-based motion graphics legible at these low resolutions. In addition, the compression codecs used for streaming video usually introduce a lot of artifacts, which can make text even harder to read. You should discuss these issues with the director or producer as early as possible. Some possible solutions include oversize motion graphics and voice-over reiteration of whatever information

Figure 17.1
Frame 53 from sample footage at 2X magnification.

the motion graphics are supposed to convey. You will probably not be able to use such common motion graphic conventions as streamers or subtitles; you will have to rely on larger text that intermittently covers most of the screen.

Streaming video is, like most video technology, changing rapidly. As of this writing, the market leader in streaming video is RealNetworks (**www.real.com**), publishers of RealSystem G2 software including RealPlayer, RealProducer G2, and RealSystem G2 Basic Server. The player, encoder, and basic server are free for downloading from the company's Web site. By encouraging free downloads, RealNetworks has put over 65 million RealPlayer copies on users' desktops. Multiple-stream servers and more advanced creation and distribution tools cost a few hundred dollars, a reasonable outlay for small companies or educational institutions. The software is a minor part of the budget for setting up streaming video servers. If you own Adobe Premiere, you already have a version of the player, which is located in the Real directory of Premiere's installation CD-ROM. Real products can produce compression ratios as high as 500:1, resulting in a 20Kbps data stream. This is well within the limits of a 28.8Kbps modem connection. Figures 17.2 through 17.7 show the image quality possible at varying levels of streaming video compression using the RealProducer G2 software encoder.

Figure 17.2
A 720x486 Cinepak AVI clip, compressed at a ratio of 368:1 for LAN bandwidth of 150Kbps, plays at 11.6 fps. Note that compression artifacts are large enough to blot out most facial features and the corner logo is illegible, while portions of the background that do not move show some fine details.

Figure 17.3

720x486 uncompressed AVI clip, resized to 640x480 and compressed at a ratio of 450:1 for LAN bandwidth of 150Kbps, plays at 12.6 fps. The image is overwhelmed by artifacts; only gross movement is visible. Faces are nearly featureless blobs, and the corner logo is almost undetectable.

Figure 17.4

720x486 uncompressed AVI, resized to 320x216 and compressed at a ratio of 146:1 for LAN bandwidth of 150Kbps, plays at 16.7 fps. Note that simply resizing the clip allows for much more detail and a lower compression ratio for a given bandwidth. The corner logo is nearly legible, and facial features and background details are discernable.

Figure 17.5
720x486 Cinepak AVI compressed at a ratio of 2700:1 for 28.8 modem bandwidth of 20Kbps, plays at 9.7 fps. This clip is a waste of time and effort; all you can see are some colored blurs. It's just not possible to push full-frame video through a 28.8 modem, because the compression ratio goes so high above the 500:1 limit for acceptable video.

Figure 17.6
320x216 Cinepak-compressed AVI, compressed at a ratio of 542:1 for 28.8 modem bandwidth of 20Kbps, plays at 10.8 fps. Again, compression higher than 500:1 is unacceptable.

Figure 17.7
320x216 Cinepak-compressed AVI, compressed at a ratio of 154:1 for LAN bandwidth of 150Kbps, plays at 17.4 fps. Although fine details are still lost to compression artifacts, this is an acceptable video quality and frame rate for most Internet viewing.

Some of the other streaming video software currently on the market includes Microsoft's ActiveMovie, Netshow, and Media Player (**www.microsoft.com**); Apple's QuickTime 4 (**www.apple.com**); Macromedia's Shockwave (**www.shockwave.com**); and GEO Interactive's Emblaze (**www.emblaze.com**). For the latest information, I recommend that you conduct some research on the Internet and test all the available demos and freeware before you choose any commercial streaming video software. This market is too volatile to pick a winner even a few months in advance. Also, with Microsoft in the market, you never know who's going to be bought out.

Downloadable Internet Video

An easier alternative to streaming video is to simply load video clips on a Web site so people can download them to view later. This bypasses the need for special streaming Web servers. Web distribution requires videos to be assembled in MPEG, AVI, QuickTime, or some other common video format. Image sequences are *not* an acceptable way to distribute video on the Internet. Some browsers can start playing back a video clip while still downloading the rest of it, emulating streaming video, but that function depends on which browser is being used and what plug-ins have been installed. It's best not to assume anything if you want your videos to be viewable by as many people as possible. Most video-heavy Web sites include links to sites where you can download the necessary video plug-ins or players.

As with streaming video, file size is very important in downloadable video because your audience may be using anything from a 28.8 modem to a fiber-optic backbone. Your most flexible options are to have several sizes of each clip, use the most common codecs, and label everything clearly so your audience can choose for themselves. The most common size for Internet video is half-resolution. If you are downsampling the entire frame, use an even divisor (720 divides evenly into 360, 240, or 180) for your horizontal resolution and keep the vertical resolution proportional. This reduces round-off errors in the downsampling operation and minimizes artifacts, while preserving (as much as possible) fine details in the reduced video.

The framing you use for SDTV is not necessarily the best framing for downloadable video. For one thing, you don't have to worry about text-safe or action-safe areas; the entire frame is always visible. You can put image and text right out in the corners and it won't get lost. Second, you are not bound by the 4:3 or 16:9 aspect ratios of a hardware-based video system. If your source video never uses the outer two-thirds of the frame, you can crop it to a 1:1.5 portrait aspect ratio. This is an especially useful approach for talking heads. Third, an "artistic" framing in which the majority of the screen is occupied by irrelevant background is inappropriate for the Internet. When every pixel has to be folded, bent, spindled, and mutilated to fit through a narrow pipeline, you can't afford to waste any. Save your widescreen framing for stills or other delivery media, and keep your Internet frames full of foreground content. Fourth, camera motion is anathema to efficient Internet video. If possible, you should stabilize your footage. If the conversion from a widescreen framing to a narrower one requires pan-and-scan, try to do it with cuts rather than pans. These techniques will greatly reduce the frame-to-frame deltas that bloat even the most thoroughly compressed video.

The popularity of various codecs for Internet video changes over time, but more slowly than the cutting edge of this technology. There are a lot of old video clips out there, and many people are slow to add the latest codec to their browser. For the widest distribution of your videos, I recommend compressing with a common codec that has been in popular use for a while. The Cinepak codec is effective for both AVI and QuickTime formats, and I highly recommend it. The test footage, downsampled from 720×486 to 360×243, was compressed using Cinepak at 50 percent image quality from 169MB to 1.38MB for AVI and to 1.68MB for QuickTime.

Web Page Issues

Many Internet users pay for their access by the minute or have slow connections that make downloading large video clips time-consuming. To be polite, you should give your audience as much information as possible before they start downloading so they can choose when or whether to download your clips. You should never embed a video clip in your home page. You should instead use a thumbnail image of a representative frame from the video as a link to the page containing the video. In addition, you should use the <ALT> tag to include the file size. For example, this line defines a graphical link to download an MPEG clip:

```
<A HREF="MortyB.mpg"><IMG SRC="MortyB.gif" ALT="370K MPEG of Morty"></A>
```

When the reader passes the mouse cursor over the image link, the ALT message informs the reader what the file size, type, and subject are before he or she starts downloading. This can save your readers a lot of wasted time and bother, and it can spare you a lot of complaints.

If you are publishing AVI, MPEG, or QuickTime files on a Web site, one of the simplest ways of adding video clips to a Web page is with the <EMBED> tag. For example, the following lines produce a complete HTML page that loads an AVI file from the current directory with a resolution of 360x243, padded to 289 with 46 extra pixel rows to allow space for the Internet Explorer control bar:

```
<HTML>
<HEAD>
<TITLE>Close-Up Explosion</TITLE>
</HEAD>
<CENTER>
<EMBED SRC="CINEPAKB.AVI" HEIGHT=289 WIDTH=360>
</CENTER>
</BODY>
</HTML>
```

This is a simple, reliable way of displaying your video clips in both Internet Explorer and Netscape Navigator. Figure 17.8 shows this HTML page loaded into both browsers.

Embedding video clips in HTML pages is also a handy way of keeping track of archive footage. For example, you could keep about five and a half minutes of high-quality clips of your best work on a CD-ROM, with a thumbnail index page linked to separate pages for each clip. This is a convenient place to record important details such as who worked on the project, the client's name and contact information, who owns the intellectual property rights to the elements and the

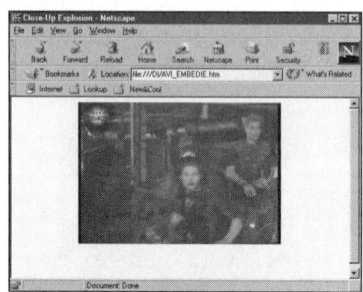

Figure 17.8
Screenshots of a half-size AVI clip as it appears in the Microsoft Internet Explorer and Netscape Navigator browsers.

finished comp, and any technical information that might be useful later. This is also a good way of having a complete but compact form of your personal or studio demo reel.

Local Computer Playback

There are a variety of reasons to deliver video through a computer. Videogame cut scenes, interactive instructional videos, and choose-your-own-ending dramatic works are just a few. In many cases, the quality of video playback on a new desktop computer can be better than VHS videotape. Direct playback on the computer depends on the system's bus speed, CD-ROM drive speed, available RAM, video display card, and sometimes hard drive space. As far back as 1995, the MPC III specifications included 4X CD-ROM, 44 kHz stereo sound, Pentium 75 MHz or better, and MPEG-1 playback support. That was just about good enough to mimic second- or third-generation VHS tape quality. New machines in 1999 typically have bus speeds of 100 MHz or higher, 40X CD-ROMs, DVD/MPEG-2 playback support, and video display cards optimized for the high refresh rates of videogames. The "bottleneck" in the pipeline for playing back video from a CD-ROM is usually at least 1.5MB per second, enabling standard television resolutions at full frame rate with a moderately efficient codec. The catch is, how do you produce video that can take advantage of all this technology?

The first step is choosing delivery media. The most cost-effective delivery media for shorter video formats is CD-ROM. You can pack a few minutes of full-screen, high-quality video onto a single CD-ROM, or more than an hour of lower-quality half-resolution video. You can make one-off or short run CDs for a few dollars each with a CD-R drive that costs less than $300. If you need higher volume, you can find CD-ROM duplicators that will turn out hundreds or thousands of copies of the master CD-R for under 50 cents a pop. If you have so much footage that a half dozen or so CD-ROMs aren't enough to hold it, you may want to consider the expense of having a DVD mastered and duplicated. As of this writing, DVD mastering is not yet cost-effective for the hobbyist, freelance artist, or small studio. Other possible delivery media include removable media such as Zip or Jaz disks, but their blank-media costs are generally too high for anything but in-house distribution.

Second, choose a file format. Your decision should take into account the platforms and operating systems of your audience. Do you care whether Windows, Mac, Unix, BeOS, or Amiga users can view your videos? If yes, you need either to use a video file format that everyone can view or to provide duplicate videos in enough formats to cover all the possibilities. AVI, or Audio Video Interleaved, is the default video format on Windows machines and can also be played back by newer Mac OS systems. It is not well-supported in Unix environments. QuickTime can be played by Windows, Mac OS, and some Unix systems. MPEG-1 can be played back by anything; I wouldn't be surprised to find an MPEG-1 player for the Altair.

Once you've settled on a file format, the next step in creating computer-playable video is choosing a compression codec. Even with bandwidth in excess of 1.5MBps, you'll need to compress the video stream quite a bit before you can get it to play back without dropped frames. A number of viable video codecs are available that can do the job, but they each have trade-offs. As a basis for comparison, the uncompressed AVI of the example footage weighs in at 159MB. The image quality is essentially identical to the original stills, as shown in Figure 17.9, but the video plays back at 9.56 fps.

One of the most popular (and deservedly so, in my opinion) codecs is Cinepak. You can get impressive file compression with very high-quality settings with Cinepak. Set for 95 percent quality, the reference AVI file squashed down to 9.88MB, a 16:1 compression (see Figure 17.10). On a PII 400 MHz equipped with the ATI All-In-Wonder card, both the ATI Player NT 5 and Microsoft Media Player can play back this video clip at 28.92 fps, just shy of recordable. The Cinepak codec for Windows shows compression artifacts in the form of *banding*, but not as prominently as the Cinepak codec for QuickTime.

The Microsoft Video 1 codec is neither as robust nor as efficient as Cinepak. The same level of quality compressed the sample footage only to 58.6MB, a compression ratio of 2.7:1 (see Figure 17.11). This clip also consistently crashed Media Player, but played back on the ATI Player at approximately 17 fps.

I used Tom Holusa's AVI2MPEG encoder to create a video-only MPEG-1 clip based on the uncompressed AVI. With data stream settings of 150Kbps, this yielded a file size of 916K, for a compression ratio of 173:1. This file played back on both ATI Player NT 5 and Microsoft Media Player at

Figure 17.9
Frame 53 of uncompressed AVI at 2X magnification.

Figure 17.10
Frame 53 of Cinepak-compressed AVI, 95 percent quality, at 2X magnification.

Figure 17.11
Frame 53 of Microsoft Video 1-compressed AVI, 95 percent quality, at 2X magnification.

29.83 fps, close enough to dump to tape for short pieces. File size savings from basing the MPEG-1 compression on Cinepak or other AVI codecs were not significant enough (plus or minus 1 percent) to justify the double compression. As Figure 17.12 shows, the compression artifacts of MPEG-1 bring the D-1 quality images down to approximately a second- or third- generation VHS tape. However, repeating the encoding with the stream set for 500Kbps produced a file size of 2.3MB and a playback speed of only 25 fps. The image quality difference (see Figure 17.13) shows how much you can gain by tweaking a setting or two. If you choose to deliver MPEG video, you should encode at the delivery system's best sustainable playback bandwidth.

MPEG-2 relies (as of this writing) on hardware compression. The inexpensive entry-level boards perform single-pass encoding that leaves artifacts similar to but significantly smaller than the MPEG-1 encoding shown in Figure 17.13. More-expensive MPEG-2 encoders make multiple passes to maximize compression and minimize artifacts. If you plan to distribute your comps via MPEG-2 or DVD, you should thoroughly research the available options before investing in hardware or software. This is a very fast-moving sector of the video industry, and what was hot six months ago is a dog today.

The QuickTime file format has at least one codec in common with AVI, plus several others. The QuickTime Cinepak codec set for 95 percent quality compressed the sample footage down to 7.93MB, for a 20:1 ratio. This file plays back in the QuickTime MoviePlayer at 28.28 fps, but it shows more prominent banding than the same codec applied to the AVI clip.

Figure 17.12
Frame 53 of 150 Kbps MPEG-1 based on uncompressed AVI, at 2X magnification.

Figure 17.13
Frame 53 of MPEG-1 compressed for delivery at 500 Kbps.

Figure 17.14
Frame 53 of QuickTime video compressed with the Cinepak codec at 95 percent quality, at 2X magnification.

Repeating the QuickTime compression with the Sorenson codec yielded a 12.4MB file, for a lower compression ratio of only 13:1. This clip also plays back more slowly, at approximately 16 fps. The advantage of the Sorenson codec is that banding is much less prominent, as shown in Figure 17.15, so the image quality is significantly improved. Depending on your delivery system's parameters, you might get better image quality with higher Sorenson compression than with lower Cinepak compression.

I had interestingly mixed results when I tested the DV codec for QuickTime. The compression ratio was only so-so, less than 9:1 with an 18.1MB output. However, the playback rate was right on the money, precisely 29.97. On the other hand, the playback is very blurred. To make matters even more confusing, individual screen prints are sharp, as Figure 17.16 shows. One would hope that the better image quality is what would be transferred to any DV device through an IEEE-1394 port.

Whatever combination of delivery media, file format, and codec you use, make sure you keep a backup of your uncompressed footage. It's very likely that you will want to distribute it at some future date in a format and codec that doesn't even exist yet. You will get the worst-possible results if you try to convert from one encoded video to another codec; the difference between the old and new sampling patterns will create really ugly moiré patterns and other artifacts.

Figure 17.15
Frame 53 of QuickTime video compressed with Sorenson codec at 95 percent quality, at 2X magnification.

Figure 17.16
Frame 53 of QuickTime video compressed with the DV codec at 2X magnification.

Output To Tape

As with the previous methods of distribution, dumping your finished comp to videotape requires a system with enough bandwidth to push out the video signal without clogging up. The less compression in that signal, the wider the bandwidth you'll need, and (generally) the more expensive your system will become. In addition, you need the right output circuitry and connectors to suit the VTR or other recording devices you want to use.

All-In-Wonder

The least-expensive option for tape recording video from your computer is an NTSC video output card such as ATI's All-In-Wonder 128, shown in Figure 17.17. This card has breakout cables that provide composite and S-Video connectors. As I mentioned in Chapter 5, the ATI Player software doesn't support NTSC input or output under Win NT. However, under Windows 98, the software enables you to tweak the NTSC output to correct the image's color, geometry, and centering. This card also has hardware acceleration for MPEG playback. Based on my tests, it doesn't do too badly on AVI playback either. The video playback rate depends on your system's bus, RAM, and hard drive speeds. For output to tape, you need to compress an AVI or MPEG stream until it can play back consistently at 29.97 fps. This system does not enable precise locking of frame rate, so it's a hit-or-miss proposition. (Hey, what do you expect from a card that costs less than $200?)

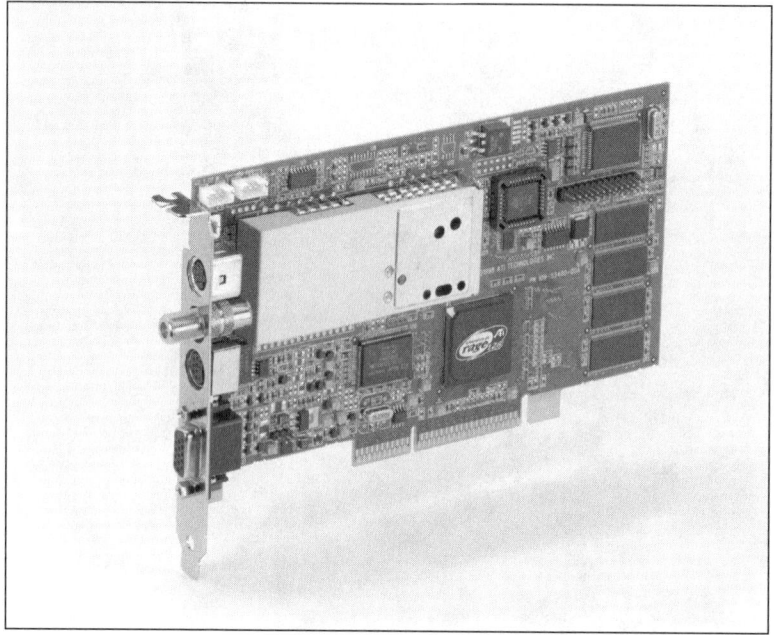

Figure 17.17
ATI All-In-Wonder 128 video display card with NTSC S-Video output.

The output looks comparable to VHS, in between Figures 17.12 and 17.13. This may be good enough for personal projects or a student demo reel, making the ATI card a good choice for students and hobbyists who simply need an affordable way to output short comps to VHS. For professionals, the ATI card may only be suitable for low-fidelity consumer productions, such as wedding or home video touch-up or effects comps. You may be able to remove Uncle Al from his inconvenient position behind the bride and groom or add some fancy titles or transitions, but you're going to incur some hefty quality losses at the same time.

FASTER PLAYBACK

If the video clip you are dumping is small enough, you may get faster playback by creating a RAM disk and playing back the clip from RAM. This takes the hard drive out of the loop but still requires a fast system bus and video card.

The next step up in price and performance is hardware designed specifically to play back video for recording to tape. This is the output side of the representative input systems described in Chapter 5: FAST's DV Master Pro, DPS's Perception RT3DX, and NewTek's Video Toaster NT. These systems are each designed as a complete input/output solution for video.

DV Master Pro

FAST Multimedia's DV Master Pro is a DV-based system that relies on a system hard drive for playback. The card has two external and one internal IEEE-1394 input and output connectors, and the breakout box has connectors for component and S-Video. This system compressed the sample footage from 159 down to 18.2MB, for a compression ratio of 8.7:1. The playback rate was a steady 29.97 fps, with image quality as shown in Figure 17.18. The bundle includes in:sync's Speed Razor editing software, so you can edit your comps, assemble them with other footage, sync the audio, and output a complete production. The software detects when the system bandwidth is inadequate to maintain the frame rate and issues an alert message with some helpful advice about the problem. In the case of a full or sluggish HDD, the message recommends clearing space or optimizing the HDD. This is helpful and well thought out, unlike other systems that require you to monitor your frame rate on playback or search recorded video for dropped frames.

The only nagging problem I found with playback to tape from the DV Master was that DV clips rendered from eyeon Software's Digital Fusion, Discreet's edit*, Adobe After Effects, or Adobe Premiere with DV-NTSC codecs did not play back directly in either Speed Razor or the DV Manager playlist application bundled with the hardware. Each application's DV output would load without trouble in each of the other compositing applications. A simple workaround for this problem is to render an image sequence from your compositing software, then use Speed Razor to assemble

Figure 17.18
DV Master Pro output image.

the sequence into a DV clip for playback. However, this lack of open systems interoperability is annoying, especially considering the DV Master Pro's $3,000 price tag. Aside from that, if you have already invested in DV equipment, this system may be your best choice.

Perception RT3DX

One of the most cost-effective solutions for a small studio or independent artist who needs to dump truly broadcast-quality digital art to tape on a regular basis is the DPS Perception RT3DX (or any higher product in the DPS line), shown in Figure 17.19. These systems are designed to work directly with broadcast equipment and are in daily use in some of the most demanding production environments you can imagine. The Perception includes a rugged, rack-mountable breakout box with output connectors for component, S-Video, and composite, along with multiple D-1 BNCs for dual-stream work plus stereo sound. This system is a real workhorse, and you'd be challenged to find something it can't handle.

Figure 17.19
DPS Perception RT3DX.

Once the Perception is set up, it's also the easiest hardware to run. As I mentioned in Chapter 5, the DPS software includes a virtual file system that makes the dedicated HDDs appear to contain folders full of image sequences in nearly every common file format. This enables you to access digitized video in almost any compositing software, transparently, without worrying about which file format suits each piece of your workflow. This is an excellent example of successful open systems design. The actual playback from the dedicated drives is an M-JPEG stream with a compression ratio of 5:1, so your comps shouldn't suffer much in the transfer. Your timing should also survive intact; because the Perception boards directly control the HDDs, the video outputs are rock-solid 29.97 fps with no dropped frames and excellent image quality, as shown in Figure 17.20. You'll have no worries about bandwidth, either, because this hardware has plenty to spare and doesn't borrow any from the rest of your system. The Perception is the only video system I've been able to test that is truly multitasking. You can run other applications while dumping video to tape without degrading the output color, resolution, or frame rate. At roughly the same price as the DV Master Pro, the Perception gives more value for the money, unless you really need direct DV I/O ports.

Video Toaster NT

NewTek's Video Toaster NT (Figure 17.21) is designed to output uncompressed ITU-R-601 video, but requires a drive or striped array that can sustain at least 22MBps transfer rate. If the drive hesitates, no frames are dropped, but the playback slows. As long as the drive keeps up, the output rate is a solid 29.97 fps. The Toaster does not monopolize the video HDDs, which enables you

Figure 17.20
M-JPEG frame from Perception RT3DX.

Figure 17.21
NewTek Video Toaster NT card.

to use them for other purposes when they're not full of video clips. The VTNT doesn't even dictate what type of drive you can use—SCSI, IDE, whatever, as long as it has a sustained data transfer rate of at least 22MBps. The most cost-effective way to achieve this data rate is to use Windows NT's striping utility to make the computer see several smaller, slower HDDs as one large, fast HDD. For example, if you have four HDDs that can each sustain 6MBps, you can stripe them into one virtual HDD that can sustain 24MBps. This enables you to use slower, less expensive HDDs. Setting up the striped HDD array is easy too. If you haven't done it before, the VTNT manual includes a step-by-step guide that had my system dumping comps to tape less than an hour after I opened the box.

The image quality from this system is also excellent, because there are no compression artifacts (see Figure 17.22). One minor quibble is that the Toaster's connectors are all BNC cable-ends rather than a nice, neat breakout box, so changing connections is a matter of chasing big black snakes around the floor. NewTek is working on an affordable 16-input switcher, and I recommend you add it to your shopping list if you're considering a Toaster. I/O options are also available for SDI and DV. The Video Toaster NT bundle includes an optimized version of in:sync's Speed Razor editing software, so you can edit your comps, assemble them with other footage, sync the audio, and output a complete production. Taking into account the $2,995 price, plus the bundled Aura paint and compositing and LightWave 3D graphics software, the Toaster is an excellent end-to-end choice for the small studio or individual artist who wants to produce videos.

The most significant disadvantage to the Toaster is that playback requires the footage to be in the proprietary RTV file format. All three bundled applications are optimized to work with it, but the RTV format is not used by any other compositing software. If you want to use other compositing tools, you have to convert RTV footage to a compatible file format through Aura, LightWave, or

Figure 17.22
Video Toaster NT uncompressed D-1 output.

Speed Razor, then repeat the process in reverse to get the finished comp back to the RTV format for real-time playback. This is a little annoying if you are trying to pop back and forth between applications, but it doesn't affect image quality as long as you don't use any compression in any of the file format conversions.

Recording Options

Your choice of recording media can either preserve the work you put into your comps or toss it all in the trash. You should choose the best format you can get your hands on. Don't go cheap on the media either. For both analog and digital tape formats, the wider the tape and the faster the tape speed, the better. The wider the track and the more tape you run past the recording heads per second, the more robust the recorded signal will be and the lower your chances of losing data to dropouts.

The trade-off is that using more tape is more expensive and reduces the time you can fit on a single cassette. However, digital compositing is such a time-consuming, labor-intensive process that tape costs are usually negligible in proportion to the rest of the costs for a shot.

Analog Recording Options

A good rule of thumb for analog formats is to record your master tape at least one step higher in quality than your distribution medium. Any analog medium incurs generational losses—that is, a copy of a copy of a copy doesn't look nearly as good as the original. If your master tape is at least one step higher in recording quality than your distribution format, it will go a long way toward counteracting that generational loss. For example, if you plan to distribute a production on VHS tape, your master should be at least S-Video quality or higher. On the other hand, if a production will be distributed only on VHS, it's overkill and a waste of money to master it on Digital HD. One way to choose an analog format for mastering tape is to contact your duplication service. If you tell them to what format you want it duplicated, they can tell you what master format they prefer for it. These are the people with the most experience, and they'll have to work with your choice in the end, so you should be able to rely on their advice.

If you are making a one-off tape for personal use, you can simply run a composite output to a consumer VHS deck. However, this will give you muddy colors, a maximum of about 350 lines of resolution, and a high rate of dropouts and other tape-induced artifacts. It will look lousy on anything better than a medium-grade 13-inch TV. The tape will also wear out faster, because most consumer-grade VHS tape is the cheapest media the manufacturers produce. This level of output is definitely not suitable for further duplication. This is not a good level of quality to show off your comps; even good comps look bad. However, if you're a starving student and this is the only way to dump your demo reel to tape, you can make it work. Just make sure your interviewer is aware of the restrictions on your tape output and doesn't blame your lack of compositing skills for the bad color control and crawly edges.

You can dramatically improve the quality of your VHS recording by using S-VHS. S-VHS decks will also record standard VHS tapes, and they are very affordable. Think of the price difference between the VHS and S-VHS deck as an upgrade to your computer's video output capabilities. The colors in your comps will remain more nearly true to what you saw on your workstation, the grayscales will be sharper, and you'll get between 25 and 50 additional lines of resolution. You can even use an S-VHS master to have VHS copies duplicated, although I don't recommend it. Whichever VHS or S-VHS option you choose, select the best-quality tape for your master. If you are making demo reels to send out, they should also be on the best-quality VHS tape, but make sure they are just long enough to hold your demo reel. If you send a tape that's over half an hour long, odds are good that someone will use it to record their favorite TV shows. You can buy standard short-length (5-, 10-, 15-minute) VHS tapes in bulk from a number of vendors (**neemannmedia.com**, **vhsduplication.com**, **camaudio.com**, and so on). If you are serious about getting into the digital compositing business, you should consider a case of short VHS tapes as an investment in your career, just like a box of résumé paper.

You will get marginally better results if you record your S-Video master to Hi8, a common camcorder format. I've been very happy with the transfers to VHS I've made from my Hi8 camcorder through an S-VHS deck. Again, this is fine for personal use and for cost-limited student demo reels, but I don't believe it's good enough for the paying customers. Also, the narrow and relatively low-speed Hi8 format is more prone to dropouts than more robust formats. I don't recommend Hi8 for archive tapes or for masters that will be used for bulk duplication.

For professional work or archival tapes, you should record a master tape on an uncompressed component medium whenever possible. Compression will almost always introduce some loss, and combining video signal components into either S-Video or composite signals will muddy the colors and blur the grayscales irretrievably. Even if you can't afford to own the necessary D-1 or D-5 recording deck, you can rent them to record your master tape, then create dubs to compressed or composite formats from the uncompressed masters. If your workstation can be lugged down to the rental shop, you can even bypass the deposit and insurance charges by making the transfer right there.

If you can't find a suitable VTR for rent in your area, talk to the nearest studio that uses one and find out what they'd charge you to make a transfer from your workstation. If you are starting up a small studio, they may be willing to make regular arrangements that benefit you both. You get the best-quality output for your comps, and they make a little more money to help pay off their expensive gear. If your work looks good, they may also throw the occasional job your way or subcontract you for the occasional comp they don't have the time or expertise to do in-house. Remember that every contact you have with a vendor is a chance to generate more business.

Digital Recording Options

Choosing to record digital S-Video or composite would be less than smart, because your comps are rendered in either RGB or YUV digital color space. Squashing that perfectly clean color signal into S-Video or composite is a complete waste. If you are going to the expense of recording digitally, you should only consider digital component video. For the same reasons, you should try to record with the best sampling pattern; 4:2:2 is the minimum you should accept. Formats such as DVCPRO that drop to 4:1:1 may be acceptable for some so-called "professional" uses, but your comps should demand a higher quality of sampling.

If possible, you should choose a larger tape format, wide enough and fast enough to give you a robust signal. Despite all the advances in technology, tape is not perfect: Digital dropouts do happen. If you consider that a video frame is typically held on the space about the width of a human hair and that the read/write heads are spinning at about 9,000 RPM, you can see that dust or tape flaws can easily cause dropouts. Given the choice between the ¼-inch DVCPRO50, the ½-inch Panasonic D-5, and the ¾-inch Sony D-1, which tape would you trust with your best work?

Digital tape formats have an additional layer of protection that analog machines don't. The error correction circuitry in digital machines can detect a dropout and substitute data from adjacent blocks to fill the gap. If the dropout is small, you won't even see it. If the dropout is larger, you may see a correction as large as an entire freeze-frame that lasts until the uncorrupted signal resumes.

If you are recording to digital tape for professional use, the lowest you should go is DVCPRO50 (*not* just DVCPRO!). This format offers 4:2:2 signal processing and a 3.3:1 compression ratio. This is relatively low compression, and differences from the original uncompressed images are barely visible. If you can't afford D-1 or D-5, DVCPRO50 is not a bad compromise. DVCPRO50 decks, such as the Panasonic AJ-D950A shown in Figure 17.23, are expensive for a small studio or individual artist, but not out of the ballpark for a medium-sized studio or a rental shop. This deck lists for $25,000, and records at 67 millimeters per second of ¼-inch metal particle tape.

A better choice is the D-5 format. This is uncompressed component video, so you don't have to worry about any image quality loss other than tape dropouts. Because this format records to ½-inch tape at 167 millimeters per second, the recording should be robust enough that you don't have to worry much about dropouts either. You can fit up to two hours on a tape, and the high bandwidth means you can convert some D-5 decks to HDTV. You'll pay high for the peace of mind: The Panasonic AJ-D580H deck, shown in Figure 17.24, originally listed for $75,000; and even at overstock and used sales, the best price I've found is $28,000.

The D-1 format is the undisputed top of the heap in standard definition video recording. It was the first digital videotape standard and is used primarily in specialized post-production applications where the image quality has to be perfect. It should come as no surprise that recording

Figure 17.23
Panasonic AJ-D950A DVCPRO50 VTR.

Figure 17.24
Panasonic AJ-D580H D-5 VTR.

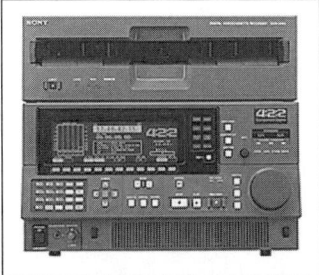

Figure 17.25
Sony DVR2100 D-1 VTR.

equipment for this format is also some of the most expensive available. Even when they are available used, D-1 equipment such as the Sony DVR2100 (see Figure 17.25) can run $64,000 or more. For your money, you'll get uncompressed component video sampled at 4:2:2 and recorded at 286 millimeters per second onto ¾-inch tape. If you're fortunate enough to find a studio that has one, expect to pay $200 or so per hour for the use of it.

Moving On

This chapter has provided you with the information you need to make the right choices for computer hardware, media, and recording equipment to preserve your comps at their best quality for multimedia, online, home, and broadcast video. The next chapter expands on this information to cover the unique issues of high-definition television, film, and electronic cinema.

THE BIG SCREEN

This chapter is the final step on the digital compositing path to the big time, the big bucks, the big screen. If you can make it here, you can make it anywhere. Your comps have to look good on screens so large that every pixel is several inches square, in front of audiences with trained eyes and high expectations. If you want to succeed on the big screen, you have to understand how that screen works. HDTV, film, and e-cinema media pose special problems that have a major effect on the appearance of your comps. You need to understand the idiosyncrasies of these media so that you can create the best-possible comps. If you don't know the limits and demands of these media, you might choose tools or techniques that work for standard video but look like junk on the big screen.

Until recently, film was the undeniable top end of special effects work by a huge margin. That margin has narrowed significantly with the ongoing conversion of broadcast television to *high definition television*. The difference between the best HDTV and the worst 35mm feature film is now less than the difference between the best and worst film projection standards. Sloppy film projection can sabotage the brightness, contrast, and resolution advantages of that medium, and exemplary digital projection can maximize the video equipment's performance. In other words, HDTV done right can look better than feature film done wrong. In addition, a number of technologies have come together in the last few years to make transfers from film to HDTV, or vice versa, much cheaper and with better results. The divide between video and film is narrowing and may soon be erased completely. The latest developments in electronic cinema, or *e-cinema,* are the precursors of the completely digital, film-quality processes that will soon become the new theatrical cinema standards.

Part of your responsibility as a digital compositor is to create art that can be transferred to whatever new standards become available. Knowing which production process to use can make the difference between losing your shirt and running your production into a dead end, or making money and distributing to every format that develops. If you choose a production process or recording format that makes transfers difficult, expensive, or lossy, you risk painting yourself into a very expensive corner. If you choose processes and formats with maximum compatibility, you will be able to adapt your production to any new format inexpensively and with the best quality.

High Definition Television

At the time of this writing, HDTV has not yet settled into a single format for use in the United States. The networks and major content producers have largely chosen up sides, but there is no clear winner (or loser) as yet. By the time you read this, the dust may have settled. Despite this uncertainty, I believe there are choices you can make that will guarantee your comps' success in any HDTV format.

The first choice you need to make is when to buy. You should know your clients. Do they really need HDTV? Can you generate a reasonable return on investment (ROI) from HDTV equipment purchases? Unless you can make a very solid business case for an immediate purchase, you should practice with rental equipment to get your feet wet and to buy time for prices to drop. As of this writing, HD equipment prices are as high as they are ever going to be. If you can temporarily shoot HD projects with rental equipment, that puts off the day you have to commit to purchasing that equipment. By that time, prices will be down, you'll have more choices, and you'll have the experience from the rental equipment to help you make well-informed purchase decisions. You may even be able to pick up bargains from early adopters who overspent and went under.

Before you see your first frame of HDTV footage, you should be aware of preproduction and shooting changes necessary to this format. The higher level of detail means that all your production values need to be higher. Those "minor" flaws in makeup, set dressing, and costume will become glaringly obvious in HDTV. For example, it's traditional for set designers and construction crew to incorporate in-jokes and other graffiti into a show's sets, small enough that they are not legible in the final production. At least one studio I know has had to redress a complex spacecraft interior set because the high-tech graffiti was perfectly legible on HDTV. Everybody connected with a production needs to be aware of the differences between SDTV and HDTV, or gremlins like this will take a bite out of the budget and schedule when you can least afford it. How would you like to do a track-and-blur on every bit of inconveniently legible graffiti in every interior shot of an entire production? Ouch! To play it safe, you should budget production costs as if for film on your first few HDTV projects and adjust the budgets downwards if necessary. That's a lot safer than budgeting for SDTV and having to adjust upwards!

Behind the camera, experienced SDTV directors, DPs, and camera operators who are new to HDTV will need to practice composing shots for both 16:9 and for possible conversion to the standard 4:3 box. There are two other new limits on the camera: no swish pans and no extreme close-ups. Early adopters have found that HDTV's higher-quality images encourage people to sit closer to the screen, creating a more immersive environment for your audience. Extreme close-ups are overwhelming, and swish pans can make viewers motion sick. The larger frame makes the director's storytelling job a little different. The 4:3 box enabled the director to restrict the audience's view, to tell a story with more control. The larger 16:9 frame allows the audience to decide what to watch. The director has to make allowances for that, or viewers may miss important story elements. Editing needs to make allowances too; whenever you cut in HDTV, the viewer needs an extra beat to scan the screen and make sense of the new point of view. Editing that is too fast will disorient the viewer.

Digital compositing, along with other postproduction effects work, has to balance a paradox. The center of the shot will be visible in SDTV's 4:3 ratio, and the edges of the screen will only be visible in 16:9 HDTV and film transfers. However, the wider formats are the ones that will most clearly show any flaws in the comps or other effects. The director can frame "4:3 safe" shots that keep the 16:9 edges unimportant to the story line, but you have no such shortcuts: Every HDTV comp has to be perfect across the entire frame. Welcome to the next level.

HDTV Hardware Selection

The quality of high definition television recording is controlled by the same factors as standard definition: bandwidth, compression, sampling, and media. You need to check the same specifications on compression ratio, tape widths and speed, and sampling frequency, pattern, and depth to judge the quality of the recording medium and hardware. The most significant difference is that all the numbers relating to bandwidth are much higher, mostly on the order of a factor of 4. If the production needs to be shown in HDTV, don't go cheap and try to produce in anything lower, then try to up-res the footage in post. It just won't look as good, no matter what equipment or software you use. If you need HDTV playback, you should record, post, and output in full HDTV.

At this time, there is a push to standardize HDTV on 1920×1080×24p. This is one of the standard HDTV resolutions, so that part is no surprise. The most significant change from NTSC SDTV is from 29.97 to 24 fps. The ATSC digital TV standard covers multiple frame rates, including 24 fps, so this choice fits within the available standards. The particular advantage of 24p is that it bypasses the necessity for 3:2 pull-down from film sources, and the reverse 2:3 pull-up to go back to film. Therefore, 1920×1080×24p can be output to film or downconverted to most other HDTV and SDTV formats easily, including 480i@24, 480p@60, 720p@60, and 1080i@30. Telecine for this format would be done at the highest resolution, and lower-quality formats downconverted from that master. Because 24p is progressive rather than interlaced, it can also be compressed more efficiently using MPEG-2. In short, if you create your work in 1920×1080×24p, you maintain simple and inexpensive compatibility with nearly every common film or video format. If you can capture at 24p, you can shift all the conversion issues downstream and perform all your digital compositing work in full-frame 24 fps, enabling you to use the same tools for film, HDTV, and SDTV. That can make an enormous difference to your workflow and your investment in your toolbox.

By the time you read this, Sony and other manufacturers should be shipping a number of new HDTV cameras, VTRs, and other production equipment, including 24p digital cinematography gear. At this time, you have relatively few choices between top-end machines suitable for recording your HDTV comps.

The Sony HDW500 VTR (see Figure 18.1) records a 1920×1080i (16:9) 10-bit digital component SMPTE-292M HD serial data stream through HD-SDI inputs with a bit rate of 1.5 Gbps at either 59.94 or 60 fields per second. This is an interlaced signal; the 24p version is due from Sony sometime in 2000. Visit **http://bpgprod.sel.sony.com** for details. Note that the color sampling depth for this deck is component and 10 bits per channel rather than 8. This isn't quite as good as some film scanners, but it's a significant step up from SDTV, and it will make a difference in the color quality of your comps. There is also an option for a downconverter to produce SDTV output. Currently, this deck is available for rental in major markets for upwards of $750.00 per day. The purchase price? If you have to ask, you can't afford it.

The Panasonic AJ-HD2700 VTR (see Figure 18.2) records a 10-bit digital component SMPTE-292M HD serial data stream sampled 4:2:2 at 74.25 MHz. Using advanced JPEG intra-field compression

Figure 18.1
Sony HDW500 digital HDTV videotape recorder.

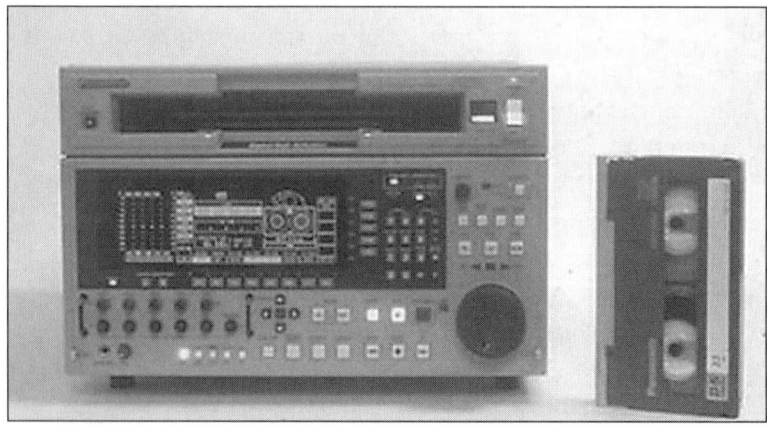

Figure 18.2
Panasonic AJ-HD2700 digital HDTV videotape recorder, and tape.

at a 5:1 ratio, this deck fits the HD digital video onto standard 1/2-inch D-5 tape running at 167 millimeters per second. You can record up to 124 minutes onto a single large cassette and select 1035i, 1080i, or 720p mode. This deck has already become a studio standard and was used to feed Texas Instruments' DLP Cinema presentation of Disney's *Tarzan* (see details under "E-Cinema," later in this chapter).

Film Recorders

Even after e-cinema systems have proven themselves, there is going to be a long period when many 35mm film projectors are still in use. And if you listen to Kodak and other film industry technologists, there's plenty of room for improvement in film stocks. If the order-of-magnitude improvements in color, resolution, and contrast that they predict ever materialize, they will go a long way toward prolonging a side-by-side existence for both electronic and film cinema. With that in mind, a digital compositor working today needs to be familiar with the existing needs of film recording technology. It's going to be around for a while.

Film has high resolution, random grain, wide contrast, and a continuous, nearly infinite color space. It has a fixed frame rate of 24 fps that is in use worldwide, as are the handful of common apertures or aspect ratios. What this means for digital compositors is that for film work you need to output your comps in the highest resolution and color depth that your workstation can handle, but you don't have to worry about interlace. If you have to match other film footage, you'll need to add grain to any elements that were smoothed out during compositing or any CGI elements that never had grain to begin with.

One big advantage to film output is that recorders don't need the data in real time, so your workstation does not have to have huge bandwidth or expensive output hardware. As long as you can dump the images to Exabyte, Jaz, CD-R, removable HDD, or whatever digital media your service bureau prefers, you can take hours to record each frame. Oddly, this makes the slowest workstation nearly equal to the fastest, at least for final data transfer to film. Rendering at film resolution—that's another story. Measuring by file size alone, you're talking about the difference between rendering a 1MB SDTV frame and a 12MB 2K Cineon frame.

Kinescope

The simplest and oldest way of transferring digital images to film is the *kinescope*. Basically, you point a single-frame-capable film camera at a high-resolution monitor, defocus the monitor slightly to hide the pixel grid, and film the frames as they are displayed one-by-one on screen. When the kinescope is home-built, this low-budget approach is even more reasonable today for student and independent projects because you can find bargains on old 16mm or 35mm animation cameras and the latest monitors have flatter, higher-resolution displays. It's up to the operator to watch the lens and monitor settings for brightness, color balance, focus, and exposure, which need to be consistent or the film will show obvious fluctuations. Because of these quality control problems, for any distribution more serious than minor film festivals, you need to make the transfer with a film recorder.

CRT Film Recorders

Cathode-ray tube, or CRT, film recorders are essentially a fine-tuned version of pointing a camera at a monitor. The CRT itself has at least 2K resolution, and the camera is a precisely registered film transport and exposure system that guarantees each frame will be placed and exposed exactly like the frames before and after it. The most popular recorder design uses a monochromatic (black-and-white) high-resolution CRT. This makes it easier to get higher resolution, because you only have one set of phosphors in the tube rather than three. To expose colors, a color wheel containing filters for red, green, and blue rotates between the camera lens and CRT. The camera takes three exposures for each frame, one for each color filter. The exposure process is time-consuming, as much as 40 seconds per frame on some of the older film recorders. The camera is often an adapted animation stand camera. The industry-standard Oxberry pin-registered animation camera, shown mounted on a recent-model film recorder in Figure 18.3, is popular.

CRT film recorders are more affordable than other types due to their relative simplicity. However, the precision engineering that goes into fine-tuning even simple technologies runs their prices into the hundreds of thousands of dollars. Only the largest studios with constant film output needs can make a good business case for buying a film recorder plus hiring a skilled operator. Most studios and independent producers use service bureaus for film recording. If turnaround time is not critical, the slower CRT film recorders will usually bring bargain rates of under $2.00 per recorded frame. Most major metropolitan areas will have at least one service bureau with a CRT film recorder.

Laser Film Recorders

Laser film recorders can be more precise than CRT-based film recorders because lasers can expose smaller spots on the film, producing less grainy, sharper images. Lasers are also brighter, enabling the use of less sensitive, lower-grain intermediate film stocks rather than grainier camera stocks. However, laser film recorders are more expensive than CRT film recorders.

The largest effects houses and film studios develop their own technology in-house. For example, Pixar Animation Studios co-founder and Director of Photo Sciences David DiFrancesco received his second Academy of Motion Pictures Arts and Sciences Scientific and Technical Academy Award in 1999 for work that led up to the new PixarVision Laser Film Recorder. DiFrancesco has been working on the use of solid-state lasers to record on motion picture materials since 1986. The PixarVision recorder exposes the film to all three colors simultaneously rather than sequentially, resulting in a speed of 8 seconds per frame. PixarVision also uses solid-state lasers, eliminating the crosstalk problems of the gas lasers used in other laser film scanners.

> *"This means that when you expose in the red channel, you don't get any blue exposure, and likewise, when you expose in blue you don't get any green. That's very important for densities under one, so you don't get muddy-looking shadows. You get higher-quality color reproduction."*
> —David DiFrancesco, Pixar Animation Studios

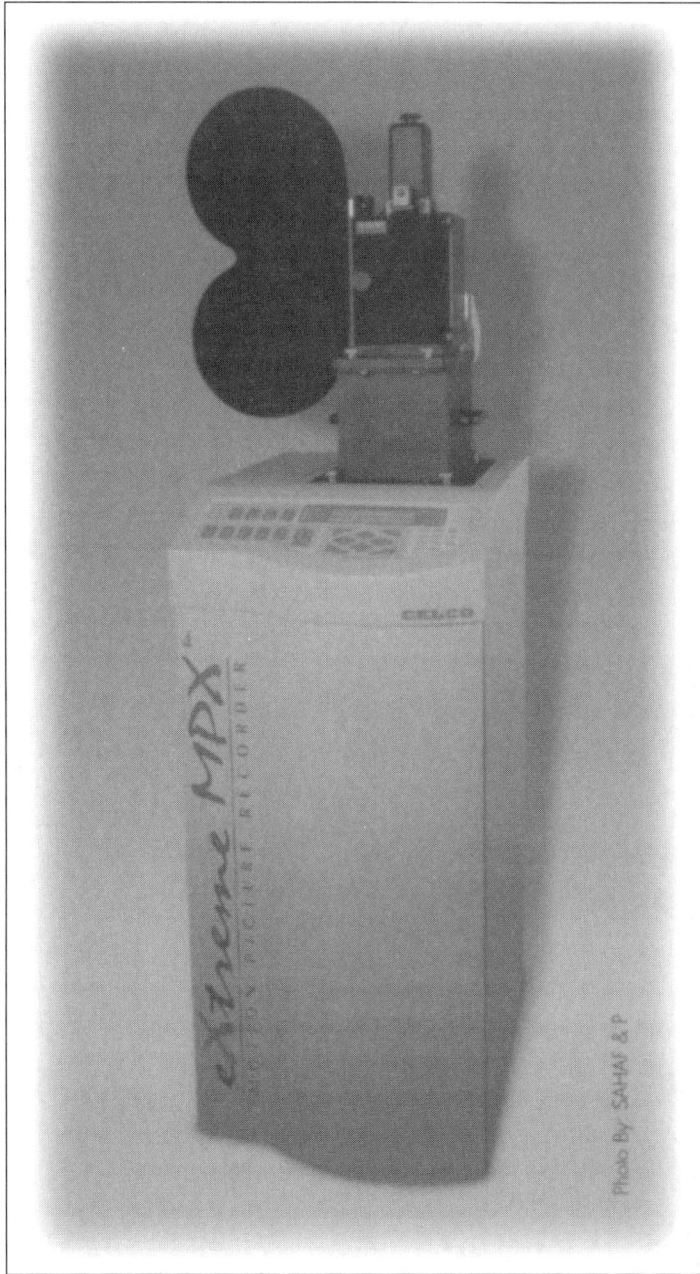

Figure 18.3
CELCO Extreme MPX film recorder with an Oxberry camera.

Solid-state lasers are also easier to use and maintain, because they don't require special power supplies or cooling systems and can simply be unplugged and replaced. The PixarVision scanner can print to virtually any film stock, including print stock. The scanner was used to print Pixar's

1998 film, *A Bug's Life*, and to print 1999's *Toy Story 2*. The film recorder was developed for internal use, and at this time, Pixar has no plans to make it available for sale.

There are several laser film recorders currently on the market. These are high-end, expensive machines in a very competitive market, so specifications and features change rapidly. One of the newest laser film recorders at the time of this writing was the ARRILaser, shown in Figure 18.4.

The laser film recording process starts with loading the film into the supply magazine of the recorder. Figure 18.5 shows the film path used in the ARRILaser. Note the supply magazine, camera, film shuttle, and take-up magazine.

Three solid-state lasers, one each for red, green, and blue, are behind a heat wall in the optics module (see Figure 18.6) to shield the rest of the scanner from their waste heat. Temperature control is important for film scanners, as for most precision equipment, so most facilities keep them in a climate-controlled room. The three laser beams are adjusted for intensity by the attenuators, which are neutral-density filters that compensate for differences in film stock sensitivity or for drifts in beam strength. Each beam then passes through an acousto-optical modulator (AOM). The AOMs modulate the intensity of the beams according to the data stream,

Figure 18.4
ARRILaser film recorder.

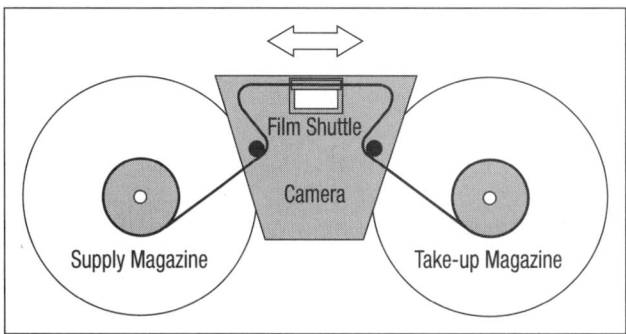

Figure 18.5
ARRILaser film path.

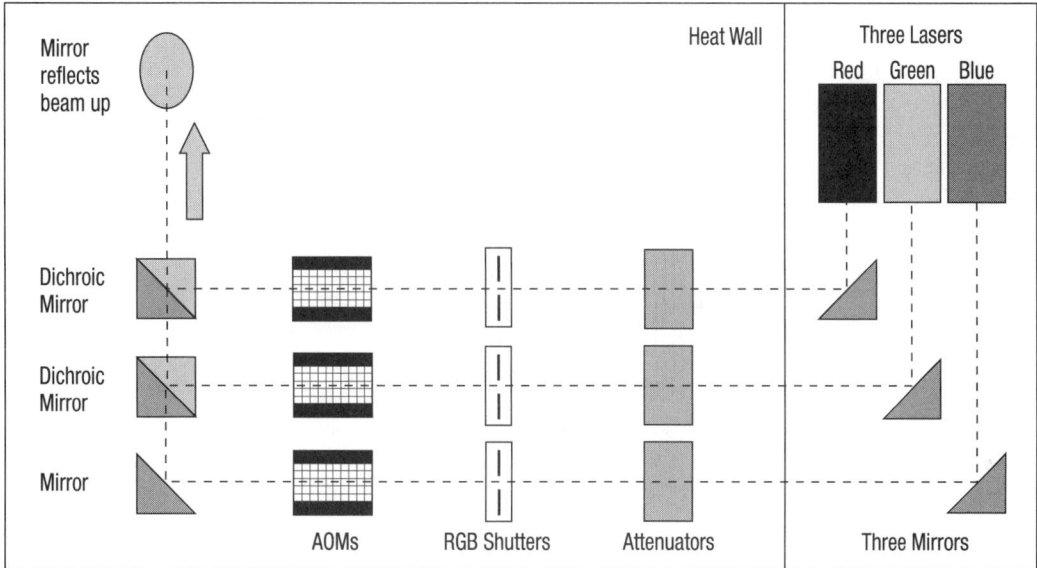

Figure 18.6
ARRILaser optics module schematic.

controlling how strongly each color will be recorded onto the film. From the AOMs, the beams are combined by a set of dichroic mirrors and finally are reflected up to the scanner module.

The scanner module (see Figure 18.7), guides the tricolor laser beam to the film. Lenses focus the beam, and a motorized prism deflects the beam to scan lines across the film.

Figure 18.8 shows how the deflected tricolor laser beam and the film shuttle's motion combine to expose the entire film frame. The scanning beam moves vertically at a very high speed, recording each line of the image. The film shuttle moves more slowly and horizontally, so that each pass of the vertical beam is precisely aligned to a new line of unexposed film. In only a few seconds, the combined motion of the shuttle and beam can record an entire full-aperture frame at 4K resolution.

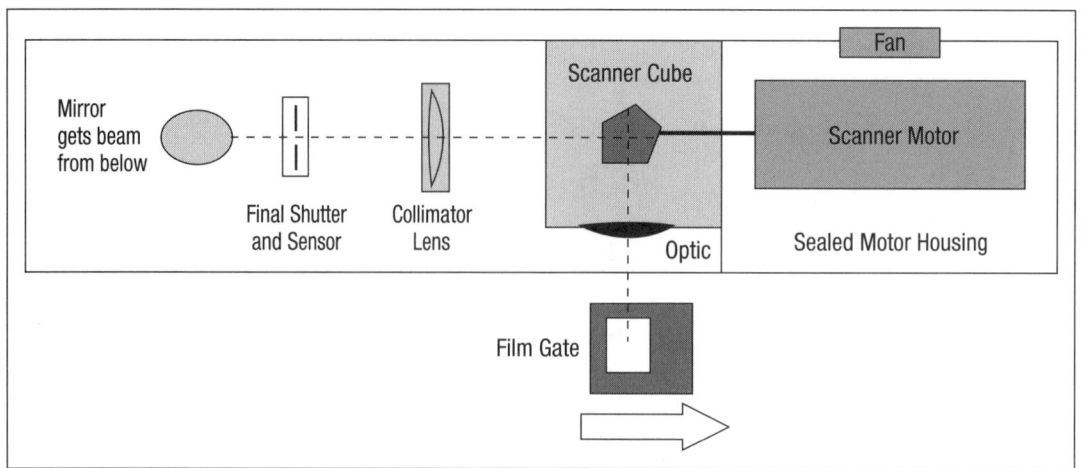

Figure 18.7
ARRILaser scanner module schematic.

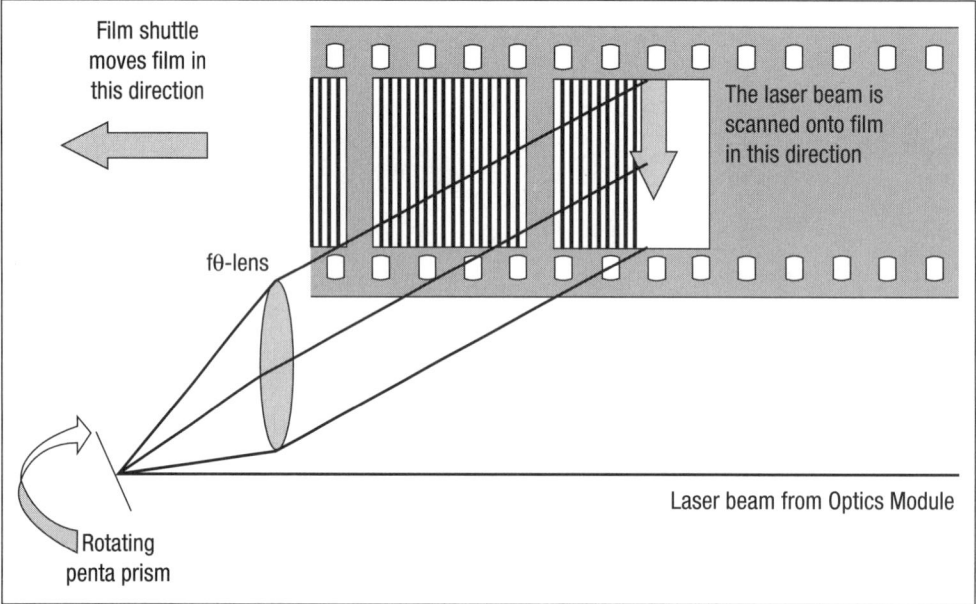

Figure 18.8
ARRILaser exposure process.

The film shuttle is only one part of the film transport. Figure 18.9 shows the four phases of the film transport cycle. First, the frame is positioned with two registration pins, mounted on the film gate, that precisely locate the film to prevent any unwanted frame-to-frame motion. When the film is locked in place, the film shuttle moves four perforations (one frame) to the right at a precisely controlled rate, synchronized with the laser beam scanning.

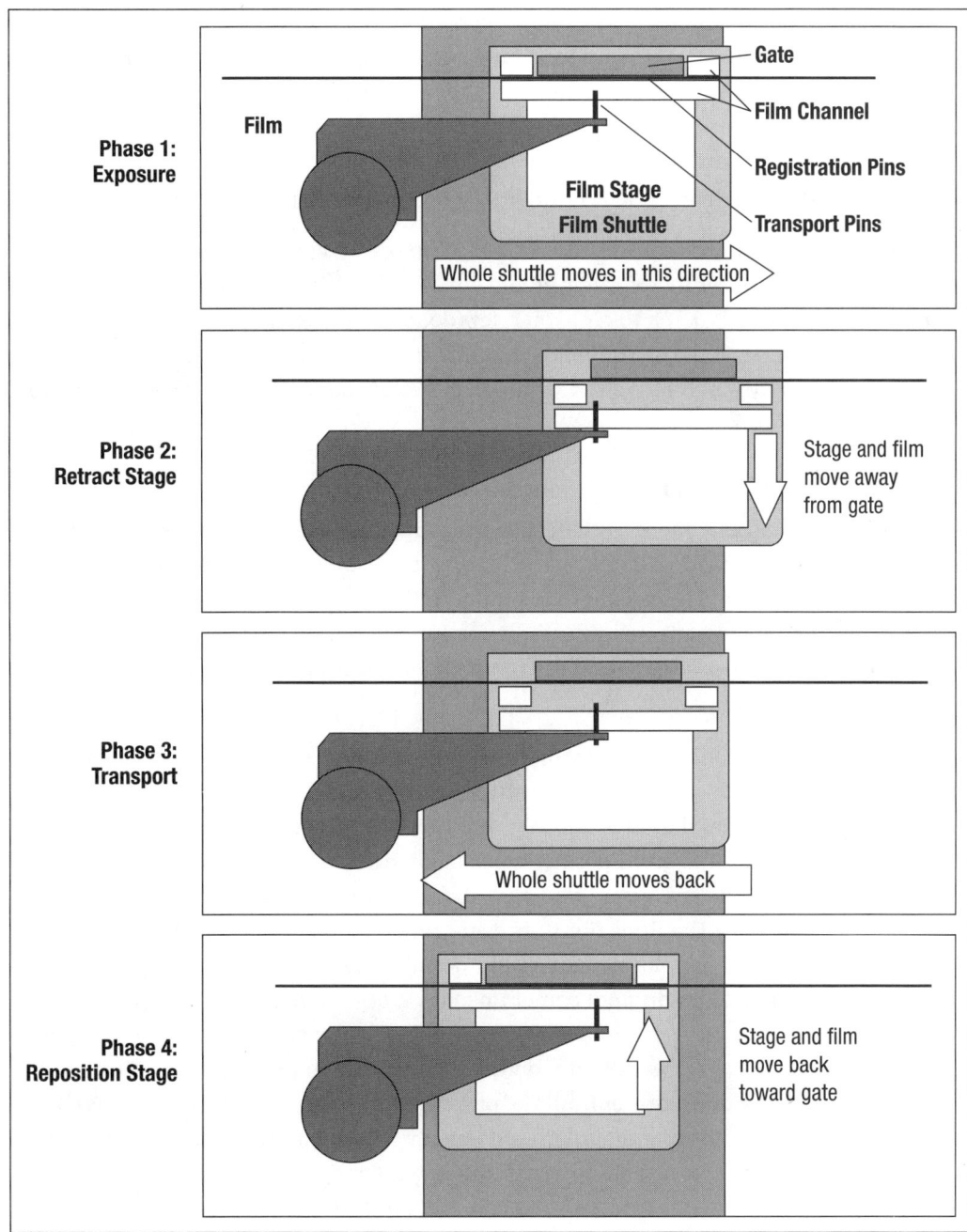

Figure 18.9
Four phases of film transport in the ARRILaser film recorder.

In the second phase, after the frame is completely exposed, the film shuttle stops and the film stage moves away from the gate, removing the film from the registration pins and transferring it to the stationary transport pins. This keeps the film stationary during the third phase, when the film shuttle returns to its starting position at the left. From this position, the film shuttle moves toward the film gate in the fourth phase, picking the film off the transport pins and moving it onto the registration pins. Once the film is registered, a new exposure phase can begin.

Although advances in laser film recording have speeded up the process considerably, it still takes a relatively long time to transfer long-format productions to film. It's also expensive: Even the lowest-quality film recording is going to cost you a few dollars per frame, and top-end recording can be over $5.00 per frame. You will also have to search a little harder to find service bureaus that use the highest-quality machines, but if you're in either the Los Angeles or New York metro areas, you can take your pick.

Electron Beam Recorder

A relatively new and potentially more cost-effective way of getting your digital files to film is the electron beam recorder, or EBR. This device uses electrons rather than photons to record an image, so no optics are necessary. The difference is similar to the inherent difference between the sharpness of an electron microscope image and the fuzziness of a light microscope image. Electrons don't scatter in the film emulsion, and the result is that the image on film is unlimited either by optics or by its own halation.

Because electrons have no color, black-and-white film is used. Sony Pictures' High Definition Center (SPHDC) is one of the few shops that uses this process, but their results have been very promising. Because very fine resolution is possible with an electron beam, the image quality is exceptionally good on 35mm fine-grain positive stock (Sony uses Fuji 71337). To get color, you output color separations for the red, green, and blue channels, and each channel is printed to a separate black-and-white film. The three films are step-printed on an optical printer to an MOS color negative (Kodak 5245). The color negative is hard-matted to 1.77:1. The negative is developed, with quality very close to an original camera negative, and an MOS one light print is struck. If you need them, you can have many apparently original print negatives struck, each with identical high quality. This gives EBR film a visible advantage in projection, because most theater prints are two generations farther from the original. As of this writing, SPHDC was charging $1.30 per frame for transfers from digital files. If you are coming from HDTV video, SPHDC will handle the conversion to film resolution and frame rates. For details, visit the Sony Pictures High Definition Center Web site at **www.spe.sony.com/Pictures/Hidef/sphweb.htm**.

E-Cinema

Electronic cinema, or *e-cinema,* is a system of projecting cinema-quality images directly from digital data without the use of film. E-cinema poses special problems for digital compositors. Several attributes of conventional 35mm film projection work together to hide small details.

Grain masks imperfections; e-cinema has no grain. Projected film can weave and jitter, which combines with the lower refresh rate and (possibly) incorrectly set optics to degrade its effective resolution; e-cinema is rock-steady. Film collects damage, dirt, and fades; e-cinema is digitally identical from first to last show. Acceptable film print resolution for feature film is 2K, or 2048 lines of resolution. This is partly the result of theater prints being several generations removed from the original footage. One of the advantages of digital cinematography is that it has no generational losses, so it can preserve every bit of its lower resolution and end up looking just as good as fourth-generation film on the big screen. Also, electronic projectors can run at higher refresh rates, effectively increasing brightness while reducing visible flicker.

Whenever a medium has imperfections, the audience comes to expect them and allows the artist more leeway. The more perfect the medium, the more perfect the work the artist has to produce. Even at the current stage of e-cinema development, the audience response has been clear. As with HDTV, even for nonprofessionals, the difference between film and e-cinema is noticeable. One group of viewers of the e-cinema presentation of *Star Wars: The Phantom Menace* remarked that the CGI shots looked "like a video game." Comments on the e-cinema quality of *Shakespeare in Love* also pointed out flaws in makeup, sets, or props that had gone unnoticed in the film presentation. In order to make audiences buy into a shot shown in e-cinema, the comp is going to have to be absolutely perfect.

The technical challenges of e-cinema are significant. From 5,000 to 10,000 lumens are required from the e-cinema projector to provide the same brightness of image as a conventional 35mm film projector. The image contrast ratio needs to be higher too, which means the luminance sampling depth needs to be at least 10 bits and preferably 12. At least 1,500 vertical lines of resolution are necessary to make a digital image difficult to distinguish from a film image. As of this writing, only two manufacturers have systems that meet theatrical film standards.

The Hughes-JVC (**www.hjt.com**) projector (see Figure 18.10) puts out 10,000 lumens, projecting images at up to 2000×1280 resolution, with contrast greater than 1500:1. It can accept RGBHV, digital serial 4:2:2, RGB analog, composite, Y/C, and component inputs in NTSC, PAL, and SECAM. Its heart is a light modulator composed of three proprietary image light amplifiers (ILAs), a 100 percent solid-state liquid crystal light valve. The ILA processes and amplifies the image from a CRT and adjusts color, contrast, and brightness to match the look, tone, and texture of film footage. The current CRT is limited to 2K resolution, but the ILA itself is capable of 4K resolution, so this system has a clear upgrade path. The projector's light source is a standard 7,000-watt xenon arc lamp. The list price on this projector is $250,000. Hughes-JVC has partnered with QUALCOMM to form CineComm Digital Cinema, L.L.C., chartered to "provide a full turn-key system for movie delivery and exhibition." CineComm provided half the projectors for e-cinema showings of *Star Wars: The Phantom Menace* in 1999.

The other projectors for the *Star Wars* e-cinema presentations used Texas Instruments' (**www.ti.com/dlp**) Digital Light Processing (DLP) imaging technology, shown in Figure 18.11.

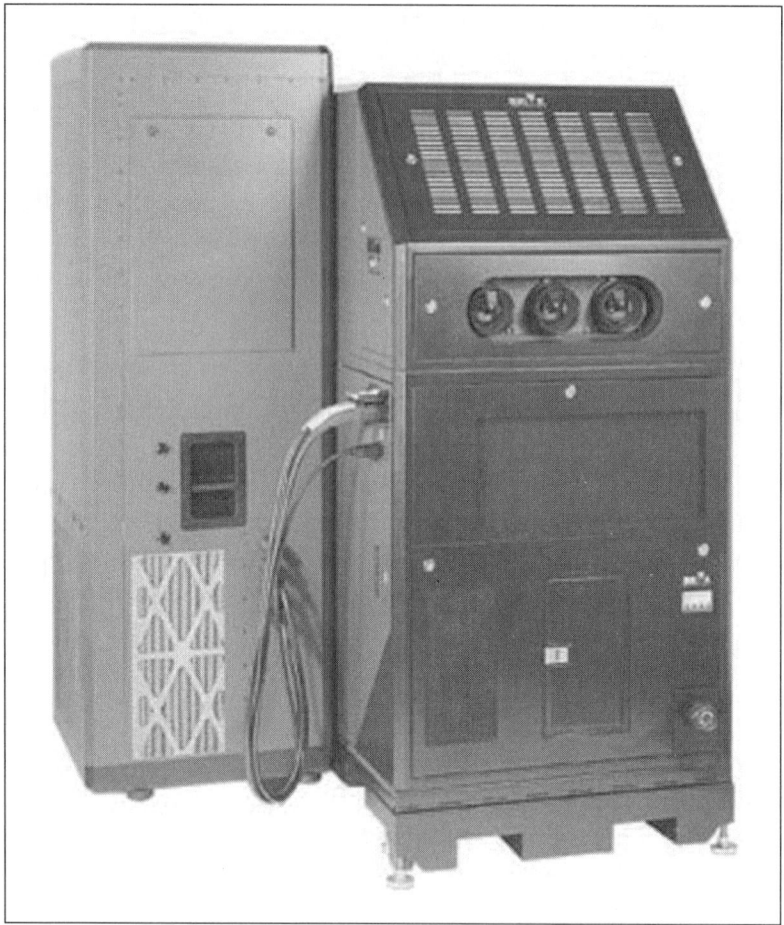

Figure 18.10
Hughes-JVC projector.

The core of this technology is the Digital Micromirror Device (DMD) shown in Figures 18.12 and 18.13. This technology is limited to the actual pixel resolution of the device, so higher-resolution images depend on the development of higher-resolution DMDs. TI has already produced a 16:9 ratio DMD with 1920×1080 resolution on a trial basis, so we can expect to see 1600×1200 or even 2000×1500 DMDs in the not-too-distant future. The DMD is a matrix of microscopic mirrors that rapidly switch on or off more than 5,000 times per second, creating an image in the light beam that reflects off the DMD's surface.

DLP-based projectors can use up to three DMDs in one system. A three-chip system utilizes a prism to split and recombine color. Filters deposited on the surface of the prism split the light into red, green, and blue components, as shown in Figure 18.14. Each of the primary colors is assigned to its own DMD, which reflects monochromatic light back into the prism, where it is recombined and projected onto a screen.

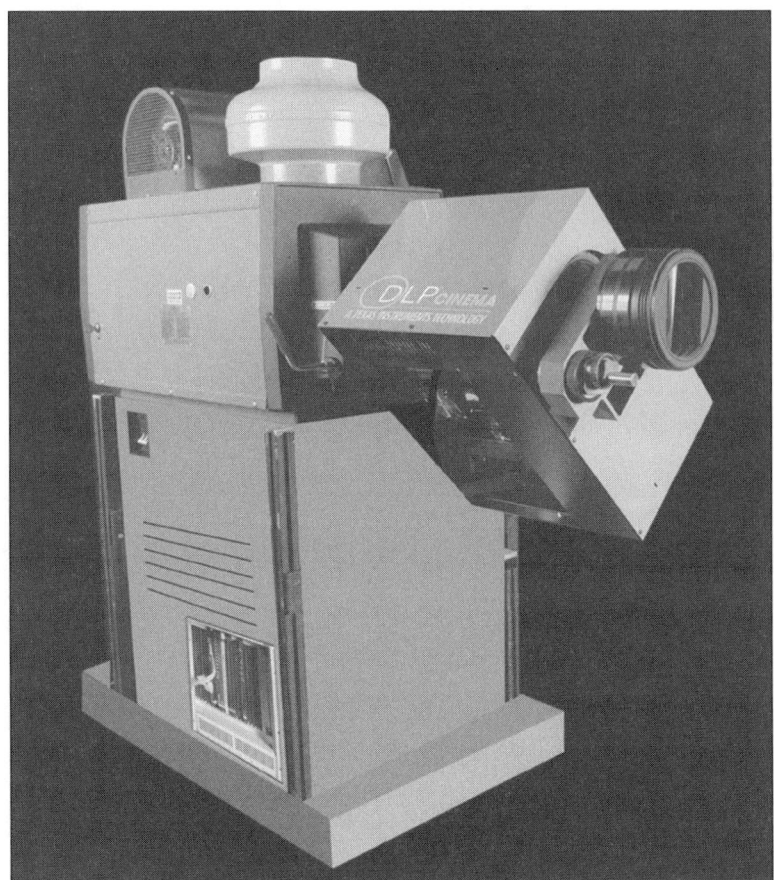

Figure 18.11
Texas Instruments' Digital Light Processing projector.

Figure 18.12
Digital Micromirror Device chip with SXGA resolution of 1280×1024, containing 1,310,720 mirrors.

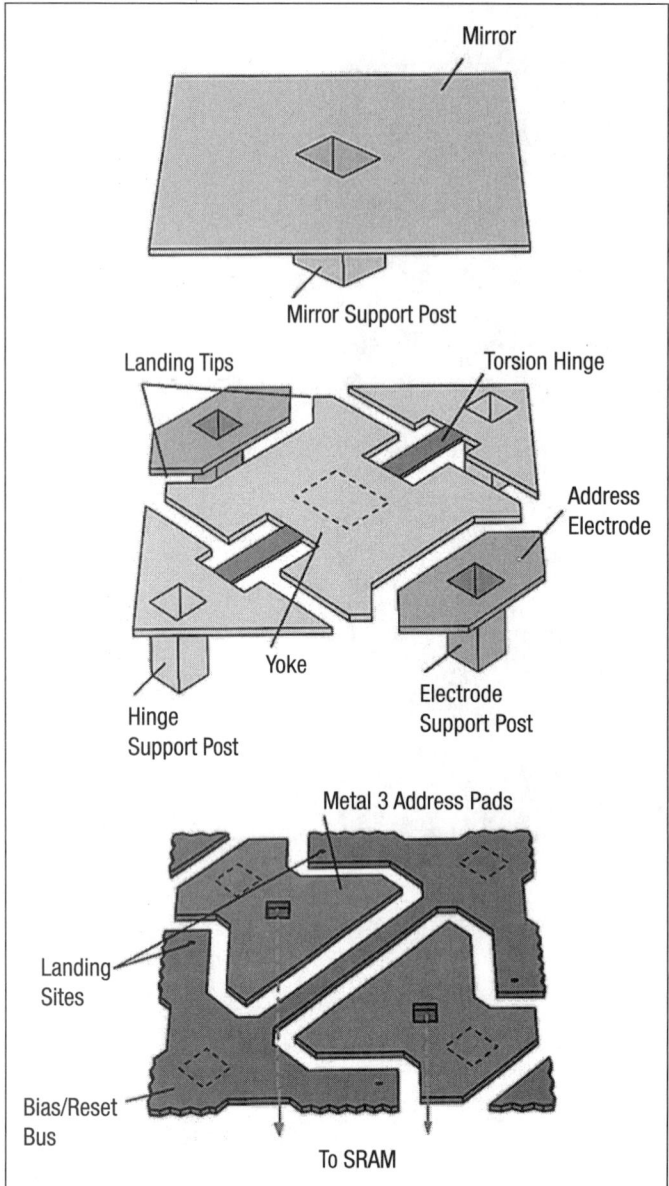

Figure 18.13

DMD™ Architecture: Exploded view of an individual mirror on a DMD. Each 16 µm2 mirror on a DMD consists of these three physical layers and two "airgap" layers. The airgap layers separate the three physical layers and allow the mirror to tilt +10 or –10 degrees.

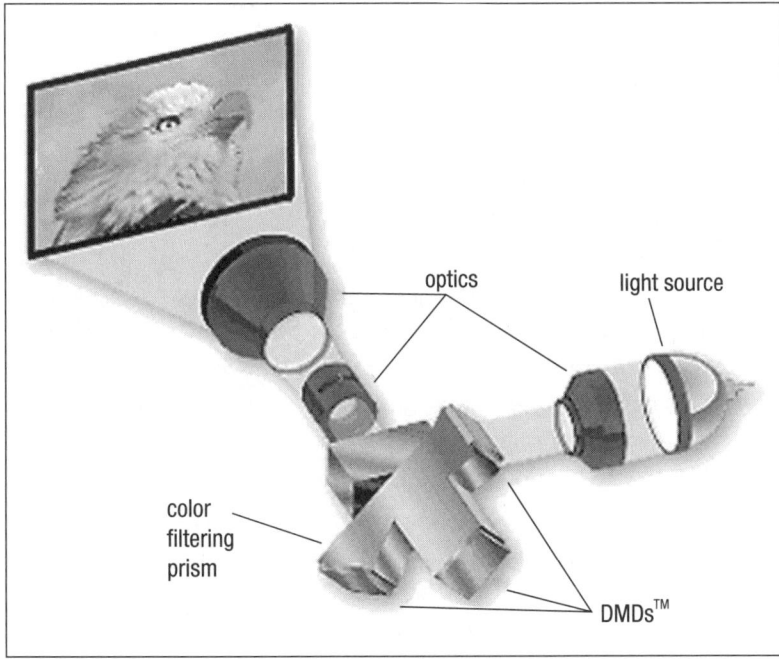

Figure 18.14
White light is split into the primary colors. Each color is directed to its own DMD for the entire frame time, producing greater brightness than that displayed in color-sequential systems.

E-cinema technology is already being accepted at the highest levels of the special effects industry. At ShoWest in Las Vegas on March 11, 1999, George Lucas announced his plans to shoot *Star Wars* prequels 2 and 3 with digital cameras, edit and post digitally, and screen them digitally. In April, at NAB '99, Sony and Panavision announced an agreement to develop filmless, digital cameras for Lucasfilm. The first production-ready prototype camcorders were expected to be delivered to Lucasfilm in the fall of 1999 for testing with Panavision lenses.

Multiplex cinema owners are not likely to start ripping out their film projectors immediately, but the demonstrations of e-cinema to date have been impressive. The remaining technical questions are only of time. The financial questions are a matter of allocating the changeover costs between the cinema owners who need the expensive new projectors and the film distributors who stand to save large amounts of money on distribution costs. This changeover affects your future as a digital compositor, but fortunately, it seems to be a positive outlook. Your work will come under closer scrutiny, and that's an opportunity to hone your craft and show what you can do.

TEXAS INSTRUMENTS DLP CINEMA PRESENTATION OF *TARZAN* FROM WALT DISNEY PICTURES

Source: The movie was transferred from digital source data generated by the Walt Disney Feature Animation's in-house digital production process, CAPS, directly to HD/D-5 format with no intermediate film element. Color timing was modified using a DaVinci 2K color corrector. The transfer was supervised by Disney Feature Animation, Buena Vista Home Entertainment WorldwideTechnical Services, and Entertainment Technology Consultants.

Resolution: The DLP Cinema prototype projector uses three TI Digital Micromirror Devices™ (DMD), each with an array of 1280×1024 microscopic aluminum mirrors for a total of nearly 4 million mirrors. Each mirror is 16 mm square with a 1 mm space between each. The imaging mirror array is within 1 mm of the size of a Cinemascope™ film print image. The movie is projected through a custom 1.5:1 anamorphic projection lens to create the 1.85:1 image on screen. The anamorphic lens was manufactured by ISCO-Optic of Germany.

Contrast: The DLP Cinema prototype projector produces a sequential contrast ratio of 1000:1.

Storage: The picture information was compressed and stored using a Panasonic Digital High Definition Recorder (AJ-HD2700). This unit performs a relatively mild 5:1 compression of the data, using an advanced JPEG intra-field adaptive compression scheme. As an entire digital cinema production, distribution, and exhibition infrastructure develops, other storage technologies will be tested, and more-robust nonlinear storage technologies are expected to be adopted.

Pixel Data: The image data is stored at 10 bits/component (Y/Cb/Cr) in 4:2:2 format. Because the DMD is a linear display device (i.e., it has no gamma characteristic as does a CRT), the data is gamma-corrected and converted to linear RGB data. Each DMD displays 14 bits/color, linear data.

Frame Rate: The TI DLP Cinema prototype projector displays at the standard film rate of 24 fps. Because the DMD is not scanned like a CRT but is a virtually continuous display device, the display can be driven at 24 fps with no objectionable flicker.

Shutter Rate: Unlike a film projector, DLP Cinema technology does not involve the use of a shutter. Because there is no film being mechanically pulled through a film gate, there is no need to douse the light. This results in a continuous flicker-free display and a more efficient use of the lamp output.

Lamp: The prototype DLP Cinema projector uses a standard film projector lamp housing provided by Strong International with a custom lamp reflector. A standard 4 KW Xenon lamp made by Osram is being used, producing approximately 10,000 lumens. This yields a screen luminance of approximately 12.5 ftL, which is roughly equivalent to the current Society of Motion Picture and Television Engineers (SMPTE) specification for nominal screen luminance. Greater than 80 percent brightness uniformity is achieved on screen.

Audio: The audio information is stored as 16-bit uncompressed PCM data on a Tascam MMR-8 hard disk-based digital audio recorder. Six of the eight available channels are used for left, center, right, right-surround, left-surround, and low-frequency effects. A timecode signal from the AJ-HD2700 is used to synchronize the audio to the picture.

—Courtesy of Texas Instruments Inc.

Moving On

This chapter has provided you with the information you need to make the right choices for recording equipment and media to preserve your comps at their best quality for HDTV, film, and e-cinema. That's the last of the technical information you will need to master to be a successful digital compositor. However, there's more to being a success than mastering your art; business skills are important too. The next chapter contains information you can use to manage your career in digital compositing, whether you are trying to break into the business, stay employed, or start your own studio.

PART VII

THE BUSINESS SIDE OF COMPOSITING

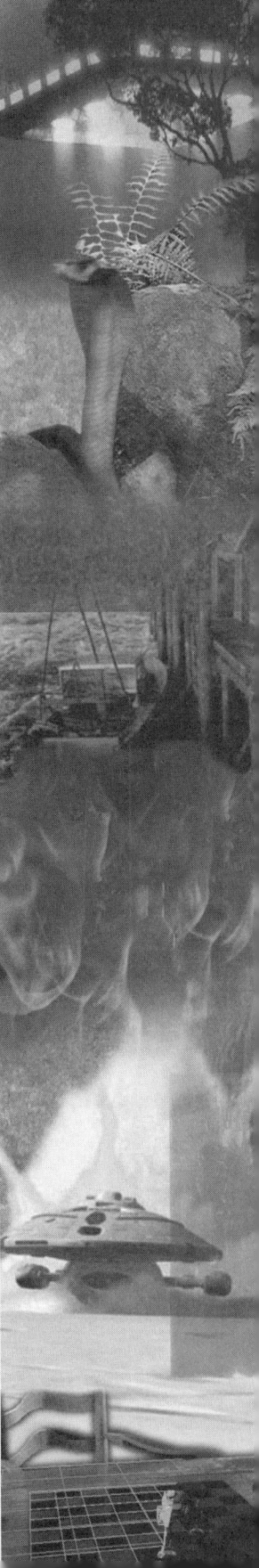

CHAPTER 19

TAKING CARE OF BUSINESS

When you are trying to break into the business, you need to know what employers are looking for and where to find industry information. After you land a job, you need to know how to keep it and how to avoid being exploited or disabled. You need to know even more if you want to start and run your own studio.

Starting Out

This chapter contains information you can use to start or continue your career in digital compositing. This information is as accurate as I could make it; but this industry is moving fast, and the details change all the time. I encourage you to double-check any critical information before taking irrevocable actions—like mailing your last copy of your demo reel to an out-of-date address.

> *"Happiness lies in being privileged to work hard for long hours in doing whatever you think is worth doing."*
> —Robert A. Heinlein

Compositing is not a career choice you should make lightly or on the spur of the moment. Most successful compositors I have interviewed have always had an interest in the visual arts, and many have spent years developing their skills. If you have been attracted to digital compositing by recent publicity on high salaries and many job opportunities, think again—this is a job you do because you love it, not because you get paid a lot to do it. The "high" salaries are not enough to compensate you for long hours and grueling work if you do not sincerely love what you are doing. Moreover, those high paychecks are the very top of the field; there are many more journeymen compers who make a decent living but who are not bringing home six-figure salaries.

Self-Education

Trying to teach yourself digital compositing is not an easy road. There are few proven paths to a successful career. Most of the time, you will have to rely on the contacts you make and the feedback you receive from your fellow students and colleagues. It is not a career choice for the weak or fainthearted.

Fortunately, there are more resources for the self-taught compositor today than at any previous time. This book and others like it, focusing on one or more software packages, are good places to start. Books on compositing and visual effects (see the Bibliography) are excellent sources of information, if you do not mind translating their techniques into something you can do in your software. For more timely information, there are magazines and professional journals in a variety of related fields. These are the journals I use (and contribute to) myself—long on information, short on fluff, and generally reliable to get the story straight:

ACM Transactions On Graphics

ACM Transactions On Graphics is a quarterly academic research journal dealing with the algorithms and other theoretical arcana behind graphics programming. Techniques first published here sometimes take years to show up in commercial desktop software. Smart technical staffs read this journal and work out their own implementations to stay ahead of the commercial pack.

www.acm.org/pubs/tog
ISSN: 0730-0301

Computer Graphics Magazine

Computer Graphics is a sister publication to *Transactions*. The contents are more about implementations and tutorials, and the annual SIGGRAPH Conference Proceedings are always a worthwhile collection of eye candy and solid information.

Association for Computing Machinery
11 West 42nd Street
New York, NY 10036
www.siggraph.org
ISSN: 0097-8930

Cinefex Magazine

Cinefex is the trade journal of the feature film special-effects community. Slick and heavily illustrated, this quarterly publishes long, in-depth, nuts-and-bolts articles on f/x techniques. Bluescreen, match moves, CGI, you name it—if it ends up on the big screen, *Cinefex* shows how it is done. Even the issues that do not include compositing articles have lots of useful information on related topics, and the advertiser's index reads like a Who's Who of houses you would like to work for.

Cinefex
P.O. Box 20027
Riverside, CA 92516
Phone: 800-434-3339
www.cinefex.com
ISSN: 0198-1056

Computer Graphics World

Computer Graphics World covers pretty much what the title says. You will find articles here about hardware, software, and other technical issues, and the industry news leans more toward hardware and software vendors than effects houses. The downside is that space constraints force tutorials to be less detailed than one would prefer.

CGW
10 Tara Blvd., 5th Floor
Nashua, NH 03062-2801
www.cgw.com
ISSN: 0271-4159

Keyframe Magazine

Keyframe Magazine is dedicated to LightWave, Aura, and Inspire enthusiasts. I am the editor, but even if I were not, I would encourage you to subscribe to this magazine. Every issue has at least one Aura tutorial, usually from the people at NewTek who work with it every day and have the inside track on new features.

DMG Publishing
2763 West Avenue L, Suite 162
Lancaster, CA 93536
Phone: 888-778-WAVE
www.keyframemag.com

Post

Post is a post-production trade journal useful primarily for news on who is doing what. You should at least scan the promotional and help-wanted ads scattered throughout the magazine for production houses that may want to hire you.

Testa Communications
25 Willowdale Avenue
Port Washington, NY 11050
Phone: 516-767-2500
Fax: 516-767-9335

DCC Magazine

DCC Magazine is a large-format trade journal for digital content creation, covering film, video, and multimedia. This magazine, published by Advanstar, has gone through a number of mergers and other major changes in the last year or two. As of this writing, it seems to be settling into lots of industry news, several decent reviews, and a few tutorials, and a little less than half advertising space per issue. I recommend it as the best single source to keep track of technologies and related news pertinent to digital compositing.

201 Sandpointe Ave., Suite 600
Santa Ana, CA 92707
Phone: 714-513-8400
Fax: 714-513-8612
www.dccmag.com

DV Magazine

DV Magazine covers digital video and related technologies, with a mix of reviews, feature articles, and a handful of tutorials in each issue. A little over half ads, it's published by Miller Freeman. DV has less industry news, but more depth and technical accuracy than DCC, and I think the tutorials are more reliably worthwhile. The Web site is worth a visit, especially for the archive of past tutorials.

411 Borel Ave., Suite 100
San Mateo, CA 94402
Phone: 650-358-9500
Fax: 650-358-8891
www.dv.com
ISSN: 1075-251X

Just The FAQs, Ma'am

A FAQ, or Frequently Asked Questions, is a document containing questions and answers that are often asked of a discussion group or help desk. Just about every major newsgroup, mailing list, or Web site has a FAQ. Smart vendors compile their own FAQs for technical support and make them freely available via the Internet.

Reading FAQs has to be the easiest, cheapest way in the history of the world to fake being an expert. Contrariwise, jumping into a newsgroup or mailing list and asking the number one question from that group's FAQ instantly labels you as a dweeb too dumb to pour sand out of a boot.

Schools

Choosing to attend a school to learn digital compositing is a big decision. You will be dedicating several years (depending on the program) and anywhere from a few thousand to a few tens of thousands of dollars. Make sure that you will be getting your time and money's worth.

The most important factor in choosing a school is the faculty. You are better off with great teachers and lousy equipment than with lousy teachers and state-of-the-art computers. Any dealer can sell you the hardware and software. Experienced compositors who can also teach are much more difficult to find. If possible, use your network contacts to find teachers with solid reputations, then get into whatever program they are teaching. If you take this approach to its logical extreme, you might consider tracking down a really good compositor and negotiating private lessons or an internship.

Your best resource in making this decision is the school placement office. Media schools like to brag about the studios that have hired their students, so ask for the names and contact information of well-placed graduates. Most compositors will be happy to discuss their educational adventures, such as which teachers to seek out, which ones to avoid, and pitfalls in the curriculum that you should sidestep. If a school cannot give you the names of at least three graduates who are employed as compositors, and who speak well of the school, look elsewhere. There are entirely too many get-rich-quick media schools springing up, and I have heard some nasty horror stories from their graduates. Graduates of one large "diploma mill" have told me that the school *rescinds the diplomas* of graduates who publicly criticize it!

I recommend against the "vocational guide" type of book that does a once-over-lightly of an industry, then ranks or recommends schools. In digital compositing, information older than a semester or two is dangerous. The best faculty may have left, and the remaining program may be a waste of your time and money. A more timely resource is the Visual Effects Society's schools page, with direct links to schools and to other lists of schools: **www.visualfx.com/schools.htm**.

You might also benefit from the VES education conference/seminar program. Information is available at: **www.visual-effects-society.org/resources/education_rs.html**.

There is a strong correlation between traditional art training and success as a digital compositor. The top practitioners in the field mostly have fine arts degrees, often in parallel with computer science or film school credentials. With this in mind, you should examine a potential school's accreditation and certifications carefully; remember that the ability to confer undergraduate and/or graduate degrees in fine arts is essential. If a school cannot maintain its accreditation to award fine arts degrees, the odds are against your getting an adequate education there. There are a few good "trade schools" that provide excellent training without awarding a fine arts degree, but those are the fortunate exceptions to the rule.

Practice

Practice, practice, practice! A compositor composites! Whether you are in school or studying on your own, you should try to composite something every day, for as many hours as you can afford. Keep raw elements handy, so you can just load them up and start compositing whenever you have the time. If you do not have original footage to work with, go back and recomp any of the project footage from the CDs included with this book. The more practice you have on the basics, the more easily you will be able to composite the hard stuff. Set a goal for yourself to composite a certain number of shots per week. Over time, you will get faster. Raise the goal and keep challenging yourself. Resist the temptation to slap together schlock just to make your goal. You should insist on every shot being the best you can do at that time. Do not throw away any of your finished practice efforts—these comps are a record of your progress. Append everything to your archive reel, so you can show it to mentors, fellow students, and potential employers.

Some schools do not emphasize building a demo reel. You might complete years of study and only have a few minutes of completed shots to show for it. However, if you composite something every day, completing as little as 10 seconds a week will enable you to assemble a 10-minute archive reel in just over a year. If you have three times as much work to show as the other candidates for a job, you will definitely have an advantage. Get to work on it!

Best Foot Forward: Your Demo Reel

Completing the step-by-step projects in this book will not get you a job. You need to go beyond this and put together a presentation that tells potential employers that you can comp any shot they hand you. This presentation will be your demo reel.

You should keep all your material, including textbook exercises, on an archive reel. Keep copies of the separate elements of each shot, too; you want to be able to show the raw materials you had to work with and the problems you solved. You can take this archive reel to an interview, where you may have the opportunity to discuss your learning experiences and techniques. All those bits and pieces of work in progress will help convince a potential employer that you actually did the work on your demo reel.

For your demo reel, select at least three minutes of your best work from your archive reel. Your demo shots should go well beyond any tutorial you may have read. As a digital compositor, you will be expected to solve new problems, not just use others' solutions. Show that you understand your tools well enough to push their limits. You can get by with less than three minutes if your work is very good, but you should have a reasonable explanation ready if you have less than two minutes. Do not go over five minutes. Reviewers will have decided in the first few minutes whether they want to talk to you—anything over five minutes is probably not going to be looked at.

Put your absolute best 10 to 30 seconds of compositing at the beginning of your reel. At least one supervisor told me he would hit the fast-forward button if he does not see something interesting in the first 10 seconds. Remember, these people sometimes have several hundred reels to go through, so do not waste their time or test their patience.

If you have a lot of material you want to show, resist the urge to do an MTV-style montage of fast cuts. Some reviewers will not mind this, but it annoys others, and you do not want to risk that. If at all possible, arrange your pieces in some logical order to minimize the jarring effect of cuts.

Put your name and contact information at the beginning and end of your reel. Keep your titles simple and legible, and if possible, make them into a digital-compositing showpiece. Do not put a date on your reel, and do not explain what software you used to make your comps either. Some houses will automatically turn you down if you do not use their favorite software. On the other hand, if you apply to a house that relies on the same software you used to produce your reel, it is pretty easy to put an explanatory printed insert in the cassette case. Your philosophy should be to let your work speak for itself—don't give the reviewer any irrelevant information they could use to weed you out. One exception to this is credit for others' work. Make sure that everybody who contributed to the work on your reel is credited on the insert, with details of who did what on which pieces. It's far better to volunteer this information up front than to be answering awkward questions at an interview.

Depending on how good your material is and how paranoid you are, you may want to rig your demo reel so unscrupulous persons can lift nothing from it. One simple technique is to run a SMPTE timecode window across the bottom of the screen. Another is to imbed your name somewhere in the frame in a way that is hard to remove. If you choose to do this, make sure that the "protection" you employ does not protect you from becoming employed. Keep it as unobtrusive as you can.

Effects houses will be looking for some very specific elements in your reel. They want to see that you can do the work you are applying for—not just that you have the potential to be able to do it someday. If your demo reel does not show what they are looking for, you can expect a polite letter to the effect that "We have no requirement for your services at this time."

If you want to be a digital compositor, then show digital compositing in your demo reel. The supervisors who review your reel will be looking for a clear understanding of rig removal, matte extraction, tracking, and the other compositing concepts you have worked through in this book. Beyond that, they will be looking at the whole effect of your work. Is the comp seamless? Do the effects shout out to be noticed, or do they blend invisibly into the shot? Did you match the lighting, or do the elements seem to be thrown together like a bad collage? Make sure that your video transfer is clean. If the video is full of static and dropouts, the viewer will not be able to accurately judge the quality of your work. You may want to include prints of some of your best images, as you can get better quality than videotape, and the reviewer can examine them at leisure.

If you are sending tapes to studios in the U.S., record your demo reel on standard VHS videotapes. You can buy inexpensive 10- or 15-minute videotapes in bulk at very reasonable prices. (The short length keeps people from taping soap operas over your reel.) That's what everybody in the industry uses, and if you are the only one in the stack with a CD-ROM, Zip, or floppy disk, reviewers are unlikely to make the extra effort to look at your work. Even if they do, they are going to expect more from you than from the tapes that made their job a little easier.

A good rule of thumb is to pretend that the reviewer is busy, irresponsible, disorganized, and forgetful. Make your reel fast and easy to view, hard to lose, and easy to remember and to locate on a crowded shelf or in a box of other tapes. Rewind the tape before you send it, and pop out the no-erase tabs. Unique or colorful labels with your name and contact information on the spine, face, and ends of the cassette will help. If your tape has a label and the rest of the shelf is just blank black plastic, you have improved your chances. Remember, it can take months before a busy studio gets to your reel, or they may be keeping you in mind for an upcoming job. Make sure that they can find your reel when they remember you.

You can also jog the reviewer's memory by putting a thumbnail image on your demo reel labels. A memorable element from the reel is best, but a personal logo or other simple graphic will work too. Use the same graphic on any cover or follow-up letters you send. You are sending your reel to people with good visual memories and perhaps only so-so verbal skills. Make it easy for them to remember and then identify your reel.

Quality, Not Quantity

What you leave off your demo reel is at least as important as what you put on. You are only as good as the worst piece on your reel. If you want to be employed as a digital compositor, leave the cheesy effects and old tutorial projects on your archive reel. And even if it looks like good digital compositing, leave off the clichéd effects. Unless you can bring something original to the old standbys, you are better off without them.

> You are only as good as the worst piece on your reel.

Never put the results of an exercise or tutorial on your demo reel. (That includes the projects in this book.) Supervisors or directors at effects houses have seen every demo, exercise, and tutorial a zillion times by the time they get to your tape, and you can guarantee an instant ejection and trashing if you put a "transporter beam" or similar over-used demo on your reel. Keep your reel original.

It should go without saying that *original* means your own work, but some people apparently are still not getting the message. Digital compositing is a relatively small professional community, and everybody sees the good demo reels eventually. I have heard similar stories from just about every reviewer about really stupid plagiarists who assemble "their" demo reels from other people's. It is especially stupid when the reviewer finds his or her own work, or a friend's, with the plagiarist's name on it. Of course, the reviewer immediately tells all their industry friends about it, and the plagiarist cannot get work anywhere. Plagiarism is an excellent way to cut your career off at the knees. Don't do it.

As stated in Chapter 1, one of the most liberating things about desktop digital-compositing software is that you really *can* do it all. Software tools are available that can assist in digitizing, creating CGI elements, compositing, audio and video mixing and editing, title design, and film or video recording. The question is, do you want to handle it all?

It may be to your advantage to work with a complementary partner or group to produce a joint demo reel. If your talents are in graphics and design, working with a cinematographer can build a reel that is more coherent and entertaining, and that demonstrates you work well as part of a team. As a compositor, you will find that working with higher-quality elements gives your reel an extra polish that puts it above the competition's.

Whatever your approach, if you follow this book's guidelines in putting together a solid, professional-quality demo reel, you will have a good chance of landing a job interview.

So, how can you improve your chances? Sending in a demo reel "cold" is a common approach, but this has some drawbacks because the most popular studios receive hundreds of reels. At some studios, a secretary filters out the absolute trash before any of the creative or supervisory staff get to see it. This can occasionally result in a reel being trashed for reasons having nothing to do with the talent of the compositor—the "filters" simply do not know what they are doing.

If you are sending a demo reel, it is a good idea to get the email address, fax, or phone number of a senior effects supervisor or director at the studio and send them a polite message that you would like to send in your reel. If they agree, tell them exactly when you are sending it, and if they give you permission, add their name to the Attention line. This way, the reel is more likely to be put aside for someone who knows what he or she is looking at, and the person you contacted may even ask to see the reel before the filter gets to it.

Remember that your contact person is doing you a favor. Be polite. Do not call the person at home. Do not nag. Send a follow-up thank-you note. And never broadcast whatever personal contact information he or she gives you.

Résumé, Portfolio, And Cover Letter

Do include a résumé and cover letter with your demo reel. Keep it businesslike, neat, and correct. If you submit a résumé with typos, it doesn't speak well for your attention to details. Run a spellchecker—that is what word processors are for. Creative layouts are okay, but make sure that both the letter and résumé are easy to read. Some supervisors are getting along in years, and their eyes are not what they used to be. Tiny or confusing typography is counterproductive.

Stress your schooling and/or industry experience. Include your outside interests, especially pursuits like photography, animation, or painting that contribute to your talents as a compositor. The better studios have gotten past the sweatshop mentality and are looking for people with balanced lives. The burnout rate on workaholics is too high to support in the long run.

In your cover letter, stress the position you are applying for and why you want it. Show that you understand what the job entails and why you want to work for this particular studio.

If you have other artwork, sending in a duplicate portfolio is acceptable to many studios. Call or write ahead to make sure that it is OK and, if possible, put as much of it on your video demo reel as possible. The simplest approach is to do a pan-and-scan coverage of your 2D art or sculptures, with close-ups of the fine details. With a little extra work, you can make this an attractive exercise in compositing and editing as well. If you do send a portfolio, make sure that it is a duplicate. Color photocopies are perfectly acceptable, and most studios cannot guarantee to return materials. Never send your only copy of anything.

Interviews

You got the call to come in for an interview. Great! Now calm down. That is the first rule in surviving an interview. Yes, it is a stressful part of life, but nobody has ever been executed for a poor interview in this business. You will live through it.

Right now, you are in a very good position for doing well in an interview. The demand for competent, talented digital compositors is still high, and most production studios are doing anything they can to lure new hires. That puts more control in your hands (just don't abuse it), so relax and just be yourself. The interviewer has every reason to try to hire you—he or she will be looking for reasons to hire you, not to turn you away.

If the interview requires air travel, the company should arrange and pay for your travel and lodging. Never fly to an interview on your nickel; if the company won't pick up the tab, they aren't serious. If it is just a short drive or a cross-town trip, you will be expected to handle it on your own.

Most effects houses are very casual places, and the few that aren't are nasty places to work. Typical attire is jeans and T-shirts. If you show up for an interview in a suit or other business attire, that's two-and-a-half strikes against you. I know several people who were hired after interviewing in ripped jeans and grungy T-shirts, but that's pushing it a little. Casual but clean is your best bet.

You probably were asked to come in for an interview because of your demo reel. If your reel was an accurate representation of your talents, the interview is going to be relatively easy for you. The interviewer will probably ask some technical questions about your work and may ask to see some rough work-in-progress examples from your archive or story reel. This is just a check to make sure that you actually did the work on your reel.

Your interview materials should include examples of every step in the process for your demo reel: storyboards, production and reference photos, raw footage, construction of CGI elements, extracted mattes, test renders, and so on. This is where your archive reel comes in. If possible, make prints of key frames from each element of your best comps. Prepare to be interviewed with or without a VTR handy. Don't just whip your prints or archive reel out first thing—that is a little pushy, and there is always the chance you will show them something they do not like. Just keep your portfolio case or briefcase in plain sight and wait for the interviewer to ask to see it. If the interviewer asks a technical question about something on your demo reel that is best explained by one of the prints or archive reel, go ahead and show it.

Aside from the technical interview, interviewers will be trying to assess whether you will fit in with other employees. I've heard stories from several studios about very good technical hires that just didn't work out. The persons in question could do the work and were, in fact, very talented; they just couldn't work well with the other members of the team or in that particular studio's culture.

The interview is also a chance for you to ask questions about the working environment. In most shops, the interview includes a tour of the facilities and introductions to many of the other team members. Use this time to ask questions about the work environment. How much creative input do people in your position have? Who will you be reporting to? How long does a typical project last? What is your potential career path within the studio? What is a typical day like? How long do people work, and at what hours? Is the daily routine regimented or free-form? Is there a lot of informal cross-pollination of ideas, or do people pretty much stay in their cubicles? Where do people go for lunch? Is the local takeout any good, or do a lot of people pack lunches? This is not as trivial as it sounds—you will be spending an hour a day (at least) with these people at one or more meals, and if the gang's favorite takeout is something you are violently allergic to, you will be miserable.

Look at the cartoons and other art on the walls, especially the work areas of people who will be working closely with you. If you see nothing on the walls and the interviewer tells you "Dilbert" and *South Park* have been banned from the facility, look for work elsewhere. In the same vein, if the interior looks as though it was inspired by the Marquis de Sade, you may be happier elsewhere.

Getting Hired

So you get a phone call, or the interviewer asks when you can start. Congratulations! But don't quit your current job just yet. Think about the offer at least overnight. They shouldn't get upset if you tell them you need to sleep on it. Also, you should ask for a letter or fax, on company letterhead, spelling out the terms of their offer. I learned this one the hard way: I accepted a verbal offer of employment from a fairly large company, relocated across the continent, then was informed that the position had been eliminated in a reorganization. Nothing was in writing, so I didn't have a leg to stand on, legally. Don't let that happen to you—get the offer in writing!

Are they offering enough compensation, both pay and benefits? Will you be able to cover your living expenses plus savings, IRAs, and other financial needs? Nothing's wrong with making a counteroffer if their offer is too low. Benefits like vacation time, overtime, and comp time are negotiable too. Unless the studio is very large and has ironclad labor contracts, everything is on the table. If your annual two-week trip to Yosemite is more important than an extra $3,000 in salary, negotiate for the extra time off.

If you are relocating, you must take into account your new cost of living. If you are accustomed to life in rural New England and you accept a new job in Los Angeles, you will be in for a shock: Car insurance, rent or mortgage payments, utility bills, restaurant meals—just about everything—costs more, a lot more. Additionally, you will have to buy some things you never needed before, such as serious security systems and electrostatic air filters. Make sure that your new job will compensate you enough to cover these expenses.

Before you sign an employment contract, read it carefully and run it past a good entertainment lawyer. Not the family lawyer; you need an entertainment specialist. There are some serious land mines in entertainment law that can make your life miserable if you are not aware of them. For example, some studios insist on a noncompete clause, which means that if you quit, you cannot work anywhere else in the industry for a number of years. There is some question as to whether this practice is even legal, but the threat of a lawsuit can definitely dampen your chances of being hired elsewhere. Even if you decide to go ahead and sign a restrictive contract, you should at least know what you are in for.

Not Getting Hired

So you don't get a phone call. Don't just sit there; send out more demo reels! The best way to wait for that one perfect job is to go out searching for others. The worst way is to sit by the phone waiting for the call that never comes. At the end of each interview, ask when you can expect to hear from them again. Wait this amount of time before you call, but then you should definitely call them back. Remember that the people who looked at your demo reel and who interviewed you are also the ones doing the work, and they do get swamped. Dealing with clients takes precedence over hiring new staff, but that does not mean they do not want you. Jogging their memory can make a big difference in how long it takes to hire you, or it will at least let you know that you should be looking elsewhere. You may also be just the right person for a job opening they will have in six months, so stay in touch.

> "Press on—nothing can take the place of persistence. Talent will not; nothing is more common than unsuccessful men with talent. Genius will not; unrewarded genius is almost a proverb. Education will not; the world is full of educated derelicts. Perseverance and determination alone are omnipotent."
> —Calvin Coolidge

If you get a definite turndown, don't take it personally and don't give up. Use this opportunity to ask the interviewer (politely, of course) for a critique of your demo reel and/or interview. If the decision was based on the quality of your work, ask what you need to improve and for advice about additional training or practice. If the decision was based on personal compatibility, ask if they can recommend any shops that might be more suitable. The effects community is a relatively small one, and most of the players know one another. It never hurts to ask for a referral.

Networking

Speaking of referrals, you should try to build up your list of contacts in the business. Keep track of everybody who has seen your demo reel, interviewed you, or spoken with you at SIGGRAPH or other gatherings. If possible, collect their email and other contact information, and keep it up-to-date. Get on the Internet, if you aren't already there. The minimum service packages available from most Internet service providers are very reasonable and consitute a worthwhile investment. Watch the industry press and monitor the appropriate mailing lists and Usenet newsgroups for announcements or gossip about upcoming projects, and use this contact information to let them know you are available. Whenever you update your demo reel, send out notices to the appropriate people, asking if they'd like to see it.

This is very important: Do *not* simply add all these people to a personal mailing list and send them a lot of trivial form-letter email. When you have new information to distribute, send an individual email to each person. If you reuse most of the text, at least make enough changes that the message is not an obvious form letter. Unless you are already on a first-name basis with the recipient, make your emails as formal and structured as a cover letter for a résumé. Keep the message brief, make your points clearly and succinctly, and be polite. Each message you send to a potential employer is the same as showing up on their doorstep unannounced—you better have a good reason for doing so, and it had better be in their best interests to hear what you have to say. Being an inconsiderate nag can get you on everybody's filter list, meaning they will never listen to you again. Use your best judgment.

If you want to survive in this business, stay in touch with your colleagues. The effects business is still project-based; only the largest studios (and not all of those) keep everybody on staff when there is no paying work for them. Some compositors follow the work, staying at a studio through a project, then moving on to another project at another studio. Others may stay at a studio for years, working on whatever comes by and hanging on through the dry spells. For either approach, it is a good idea for you to stay informed about who is working where, on what project, and for how long. Even a large studio may have to suddenly cancel a project and lay people off, for business reasons having nothing to do with the merits of the project. If you are well connected and up-to-date, you will be able to find another job immediately. If you have been out of the loop for awhile, however, you will have a harder time of it.

Mentoring

Whether you are a student, self-teacher, amateur, or professional, you can use a good mentor. Mentoring can include occasional career advice, a fresh pair of eyes to critique your work, frequent tutoring, and even collaboration. It depends on what you need and what your mentor can provide. There are a lot of ways a more experienced person can assist your growth as a compositor.

Finding a mentor will take some effort. If you are working in an effects house, you may have coworkers willing to act as mentors. If you are a student, one of your teachers may be able to give you the extra time outside of class. If you are on your own, try meeting senior effects people through the following networking resources. If you hit it off with one of them, ask if they'd be willing to mentor you.

SIGGRAPH

SIGGRAPH is the Special-Interest Group of the Association for Computing Machinery (ACM) that deals with computer graphics, from scientific visualization to entertainment. The annual SIGGRAPH conference is the major CGI event of the year. If you are at all interested in computer graphics as a profession (or even a serious hobby), do not miss it. This is where the software and hardware vendors and studios pull out the stops. SIGGRAPH is held in Southern California every other year, and the alternate years rotate from city to city. SIGGRAPH '98 was held in Orlando, Florida. You can find future venues at the SIGGRAPH Web site. Don't miss it! For information on the SIGGRAPH conference, contact the following:

Association for Computing Machinery
11 West 42nd Street
New York, NY 10036
www.siggraph.org

Visual Effects Society

The Visual Effects Society is an organization for experienced professional effects people. You have to have been in the business for five years, and have two current members vouch for you, to become a member.

> *"The Visual Effects Society is an organization comprised of visual effects professionals who desire to honor, advance, and promote visual effects for its membership and the industry as a whole. The goals of the Visual Effects Society are to promote continuous public and business awareness about the visual effects industry, to support combined technology research and development, to design and implement educational programs for talent development and public understanding, to establish an awards program to acknowledge creativity from the various skilled disciplines which are utilized in the creation of visual effects, and to address any other issues deemed important by its membership and Board of Directors."*
> *—Quoted from the VES Mission Statement*

As of this writing, VES has over 400 individual members. Corporate members include CBS Animation Group, Cinesite, Digiscope, Digital Domain, Dream Quest Images, Dream Theater, DreamWorks Animation, Flat Earth Productions, Industrial Light + Magic, Pixel Magic/OCS Freezeframe, Pacific Data Images, Pacific Title/Mirage Studio, and View Studio. VES sponsors special events for members, including presentations and discussions with some of the top artists in the field. Most of the activities are located in the Los Angeles area. If you can get a job with a member studio (or convince your current employer to join), attending VES functions can greatly improve your networking opportunities.

You can contact VES at the following:

Visual Effects Society
15118 Valley Vista Blvd.
Sherman Oaks CA 91403
Phone: 818-789-7083
Fax: 818-789-7085
Tom Atkin, Executive Director
visual.effects.society@worldnet.att.net
www.visual-effects-society.org/main.html

VFXPro: The Daily Visual Effects Resource

VES and Creative Planet have cosponsored VFXPro, a Web site with some of the best information available on the visual effects community. Interviews, job postings, industry news, and tutorials combine to create one of the best online resources I know of for digital compositors. You should make VFXPro one of your top bookmarks and visit it at least a few times a week, at **http://VFXPro.com/**.

If you have the talent and you have followed the preceding guidelines, you should be well on your way to landing a job in digital compositing. The next section has some tips for coping with your working life when you are employed in someone else's studio.

Being An Employee

If you have landed your first compositing job, congratulations! You are on your way in a career with lots of opportunities for personal growth, increasing public recognition, and artistic satisfaction—not to mention that at least some of your work will be just plain fun. Seeing your work in public for the first time, whether in a video game, on TV, or on the silver screen, will be a rush you will not forget. Most digital artists I have talked to still get opening-night jitters when they attend premieres—it is a thrill that will not fade, as long as you care about your work.

> *"It is fun, and if you can't appreciate the creative joy of doing it, then probably you should be doing something else."*
> *—Eric Jurgenson, Video Workshop*

Now What Do I Do?

So, what is your job? No matter what your job title or description reads, your number one job is getting the work done. That means doing your assigned work, plus working well with others, taking direction, and understanding how the rest of the studio works. You are not a cog in a machine—you are a voice in the chorus, a creative artist who collaborates with professional colleagues to produce great digital compositing. The better you understand others' work, the better you can do your own.

Whenever possible, find out how you can make your coworkers' jobs easier. If others are depending on your work, ask what they need from you. If some small additional task on your part makes their part much easier, do it. Conversely, you should tactfully let coworkers know how to make your job easier. One way to do this is to show polite interest in the jobs of people who provide footage, CGI elements, and other materials for your job. If the studio has been running successfully for a while, you will probably find out that they are way ahead of you on labor-saving tricks. However, once in a while, you will find they are spending a lot of effort on something that is not crucial. Handle this diplomatically. As a general rule, make positive reports and compliments in a personal way, but try to put negative reports and critiques in as objective a form as possible. It's just human nature— nobody enjoys criticism, even when it's constructive.

Understanding exactly where the studio priorities are is of vital importance to your career and your current project. It is not unreasonable that two weeks of your time may very well be less expensive than two days (or even two hours) of someone else's. I ran into this situation a few years ago when I was coordinating materials from about 60 individuals for a corporate project. I was presented with more than 20 different file formats, which meant I would have to spend a lot of time translating them to a single common format. I tried to impose some file format standards. The project director took me aside and very reasonably explained that it was more time- and cost-effective for one person (me) to be stuck doing a week's worth of translating than to retrain 60 other employees who all had more technically demanding work to do. Sometimes doing tedious, apparently stupid work is the most effective use of your time on a project. It is nothing personal, so do not take it that way. Remember your position. You will be starting off on a very low rung and should not try to act like you are a director. Entry-level positions, even well-paid ones, are for people who are there to learn.

One of the best things about the digital-compositing business is that after you are on the job, nobody cares whether you graduated from a premier school or you taught yourself. The majority of effects studios are well-run businesses where hard work and talent are rewarded. In fact, most are complete meritocracies; it is only your work they notice. Make sure that your work says the right things about you: good, solid, on time, and with no unpleasant strings attached. If you do magnificent work but are a prima donna, every time the director sees one of your shots, he is going to remember the temper tantrum you threw while working on it. On the other hand, if you put in a lot of extra effort to make an excellent shot, every time the director sees it, she will remember you in the best-possible way. Give your employer good value for value received. Work for the hours you are paid and give the best efforts that your talents, skills, and full attention can produce. Make them glad they hired you.

Make Your Boss Look Good

One of the smartest things you can do on your first job is to make your boss look good. If there is a problem on the project, resist the urge to blurt out the solution to all and sundry. Instead, see your supervisor privately, and float your idea as a possible solution. If it is not viable for some reason, you have not embarrassed yourself. If it is a good idea, your supervisor can help you develop it and can share in the credit. This is good for both of you—your boss gets a solution, and you get your boss's good will. If your boss chooses to take full credit for your idea, I suggest that you let it slide as long as this is your first job. Think of it as part of paying your dues. As I mentioned previously, the effects community is a small one. A good recommendation from an experienced supervisor is worth a lot. You will have lots of good ideas throughout your career, so one idea is a small price to pay to start your career on the right foot.

Most of the supervisors and managers you will work for will be reasonable people who are great to work for and helpful to your career. A small percentage of supervisors can be more difficult. If you are working for one of them, you will have to show more self-control and be more solidly centered. Don't be a prima donna, but don't be a doormat either. Getting a paycheck doesn't mean they own you, just as being an artist doesn't mean you should abuse or rip off your employer. Be honest, reasonable, and fair, as long as your employer is the same.

It is to your advantage to build a reputation of reliability. The first rule is: Do not promise what you cannot deliver. You are not making a sales pitch to a client; you are telling your boss what you can and cannot do. It is not good for anyone if you bite off more than you can chew. Of course, we all make mistakes sometime. If you cannot deliver on a promise, go to your supervisor as soon as you have identified the problem. Work with your supervisor to find a solution. Don't just throw it in his lap and run away. And don't wait until two seconds before the deadline to ask for help.

> *"Och, laddie, ye've got a lot to learn about being a miracle worker."*
> —Capt. Montgomery Scott, UFP, Ret.

When you are being asked to do a job that you are unsure of, be willing to say, "I don't know." And be just as willing to say, "I can try to find out." If you have a really bad feeling about a job or if you can see major problems, don't just say "No." Instead say, "We can do it that way, but it will cost *x* dollars and take *y* days extra." It is the supervisor's, director's, or producer's job to make the call. It is your job to provide them with your best professional assessment, then carry out their decision.

Most large studios have a cadre of "suits," the business school graduates, attorneys, and financiers that make the business decisions. If you are lucky (or simply did your research), the suits at your studio also have a background in or at least a solid personal liking for motion pictures and storytelling. The best situation is where former effects artists have built their own studio, so the top executives once had your job and understand both the creative and business side of special effects. If you are stuck in a studio managed by suits who do not understand filmmaking, special effects, or art in any form, you are probably not going to have a long and happy career there.

Despite this, your career survival depends on your ability to cooperate with suits. Don't bite the hand that feeds you. The suits in your studio are the people who make your paycheck show up on time. If they were not out there, meeting with clients and hustling for projects to keep you and your buddies busy, you would be out looking for another job. The bottom line is that suits who may know little or nothing about the creative process can nevertheless green-light or kill projects. It is a classic example of the Golden Rule: He who has the gold makes the rules. If you antagonize the wrong suit, you can find yourself unemployed (the project was killed) or doing scut work (the project was bastardized), with a bunch of your coworkers alongside you. This does not mean you should grovel—just that you have to make your observations, criticisms, and suggestions in polite form, through proper channels, and in language the suits can understand.

Most suits are not inherently bad people. They do not enjoy producing schlock any more than you do. Many of them have years of training and experience in the financial and business side of special effects, and their expertise is a valid contribution to the production. To get where they are, odds are that they put in a lot of time, are very talented or very lucky, or have serious connections. Any one of these cases is sufficient reason for you to treat them with a modicum of respect. If they are making decisions that make your job harder, you should discuss that fact, privately, with your supervisor. If you point out that a change they have asked for will require weeks of expensive overtime and a missed delivery date, they will most likely see reason. If you rant and rave and call them names, you will do yourself more harm than good, and they are not likely to listen to you in the future. Be professional, be reasonable, and if the suits will not reciprocate, keep your demo reel and résumé updated—you will probably need them sooner rather than later.

Maintaining Your Space—And Yourself

If you are a typical compositor, you will spend more time at work than away from it. With that in mind, make sure that you are going to be comfortable. Windows? What windows? Get used to the idea of not seeing the sun very much. Sunlight glaring off your monitor's screen and the cost of commercial office space mean you will usually be working in a windowless cubicle or sharing a room with other compositors.

Make sure that you take care of yourself physically. Compositors, like other computer workers, are prone to repetitive stress injury (RSI), including carpal tunnel syndrome, DeQuervain's, and related maladies. Set up your workstation to provide proper support, and if you have already injured yourself, follow the directions of your therapist. Many digital artists use wrist braces and ergonomic supports. Get a good chair with proper back support. After searching unsuccessfully for decent workstation furniture, I finally designed and built my own. It is a standing-height work surface for my keyboard and tablet, with my monitor at eye level, and a matching draftsman's stool. I alternate standing and sitting on about a 20-minute cycle to keep from stiffening up over the course of a 16-hour workday.

Take especially good care of your eyes. Staring at a monitor for hours can exhaust the focusing muscles of your eyes, getting them in a rut that can affect your ability to change focus rapidly. Try to have a brightly colored object within view at least 20 feet away, and periodically (every 15 minutes or so) look up and focus your eyes on it. Looking out a window is best, but, if your work area is too enclosed, set up a mirror on the far wall to double your line of sight. If you ever question the effect your job is having on your vision, talk to your optometrist or ophthalmologist.

Even if you love your job, you need to keep a balanced perspective. Set aside some time, on a regular basis, to keep up your personal life.

> *"This whole process, no matter how wonderful computers are, can make people crazy."*
> — Rita Street, editor of Film & Video Magazine.

Collecting Your Due

The intangible rewards of a job you love are wonderful, but you have to pay the bills too. Never work for free. Negotiate comp time, overtime pay, a percentage of the project, or even stock options, but do not agree to work uncompensated overtime. If there is a real crunch to finish an important job, management should at least agree to give you an equivalent amount of time off (with pay) after the crunch is over.

Mandatory unpaid overtime happens to be against the law. The Fair Labor Standards Act (FLSA), passed in 1938 and enforced by the U.S. Department of Labor, requires premium pay for work in excess of 40 hours per week. If management attempts to end-run this law by telling you that you are salaried and therefore exempt, here are some of the other criteria the Department of Labor will apply: setting work schedules; requiring employees to keep time sheets; docking pay for partial days worked; paying overtime for "extra" hours worked; reporting pay on an hourly basis; and using the same disciplinary system for exempt and nonexempt employees. Essentially, if the studio wants you to work and be paid like management, they have to treat you like management. Penalties are serious, including back pay and punitive damages.

Usually, employers who try to require unpaid overtime are simply new to running a business and do not understand the situation. Once in a great while, you will have an employer who knowingly and systematically breaks this law. I suggest you find work elsewhere and perhaps send a letter to the Department of Labor after you are safely employed again.

Benefits

Take advantage of company benefits that improve your quality of life. When you are hired, the HR (Human Resources) department should provide you with a list of official benefits. At least one shop has an on-site masseur, which is great for muscle cramps and RSI, the digital artists' occupational hazards. If you wear corrective lenses and have optical health insurance, you should consider getting the new prescription glasses designed especially for computer work. Some studios also have discount purchase programs for everything from movie tickets to groceries to computers. Take advantage of what you can, and if you think of a good benefit for you and your coworkers, suggest it. Good benefits are cost-effective ways for your employer to stay competitive, and they'll usually appreciate your suggestions.

Even if this is your first job as a compositor, you should start planning for your retirement. There are entirely too many horror stories of traditional effects artists dying broke because they did not plan for retirement. Do not let that happen to you. The nature of the business is that you will probably move around a lot, being a "project gypsy," or being head-hunted from one studio to the next as your skills and reputation improve. There is also the fact that digital compositing is still a young profession, and even the oldest effects shops have not been around very long. Shops tend to open, have a more or less successful run, then close, just like any other small business. If your career is going to last 25 to 40 years, you cannot count on retiring from the first studio you work for.

The ephemeral nature of the industry means you need a retirement plan that you can take with you. Plans administered through a union are one option. IRAs and other savings plans that you run for yourself are another. In my opinion, Social Security will probably be broke or completely overhauled by the time you can collect from it, so do not count on that. If you have no idea how to invest money over the long term, I suggest you consult a personal financial planner. Your banker or insurance agent may be able to help, but they will have an understandable bias toward the products that they will try to sell you.

My personal recommendation is investment in income properties like real estate or intellectual property. If you build up a portfolio of marketable assets, you can practically guarantee a steady cash flow from leasing or licensing without having to work very hard after your retirement. This is the strategy followed by some of the wealthiest people in the entertainment business. For details on how this works, I recommend *Fortune* magazine.

Screen Credit

There is one benefit you will probably not be able to negotiate for your first job, but you should get it as soon as you can and then never let it go: screen credit. This is not just about vanity; it is about money. If you have a string of screen credits on your résumé, and the people who watch credits (most of the industry, plus the fans) recognize your name, that is worth serious cash when you negotiate your next contract. It is also the way your name gets attached to the industry's awards—they go to the people named in the credits, not necessarily the people who did the work. If you are ever going to cash in on your professional reputation, make the lecture circuit, try to get an independent project green-lighted, or publish your memoirs or even a technical book, your screen credits are even more important than your demo reel. You should start collecting screen credits as soon as you have the leverage to demand them; you do not need to wait until your current contract is up.

Renegotiation Is Not A Bad Thing

After you have been working for a while, and especially if you are doing exemplary work, it's a good idea to think about changes you would like to make. More money is always nice, but think about additional vacation time, company sponsorship of private projects, or more creative input/control. Everything is subject to renegotiation, but you have to be willing to leave for greener pastures if management will not give you what you need. Do not even think about trying to bluff; they will call you on it every time.

Professional Development

Digital compositing is an art that you will never completely master. It is a lifelong pursuit, a process of honing your skills toward a perfection you can reach for but never grasp. There is always something new to learn, some new method or fine-tuning of an older method that will get you closer to your goal. You should always be developing your skills and professional knowledge. Never rest on your laurels. Always be learning, always be curious about what is around the bend, technically and cinematically.

The resources listed earlier in this chapter will continue to serve you well throughout your career. Learn from others' work at every opportunity. See every film or TV program that includes digital compositing, and collect laser disks (or DVDs) of the best examples. Try to keep up on the literature, keep an eye on the most useful listservs and newsgroups, and don't miss SIGGRAPH if at all possible.

If traditional art training will help you hone your skills, you should investigate the opportunities available in your community. Most art schools have open life-drawing classes where you can practice for a small fee. Classes in related disciplines such as sculpture, photography, or filmmaking may be available too. Opportunities tend to be more plentiful in larger cities, but you can find an art teacher willing to tutor in even the smallest town. If you are a union member, the local chapter may offer classes or referrals to other members who can be of assistance. Keep an eye out for special seminars as well.

You should habitually pull out all the stops on your tools. Learn absolutely everything you can do with the software and hardware you have access to. Go beyond the manuals, books like this one, and the conventional solutions others rely on. Find new solutions to problems that have not even been recognized yet. When you have the time and budget to make your own projects, the intimate familiarity with your tools that you've gained will pay you back manyfold.

The path you follow to develop yourself depends entirely on the type of work you like to do. If you enjoy being a generalist, you may want to stay with smaller studios. Conversely, if you are working for a larger studio, you may find it difficult to get assignments outside your narrow job description.

> "Being responsible for it all is the norm in the small startups, with the luxury of specialization arriving only as the shop scales up over time. Specialization is more to the studio's advantage than to the individual's. Production roles become apprenticeship rungs on a ladder that's hard to climb inside just one studio. A three-year contract is to keep your slot occupied, not to assure you a chance to find the place in production where your strengths can best be utilized."
> — Ken Cope

You may choose to stick with one studio through many projects or follow the most interesting work from studio to studio. You may decide to remain a compositor, or with experience, you may find that you prefer to supervise, direct, or produce. If you cannot find personal satisfaction at any studio, you may even choose to branch out on your own.

Side Projects

Odds are good that you became interested in special effects because you want to tell stories, to make your own movies. At some time in your career, you are going to want to take on a side project, a personal film to scratch the storytelling itch you cannot indulge at your regular job. Some studios are very supportive of side projects, even providing facilities, budgets, and personnel to assist you. Others do not support side projects, but do not forbid them either. Some studios actively discourage side projects with a myriad of sanctions, legal and otherwise.

Despite what your employer or their lawyers may say, what you do on your time is yours, unless your contract states something to the contrary. If you develop valuable ideas—graphic designs, scripts, any kind of intellectual property—you should be very careful not to use any company resources. If you so much as borrow a company pencil, the company may have a legal claim on the properties that you develop. If you do it on your own time, in your own place, on your own equipment, it belongs to you. Just make sure that you can prove all this in a court of law.

This is why it is important to own your equipment and software. With appropriate tools at home, you can pursue side projects without official support or sanctions. You can choose to use the same software tools as in your regular job or branch out and experiment with other solutions. In either case, the skills you hone at home will make you a better compositor at work too. Reasonable companies understand this and encourage it. If your company does not, you might want to reexamine your reasons for continuing to work there.

Even if you are deliriously happy with your current position, you should continually update your demo reel and résumé. Every time you finish a nice shot, especially when you wrap up a major project, add those bits to your archive reel. If the new material justifies it, update the editing of your demo reel. You never know when an opportunity is going to knock, and a prepared demo reel can make the difference between grabbing the brass ring and missing it clean.

I hope I have provided you with some sound advice that will make your first compositing job a little easier. If you have been in the business for a while or are just curious about your future options, the next section describes some of the advantages and pitfalls of going into the visual effects business for yourself.

Running Your Own Shop

If you really love doing the best work you can, making your creative decisions, setting your rules, and working on your own schedule, you may want to work for yourself.

"Cheaper tools do enable people to go off on their own, but it is the artist who drives the tools that actually gets the work done."
—Guy Griffiths, Director of Technology, Cinesite

Working for yourself is potentially the most rewarding career path for a compositor, both financially and creatively. However, being a great compositor doesn't automatically qualify you to run a business. It requires a set of skills, talents, and attitudes that can be very different from the creative side of effects work. If you do not have these qualities, you are better off working in another person's shop.

Working as an independent is not the best option for every compositor. Being an employee of an effects house has several advantages: You do not have to manage the business, you can concentrate on your compositing, and you (usually) get a steady paycheck and benefits. The pay, however, can be a fraction of what you could make on your own.

Independent compositors are generally freelancers, subcontractors, or consultants. To succeed as an independent, you need the basic know-how of any successful small-business owner: accounting and finance, customer relations, legal risk management, and estimating, for starters. As a person, you need to be self-starting, diplomatic, persistent, entrepreneurial, thorough, and organized. That is all in addition to your skills and talent as a compositor. Do you see why most compositors are not in business for themselves?

Freelance compositing is usually a work-for-hire proposition, which means you are essentially a temporary employee on a project basis. Freelancing can make you very good money, but you will also have to market your services and pay more attention to business matters than a regular employee would.

Being a subcontractor is like running your own production house, with a little less responsibility and a lot less creative control. Your client, the main contractor on the project, will hand you a piece of work and tell you when the finished product is due. Where, when, and how you do the work is usually up to you. With this freedom comes added risk—if you do not deliver as contracted, the client (and sometimes even their client) can sue you for damages. Think about production insurance, and do not promise what you cannot deliver.

Being a consultant can be lucrative and relatively low-risk, but you need a solid reputation and a lot of friends and colleagues in the business who know the quality of your work and will recommend you when a problem arises. Do not plan to start off as a successful visual effects consultant. You can only get there after a lot of solid professional work and sustained networking.

"The most important thing for me when I go to a post house is whether the individuals have film experience. Film work requires greater attention to detail than commercials or television, and takes longer to complete."
—Eric Henry, Visual Effects Supervisor, Blue Sky/VIFX

Running a production house is the next rung up the ladder. To succeed at this level, you need a reputation that will bring in clients, the management and people skills to attract and retain talented personnel, and the discipline and tenacity to keep it all running smoothly. The financial rewards can be huge, in proportion to the risks you run while building up your studio. The less-tangible rewards are good too. If your studio wins an award, you can be the one on stage stammering through a laundry list of thank-yous.

Growing A Business

More than half of all small-business start-ups fail in the first three years. It is up to you to make sure that you are not one of them. One of the most sensible strategies is detailed in a book I highly recommend, Paul Hawken's *Growing a Business*. Its central concept is that each business has an optimal growth rate and path, and attempting to hurry or force it will only cause trouble. If you read this book and think carefully about your business, the next logical growth opportunity will usually become obvious.

Setting Goals

Whether or not you read Paul Hawken's book, you should keep an eye on your goals. Set a goal for your business. It should not sound like one of those pompous corporate mission statements. Instead, it should be something that is personally important to you. "Create the best digital compositing in the tristate area," "make enough money to retire by age 40," or "prove to my parents that I'm not a waste of space" are all perfectly good goals, although you might not want to put those last two on your company letterhead.

After you make a goal for yourself, make a list of tasks you need to accomplish to reach your goal. Write the goal across the top of the page, and list the tasks under it. Don't get stressed out about making a perfect or exhaustive list. Again, these should be simple statements describing milestones to your goal. If your goal is to produce award-winning effects, you need to work at tasks such as "study and learn from other compositors," "finish comps to the best of my ability," and "practice and improve my compositing skills every day." Keep this list of tasks where you can refer to it. If your workspace is private or you do not mind clients reading your list, you might put it on the wall where you can see it as you work.

> *Be careful what you wish for; you just might get it!*

When you need to make a decision about your business—a new project to accept or decline, a software or hardware purchase, an offer to include your work in an exhibition, whether to hire employees—refer to your goals and your list of tasks. Which choice will get you closer to your goal? Are you making progress on the tasks? Is your goal still the one you want, and do you still believe these tasks will get you there? Over time, your tasks and even your goal will change. This is a natural part of the growth of your business. The important thing is that you are constantly aware of your goal, so you can work toward it without wasting yourself on distractions and tangents.

Personnel

You are it. Until you have signed contracts for work you simply do not have time to do, you should be your only employee. Once you have a surplus, you can think about hiring independent contractors to pick up the slack. There are very good reasons many businesses are choosing to use contractors rather than employees—it is just too expensive to keep full-timers around, costing you salary, benefits, and overhead if they are not working full-time on projects. On top of that, you have the problems of recruiting, training, and retaining good talent in a field that is absolutely vicious about headhunting.

Independent contractors are a good compromise between your one-person shop and the next ILM. You can bring them together for a large project, and if you can keep the projects coming in, you can keep the team together. You will have to pay careful attention to the legalities, however. The IRS has been clamping down on employers who just re-label everyone a contractor. If they are supposed to be independent, you have to treat them as independent—which means you cannot dictate when and how they work and just what they are supposed to turn in. You need to be comfortable with delegating authority and trusting your contractors to deliver on time. If you cannot, you are probably better off sticking with solo work or growing your business through a partnership with other effects artists.

Financing Your Business

We live in a capitalist society. So, whatever your personal beliefs, you need to be conversant with and competent in financial matters, or your business will not survive.

The first step is to calculate the bare necessities for your business. This means figuring out just what you need to create the products your clients will pay for. It does not include luxuries such as new office furniture, top-of-the-line entertainment systems, or a new car, even though you can make a case for those items being business expenses. When you are starting a new business, you should start on a shoestring. It keeps your mind focused, minimizes distractions, and keeps you in touch with financial reality. It also minimizes the financial fall you may take if your business fails and maximizes your profit margin if you succeed.

Your bare necessities will probably include a space to work, a computer, at least one software package capable of digital compositing, a means of importing raw footage, and a means of delivering the finished comps to your clients. That's it. Everything else is extra, and you should avoid adding anything to your necessities list unless it can pay for itself immediately. You need furniture? Stack boards and milk crates, or visit the local thrift or secondhand shops. You need office supplies? Buy them as needed for specific projects until you can justify maintaining an inventory. If you go out and buy a filing cabinet, file folders, stapler, printer, paper, letterhead, business cards, answering machine, tape dispenser, paper clips, matching envelopes, et cetera ad nauseam, you will tie up hundreds of dollars before you even have a client. You do not need to instantly re-create the office environment you chose to leave!

Do Not Waste, But Do Not Skimp

Your computer should run well, with enough free memory and mass storage that you are not wasting creative time trying to coax an overtaxed machine. If there are software tools that will honestly make you more productive, find a way to finance them as reasonably as possible. Some tools are valuable enough that you can make a good business case for charging them to your credit card—but keep in mind that it takes a pretty big return to justify investment at a 17-percent interest rate.

Your computer, input and output hardware, and primary software package will probably be your largest start-up costs. If your cash flow is tight, consider leasing your computer. If you add up all the lease payments, this probably seems very expensive. Look at it another way: Instead of having several thousand dollars tied up in a piece of equipment, you pay a few hundred dollars per month for the same capability while using that big chunk of money as working capital. This might enable you, for example, to rent a broadcast-quality VTR to do your video transfers, where you might otherwise have had to work with prosumer- or consumer-grade hardware. This option means you can charge more for the job with a smaller investment. Leasing is not completely risk-free. You should make sure there is an escape clause that enables you to get out of the lease if your business doesn't fly, and don't neglect insurance on the equipment.

When you start calculating cost/benefit ratios and getting quotes on equipment and services, you should consider how you want to make the transition from your current job to running your own business. If you have an inexpensive home workspace, you are not risking much. You can experiment, working evenings and weekends as a compositor while maintaining your day job. You can track your expenses, and when the compositing is bringing in enough to pay your bills, you can drop the day job and composite full-time. If compositing never does bring in enough to support you, you still have the day job, and you have not wasted a lot of time and money in setting up a home office.

On the other hand, if you sink your savings into a lease on commercial office space and buy new furniture and the latest top-of-the-line compositing workstations, a failing business could push you into bankruptcy. This is why you should start a business on your own, financially. Do not borrow, do not go looking for venture capital, and do not take on well-heeled silent partners. One of the worst mistakes you can make is being in debt to people who do not understand the effects business. Borrowing puts you in the hole from the first minute. Interest starts accruing before you even have clients. Venture capitalists are not in business to sponsor the development of great visual effects; they are in it to make money as quickly as possible. If you do not produce, they will have no compunctions about auctioning off your assets and suing you for their losses. Silent partners are rarely either silent or truly partners. Sooner or later, they will stick their noses into the business, and you will then find out that the people who kick in the cash expect to dictate how the business is run.

Your number one asset is your talent as a compositor. No amount of cash can compensate for a lack of talent, but talent can demand lots and lots of cash, if you handle it right. You are the only person who should be in control of your business.

Pricing

After you decide to take the plunge and composite full-time, it is even more important to have a clear financial picture of your business. The longer you have been compositing part-time, the better your baseline of financial records. You need to add up all your fixed expenses: rent, leases, service contracts, utilities, telephone, finance charges, insurance—the whole nine yards. This is your overhead, the amount you have to bring in just to keep breathing. Add on what you need to match the discretionary income you are used to or want to get used to. Don't delude yourself into believing that you can live like a king, with clients paying the bills, or that you can live really cheaply, to keep your expenses low. Be as realistic as possible, and don't forget to include whatever you have been contributing to your savings or retirement plan. Increase this figure by your new withholding rate, including Social Security, income taxes, and all the other fun stuff you would rather not have to pay. This total is your nut, what you need to collect from clients in order to break even and maintain your standard of living.

The production expenses go on top of this and are based on what the job actually requires in addition to your overhead. Extra equipment rental, blank media, subcontracted services, couriers, insurance riders—all the stuff that you have been learning about while you have been part-timing. These figures are going to be different for every job you do and are the ones most likely to change during a project, due to client decisions or unforeseen problems.

Now that you know what you need to charge for your work, you have to decide how to bill it to your clients. My personal preference is to quote an hourly rate only for very small jobs, a daily rate for projects taking up to two weeks, and my lowest rate for projects over two weeks. For the shorter projects, I pad out my time to compensate for the sales and client setup time, which seems to be nearly the same for tiny jobs as it is for big ones. Remember that every minute you spend meeting with, traveling to, or telephoning your client is also part of your working time. If you can't get away with billing every minute of that time directly, you need to find some way to cover it in the project's overhead or you will be losing money.

Business Is Business

For details on invoices, collections, taxes, and accounting practices, I highly recommend Bernard B. Kamoroff's book *Small-Time Operator*. In my opinion, it is the best single source on the administration of small businesses, just as Hawken is best on small-business philosophy.

Even if you are just starting out as a compositor, resist the temptation to do work "on spec," or for free, just to build up your demo reel or reputation. If the potential client is a nonprofit organization, insist on some sort of compensation, whether it is free tickets or other services, access to equipment, or a tax-deductible receipt for services rendered (calculated at your full rates, of course). If the client is a for-profit, insist on a cut of the gross, barter for services or product, or a contract for your standard rates. Any other arrangement will most likely add your name to the long list of digital artists who have been ripped off by unscrupulous or inexperienced clients. If you really need the advertising, I suggest you do a pro bono PSA (public service announcement) for a local nonprofit or charity that will arrange to give it a lot of airtime. This work goes under the accounting category of promotional business expense, so you at least earn a nice tax deduction.

Insurance

Working for yourself is enough of a risk; you do not need to raise the stakes by neglecting to insure yourself against problems that are beyond your control. You should maintain insurance on yourself, your family, and your possessions as if you were still working for someone else. Most homeowners or renters insurance will not cover the replacement costs of computers adequate for professional digital compositing, so you should consider additional insurance appropriate to your business. Ask your current insurance agent if you can add a computer rider to your current policies. You may be able to get a better deal than with a completely separate policy.

Take a careful look at your assets. Your computer(s), software, reference books, videos, and AV and office equipment are important to your business. If you lose them to theft or disaster, you need to replace most of them before you can continue generating income. One approach is to insure everything for replacement value and keep an updated list of your business assets on file with your insurance agent. You might also consider operational insurance that will pay for emergency leases on critical equipment until you can purchase your own replacements. The cheapest computer insurance is a regular set of system backups, stored offsite so you can get your new or repaired system up and running as quickly as possible.

Do not neglect insurance on yourself in addition to the standard life, health, and disability. If your business depends on your talents and performance, you may want to consider key-person insurance sufficient to keep your business going if you are ever laid up and unable to perform. You should maintain a baseline of insurance on yourself and your business assets from the start. Figure the insurance premiums into your overhead, because they do not change according to the amount of income the business brings in. There are other forms of insurance that you should research and price before you actually need them. If a particular project is going to require you to purchase additional insurance, you need to include those charges in calculating your bid.

If you are doing film or television work, you should consult an insurance broker or agency that specializes in production insurance. They are familiar with your needs and will be able to point out contingencies and risks you might not have considered. They will also be able to quote reasonable rates. An ordinary small-business insurance agent might respond to your list of expensive electronics with a disproportionately high premium. If a production requires you to lease equipment in addition to your usual layout, you should get riders or additional policies to cover them from the time you accept delivery to the time you return them. If you rent rather than buy a piece of equipment, odds are that it will be too expensive for you to replace easily.

If your product is going to be shown in public, you should consider Errors and Omissions (E&O) insurance. This covers you against libel, slander, and copyright or trademark infringement. It does not give you permission to infringe on people, but it does protect you against honest mistakes. If you have employees, make sure that they are covered in the policy too. Getting E&O insurance usually means having a good entertainment attorney help you fill out the forms, so the expense includes the policy's premium plus your attorney's fees.

If you are making the leap to film or high-end video production, you may want to insure negatives, master tapes, or other original elements. You may also want insurance against flawed equipment, processing, or media. Remember the disclaimers on videotapes? If a bad tape drops out in the middle of your final delivery, the manufacturer will not do anything more than hand you a new blank tape. If a deadline, payment, or original element is at risk, always keep duplicates, but buy the insurance too.

If the amount of work requires you to hire independent subcontractors or employees, you will have a lot of insurance regulations to comply with. Depending on where you work, you may have to pay for state disability benefits, Worker's Compensation, Social Security, and so on. One more reason to think long and hard before hiring employees.

Advertising

If you are working freelance or subcontracting, get yourself a good agent. An agent only makes money if you do, and a good one will get you far more than you could negotiate for yourself. Agents also network for you, keeping track of where the work is and who is doing what—an invaluable resource when you are hired project-by-project. If you are a consultant, you are probably going to be doing your own networking, although having an agent might not hurt.

If you are running your own studio, you need to get your name and services in front of the people who write the checks. My own experience has been that word-of-mouth advertising has the best return on investment. This does not mean sitting in your office and waiting for friends to throw you work. It means making sure that all your friends, acquaintances, colleagues, and clients have current copies of your demo reel, business card, brag sheet, and schedule of services. Take your best contacts out to lunch now and then (networking, remember?), and let them know you will appreciate any business they can throw your way. This is also crucial to planning for growth. You need to stay in touch with people who can supply you with labor, expertise, and equipment when you get a large or rush job that is beyond your capacities. If you have a solid network of colleagues, you can put together a larger production team much more rapidly and with a better chance of success.

If you really feel you must advertise conventionally, do try to keep your expenses down, and target your ads to the market you are trying to reach. Direct mail, ads in industry newsletters, and bartered services for advertising (especially for local-access cable TV or your neighborhood movie theater) are low-budget strategies that have a good chance of paying off.

Protecting Yourself

It is a sad fact that few in this industry do not have a horror story about a client or employer who exploited them. This doesn't mean there are a lot of dishonest clients out there. The real villains are few and far between, and they quickly develop reputations in the industry. You can avoid them by using your network of colleagues to do your background check. A more common problem is the client who doesn't understand the business, gets in over his head, and then decides that stiffing the compositor is a viable solution to his problem. It is up to you to protect yourself from this kind of unpremeditated rip-off.

Disclaimer: I'm not an attorney, and nothing in this book constitutes legal advice. This information is based on my personal experience and that of the compositors I have interviewed. Every situation is different, and although I believe these tips can be useful, you should definitely consult your attorney before agreeing to do anything for a client.

Dealing With Clients

Ah, clients. Where would digital artists be without clients? Broke and unemployed, but probably less stressed.

The client/artist relationship is a simple one. They have money, which you need. You can create effects, which they want. Try not to lose sight of this basic fact, especially when a difficult client's head games cloud the issue.

The best way to deal with client problems is to prevent them from occurring. Make sure that you have a good contract that spells out all the details. Nothing is impossible, just expensive. If the client is willing to pay for it, you should be willing to do it. If a particular piece of work is going to be unpleasant, quote them a high price and a long delivery schedule. If they are willing to pay your asking price, at least you will be compensated well for work you do not enjoy.

If an approval deadline is approaching and you have not heard from the client, call them. Stay in touch. More client delays are due to oversight than intentional stonewalling or indecision. Make sure that the client knows the deadline is coming up and that you are ready to go. When your deadlines are looming, do not talk to the client. Filter your incoming calls with an answering machine, and reply to the client's answering machine after-hours, when you will not have to speak to the client directly. Every time you interact with the client, they see it as an opportunity to make changes. Even if you convince them not to make changes, those negotiations are coming out of your production time. Stick to the approvals spelled out in your contract, and don't let the client micromanage you.

When you are presenting materials for approval, make sure that there is one obvious glitch to fix. Clients are like editors; they need to feel useful. Don't bring other problems to their attention; just fix them. Pointing out a problem to a client can get them started on a whole chain of revisions. Anticipate changes you think the client will request, but if you finish them ahead of time, hold the changes in reserve. In fact, you should always hold work in reserve. If you finish work ahead of schedule, do not try to deliver it. The client will just ask for more changes, right up to the original deadline. Deliver work exactly when it's due, no sooner and no later.

Dealing with a client when a problem occurs is the acid test of your diplomacy skills. Even the best clients can be difficult, just because they do not understand your business or your problems. If the client is reasonable, your best approach is to explain the problem—and your proposed solution—in plain English and with just enough detail to get your point across. If the client is unreasonable, your only defense is your contract.

Remember, they have money, which you need. You can create effects, which they want. If they are difficult, pad the bid on the next job enough to pay for the aggravation. If a client becomes more trouble than they are willing to pay for, just politely turn down the job.

Contracts

A contract is simply an agreement between people to do things for each other. You agree to give me videotape with a certain effects sequence on it, and I agree to give you a certain amount of money. That is the principle, anyway. Contracts get complicated when the job, your risks, or the client's wishes get complicated. But complex or simple, you need to understand and stick with the essentials of contracts.

A good contract should be all or nothing: If you are not willing to put everything in writing, you should not have a contract at all. A good contract must spell out the precise terms of the entire relationship between the people involved. Leaving anything out or relying on verbal agreements, handshakes, or memoranda is just begging for trouble. If a negotiating point is important enough for the client or you to agree to it, it is important enough to write into the contract. If changes in the relationship require changes to the contract, you should amend it in writing too. There is standard contract language that spells out exactly how you can make agreed-on changes, ranging from initialed handwritten notes on the original contract to the renegotiation and redrafting of the whole thing.

I have signed contracts with people who would rather have seen me arrested and jailed. We were able to build all our expectations into the contracts in sufficient detail that, despite extreme personal differences, we were able to deal with each other in a businesslike way, so that each of us gave and received a fair deal. The product was delivered on time and within budget, and I got paid in full, with no lawsuits, threats, or unpleasantness. Contracts are a good thing.

Family Business Is Still Business

A contract is even more important when you are doing business with family or friends. Spelling out all the details ahead of time can save you major headaches, loss of friendship, and even broken families. If you find out during negotiation that the other parties cannot or will not agree to terms that you find necessary, it is better to call off the deal right then, with no hard feelings and no losses on either side. After you have a contract, you have to stick with it, or you risk losing your business.

So, what should a good effects production contract include? The first items are the ground rules for the contract: who the parties are, what the purpose of the contract is, how the contract can be modified, and under what laws the contract will be enforced (usually the state or country where you live). This is all standard legal stuff.

The next critical item is the escape clause. This is an explicit description of how each party can cancel the contract without getting sued. You need one of these to protect yourself in case you get sick or otherwise cannot complete the project, or if the client becomes completely unreasonable. The client needs this clause in case the project becomes unnecessary, their business changes, or you become completely unreasonable. In either case, you need a set of rules that determines when the contract can be canceled, how each party notifies the other about cancellation, whether or how much you get paid for work already performed, and what completed work, if any, you turn over to the client. A worst-case starting point is for you to keep all your work, return any money the client has paid you, and call it even. It is up to you and your attorney to negotiate better terms, like guarantees of payment for out-of-pocket expenses and work already completed.

Next is the description of the work you will perform, usually described in terms of deliverables. This can include videotapes, film, prints, data files, or just about any other tangible media. The more specific the description, the better for you. If the contract reads "videotape," and you budget for VHS but the client insists that you deliver on BetacamSP, you will probably end up eating the bill for the more expensive master.

You need to be very specific about working files too. It is in your interest to deliver only the finished product and to retain all working files. This way, if the client wants to reuse any of the elements, they have to contract with you. If the client will not agree to let you keep the working files, charge extra for the buyout (see the "Intellectual Property" section later in this chapter). Deliverables can come from the client as well. If you need their logo, stock footage, or other proprietary data, the client has to provide it before you can get started. Again, be very specific. If all you have is a CD-ROM drive, that 9-track tape they hand you can blow your budget.

Compensation is another set of clauses you need to scrutinize closely. You should never start a job for less than 25 percent of the total, and if you will have extra expenses, you should get that money up front. It is common to get 50 percent up front, 25 percent at the halfway point, and the final 25 percent on delivery. Here is an important safety tip: Never hand over the final tape, print, or film until you have payment in hand. If the client insists on seeing the final product before paying you, give them an approval tape with SMPTE timecode across the bottom. They will be able to see the whole piece; they just cannot broadcast it. When they pay you, give them the tape without the timecode.

Do You Like Getting Paid?
Never hand over the final deliverable until you have payment in hand.

That brings up the subject of schedules. Most clients will insist that the final deliverable be in their hands by a particular date and time. In fact, ridiculously short schedules are the norm in this business. Television work needs to make a scheduled airdate, and feature films have to meet a release schedule. In either case, clients will be much less concerned about providing you with the data or approvals you need. It is up to you to make a contract that will keep everybody on schedule or compensate you when the client ignores it.

The first item should be your start date. Make it a dependency—you agree to start work the day you receive all the client's promised deliverables. That puts the ball in their court. If they delay the project, it is not your fault. In fact, you should consider making every date in the schedule a dependency. Your deadlines should be something like "20 business days following receipt of approved storyboards," rather than "no later than February 12." This encourages the client to keep track of the project and can dramatically reduce your stress levels. If waiting for the client may cost you money (loss of other opportunities, storage fees, rentals, and so forth), include a schedule of additional charges to make up your losses. Time is money, after all. And turnabout is fair play. Expect the client to insist on late-delivery penalties, ranging from progressive forfeiture of your fee to a whopping payment to them if you make them miss a TV advertising slot. Do not sign anything that could wipe out your business, unless you really enjoy high-stakes gambling.

The potentially stickiest part of the contract is the schedule of approvals. It is rare for a client to simply tell you what they want, hand you the money, and accept what you deliver. Most clients will want to see work in progress, and all of them will want to make changes. To save time, money, and sanity all around, all parties should agree on these approvals and schedule them in the contract, then stick to them. Typical approvals for digital compositing include storyboards, CGI element design, test renderings, and final comp, not necessarily in that order. The client must sign off on each of these deliverables before you do any more work. If you are halfway through final rendering and they want to change the CGI element design, you have just wasted a lot of effort. If you suspect (or know, from prior experience) that certain clients will drag their feet on approvals, add on "held work" fees that are high enough to compensate you for your waiting time. If a client wants to make changes after approvals, your contract should spell out exactly what fees must be paid for you to do the work over. You will not be able to tell the client they cannot make changes, so you have to make it in their own financial interest to keep their vacillation to a minimum.

Intellectual Property

Intellectual property is a legal category that includes copyrights, patents, and trademarks. If you are creating anything, you will be dealing with at least one of these critters. Unless you invent a new process or gadget, you will not be concerned with patents. Most commonly, you will be dealing with the copyrights for the effects sequences you produce.

Copyrights are used for artistic, literary, dramatic, or musical works. You, as the creator, have secured copyright protection the moment you record a work in a fixed form. That includes drawings, renderings, videotape, film—you get the idea. It is not necessary for you to register a work for you to have copyright protection, but registration does beef up the protection. Secured copyright gives you the exclusive right to display or perform the work or to reproduce and distribute copies to the public. Nobody else can do this, legally, without your permission. Like patents, a copyright is a license to sue rather than a guarantee of compliance.

To register a copyright, you must first get a copy of the appropriate forms from the Register of Copyrights in Washington, DC. Each type of copyrightable work has a different form; make sure that you get the right one. The forms are very simple—mostly your contact information and a description of the work. When you have completed the forms, you send the form, copies of the work (not your only original!), and a filing fee (usually $20) to the Copyright Office. You do not have to register right away, but like most forms of legal protection, it is a good idea. After a few months, you will receive official notice that your copyright has been registered.

Whenever you create a new work, you should immediately tag it with the standard copyright notice; for example, Copyright © 1999 Douglas A. Kelly. Displaying this notice does not make a legal difference, but it might persuade the more timid plagiarists to steal elsewhere. One odd bit for the notice: If you are copyrighting a revised work, the date should be hyphenated to include both first and most recent copyright dates. For example, Copyright (c) 1994-1999 Douglas A. Kelly would be appropriate for a book published in 1999 that included material I first copyrighted in 1994. This is for tracking the expiration of copyright, which is measured from the earlier date. Something you create yourself is copyrighted for your lifetime plus 50 years. Something you hire or contract for, and for which you buy out the copyright of the creator, is good for 75 years.

If you are creating copyrightable works as an employee or under a work-for-hire contract, your employer retains the copyright. If you are an independent contractor, you retain copyright unless your contract specifically states otherwise. Do not just give this away, for goodwill or any other purpose. If your client insists on retaining the copyrights, make sure that they pay you extra for it. For this agreement, as well as for most other contract negotiations, have an attorney who will negotiate the best deal for you.

If a client tries to grab your copyrights without paying extra, you have a number of big sticks you can wave. A registered copyright permits you to file a federal copyright-infringement suit, which would be very expensive for your client to fight. Second, if they have been accounting for you as an independent contractor and now they claim you are an employee (so they can keep your copyrights), they may be in big trouble with the IRS for evading employer taxes.

Choosing An Attorney

Yes, you need an attorney. Starting your own effects business without a lawyer is like walking around the Old West without a six-gun—you are just begging to be robbed. *Never* sign a contract without having qualified legal counsel review it, especially if you want to remain on good terms with the other parties to the agreement. A good attorney will draft a contract in which everything is spelled out as clearly as possible. Cobbling something together on your own, or worse yet, blindly signing something the other party drafted, is a recipe for disaster. A bad contract can literally cripple your business, stop your career, and generally ruin your life. A good contract can save you from even the worst run of bad luck or broken promises. I usually draft my own contracts, but I still run them past my attorney and cheerfully pay his fee. It is the cheapest form of business insurance you will ever buy.

Just as you would not choose a dermatologist to treat a brain tumor, do not go to the family lawyer when you need an entertainment law specialist. Family law, or even standard business practice, is a far cry from what you will be doing. Furthermore, make sure that the entertainment attorney knows the specifics of effects production contracts and has successfully represented special-effects artists. This is a highly specialized niche of the entertainment industry, and there are issues common to effects that rarely crop up in other parts of the industry. I have seen a contractor's attorney actually revise a production subcontract in my favor, just because he did not know the business well enough to look out for his client's interests.

Word of mouth is probably your best bet for locating a competent entertainment attorney. Even if you search through bar association listings, you will finally be relying on personal recommendations to narrow down your search. This is another area where your professional networking will pay off. The wider your circle of colleagues, the more opinions and experience you will be able to draw on in selecting an attorney.

After you have a name, call for an appointment to discuss your needs. Make sure that the initial meeting is free. You should never retain an attorney or agree to pay any kind of fee without that first face-to-face meeting. I have been burned on this point myself. I once paid an up-front fee to an attorney and was thereafter foisted off on a series of assistants and never saw the attorney again. Needless to say, I changed representation almost immediately, but my fee was gone.

In hindsight, I could have saved that fee by doing a little basic research and asking a few pertinent questions. Where did the attorney go to law school? What is her specialty, and how long has she been practicing it? How many other clients does she have? (That's an important one; if she has hundreds, it is a bucket shop and you will be lucky just to get your calls returned.) Can you have a few clients' names as references? After your meeting, call these references and ask their opinion of the attorney. Does the attorney return phone calls promptly? Does she answer questions understandably, or give you the brush-off? Have the contracts been well-written? Has the attorney been conscientious in preventing trouble before it happens? When trouble does happen, has her in-court representation been successful?

The factual, professional part of the meeting is only half the issue. You should also find out if you and the attorney will be able to trust each other and work together. One of the worst mistakes you can make in any business is to hide something from your attorney, and one of the most unpleasant things that can happen is to be stuck with untrustworthy or offensive counsel during a difficult legal process. The best lawyer in the business is useless if you cannot share critical information with her. Unfortunately, an attorney will rarely give away the fact that she is unreliable or obnoxious in the first meeting. You will just have to go with your instincts. If you feel something is not right, trust that feeling and seek counsel elsewhere.

When you are satisfied with an attorney's credentials and personality, you can secure her services by signing a retainer agreement. This can be a straight fee-for-services contract, a percentage of your net income, or a combination of the two. You can find out more about comparable fee schedules and percentage arrangements by contacting your state's bar association. If you do not have many contracts to review or draft, the flat rate is probably best. If the number of contracts picks up, you may find it more cost-effective to cut your attorney in for a share of the net in exchange for as-needed legal counsel.

Legal Self-Care

Retaining a good entertainment attorney is no excuse to ignore the legal aspects of your business. The more you know, the safer you are. At the least, you will be better able to judge when to call your lawyer.

There are a number of resources specifically designed for the legal needs of the small-business operator. One of the best is Nolo Press, an organization dedicated to legal self-help for individuals and small organizations. If you have access to the Internet, I highly recommend Nolo's Web site at: **www.nolo.com/index.html**.

Another source of excellent free advice and lots of links to pertinent books is Nolo's Small Business index: **www.nolopress.com/ChunkSB/SB.index.html**.

These books are well-written, thorough, and easy to read. Most of them include tear-out forms for the most common business needs. It has been my experience that if you read the appropriate Nolo Press books, you will be almost as well prepared as your attorney.

When It Is Not Fun Anymore

Most small-business owners will reach a point when they question getting into the business. That feeling is perfectly natural and just means you have been working too hard for too long. Take a break. Pace yourself. It is good to work hard, but you also need to take full days away from work on a regular basis. Between jobs, right after sending a deliverable to a client, when you have hit a creative block—whenever the "fresh" mind will do you the most good.

If you are dissatisfied with your career choice over a longer period of time, perhaps it is the work you are doing. If the work is just a succession of jobs for clients, sustaining your enthusiasm can be very difficult. Think about developing your own content, working on your own films, or otherwise having a purely personal creative project. Some of the best studios in the business do this for their employees, encouraging them to experiment, learn, and recharge their creative batteries between commercial projects. The results may not be commercially viable, but you can always submit them to the screening rooms at SIGGRAPH or film festivals. If nothing else, it is a rewarding hobby that also provides a nice tax deduction.

Moving On

This chapter provided a quick overview of some of the most critical career and business issues facing digital compositors. I hope some of this advice will save you the painful lessons others have learned the hard way and make your experiences that much easier. I also hope you will find encouragement here, and go out and build your career. Good luck!

APPENDIX A

WHAT'S ON THE CD-ROMS

This appendix presents a summary guide to the two CD-ROMs for *Digital Compositing In Depth*. These CD-ROMs also contain HTML versions of this text (INDEX.HTM) that you can open with any Web browser.

If you have questions, problems, or if you just want to chat, email me at **dakelly@earthlink.net**. For online updates to this book, plus news about my other projects, browse **http://home. earthlink.net/~dakelly**.

The CD-ROMs' Contents

Because this book's digital files are spread across two CD-ROMs, you need to be aware of which files are on which disk. If you can't find a file for a particular project, try searching the other disk. If you need to use files from both CD-ROMs in the same project (and your system doesn't have two CD-ROM drives), you can copy the smaller files from one CD-ROM to a temporary folder on your system's hard drive and keep the CD-ROM containing the larger files in your CD-ROM drive.

CD-ROM 1 Contents

CD-ROM 1 is (mostly) devoted to software—shareware, tryout software, other kinds of demos, and documentation, along with samples of images and frames.

The eyeon Folder

• A link to a file to install the demo version of Digital Fusion 2.52. The eyeon folder also contains the CFLT_UV_BLEND.flt YUV sampling filter used in Chapter 9.

The Discreet Folder

• A link to a text file about these demos.

• A link to a file to install effect* for Intel.

• A link to a file to install paint* for Intel.

Note: Installing the demo software also installs tutorial files and footage.

The Adobe Folder

- A link to a file to install After Effects tryout.

The Chalice Folder

- A link to Chalice tutorial PDFs.
- A link to miscellaneous footage files.

The Ultimatte Folder

- A link to open and read the Ultimatte Overview in Acrobat PDF format.
- A link to open and read the Ultimatte drivers README file.
- A link to a file to install Ultimatte plug-ins for Intel.
- A link to open and read the Ultimatte Digital Fusion manual in Acrobat PDF format.
- A link to a file to install Ultimatte plug-ins for eyeon Digital Fusion.
- A link to open and read the Ultimatte After Effects manual in Acrobat PDF format.
- A link to a file to install Ultimatte plug-ins for Adobe After Effects.
- A link to open and read the Ultimatte Premiere manual in Acrobat PDF format.
- A link to a file to install Ultimatte plug-ins for Premiere for Windows.
- A link to open and read the Ultimatte Speed Razor manual in Acrobat PDF format.
- A link to a file to install Ultimatte plug-ins for Discreet edit*.
- Browse the Ultimatte/Images/TARGAS/ folder.
- Browse the Ultimatte/WINDOWS/SAMPLES/ folder.

The Zbig Folder

- A link to a file to install a demo of Zbig for Intel.
- A link to Zbig Help, in HTML format, including Contents, Introduction, Chapter 1, Chapter 2, Chapter 3, Chapter 4, Chapter 5, Registration, and Support.

The DigiEffects Folder

- A link to a file to install a demo of CineLook for Windows NT.
- A link to open and read the CineLook NT Broadcast User Guide in PDF format.
- A link to open and read the About DigiEffects text file.

The Artbeats Folder

- A link to open and read About the Clips in HTML format.

- The CeilFire folder contains a 209-frame looping clip of a ceiling on fire, suitable for luma keying.

- The Gs134 folder contains 134 RGB frames of muzzle blast from an M-16 automatic rifle.

- The Gs134m folder contains the matching matte footage for the Gs134 footage.

The ChessN And ChessP Folders

These directories contain the chessboard motion control footage.

- The ChessN folder contains 276 frames of footage shot with a motion controlled camera rig. This provides a 'clean plate' for rig removal and other compositing effects, and also provides camera motion data for CGI software to create matching footage such as the Walker robot.

- The ChessP folder contains matching footage for the ChesN sequence with the chess pieces on the board. This provides foreground footage for compositing operations using ChesN as a clean plate.

The Walker And WalkerM Folders

- The Walker folder contains 276 RGB frames of a CGI rendered walking robot crossing the chessboard shown in the ChessN footage.

- The WalkerM folder contains 276 grayscale frames of alpha channel to match the walking robot.

The Titles Folder

- The Titles folder contains the images used in the main title sequence tutorial in Chapter 8.

The Match Folder

- This folder contains frame 135 of the tracking and match move footage used in tutorials in Chapters 11 and 12.

Miscellaneous Tutorial Files

The following folders provide data files, object files, and images that you will use in projects in Chapters 6, 8, and 12:

- The Motions folder contains the motion control camera data files, in ASCII and LightWave .MOT formats, in original and metric conversions.

- The Objects folder contains the porch, lamp, and other object files used in Chapters 6 and 12.

- The Scenes folder contains an optional LightWave character animation scene that can be used in Chapter 12.

The MatchMover Folder

- A link to a file to install the demo version of RealViz MatchMover.

- A link to open and read the tutorial for the demo version of RealViz MatchMover, in PDF format.

- A link to open and view the Orbital.avi video clip.

The Momentum Folder

- A link to open and view the Cobra.mov QuickTime video clip from Momentum Animation's match-move, shadow and lighting match, and character animation case study of the Jurong Cobra television advertisement.

Miscellaneous Root Folder Files

- Gship.TGA is a single RGBA image of a CGI element with integrated alpha channel, used in a multilayer compositing project.

- CU_Expld.TGA is a single frame from live-action footage, used in a filtering project.

CD-ROM 2 Contents

Although you will find several links to demo software on this CD-ROM, most of the space is used to provide single images and footage for projects found throughout the book.

The BeamdnBG Folder

- 50 frames of clean plate background footage for the Beamdown footage, used in rig removal projects in several chapters.

The Beamdown Folder

- 226 frames of live action footage on the same set as the BeamdnBG footage, used in rig-removal projects in several chapters.

The Box Folder

- 203 frames of live action footage, used in stabilizing, filtering, and rig-removal projects in several chapters.

The CineGirl Folder

- A dozen frames of bluescreen live action, in 2K-resolution full-frame Cineon format, scanned from 35mm motion picture film.

The CineVort Folder

- A single frame of an alternate take of the Box footage, in 2K-resolution full-frame Cineon format, scanned from 35mm motion picture film.

The GirlSide Folder

• 181 frames of live-action bluescreen footage, used in bluescreen and rig-removal projects in several chapters.

The Jump Folder

• 103 frames of live-action footage, used in luma key and timing projects in several chapters.

The Shake Folder

• A link to read the manual and tutorials for Shake 2.1 in HTML format.

• A link to download a 15-day trial version of Shake 2.1 from the Nothing Real Web site.

The Tshipbg Folder

• 151 frames of a CGI background, used in a multilayer compositing project.

The Tshipfg Folder

• 91 frames of a CGI foreground element, used in a multilayer compositing project.

The TshipfgM Folder

• 91 frames of matching alpha channel for the Tshipfg CGI foreground element, used in a multi-layer compositing project.

The Tshipmg Folder

• 151 frames of a CGI middle ground element, used in a multilayer compositing project.

TshipmgM Folder

• 151 frames of matching alpha channel for the Tshipmg CGI middle ground element, used in a multilayer compositing project.

• The Refs folder contains an NTSC color bar TGA image and a 1-kHz tone WAV file that you may find useful for marking the beginning of your productions. It also contains the Credits.txt file used in the end credits scroll tutorial in Chapter 8 and a 2k Cinean-format referenc frame for film production.

Technical Support From The Coriolis Group

Technical support is available for installation-related problems from 8 a.m. to 5 p.m., Mountain Standard Time, Monday through Friday.

Phone: (800) 410-0192
Fax: (480) 483-0193
techsupport@coriolis.com
www.coriolis.com

Please send written inquiries to:

The Coriolis Group
14455 N. Hayden Rd.
Suite 220
Scottsdale, AZ 85260

Limits Of Liability & Disclaimer Of Warranty

Although the author and publisher have taken every precaution when preparing this disk, they make no expressed or implied warranty of any kind and assume no responsibility for errors or omissions. No liability is assumed for incidental or consequential damages in connection with or arising out of the use of the information or programs contained herein.

Some of the software on this CD-ROM is shareware; you may be required to pay additional charges to the software vendor for registration and continued use. See individual programs' readme files for more information.

Appendix B
Bibliography

Ablan, Dan. *LightWave Power Guide*. New Riders Press, Indianapolis, IN: 1996. ISBN: 1-56205-633-6. Good general coverage of LightWave 5.0's features, with excellent tutorials and a few items on character animation.

Ablan, Dan, Patrik Beck, Mike Desantis, Bill Fleming, and Bob Hood. *Inside LightWave 3D*. New Riders Press, Indianapolis, IN: 1997. ISBN: 1-56205-799-5. A major improvement over Ablan's previous book, with much more professional-level detail and contributions by a handful of other LightWave experts. If you own the software, you should definitely own this book, especially because the official 5.5 manuals have fewer tutorials than the older versions.

Adobe. *Classroom in a Book: Adobe Premiere 5.0*. Adobe Press, Berkeley, CA: 1998. ISBN: 1-56830-467-6. Premiere is often the first stepping-stone to digital compositing, even though its comping tools are limited. The official guide to the software, this book includes adequate tutorials on motion graphics, titles, and rudimentary matte work. If you already have a copy of Premiere, this book helps you get more out of your investment.

Adobe. *Classroom in a Book: Adobe After Effects 4*. Adobe Press, Berkeley, CA: 1999. ISBN: 0-201658-91-7. If you use After Effects, you should work through every exercise in this book. If you don't, you can't say you really know how to use AE. Next to the manuals, this is the most important documentation you can have for the software.

Arijon, Daniel. *Grammar of the Film Language*. Silman-James Press, Hollywood, CA: 1991. ISBN: 1-879505-07-X. An exhaustive guide to the visual narrative techniques that form the "language" of filmmaking regarding the positioning and movement of players and cameras, as well as the sequence and pacing of images. Heavily illustrated with line drawings, this book has been in print for nearly 20 years in several languages. If you need to understand what a director is telling you, you need to read this book. Highly recommended.

Bayes, Steve. *The Avid Handbook*. Focal Press, Boston, MA: 1998. ISBN: 0-240-80347-7. If an Avid is part of your studio's workflow, you will benefit from a basic understanding of the system. This book is an adequate introduction of the processes preceding and following your digital compositing. Readable, concise, and well organized.

Blacker, Irwin R. *The Elements of Screenwriting*. Collier Books, New York, NY: 1986. ISBN: 0-02-000220-3. If you anticipate being a visual effects supervisor and participating in preproduction planning, you need to be able to read a script accurately and with a sharp eye for effects sequences. This book is one of the best sources, and certainly the most compact, about writing for film or video.

Brinkmann, Ron. *The Art and Science of Digital Compositing*. Morgan Kaufmann, New York, NY: 1999. ISBN: 0-12-133960-2. **If you buy only one other book on digital compositing, this should be it.** This is an excellent introduction to the theory and general practice of digital compositing at the feature-film level. Brinkmann has impeccable credentials and an impressive credits list, and he has been teaching digital compositing worldwide for years. He is also involved in the ongoing development of the Shake line of software at Nothing Real, so he speaks with experience from all sides of the business. This book is deliberately software-free, but the author does include a very useful appendix on comparing features to select your own digital compositing software.

Browne, Steven E. *Nonlinear Editing Basics: Electronic Film and Video Editing*. Focal Press, Boston, MA: 1998. ISBN: 0-240-80282-9. This book has some useful technical information pertaining to film and video editing, but the information on compositing and special effects is woefully out-of-date to the point of being harmful. If you consult this book, double-check the facts with another source before you commit to anything.

Chan, Alan. *The FX Kit for LightWave*. Lightspeed, Lancaster, CA: 1995. Writing and publication quality are spotty, but this 300+ page collection of tutorials (and its version 5.0 Addendum) is a useful supplement to the NewTek 5.0 and 5.5 manuals for lighting, modeling, and animating CGI elements.

Cook, David A. *A History of Narrative Film*. 3rd ed. W. W. Norton, New York, NY: 1996. ISBN: 0-393-96819-7 (pbk.). Good basic history of film, especially cinematic technique and influences.

De Leeuw, Ben. *Digital Cinematography*. Academic Press, San Diego, CA: 1997. ISBN: 0-12208-875-1. Excellent coverage of lighting and camera work for CGI, tied to the real-world equivalents. Profusely illustrated.

Hawken, Paul. *Growing a Business*. Simon & Schuster Books, New York, NY: 1988. ISBN: 0-67167-164-2. The best single source on how to start and grow a small business. Learn from other people's mistakes; and save yourself a lot of pain, money, and time.

Hayward, Stan. *Scriptwriting for Animation*. Focal Press, Boston, MA: 1978. ISBN: 0-24050-967-6. Animation here means 2D cel work, but there are some useful tips that particularly apply to hand-painted composited effects. Out of print; check your local library.

Itten, Johannes. *The Elements of Color*. John Wiley & Sons, New York, NY: 1970. ISBN: 0-471-28929-9. Standard reference for art classes. If you need help on color correction, balance, or lighting, this chunk of theory may be what you need.

Kamoroff, Bernard B. *Small Time Operator: How to Start Your Own Small Business, Keep Your Books, Pay Your Taxes, and Stay Out of Trouble!* 6th ed. Bell Springs Publishing, Willits, CA: 1999. ISBN: 091751-015-1. Precisely what the title says. 'Nuff said.

Katz, Steven D. *Film Directing: Shot by Shot*. Michael Wiese Productions, Studio City, CA: 1991. ISBN: 0-941188-10-8. Excellent resource on the creation and use of storyboards for directing a film. As with Blacker's book on scripting, this is essential groundwork if you plan to supervise or need to participate in preproduction planning.

Katz, Steven D. *Film Directing—Cinematic Motion: A Workshop for Staging Scenes*. Michael Wiese Productions, Studio City, CA: 1992. ISBN: 0-941188-14-0. Less important (for effects work, anyway) resource on the actual composition and framing techniques used in directing a film. Discussions on staging, choreography, blocking, and so on are included, along with meaty interviews with professionals such as John Sayles and Ralph Singleton. A good complement to Arijon's book, with a different perspective.

Kelly, Doug. *Character Animation In Depth*. The Coriolis Group, Scottsdale, AZ: 1998. ISBN: 1-56604-771-4. One of my books, surveying all the available character animation software. If you need to create animated CGI characters as elements for your comps, you need this book. Also available in Japanese.

Kelly, Doug. *LightWave 3D 5 Character Animation F/X*. Ventana Press: 1997. ISBN: 1-56604-532-0. One of my books, including some of the information in *Character Animation In Depth*, but with more detail on specific LightWave procedures. Also available in Japanese and Chinese.

Lasseter, John and Steve Daly. *Toy Story: The Art and Making of the Animated Film*. Hyperion Press, New York, NY: 1995. ISBN: 0-7868-6180-0. A wonderful collection of production art and interviews with its principal creators, both at Pixar and Disney. A must-have for 3D CGI enthusiasts and professionals. The sections on preproduction planning, surfacing, and lighting are priceless.

Lewis, Verin G. "Storyboarding." *3D Artist*, 18 (1995): 32-33. P.O. Box 4787, Santa Fe, NM. Irregular. ISSN: 1058-9503. This article presents a concise argument for the necessity of storyboarding commercial 3D animation and a brief overview of storyboard production. When you consider that advertising is the bread and butter of most small shops and freelancers, this is worth hunting down.

LightWave 3D Book: Tips, Techniques, and Ready-to-Use Objects. Miller Freeman Books, San Francisco, CA: 1997. ISBN: 0-879304-55-3. A collection of 100 tutorials from *LightWavePro* magazine. Worth acquiring, even though there isn't much on versions later than 5. It includes a CD-ROM of objects, scenes, and other goodies.

London, Barbara and John Upton. *Photography.* 5th ed. Harper Collins, New York, NY: 1994. ISBN: 0-673-52223-7. Useful for chapters on lighting, composition, color, lenses, and film vocabulary. Excellent background for digital compositing.

Malkiewicz, Kris. *Film Lighting: Talks with Hollywood's Cinematographers and Gaffers.* Prentice-Hall Press, New York, NY: 1986. ISBN: 0-671-62271-4 (pbk.). This is the working expertise of an impressive collection of lighting professionals. Not exactly an easy read, but lots of information is provided. Derived almost entirely from live-action production, a lot of the hardware specifics won't apply to digital compositing, but the principles are the same. You need to understand the real-world light sources in order to tweak or fake them in software.

Martino, Stephen Michael. *Storyboard Design for Computer-Generated Animation.* Master's thesis. Ohio State University, Columbus, OH: 1989. Well written and adequately illustrated, this is one thesis that won't put you to sleep. The author had previously worked as a designer and animator at Cranston/Csuri in Columbus and as a director at Metrolight Studios in Los Angeles. Storyboard examples include Dow "Scrubbing Bubbles," and KTLA, NBA, and HBO logos, among others. Solid practical advice on dealing with clients, too. Again, priceless if you plan to supervise effects or need to participate in preproduction planning.

Murch, Walter. *In the Blink of An Eye.* Silman-James Press, Los Angeles, CA: 1995. ISBN: 1-87950-523-1. An excellent book on editing. If you are a freelance artist, work in a small studio, or simply want to understand why the director and editor chopped up your shots or asked you to stretch them, you will learn a lot from this book.

Pintoff, Ernest, et al. *The Complete Guide to Animation and Computer Graphics Schools*: 1995. ISBN: 0-82302-177-7. Useful, but out-of-date and out-of-print. Double-check phone numbers, addresses, placement rates, accreditations, and policies before you mail out any applications or make other expensive plans.

Ruff, Barry, et al. *Softimage 3D Design Guide: Everything You Need to Master 3D Modeling and Animation with Microsoft's Softimage.* The Coriolis Group, Scottsdale, AZ: 1997. ISBN: 1-57610-147-9. An excellent book on Softimage 3.8. A very dense book, with a great deal of useful information about software that is covered by few other third-party books.

Vaz, Mark Cotta and Patricia Rose Duignan. *Industrial Light + Magic: Into the Digital Realm.* Ballantine Books/Del Rey, New York, NY: 1996. ISBN: 0-345-38152-1. In the decade covered by this book, ILM invented or developed nearly every digital compositing process used today. This book does not describe the intricate details of the work, but adequately covers the history of

ILM's transition from optical to digital special effects. The photos and narrative text are great, but the most valuable content of this book is the spirit of problem solving communicated through the many interviews with ILM staff.

Weil, Jerry, Neil Eskuri, Andy Kopra, John McLaughlin, and Kathy White. "Tricks of the Trade: Computer Graphics Production." *ACM SIGGRAPH Course Notes 5* (1995). P.O. Box 12114, New York, NY 10257. Annual. A gold mine of production rules of thumb, collected from technical directors at different production houses. Recommended for TDs, animation supervisors, and anyone else who needs to produce CGI elements on time and within budget.

Wilson, Steven S. *Puppets and People.* Tantivy Press, London: 1980. ISBN: 0-498-02312-5. A history and filmography, with a smattering of basic nuts and bolts for the motion picture techniques of optically compositing live-action with stop-motion puppets. Examines the work of Willis O'Brien, Ray Harryhausen, Phil Tippett, and others. Lots of photos; and, because the physical models tend to decay or be salvaged for parts, this is a collection of information hard to find elsewhere. Worth looking for, if only to use the extensive bibliography pointing to primary sources in the industry press.

Zaloom Mayfield Productions, prod. *The Making of Jurassic Park.* MCA Universal Home Video, Universal City, CA: 1995. ISBN: 0-7832-0889-8. Laserdisc. A good collection of behind-the-scenes information and interviews, featuring Steven Spielberg, Stan Winston, Phil Tippett, Dennis Muren, Michael Lantieri, Mark Dippe, Steve Williams, and others. Includes a sequence on the techniques used for move-matching CGI elements to live-action footage from a moving camera. Originally broadcast on NBC. The laserdisc edition has even more production stills, plus home movies of preproduction meetings. Spielberg at work, with the top VFX supervisors in the business, is a glimpse of Hollywood reality that is worth tracking down.

GLOSSARY

16mm—A smaller film size for educational and film festival use.

35mm—The standard film size for motion pictures in wide release.

Academy field ratio—A standardized ratio for the film frame. Created in 1930, it began at 1:1.33 (height vs. width), it currently stands at 1:1.85.

Academy leader—A length of film appended at the beginning of a reel to assist the projectionist in framing and focusing.

algorithm—A procedure or set of rules for solving a problem. An algorithm is implemented by a programmer to create software.

aliasing—The stair step pattern seen along the edge of a curve or diagonal border when presented in a raster display, as in a computer monitor or print. See *anti-aliasing*.

alpha—In software, the first draft of a computer program, before the faults have been corrected.

alpha channel—A grayscale or black-and-white image used as a matte in compositing.

analog—A signal or value that can change smoothly and continuously without discrete breaks. Compare to *digital*.

animation—Any technique that make inanimate objects move on the screen.

anti-aliasing—A technique for blending color values near an aliased border to visually smooth it out for raster display. In most 3D software, this requires rendering multiple passes and blending aliased areas.

aperture (lens aperture)—In cinematography, the size of the lens opening divided by the focal length, expressed as an f-stop, e.g., f/8, f/11.

articulate matte—A matte that changes shape over the course of a shot. See also *rotoscope matte*.

artifact—A visible flaw created by a process or operation other than the original photography.

aspect ratio—The ratio of width to the height of a film frame. In computer graphics, it also refers to the ratio of the resolution and takes into account the aspect ratio of the individual pixels.

AVI—Audio Video Interleaved, a playback format designed for the Microsoft Windows operating systems.

back light—See *rim light*.

back projection—In cinematography, projecting footage onto a screen placed behind the action as a means of compositing in the camera.

background—An image or sequence rendered behind all the objects in a scene.

background plate—See *clean plate*.

backplane—An object sized and positioned to act as a background.

banding—Borders between areas of similar color or brightness, visible because the image does not contain enough colors (see *bit depth*) to shade the border more smoothly. Dithering can make banding less noticeable.

bandwidth—Maximum amount of data that can pass through a system in a given length of time.

bank—Rotation on the front-to-back horizontal axis.

bar sheet—Diagrams similar to sheet music, used to set the broad timing for long sequences of animation.

batch—The repeated application of an operation to a series of images or other data, generally controlled by a small bit of code called a batch file.

beta (software)—The next generation of software after alpha, ideally with fewer faults but not yet ready for public release.

beta tester—An optimist who believes he or she can do production work with faulty software. One who tests beta software.

Betacam—A family of VTR formats developed by Sony.

BG—In cinematography, abbreviation for background.

bit—The smallest unit of information processed by a digital computer, a 1 or 0. Bits are grouped into bytes.

bit depth—The levels of detail possible in a digitized sample. 8-bit images have 256 levels, 10-bit images have 1,024.

blacks—Opaque black backing materials used to prevent background light from bleeding through bluescreen materials.

bleed—Smearing effect at the border between overly saturated colors, especially in NTSC video.

blocking—In stage or cinema direction, setting marks or positions for actors in a scene.

bluescreen—An evenly illuminated background screen frequently (but not always) colored blue that is used in chroma keying. See also *chroma key*.

bounce light—Light that is reflected from other surfaces before hitting the subject. Bounce light from a bluescreen creates spill.

bracketing—Empirically deriving a solution by progressively redefining the range of a variable.

bug—An error in computer software that produces an unintended result. Also referred to as a *fault* or glitch.

byte—A group or word of bits, a unit of digital data. Computer file sizes are usually measured in thousands (KB) or millions (MB) of bytes.

calibrated monitor—One that includes a feedback sensor and special stabilizing circuitry to keep the displayed colors as precise as possible.

camera—A machine designed to expose photosensitive film to a focused image for a controlled period of time, to create an image on the film. In cinematography, a machine to perform this operation repeatedly for successive frames to create a motion picture. In video, a sensor array is substituted for the film. In most 3D software, the point from which the scene is rendered, emulating a physical camera.

camera animation—Animation performed exclusively with the camera, as pans, dollies, zooms, or other changes, while photographing a scene or image with no other action.

camera back—The part of the camera that holds the film. Motion picture and film recorder camera backs can hold many feet of film. Also called a *magazine*.

camera body—The main part of the camera between the back and the lens, containing the shutter and film transport. Film recorder and stop-motion camera bodies have very accurate pin registration for the film sprocket holes, to ensure that each image is recorded in precisely the same position.

CCD—Charge-coupled device, the technology used in sensor chips for digital and solid-state video cameras.

center of gravity—Abbreviated CG, the center of an object's balance.

CGI—Computer Generated Imagery, any graphic image created with the assistance of a computer.

channel—A subset of an image or signal specific to a color or grayscale element. For example, an RGBA color image is composed of red, green, blue, and alpha channels.

character—In CGI, an object that displays volition and personality in a scene.

character animation—In CGI, the process of timing and posing a character object to create the illusion of life.

character model—In CGI, an object or collection of objects to be animated as a character.

chatter—A temporal, or time-based, artifact of a roughly applied operation that fluctuates in a repeating pattern.

chroma—The intensity or saturation of a color. Also known as chrominance.

chroma crawl—Temporal artifact in video caused by using high-saturation adjacent colors that are opposite in hue, e.g., yellow-blue or red-green in NTSC video.

chroma key—Keying a composite layer by color, typically blue or green. See also *bluescreen*.

Cineon—A digital file format developed by Kodak specifically for film scanning, manipulation, and recording.

clean plate—A live-action shot with no actors in it, to be used in compositing.

climax—In drama, the most important crisis in the story.

clipping—Changing values above or below a certain range to the limits of that range.

close-up—Literally, a shot of the subject face alone. Generally, considered to be any close shot.

code—Part of a program as written by a programmer. "Fixing that fault only took a few lines of code."

codec—Contraction of compression/decompression, an implementation of a compression algorithm for storing and playing back video or audio. Examples include Cinepak, Indeo, and Sorenson.

color depth—The number of bits used to store color information for each pixel in an image. 1-Bit is black and white, 8-bit can be color or grayscale having 256 different values, 24-bit has 8-bit values for red, green, and blue, approximating the color depth of a television screen.

color key—See *chroma key*.

colorist—Specialist responsible for color correction during telecine or film transfer processes.

color space—A system for representing color values by numbers.

complementary matte—The reverse of a primary matte, used to control operations that do not have an invert function.

commercial—A brief advertisement, generally intended for television. Typically 15, 30, or 60 seconds in length. Also known as a spot or ad.

component—Video signal run through separate conductors for luma and color elements.

composite—Video signal run through a single wire.

compositor—A person who creates composites.

compression—Removing redundant information from a data file to make it smaller, often used for storing or playing back images and animations. Different algorithms and software have different definitions of "redundant."

computer—A machine capable of running a program to produce the intended result. A machine that can't run a program correctly is sometimes referred to as a boat anchor, e.g., "Your 286 is a boat anchor as far as LightWave is concerned."

computer animation—Animation timed and posed by a human and inbetweened and rendered by a computer. If a non-animator is ignorant enough to say something like, "The computer does all the work," the nearest animator is entitled to whup them upside the head with a blunt instrument.

computer graphics—See *CGI*.

conflict—In drama, the collision between character and circumstance that drives the story.

contouring—A process of image enhancement that accentuates differences in levels at transitions. See *banding*.

convolve—Spatial convolution filter.

coordinates—In geometry and CGI, a set of numbers that describes a location from the origin of the local system. In most 3D software, XYZ coordinates are used to describe the location of an object in world coordinates, and the location of each point in an object's local coordinates.

coverage—Additional camera angles and setups filmed to give the editor more leeway in assembling the final cut.

crane—Vertical movement of the camera. Also referred to as a boom.

crawl—Very slow camera (also called creep) move intended to build tension, or horizontal movement of text across the screen..

creeping titles—Titles that move across the screen—typically from bottom to top—which makes it easier for the audience to read credits that are displayed briefly. Also called rolling titles.

crisis—In drama, a decision point where a character's actions determine the direction of the story.

crossing the line—Shifting the camera to the opposite side of the line of action, which can confuse the audience if not handled carefully.

CRT—Acronym for cathode ray tube, a common type of computer or video display.

CU—In cinematography, close up. See also *close-up*.

cut—The act of switching from one shot to another through the editing process.

cutting height—In cinematography, the height where the bottom of the frame intersects the actor(s).

cutting on the action—Changing from one camera position to the next during the character's action. This relieves the visual jar, since the audience focuses its attention on the action, not the shot composition.

cyclorama—A set with curves at the joining of walls or floor to reduce shadows and to remove depth cues from the perspective created by visible edges, often painted for use as a bluescreen. Also known as cyc.

delta—A change in color or luminance values for each pixel from one frame of an animation to the next. Large deltas make animations more difficult to compress for direct computer playback.

depth of field—The distance between the points where objects come into focus.

desaturate—Reduce or wash out the chroma values of an image while preserving the luma values. Extreme desaturation produces a grayscale image.

dialogue—Any soundtrack, script, or storyboard incorporating an actor's vocal performance.

difference key—A matte created by subtracting the values of one image from those of another.

digital—A signal or value which is broken up into discrete samples that are given numerical values. Contrast with *analog*.

digitizer—A device, often a computer peripheral, for converting analog signals to digital data. In CGI, typical source materials are 3D models, film or video footage, or still images.

dilate—An operation that enlarges the brighter areas of the image and shrinks the darker areas.

direct to video—A growing market segment of videotape sales and rentals, of films that have never been theatrically released. A potential opportunity for independent filmmakers.

director—The person who oversees the big picture of the production, and who generally has final creative control over the look, story, timing, and editing of an animated film.

display buffer—A section of RAM that contains the current image.

dissolve—A special effect shot transition where the first shot gradually fades out and is replaced by the second shot fading in. See *wipe*.

dither—Scattering pixels of one value over the border into an area of a different value, to visually blend the two areas together. See *banding*.

dolly—Camera move as if on a dolly, a truck, or another horizontally mobile platform. Also referred to as track or truck.

drop shadow—A contrasting copy of a graphic or text that is slightly larger and sometimes slightly offset to create a consistent visual contrast over varying background colors.

e-cinema—See *electronic cinema*.

ECU—In cinematography, extreme close up. See also *close-up*.

edge—A line connecting two points, the boundary between one polygon and the next.

edge matte—A matte containing only the outline or boundaries of the subject.

editor, film editor—The person who assembles shots in sequence and synchronizes the soundtrack(s) according to the director's instructions.

effects—See *special effects animation*.

effects animation—Animation created to mimic phenomena such as fire, smoke, clouds, rain, or anything else that moves but is not a character or prop.

effects track—A soundtrack containing sound effects, rather than music or dialogue.

electronic cinema—Digital or electronic projection systems that approach or match the image quality of theatrical 35mm film systems.

elevation—A side or front view of a set design.

ELS—In cinematography, extreme long shot.

encoder—A device that converts a signal to another form. Commonly, a computer-to-broadcast video converter. Also called a scan converter.

ergonomics—Design of objects to fit the user's shape and actions; to prevent injury and to increase comfort and efficiency.

erode—An operation that shrinks the brighter areas and enlarges the darker areas of an image.

establishing shot—Shows the audience the general environment in which the action will take place.

executive—As in executive producer, one who makes financial decisions about a production. See also *suit*.

exposition—In drama, necessary background information communicated to the audience, usually by dialogue, sometimes by a title sequence or insert shot, that would be difficult or impossible to convey by a character's actions.

expression—Short for "mathematical expression." Using one object or control to manipulate another object or control by way of an algorithm or set of rules.

eyelights—In cinematography, lights set up specifically to bring out a highlight spot in an actor's eyes.

fade—A dissolve to or from a solid color, usually black or white.

fade in—The process where an image gradually appears from a blackened screen by lightening up to scene.

fade out—The opposite of *fade in*.

fair use—The doctrine of copyright prevalent in the U.S., that a free duplicate of a copyrighted work may be made for personal educational use.

fault—An error in a computer program that produced unwanted or unintentional results. Less scrupulous developers may document the behavior of a fault and call it a feature.

FG—In cinematography, foreground.

fill light—A light used to soften shadows and make hidden details visible without washing out the key light.

film grain—Tiny imperfections in an image produced by the crystals in film emulsion.

film recorder—A system that uses a camera to record digital images from a high-resolution CRT or laser. For motion picture film, the camera must have a pin-register film transport.

filter—An algorithm used to sample and modify an image pixel by pixel.

flicker fusion—The visual phenomenon that blends a rapid series of still images into the illusion of continuous motion. The frame rate at which flicker fusion occurs varies widely, from as low as 15 fps to over 100 fps. See also *Showscan*.

focal length—The length of a camera lens assembly, measured from the rear nodal point to the focal plane. After all, it's not the size of the lens, it's how you use it.

focal plane—The plane behind the camera lens where the image is in sharpest focus. Also known as the film plane.

focus—The sharpness and clarity of an image.

focus pull—Animating the depth of field to match the area of sharp focus to an object's movement.

foley—Sound effects recording by professional noisemakers.

footage—In cinematography, exposed film from a camera, measured in feet.

fps—Abbreviation of frames per second, the rate at which images are projected to create the illusion of motion, in film, video, or other media. See also *frame rate*.

frame—In cinematography, the boundaries of the projected image.

frame rate—The speed at which separate images are viewed in a motion picture or other device for creating the illusion of motion. See also *sound speed*, *silent speed*, *flicker fusion*, *fps*.

frame-accurate—A VTR with a tape transport that can accurately record a single frame or field at a time. Used until recently to record animation to tape, now largely replaced by digital recorders.

fringe—An outline of a different color (usually brighter) along the edge of a matte. The fringe is also known as the *matte line*.

front projection—Projecting an image into a scene from the front, used to composite in the camera. Contrast with *rear projection*.

function curve—Long form of fcurve. A spline used to animate a function.

garbage matte—A simple matte designed to block complex noise or garbage that would otherwise interfere with a more elaborate or sensitive matte process.

good take—A live action shot or soundtrack recording good enough to be used.

graphics—See *CGI*.

gray card—A flat object with calibrated gray colored surface, used to adjust or measure lighting levels.

hardware—Computer equipment that you can see and touch, in contrast to software, which is intangible.

Hi-8—A consumer video format developed by Sony and popular for camcorders, providing higher image quality than 8mm or VHS.

hidden line removal—An algorithm that removes lines not visible to the camera from a wireframe rendering, producing a cleaner image.

hit—A musical beat or sound effect used to synchronize the action.

hold—A pose or shot repeated over a number of frames.

in-camera effect—A double exposure, matte, or other special effect performed in the camera with the original film.

index of refraction—A number representing how much a material bends or refracts the light passing through it.

inertia—The tendency of objects to keep doing what they've been doing.

input—Communicating information to a computer.

input devices—Peripherals designed to make it easier to communicate information to a computer. Common examples include the mouse, keyboard, pen and tablet, scanner, and digitizer.

insert shot—A shot filmed or rendered separately from the master shot, usually a close-up for exposition or from a character's POV, and edited into the main shot.

inter-cut—Shots edited together in a sequence.

iris—A device that controls the amount of light entering a camera. Also, the colored portion of the eye surrounding the pupil.

iris out—In cinematography, a transition in which a circular matte shrinks until the entire frame is obscured. *Iris in* is the reverse.

joystick—An input device usually relegated to games, but occasionally useful in CGI.

kernel—A pattern of pixels surrounding the current pixel, used for sampling by some filters.

key—See *matte, chroma key*.

key light—The primary light in a scene, providing most of the illumination.

key sounds—Points in the soundtrack used to match the animation, e.g., footsteps.

keyframe animation—Setting key poses and interpolating between the keys to create animation. Contrast with *procedural animation*.

kinescope—Simplest and oldest way of transferring digital images to film; a single-frame-capable film camera pointed at a high-resolution monitor.

lateral—A sideways camera move.

level—Status in an animated character's hierarchy, determining when in the animation process a part is posed. Generally, the root of the hierarchy is posed first, and the extremities last.

line of action—In cinematography, the main line (or slalom) of the action. The camera should stay on one side of the line of action during a sequence, to avoid confusing the audience.

linear—A sampling system in which increments between values are evenly distributed. Also referred to as the lin. Compare to *logarithmic*.

lip sync—Coordinating a character's facial animation to a sound track to create the illusion that the character is speaking.

live action—Footage shot in the real world.

local coordinates—In most 3D software, XYZ values are calculated from the pivot of an object, rather than the origin of the entire virtual world.

lockdown—In puppet animation, a fastener inserted into a puppet's foot to keep it in place on the set. In cinematography, securing the camera so it does not move during a shot. In most 3D software, setting several identical values with linear interpolation in adjacent frames of a motion graph, to prevent any undesired movement.

logarithmic—A sampling system in which increments between values are progressively larger toward the extremes of the sampling range. Also known as log. Compare to *linear*.

long shot—A shot in which the entire figure, as well as a good deal of the background, is visible.

LS—In cinematography, long shot.

luma key—Similar to chroma key, but composites images based on luminance or brightness rather than color.

mask—A type of matte used to restrict an effect to a particular area of the screen.

master shot—A shot that establishes the entire environment of a sequence, laying out a visual map for the audience. A camera setup wide enough to encompass an entire scene, designed to be intercut with closer shots.

match—See *move matching* and *dissolve*.

match dissolve—A dissolve from one image to a similar image, to show the passage of time or other gradual change or to smooth the transition.

matte—An image used to control the transparency of another image for compositing. Also known as *key*.

matte line—The edge between a matte painting and the live-action area. See *fringe*.

matte painting—A two-dimensional image created at least partly by painting rather than photographic techniques, and composited with other elements to create illusions of depth and scale.

MCU—In cinematography, medium close up. Also called medium close shot.

memory color—Colors that are so well-known that most people can immediately detect any difference from the standard (such as Coca-Cola red).

mocap—Motion capture, the recording of an actor's movements in real-time for application to computer-generated effects.

modeling—In CGI, creating objects by manipulating points, edges, and faces.

motion blur—Motion occurring while the camera shutter is open produces a blurred image; CGI can reproduce this effect by rendering and compositing images of a moving object's position between frames.

mouse—Input device, common but not well suited to most artwork. See also *pen* and *tablet*.

move matching—Matching the CGI camera movements and settings to live action footage in order to render CGI elements that will merge seamlessly with the live action.

MPEG—A lossy compression format popular for direct computer playback of animation and live action.

multiplane camera—An animation camera stand designed to hold and independently move multiple layers of artwork, simulating perspective shifts and depth of field.

MS—In cinematography, medium shot.

noodle—Tweaking settings back and forth and repeatedly creating previews long past the point of diminishing returns.

normalize—Converting different bit depths to the range 0.0 through 1.0.

NTSC—National Television Standards Committee. The standard for television signals broadcast in the U.S.

omniscient observer—In cinematography, a camera directed as if it were an invisible, all-seeing actor in a scene.

on-axis cut—Abrupt change in camera setup on the long axis of the lens, either closer to or farther from the subject.

one-shot—One subject fills the frame. Also referred to as a single.

optical printer—A machine that produced a film print by combining two or more prints, used for transitions and other compositing effects.

opticals—Effects produced by an optical printer.

orbit—An elliptical camera move roughly centered around the subject.

origin—The center of the coordinate system, where X, Y, and Z all equal 0.

OTS—In cinematography, over the shoulder.

out of sync—Soundtrack running behind or ahead of the animation.

out take—A shot that is not included in the final print of the film.

PAL—Phase Alternating Line. A standard for television signals broadcast in the U.K. and Europe.

palette—The range of colors available to a display device. A 24-bit palette can reproduce as many shades of color as the average person can see.

pan—Abbreviation of panorama. Horizontal camera rotation around a fixed point; a Y-axis rotation.

pan, truck—A pan executed by moving the camera sideways rather than rotating it.

pan, zip—A caricatured camera motion representing a fast stop, as if the entire camera is vibrating rapidly.

pattern recognition—Algorithms that use a defined matrix of pixel values to identify a similar matrix of pixel values within an image.

pen and tablet—A more artist-friendly substitute for the standard computer mouse, which simulates the behavior of a pen on paper. Also called a stylus.

peripherals—Additional equipment for a computer, e.g., external hard drives, pen and tablet, film recorder, or digitizer.

persistence of vision—See *flicker fusion*.

phoneme—The shape of the mouth when pronouncing a particular sound. Also known as mouth action or phonic shape.

pin registration—Securing the film precisely in an animation camera or film recorder with a set of pins, to ensure that each frame is registered exactly like all the others.

pitch—In most 3D software, the left-to-right rotational axis. A character's head nods on the Pitch axis. Also, the presentation of a storyboard, related to a salesperson's presentation.

pixel—Contraction of Picture Element. The smallest individual dot visible on a computer monitor. Rows and columns of pixels together make an image.

plan—A top or overhead view of a set design.

point—One set of XYZ coordinates that defines the end or intersection of an edge. Also referred to as the *vertex*.

point of view—See *POV*.

polygon—A surface defined by three or more edges and three or more points. Also known as face or surface.

POV—Abbreviation of point of view. A camera directed to show the scene as it would appear to one of the characters.

precomposition—The rendering of a partial composition to conserve resources in a larger composition. Also referred to as precomp.

premise—A very brief summary of the point of a story, generally a sentence or two at the most.

premultiplied—An image in which each color channel is changed by being multiplied by the alpha channel.

preview—A rapidly rendered part of an animation, created as a test.

procedural animation—Movement or other animation that is controlled by an algorithm, e.g., Dynamic Realities' Impact plug-in. Contrast with *keyframe animation*.

propeller head—A term applied to CGI artists who come from a more technical, especially computer science, background. Can be comradely or pejorative, depending on usage.

proxy—See *thumbnail*.

pull-back—See *zoom*.

push-in—See *zoom*.

quant error—Quantization error, a rounding error during digitization resulting from the digital values available not exactly matching the actual value of the signal.

RAM—Random Access Memory, the type of memory used to hold program information for fast access. Equivalent to having information on your desk, rather than filed in a drawer. CGI requires a lot of RAM.

raster—Data generated or displayed one row of points at a time, adding rows to create a matrix or image. In CGI, the data is usually an image or scanner dataset.

raytracing—A class of CGI rendering algorithms that calculates the value of each pixel by mathematically tracing the path of a ray from the pixel through all the reflections and refractions it would encounter in a scene.

real-time—"Live" or in a 1:1 temporal ratio, in contrast to animation or computer time.

rear projection—Projecting images or sequences on a screen behind the actors in a scene, to composite the image and live action in the camera.

region of interest—A specific area where the mathematical operations of a composition will be especially critical or time-consuming.

rendering—The process of applying one or more operations to an image.

resolution—The number of pixels in an image, usually expressed as the width by the height, e.g., 720×486.

rev. (revision)—In software, a new or improved edition of a program, presumably superior to, or at least not as flawed as, the preceding revision.

reveal—Moving the camera to gradually expose more of a scene.

reverse angle—Cutting from one camera angle to another nearly 180 degrees from the first.

rig removal—Using a variety of compositing techniques to delete unwanted elements such as safety rigging, microphones, or crew members from an image.

rim light—A light used to highlight the edges or rim of the subject.

room tone—The ambient or background sound and acoustic nature of a space where recording is done. Room tone is recorded for dubbing into blank spaces in the track, since the audience would notice completely blank spots in the soundtrack.

rotoscope—A technique originally patented by the Fleischer studio, in which live action footage was traced over to create cel animation.

rotoscope matte—A matte or mask in which control points are manually animated frame by frame.

rough cut—The first complete edit of the film, which still needs to be fine tuned.

RSI, RMI, CTS—Repetitive Stress Injury, Repetitive Motion Injury, Carpal Tunnel Syndrome. These occupational hazards of CGI workers (and most others who work extensively with computers) can permanently disable the victim's hands. Prevention is the best cure.

sampling rate—The number of divisions per unit of time in a digital signal. A higher rate generally produces a higher quality signal.

scene—In 3D software, a file containing all the camera, object, and rendering settings necessary to create a series of images. In cinematography, a collection of shots in the same set and in a close temporal series.

script—The written plan for a film, including dialogue and some stage direction. The precursor to the storyboard.

sequence—A number of shots, in order, that tells part of the story.

set—The place where a scene is filmed.

setup—In cinematography, the positions of actors and camera; in CGI, the links, constraints, and expressions created to make animation of a character easier.

short—Film with running time between 2 to 20 minutes. Classic cartoon shorts usually ran between 6 and 7 minutes.

shot—The basic unit of film. A continuously exposed unedited piece of film. In CGI, an uncut sequence of frames.

shot volume—The space contained in the pyramid formed by the lens (the apex) and the four corners of the frame. The apparent volume of the shot ends at the central object or character.

Showscan—A projection system combining 65 fps frame rate and a wide-screen format to enhance perceived realism.

SIGGRAPH—The Association for Computing Machinery's Special Interest Group on Computer Graphics.

sightlines—An actor or character's line of vision, from the center of the eyeball through the pupil to the point being observed.

silent speed—16 fps, the minimum required to prevent strobing.

slalom—The path followed by any system, natural or machine, that can correct its movement toward a goal.

software—The set of instructions, or programs, used to control a computer.

softbox—A type of diffuse light source.

sound effects—See *foley*.

sound speed—24 fps.

soundtrack—The dialogue, music, and sound effects from a film.

special effects animation—Smoke, water, or other non-character visual effects, generally animated in most 3D software by a specially designed plug-in.

spill—Colored light reflected from backgrounds, especially bluescreen, onto foreground objects. Spill removal is important for bluescreen compositing.

Sprocket hole—An evenly spaced series of holes matching the sprocket that pulls film through a camera or projector.

stabilize—The process of removing apparent camera motion from footage, generally through the use of pattern recognition and tracking.

still shot—A shot in which the camera does not move. Also referred to as a *lockdown*.

story reel—An animation composed of story sketches synchronized to the soundtrack. Usually, each sketch is replaced with finished sequences as production proceeds.

storyboard—A sequence of story sketches depicting the major actions and layout for each shot. Often pinned to a large board or wall for group review and critique.

streaming video—Compressed video signal transmitted through the Internet and played back in real-time.

strobing—Changes between frames that are too extreme, which catch the audience's eye and destroy the illusion of smooth movement.

stroboscopic photography—Capturing a series of images on a single film frame by leaving the shutter open and firing a sequence of flashes or strobes, often used to capture a complex or rapid motion.

stylus—See *pen* and *tablet*.

suit—Decision-maker who wears a business suit. Generally, the antithesis and nemesis of a creative artist or studio.

super black—A luma value of 0 IRE rather than the 7.5 IRE of a legal NTSC signal.

sweatbox—Projection room in an animation studio used to review and critique animation. Term originated at Disney studios due to lack of air conditioning, and was retained and used elsewhere due to the animator's stress levels during critiques.

sync—Short for synchronization, the matching of sound to action on film or videotape.

synchronization—See *sync*.

synopsis—A brief summary of a script.

tablet—See *pen* and *tablet*.

telecine—A machine or process for transferring film to video.

telephoto lens—A camera lens assembly constructed so its focal length is significantly longer than its physical length.

television cutoff—The outside border of the television image that is visible on studio monitors but is not displayed by many home televisions.

television safe-titling—The area within the television image that is safe for titles and other written communication.

temporal artifacts—Tiny changes between frames that make edges crawl or pop.

three-shot—Three subjects fill the frame.

thumbnail—A smaller version of an image, used for convenience or to conserve computer memory or bandwidth. Also referred to as a proxy.

tie-down—In traditional 3D animation, usually a threaded rod with a keyed head that locks into the bottom of a character's foot. The animator passes the rod through a hole in the stage and tightens it down with a wingnut, securing the puppet in place.

tilt—Vertical equivalent of pan. See *pan*.

time encoding—Adding time code to a videotape to enable accurate measurement and reference down to the frame and field. Generally, time encoding uses the SMPTE standard HH:MM:SS:FF.

tracking—A process to extract the movement of an object, generally by using pattern recognition.

transcode—Changing data from one codec to another.

transfer—In cinematography, a moving object carries the audience's attention across the frame. Also referred to as hand-off. In editing, duplicating images or sound from one media format to another.

transform—An element's change in shape or size. Contrast with *translate*.

transition—In drama, a visible change from one dominant emotional state to another. In editing or cinematography, the effect or cut used between shots.

translate—In CGI, to change position. In general computer usage, changing data to a different file format, as when importing a JPG or TIF file and saving it in another image format.

transport—The mechanism in a VTR used to move the tape past the recording and playback heads. A very accurate and expensive transport can reliably position the tape to within one frame, enabling single-frame recording for animation.

treatment—A short form of a script, used by some studios when considering a production.

triplet—Series of three numbers that when all three are equal is referred to by a single number.

trompe l'oeil—A painting style with photographically realistic detail and perspective; literally, "deceive the eye."

trucking, truck pan—See *dolly*.

tweak—To make fine adjustments or changes to settings. See also *noodle*.

two-shot—Two subjects fill the frame. Also referred to as a double.

U-matic—An industrial videotape format, rarely used in consumer or entertainment venues.

union shop—A studio or production house that has signed an agreement with a union to hire only members of that union. Non-union workers can (sometimes) still get a job there, but may have to join the union to keep it.

user friendly—A matter of opinion regarding the utility of computer software, as people have different cognitive and working styles. Hostile for some is friendly for others.

vector graphics—Images drawn on a screen by lines connecting points. Good for outlines and wireframes, not good for color images of solid objects.

vertex—In most 3D software, a point.

VGA-to-NTSC converter—An adapter that converts the VGA output of a computer to the NTSC standard video signal used by most video equipment. Inexpensive ones have inferior video signals; you should test them before buying or renting. See also *encoder*.

VHS—A consumer-grade videotape format using half-inch tape in a cassette, having a maximum resolution of approximately 400 lines.

visual jar—A sudden change in shot volume or camera orientation that momentarily disorients the audience.

voice track—The part of the sound track that contains dialogue.

voice-over—An offscreen voice dubbed over footage, which does not need to be lip synched. A fast and cheap way to make changes after animation is completed.

VTR—Video Tape Recorder.

WAV—A file format for digitized sound, commonly used with the Microsoft Windows operating systems.

wedge—Sequence of images with progressive changes in color, brightness, and contrast settings, shot as a test for making adjustments.

wide angle lens—A lens having a focal length shorter than the diagonal measure of the image at the focal plane.

wide-screen—A film format designed for a higher aspect ratio, producing panoramic images.

wild wall—A wall or other object in a set that can be deleted or moved when not in camera range to make room for lighting or camera movement.

wipe—A special effect shot transition where the first shot is gradually replaced by the second shot, with a relatively sharp dividing line. A wipe can go from any direction, but typically moves top-to-bottom or left-to-right. See *dissolve*.

wipe the frame—Passing a foreground object in front of the camera at the moment of a cut, usually used to smooth a transition.

wire frame—An abbreviated representation of an object, showing just the edges defining the object's polygons. Computers can draw wireframes very fast, so they are widely used for previews and tests.

workstation—Marketing term for a more powerful personal computer system. Also, a person's work area.

world coordinates—A coordinate system of measuring translation from a single origin for all items.

WS—In cinematography, wide shot.

XYZ—Coordinate axes of three-dimensional space; in most 3D software, the Y-axis is up-and-down, the Z axis is front-to-back, and the X axis is side-to-side.

Z-channel—Changes the luminance based on the distance from the camera. Also referred to as Z-buffer.

zip pan—See *pan, zip*.

zoom—Using a lens capable of various focal lengths in order to change a shot. Zooming in (changing a zoom lens from wide angle or normal to telephoto) is known as a *push-in*. Zooming out (the opposite of push-in) is known as *pull-back*.

INDEX

Bold numbers indicate a figure that illustrates
the index entry

16mm, 565
2K, 59, 89, 91, 250-251
35mm film, 59, 91, 251, 561, 565, 572
3D Studio MAX (software), 37-40, 401
4:1:1 sampling, 557
4:2:0 sampling, 71-**72**
4:2:1 sampling, 71-**72**
4:2:2 sampling, 71-**72**, 229-232, 441-445, 557
4:4:4 sampling, 71
4K, 59, 91

A

Academic degrees. *See* Education.
Accuracy, mathematical, 48
Add. *See* Operations.
After Effects (software), 13, 16-17, 20, 49-50, 54,
  74-79, 103-104, 108-111, 244-246, 254-259,
  270-272, 358, 369-**370**, 377, 384, 399, 407,
  418-421, 434, 442, 450-452, 460-461, 485-**488**,
  495-**496**, 514
    Difference Matte, 236-240
    Echo effect, 419-**421**, 507
    Effect Mask, 280-283, 300-303, 306-**308**
    Film and, 254-259
    Frame Blending, 490-**491**
    Gamma, 255
    Mask Shape, 300-303
    Motion Blur, 419-**421**
    Motion Math, **467**-469
    Motion Tracker, 332-334
    Motion Stabilizer, 340-**342**
    Production Bundle, 340

Time Layout, 312-**314**, **370**, 480-481,
  502-**505**, 510-**512**, 514-515
Ultimatte Screen Correction, 244-246
Aliasing, **155-156**
Allardice, John, 34-35. *See also*
  Foundation Imaging.
Alpha channel, 61, 136, 165-173, 521.
  See also Matte.
Alt.movies.visual-effects newsgroup, 42-**43**
Amiga. *See* Operating systems.
Amirah, 225-227
Analog, 19, 57-58, 555-557
Animation,
    Keyframe, 190-192, 198-199, 265-266,
      276-279, 281-**283**, 288-305, 317, 319,
      330-331, 334, 344, 349, 380, 391-398,
      409-410
    Spline, 507-511, 513-514
Animation:Master (software), 108-111
Animator, 33
Aperture (lens aperture), 97, 101
Approvals, 615
ARRILaser, **568**-572. *See also* Film recorder.
Art director, 27
Artbeats Software Inc., **174**-175
Articulate matte. *See* Matte, Articulate.
Artifacts
    Compression, 155-**156**, 535-559
    Temporal, 160
Aspect ratio, 59-**60**, 541, 562-563
ATI All-In-Wonder PRO, 74, 320, 549-**550**
Atmosphere, 151
Attorney, 616-618
Aura (software), 52-53, 240, 259, 334, 340,
  359, 377, 384, 400, 407, 422-**424**, 434, 442,
  469-**471**, 528, 532-534, 554
    Eraser, 283-284

    Keyframer, 469-**471**
    Reverse Selection, 481-**482**
AVI, 540-546, 549
AVI2MPEG (software), 544, **546-547**
Awards, 16

B

Babylon 5, 16
Back light, 97
Baker, Stephen, 74-79
Banding, 61, 157-158, 544
Bandwidth, 523, 535-559
Barnes, Jeff, 23
Binary numbers, 60
Bit, 60
Bit depth, 60-61
Blacks, 95. *See also* Bluescreen.
Bleed, 433
Bloom, Steve, 37
Bluescreen, 74-79, 95-100, 136, **138**, 179-188, 232-233, 521
Blur, 147, 405
Bonchune, Rob, 34-35. *See also* Foundation Imaging.
Bond, Christopher, 7, 9-12, 37-40, 225-227
Booth monkeys, 42
Boris FX (software), 43-44
Bracketing, 278-279, 394
Brainstorming, 36
Brinkmann, Ron. *See* Shake.
Bullet list, 41, 46-49
Burg, Steve, 460-461. *See also* Foundation Imaging.
Burns, Debbie, 102-105
Byte, 60

C

C-Reality, 86-**87**
Cache, 524-**525**
Calibrated monitor. *See* Workstation.

Camera, 94-95, 363, 413, 449, 483, 562-563
    animation, 105, 319, 409-410, 460-461
    crew, 27-28, 94-95, 101, 319, 414
    First Assistant, 28
    lockdown, 100, 319-321, 336, 461-462, 541
    Motion Control. *See* Motion control camera.
    Multiplane, 462
    notes on motion, 31
    operator, 28, 319, 462, 562
    Second Assistant, 28
Career ladder, 5, 583
Carpenter, Russell, 28-32
Case studies, 7, 102-105, 108-111
CCD, 86-88, 91
CD-ROM, 543
CGI, 28-32, 37-40, 103, 108-111, 116-**125**, 151,
    165-173, 344, 349, 359, 363, 379-410, 434, 450-452, 473-474, 565
Chalice (software), 54, 240, 246, 260, 334-335, 341, 377, 400, 408, 435, 442, 470
    Disk Input Node, 482
    Expression Language, 377, 408
    Film and, 260
    Ultimatte Classic Screen Correction, 246
    Ultimatte Roto Screen Correction, 246
Changes, last minute, 6, 615. *See also* Clients.
Channels, 60-61, 131-**133**, 323-324, **326**, 349
Chatter, 270, 279, 287, 294, 394
Christiansen, Mark, 93
Chroma crawl, 208, 212
Chroma key. *See* Bluescreen.
Cineon, 250-263
Cinematographer. *See* DP.
Cinepak codec, **537**, 539-541
Cintel, 85
Clavadetscher, Charlie, 386. *See also* ILM.
Clean plate, 95, 100, 105, 119, 136, **139**, 234-247, 273, 309-315, 363-374, 414, 520-521
Clients, 5-6, 10, 13, 19-22, 36, 528, 535, 557, 609, 612-613

CMYK, 60. *See also* Color space.

Cobra, Jurong, **108-111**

Codec, 541, 543-548. *See also* Cinepak, Microsoft Video 1, MPEG, Sorenson.

Color balance, 427

Color bars. *See* NTSC.

Color correction, 88, 413, 427-447

Color depth, 61

Color key. *See* Bluescreen.

Color sampling, **437-438**

Color space, 48, 60-61

    Conversion, 438-445

Colorist, 33-34, 86, 88. *See also* Telecine operator.

Commotion (software), 54, 240-242, 260-262, 284, 335, 342, 359, 372, 377, 384, 400-401, 408, 435, 492

    Difference Matte, 241-242

    Film and, 260-262

    Frame Time Adjust, 482-483, 485, 488, 495, 512-513, 515-516

    ICE Blur filter, 443

    Rotospline, 303, 308

    SuperClone, 313-314

Compensation, 601-603, 609-610, 614

Component, 70

Composite, 70

Compression, 61-62, 73, 535-559

    Artifacts, **156**, 520

Computer Café, 22-24

Computer, basic skills, 9

Contact, 20

Contouring. *See* Banding.

Contracts, 593-594, 602-603, 612-618

Contrast, 427

Convolve. *See* Filters, Convolve.

Coolidge, Calvin, 594

Cope, Ken, 603

Copyright. *See* Intellectual Property.

Creative opportunities, 36, 593

Credits, 209-**216**, 602. *See also* Text.

CREDITS.TXT, 210

Creeping titles. *See* Text.

Crooke, Dylan, **12**-15, 102-105, 108-111

CRT, 566

Cyclorama, 97

D

D-1, 552, 557-**559**

D-5, 557-**558**

Deadlines, 6, 111, 519-520, 522, 612-613, 615

Defocus, 147

Deja.com, 42-**43**

Delta, 80

Demo reel, 8, 12, 16, 23, 556, 583, 588-592, 604

Demo software. *See* Software, evaluating.

Destabilize, 374-379, 401-409, 522. *See also* Stabilize.

Difference key, 136

DiFrancesco, David, 566

DiGiorgio, Dominic, 102-105, 108-111

Digital, 57-58, 557-559

Digital artist, 32

Digital compositing, definition, 129

Digital Fusion (software), 32, 51-52, 162-164

    Adjust To Legal, **434**

    BézierSpline, 191-**192**, 198-**199**

    Blur filter, 316-**317**, 405

    Brightness/Contrast tool, 190-192, 445-**446**

    Channel Booleans tool, 169

    Color Gain tool, **445**

    Color Space Control, 438-442

    Corner Tracker, 401-**403**

    Dent tool, 315-**316**

    Difference Keyer tool, 235-236

    Displace Warp tool, 316-**318**

    Dissolve tool, 192-**194**

    Effect Mask, 192-**197**, 228-**229**, 273-280, 288-300, 305-**306**, 309, 364

    Expression, 464-466

    Film and, 250-254

    Glow tool, 219-**220**

    Luma Keyer tool, 174-**178**

    Matte Control tool, 521

    Merge tool, 171, 309

Path, 327-332, 381-382

Perspective Positioner, **404-405**

Preferences, 524-**525**

Preview, 171

Reverse Box, 478

Safe Title Area, 210, 217

Spline Editor, **415-416**, 507-**509**

Stabilizer tool, 352-358

Steady Position, 337-340

Time Speed tool, 417-**418**, 478-**479**, 483-**484**, 486, 489-**490**,497-**502**, **506**-507

Time Stretcher, **509**-510

Tracker, 323-332, 381-382, 414

Text tool, 209-224

Transform tool, 197-199

Ultimatte Screen Correction tool, 243-**244**

Ultra Keyer tool, 180-188

Unsteady Position, **375-376**

Digital Light Processing (DLP), 573-578. *See also* E-cinema.

Digital media, 67

Digital Micromirror Device (DMD), 574-578. *See also* E-cinema.

Digital video, 70, 81

Digitizers, 58, 74-84

Dilate, 153-**154**

Dippe, Mark A. Z., 346. *See also* ILM.

Director, 26-27, 94, 319-320, 363, 380, 462, 477, 522, 536, 562

Director of Photography. *See* DP.

Dissolve, 151

Dither, 157-**158**

Downsampling, 540-541

DP (Director of Photography), 27-28, 94, 363, 562, 591

DPS Perception RT3DX, 83-84

Drop shadow, **218-219**

Dropped frames, 414-418

DV Master Pro, 81, 548-**549**, **551**-552

DVCPRO, DVCPRO50, 557-558

DVD, 543, 546

E

Ebner, David, 23

E-cinema, 450, 561, 572-579

E-mail, 595

EBR. *See* Electron Beam Recorder.

Edge matte. *See* Matte, Edge.

Edge enhancement, camera, 95

Education, 4, 7-8, 11, 14-15, 18, 22-24, 584-588, 603. *See also* Training.

effect* (software), 50-51, 242, 262, 336, 401, 408-409, 424-**426**, 435, 443, 471, 483, 486, 488-489, 505, 507, 513-514

    Blend effect, **426**

    Effect Mask, 284-286

    Frame Blending, 492-**493**, 496-497

    Freeform Mask, **304**-305, 308-309, 372-**373**

    Stabilize 1 Point, 342-344, 377-**379**

    Stabilize 2 Points, 359-362, 408-409

    Timeline, 314-315, 372-**373**, 516

    Tracker, 342-344, 359-362, 384-385

Electric Image (software), 384, 401

Electron Beam Recorder, 572. *See also* Film recorder.

Electronic cinema. *See* E-cinema.

Emblaze, 540

Encoder, 544, **546-547**

Ergonomics, 600-601

Erode, 153-**154**, 247

Evans, Stephen, 102-105, 108-111

Executive producer, 26

Experience, 4-5, 93. *See also* Training, Education.

Expressions, 48, 463-466

F

Fade, 151, **153**, 190-192

Fair use. *See* Intellectual property.

Fame, 597

Fast motion, 483-486

Features. *See* Bullet list.

File formats, 63-67

File size, 61-62
Film, 250-263, 522, 561
    festivals, 14-15
    grain, 88, **90**, 227-228, 250-263, 318, 405, 413, 449-450, 472, 477, 521, 565
    recorder, 565-572
    scanning. *See* Scanning, film.
    stock, 94
Film-to-video, 47, 67. *See also* Telecine.
Filter, 48, **145-149**, **189-190**
    Blur, 318, 405
    Convolve, 143
    Gaussian, 147-**148**
    Impulse, 143, **146**
    Median, **146**
    Mitchell, 147-**148**
    Sharpening, **147**
    Sinc, 147, **149**
    Spatial, 143
Finances, 607-609
FireWire, 70, 81
Flat Earth Productions, 16
Floating-point values, 48, 130
Flying spot scanner, 85-86
Footage
    Evaluating, 6, 93-94, 519-523
    Tutorial, 45-46, 164, 170
    Looping, 176
Formats. *See* File formats.
Foundation Imaging, 15-17, 34-35, 450-452, 460-461
Fps, 34
Frantic Films, 7, 9-12, 37-40, 225-227
Freeze frame, 477
Fringe, 155, **157**, 184-**186**. *See also* Matte Line.

G

Gaffer. *See* Lighting, set.
Gamma, 251, 255, 260-**261**, 432-**433**
Garbage matte. *See* Matte, Garbage.
GB (gigabyte), 60

Geometric transformation. *See* Transform.
Geri's Game, 15
Goals, 37, 606
Goodman, Jason, 74-79
Gray card, 429
Griffiths, Guy, 605
Growing A Business, 606

H

Haley, Paul, 270-272, 287-288
Hard disk drives, 81-83, 520, 524-528, 553-554
Hardware. *See* Workstation.
Hawken, Paul, 606
HDTV, 19, 59, 67-68, 522, 558, 561-565
Heinlein, Robert A., 583
Henry, Eric, 605
Hi-8, 556
Hibsher, David, 28-32
Highlights, keying out, 250
History of compositing, 3, 5, 22
Hitch, Sherry, **15**-17, 34-35, 450-452, 460-461
    See also Foundation Imaging.
HLS, 60. *See also* Color space.
Hollander, Richard, 10
Holoset, **99**-100
Holusa, Tom, 544
Hook, 474
Honn, Ron, 23
HSB, 60. *See also* Color space.
HTML, 541-543. *See also* Web.
Hughes-JVC projector, 573-**577**.
    See also E-cinema.

I

ICE accelerator, 20
IEEE-1394, 70, 81, 551
IFF format, 78-79
ILM (Industrial Light + Magic), 5, 380, 385-386, 409
Imagica IMAGER XE film scanner, 91-92

Independence Day, 13
Innovation, 4-5, 14
Input, 47, 522-523
Insurance, 610-611
Intellectual property, 614-618
Interconnectivity, 44
Internet, 14, 536-543
Interns, 10
Interpolation, 296, 395, 417-418, 489-497
Interview, 9, 14, 23
Invisible effects, 10
Irez CapSure, 74-79
IRE. *See* NTSC.

J

Jargon, 9
Job interview, 592-593
Job requirements, 3
Job satisfaction, 7, 17, 21
Jones, Chris, 102-105
Jurassic Park, 16, 101, 379-380, 409
Jurgenson, Eric, 17-22, 270-272, 287-288, 597
Just A Minute, 225-227

K

K (kilobyte), 60
Kamoroff, Bernard, 609
Key, 136. *See also* Bluescreen, Luma key,
    Difference key.
Keyframe animation.
    See Animation, Keyframe.
Kinescope, 565
Kuper (software), 112, **114**-115, 118
Kutchaver, Kevin, 16
King, Stephen, 10, 37-40
Kutchaver, Kevin, 16

L

Laser, 566. *See also* Film recorders.
Lawyer, 616-618

Lay, Tony, 104
Legal colors. *See* NTSC.
Leonard, Christle, 225-227
Light meter, 97
Lighting, set, 74-79, 95-101
Lighting reference objects, 106-108
LightWave (software), 30-32, 34-35, 74-79,
    102-105, 117-124, 165, 386-400, 405,
    528-532, 554
LightWave motion file, **115**-116, 381-384
Liman, Doug, 28-32
Linear color space, 61
Listserv. *See* Mailing lists.
Logarithmic color space, 61
Lossless. *See* Compression.
Luma key, 136, **138**, 174-**178**
LZW compression, 62. *See also* Compression.

M

M-JPEG, **553**
Macca Strewth, 14
MacOS. *See* Operating systems.
Macrae, Ian, 102-105
Mailing lists, 43-44
Maine Video Systems, 18
Markers. *See* Reference points.
Mask, 108-111, 143-**144**, 192-**197**, 228-**229**,
    273-286
    Animating, 275-279
    Soft Edge, 275, 299
Master Class, 7
Match lighting, 102-105, 108, 119-**125**,
    450-452
Match move, 5, 31, 102-105, 108-111, 344,
    349-351, 359, 374-401
Mathematical expressions. *See* Expressions.
Mathematical operations. *See* Operations.
Matte, 47, 133-137, 247
    Articulate, 137, **140**
    Complementary, **141**
    Difference, 136, **140**
    Edge, 141-143, 153

Garbage, 141-**142**, 227-**228**, 450-452, 520-521

Line, 155, **157**, **159**, 184-**186**, 452

Painting, 317-318, 449-**475**

Rotoscope, 32, 100, 141, 287-309, **371**, 452

Static, 137, 315

Traveling, 137

MB (megabyte), 60

Media Player, 540

Meetings, 36-37

Megabyte. *See* MB.

Memory, 524-528

Memory color, 429

Mentors, 16, 595. *See also* Training, Education.

Microsoft Video 1, 544-**545**. *See also* Codec.

Mighty Joe Young, 94

Mocap. *See* Motion capture.

Modeling, 102

Momentum Animations, 12-15, 102-105

Monitors, 427-428

Motion blur, 497-**505**

Motion capture, 34

Engineer, 34

Motion-control camera, 28, 100, **112**-117, 272

Motion control operator, 28, 272

Move matching. *See* Match move.

MPEG, 79-81, 540-**547**, 549, 563

Multimedia Software Design, 74-79

Multiplane camera. *See* Camera, multiplane.

Murphy, George, 409. *See also* ILM.

Mystic Knights of Tir Na Nog, 16, 450-452. *See also* Foundation Imaging.

N

Network, 520, 523

Games, 524

Networking, 594-595, 611

Neutral colors, 428, **430**

Nibley, Chris, **112**, 165-167, 272

Noise, 247-249, 405, 440-445, 472, 521

Normalized values, 130, 432

Notes, shooting, 31, 100, **349**, 380

NT. *See* Operating systems.

NTSC, 67-68, 428, 430-**431**, 433-437

O

Old Mill, The, 462

Operating systems, 44-45, 91, 524-528, 543

Operations, 46-47, 129-131

Add, 46, **130**

Over, 46, 133, **135**, 171

Optimization, 49, 519

Out Of Screen, 270-272

Output, 47, 522-523, 528, 535-559

Over. *See* Operations.

Oversize framing. *See* Uncrop.

Oz Encounters, 13, **102-105**

P

PAL, 67

paint* (software), 50-51

Pan. *See* Transform, Pan.

Parallax, 392, 461-462, 466, 468

Path, 320

Pattern recognition, 320-336

Perception RT3DX, **552-553**

Persistence, 594

Perspective, 461-462, 466

Peter Pan, 462

Photography, principal, 5-6, 93-101, 103-105, 108-109, 112-116, 119, 125, 413

Photoshop (software), 13-14, 16, 364-**367**, 427, 450-**459**

Pigsfly.com, 43-44

Pin registration, 100

Pixar, 14, 566-568

Pixel, 58-59

Plagiarism, 590

Planning, preproduction, 5, 30, 102-105, 519-520

Plug-ins, software, 48, 263-265, 540. *See also* Ultimatte, Zbig.

Portfolio, 8-9, 11. *See also* Demo reel.

PostScript. *See* Text.

Practice, 4, 6, 8, 11, 14, 21, 23, 587-588.
See also Training, Education.

Precomposition, 49, 170, 495, 519-523

Preferences, 524-**525**

Preissler, Suzanne, 28-32

Premiere (software), 537

Premultiplied, 157, **159**

Problem-solving, 5-6, 9, 93, 153, 155-160,
519, 522

Producer, 26, 536

Production team, 25-28

Production assistant (PA), 28, 34

Propeller head. *See* Technical Director.

Pugh, Steve, 16, 34-35. *See also*
Foundation Imaging.

Q

Quant error, 71-73

QuickTime, 540-544, 546-548

R

RAM, 524-528, 550

Real (software), **537-540**

Reference image, 431. *See also* Color.

Reference frame, 350, 356-357, 392

Reference points, 100-104, 108-111, 116-117

Reflection maps, environment, 105

Region of interest, 49, 143, 227

Rendering, 131, 519, 522-523, 528

Research, online, 42-44, 64-67

Resolution, **59**

Responsibility, 6

Reverse motion, 477-483

Reviews, software, 42

RGB, 60. *See* Color space.

Rig removal, 5, 103, 108-111, 269-286, 363-374,
414, 520-521

Rigging. *See* Lighting, set.

Ringing, 147, 157-**158**

Rotoscope matte. *See* Matte, Rotoscope.

Rotoscope, 100, 287

Rounding error. *See* Quant error.

Roy, Beth, 460-461. *See also*
Foundation Imaging.

RSI (Repetitive Stress Injury), 600

RTV format, 528-534, 554-555

S

S-Video, 70, 549, 552, 556

S-VHS, 556

Safety margin. *See* Uncrop.

Saint Patrick, **460-461**. *See also*
Foundation Imaging.

Sampling, 71-**72**, 229-232, 548
rate, 57-58

Saturated colors, 427

Scaling. *See* Transforms.

Scanner operator, 33-34. *See also*
Telecine operator.

Scanning, film, 89-**92**, 250, 414

Schools. *See* Training, Education.

Scott, Montgomery, 599

Screen correction, 74-79, 95, 233-247

SDI, 70

Sesame Street, 10

Set extension, 28-32, 450-**452**, **460-461**

Settings, saving, 266

SFX 200T (film), 94

SGI. *See* Operating systems.

Shadow surfaces, 101, 105, 116-**118**, 351, 386

Shake (software), 53, 243, 262, 286, 344, 362,
374, 379, 385, 401, 409, 443-445, 471
CameraShake function, 410
ColorX node, 444-445
Common function, 243
Film and, 262
QuickShape, 305, 309
RGBToYIQ node, **444**
TimeX function, 483
VideoSafe node, 435
YIQToRGB node, **444**

Shermis, Boyd, 10

Shockwave, 540

Shoot. *See* Photography, principal.

SIGGRAPH, 4, 10, 594, 596

Silence of the Lambs, 209

Slow motion, 477, 483, 486-493

Small-Time Operator, 609

Smith, Emile, 34-35. *See also*
   Foundation Imaging.

SMPTE, 68. *See also* Timecode.

Softbox, 97

Software
      evaluating, 41-49, 263-265
      Developer Kit (SDK), 48

Sorenson, **548-549**. *See also* Codecs.

Specialization, 5

Speed Razor (software), 43-44, 81, 528, 551,
   554-555

Spielberg, Steven, 380, 388

Spill, **96**-97, 99

Spirit DataCine, 86-88

Squires, Scott, 380. *See also*
   Commotion (software).

Stabilize, 47, 108-111, 310, 336-362.
   See also Destabilize.
      Single-point, 336-344, 522
      Multiple-point, 344-362, 522

Static matte. *See* Matte, Static.

Storm Of The Century, 10, 37-40

Story meeting, 36

Storyboard, 6, 103-104
      Artist, 27
      Session, 36

Stranahan, Ken, 28-32

Stranahan, Lee, 28-32

Streaming video, 536-**540**

Street, Rita, 601

Strobing, **506**-507

Studio, running your own, 18-19, 44-45, 93,
   604-606

Subcontracting, 607

Suits, 599-600

Sun angle, 95. *See also* Lighting, set.

Super black, 435-437

Supervising compositor, 32, 36

Supervisor. *See* VFX Supervisor.

Suskin, Mitch, 16, 34-35. *See also*
   Foundation Imaging.

Sync, 136

Sysop (System Operator), 523

T

Talent, 3, 5, 7-8, 11, 21, 23

Talking Cow, 287-288

Task list, 519-520, 606

TD. *See* Technical Director.

Team player, 33

Technical Director (TD), 33

Telecine, 85-**90**, 250-251, 414
      Operator, 33-34, **89**

Temporal artifacts. *See* Artifacts, Temporal.

Terabyte, 60

Teska, John, 34-35. *See also*
   Foundation Imaging.

Testing. *See* Software, evaluating.

Testimonials, 42

Texas Instruments DLP, 573-578.
   See also E-cinema.

Text burn-in, 7

Text, 49, 203-224, 536-537, 589.
   See also Timecode.
      Design principles, 204-209
      Dissolve, 220-224
      Drop shadow, 218-219
      Outline, 219-220
      Safe area, 209

The November Men, 210-216

Thornton, Ron, 16

Time-shifting, 310-315, 363, 372

Timecode, 68, 216-224, 588, 614

Timing, 47

Titles. *See* Text.

Tools, compositing. *See* After Effects, Aura,
   Chalice, Commotion, Digital Fusion,
   effect*, Shake.

Tools, evaluating and choosing, 7

Tools, high-end, 6

Tracking, 13, 47, 108-111, 320-336, 349-**350**, **354**, 380, 391

Trainees. *See* Interns.

Training, 3-4, 7-8, 11, 586-587. *See also* Education.

Transform, 48, 149-**152**, 197-200
    Flip, 149-**150**, 197-**198**, 318
    Flop, 149-**150**
    Multiplane pan, 151-**152**, 201-**204**, 462-471
    Pan, 149, 199
    Rotate, 344, 350
    Size, 199, 344, 350
    Translate, 344, 350

Translate. *See* Transform.

Traveling matte. *See* Matte, Traveling.

Triplet, 428, 432

Trompe l'oeil, 450

TrueType. *See* Text.

U

Ultimatte (software), 74-79, 89, 97, 243-247, 264-265

Ultraviolet (UV) light, 97

Uncrop, 344-**342**,346-**348**, 351-**352**, 359

Usenet, 42-**43**

V

VFX Research & Development, 33

VFX Supervisor, 5-6, 8-12, 22, 27, 93-94, 125, 320, 380, 519, 522, 528, 598-599, 605

VFXPro, 4, 597. *See also* Visual Effect Society.

VHS, 550, 556, 588

Video tap, 95

Videotape, 549, 555-559, 588

Video Toaster NT, 74-79, 82, 528-534, 553-**555**

Video Workshop, 17-22, 270-272, 287-288

VistaVision, 89, 91, 346, 409

Visual effects art director, 27

Visual effects producer, 26

Visual Effects Society, 596-597

Visual effects supervisor. *See* VFX Supervisor.

Voyager, 34-35

W

Walker, 165-173

Waveform, **58**

Web, 540-543

Wedge, 427-428

White balance, 95

Williamson, Tom, 22-24

Windows. *See* Operating systems.

Wireframe, **390**, 395

Wire removal, 309

Workflow, 5, 10, 13, 22, 36, 519-523, 593, 598, 601

Working conditions. *See* Workflow.

Workstation, 428, 523, 600-601, 608

World's Greatest Commercials, 12

Writer, 27

Y

YIQ, 60. *See also* Color space.

YUV, 60, 229-232, 440-442. *See also* Color space.

YUV9, 71

Z

Zbig (software), 264

Z-channel, 151, **153**

Zorniak, Ken, 10

COLOPHON

From start to finish, The Coriolis Group designed *Digital Compositing In Depth* with the creative professional in mind.

The cover was produced on a G3 Macintosh, using QuarkXPress 3.3 for layout compositing. Text imported from Microsoft Word was restyled using the Futura and Trajan font families from the Adobe font library. It was printed using four-color process and spot UV coating.

Select images from the color studio were combined with new figures to form the color montage art strip, unique for each Creative Professionals book. Adobe Photoshop 5 was used in conjunction with filters to create the individual special effects.

The color studio was assembled using Adobe Pagemaker 6.5 on a G3 Macintosh system. Images in TIFF format were color corrected and sized in Adobe Photoshop 5. It was printed using four-color process.

The interior layout was built in Adobe Pagemaker 6.5 on a G3 Macintosh. Adobe fonts used include Stone Informal for body, Avenir Black for heads, and Copperplate 31ab for chapter titles. Adobe Photoshop 5 was used to process grayscale images, lightening the original files to accommodate for dot gain. Text originated in Microsoft Word.

Imagesetting and manufacturing were completed by Hart Graphics, Austin, TX.